SIXTH
EDITION

STUDENT
SOLUTIONS MANUAL

Mark Mc Combs

Michael Sullivan

COLLEGE ALGEBRA

Prentice
Hall

Upper Saddle River, NJ 07458

Editor in Chief: Sally Yagan
Associate Editor: Dawn Murrin
Assistant Managing Editor: John Matthews
Production Editor: Wendy A. Perez
Supplement Cover Manager: Paul Gourhan
Supplement Cover Designer: PM Workshop Inc.
Manufacturing Buyer: Lisa McDowell

© 2001 by Prentice Hall
    Upper Saddle River, NJ 07458

Printed in the United States of America

10 9 8 7 6 5 4 3 2 1

ISBN 0-13-092452-0

Prentice-Hall International (UK) Limited, London
Prentice-Hall of Australia Pty. Limited, Sydney
Prentice-Hall Canada, Inc., Toronto
Prentice-Hall Hispanoamericana, S.A., Mexico
Prentice-Hall of India Private Limited, New Delhi
Pearson Education Asia Pte. Ltd., Singapore
Prentice-Hall of Japan, Inc., Tokyo
Editora Prentice-Hall do Brazil, Ltda., Rio de Janeiro

Contents

Chapter 4   Polynomial and Rational Functions

Chapter 5   The Zeros of a Polynomial Function

Chapter 6   Exponential and Logarithmic Functions

Chapter 7   The Conics

Chapter 8   Systems of Equations and Inequalities

Chapter 9   Sequences; Induction; The Binomial Theorem

Chapter 10   Counting and Probability

Appendix   Graphing   Utilities

Preface

The Student's Solutions Manual to accompany College Algebra, 6th Edition by Michael Sullivan and Michael Sullivan, III contains detailed solutions to all of the odd-numbered problems in the textbook. TI-83 graphing calculator screens have been included to demonstrate the use of the graphics calculator in solving and in checking solutions to the problems where requested. Every attempt has been made to make this manual as error free as possible. If you have suggestions, error corrections, or comments please feel free to write to me about them.

A number of people need to be recognized for their contributions in the preparation of this manual. Thanks go to Sally Yagan, Dawn Murrin and Audra Walsh at Prentice Hall. Thanks also to Rachelle DeCoste, Kyle Kneisl, Laura Stevens and Scott Young for thoroughly checking the solutions for errors.

I especially wish to thank my mother, Sarah, and my brothers, Kirk and Doug, for their unwavering support and encouragement.

Finally, I want to thank Lily for her invaluable help in formatting the manual.

Mark A. McCombs
Department of Mathematics
Campus Box 3250
University of North Carolina at Chapel Hill
Chapel Hill, NC 27599
mccombs@math.unc.edu

Review

R.1 Real Numbers

1. (a) $\{2, 5\}$
   (b) $\{-6, 2, 5\}$
   (c) $\left\{-6, \dfrac{1}{2}, -1.333\ldots, 2, 5\right\}$
   (d) $\{\pi\}$
   (e) $\left\{-6, \dfrac{1}{2}, -1.333\ldots, \pi, 2, 5\right\}$

3. (a) $\{1\}$
   (b) $\{0, 1\}$
   (c) $\left\{0, 1, \dfrac{1}{2}, \dfrac{1}{3}, \dfrac{1}{4}\right\}$
   (d) None
   (e) $\left\{0, 1, \dfrac{1}{2}, \dfrac{1}{3}, \dfrac{1}{4}\right\}$

5. (a) None
   (b) None
   (c) None
   (d) $\left\{\sqrt{2}, \pi, \sqrt{2}+1, \pi+\dfrac{1}{2}\right\}$
   (e) $\left\{\sqrt{2}, \pi, \sqrt{2}+1, \pi+\dfrac{1}{2}\right\}$

7. (a) 18.953
   (b) 18.952

9. (a) 28.653
   (b) 28.653

11. (a) 0.063
    (b) 0.062

13. (a) 9.998
    (b) 9.998

15. (a) 0.429
    (b) 0.428

17. (a) 34.733
    (b) 34.733

19. $3 + 2 = 5$

21. $x + 2 = (3)(4)$

23. $3y = 1 + 2$

25. $x - 2 = 6$

27. $\dfrac{x}{2} = 6$

29. $9 - 4 + 2 = 5 + 2 = 7$

31. $-6 + 4 \cdot 3 = -6 + 12 = 6$

33. $4 + 5 - 8 = 9 - 8 = 1$

35. $4 + \dfrac{1}{3} = \dfrac{12+1}{3} = \dfrac{13}{3}$

37. $6 - [3\cdot5 + 2\cdot(3-2)]$
    $= 6 - [15 + 2\cdot(1)]$
    $= 6 - 17 = -11$

39. $2\cdot(3-5) + 8\cdot2 - 1$
    $= 2\cdot(-2) + 16 - 1$
    $= -4 + 16 - 1$
    $= 12 - 1 = 11$

41. $10 - [6 - 2\cdot2 + (8-3)]\cdot2$
    $= 10 - [6 - 4 + (5)]\cdot2$
    $= 10 - [2 + 5]\cdot2$
    $= 10 - 7\cdot2 = 10 - 14 = -4$

1

43. $(5-3)\dfrac{1}{2} = (2)\dfrac{1}{2} = 1$

45. $\dfrac{4+8}{5-3} = \dfrac{12}{2} = 6$

47. $\dfrac{3}{5} \cdot \dfrac{10}{21} = \dfrac{2}{7}$

49. $\dfrac{6}{25} \cdot \dfrac{10}{27} = \dfrac{4}{15}$

51. $\dfrac{3}{4} + \dfrac{2}{5} = \dfrac{15+8}{20} = \dfrac{23}{20}$

53. $\dfrac{5}{6} + \dfrac{9}{5} = \dfrac{25+54}{30} = \dfrac{79}{30}$

55. $\dfrac{5}{18} + \dfrac{1}{12} = \dfrac{10+3}{36} = \dfrac{13}{36}$

57. $\dfrac{1}{30} - \dfrac{7}{18} = \dfrac{3-35}{90}$
$= -\dfrac{32}{90} = -\dfrac{16}{45}$

59. $\dfrac{3}{20} - \dfrac{2}{15} = \dfrac{9-8}{60} = \dfrac{1}{60}$

61. $\dfrac{\tfrac{5}{18}}{\tfrac{11}{27}} = \dfrac{5}{18} \cdot \dfrac{27}{11} = \dfrac{15}{22}$

63. $6(x+4) = 6x + 24$

65. $x(x-4) = x^2 - 4x$

67. $(x+2)(x+4)$
$= x^2 + 4x + 2x + 8$
$= x^2 + 6x + 8$

69. $(x-2)(x+1)$
$= x^2 + x - 2x - 2$
$= x^2 - x - 2$

71. $(x-8)(x-2)$
$= x^2 - 2x - 8x + 16$
$= x^2 - 10x + 16$

73. $(x+2)(x-2)$
$= x^2 - 2x + 2x - 4$
$= x^2 - 4$

75. $2x + 3x$
$= x(2+3)$
$= x(5) = 5x$

77. $2(3 \cdot 4)$ means the same thing as $3 \cdot 4 + 3 \cdot 4 = 12 + 12 = 24$
$(2 \cdot 3) \cdot (2 \cdot 4)$ means the same thing as $(3+3) \cdot (4+4) = (6)(8) = 8 + 8 + 8 + 8 + 8 + 8 = 48$

79. Subtraction is not commutative; for example: $1 - 4 = -3$, but $4 - 1 = 3$.

81. Division is not commutative; for example: $\dfrac{6}{2} = 3$, but $\dfrac{2}{6} = \dfrac{1}{3}$.

83. The Symmetric Property of Equality implies that if $2 = x$, then $x = 2$.

85. There are no real numbers that are both rational and irrational, since an irrational number, by definition, is a number that cannot be expressed as the ratio of two integers.

   Every real number is either a rational number or an irrational number, since the decimal form of a real number either involves an infinitely repeating pattern of digits or an infinite, non-repeating string of digits.

87. Let $x = 0.\overline{9} \rightarrow 10x = 9.\overline{9}$,   Now compute $10x = 9.\overline{9}$
$$\underline{- \ x = 0.\overline{9}}$$
$$9x = 9 \rightarrow x = 1$$

   So 0.99999…….. equals 1.

Review

R.2 Algebra Review

1.

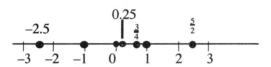

3. $\dfrac{1}{2} > 0$

5. $-1 > -2$

7. $\pi > 3.14$

9. $\dfrac{1}{2} = 0.5$

11. $\dfrac{2}{3} < 0.67$

13. $x > 0$

15. $x < 2$

17. $x \le 1$

19. Graph on the number line: $x \ge -2$

21. Graph on the number line: $x > -1$

23. $d(C,D) = d(0,1) = |1 - 0| = |1| = 1$

25. $d(D,E) = d(1,3) = |3 - 1| = |2| = 2$

27. $d(A,E) = d(-3,3) = |3 - (-3)| = |6| = 6$

29. $x + 2y = -2 + 2 \cdot 3 = -2 + 6 = 4$

31. $5xy + 2 = 5(-2)(3) + 2 = -30 + 2 = -28$

33. $\dfrac{2x}{x - y} = \dfrac{2(-2)}{-2 - 3} = \dfrac{-4}{-5} = \dfrac{4}{5}$

35. $\dfrac{3x + 2y}{2 + y} = \dfrac{3(-2) + 2(3)}{2 + 3} = \dfrac{-6 + 6}{5} = \dfrac{0}{5} = 0$

37. $|x + y| = |3 + (-2)| = |1| = 1$

39. $|x| + |y| = |3| + |-2| = 3 + 2 = 5$

41. $\dfrac{|x|}{x} = \dfrac{|3|}{3} = \dfrac{3}{3} = 1$

43. $|4x - 5y| = |4(3) - 5(-2)| = |12 + 10| = |22| = 22$

45. $||4x| - |5y|| = ||4(3)| - |5(-2)|| = ||12| - |-10|| = |12 - 10| = |2| = 2$

47. $\dfrac{x^2 - 1}{x}$ Part (c) must be excluded.

The value $x = 0$ must be excluded from the domain because it causes division by 0.

49. $\dfrac{x}{x^2 - 9} = \dfrac{x}{(x - 3)(x + 3)}$ Part (a) must be excluded.

The values $x = -3$ and $x = 3$ must be excluded from the domain because they cause division by 0.

51. $\dfrac{x^2}{x^2 + 1}$ None of the given values are excluded. The domain is all real numbers.

53. $\dfrac{x^2 + 5x - 10}{x^3 - x} = \dfrac{x^2 + 5x - 10}{x(x - 1)(x + 1)}$ Parts (b), (c), and (d) must be excluded.

The values $x = 0$, $x = 1$, and $x = -1$ must be excluded from the domain because they cause division by 0.

55. $\dfrac{4}{x - 5}$ Domain $= \{x | x \neq 5\}$ 57. $\dfrac{x}{x + 4}$ Domain $= \{x | x \neq -4\}$

59. $C = \dfrac{5}{9}(F - 32) = \dfrac{5}{9}(32 - 32) = \dfrac{5}{9}(0) = 0$

61. $C = \dfrac{5}{9}(F - 32) = \dfrac{5}{9}(77 - 32) = \dfrac{5}{9}(45) = 25$

63. $A = l \cdot w$ 65. $C = \pi \cdot d$ 67. $A = \dfrac{\sqrt{3}}{4} \cdot x^2$

69. $V = \dfrac{4}{3}\pi \cdot r^3$ 71. $V = x^3$

73. (a) If $x = 1000$, $C = 4000 + 2x = 4000 + 2(1000) = 4000 + 2000 = \$6000$
    (b) If $x = 2000$, $C = 4000 + 2x = 4000 + 2(2000) = 4000 + 4000 = \$8000$

75. $|x - 115| \leq 5$
    (a) $|x - 115| = |113 - 115| = |-2| = 2 \leq 5$ 113 volts is acceptable.
    (b) $|x - 115| = |109 - 115| = |-6| = 6 \nleq 5$ 109 volts is _not_ acceptable.

77. $|x - 3| \leq 0.01$
    (a) $|x - 3| = |2.999 - 3| = |-0.001| = 0.001 \leq 0.01$ A radius of 2.999 centimeters is acceptable.
    (b) $|x - 3| = |2.89 - 3| = |-0.11| = 0.11 \nleq 0.01$ A radius of 2.89 centimeters is _not_ acceptable.

79. $\dfrac{1}{3} = 0.333333\ldots > 0.333$ $\dfrac{1}{3}$ is larger by approximately $0.0003333\ldots$

81. No.

83. Answers will vary.

Review

R.3   Geometry Review

1. $a = 5, \ b = 12, \ c^2 = a^2 + b^2 = 5^2 + 12^2 = 25 + 144 = 169 \ \rightarrow \ c = 13$

3. $a = 10, \ b = 24, \ c^2 = a^2 + b^2 = 10^2 + 24^2 = 100 + 576 = 676 \ \rightarrow \ c = 26$

5. $a = 7, \ b = 24, \ c^2 = a^2 + b^2 = 7^2 + 24^2 = 49 + 576 = 625 \ \rightarrow \ c = 25$

7. $5^2 = 3^2 + 4^2 \ \rightarrow \ 25 = 9 + 16 \ \rightarrow \ 25 = 25$
The given triangle is a right triangle. The hypotenuse is 5.

9. $6^2 = 4^2 + 5^2 \ \rightarrow \ 36 = 16 + 25 \ \rightarrow \ 36 \neq 41$
The given triangle is not a right triangle.

11. $25^2 = 7^2 + 24^2 \ \rightarrow \ 625 = 49 + 576 \ \rightarrow \ 625 = 625$
The given triangle is a right triangle. The hypotenuse is 25.

13. $6^2 = 3^2 + 4^2 \ \rightarrow \ 36 = 9 + 16 \ \rightarrow \ 36 \neq 25$
The given triangle is not a right triangle.

15. $A = l \cdot w = 4 \cdot 2 = 8 \text{ in}^2$ 17. $A = \dfrac{1}{2} b \cdot h = \dfrac{1}{2}(2)(4) = 4 \text{ in}^2$

19. $A = \pi r^2 = \pi (5)^2 = 25\pi \text{ m}^2$ $C = 2\pi r = 2\pi (5) = 10\pi \text{ m}$

21. $V = lwh = 8 \cdot 4 \cdot 7 = 224 \text{ ft}^2$

23. $V = \dfrac{4}{3}\pi r^3 = \dfrac{4}{3}\pi \cdot 4^3 = \dfrac{256}{3}\pi \text{ cm}^3$ $S = 4\pi r^2 = 4\pi \cdot 4^2 = 64\pi \text{ cm}^2$

25. $V = \pi r^2 h = \pi (9)^2 (8) = 648\pi \text{ in}^3$

27.   The diameter of the circle is 2, so its radius is 1. $A = \pi r^2 = \pi (1)^2 = \pi$ square units

29.   The diameter of the circle is the length of the diagonal of the square.
$d^2 = 2^2 + 2^2 = 4 + 4 = 8 \ \rightarrow \ d = \sqrt{8} = 2\sqrt{2}$ $r = \sqrt{2}$
The area of the circle is: $A = \pi r^2 = \pi \left(\sqrt{2}\right)^2 = 2\pi$ square units

31. The total distance traveled is 4 times the circumference of the wheel.
Total distance $= 4C = 4(\pi d) = 4\pi \cdot 16 = 64\pi = 201.1$ inches

33. Area of the border = area of EFGH – area of ABCD $= 10^2 - 6^2 = 100 - 36 = 64$ ft^2

35. Area of the window = area of the rectangle + area of the semicircle.
$$A = (6)(4) + \frac{1}{2} \cdot \pi \cdot 2^2 = 24 + 2\pi = 30.28 \text{ ft}^2$$
Perimeter of the window = 2 heights + width + one-half the circumference.
$$P = 2(6) + 4 + \frac{1}{2} \cdot \pi(4) = 12 + 4 + 2\pi = 16 + 2\pi = 22.28 \text{ feet}$$

37. Convert 20 feet to miles, and solve the Pythagorean theorem to find the distance:

$$20 \text{ feet} = 20 \text{ feet} \cdot \frac{1 \text{ mile}}{5280 \text{ feet}} = 0.003788 \text{ miles}$$
$$d^2 = (3960 + 0.003788)^2 - 3960^2 = 30$$
$$d \approx 5.477 \text{ miles}$$

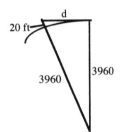

39. Convert 100 feet to miles, and solve the Pythagorean theorem to find the distance:
$$100 \text{ feet} = 100 \text{ feet} \cdot \frac{1 \text{ mile}}{5280 \text{ feet}} = 0.018939 \text{ miles}$$
$$d^2 = (3960 + 0.018939)^2 - 3960^2 = 150$$
$$d \approx 12.247 \text{ miles}$$
Convert 150 feet to miles, and solve the Pythagorean theorem to find the distance:
$$150 \text{ feet} = 150 \text{ feet} \cdot \frac{1 \text{ mile}}{5280 \text{ feet}} = 0.028409 \text{ miles}$$
$$d^2 = (3960 + 0.028409)^2 - 3960^2 = 225$$
$$d \approx 15 \text{ miles}$$

41. Given a rectangle with perimeter = 1000 feet, the largest area will be enclosed by a square with dimensions 250 by 250 feet.   That is, the area $= 250^2 = 62500$ square feet.

A circular pool with circumference = 1000 feet yields the equation : $2\pi r = 1000 \rightarrow r = \dfrac{500}{\pi}$

The area enclosed by the circular pool is: $A = \pi r^2 = \pi \left(\dfrac{500}{\pi}\right)^2 = \dfrac{500^2}{\pi} \approx 79577.47$ square feet

Therefore, a circular pool will enclose the most area.

Review

R.4 Integer Exponents

1. $4^2 = 16$

3. $4^{-2} = \dfrac{1}{4^2} = \dfrac{1}{16}$

5. $-4^{-2} = -\dfrac{1}{4^2} = -\dfrac{1}{16}$

7. $4^0 \cdot 2^{-3} = 1 \cdot \dfrac{1}{2^3} = 1 \cdot \dfrac{1}{8} = \dfrac{1}{8}$

9. $2^{-3} + \left(\dfrac{1}{2}\right)^3 = \dfrac{1}{2^3} + \dfrac{1^3}{2^3} = \dfrac{1}{8} + \dfrac{1}{8} = \dfrac{1}{4}$

11. $3^{-6} \cdot 3^4 = 3^{-6+4} = 3^{-2} = \dfrac{1}{3^2} = \dfrac{1}{9}$

13. $\dfrac{\left(3^2\right)^2}{\left(2^3\right)^2} = \dfrac{3^4}{2^6} = \dfrac{81}{64}$

15. $\left(\dfrac{2}{3}\right)^{-3} = \dfrac{1}{\left(\dfrac{2}{3}\right)^3} = \dfrac{1}{\dfrac{2^3}{3^3}} = \dfrac{3^3}{2^3} = \dfrac{27}{8}$

17. $\dfrac{2^3 \cdot 3^2}{2^4 \cdot 3^{-2}} = \dfrac{2^3}{2^4} \cdot \dfrac{3^2}{3^{-2}} = 2^{3-4} \cdot 3^{2-(-2)} = 2^{-1} \cdot 3^4 = \dfrac{1}{2} \cdot 81 = \dfrac{81}{2}$

19. $\left(\dfrac{9}{2}\right)^{-2} = \dfrac{1}{\left(\dfrac{9}{2}\right)^2} = \dfrac{1}{\dfrac{9^2}{2^2}} = \dfrac{2^2}{9^2} = \dfrac{4}{81}$

21. $\dfrac{2^{-2}}{3} = \dfrac{\dfrac{1}{2^2}}{3} = \dfrac{\dfrac{1}{4}}{3} = \dfrac{1}{4} \cdot \dfrac{1}{3} = \dfrac{1}{12}$

23. $\dfrac{-3^{-1}}{2^{-1}} = \dfrac{-\dfrac{1}{3}}{\dfrac{1}{2}} = -\dfrac{1}{3} \cdot \dfrac{2}{1} = -\dfrac{2}{3}$

25. $x^0 y^2 = 1 \cdot y^2 = y^2$

27. $x\,y^{-2} = x \cdot \dfrac{1}{y^2} = \dfrac{x}{y^2}$

29. $\left(8x^3\right)^{-2} = \dfrac{1}{\left(8x^3\right)^2} = \dfrac{1}{8^2 \cdot x^6} = \dfrac{1}{64x^6}$

31. $-4x^{-1} = -4 \cdot \dfrac{1}{x} = -\dfrac{4}{x}$

33. $3x^0 = 3 \cdot 1 = 3$

35. $\dfrac{x^{-2} y^3}{x\,y^4} = \dfrac{x^{-2}}{x} \cdot \dfrac{y^3}{y^4} = x^{-2-1} y^{3-4} = x^{-3} y^{-1} = \dfrac{1}{x^3} \cdot \dfrac{1}{y} = \dfrac{1}{x^3 y}$

37. $x^{-1} y^{-1} = \dfrac{1}{x} \cdot \dfrac{1}{y} = \dfrac{1}{xy}$

39. $\dfrac{x^{-1}}{y^{-1}} = \dfrac{\frac{1}{x}}{\frac{1}{y}} = \dfrac{1}{x} \cdot \dfrac{y}{1} = \dfrac{y}{x}$

41. $\left(\dfrac{4y}{5x}\right)^{-2} = \dfrac{1}{\left(\frac{4y}{5x}\right)^2} = \dfrac{1}{\frac{(4y)^2}{(5x)^2}} = \dfrac{(5x)^2}{(4y)^2} = \dfrac{5^2 \cdot x^2}{4^2 \cdot y^2} = \dfrac{25x^2}{16y^2}$

43. $x^{-2}y^{-2} = \dfrac{1}{x^2} \cdot \dfrac{1}{y^2} = \dfrac{1}{x^2 y^2}$

45. $\dfrac{x^{-1}y^{-2}z^3}{x^2 y z^3} = \dfrac{x^{-1}}{x^2} \cdot \dfrac{y^{-2}}{y} \cdot \dfrac{z^3}{z^3} = x^{-1-2}y^{-2-1}z^{3-3} = x^{-3}y^{-3}z^0 = \dfrac{1}{x^3} \cdot \dfrac{1}{y^3} \cdot 1 = \dfrac{1}{x^3 y^3}$

47. $\dfrac{(-2)^3 x^4 (yz)^2}{3^2 xy^3 z^4} = \dfrac{-8x^4 y^2 z^2}{9xy^3 z^4} = \dfrac{-8}{9} x^{4-1} y^{2-3} z^{2-4} = \dfrac{-8}{9} x^3 y^{-1} z^{-2} = \dfrac{-8}{9} x^3 \cdot \dfrac{1}{y} \cdot \dfrac{1}{z^2} = \dfrac{-8x^3}{9yz^2}$

49. $\dfrac{\left(\frac{x}{y}\right)^{-2} \cdot \left(\frac{y}{x}\right)^4}{x^2 y^3} = \dfrac{\frac{y^2}{x^2} \cdot \frac{y^4}{x^4}}{x^2 y^3} = \dfrac{y^6}{x^6} \cdot \dfrac{1}{x^2 y^3} = \dfrac{y^3}{x^8}$

51. $\left(\dfrac{3x^{-1}}{4y^{-1}}\right)^{-2} = \dfrac{1}{\left(\frac{3x^{-1}}{4y^{-1}}\right)^2} = \dfrac{1}{\frac{(3x^{-1})^2}{(4y^{-1})^2}} = \dfrac{(4y^{-1})^2}{(3x^{-1})^2} = \dfrac{4^2 y^{-2}}{3^2 x^{-2}} = \dfrac{16 \cdot \frac{1}{y^2}}{9 \cdot \frac{1}{x^2}} = \dfrac{16}{9} \cdot \dfrac{x^2}{y^2} = \dfrac{16x^2}{9y^2}$

53. $\dfrac{\left(xy^{-1}\right)^{-2}}{xy^3} = \dfrac{x^{-2}y^2}{xy^3} = \dfrac{x^{-2}}{x} \cdot \dfrac{y^2}{y^3} = x^{-2-1}y^{2-3} = x^{-3}y^{-1} = \dfrac{1}{x^3 y}$

55. $\left(\dfrac{x}{y^2}\right)^{-2} \cdot \left(y^2\right)^{-1} = \dfrac{x^{-2}}{\left(y^2\right)^{-2}} \cdot \dfrac{1}{y^2} = \dfrac{x^{-2}}{y^{-4}y^2} = \dfrac{x^{-2}}{y^{-2}} = \dfrac{\frac{1}{x^2}}{\frac{1}{y^2}} = \dfrac{y^2}{x^2}$

57. If $x = 2$, $2x^3 - 3x^2 + 5x - 4 = 2 \cdot 2^3 - 3 \cdot 2^2 + 5 \cdot 2 - 4 = 16 - 12 + 10 - 4 = 10$
    If $x = 1$, $2x^3 - 3x^2 + 5x - 4 = 2 \cdot 1^3 - 3 \cdot 1^2 + 5 \cdot 1 - 4 = 2 - 3 + 5 - 4 = 0$

59. $\dfrac{(666)^4}{(222)^4} = \left(\dfrac{666}{222}\right)^4 = 3^4 = 81$

61. $(8.2)^6 \approx 304{,}006.671$

63. $(6.1)^{-3} \approx 0.004$

65. $(-2.8)^6 \approx 481.890$

67. $(-8.11)^{-4} \approx 0.000$

69. $454.2 = 4.542 \times 10^2$

71. $0.013 = 1.3 \times 10^{-2}$

73. $32,155 = 3.2155 \times 10^4$

75. $0.000423 = 4.23 \times 10^{-4}$

77. $6.15 \times 10^4 = 61,500$

79. $1.214 \times 10^{-3} = 0.001214$

81. $1.1 \times 10^8 = 110,000,000$

83. $8.1 \times 10^{-2} = 0.081$

85. $4 \times 10^8 = 400,000,000$ meters

87. $5 \times 10^{-7} = 0.0000005$

89. $0.0005 = 5 \times 10^{-4}$

91. $64,000,000 \cdot 30 = \left(6.4 \times 10^7\right)\left(3 \times 10^1\right) = 19.2 \times 10^8 = 1.92 \times 10^9$

93. $186,000 \cdot 60 \cdot 60 \cdot 24 \cdot 365 = \left(1.86 \times 10^5\right)\left(6 \times 10^1\right)\left(6 \times 10^1\right)\left(2.4 \times 10^1\right)\left(3.65 \times 10^2\right)$
$$= 586.5696 \times 10^{10} = 5.865696 \times 10^{12}$$

95. Answers will vary.

Review

R.5 Polynomials

1. $2x^3$ Monomial; Variable: x; Coefficient: 2; Degree: 3

3. $\dfrac{8}{x}$ Not a monomial.

5. $-2xy^2$ Monomial; Variable: x, y; Coefficient: –2; Degree: 3

7. $\dfrac{8x}{y}$ Not a monomial

9. $x^2 + y^2$ Not a monomial.

11. $3x^2 - 5$ Polynomial; Degree: 2

13. 5 Polynomial; Degree: 0

15. $3x^2 - \dfrac{5}{x}$ Not a polynomial.

17. $2y^3 - \sqrt{2}$ Polynomial; Degree: 3

19. $\dfrac{x^2 + 5}{x^3 - 1}$ Not a polynomial.

21. $(x^2 + 4x + 5) + (3x - 3) = x^2 + (4x + 3x) + (5 - 3) = x^2 + 7x + 2$

23. $(x^3 - 2x^2 + 5x + 10) - (2x^2 - 4x + 3) = x^3 - 2x^2 + 5x + 10 - 2x^2 + 4x - 3$
$$= x^3 + (-2x^2 - 2x^2) + (5x + 4x) + (10 - 3)$$
$$= x^3 - 4x^2 + 9x + 7$$

25. $\left(6x^5 + x^3 + x\right) + \left(5x^4 - x^3 + 3x^2\right) = 6x^5 + 5x^4 + 3x^2 + x$

27. $(x^2 - 3x + 1) + 2(3x^2 + x - 4) = x^2 - 3x + 1 + 6x^2 + 2x - 8 = 7x^2 - x - 7$

29. $6(x^3 + x^2 - 3) - 4(2x^3 - 3x^2) = 6x^3 + 6x^2 - 18 - 8x^3 + 12x^2 = -2x^3 + 18x^2 - 18$

31. $\left(x^2 - x + 2\right) + \left(2x^2 - 3x + 5\right) - \left(x^2 + 1\right) = x^2 - x + 2 + 2x^2 - 3x + 5 - x^2 - 1$
$$= 2x^2 - 4x + 6$$

33. $9\left(y^2 - 3y + 4\right) - 6\left(1 - y^2\right) = 9y^2 - 27y + 36 - 6 + 6y^2 = 15y^2 - 27y + 30$

35. $x(x^2 + x - 4) = x^3 + x^2 - 4x$

37. $-2x^2(4x^3 + 5) = -8x^5 - 10x^2$

39. $(x + 1)(x^2 + 2x - 4) = x(x^2 + 2x - 4) + 1(x^2 + 2x - 4)$
$$= x^3 + 2x^2 - 4x + x^2 + 2x - 4$$
$$= x^3 + 3x^2 - 2x - 4$$

41. $(x + 2)(x + 4) = x^2 + 4x + 2x + 8 = x^2 + 6x + 8$

43. $(2x + 5)(x + 2) = 2x^2 + 4x + 5x + 10 = 2x^2 + 9x + 10$

45. $(x - 4)(x + 2) = x^2 + 2x - 4x - 8 = x^2 - 2x - 8$

47. $(x - 3)(x - 2) = x^2 - 2x - 3x + 6 = x^2 - 5x + 6$

49. $(2x + 3)(x - 2) = 2x^2 - 4x + 3x - 6 = 2x^2 - x - 6$

51. $(-2x + 3)(x - 4) = -2x^2 + 8x + 3x - 12 = -2x^2 + 11x - 12$

53. $(-x - 2)(-2x - 4) = 2x^2 + 4x + 4x + 8 = 2x^2 + 8x + 8$

55. $(x - 2y)(x + y) = x^2 + xy - 2xy - 2y^2 = x^2 - 3xy - 2y^2$

57. $(-2x - 3y)(3x + 2y) = -6x^2 - 4xy - 9xy - 6y^2 = -6x^2 - 13xy - 6y^2$

59. $(x - 7)(x + 7) = x^2 - 7^2 = x^2 - 49$

61. $(2x + 3)(2x - 3) = (2x)^2 - 3^2 = 4x^2 - 9$

63. $(x + 4)^2 = x^2 + 2 \cdot x \cdot 4 + 4^2 = x^2 + 8x + 16$

65. $(x - 4)^2 = x^2 - 2 \cdot x \cdot 4 + 4^2 = x^2 - 8x + 16$

67. $(3x + 4)(3x - 4) = (3x)^2 - 4^2 = 9x^2 - 16$

69. $(2x - 3)^2 = (2x)^2 - 2(2x)(3) + 3^2 = 4x^2 - 12x + 9$

71. $(x + y)(x - y) = (x)^2 - (y)^2 = x^2 - y^2$

73. $(3x + y)(3x - y) = (3x)^2 - (y)^2 = 9x^2 - y^2$

75. $(x + y)^2 = x^2 + 2xy + y^2$

77. $(x - 2y)^2 = x^2 + 2(x \cdot (-2y)) + (2y)^2 = x^2 - 4xy + 4y^2$

79. $(x - 2)^3 = x^3 - 3 \cdot x^2 \cdot 2 + 3 \cdot x \cdot 2^2 - 2^3 = x^3 - 6x^2 + 12x - 8$

81. $(2x+1)^3 = (2x)^3 + 3(2x)^2(1) + 3(2x) \cdot 1^2 + 1^3 = 8x^3 + 12x^2 + 6x + 1$

83. Divide:

$$4x^2 - 3x + 1$$
$$x \overline{)4x^3 - 3x^2 + x + 1}$$
$$\underline{4x^3}$$
$$-3x^2 + x + 1$$
$$\underline{-3x^2}$$
$$x + 1$$
$$\underline{x}$$
$$1$$

Check:

$(x)(4x^2 - 3x + 1) + (1)$

$= 4x^3 - 3x^2 + x + 1$

The quotient is $4x^2 - 3x + 1$; the remainder is 1.

85. Divide:

$$4x^2 - 11x + 23$$
$$x + 2 \overline{)4x^3 - 3x^2 + x + 1}$$
$$\underline{4x^3 + 8x^2}$$
$$-11x^2 + x$$
$$\underline{-11x^2 - 22x}$$
$$23x + 1$$
$$\underline{23x + 46}$$
$$-45$$

Check:

$(x + 2)(4x^2 - 11x + 23) + (-45)$

$= 4x^3 - 11x^2 + 23x + 8x^2 - 22x + 46 - 45$

$= 4x^3 - 3x^2 + x + 1$

The quotient is $4x^2 - 11x + 23$; the remainder is –45.

87. Divide:

$$4x - 3$$
$$x^2 \overline{)4x^3 - 3x^2 + x + 1}$$
$$\underline{4x^3}$$
$$-3x^2 + x + 1$$
$$\underline{-3x^2}$$
$$x + 1$$

Check:

$(x^2)(4x - 3) + (x + 1)$

$= 4x^3 - 3x^2 + x + 1$

The quotient is $4x - 3$; the remainder is $x + 1$.
Check:

$(x^2)(3x + 1) + (x - 2)$

$= 3x^3 + x^2 + x - 2$

The quotient is $3x + 1$; the remainder is $x - 2$.

89.   Divide:

$$\require{enclose}
\begin{array}{r}
4x - 3 \\
x^2 + 2 \enclose{longdiv}{4x^3 - 3x^2 + x + 1} \\
\underline{4x^3 \quad\quad + 8x} \\
-3x^2 - 7x \\
\underline{-3x^2 \quad\quad -6} \\
-7x + 7
\end{array}$$

Check:

$(x^2 + 2)(4x - 3) + (-7x + 7)$

$= 4x^3 - 3x^2 + 8x - 6 - 7x + 7$

$= 4x^3 - 3x^2 + x + 1$

The quotient is $4x - 3$; the remainder is $-7x + 7$.

91.   Divide:

$$\begin{array}{r}
2 \\
2x^3 - 1 \enclose{longdiv}{4x^3 - 3x^2 + x + 1} \\
\underline{4x^3 \quad\quad\quad -2} \\
-3x^2 + x + 3
\end{array}$$

Check:

$(2x^3 - 1)(2) + (-3x^2 + x + 3)$

$= 4x^3 - 2 - 3x^2 + x + 3$

$= 4x^3 - 3x^2 + x + 1$

The quotient is 2; the remainder is $-3x^2 + x + 3$.

93.   Divide:

$$\begin{array}{r}
2x - \dfrac{5}{2} \\
2x^2 + x + 1 \enclose{longdiv}{4x^3 - 3x^2 + x + 1} \\
\underline{4x^3 + 2x^2 + 2x} \\
-5x^2 - x \\
\underline{-5x^2 - \dfrac{5}{3}x - \dfrac{5}{2}} \\
\dfrac{3}{2}x + \dfrac{7}{2}
\end{array}$$

Check :

$(2x^2 + x + 1)(2x - \dfrac{5}{2}) + \left(\dfrac{3}{2}x + \dfrac{7}{2}\right)$

$= 4x^3 - 5x^2 + 2x^2 - \dfrac{5}{2}x + 2x - \dfrac{5}{2} + \dfrac{3}{2}x + \dfrac{7}{2} = 4x^3 - 3x^2 + x + 1$

The quotient is $2x - \dfrac{5}{2}$; the remainder is $\dfrac{3}{2}x + \dfrac{7}{2}$.

95. Divide:

$$x - 1 \overline{\smash{\big)}\, -4x^3 + x^2 + 0x - 4}$$

quotient: $-4x^2 - 3x - 3$

$$\begin{array}{r} -4x^2 - 3x - 3 \\ x-1 \overline{\smash{\big)} -4x^3 + x^2 + 0x - 4} \\ \underline{-4x^3 + 4x^2} \\ -3x^2 \\ \underline{-3x^2 + 3x} \\ -3x - 4 \\ \underline{-3x + 3} \\ -7 \end{array}$$

Check:

$(x-1)(-4x^2 - 3x - 3) + (-7)$
$= -4x^3 - 3x^2 - 3x + 4x^2 + 3x + 3 - 7$
$= -4x^3 + x^2 - 4$

The quotient is $-4x^2 - 3x - 3$; the remainder is –7

97. Divide:

$$\begin{array}{r} x^2 - x - 1 \\ x^2 + x + 1 \overline{\smash{\big)} x^4 + 0x^3 - x^2 + 0x + 1} \\ \underline{x^4 + x^3 + x^2} \\ -x^3 - 2x^2 \\ \underline{-x^3 - x^2 - x} \\ -x^2 + x + 1 \\ \underline{-x^2 - x - 1} \\ 2x + 2 \end{array}$$

Check:

$(x^2 + x + 1)(x^2 - x - 1) + 2x + 2$
$= x^4 + x^3 + x^2 - x^3 - x^2 - x - x^2 - x - 1 + 2x + 2$
$= x^4 - x^2 + 1$

The quotient is $x^2 - x - 1$; the remainder is $2x + 2$.

99. Divide:

$$\begin{array}{r} x^2 + ax + a^2 \\ x - a \overline{\smash{\big)} x^3 + 0x^2 + 0x - a^3} \\ \underline{x^3 - ax^2} \\ ax^2 \\ \underline{ax^2 - a^2 x} \\ a^2 x - a^3 \\ \underline{a^2 x - a^3} \\ 0 \end{array}$$

Check:

$(x - a)(x^2 + ax + a^2) + 0$
$= x^3 + ax^2 + a^2 x - ax^2 - a^2 x - a^3$
$= x^3 - a^3$

The quotient is $x^2 + ax + a^2$; the remainder is 0.

101.

$$\frac{x^3 - 2x^2 + 3x + 5}{x + 2} = ax^2 + bx + c + \frac{d}{x + 2}$$

In order to find $a + b + c + d$, we do the long division and then look at the coefficients of the quotient and remainder.

$$
\require{enclose}
\begin{array}{r}
x^2 - 4x + 11 \\
x+2 \enclose{longdiv}{x^3 - 2x^2 + 3x - 5} \\
\underline{x^3 + 2x^2} \\
-4x^2 + 3x - 5 \\
\underline{-4x^2 - 8x} \\
11x - 5 \\
\underline{11x + 22} \\
-27
\end{array}
$$

therefore,

$$\frac{x^3 - 2x^2 + 3x + 5}{x + 2} = x^2 - 4x + 11 + \frac{-27}{x + 2}$$

$$a + b + c + d = 1 - 4 + 11 - 27 = -19$$

103. When we add two polynomials $p_1(x)$ and $p_2(x)$, where the degree of $p_1(x) \neq$ the degree of $p_2(x)$, each term of $p_1(x)$ will be added to each term of $p_2(x)$. Since only the terms with equal degrees will combine via addition, the degree of the sum polynomial will be the degree of the highest powered term overall, that is, the degree of the polynomial that had the higher degree.

105. Answers will vary.

Review

R.6 Factoring Polynomials

1. $3x + 6 = 3(x + 2)$

3. $ax^2 + a = a(x^2 + 1)$

5. $x^3 + x^2 + x = x(x^2 + x + 1)$

7. $2x^2 - 2x = 2x(x - 1)$

9. $3x^2y - 6xy^2 + 12xy = 3xy(x - 2y + 4)$

11. $x^2 - 1 = x^2 - 1^2 = (x - 1)(x + 1)$

13. $4x^2 - 1 = (2x)^2 - 1^2 = (2x - 1)(2x + 1)$

15. $x^2 - 16 = x^2 - 4^2 = (x - 4)(x + 4)$

17. $25x^2 - 4 = (5x - 2)(5x + 2)$

19. $x^2 + 2x + 1 = (x + 1)^2$

21. $x^2 + 4x + 4 = (x + 2)^2$

23. $x^2 - 10x + 25 = (x - 5)^2$

25. $4x^2 + 4x + 1 = (2x + 1)^2$

27. $16x^2 + 8x + 1 = (4x + 1)^2$

29. $x^3 - 27 = x^3 - 3^3 = (x - 3)(x^2 + 3x + 9)$

31. $x^3 + 27 = x^3 + 3^3 = (x + 3)(x^2 - 3x + 9)$

33. $8x^3 + 27 = (2x)^3 + 3^3 = (2x + 3)(4x^2 - 6x + 9)$

35. $x^2 + 5x + 6 = (x + 2)(x + 3)$

37. $x^2 + 7x + 6 = (x + 6)(x + 1)$

39. $x^2 + 7x + 10 = (x + 2)(x + 5)$

41. $x^2 - 10x + 16 = (x - 2)(x - 8)$

43. $x^2 - 7x - 8 = (x + 1)(x - 8)$
$x^2 - 2x - 8 = (x + 2)(x - 4)$

45. $x^2 + 7x - 8 = (x + 8)(x - 1)$

47. $2x^2 + 4x + 3x + 6 = 2x(x + 2) + 3(x + 2) = (x + 2)(2x + 3)$

49. $2x^2 - 4x + x - 2 = 2x(x - 2) + 1(x - 2) = (x - 2)(2x + 1)$

51. $6x^2 + 9x + 4x + 6 = 3x(2x + 3) + 2(2x + 3) = (2x + 3)(3x + 2)$

53. $3x^2 + 4x + 1 = (3x + 1)(x + 1)$

55. $2z^2 + 5z + 3 = (2z + 3)(z + 1)$

57. $3x^2 - 2x - 8 = (3x + 4)(x - 2)$

59. $3x^2 - 2x - 8 = (3x - 4)(x + 2)$

61. $3x^2 + 14x + 8 = (3x + 2)(x + 4)$

63. $3x^2 + 10x - 8 = (3x - 2)(x + 4)$

65. $x^2 - 36 = (x - 6)(x + 6)$

67. $2 - 8x^2 = 2(1 - 4x^2) = 2(1 - 2x)(1 + 2x)$

69. $x^2 + 7x + 10 = (x + 2)(x + 5)$

71. $x^2 - 10x + 21 = (x - 7)(x - 3)$

73. $4x^2 - 8x + 32 = 4(x^2 - 2x + 8)$

75. $x^2 + 4x + 16$ is prime because there are no factors of 16 whose sum is 4.

77. $15 + 2x - x^2 = -(x^2 - 2x - 15) = -(x - 5)(x + 3)$

79. $3x^2 - 12x - 36 = 3(x^2 - 4x - 12) = 3(x - 6)(x + 2)$

81. $y^4 + 11y^3 + 30y^2 = y^2(y^2 + 11y + 30) = y^2(y + 5)(y + 6)$

83. $4x^2 + 12x + 9 = (2x + 3)^2$

85. $6x^2 + 8x + 2 = 2(3x^2 + 4x + 1) = 2(3x + 1)(x + 1)$

87. $x^4 - 81 = (x^2 - 9)(x^2 + 9) = (x - 3)(x + 3)(x^2 + 9)$

89. $x^6 - 2x^3 + 1 = (x^3 - 1)^2 = \left[(x - 1)(x^2 + x + 1)\right]^2 = (x - 1)^2(x^2 + x + 1)^2$

91. $x^7 - x^5 = x^5(x^2 - 1) = x^5(x - 1)(x + 1)$

93. $16x^2 + 24x + 9 = (4x + 3)^2$

95. $5 + 16x - 16x^2 = -(16x^2 - 16x - 5) = -(4x - 5)(4x + 1)$

97. $4y^2 - 16y + 15 = (2y - 5)(2y - 3)$

99. $1 - 8x^2 - 9x^4 = -(9x^4 + 8x^2 - 1) = -(9x^2 - 1)(x^2 + 1) = -(3x - 1)(3x + 1)(x^2 + 1)$

101. $x(x + 3) - 6(x + 3) = (x + 3)(x - 6)$

103. $(x + 2)^2 - 5(x + 2) = (x + 2)[(x + 2) - 5] = (x + 2)(x - 3)$

105. $(3x-2)^3 - 27 = \left[(3x-2)-3\right]\left[(3x-2)^2 + 3(3x-2)+9\right]$
$= (3x-5)(9x^2 - 12x + 4 + 9x - 6 + 9) = (3x-5)(9x^2 - 3x + 7)$

107. $3(x^2 + 10x + 25) - 4(x+5) = 3(x+5)^2 - 4(x+5)$
$= (x+5)[3(x+5)-4] = (x+5)(3x+15-4) = (x+5)(3x+11)$

109. $x^3 + 2x^2 - x - 2 = x^2(x+2) - (x+2) = (x+2)(x^2-1) = (x+2)(x-1)(x+1)$

111. $x^4 - x^3 + x - 1 = x^3(x-1) + (x-1) = (x-1)(x^3+1) = (x-1)(x+1)(x^2-x+1)$

113.

Factors of 4	1, 4	2, 2	−1, −4	−2, −2
Sum	5	4	−5	−4

None of the sums of the factors is 0, so $x^2 + 4$ is prime.

115. Answers will vary.

Review

R.7 Rational Expressions

1. $\dfrac{3x+9}{x^2-9} = \dfrac{3(x+3)}{(x-3)(x+3)} = \dfrac{3}{x-3}$

3. $\dfrac{x^2-2x}{3x-6} = \dfrac{x(x-2)}{3(x-2)} = \dfrac{x}{3}$

5. $\dfrac{24x^2}{12x^2-6x} = \dfrac{24x^2}{6x(2x-1)} = \dfrac{4x}{2x-1}$

7. $\dfrac{y^2-25}{2y^2-8y-10} = \dfrac{(y+5)(y-5)}{2(y^2-4y-5)} = \dfrac{(y+5)(y-5)}{2(y-5)(y+1)} = \dfrac{y+5}{2(y+1)}$

9. $\dfrac{x^2+4x-5}{x^2-2x+1} = \dfrac{(x+5)(x-1)}{(x-1)(x-1)} = \dfrac{x+5}{x-1}$

11. $\dfrac{x^2+5x-14}{2-x} = \dfrac{(x+7)(x-2)}{2-x} = \dfrac{(x+7)(x-2)}{(-1)(-2+x)} = \dfrac{(x+7)(x-2)}{(-1)(x-2)} = -(x+7)$

13. $\dfrac{3x+6}{5x^2} \cdot \dfrac{x}{x^2-4} = \dfrac{3(x+2)}{5x^2} \cdot \dfrac{x}{(x-2)(x+2)} = \dfrac{3}{5x(x-2)}$

15. $\dfrac{4x^2}{x^2-16} \cdot \dfrac{x-4}{2x} = \dfrac{4x^2}{(x-4)(x+4)} \cdot \dfrac{x-4}{2x} = \dfrac{2x}{x+4}$

17. $\dfrac{4x-8}{-3x} \cdot \dfrac{12}{12-6x} = \dfrac{4(x-2)}{-3x} \cdot \dfrac{12}{6(2-x)} = \dfrac{4(x-2)}{-3x} \cdot \dfrac{2}{(-1)(x-2)} = \dfrac{8}{3x}$

19. $\dfrac{x^2-3x-10}{x^2+2x-35} \cdot \dfrac{x^2+4x-21}{x^2+9x+14} = \dfrac{(x-5)(x+2)}{(x+7)(x-5)} \cdot \dfrac{(x+7)(x-3)}{(x+7)(x+2)} = \dfrac{x-3}{x+7}$

21. $\dfrac{\left(\dfrac{6x}{x^2-4}\right)}{\left(\dfrac{3x-9}{2x+4}\right)} = \dfrac{6x}{x^2-4} \cdot \dfrac{2x+4}{3x-9} = \dfrac{6x}{(x-2)(x+2)} \cdot \dfrac{2(x+2)}{3(x-3)} = \dfrac{4x}{(x-2)(x-3)}$

23. $\dfrac{\left(\dfrac{8x}{x^2-1}\right)}{\left(\dfrac{10}{x+1}\right)} = \dfrac{8x}{x^2-1} \cdot \dfrac{x+1}{10} = \dfrac{8x}{(x-1)(x+1)} \cdot \dfrac{x+1}{10} = \dfrac{4x}{5(x-1)}$

25. $\dfrac{\left(\dfrac{4-x}{4+x}\right)}{\left(\dfrac{4x}{x^2-16}\right)} = \dfrac{4-x}{4+x}\cdot\dfrac{x^2-16}{4x} = \dfrac{4-x}{4+x}\cdot\dfrac{(x+4)(x-4)}{4x} = \dfrac{(4-x)(x-4)}{4x} = \dfrac{-(x-4)^2}{4x}$

27. $\dfrac{\left(\dfrac{x^2+7x+12}{x^2-7x+12}\right)}{\left(\dfrac{x^2+x-12}{x^2-x-12}\right)} = \dfrac{x^2+7x+12}{x^2-7x+12}\cdot\dfrac{x^2-x-12}{x^2+x-12} = \dfrac{(x+3)(x+4)}{(x-3)(x-4)}\cdot\dfrac{(x-4)(x+3)}{(x+4)(x-3)} = \dfrac{(x+3)^2}{(x-3)^2}$

29. $\dfrac{\left(\dfrac{2x^2-x-28}{3x^2-x-2}\right)}{\left(\dfrac{4x^2+16x+7}{3x^2+11x+6}\right)} = \dfrac{2x^2-x-28}{3x^2-x-2}\cdot\dfrac{3x^2+11x+6}{4x^2+16x+7} = \dfrac{(2x+7)(x-4)}{(3x+2)(x-1)}\cdot\dfrac{(3x+2)(x+3)}{(2x+7)(2x+1)}$

$= \dfrac{(x-4)(x+3)}{(x-1)(2x+1)}$

31. $\dfrac{x}{2}+\dfrac{5}{2} = \dfrac{5+x}{2}$

33. $\dfrac{x^2}{2x-3}-\dfrac{4}{2x-3} = \dfrac{x^2-4}{2x-3} = \dfrac{(x+2)(x-2)}{2x-3}$

35. $\dfrac{x+1}{x-3}+\dfrac{2x-3}{x-3} = \dfrac{x+1+2x-3}{x-3} = \dfrac{3x-2}{x-3}$

37. $\dfrac{3x+5}{2x-1}-\dfrac{2x-4}{2x-1} = \dfrac{(3x+5)-(2x-4)}{2x-1} = \dfrac{3x+5-2x+4}{2x-1} = \dfrac{x+9}{2x-1}$

39. $\dfrac{4}{x-2}+\dfrac{x}{2-x} = \dfrac{4}{x-2}-\dfrac{x}{x-2} = \dfrac{4-x}{x-2}$

41. $\dfrac{4}{x-1}-\dfrac{2}{x+2} = \dfrac{4(x+2)}{(x-1)(x+2)}-\dfrac{2(x-1)}{(x+2)(x-1)} = \dfrac{4x+8-2x+2}{(x+2)(x-1)} = \dfrac{2x+10}{(x+2)(x-1)}$

$= \dfrac{2(x+5)}{(x+2)(x-1)}$

43. $\dfrac{x}{x+1}+\dfrac{2x-3}{x-1} = \dfrac{x(x-1)}{(x+1)(x-1)}+\dfrac{(2x-3)(x+1)}{(x-1)(x+1)} = \dfrac{x^2-x+2x^2-x-3}{(x-1)(x+1)}$

$= \dfrac{3x^2-2x-3}{(x-1)(x+1)}$

45. $\dfrac{x-3}{x+2}-\dfrac{x+4}{x-2} = \dfrac{(x-3)(x-2)}{(x+2)(x-2)}-\dfrac{(x+4)(x+2)}{(x-2)(x+2)} = \dfrac{x^2-5x+6-(x^2+6x+8)}{(x+2)(x-2)}$

$= \dfrac{x^2-5x+6-x^2-6x-8}{(x+2)(x-2)} = \dfrac{-11x-2}{(x+2)(x-2)}$

47. $\dfrac{x}{x^2-4}+\dfrac{1}{x}=\dfrac{x^2+x^2-4}{(x)(x^2-4)}=\dfrac{2x^2-4}{(x)(x^2-4)}=\dfrac{2(x^2-2)}{(x)(x-2)(x+2)}$

49. $x^2-4=(x+2)(x-2)$
$x^2-x-2=(x+1)(x-2)$
$\therefore$ LCM is $(x+2)(x-2)(x+1)$

51. $x^3-x=x(x^2-1)=x(x+1)(x-1)$
$x^2-x=x(x-1)$
$\therefore$ LCM is $x(x+1)(x-1)$

53. $4x^3-4x^2+x=x(4x^2-4x+1)=x(2x-1)(2x-1)$
$2x^3-x^2=x^2(2x-1)$
$\qquad x^3$
$\therefore$ LCM is $x^3(2x-1)^2$

55. $x^3-x=x(x^2-1)=x(x+1)(x-1)$
$x^3-2x^2+x=x(x^2-2x+1)=x(x-1)^2$
$\qquad x^3-1=(x-1)(x^2+x+1)$
$\therefore$ LCM is $x(x+1)(x-1)^2(x^2+x+1)$

57. $\dfrac{x}{x^2-7x+6}-\dfrac{x}{x^2-2x-24}=\dfrac{x}{(x-6)(x-1)}-\dfrac{x}{(x-6)(x+4)}$
$\qquad\qquad =\dfrac{x(x+4)}{(x-6)(x-1)(x+4)}-\dfrac{x(x-1)}{(x-6)(x+4)(x-1)}$
$\qquad\qquad =\dfrac{x^2+4x-x^2+x}{(x-6)(x+4)(x-1)}=\dfrac{5x}{(x-6)(x+4)(x-1)}$

59. $\dfrac{4x}{x^2-4}-\dfrac{2}{x^2+x-6}=\dfrac{4x}{(x-2)(x+2)}-\dfrac{2}{(x+3)(x-2)}$
$\qquad\qquad =\dfrac{4x(x+3)}{(x-2)(x+2)(x+3)}-\dfrac{2(x+2)}{(x+3)(x-2)(x+2)}$
$\qquad\qquad =\dfrac{4x^2+12x-2x-4}{(x-2)(x+2)(x+3)}=\dfrac{4x^2+10x-4}{(x-2)(x+2)(x+3)}$
$\qquad\qquad =\dfrac{2(2x^2+5x-2)}{(x-2)(x+2)(x+3)}$

61. $\dfrac{3}{(x-1)^2(x+1)}+\dfrac{2}{(x-1)(x+1)^2}=\dfrac{3(x+1)+2(x-1)}{(x-1)^2(x+1)^2}=\dfrac{3x+3+2x-2}{(x-1)^2(x+1)^2}$
$\qquad\qquad =\dfrac{5x+1}{(x-1)^2(x+1)^2}$

63. $\dfrac{x+4}{x^2-x-2} - \dfrac{2x+3}{x^2+2x-8} = \dfrac{x+4}{(x-2)(x+1)} - \dfrac{2x+3}{(x+4)(x-2)}$

$= \dfrac{(x+4)(x+4)}{(x-2)(x+1)(x+4)} - \dfrac{(2x+3)(x+1)}{(x+4)(x-2)(x+1)}$

$= \dfrac{x^2+8x+16-(2x^2+5x+3)}{(x-2)(x+1)(x+4)} = \dfrac{-x^2+3x+13}{(x-2)(x+1)(x+4)}$

65. $\dfrac{1}{x} - \dfrac{2}{x^2+x} + \dfrac{3}{x^3-x^2} = \dfrac{1}{x} - \dfrac{2}{x(x+1)} + \dfrac{3}{x^2(x-1)} = \dfrac{x(x+1)(x-1)-2x(x-1)+3(x+1)}{x^2(x+1)(x-1)}$

$= \dfrac{x(x^2-1)-2x^2+2x+3x+3}{x^2(x+1)(x-1)} = \dfrac{x^3-x-2x^2+5x+3}{x^2(x+1)(x-1)} = \dfrac{x^3-2x^2+4x+3}{x^2(x+1)(x-1)}$

67. $\dfrac{1}{h}\left(\dfrac{1}{x+h} - \dfrac{1}{x}\right) = \dfrac{1}{h}\left(\dfrac{1\cdot x}{(x+h)x} - \dfrac{1(x+h)}{x(x+h)}\right) = \dfrac{1}{h}\left(\dfrac{x-x-h}{x(x+h)}\right) = \dfrac{-h}{hx(x+h)} = \dfrac{-1}{x(x+h)}$

69. $\dfrac{\left(1+\dfrac{1}{x}\right)}{\left(1-\dfrac{1}{x}\right)} = \dfrac{\left(\dfrac{x}{x}+\dfrac{1}{x}\right)}{\left(\dfrac{x}{x}-\dfrac{1}{x}\right)} = \dfrac{\left(\dfrac{x+1}{x}\right)}{\left(\dfrac{x-1}{x}\right)} = \dfrac{x+1}{x}\cdot\dfrac{x}{x-1} = \dfrac{x+1}{x-1}$

71. $\dfrac{\left(x-\dfrac{1}{x}\right)}{\left(x+\dfrac{1}{x}\right)} = \dfrac{\left(\dfrac{x^2}{x}-\dfrac{1}{x}\right)}{\left(\dfrac{x^2}{x}+\dfrac{1}{x}\right)} = \dfrac{\left(\dfrac{x^2-1}{x}\right)}{\left(\dfrac{x^2+1}{x}\right)} = \dfrac{x^2-1}{x}\cdot\dfrac{x}{x^2+1} = \dfrac{(x-1)(x+1)}{x^2+1}$

73. $\dfrac{\left(\dfrac{x+4}{x-2} - \dfrac{x-3}{x+1}\right)}{x+1} = \dfrac{\left(\dfrac{(x+4)(x+1)}{(x-2)(x+1)} - \dfrac{(x-3)(x-2)}{(x+1)(x-2)}\right)}{x+1} = \dfrac{\left(\dfrac{x^2+5x+4-(x^2-5x+6)}{(x-2)(x+1)}\right)}{x+1}$

$= \dfrac{10x-2}{(x-2)(x+1)}\cdot\dfrac{1}{x+1} = \dfrac{2(5x-1)}{(x-2)(x+1)^2}$

75. $\dfrac{\left(\dfrac{x-2}{x+2} + \dfrac{x-1}{x+1}\right)}{\left(\dfrac{x}{x+1} - \dfrac{2x-3}{x}\right)} = \dfrac{\left(\dfrac{(x-2)(x+1)}{(x+2)(x+1)} + \dfrac{(x-1)(x+2)}{(x+1)(x+2)}\right)}{\left(\dfrac{x^2}{(x+1)(x)} - \dfrac{(2x-3)(x+1)}{x(x+1)}\right)} = \dfrac{\left(\dfrac{x^2-x-2+x^2+x-2}{(x+2)(x+1)}\right)}{\left(\dfrac{x^2-(2x^2-x-3)}{x(x+1)}\right)}$

$= \dfrac{\left(\dfrac{2x^2-4}{(x+2)(x+1)}\right)}{\left(\dfrac{-x^2+x+3}{x(x+1)}\right)} = \dfrac{2(x^2-2)}{(x+2)(x+1)}\cdot\dfrac{x(x+1)}{-(x^2-x-3)}$

$= \dfrac{2x(x^2-2)}{-(x+2)(x^2-x-3)}$

77. $\quad 1 - \dfrac{1}{\left(1 - \dfrac{1}{x}\right)} = 1 - \dfrac{1}{\left(\dfrac{x-1}{x}\right)} = 1 - 1 \cdot \dfrac{x}{x-1} = \dfrac{x - 1 - x}{x - 1} = \dfrac{-1}{x-1}$

79. $\qquad \dfrac{1}{f} = (n-1)\left(\dfrac{1}{R_1} + \dfrac{1}{R_2}\right)$

$\qquad \dfrac{R_1 \cdot R_2}{f} = (n-1)\left(\dfrac{1}{R_1} + \dfrac{1}{R_2}\right) R_1 \cdot R_2$

$\qquad \dfrac{R_1 \cdot R_2}{f} = (n-1)\left(R_2 + R_1\right)$

$\qquad \dfrac{f}{R_1 \cdot R_2} = \dfrac{1}{(n-1)\left(R_2 + R_1\right)}$

$\qquad f = \dfrac{R_1 \cdot R_2}{(n-1)\left(R_2 + R_1\right)}$

$\qquad f = \dfrac{0.1(0.2)}{(1.5-1)(0.2+0.1)} = \dfrac{0.02}{0.5(0.3)} = \dfrac{0.02}{0.15} = \dfrac{2}{15}$

81. $\quad 1 + \dfrac{1}{x} = \dfrac{x+1}{x} \to a = 1, b = 1, c = 0$

$1 + \dfrac{1}{\left(1 + \dfrac{1}{x}\right)} = 1 + \dfrac{1}{\left(\dfrac{x+1}{x}\right)} = 1 + \dfrac{x}{x+1} = \dfrac{x+1+x}{x+1} = \dfrac{2x+1}{x+1} \to a = 2, b = 1, c = 1$

$1 + \dfrac{1}{1 + \dfrac{1}{1 + \dfrac{1}{x}}} = 1 + \dfrac{1}{\left(\dfrac{2x+1}{x+1}\right)} = 1 + \dfrac{x+1}{2x+1} = \dfrac{2x+1+x+1}{2x+1} = \dfrac{3x+2}{2x+1} \to a = 3, b = 2, c = 1$

$1 + \dfrac{1}{1 + \dfrac{1}{1 + \dfrac{1}{1 + \dfrac{1}{x}}}} = 1 + \dfrac{1}{\left(\dfrac{3x+2}{2x+1}\right)} = 1 + \dfrac{2x+1}{3x+2} = \dfrac{3x+2+2x+1}{3x+2} = \dfrac{5x+3}{3x+2} \to a = 5, b = 3, c = 2$

If we continue this process, the values of *a*, *b* and *c* produce the following sequences:

$\quad a : 1, 2, 3, 5, 8, 13, 21, \dots$

$\quad b : 1, 1, 2, 3, 5, 8, 13, 21, \dots$

$\quad c : 0, 1, 1, 2, 3, 5, 8, 13, 21, \dots$

In each case we have the *Fibonacci Sequence*, where the next value in the list is obtained from the sum of the previous 2 values in the list.

83. Answers will vary.

Review

R.8   Square Roots; Radicals

1. $\sqrt{25} = 5$

3. $\sqrt[3]{27} = 3$

5. $\sqrt[3]{-64} = -4$

7. $\sqrt{\dfrac{1}{9}} = \dfrac{1}{3}$

9. $\sqrt{25x^4} = 5x^2$

11. $\sqrt[3]{8(1+x)^3} = 2(1+x)$

13. $\sqrt{8} = \sqrt{4 \cdot 2} = 2\sqrt{2}$

15. $\sqrt{50} = \sqrt{25 \cdot 2} = 5\sqrt{2}$

17. $\sqrt[3]{16} = \sqrt[3]{8 \cdot 2} = 2\sqrt[3]{2}$

19. $\sqrt[3]{-16} = \sqrt[3]{-8 \cdot 2} = -2\sqrt[3]{2}$

21. $\sqrt{\dfrac{25x^3}{9x}}, x \neq 0 \quad = \sqrt{\dfrac{25x^2}{9}} = \dfrac{5}{3}|x|$

23. $\sqrt[4]{x^{12}y^8} = \sqrt[4]{\left(x^3\right)^4\left(y^2\right)^4} = x^3 y^2$

25. $\sqrt{36x} = 6\sqrt{x}$

27. $\sqrt{3x^2}\sqrt{12x} = \sqrt{36x^2 \cdot x} = 6x\sqrt{x}$

29. $\dfrac{\sqrt{3xy^3}\sqrt{2x^2y}}{\sqrt{6x^3y^4}}, x > 0, y > 0 \quad = \sqrt{\dfrac{\left(3xy^3\right)\left(2x^2y\right)}{6x^3y^4}} = \sqrt{\dfrac{6x^3y^4}{6x^3y^4}} = \sqrt{1} = 1$

31. $\sqrt{\dfrac{16y^4}{9x^2}}, x > 0, y \geq 0 \quad = \dfrac{4y^2}{3x}$

33. $\left(\sqrt{5}\sqrt[3]{9}\right)^2 = 5\sqrt[3]{81} = 5\sqrt[3]{27 \cdot 3} = 5 \cdot 3\sqrt[3]{3} = 15\sqrt[3]{3}$

35. $\sqrt{\dfrac{2x-3}{2x^4+3x^3}}\sqrt{\dfrac{x}{4x^2-9}}, x > \dfrac{3}{2}$

$= \sqrt{\dfrac{2x-3}{2x^4+3x^3} \cdot \dfrac{x}{4x^2-9}} = \sqrt{\dfrac{2x-3}{x^3(2x+3)} \cdot \dfrac{x}{(2x+3)(2x-3)}} = \sqrt{\dfrac{1}{x^2(2x+3)^2}} = \dfrac{1}{x(2x+3)}$

37. $\sqrt{\dfrac{x-1}{x+1}}\sqrt{\dfrac{x^2+2x+1}{x^2-1}}, x > 1$

$$= \sqrt{\dfrac{x-1}{x+1}\cdot\dfrac{x^2+2x+1}{x^2-1}} = \sqrt{\dfrac{x-1}{x+1}\cdot\dfrac{(x+1)^2}{(x-1)(x+1)}} = \sqrt{\dfrac{(x+1)^2}{(x+1)^2}} = \sqrt{1} = 1$$

39. $3\sqrt{2}+4\sqrt{2}=7\sqrt{2}$

41. $-\sqrt{18}+2\sqrt{8}=-\sqrt{9\cdot2}+2\sqrt{4\cdot2}=-3\sqrt{2}+4\sqrt{2}=\sqrt{2}$

43. $5\sqrt[3]{2}-2\sqrt[3]{54}=5\sqrt[3]{2}-2\sqrt[3]{27\cdot2}=5\sqrt[3]{2}-6\sqrt[3]{2}=-\sqrt[3]{2}$

45. $\sqrt{8x^3}-3\sqrt{50x}, x \geq 0$

$$\sqrt{4\cdot2x^3}-3\sqrt{25\cdot2x}=2x\sqrt{2x}-15\sqrt{2x}=\sqrt{2x}(2x-15)$$

47. $\sqrt[3]{16x^4y}-3x\sqrt[3]{2xy}+5\sqrt[3]{-2xy^4}=\sqrt[3]{8\cdot2x^4y}-3x\sqrt[3]{2xy}-5y\sqrt[3]{2xy}$

$$=2x\sqrt[3]{2xy}-3x\sqrt[3]{2xy}-5y\sqrt[3]{2xy}=\sqrt[3]{2xy}(2x-3x-5y)=\sqrt[3]{2xy}(-x-5y)$$

49. $\left(3\sqrt{6}\right)\left(4\sqrt{3}\right)=12\sqrt{18}=12\sqrt{9\cdot2}=36\sqrt{2}$

51. $\sqrt{3}\left(\sqrt{3}-4\right)=3-4\sqrt{3}$

53. $3\sqrt{7}\left(2\sqrt{7}+3\right)=6\cdot7+9\sqrt{7}=42+9\sqrt{7}$

55. $\left(\sqrt{2}-1\right)^2=\left(\sqrt{2}\right)^2-2\sqrt{2}+1=2-2\sqrt{2}+1=3-2\sqrt{2}$

57. $\left(\sqrt[3]{2}-1\right)^3=\left(\sqrt[3]{2}\right)^3-3\left(\sqrt[3]{2}\right)^2+3\left(\sqrt[3]{2}\right)-1=2-3\left(\sqrt[3]{2}\right)^2+3\left(\sqrt[3]{2}\right)-1$

$$=1-3\left(\sqrt[3]{2}\right)\left(\sqrt[3]{2}-1\right)$$

59. $\left(2\sqrt{x}-3\right)\left(2\sqrt{x}+5\right), x \geq 0 \qquad = 4x-6\sqrt{x}+10\sqrt{x}-15=4x+4\sqrt{x}-15$

61. $\sqrt{1-x^2} - \dfrac{1}{\sqrt{1-x^2}}, -1 < x < 1 \quad = \dfrac{\sqrt{1-x^2} \cdot \sqrt{1-x^2} - 1}{\sqrt{1-x^2}} = \dfrac{1-x^2-1}{\sqrt{1-x^2}} = \dfrac{-x^2}{\sqrt{1-x^2}} \cdot \dfrac{\sqrt{1-x^2}}{\sqrt{1-x^2}}$

$$= \dfrac{-x^2\sqrt{1-x^2}}{(1+x)(1-x)}$$

63. $\dfrac{2}{\sqrt{5}} \cdot \dfrac{\sqrt{5}}{\sqrt{5}} = \dfrac{2\sqrt{5}}{5}$

65. $\dfrac{8}{\sqrt{6}} \cdot \dfrac{\sqrt{6}}{\sqrt{6}} = \dfrac{8\sqrt{6}}{6} = \dfrac{4\sqrt{6}}{3}$

67. $\dfrac{1}{\sqrt{x}}, x > 0 \quad \dfrac{1}{\sqrt{x}} \cdot \dfrac{\sqrt{x}}{\sqrt{x}} = \dfrac{\sqrt{x}}{x}$

69. $\dfrac{3}{5+\sqrt{2}} \cdot \dfrac{5-\sqrt{2}}{5-\sqrt{2}} = \dfrac{3(5-\sqrt{2})}{25-2} = \dfrac{3(5-\sqrt{2})}{23}$

71. $\dfrac{3}{4+\sqrt{7}} \cdot \dfrac{4-\sqrt{7}}{4-\sqrt{7}} = \dfrac{3(4-\sqrt{7})}{16-7} = \dfrac{3(4-\sqrt{7})}{9} = \dfrac{4-\sqrt{7}}{3}$

73. $\dfrac{\sqrt{5}}{2+3\sqrt{5}} \cdot \dfrac{2-3\sqrt{5}}{2-3\sqrt{5}} = \dfrac{\sqrt{5}(2-3\sqrt{5})}{4-9\cdot5} = \dfrac{\sqrt{5}(2-3\sqrt{5})}{4-45} = \dfrac{\sqrt{5}(2-3\sqrt{5})}{-41} = \dfrac{2\sqrt{5}-15}{-41}$

75. $\dfrac{\sqrt{3}-\sqrt{2}}{\sqrt{3}+\sqrt{2}} \cdot \dfrac{\sqrt{3}-\sqrt{2}}{\sqrt{3}-\sqrt{2}} = \dfrac{3-2\sqrt{3}\sqrt{2}+2}{3-2} = 5-2\sqrt{6}$

77. $\dfrac{1}{\sqrt{x}+2}, x \geq 0 \quad \dfrac{1}{\sqrt{x}+2} \cdot \dfrac{\sqrt{x}-2}{\sqrt{x}-2} = \dfrac{\sqrt{x}-2}{x-4}$

79. $\sqrt{2} \approx 1.41$

81. $\sqrt[3]{4} \approx 1.59$

83. $\dfrac{2+\sqrt{3}}{3-\sqrt{5}} \approx 4.88$

85. $\dfrac{3\sqrt[3]{5}-\sqrt{2}}{\sqrt{3}} \approx 2.14$

87. (a) $V = 40(12)^2 \sqrt{\dfrac{96}{12}-0.608} \approx 15660.422$ gallons

(b) $V = 40(1)^2 \sqrt{\dfrac{96}{1}-0.608} \approx 390.68$ gallons

(b) $v = \sqrt{64\cdot16+0^2} = \sqrt{1024} = 32$ feet per second

89.　　$T = 2\pi\sqrt{\dfrac{64}{32}} = 2\pi\sqrt{2} \approx 8.89$ seconds

91.　　$T = 2\pi\sqrt{\dfrac{64}{\left(\dfrac{8}{12}\right)}} = 2\pi\sqrt{96} \approx 61.56$ seconds

93.　　if $a = -5$, then $\sqrt{a^2} = \sqrt{(-5)^2} = \sqrt{25} = 5 \neq a$.

Since we use the principal square root, which is always non-negative,

$$\sqrt{a^2} = \begin{cases} a & \text{if } a \geq 0 \\ -a & \text{if } a < 0 \end{cases}$$

which is the definition of $|a|$, so $\sqrt{a^2} = |a|$.

Chapter R

Review

R.9 Rational Exponents

1. $8^{2/3} = \left(2^3\right)^{2/3} = 2^2 = 4$

3. $(-27)^{1/3} = \left((-3)^3\right)^{1/3} = -3$

5. $(4)^{-3/2} = \left(2^2\right)^{-3/2} = (2)^{-6/2} = (2)^{-3} = \dfrac{1}{2^3} = \dfrac{1}{8}$

7. $9^{-3/2} = \left(3^2\right)^{-3/2} = 3^{-3} = \dfrac{1}{3^3} = \dfrac{1}{27}$

9. $\left(\dfrac{9}{4}\right)^{3/2} = \left(\dfrac{3^2}{2^2}\right)^{3/2} = \dfrac{3^{6/2}}{2^{6/2}} = \dfrac{3^3}{2^3} = \dfrac{27}{8}$

11. $\left(\dfrac{4}{9}\right)^{-3/2} = \left(\dfrac{2^2}{3^2}\right)^{-3/2} = \dfrac{2^{-6/2}}{3^{-6/2}} = \dfrac{2^{-3}}{3^{-3}} = \dfrac{3^3}{2^3} = \dfrac{27}{8}$

13. $4^{1.5} = 4^{3/2} = \left(2^2\right)^{3/2} = 2^{6/2} = 2^3 = 8$

15. $\left(\dfrac{1}{4}\right)^{-1.5} = \left(\dfrac{1}{4}\right)^{-3/2} = 4^{3/2} = \left(2^2\right)^{3/2} = 2^{6/2} = 2^3 = 8$

17. $\left(\sqrt{3}\right)^6 = \left(3^{1/2}\right)^6 = 3^{6/2} = 3^3 = 27$

19. $\left(\sqrt{5}\right)^{-2} = \left(5^{1/2}\right)^{-2} = 5^{-2/2} = 5^{-1} = \dfrac{1}{5}$

21. $3^{1/2} \cdot 3^{3/2} = 3^{1/2+3/2} = 3^2 = 9$

23. $\dfrac{7^{1/3}}{7^{4/3}} = 7^{1/3-4/3} = 7^{-3/3} = 7^{-1} = \dfrac{1}{7}$

25. $2^{1/3} \cdot 4^{1/3} = (2 \cdot 4)^{1/3} = 8^{1/3} = \left(2^3\right)^{1/3} = 2^{3/3} = 2^1 = 2$

27. $\sqrt[4]{3} \cdot \sqrt[4]{27} = \sqrt[4]{3 \cdot 27} = \sqrt[4]{81} = 81^{1/4} = \left(3^4\right)^{1/4} = 3^{4/4} = 3^1 = 3$

29. $\left(\sqrt[4]{2}\right)^{-4} = \left(2^{1/4}\right)^{-4} = 2^{-4/4} = 2^{-1} = \dfrac{1}{2}$

31. $\left(\sqrt[3]{6}\right)^2 = \left(6^{1/3}\right)^2 = 6^{2/3} = \sqrt[3]{6^2} = \sqrt[3]{36}$

33. $\sqrt{2}\ \sqrt[3]{2} = 2^{1/2} \cdot 2^{1/3} = 2^{1/2+1/3} = 2^{5/6} = \sqrt[6]{32}$

35. $\sqrt[8]{x^4} = \left(x^4\right)^{1/8} = x^{4/8} = x^{1/2}$

37. $\sqrt{x^3}\ \sqrt[4]{x} = x^{3/2} \cdot x^{1/4} = x^{3/2+1/4} = x^{7/4}$

39. $x^{3/2} \cdot x^{-1/2} = x^{3/2-1/2} = x^1 = x$

41. $\left(x^3 y^6\right)^{1/3} = \left(x^3\right)^{1/3}\left(y^6\right)^{1/3} = x y^2$

43. $\left(x^2 y\right)^{1/3}\left(x y^2\right)^{2/3} = x^{2/3} y^{1/3} x^{2/3} y^{4/3} = x^{4/3} y^{5/3}$

45. $\left(16 x^2 y^{-1/3}\right)^{3/4} = \left(2^4 x^2 y^{-1/3}\right)^{3/4} = 2^3 x^{3/2} y^{-1/4} = \dfrac{8 x^{3/2}}{y^{1/4}}$

47. $\left(\dfrac{x^{2/5} y^{-1/5}}{x^{-1/3}}\right)^{15} = \left(\dfrac{x^{2/5} x^{1/3}}{y^{1/5}}\right)^{15} = \dfrac{x^{30/5} x^{15/3}}{y^{15/5}} = \dfrac{x^6 x^5}{y^3} = \dfrac{x^{6+5}}{y^3} = \dfrac{x^{11}}{y^3}$

49. $\dfrac{x}{(1+x)^{1/2}} + 2(1+x)^{1/2} = \dfrac{x + 2(1+x)^{1/2}(1+x)^{1/2}}{(1+x)^{1/2}} = \dfrac{x + 2(1+x)}{(1+x)^{1/2}} = \dfrac{x + 2 + 2x}{(1+x)^{1/2}} = \dfrac{3x + 2}{(1+x)^{1/2}}$

51. $2x\left(x^2+1\right)^{1/2} + x^2 \cdot \dfrac{1}{2}\left(x^2+1\right)^{-1/2} \cdot 2x = 2x\left(x^2+1\right)^{1/2} + \dfrac{x^3}{\left(x^2+1\right)^{1/2}}$

$= \dfrac{2x\left(x^2+1\right)^{1/2} \cdot \left(x^2+1\right)^{1/2} + x^3}{\left(x^2+1\right)^{1/2}} = \dfrac{2x\left(x^2+1\right)^{1/2+1/2} + x^3}{\left(x^2+1\right)^{1/2}} = \dfrac{2x\left(x^2+1\right)^1 + x^3}{\left(x^2+1\right)^{1/2}}$

$= \dfrac{2x^3 + 2x + x^3}{\left(x^2+1\right)^{1/2}} = \dfrac{3x^3 + 2x}{\left(x^2+1\right)^{1/2}} = \dfrac{x\left(3x^2+2\right)}{\left(x^2+1\right)^{1/2}}$

53. $\sqrt{4x+3} \cdot \dfrac{1}{2\sqrt{x-5}} + \sqrt{x-5} \cdot \dfrac{1}{5\sqrt{4x+3}}, x > 5$

$= \dfrac{\sqrt{4x+3}}{2\sqrt{x-5}} + \dfrac{\sqrt{x-5}}{5\sqrt{4x+3}} = \dfrac{\sqrt{4x+3} \cdot \sqrt{4x+3} + \sqrt{x-5} \cdot \sqrt{x-5}}{10\sqrt{x-5}\sqrt{4x+3}}$

$= \dfrac{4x+3+x-5}{10\sqrt{(x-5)(4x+3)}} = \dfrac{5x-2}{10\sqrt{(x-5)(4x+3)}}$

55. $$\frac{\left(\sqrt{1+x}-x\cdot\dfrac{1}{2\sqrt{1+x}}\right)}{1+x}=\frac{\left(\sqrt{1+x}-\dfrac{x}{2\sqrt{1+x}}\right)}{1+x}=\frac{\left(\dfrac{2\sqrt{1+x}\sqrt{1+x}-x}{2\sqrt{1+x}}\right)}{1+x}$$

$$=\frac{2(1+x)-x}{2(1+x)^{1/2}}\cdot\frac{1}{1+x}=\frac{2+x}{2(1+x)^{3/2}}$$

57. $$\frac{(x+4)^{1/2}-2x(x+4)^{-1/2}}{x+4}=\frac{\left((x+4)^{1/2}-\dfrac{2x}{(x+4)^{1/2}}\right)}{x+4}=\frac{\left((x+4)^{1/2}\cdot\dfrac{(x+4)^{1/2}}{(x+4)^{1/2}}-\dfrac{2x}{(x+4)^{1/2}}\right)}{x+4}$$

$$=\frac{\left(\dfrac{x+4-2x}{(x+4)^{1/2}}\right)}{x+4}=\frac{-x+4}{(x+4)^{1/2}}\cdot\frac{1}{x+4}=\frac{-x+4}{(x+4)^{3/2}}$$

59. $$\frac{\left(\dfrac{x^2}{(x^2-1)^{1/2}}-(x^2-1)^{1/2}\right)}{x^2},x<-1\ \text{ or }\ x>1$$

$$=\frac{\left(\dfrac{x^2-(x^2-1)^{1/2}\cdot(x^2-1)^{1/2}}{(x^2-1)^{1/2}}\right)}{x^2}=\frac{x^2-(x^2-1)^{1/2}\cdot(x^2-1)^{1/2}}{(x^2-1)^{1/2}}\cdot\frac{1}{x^2}$$

$$=\frac{x^2-(x^2-1)}{(x^2-1)^{1/2}}\cdot\frac{1}{x^2}=\frac{x^2-x^2+1}{(x^2-1)^{1/2}}\cdot\frac{1}{x^2}=\frac{1}{x^2(x^2-1)^{1/2}}$$

61. $$\frac{\left(\dfrac{1+x^2}{2\sqrt{x}}-2x\sqrt{x}\right)}{(1+x^2)^2},x>0$$

$$=\frac{\left(\dfrac{1+x^2-(2\sqrt{x})(2x\sqrt{x})}{2\sqrt{x}}\right)}{(1+x^2)^2}=\frac{1+x^2-(2\sqrt{x})(2x\sqrt{x})}{2\sqrt{x}}\cdot\frac{1}{(1+x^2)^2}$$

$$=\frac{1+x^2-4x^2}{2\sqrt{x}}\cdot\frac{1}{(1+x^2)^2}=\frac{1-3x^2}{2\sqrt{x}(1+x^2)^2}$$

63. $(x+1)^{3/2} + x \cdot \frac{3}{2}(x+1)^{1/2} = (x+1)^{1/2}\left(x+1+\frac{3}{2}x\right) = (x+1)^{1/2}\left(\frac{5}{2}x+1\right) = \frac{1}{2}(x+1)^{1/2}(5x+2)$

65. $6x^{1/2}\left(x^2+x\right) - 8x^{3/2} - 8x^{1/2} = 2x^{1/2}\left(3(x^2+x)-4x-4\right) = 2x^{1/2}\left(3x^2-x-4\right)$
$$= 2x^{1/2}(3x-4)(x+1)$$

67. $3\left(x^2+4\right)^{4/3} + x \cdot 4\left(x^2+4\right)^{1/3} \cdot 2x = \left(x^2+4\right)^{1/3}\left[3\left(x^2+4\right)+8x^2\right]$
$$= \left(x^2+4\right)^{1/3}\left[3x^2+12+8x^2\right] = \left(x^2+4\right)^{1/3}\left(11x^2+12\right)$$

69. $4(3x+5)^{1/3}(2x+3)^{3/2} + 3(3x+5)^{4/3}(2x+3)^{1/2}, x \geq -\frac{3}{2}$
$$= (3x+5)^{1/3}(2x+3)^{1/2}\left[4(2x+3)+3(3x+5)\right] = (3x+5)^{1/3}(2x+3)^{1/2}(8x+12+9x+15)$$
$$= (3x+5)^{1/3}(2x+3)^{1/2}(17x+27)$$

71. $3x^{-1/2} + \frac{3}{2}x^{1/2}, x > 0$

$$= \frac{3}{x^{1/2}} + \frac{3}{2}x^{1/2} = \frac{3 \cdot 2 + 3x^{1/2} \cdot x^{1/2}}{2x^{1/2}} = \frac{6+3x}{2x^{1/2}} = \frac{3(2+x)}{2x^{1/2}}$$

Review

R.R Review Exercises

1. $3 - 4 \cdot 5 + 6 = 3 - 20 + 6 = -17 + 6 = -11$

3. $\dfrac{3}{4} - \dfrac{7}{12} = \dfrac{3 \cdot 3 - 7}{12} = \dfrac{9 - 7}{12} = \dfrac{2}{12} = \dfrac{1}{6}$

5. $\dfrac{\frac{15}{2} + \frac{1}{4}}{\frac{2}{3}} = \dfrac{\frac{15 \cdot 2 + 1}{4}}{\frac{2}{3}} = \dfrac{\frac{31}{4}}{\frac{2}{3}} = \dfrac{31}{4} \cdot \dfrac{3}{2} = \dfrac{93}{8}$

7. $5^2 - 3^3 \cdot 2 = 25 - 27 \cdot 2 = 25 - 54 = -29$

9. $\dfrac{2^{-3} \cdot 5^0}{4^2} = \dfrac{5^0}{2^3 \cdot 4^2} = \dfrac{1}{8 \cdot 16} = \dfrac{1}{128}$

11.
$$\left(2\sqrt{5} - 2\right)\left(2\sqrt{5} + 2\right) = \left(2\sqrt{5}\right)^2 - 2^2 = 4 \cdot 5 - 4 = 20 - 4 = 16$$

13. $\left(\dfrac{8}{27}\right)^{-2/3} = \left(\dfrac{27}{8}\right)^{\frac{2}{3}} = \dfrac{27^{\frac{2}{3}}}{8^{\frac{2}{3}}} = \dfrac{\left(3^3\right)^{\frac{2}{3}}}{\left(2^3\right)^{\frac{2}{3}}} = \dfrac{3^2}{2^2} = \dfrac{9}{4}$

15. $\left(\sqrt[3]{3}\right)^{-3} = \left(3^{1/3}\right)^{-3} = 3^{-3/3} = 3^{-1} = \dfrac{1}{3}$

17. $\left|6 - 8^{1/3}\right| = \left|6 - \left(2^3\right)^{1/3}\right| = \left|6 - 2^{3/3}\right| = \left|6 - 2^1\right| = \left|6 - 2\right| = \left|4\right| = 4$

19. $\sqrt{\left|3^2 - 5^2\right|} = \sqrt{\left|9 - 25\right|} = \sqrt{\left|-16\right|} = \sqrt{16} = 4$

21. $\dfrac{x^{-2}}{y^{-2}} = \dfrac{y^2}{x^2}$

23. $\dfrac{\left(x^2 y\right)^{-4}}{\left(xy\right)^{-3}} = \dfrac{\left(xy\right)^3}{\left(x^2 y\right)^4} = \dfrac{x^3 y^3}{x^{2 \cdot 4} \cdot y^4} = \dfrac{x^3 y^3}{x^8 \cdot y^4} = \dfrac{1}{x^{8-3} \cdot y^{4-3}} = \dfrac{1}{x^5 y}$

25. $\dfrac{\left(\dfrac{x^2}{y}\right)^2}{\left(\dfrac{x}{y^2}\right)^3} = \dfrac{\left(\dfrac{x^{2\cdot2}}{y^2}\right)}{\left(\dfrac{x^3}{y^{2\cdot3}}\right)} = \dfrac{\left(\dfrac{x^4}{y^2}\right)}{\left(\dfrac{x^3}{y^6}\right)} = \dfrac{x^4}{y^2}\cdot\dfrac{y^6}{x^3} = x^{4-3}\cdot y^{6-2} = x^1 y^4 = xy^4$

27. $\dfrac{x^{-2}}{x^{-2}+y^{-2}} = \dfrac{\dfrac{1}{x^2}}{\dfrac{1}{x^2}+\dfrac{1}{y^2}} = \dfrac{\dfrac{1}{x^2}}{\dfrac{y^2+x^2}{x^2 y^2}} = \dfrac{1}{x^2}\cdot\dfrac{x^2 y^2}{y^2+x^2} = \dfrac{y^2}{y^2+x^2}$

29. $\left(25x^{-4/3}y^{-2/3}\right)^{3/2} = (25)^{3/2}\left(x^{(-4/3)(3/2)}\right)\left(y^{(-2/3)(3/2)}\right) = \left(5^2\right)^{3/2}\left(x^{-12/6}\right)\left(y^{-6/6}\right)$

$= \left(5^{6/2}\right)\left(x^{-2}\right)\left(y^{-1}\right) = \dfrac{5^3}{x^2 y} = \dfrac{125}{x^2 y}$

31. $\left(\dfrac{2x^{-1/2}}{y^{-3/4}}\right)^{-4} = \dfrac{(2)^{-4}\left(x^{-1/2}\right)^{-4}}{\left(y^{-3/4}\right)^{-4}} = \dfrac{(2)^{-4}\left(x^{4/2}\right)}{\left(y^{12/4}\right)} = \dfrac{x^2}{2^4 y^3} = \dfrac{x^2}{16y^3}$

33. $(2x-3)(-4x+2) = -8x^2+4x+12x-6 = -8x^2+16x-6$

35. $4\left(3x^3-2x^2+1\right) - 3\left(x^3+4x^2-2x-3\right) = 12x^3-8x^2+4-3x^3-12x^2+6x+9$

$= 9x^3-20x^2+6x+13$

37. $(2x-5)\left(3x^2+2\right) = 6x^3+4x-15x^2-10 = 6x^3-15x^2+4x-10$

39. $(x+1)(x+2)(x-3) = \left(x^2+2x+x+2\right)(x-3) = \left(x^2+3x+2\right)(x-3)$

$= x^3-3x^2+3x^2-9x+2x-6 = x^3-7x-6$

41. Divide:

$$
\begin{array}{r}
3x^2+8x+25 \\
x-3\overline{)3x^3-\ x^2+x+4} \\
\underline{3x^3-9x^2} \\
8x^2+\ x+4 \\
\underline{8x^2-24x} \\
25x+4 \\
\underline{25x-75} \\
79
\end{array}
$$

Check :

$(x-3)(3x^2+8x+25)+(79)$

$= 3x^3+8x^2+25x-9x^2-24x-75+79$

$= 3x^3-x^2+x+4$

The quotient is $3x^2+8x+25$; the remainder is 79.

43.   Divide:

$$
\begin{array}{r}
-3x^2 + 4 \\
x^2 + 1\overline{)\,-3x^4 + 0\cdot x^3 + x^2 + 0\cdot x + 2} \\
\underline{-3x^4 \qquad\quad -3x^2} \\
4x^2 \qquad +2 \\
\underline{4x^2 \qquad +4} \\
-2
\end{array}
$$

The quotient is $-3x^2 + 4$; the remainder is -2.

Check :

$(x^2 + 1)(-3x^2 + 4) + (-2)$

$= -3x^4 + 4x^2 - 3x^2 + 4 - 2$

$= -3x^4 + x^2 + 2$

45.   Divide:

$$
\begin{array}{r}
8x^2 + 24x + 62 \\
x^2 - 3x + 1\overline{)\,8x^4 + 0\cdot x^3 - 2x^2 + 5x + 1} \\
\underline{8x^4 \; - 24x^3 \; + 8x^2} \\
24x^3 - 10x^2 + 5x + 1 \\
\underline{24x^3 - 72x^2 + 24x} \\
62x^2 - 19x \quad + 1 \\
\underline{62x^2 - 186x + 62} \\
167x - 61
\end{array}
$$

Check : $(x^2 - 3x + 1)(8x^2 + 24x + 62) + (167x - 61)$

$= 8x^4 + 24x^3 + 62x^2 - 24x^3 - 72x^2 - 186x + 8x^2 + 24x + 62 + 167x - 61$

$= 8x^4 - 2x^2 + 5x + 1$ The quotient is $8x^2 + 24x + 62$; the remainder is $167x - 61$.

47.   Divide:

$$
\begin{array}{r}
x^4 - x^3 + x^2 - x + 1 \\
x + 1\overline{)\,x^5 + 0\cdot x^4 + 0\cdot x^3 + 0\cdot x^2 + 0\cdot x + 1} \\
\underline{x^5 \; + x^4} \\
-x^4 \qquad\qquad\qquad\qquad + 1 \\
\underline{-x^4 - x^3} \\
x^3 \qquad\qquad\qquad + 1 \\
\underline{x^3 + x^2} \\
-x^2 \qquad\quad +1 \\
\underline{-x^2 - x \qquad +1} \\
x \qquad +1 \\
\underline{x \qquad\quad +1} \\
0
\end{array}
$$

Check :

$(x + 1)(x^4 - x^3 + x^2 - x + 1) + (0)$

$= x^5 - x^4 + x^3 - x^2 + x + x^4 - x^3 + x^2 - x + 1$

$= x^5 + 1$

The quotient is $x^4 - x^3 + x^2 - x + 1$; the remainder is 0.

49. Divide:

$$\begin{array}{r} 3x^4 - 2x^2 + 1 \\ 2x+1{\overline{\smash{\big)}\,6x^5 + 3x^4 - 4x^3 - 2x^2 + 2x + 1}} \end{array}$$

$$\underline{6x^5 + 3x^4}$$
$$-4x^3 - 2x^2 + 2x + 1$$
$$\underline{-4x^3 - 2x^2}$$
$$2x + 1$$
$$\underline{2x + 1}$$
$$0$$

Check:

$(2x+1)(3x^4 - 2x^2 + 1) + (0)$

$= 6x^5 - 4x^3 + 2x + 3x^4 - 2x^2 + 1$

$= 6x^5 + 3x^4 - 4x^3 - 2x^2 + 2x + 1$

The quotient is $3x^4 - 2x^2 + 1$; the remainder is 0.

51. $x^2 + 5x - 14 = (x+7)(x-2)$ 53. $6x^2 - 5x - 6 = (3x+2)(2x-3)$

55. $3x^2 - 15x - 42 = (3x+6)(x-7)$

57. $8x^3 + 1 = (2x+1)\left((2x)^2 - (2x)(1) + 1^2\right) = (2x+1)(4x^2 - 2x + 1)$

59. $2x^3 + 3x^2 - 2x - 3 = x^2(2x+3) - (2x+3) = (2x+3)(x^2-1)$
$$= (2x+3)(x-1)(x+1)$$

61. $25x^2 - 4 = (5x+2)(5x-2)$

63. $9x^2 + 1$; a sum of perfect squares is always prime over the set of real numbers

65. $\dfrac{2x^2 + 11x + 14}{x^2 - 4} = \dfrac{(2x+7)(x+2)}{(x+2)(x-2)} = \dfrac{2x+7}{x-2}$

67. $\dfrac{9x^2 - 1}{x^2 - 9} \cdot \dfrac{3x - 9}{9x^2 + 6x + 1} = \dfrac{(3x+1)(3x-1)}{(x+3)(x-3)} \cdot \dfrac{3(x-3)}{(3x+1)^2} = \dfrac{3(3x-1)(x-3)}{(x+3)(3x+1)}$

69. $\dfrac{x+1}{x-1} - \dfrac{x-1}{x+1} = \dfrac{(x+1)(x+1) - (x-1)(x-1)}{(x-1)(x+1)} = \dfrac{(x^2 + 2x + 1) - (x^2 - 2x + 1)}{(x-1)(x+1)}$

$$= \dfrac{x^2 + 2x + 1 - x^2 + 2x - 1}{(x-1)(x+1)} = \dfrac{4x}{(x-1)(x+1)}$$

71. $\dfrac{3x+4}{x^2-4} - \dfrac{2x-3}{x^2+4x+4} = \dfrac{3x+4}{(x+2)(x-2)} - \dfrac{2x-3}{(x+2)^2} = \dfrac{(3x+4)(x-2) - (2x-3)(x-3)}{(x+2)^2(x-2)}$

$= \dfrac{3x^2-6x+4x-8 - (2x^2-6x-3x+9)}{(x+2)^2(x-2)} = \dfrac{3x^2-2x-8 - (2x^2-9x+9)}{(x+2)^2(x-2)}$

$= \dfrac{3x^2-2x-8-2x^2+9x-9}{(x+2)^2(x-2)} = \dfrac{x^2+7x-17}{(x+2)^2(x-2)}$

73. $\dfrac{4}{\sqrt{5}} \cdot \dfrac{\sqrt{5}}{\sqrt{5}} = \dfrac{4\sqrt{5}}{5}$

75. $\dfrac{2}{1-\sqrt{2}} \cdot \dfrac{1-\sqrt{2}}{1-\sqrt{2}} = \dfrac{2(1-\sqrt{2})}{1-(\sqrt{2})^2} = \dfrac{2(1-\sqrt{2})}{1-2} = \dfrac{2(1-\sqrt{2})}{-1} = -2(1-\sqrt{2})$

77. $\dfrac{1+\sqrt{5}}{1-\sqrt{5}} \cdot \dfrac{1+\sqrt{5}}{1+\sqrt{5}} = \dfrac{1+2\sqrt{5}+(\sqrt{5})^2}{1-(\sqrt{5})^2} = \dfrac{1+2\sqrt{5}+5}{1-5} = \dfrac{6+2\sqrt{5}}{-4} = \dfrac{-3-\sqrt{5}}{2}$

79. $(2+x^2)^{1/2} + x \cdot \dfrac{1}{2}(2+x^2)^{-1/2} \cdot 2x$

$= (2+x^2)^{1/2} + \dfrac{2x^2}{2(2+x^2)^{1/2}} = (2+x^2)^{1/2} + \dfrac{x^2}{(2+x^2)^{1/2}}$

$= \dfrac{(2+x^2)^{1/2}(2+x^2)^{1/2} + x^2}{(2+x^2)^{1/2}} = \dfrac{2+x^2+x^2}{(2+x^2)^{1/2}} = \dfrac{2+2x^2}{(2+x^2)^{1/2}} = \dfrac{2(1+x^2)}{(2+x^2)^{1/2}}$

81. $\dfrac{(x+4)^{1/2} \cdot 2x - x^2 \cdot \dfrac{1}{2}(x+4)^{-1/2}}{x+4}, x > -4$

$= \dfrac{(x+4)^{1/2} \cdot 2x - \dfrac{x^2}{2(x+4)^{1/2}}}{x+4} = \dfrac{\dfrac{2(x+4)^{1/2}(x+4)^{1/2} \cdot 2x - x^2}{2(x+4)^{1/2}}}{x+4}$

$= \dfrac{\dfrac{2(x+4) \cdot 2x - x^2}{2(x+4)^{1/2}}}{x+4} = \dfrac{\dfrac{4x^2 - x^2 + 16x}{2(x+4)^{1/2}}}{x+4} = \left(\dfrac{3x^2+16x}{2(x+4)^{1/2}}\right)\left(\dfrac{1}{x+4}\right) = \dfrac{3x^2+16x}{2(x+4)^{3/2}} = \dfrac{x(3x+16)}{2(x+4)^{3/2}}$

83. $C(x) = 3000 + 6x - \dfrac{x^2}{1000}$

   (a) $C(1000) = 3000 + 6(1000) - \dfrac{(1000)^2}{1000} = 3000 + 6000 - 1000 = \$8000$

   (b) $C(3000) = 3000 + 6(3000) - \dfrac{(3000)^2}{1000} = 3000 + 18000 - 9000 = \$12000$

85.   The total area enclosed by the window is given by

   Total Area = area of the triangle + area of the rectangle

   Total Area $= \dfrac{1}{2}(base)(height) + (length)(width)$

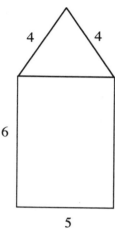

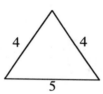

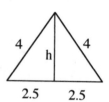

By the Pythagorean Theorem we have
$$(2.5)^2 + h^2 = (4)^2$$
$$h^2 = (4)^2 - (2.5)^2 = 16 - 6.25$$
$$h = \sqrt{9.75}$$

Total Area $= \dfrac{1}{2}(5)\left(\sqrt{9.75}\right) + (6)(5) \approx 37.81$ square feet.

The perimeter of the window $= 4 + 4 + 6 + 5 + 6 = 25$. So the wood frame requires 25 feet of wood.

87   Pond Area = area of outer circle - area of inner circle
$$= \pi(5)^2 - \pi(3)^2 = 25\pi - 9\pi = 16\pi \approx 50.27 \text{ square feet}$$

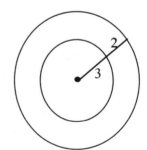

   Outer Perimeter $= 2\pi(\text{outer radius}) = 2\pi(5)$
   $= 10\pi \approx 314.16$ feet

89.   Answers will vary.

91. Since 1 day = 24 hours, we compute $\dfrac{12997}{24} = 541.54\overline{16}$.

Now we only need to consider the decimal part of the answer in terms of a 24 hour day. That is, $(0.54\overline{16})(24) \approx 13$ hours. So it must be 13 hours later than 12 noon, which makes the time 1 AM CST.

Equations and Inequalities

1.1 Equations

1.
$$7x = 21$$
$$\frac{7x}{7} = \frac{21}{7}$$
$$x = 3$$

3.
$$3x + 15 = 0$$
$$3x + 15 - 15 = 0 - 15$$
$$3x = -15$$
$$\frac{3x}{3} = \frac{-15}{3}$$
$$x = -5$$

5.
$$2x - 3 = 0$$
$$2x - 3 + 3 = 0 + 3$$
$$2x = 3$$
$$\frac{2x}{2} = \frac{3}{2}$$
$$x = \frac{3}{2}$$

7.
$$\frac{1}{3}x = \frac{5}{12}$$
$$(3)\left(\frac{1}{3}x\right) = \left(\frac{5}{12}\right)(3)$$
$$x = \frac{5}{4}$$

9.
$$3x + 4 = x$$
$$3x + 4 - 4 = x - 4$$
$$3x = x - 4$$
$$3x - x = x - 4 - x$$
$$2x = -4$$
$$\frac{2x}{2} = \frac{-4}{2}$$
$$x = -2$$

11.
$$2t - 6 = 3 - t$$
$$2t - 6 + 6 = 3 - t + 6$$
$$2t = 9 - t$$
$$2t + t = 9 - t + t$$
$$3t = 9$$
$$\frac{3t}{3} = \frac{9}{3}$$
$$t = 3$$

13.
$$6 - x = 2x + 9$$
$$6 - x - 6 = 2x + 9 - 6$$
$$-x = 2x + 3$$
$$-x - 2x = 2x + 3 - 2x$$
$$-3x = 3$$
$$\frac{-3x}{-3} = \frac{3}{-3} \rightarrow x = -1$$

15.
$$3 + 2n = 4n + 7$$
$$3 + 2n - 3 = 4n + 7 - 3$$
$$2n = 4n + 4$$
$$2n - 4n = 4n + 4 - 4n$$
$$-2n = 4$$
$$\frac{-2n}{-2} = \frac{4}{-2} \rightarrow n = -2$$

17.
$$2(3 + 2x) = 3(x - 4)$$
$$6 + 4x = 3x - 12$$
$$6 + 4x - 6 = 3x - 12 - 6$$
$$4x = 3x - 18$$
$$4x - 3x = 3x - 18 - 3x$$
$$x = -18$$

19.
$$8x - (3x + 2) = 3x - 10$$
$$8x - 3x - 2 = 3x - 10$$
$$5x - 2 = 3x - 10$$
$$5x - 2 + 2 = 3x - 10 + 2$$
$$5x = 3x - 8$$
$$5x - 3x = 3x - 8 - 3x$$
$$2x = -8$$
$$\frac{2x}{2} = \frac{-8}{2} \rightarrow x = -4$$

21.
$$\frac{3}{2}x + 2 = \frac{1}{2} - \frac{1}{2}x$$
$$\frac{3}{2}x + 2 - 2 = \frac{1}{2} - \frac{1}{2}x - 2$$
$$\frac{3}{2}x = -\frac{3}{2} - \frac{1}{2}x$$
$$\frac{3}{2}x + \frac{1}{2}x = -\frac{3}{2} - \frac{1}{2}x + \frac{1}{2}x$$
$$2x = -\frac{3}{2}$$
$$\left(\frac{1}{2}\right)(2x) = \left(-\frac{3}{2}\right)\left(\frac{1}{2}\right)$$
$$x = -\frac{3}{4}$$

23.
$$\frac{1}{2}x - 5 = \frac{3}{4}x$$
$$\frac{1}{2}x - 5 + 5 = \frac{3}{4}x + 5$$
$$\frac{1}{2}x = \frac{3}{4}x + 5$$
$$\frac{1}{2}x - \frac{3}{4}x = \frac{3}{4}x + 5 - \frac{3}{4}x$$
$$\frac{2}{4}x - \frac{3}{4}x = 5$$
$$-\frac{1}{4}x = 5$$
$$(-4)\left(-\frac{1}{4}x\right) = (5)(-4)$$
$$x = -20$$

25.
$$\frac{2}{3}p = \frac{1}{2}p + \frac{1}{3}$$
$$6 \cdot \left(\frac{2}{3}p\right) = 6 \cdot \left(\frac{1}{2}p + \frac{1}{3}\right)$$
$$4p = 3p + 2$$
$$4p - 3p = 3p + 2 - 3p$$
$$p = 2$$

27.
$$0.9t = 0.4 + 0.1t$$
$$0.9t - 0.1t = 0.4 + 0.1t - 0.1t$$
$$0.8t = 0.4$$
$$\frac{0.8t}{0.8} = \frac{0.4}{0.8} \rightarrow t = 0.5$$

29.
$$\frac{x+1}{3} + \frac{x+2}{7} = 2$$
$$(21)\left(\frac{x+1}{3} + \frac{x+2}{7}\right) = (2)(21)$$
$$(21)\left(\frac{x+1}{3}\right) + (21)\left(\frac{x+2}{7}\right) = 42$$
$$7(x+1) + (3)(x+2) = 42$$
$$7x+7+3x+6 = 42$$
$$10x+13 = 42$$
$$10x+13-13 = 42-13$$
$$10x = 29$$
$$\frac{10x}{10} = \frac{29}{10}$$
$$x = 2.9$$

31.
$$\frac{2}{y} + \frac{4}{y} = 3$$
$$y\left(\frac{2}{y} + \frac{4}{y}\right) = y(3)$$
$$2+4 = 3y$$
$$6 = 3y$$
$$\frac{6}{3} = \frac{3y}{3}$$
$$y = 2$$

and since y = 2 does not cause a denominator to equal zero, the solution set is {2}

33.
$$\frac{1}{2} + \frac{2}{x} = \frac{3}{4}$$
$$(4x)\left(\frac{1}{2} + \frac{2}{x}\right) = \left(\frac{3}{4}\right)(4x)$$
$$(4x)\left(\frac{1}{2}\right) + (4x)\left(\frac{2}{x}\right) = 3x$$
$$2x+8 = 3x$$
$$2x+8-8 = 3x-8$$
$$2x = 3x-8$$
$$2x-3x = 3x-8-3x$$
$$-x = -8$$
$$\frac{-x}{-1} = \frac{-8}{-1}$$
$$x = 8$$

and since x = 8 does not cause any denominator to equal zero, x = 8 solves the original equation.

35.
$$(x+7)(x-1) = (x+1)^2$$
$$x^2+6x-7 = x^2+2x+1$$
$$x^2+6x-7-x^2 = x^2+2x+1-x^2$$
$$6x-7 = 2x+1$$
$$6x-7+7 = 2x+1+7$$
$$6x = 2x+8$$
$$6x-2x = 2x+8-2x$$
$$4x = 8$$
$$\frac{4x}{4} = \frac{8}{4}$$
$$x = 2$$

37.
$$x(2x-3) = (2x+1)(x-4)$$
$$2x^2 - 3x = 2x^2 - 7x - 4$$
$$2x^2 - 3x - 2x^2 = 2x^2 - 7x - 4 - 2x^2$$
$$-3x = -7x - 4$$
$$-3x + 7x = -7x - 4 + 7x$$
$$4x = -4$$
$$\frac{4x}{4} = \frac{-4}{4} \rightarrow x = -1$$

39.
$$z(z^2 + 1) = 3 + z^3$$
$$z^3 + z = 3 + z^3$$
$$z^3 + z - z^3 = 3 + z^3 - z^3$$
$$z = 3$$

41.
$$\frac{x}{x-2} + 3 = \frac{2}{x-2}$$
$$(x-2)\left(\frac{x}{x-2} + 3\right) = \left(\frac{2}{x-2}\right)(x-2)$$
$$(x-2)\left(\frac{x}{x-2}\right) + (x-2)(3) = 2$$
$$x + 3x - 6 = 2$$
$$4x - 6 = 2$$
$$4x - 6 + 6 = 2 + 6$$
$$4x = 8$$
$$\frac{4x}{4} = \frac{8}{4} \rightarrow x = 2$$

but x = 2 causes a denominator to equal zero, so we must discard this answer. Therefore the original equation has no real solution.

43.
$$x^2 = 9x$$
$$x^2 - 9x = 0$$
$$x(x-9) = 0$$
$$x = 0 \text{ or } x = 9$$
The solution set is {0, 9}.

45.
$$t^3 - 9t^2 = 0$$
$$t^2(t-9) = 0$$
$$t^2 = 0$$
$$\text{or } t - 9 = 0 \rightarrow t = 0$$
$$\text{or } t = 9$$
The solution set is $\{0, 9\}$

47.
$$\frac{2x}{x^2-4} = \frac{4}{x^2-4} - \frac{3}{x+2}$$
$$\frac{2x}{(x+2)(x-2)} = \frac{4}{(x+2)(x-2)} - \frac{3}{x+2}$$
$$(x+2)(x-2)\left(\frac{2x}{(x+2)(x-2)}\right) = \left(\frac{4}{(x+2)(x-2)} - \frac{3}{x+2}\right)(x+2)(x-2)$$
$$2x = \left(\frac{4}{(x+2)(x-2)}\right)(x+2)(x-2) - \left(\frac{3}{x+2}\right)(x+2)(x-2)$$
$$2x = 4 - (3)(x-2)$$
$$2x = 4 - 3x + 6$$
$$2x = 10 - 3x$$
$$2x + 3x = 10 - 3x + 3x$$
$$5x = 10 \rightarrow \frac{5x}{5} = \frac{10}{5} \rightarrow x = 2$$

but x = 2 causes a denominator to equal zero, so we must discard this answer. Therefore the original equation has no real solution.

49.
$$\frac{x}{x+2} = \frac{3}{2}$$

$$(2)(x+2)\left(\frac{x}{x+2}\right) = \left(\frac{3}{2}\right)(2)(x+2)$$

$$(2)x = 3(x+2)$$

$$2x = 3x + 6$$

$$2x - 3x = 3x + 6 - 3x$$

$$-x = 6$$

$$\frac{-x}{-1} = \frac{6}{-1} \rightarrow x = -6$$

and since x = - 6 does not cause any denominator to equal zero, x = - 6 solves the original equation.

51.
$$\frac{5}{2x-3} = \frac{3}{x+5}$$

$$(2x-3)(x+5)\left(\frac{5}{2x-3}\right) = \left(\frac{3}{x+5}\right)(2x-3)(x+5)$$

$$(x+5)(5) = (3)(2x-3)$$

$$5x + 25 = 6x - 9$$

$$5x + 25 - 6x = 6x - 9 - 6x$$

$$25 - x = -9$$

$$25 - x - 25 = -9 - 25$$

$$-x = -34$$

$$\frac{-x}{-1} = \frac{-34}{-1}$$

$$x = 34$$

and since $x = 34$ does not cause any denominator to equal zero, $x = 34$ solves the original equation.

53.
$$\frac{6t+7}{4t-1} = \frac{3t+8}{2t-4}$$

$$(4t-1)(2t-4)\left(\frac{6t+7}{4t-1}\right) = \left(\frac{3t+8}{2t-4}\right)(4t-1)(2t-4)$$

$$(2t-4)(6t+7) = (3t+8)(4t-1)$$

$$12t^2 + 14t - 24t - 28 = 12t^2 - 3t + 32t - 8$$

$$12t^2 + 14t - 24t - 28 - 12t^2 = 12t^2 - 3t + 32t - 8 - 12t^2$$

$$14t - 24t - 28 = -3t + 32t - 8$$

$$-10t - 28 = 29t - 8$$

$$-10t - 28 - 29t = 29t - 8 - 29t$$

$$28 - 39t - 28 = -8 - 28 \quad \leftarrow \text{*} \quad error ? \quad should \quad ADD \quad 28$$

$$-39t = -36$$

$$\frac{-39t}{-39} = \frac{-36}{-39}$$

$$t = \frac{12}{13} \quad t = \frac{-29}{30}$$

and since $t = \dfrac{12}{13}$ does not cause any denominator to equal zero, $t = \dfrac{12}{13}$ solves the original equation.

55.
$$\frac{4}{x-2} = \frac{-3}{x+5} + \frac{7}{(x+5)(x-2)}$$

$$(x+5)(x-2)\left(\frac{4}{x-2}\right) = \left(\frac{-3}{x+5} + \frac{7}{(x+5)(x-2)}\right)(x+5)(x-2)$$

$$(x+5)(4) = \left(\frac{-3}{x+5}\right)(x+5)(x-2) + \left(\frac{7}{(x+5)(x-2)}\right)(x+5)(x-2)$$

$$4x + 20 = (-3)(x-2) + 7$$

$$4x + 20 = -3x + 6 + 7$$

$$4x + 20 = -3x + 13 \quad \leftarrow 2.$$

$$4x + 20 + 3x = -3x - 8 + 3x$$

$$7x + 20 = -8$$

error should subtract 13 not 8

$$7x + 20 - 20 = -8 - 20$$

$$7x = -28$$

$$\frac{7x}{7} = \frac{-28}{7}$$

$$x = -4$$

$$x = -1$$

and since $x = -4$ does not cause any denominator to equal zero, $x = -4$ solves the original equation.

57.
$$\frac{2}{y+3} + \frac{3}{y-4} = \frac{5}{y+6}$$

$$(y+3)(y-4)(y+6)\left(\frac{2}{y+3} + \frac{3}{y-4}\right) = \left(\frac{5}{y+6}\right)(y+3)(y-4)(y+6)$$

$$(y+3)(y-4)(y+6)\left(\frac{2}{y+3}\right) + (y+3)(y-4)(y+6)\left(\frac{3}{y-4}\right) = (5)(y+3)(y-4)$$

$$(y-4)(y+6)(2) + (y+3)(y+6)(3) = (5)(y+3)(y-4)$$

45

$$\left(y^2 + 6y - 4y - 24\right)(2) + \left(y^2 + 6y + 3y + 18\right)(3) = (5)\left(y^2 - 4y + 3y - 12\right)$$

$$\left(y^2 + 2y - 24\right)(2) + \left(y^2 + 9y + 18\right)(3) = (5)\left(y^2 - y - 12\right)$$

$$2y^2 + 4y - 48 + 3y^2 + 27y + 54 = 5y^2 - 5y - 60$$

$$5y^2 + 31y + 6 = 5y^2 - 5y - 60$$

$$5y^2 + 31y + 6 - 5y^2 = 5y^2 - 5y - 60 - 5y^2$$

$$31y + 6 = -5y - 60$$

$$31y + 6 + 5y = -5y - 60 + 5y$$

$$36y + 6 = -60$$

$$36y + 6 - 6 = -60 - 6$$

$$36y = -66$$

$$\frac{36y}{36} = \frac{-66}{36}$$

$$y = -\frac{11}{6}$$

and since $y = -11/6$ does not cause any denominator to equal zero, $y = -11/6$ solves the original equation.

59.
$$\frac{x}{x^2 - 1} - \frac{x + 3}{x^2 - x} = \frac{-3}{x^2 + x}$$

$$\frac{x}{(x+1)(x-1)} - \frac{x+3}{x(x-1)} = \frac{-3}{x(x+1)}$$

$$(x+1)(x-1)(x)\left(\frac{x}{(x+1)(x-1)} - \frac{x+3}{x(x-1)}\right) = \left(\frac{-3}{x(x+1)}\right)(x+1)(x-1)(x)$$

$$(x+1)(x-1)(x)\left(\frac{x}{(x+1)(x-1)}\right) - (x+1)(x-1)(x)\left(\frac{x+3}{x(x-1)}\right) = (-3)(x-1)$$

$$(x)(x) - (x+1)(x+3) = -3x + 3$$

$$x^2 - \left(x^2 + 3x + x + 3\right) = -3x + 3$$

$$x^2 - \left(x^2 + 4x + 3\right) = -3x + 3$$

$$x^2 - x^2 - 4x - 3 = -3x + 3$$

$$-4x - 3 = -3x + 3$$

$$-4x - 3 + 4x = -3x + 3 + 4x$$

$$-3 = 3 + x$$

$$-3 - 3 = 3 + x - 3$$

$$-6 = x$$

and since $x = -6$ does not cause any denominator to equal zero, $x = -6$ solves the original equation.

61.
$$3.2x + \frac{21.3}{65.871} = 19.23$$

$$3.2x + \frac{21.3}{65.871} - \frac{21.3}{65.871} = 19.23 - \frac{21.3}{65.871}$$

$$3.2x = 19.23 - \frac{21.3}{65.871}$$

$$\left(\frac{1}{3.2}\right)(3.2x) = \left(19.23 - \frac{21.3}{65.871}\right)\left(\frac{1}{3.2}\right)$$

$$x = \left(19.23 - \frac{21.3}{65.871}\right)\left(\frac{1}{3.2}\right) \rightarrow x \approx 5.91$$

63.
$$14.72 - 21.58x = \frac{18}{2.11}x + 2.4$$

$$14.72 - 21.58x - \frac{18}{2.11}x = \frac{18}{2.11}x + 2.4 - \frac{18}{2.11}x$$

$$14.72 - 21.58x - \frac{18}{2.11}x = 2.4$$

$$14.72 - 21.58x - \frac{18}{2.11}x - 14.72 = 2.4 - 14.72$$

$$-21.58x - \frac{18}{2.11}x = 2.4 - 14.72$$

$$(x)\left(-21.58 - \frac{18}{2.11}\right) = 2.4 - 14.72$$

$$\left(\frac{1}{-21.58 - \frac{18}{2.11}}\right)(x)\left(-21.58 - \frac{18}{2.11}\right) = (2.4 - 14.72)\left(\frac{1}{-21.58 - \frac{18}{2.11}}\right)$$

$$x = (2.4 - 14.72)\left(\frac{1}{-21.58 - \frac{18}{2.11}}\right)$$

$$x \approx 0.41$$

65.
$$x^2 - 7x + 12 = 0$$
$$(x - 4)(x - 3) = 0$$
$$x - 4 = 0 \rightarrow x = 4$$
$$\text{or } x - 3 = 0 \rightarrow x = 3$$
Therefore the solution set is $\{3,4\}$

67.
$$2x^2 + 5x - 3 = 0$$
$$(2x - 1)(x + 3) = 0$$
$$2x - 1 = 0 \rightarrow x = \frac{1}{2}$$
$$\text{or } x + 3 = 0 \rightarrow x = -3$$
Therefore the solution set is $\left\{-3, \frac{1}{2}\right\}$.

69.
$$x^3 = 9x$$
$$x^3 - 9x = 0$$
$$x(x^2 - 9) = 0$$
$$x(x + 3)(x - 3) = 0$$
$$x = 0$$
or $x + 3 = 0 \rightarrow x = -3$
or $x - 3 = 0 \rightarrow x = 3$
Therefore the solution set is $\{-3, 0, 3\}$.

71.
$$x^3 + x^2 - 20x = 0$$
$$x(x^2 + x - 20) = 0$$
$$x(x + 5)(x - 4) = 0$$
$$x = 0$$
or $x + 5 = 0 \rightarrow x = -5$
or $x - 4 = 0 \rightarrow x = 4$
Therefore the solution set is $\{-5, 0, 4\}$.

73. $x^3 + x^2 - x - 1 = 0$
We can factor by grouping to get

$$x^2(x + 1) - (x + 1) = 0$$
$$(x + 1)(x^2 - 1) = 0$$
$$(x + 1)(x + 1)(x - 1) = 0$$
$$x + 1 = 0 \rightarrow x = -1$$
or $x - 1 = 0 \rightarrow x = 1$
Therefore the solution set is $\{-1, 1\}$.

75. $x^3 - 3x^2 - 4x + 12 = 0$
We can factor by grouping to get

$$x^2(x - 3) - 4(x - 3) = 0$$
$$(x - 3)(x^2 - 4) = 0$$
$$(x - 3)(x + 2)(x - 2) = 0$$
$$x - 3 = 0 \rightarrow x = 3$$
or $x + 2 = 0 \rightarrow x = -2$
or $x - 2 = 0 \rightarrow x = 2$
Therefore the solution set is $\{-2, 2, 3\}$.

77.
$$ax - b = c, \quad a \neq 0$$
$$ax - b + b = c + b$$
$$ax = c + b$$
$$\frac{ax}{a} = \frac{c + b}{a}$$
$$x = \frac{c + b}{a}$$

79. $\dfrac{x}{a} + \dfrac{x}{b} = c, \quad a \neq 0, \, b \neq 0, \, a \neq -b$
$$ab\left(\frac{x}{a} + \frac{x}{b}\right) = ab \cdot c$$
$$bx + ax = abc$$
$$x(a + b) = abc$$
$$\frac{x(a + b)}{a + b} = \frac{abc}{a + b} \rightarrow x = \frac{abc}{a + b}$$

81.
$$\frac{1}{x - a} + \frac{1}{x + a} = \frac{2}{x - 1}$$
$$(x - a)(x + a)(x - 1)\left(\frac{1}{x - a} + \frac{1}{x + a}\right) = \left(\frac{2}{x - 1}\right)(x - a)(x + a)(x - 1)$$
$$(x + a)(x - 1)(1) + (x - a)(x - 1)(1) = (2)(x - a)(x + a)$$
$$x^2 - x + ax - a + x^2 - x - ax + a = 2x^2 - 2a^2$$
$$2x^2 - 2x = 2x^2 - 2a^2$$
$$-2x = -2a^2$$
$$\frac{-2x}{-2} = \frac{-2a^2}{-2} \rightarrow x = a^2$$

such that $x \neq \pm a, x \neq 1$

83.
$$x + 2a = 16 + ax - 6a$$
$$x = 4 \rightarrow$$
$$4 + 2a = 16 + a(4) - 6a$$
$$4 + 2a = 16 + 4a - 6a$$
$$4 + 2a = 16 - 2a$$
$$4a = 12$$
$$a = 3$$

85. Solving for R:
$$\frac{1}{R} = \frac{1}{R_1} + \frac{1}{R_2}$$
$$RR_1R_2\left(\frac{1}{R}\right) = RR_1R_2\left(\frac{1}{R_1} + \frac{1}{R_2}\right)$$
$$R_1R_2 = RR_2 + RR_1$$
$$R_1R_2 = R(R_2 + R_1)$$
$$\frac{R_1R_2}{R_2 + R_1} = \frac{R(R_2 + R_1)}{R_2 + R_1}$$
$$\frac{R_1R_2}{R_2 + R_1} = R$$

87. Solving for R:
$$F = \frac{mv^2}{R}$$
$$RF = R\left(\frac{mv^2}{R}\right)$$
$$RF = mv^2$$
$$\frac{RF}{F} = \frac{mv^2}{F} \rightarrow R = \frac{mv^2}{F}$$

89. Solving for r:
$$S = \frac{a}{1 - r}$$
$$S(1 - r) = \left(\frac{a}{1 - r}\right)(1 - r)$$
$$S - Sr = a$$
$$S - Sr - S = a - S$$
$$-Sr = a - S$$
$$\frac{-Sr}{-S} = \frac{a - S}{-S} \rightarrow r = \frac{S - a}{S}$$

91. Step 7 is only allowed if $x \neq 2$. But step 1 states that $x = 2$, so we have a contradiction.

93. In order to solve $\dfrac{5}{x + 3} + 3 = \dfrac{8 + x}{x + 3}$, we multiply each term by the expression

"$x + 3$"   to get $(x + 3)\left(\dfrac{5}{x + 3} + 3\right) = \left(\dfrac{8 + x}{x + 3}\right)(x + 3).$

Now, provided $x \neq -3$, we can cancel the denominators to get
$$5 + (x + 3)(3) = 8 + x$$

$$5 + 3x + 9 = 8 + x \rightarrow 2x = -6 \rightarrow x = -3$$
However, we already stated that $x \neq -3$. So we have a contradiction.

Equations and Inequalities

1.2   Setting Up Equations: Applications

1.   Let A represent the area of the circle and r the radius.
The area of a circle is the product of π times the square of the radius. $A = \pi r^2$

3.   Let A represent the area of the square and s the length of a side.
The area of the square is the square of the length of a side. $A = s^2$

5.   Let F represent the force, m the mass, and a the acceleration.
Force equals the product of the mass times the acceleration. $F = ma$

7.   Let W represent the work, F the force, and d the distance.
Work equals force times distance. $W = Fd$

9. C = total variable cost, x = number of dishwashers manufactured.
$C = 150x$

11.

Amount in Bonds	Amount in CD's	Total
x	$x - 3000$	20,000

$$x + x - 3000 = 20000$$
$$2x - 3000 = 20000$$
$$2x = 23000 \rightarrow x = 11500$$
$11,500 will be invested in bonds. $8,500 will be invested in CD's.

13.

Scott	Alice	Tricia	Total
x	$\frac{3}{4}x$	$\frac{1}{2}x$	900,000

$$x + \frac{3}{4}x + \frac{1}{2}x = 900{,}000$$
$$\frac{9}{4}x = 900{,}000$$
$$x = \frac{4}{9}(900{,}000) \rightarrow x = 400{,}000$$
Scott receives $400,000. Alice receives $300,000. Tricia receives $200,000.

15.

	Dollars per hour	Number of hours worked	Money earned
Regular wage	x	40	$40x$
Overtime wage	$1.5x$	8	$(1.5x)(8)$

$$40x + (1.5x)(8) = 442$$

$$40x + 12x = 442 \rightarrow 52x = 442 \rightarrow x = \frac{442}{52} = 8.50$$

Sandra's regular hourly wage is $8.50.

17.   Let x represent the score on the final exam and construct the table

	Test1	Test2	Test3	Test4	Test5	Final Exam	Final Exam
score	80	83	71	61	95	x	x
weight	1/7	1/7	1/7	1/7	1/7	1/7	1/7

Compute the final average and set equal to 80.

$$\left(\frac{1}{7}\right)(80 + 83 + 71 + 61 + 95 + x + x) = 80$$

Now solve for x:

$$\left(\frac{1}{7}\right)(390 + 2x) = 80$$

$$390 + 2x = 560 \rightarrow 2x = 170 \rightarrow x = 85$$

Brooke needs to score an 85 on the final exam to get an average of 80 in the course.

19.   Let x represent the original price of the house.
Then $0.15x$ represents the reduction in the price of the house.
original price – reduction = new price
$$x - 0.15x = 125,000$$
$$0.85x = 125,000 \rightarrow x = 147,058.82$$
The original price of the house was $147,058.82.
The amount of the savings is $0.15(\$147,058.82) = \$22,058.82$.

21.   Let x represent the price the bookstore pays for the book (publisher price).
Then $0.35x$ represents the mark up on the book.
The selling price of the book is $56.00.
publisher price + mark up = selling price
$$x + 0.35x = 56.00$$
$$1.35x = 56.00 \rightarrow x = 41.48$$
The bookstore pays $41.48 for the book.

23.

	Number of tickets sold	Price per ticket	Money earned
adults	x	4.75	$4.75x$
children	$5200 - x$	2.5	$(5200 - x)(2.5)$

money from adult tickets + money from children tickets = total receipts

$4.75x + (5200 - x)(2.5) = 20,335$

$4.75x + 13,000 - 2.5x = 20,335$

$$2.25x = 7335 \rightarrow x = \frac{7335}{2.25} = 3260$$

There were 3260 adult patrons.

25. l = length, w = width

$2l + 2w = 60$ Perimeter $= 2l + 2w$

$l = w + 8$ The length is 8 more than the width.

$2(w + 8) + 2w = 60$

$2w + 16 + 2w = 60$

$4w + 16 = 60 \rightarrow 4w = 44 \rightarrow w = 11$ feet, $l = 19$ feet

27. Let x represent the amount of money invested in bonds.

Then $50,000 - x$ represents the amount of money invested in CD's.

	Principle	Rate	Time (yrs)	Interest
Bonds	x	0.15	1	$0.15x$
CD's	$50,000 - x$	0.07	1	$0.07(50,000 - x)$

Since the total interest is to be $6,000, we have:

$0.15x + 0.07(50,000 - x) = 6,000$

$(100)(0.15x + 0.07(50,000 - x)) = (6,000)(100)$

$15x + 7(50,000 - x) = 600,000$

$15x + 350,000 - 7x = 600,000$

$8x + 350,000 = 600,000 \rightarrow 8x = 250,000 \rightarrow x = 31,250$

$31,250 should be invested in bonds at 15% and $18,750 should be invested in CD's at 7%.

29. Let x represent the amount of money loaned at 8%.

Then $12,000 - x$ represents the amount of money loaned at 18%.

	Principle	Rate	Time (yrs)	Interest
Loan at 8%	x	0.08	1	$0.08x$
Loan at 18%	$12,000 - x$	0.18	1	$0.18(12,000 - x)$

Since the total interest is to be $1,000, we have:

$0.08x + 0.18(12,000 - x) = 1,000$

$(100)(0.08x + 0.18(12,000 - x)) = (1,000)(100)$

$8x + 18(12,000 - x) = 100,000 \rightarrow 8x + 216,000 - 18x = 100,000$

$-10x + 216,000 = 100,000 \rightarrow -10x = -116,000 \rightarrow x = 11,600$

$11,600 is loaned at 8% and $400 is loaned at 18%.

31. Let x represent the number of pounds of Earl Gray tea.
     Then $100 - x$ represents the number of pounds of Orange Pekoe tea.

	No. of pounds	Price per pound	Total Value
Earl Gray	x	$5.00	$5x$
Orange Pekoe	$100 - x$	$3.00	$3(100 - x)$
Blend	100	$4.50	$4.50(100)$

     $$5x + 3(100 - x) = 4.50(100)$$
     $$5x + 300 - 3x = 450$$
     $$2x + 300 = 450 \rightarrow 2x = 150 \rightarrow x = 75$$
     75 pounds of Earl Gray tea must be blended with 25 pounds of Orange Pekoe.

33. Let x represent the number of pounds of cashews.
     Then $x + 60$ represents the number of pounds in the mixture.

	No. of pounds	Price per pound	Total Value
cashews	x	$4.00	$4x$
peanuts	60	$1.50	$1.50(60)$
mixture	$x + 60$	$2.50	$2.50(x + 60)$

     $$4x + 1.50(60) = 2.50(x + 60)$$
     $$4x + 90 = 2.50x + 150 \rightarrow 1.5x = 60 \rightarrow x = 40$$
     40 pounds of cashews must be added to the 60 pounds of peanuts.

35. Let r represent the speed of the current.

	Rate	Time	Distance
Upstream	$16 - r$	$\dfrac{20}{60} = \dfrac{1}{3}$	$\dfrac{16 - r}{3}$
Downstream	$16 + r$	$\dfrac{15}{60} = \dfrac{1}{4}$	$\dfrac{16 + r}{4}$

     Since the distance is the same in each direction:
     $$\frac{16 - r}{3} = \frac{16 + r}{4}$$
     $$4(16 - r) = 3(16 + r)$$
     $$64 - 4r = 48 + 3r \rightarrow 16 = 7r \rightarrow r = \frac{16}{7} \approx 2.286$$
     The speed of the current is approximately 2.286 miles per hour.

37. Let r represent the rate of the Metra commuter train.
     Then $r + 50$ represents the rate of the Amtrak train.

	Rate	Time	Distance
Metra train	r	3	$3r$
Amtrak train	$r + 50$	1	$r + 50$

     Amtrak distance = Metra distance $- 10$
     $$r + 50 = 3r - 10$$
     $$60 = 2r \rightarrow r = 30$$
     The Metra commuter train travels at a rate of 30 miles per hour.
     The Amtrak train travels at a rate of 80 miles per hour.

39.   Let t represent the time it takes to do the job together.

	Time to do job	Part of job done in one minute
Trent	30	$\dfrac{1}{30}$
Lois	20	$\dfrac{1}{20}$
Together	t	$\dfrac{1}{t}$

$$\frac{1}{30} + \frac{1}{20} = \frac{1}{t} \rightarrow 2t + 3t = 60 \rightarrow 5t = 60 \rightarrow t = 12$$

Working together, the job can be done in 12 minutes.

41. l = length of the garden

w = width of the garden

(a)   The length of the garden is to be twice its width. Thus, $l = 2w$.

The dimensions of the fence are $l + 4$ and $w + 4$.

The perimeter is 46 feet, so:

$$2(l + 4) + 2(w + 4) = 46$$

$$2(2w + 4) + 2(w + 4) = 46$$

$$4w + 8 + 2w + 8 = 46$$

$$6w + 16 = 46 \rightarrow 6w = 30 \rightarrow w = 5$$

The dimensions of the garden are 5 feet by 10 feet.

(b)   Area $= l \cdot w = 5 \cdot 10 = 50$ square feet

(c)   If the dimensions of the garden are the same, then the length and width of the fence are also the same $(l + 4)$. The perimeter is 46 feet, so:

$$2(l + 4) + 2(l + 4) = 46$$

$$2l + 8 + 2l + 8 = 46$$

$$4l + 16 = 46 \rightarrow 4l = 30 \rightarrow l = 7.5$$

The dimensions of the garden are 7.5 feet by 7.5 feet.

(d)   Area $= l \cdot w = 7.5(7.5) = 56.25$ square feet.

43.   Let t represent the time it takes for the defensive back to catch the tight end.

	Time to run 100 yards	Time	Rate	Distance
Tight End	12 sec	t	$\dfrac{100}{12} = \dfrac{25}{3}$	$\dfrac{25}{3}t$
Defensive Back	10 sec	t	$\dfrac{100}{10} = 10$	$10t$

Since the defensive back has to run 5 yards farther, we have:

$$\frac{25}{3}t + 5 = 10t$$

$$25t + 15 = 30t$$

$$15 = 5t$$

$$t = 3 \quad \rightarrow \quad 10t = 30$$

The defensive back will catch the tight end at the 45 yard line.

45.   Let x represent the number of ounces of pure water.
Then $x+1$ represents the number of gallons in the 60% solution.

	No. of gallons	Conc. of Antifreeze	Pure Antifreeze
water	x	0	0
100% antifreeze	1	1.00	1(1)
60% antifreeze	$x+1$	0.60	$0.60(x+1)$

$$0 + 1(1) = 0.60(x+1)$$

$$1 = 0.6x + 0.6 \rightarrow 0.4 = 0.6x \rightarrow x = \frac{4}{6} = \frac{2}{3}$$

$\frac{2}{3}$ gallon of pure water should be added.

47.   Let x represent the number of ounces of water to be evaporated.

	No. of ounces	Conc. of Salt	Pure Salt
Water	x	0.00	0
4% Salt	32	0.04	0.04(32)
6% Salt	$32 - x$	0.06	$0.06(32 - x)$

$$0 + 0.04(32) = 0.06(32 - x) \rightarrow 1.28 = 1.92 - 0.06x \rightarrow 0.06x = 0.64 \rightarrow x = \frac{0.64}{0.06} = \frac{32}{3}$$

32/3 ounces of water need to be evaporated.

49.   Let x represent the number of grams of pure gold.
Then $60 - x$ represents the number of grams of 12 karat gold to be used.

	No. of grams	Conc. of gold	Pure gold
Pure gold	x	1.00	x
12 karat gold	$60 - x$	$\dfrac{1}{2}$	$\dfrac{1}{2}(60 - x)$
16 karat gold	60	$\dfrac{2}{3}$	$\dfrac{2}{3}(60)$

$$x + \frac{1}{2}(60 - x) = \frac{2}{3}(60) \rightarrow x + 30 - 0.5x = 40 \rightarrow 0.5x = 10 \rightarrow x = 20$$

20 grams of pure gold should be mixed with 40 grams of 12 karat gold.

51.   Let t represent the time it takes for Mike to catch up with Dan.

	Time to run mile	Time	Part of mile run in one minute	Distance
Mike	6	t	$\dfrac{1}{6}$	$\dfrac{1}{6}t$
Dan	9	$t + 1$	$\dfrac{1}{9}$	$\dfrac{1}{9}(t+1)$

Since the distances are the same, we have:

$$\frac{1}{6}t = \frac{1}{9}(t+1) \rightarrow 3t = 2t + 2 \rightarrow t = 2$$

Mike will pass Dan after 2 minutes, which is a distance of $\frac{1}{3}$ mile.

53. Let t represent the time the auxiliary pump needs to run.

	Time to do job alone	Part of job done in one hour	Time on Job	Part of total job done by each pump
Main Pump	4	$\dfrac{1}{4}$	3	$\dfrac{3}{4}$
Auxiliary Pump	9	$\dfrac{1}{9}$	t	$\dfrac{1}{9}t$

Since the two pumps are emptying one tanker, we have:

$$\frac{3}{4} + \frac{1}{9}t = 1 \rightarrow 27 + 4t = 36 \rightarrow 4t = 9 \rightarrow t = \frac{9}{4} = 2.25$$

The auxiliary pump must run for 2.25 hours. It must be started at 9:45 a.m.

55. Let t represent the time for the tub to fill with the faucets on and the stopper removed.

	Time to do job alone	Part of job done in one minute	Time on Job	Part of total job done by each
Faucets open	15	$\dfrac{1}{15}$	t	$\dfrac{t}{15}$
Stopper removed	20	$-\dfrac{1}{20}$	t	$-\dfrac{t}{20}$

Since one tub is being filled, we have:

$$\frac{t}{15} + \left(-\frac{t}{20}\right) = 1 \rightarrow 4t - 3t = 60 \rightarrow t = 60$$

  $\therefore$ 60 minutes is required to fill the tub.

57. Burke's rate is $\dfrac{100}{12}$ meters/sec.

In 9.99 seconds, Burke will run $\dfrac{100}{12}(9.99) = 83.25$ meters.

Lewis would win by 16.75 meters.

59. Answers will vary.

Equations and Inequalities

1.3 Quadratic Equations

1. $x^2 - 9x = 0$
$x(x-9) = 0 \rightarrow x = 0$ or $x = 9$
The solution set is $\{0, 9\}$.

3. $x^2 - 25 = 0$
$(x+5)(x-5) = 0 \rightarrow x = -5$ or $x = 5$
The solution set is $\{-5, 5\}$.

5. $z^2 + z - 6 = 0$
$(z+3)(z-2) = 0 \rightarrow z = -3$ or $z = 2$
The solution set is $\{-3, 2\}$.

7. $2x^2 - 5x - 3 = 0$
$(2x+1)(x-3) = 0 \rightarrow x = -\dfrac{1}{2}$ or $x = 3$
The solution set is $\left\{-\dfrac{1}{2}, 3\right\}$.

9. $3t^2 - 48 = 0$
$3(t^2 - 16) = 0 \rightarrow 3(t+4)(t-4) = 0$
$t = -4$ or $t = 4$
The solution set is $\{-4, 4\}$.

11. $x(x-8) + 12 = 0$
$x^2 - 8x + 12 = 0$
$(x-6)(x-2) = 0 \rightarrow x = 6$ or $x = 2$
The solution set is $\{2, 6\}$.

13. $4x^2 + 9 = 12x$
$4x^2 - 12x + 9 = 0$
$(2x-3)^2 = 0 \rightarrow x = \dfrac{3}{2}$
The solution set is $\left\{\dfrac{3}{2}\right\}$.

15. $6(p^2 - 1) = 5p$
$6p^2 - 6 = 5p$
$6p^2 - 5p - 6 = 0$
$(3p+2)(2p-3) = 0 \rightarrow p = -\dfrac{2}{3}$ or $p = \dfrac{3}{2}$
The solution set is $\left\{-\dfrac{2}{3}, \dfrac{3}{2}\right\}$.

17. $6x - 5 = \dfrac{6}{x}$
$6x^2 - 5x = 6 \rightarrow 6x^2 - 5x - 6 = 0$
$(3x+2)(2x-3) = 0 \rightarrow x = -\dfrac{2}{3}$ or $x = \dfrac{3}{2}$

Since neither of these values causes a denominator to equal zero, the solution set is $\left\{-\dfrac{2}{3}, \dfrac{3}{2}\right\}$.

19.
$$\frac{4(x-2)}{x-3} + \frac{3}{x} = \frac{-3}{x(x-3)}$$

$$x(x-3)\left(\frac{4(x-2)}{x-3} + \frac{3}{x}\right) = \left(\frac{-3}{x(x-3)}\right)x(x-3)$$

$$x(x-3)\left(\frac{4(x-2)}{x-3}\right) + x(x-3)\left(\frac{3}{x}\right) = -3$$

$$x(4(x-2)) + (x-3)(3) = -3$$

$$4x^2 - 8x + 3x - 9 = -3$$

$$4x^2 - 5x - 6 = 0$$

$$(4x+3)(x-2) = 0$$

$$x = -\frac{3}{4} \text{ or } x = 2$$

Since neither of these values causes a denominator to equal zero, the solution set is $\left\{-\frac{3}{4}, 2\right\}$.

27. $\left(\frac{8}{2}\right)^2 = 4^2 = 16$

31.
$$\left(\frac{\left(-\frac{2}{3}\right)}{2}\right)^2 = \left(-\frac{1}{3}\right)^2 = \frac{1}{9}$$

21.
$$x^2 = 25 \rightarrow x = \pm\sqrt{25} \rightarrow x = \pm 5$$
The solution set is $\{-5, 5\}$.

23. $(x-1)^2 = 4$

$$x - 1 = \pm\sqrt{4}$$

$$x - 1 = \pm 2$$

$$x - 1 = 2 \text{ or } x - 1 = -2$$

$$\rightarrow x = 3 \text{ or } x = -1$$
The solution set is $\{-1, 3\}$.

25. $(2x+3)^2 = 9$

$$2x + 3 = \pm\sqrt{9}$$

$$2x + 3 = \pm 3$$

$$2x + 3 = 3 \text{ or } 2x + 3 = -3$$

$$\rightarrow x = 0 \text{ or } x = -3$$
The solution set is $\{-3, 0\}$.

29.
$$\left(\frac{\left(\frac{1}{2}\right)}{2}\right)^2 = \left(\frac{1}{4}\right)^2 = \frac{1}{16}$$

33.
$$x^2 + 4x = 21$$
$$x^2 + 4x + 4 = 21 + 4$$
$$(x+2)^2 = 25$$
$$x + 2 = \pm\sqrt{25} \rightarrow x + 2 = \pm 5$$
$$x = -2 \pm 5 \rightarrow x = 3 \text{ or } x = -7$$
The solution set is $\{-7, 3\}$.

35. $x^2 - \dfrac{1}{2}x - \dfrac{3}{16} = 0$

$x^2 - \dfrac{1}{2}x = \dfrac{3}{16}$

$x^2 - \dfrac{1}{2}x + \dfrac{1}{16} = \dfrac{3}{16} + \dfrac{1}{16}$

$\left(x - \dfrac{1}{4}\right)^2 = \dfrac{1}{4}$

$x - \dfrac{1}{4} = \pm\sqrt{\dfrac{1}{4}}$

$x - \dfrac{1}{4} = \pm\dfrac{1}{2}$

$x = \dfrac{1}{4} \pm \dfrac{1}{2} \rightarrow x = \dfrac{3}{4}$

or $x = -\dfrac{1}{4}$

The solution set is $\left\{-\dfrac{1}{4}, \dfrac{3}{4}\right\}$.

37. $3x^2 + x - \dfrac{1}{2} = 0$

$x^2 + \dfrac{1}{3}x - \dfrac{1}{6} = 0$

$x^2 + \dfrac{1}{3}x = \dfrac{1}{6}$

$x^2 + \dfrac{1}{3}x + \dfrac{1}{36} = \dfrac{1}{6} + \dfrac{1}{36}$

$\left(x + \dfrac{1}{6}\right)^2 = \dfrac{7}{36}$

$x + \dfrac{1}{6} = \pm\sqrt{\dfrac{7}{36}}$

$x + \dfrac{1}{6} = \pm\dfrac{\sqrt{7}}{6}$

$x = -\dfrac{1}{6} \pm \dfrac{\sqrt{7}}{6}$

The solution set is $\left\{-\dfrac{1}{6} + \dfrac{\sqrt{7}}{6}, -\dfrac{1}{6} - \dfrac{\sqrt{7}}{6}\right\}$.

39. $x^2 - 4x + 2 = 0$
$a = 1, \quad b = -4, \quad c = 2$

$x = \dfrac{-(-4) \pm \sqrt{(-4)^2 - 4(1)(2)}}{2(1)}$

$= \dfrac{4 \pm \sqrt{16 - 8}}{2} = \dfrac{4 \pm \sqrt{8}}{2}$

$= \dfrac{4 \pm 2\sqrt{2}}{2} = 2 \pm \sqrt{2}$

$\left\{2 - \sqrt{2}, 2 + \sqrt{2}\right\}$

41. $x^2 - 4x - 1 = 0$
$a = 1, \quad b = -4, \quad c = -1$

$x = \dfrac{-(-4) \pm \sqrt{(-4)^2 - 4(1)(-1)}}{2(1)}$

$= \dfrac{4 \pm \sqrt{16 + 4}}{2} = \dfrac{4 \pm \sqrt{20}}{2}$

$= \dfrac{4 \pm 2\sqrt{5}}{2} = 2 \pm \sqrt{5}$

$\left\{2 - \sqrt{5}, 2 + \sqrt{5}\right\}$

43. $2x^2 - 5x + 3 = 0$
$a = 2, \quad b = -5, \quad c = 3$

$x = \dfrac{-(-5) \pm \sqrt{(-5)^2 - 4(2)(3)}}{2(2)}$

$= \dfrac{5 \pm \sqrt{25 - 24}}{4} = \dfrac{5 \pm 1}{4}$

$\left\{1, \dfrac{3}{2}\right\}$

45. $4y^2 - y + 2 = 0$
$a = 4, \quad b = -1, \quad c = 2$

$y = \dfrac{-(-1) \pm \sqrt{(-1)^2 - 4(4)(2)}}{2(4)}$

$= \dfrac{1 \pm \sqrt{1 - 32}}{8} = \dfrac{1 \pm \sqrt{-31}}{8}$

No real solution.

47. $4x^2 = 1 - 2x$

$4x^2 + 2x - 1 = 0$

$a = 4, \quad b = 2, \quad c = -1$

$$x = \frac{-2 \pm \sqrt{2^2 - 4(4)(-1)}}{2(4)}$$

$$= \frac{-2 \pm \sqrt{4 + 16}}{8} = \frac{-2 \pm \sqrt{20}}{8}$$

$$= \frac{-2 \pm 2\sqrt{5}}{8} = \frac{-1 \pm \sqrt{5}}{4}$$

$$\left\{ \frac{-1 - \sqrt{5}}{4}, \frac{-1 + \sqrt{5}}{4} \right\}$$

49. $4x^2 = 9x$

$4x^2 - 9x = 0$

$a = 4, \quad b = -9, \quad c = 0$

$$x = \frac{-(-9) \pm \sqrt{(-9)^2 - 4(4)(0)}}{2(4)}$$

$$= \frac{9 \pm \sqrt{81}}{8} = \frac{9 \pm 9}{8}$$

$$\rightarrow x = \frac{9 + 9}{8} \quad \text{or} \quad x = \frac{9 - 9}{8}$$

$$x = \frac{18}{8} = \frac{9}{4} \quad \text{or} \quad x = 0$$

$$\left\{ 0, \frac{9}{4} \right\}$$

51. $9t^2 - 6t + 1 = 0$

$a = 9, \quad b = -6, \quad c = 1$

$$t = \frac{-(-6) \pm \sqrt{(-6)^2 - 4(9)(1)}}{2(9)}$$

$$= \frac{6 \pm \sqrt{36 - 36}}{18} = \frac{6 \pm 0}{18} = \frac{1}{3}$$

$$\left\{ \frac{1}{3} \right\}$$

53. $\frac{3}{4}x^2 - \frac{1}{4}x - \frac{1}{2} = 0$

$$4\left(\frac{3}{4}x^2 - \frac{1}{4}x - \frac{1}{2} \right) = (0)(4)$$

$$3x^2 - x - 2 = 0$$

$$a = 3, \quad b = -1, \quad c = -2$$

$$x = \frac{-(-1) \pm \sqrt{(-1)^2 - 4(3)(-2)}}{2(3)}$$

$$= \frac{1 \pm \sqrt{1 + 24}}{6}$$

$$= \frac{1 \pm \sqrt{25}}{6} = \frac{1 \pm 5}{6}$$

$$\rightarrow x = \frac{1 + 5}{6} \quad \text{or} \quad x = \frac{1 - 5}{6}$$

$$x = \frac{6}{6} = 1 \quad \text{or} \quad x = \frac{-4}{6} = -\frac{2}{3}$$

$$\left\{ -\frac{2}{3}, 1 \right\}$$

55.
$$4 - \frac{1}{x} - \frac{2}{x^2} = 0$$

$$(x^2)\left(4 - \frac{1}{x} - \frac{2}{x^2}\right) = (0)(x^2)$$

$$4x^2 - x - 2 = 0$$

$$a = 4, \quad b = -1, \quad c = -2$$

$$x = \frac{-(-1) \pm \sqrt{(-1)^2 - 4(4)(-2)}}{2(4)}$$

$$= \frac{1 \pm \sqrt{1 + 32}}{8} = \frac{1 \pm \sqrt{33}}{8}$$

Since neither of these values causes a denominator to equal zero, the solution set is

$$\left\{ \frac{1 + \sqrt{33}}{8}, \frac{1 - \sqrt{33}}{8} \right\}.$$

57.
$$3x = 1 - \frac{1}{x}$$

$$x(3x) = \left(1 - \frac{1}{x}\right)(x)$$

$$3x^2 = x - 1$$

$$3x^2 - x + 1 = 0$$

$$a = 3, \quad b = -1 \quad c = 1$$

$$x = \frac{-(-1) \pm \sqrt{(-1)^2 - 4(3)(1)}}{2(4)}$$

$$= \frac{1 \pm \sqrt{1 - 12}}{8} = \frac{1 \pm \sqrt{-11}}{8}$$

No real solutions.

59. $x^2 - 4.1x + 2.2 = 0$

$$a = 1, \quad b = -4.1, \quad c = 2.2$$

$$x = \frac{-(-4.1) \pm \sqrt{(-4.1)^2 - 4(1)(2.2)}}{2(1)}$$

$$= \frac{4.1 \pm \sqrt{16.81 - 8.8}}{2} = \frac{4.1 \pm \sqrt{8.01}}{2}$$

$$x \approx 3.47, x \approx 0.64$$

$$\{3.47, 0.64\}$$

61. $x^2 + \sqrt{3}x - 3 = 0$

$$a = 1, \quad b = \sqrt{3}, \quad c = -3$$

$$x = \frac{-(\sqrt{3}) \pm \sqrt{(\sqrt{3})^2 - 4(1)(-3)}}{2(1)}$$

$$= \frac{-\sqrt{3} \pm \sqrt{3 + 12}}{2} = \frac{-\sqrt{3} \pm \sqrt{15}}{2}$$

$$x \approx 1.07, x \approx -2.80$$

$$\{1.07, -2.80\}$$

67. $x^2 - 5 = 0$

$$x^2 = 5 \rightarrow x = \pm\sqrt{5}$$

$$\{\sqrt{5}, -\sqrt{5}\}$$

69.
$$16x^2 - 8x + 1 = 0$$

$$(4x - 1)(4x - 1) = 0$$

$$4x - 1 = 0 \rightarrow x = \frac{1}{4}$$

$$\left\{ \frac{1}{4} \right\}$$

71.
$$10x^2 - 19x - 15 = 0$$

$$(5x + 3)(2x - 5) = 0$$

$$5x + 3 = 0 \quad \text{or} \quad 2x - 5 = 0$$

$$\rightarrow x = -\frac{3}{5} \quad \text{or} \quad x = \frac{5}{2}$$

$$\left\{ -\frac{3}{5}, \frac{5}{2} \right\}$$

73.
$$2 + z = 6z^2$$

$$0 = 6z^2 - z - 2 \rightarrow 0 = (3z - 2)(2z + 1)$$

$$3z - 2 = 0 \quad \text{or} \quad 2z + 1 = 0$$

$$\rightarrow z = \frac{2}{3} \quad \text{or} \quad x = -\frac{1}{2}$$

$$\left\{ -\frac{1}{2}, \frac{2}{3} \right\}$$

75.
$$x^2 + \sqrt{2}x = \frac{1}{2}$$

$$x^2 + \sqrt{2}x - \frac{1}{2} = 0$$

$$2\left(x^2 + \sqrt{2}x - \frac{1}{2}\right) = (0)(2)$$

$$2x^2 + 2\sqrt{2}x - 1 = 0$$

$$a = 2, \quad b = 2\sqrt{2}, \quad c = -1$$

$$x = \frac{-(2\sqrt{2}) \pm \sqrt{(2\sqrt{2})^2 - 4(2)(-1)}}{2(2)}$$

$$= \frac{-2\sqrt{2} \pm \sqrt{8+8}}{4} = \frac{-2\sqrt{2} \pm \sqrt{16}}{4}$$

$$= \frac{-2\sqrt{2} \pm 4}{4} = \frac{-\sqrt{2} \pm 2}{2}$$

$$\left\{\frac{-\sqrt{2}+2}{2}, \frac{-\sqrt{2}-2}{2}\right\}$$

77.
$$x^2 + x = 4$$

$$x^2 + x - 4 = 0$$

$$a = 1, \quad b = 1, \quad c = -4$$

$$x = \frac{-(1) \pm \sqrt{(1)^2 - 4(1)(-4)}}{2(1)}$$

$$= \frac{-1 \pm \sqrt{1+16}}{2} = \frac{-1 \pm \sqrt{17}}{2}$$

$$\left\{\frac{-1+\sqrt{17}}{2}, \frac{-1-\sqrt{17}}{2}\right\}$$

79.
$$2x^2 - 6x + 7 = 0$$
$$a = 2, \quad b = -6, \quad c = 7$$

$$b^2 - 4ac = (-6)^2 - 4(2)(7)$$

$$= 36 - 56 = -20$$

Since the discriminant < 0, we have no real solutions

81.
$$9x^2 - 30x + 25 = 0$$
$$a = 9, \quad b = -30, \quad c = 25$$

$$b^2 - 4ac = (-30)^2 - 4(9)(25)$$

$$= 900 - 900 = 0$$

since the discriminant $= 0$, we have one repeated real solution

83.
$$3x^2 + 5x - 8 = 0$$
$$a = 3, \quad b = 5, \quad c = -8$$

$$b^2 - 4ac = (5)^2 - 4(3)(-8)$$

$$= 25 + 96 = 121$$

since the discriminant > 0, we have two unequal real solutions

85. Let w represent the width of window.
Then $l = w + 2$ represents the length of the window.
Since the area is 143 square feet, we have: $w(w+2) = 143$

$$w^2 + 2w - 143 = 0 \rightarrow (w+13)(w-11) = 0 \rightarrow w = -13 \text{ which is not practical}$$

or $w = 11$

The width of the rectangular window is 11 feet and the length is 13 feet.

87. Let l represent the length of the rectangle.
Let w represent the width of the rectangle.
The perimeter is 26 meters and the area is 40 square meters.

$$2l + 2w = 26 \quad \rightarrow \quad l + w = 13 \quad \rightarrow \quad w = 13 - l$$

$$lw = 40$$

$$l(13 - l) = 40 \rightarrow 13l - l^2 = 40 \rightarrow l^2 - 13l + 40 = 0 \rightarrow (l-8)(l-5) = 0$$

$$l = 8 \quad \text{or} \quad l = 5$$

$$w = 5 \qquad w = 8$$

The dimensions are 5 meters by 8 meters.

89. Let x represent the length of the side of the sheet metal.

$$(x-2)(x-2)(1) = 4$$
$$x^2 - 4x + 4 = 4$$
$$x^2 - 4x = 0$$
$$x(x-4) = 0 \rightarrow x = 0 \ \text{or} \ x = 4$$

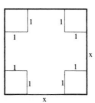

Since the side cannot be 0 feet long, the length of a side of the sheet metal is 4 feet. Hence, the dimensions of the sheet metal before the cut are 4 feet by 4 feet.

91. (a) $s = 96 + 80t - 16t^2$. The ball strikes the ground when the height = 0.
So we solve $0 = 96 + 80t - 16t^2$.

$$0 = -16t^2 + 80t + 96 \rightarrow \frac{0}{-16} = \frac{-16t^2 + 80t + 96}{-16}$$

$0 = t^2 - 5t - 6 \rightarrow 0 = (t-6)(t+1) \rightarrow t = 6 \ \text{or} \ t = -1$, we discard the negative value since t represents elapsed time. Therefore, the ball hits the ground after 6 seconds.

(b) $s = 96 + 80t - 16t^2$. The ball passes the top of the building when the height = 96.

So we solve $96 = 96 + 80t - 16t^2$.

$96 = 96 + 80t - 16t^2 \rightarrow 0 = 80t - 16t^2 \rightarrow 0 = 16t(5-t) \rightarrow t = 0 \ \text{or} \ t = 5$

We know that the ball starts ($t = 0$) at a height of 96 feet. Therefore, the ball hits the ground after 6 seconds.

93. Let x = number of boxes in excess of 150.
The total number of boxes ordered = $150 + x$
The price per box = $200 - x$
The customer's total bill = (# boxes ordered)(price per box)
$$= (150 + x)(200 - x)$$
So we need to solve the equation $(150 + x)(200 - x) = 30{,}625$.
$$30{,}000 + 50x - x^2 = 30{,}625$$

$0 = x^2 - 50x + 625 \rightarrow 0 = (x - 25)(x - 25) \rightarrow x = 25$
So the customer ordered a total of $150 + 25 = 175$ boxes.

95. Let x represent the width of the border measured in feet.
The total area is $A_T = (6 + 2x)(10 + 2x)$.
The area of the garden is $A_G = 6 \cdot 10 = 60$.
The area of the border is $A_B = A_T - A_G = (6 + 2x)(10 + 2x) - 60$.
Since the concrete is 3 inches or 0.25 feet thick, the volume of the concrete in the border is
$$0.25 A_B = 0.25 \big((6 + 2x)(10 + 2x) - 60\big)$$
Solving the volume equation:
$$0.25 \big((6 + 2x)(10 + 2x) - 60\big) = 27$$
$$60 + 32x + 4x^2 - 60 = 108$$
$$4x^2 + 32x - 108 = 0 \rightarrow x^2 + 8x - 27 = 0$$

$$x = \frac{-8 \pm \sqrt{8^2 - 4(1)(-27)}}{2(1)} = \frac{-8 \pm \sqrt{172}}{2}$$

$$\approx \frac{-8 \pm 13.11}{2} = 2.56 \text{ or } -10.56 \text{ which is not practical.}$$

The width of the border is approximately 2.56 feet.

97. Let x represent the number of centimeters the length and width should be reduced.
$12 - x = $ the new length, $7 - x = $ the new width.
The new volume is 90% of the old volume.

$$(12 - x)(7 - x)(3) = 0.9(12)(7)(3)$$

$$3x^2 - 57x + 252 = 226.8 \rightarrow 3x^2 - 57x + 25.2 = 0 \rightarrow x^2 - 19x + 8.4 = 0$$

$$x = \frac{-(-19) \pm \sqrt{(-19)^2 - 4(1)(8.4)}}{2(1)} = \frac{19 \pm \sqrt{327.4}}{2}$$

$$\approx \frac{19 \pm 18.09}{2} = 0.45 \text{ or } 18.55$$

Since 18.55 exceeds the dimensions, it is discarded.
The dimensions of the new chocolate bar are: 11.55 cm by 6.55 cm by 3 cm.

99. Let x represent the width of the border measured in feet.
The radius of the pool is 5 feet.
Then $x + 5$ represents the radius of the circle, including both the pool and the border.
The total area of the pool and border is $A_T = \pi(x + 5)^2$.
The area of the pool is $A_P = \pi(5)^2 = 25\pi$.
The area of the border is $A_B = A_T - A_P = \pi(x + 5)^2 - 25\pi$.
Since the concrete is 3 inches or 0.25 feet thick, the volume of the concrete in the border is

$$0.25 A_B = 0.25\left(\pi(x + 5)^2 - 25\pi\right)$$

Solving the volume equation:

$$0.25\left(\pi(x + 5)^2 - 25\pi\right) = 27 \rightarrow \pi\left(x^2 + 10x + 25 - 25\right) = 108 \rightarrow \pi x^2 + 10\pi x - 108 = 0$$

$$x = \frac{-10\pi \pm \sqrt{(10\pi)^2 - 4(\pi)(-108)}}{2(\pi)}$$

$$= \frac{-31.42 \pm \sqrt{2344.1285}}{6.28} = \frac{-31.42 \pm 48.42}{6.28} = 2.71 \text{ or } -12.71$$

The width of the border is approximately 2.71 feet.

101. Let r represent the speed of the current.

	Rate	Time	Distance
Upstream	$15 - r$	$\dfrac{10}{15 - r}$	10
Downstream	$15 + r$	$\dfrac{10}{15 + r}$	10

Since the total time is 1.5 hours, we have:

$$\frac{10}{15 - r} + \frac{10}{15 + r} = 1.5$$

$$10(15 + r) + 10(15 - r) = 1.5(15 - r)(15 + r)$$

$$150 + 10r + 150 - 10r = 1.5(225 - r^2) \rightarrow 300 = 1.5(225 - r^2)$$

$$200 = 225 - r^2 \rightarrow r^2 - 25 = 0 \rightarrow (r - 5)(r + 5) = 0 \rightarrow r = 5 \text{ or } r = -5$$

The speed of the current is 5 miles per hour.

103. given a quadratic equation $ax^2 + bx + c = 0$

the solutions are given by $x = \dfrac{-b + \sqrt{b^2 - 4ac}}{2a}$ and $x = \dfrac{-b - \sqrt{b^2 - 4ac}}{2a}$

adding these two values we get

$$\frac{-b + \sqrt{b^2 - 4ac}}{2a} + \frac{-b - \sqrt{b^2 - 4ac}}{2a} = \frac{-b + \sqrt{b^2 - 4ac} - b - \sqrt{b^2 - 4ac}}{2a} = \frac{-2b}{2a} = -\frac{b}{a}$$

105. The quadratic equation $kx^2 + x + k = 0$ will have a repeated solution provided the discriminant $= 0$ that is, we need $b^2 - 4ac = 0$ in the given quadratic equation

$$b^2 - 4ac = (1)^2 - 4(k)(k) = 1 - 4k^2$$

so we solve

$$1 - 4k^2 = 0 \rightarrow 1 = 4k^2 \rightarrow \frac{1}{4} = k^2 \rightarrow \pm\sqrt{\frac{1}{4}} = k \rightarrow \pm\frac{1}{2} = k$$

107. The quadratic equation $ax^2 + bx + c = 0$ has solutions given by

$$x_1 = \frac{-b + \sqrt{b^2 - 4ac}}{2a} \text{ and } x_2 = \frac{-b - \sqrt{b^2 - 4ac}}{2a}$$

The quadratic equation $ax^2 - bx + c = 0$ has solutions given by

$$x_3 = \frac{-(-b) + \sqrt{(-b)^2 - 4ac}}{2a} = \frac{b + \sqrt{b^2 - 4ac}}{2a} = -x_2$$

and

$$x_4 = \frac{-(-b) - \sqrt{(-b)^2 - 4ac}}{2a} = \frac{b - \sqrt{b^2 - 4ac}}{2a} = -x_1$$

So we have the negatives of the first pair of solutions.

109.   We need to solve the equation $\frac{1}{2}n(n+1) = 666$

$$2\left(\frac{1}{2}\right)n(n+1) = (666)(2) \rightarrow n(n+1) = 1332$$

$$n^2 + n = 1332 \rightarrow n^2 + n - 1332 = 0 \rightarrow (n+37)(n-36) = 0$$

$$n = -37 \quad \text{or} \quad n = 36$$

Since n must be a positive integer (it represents how many numbers we add together), we discard the negative value. Therefore, we conclude that $1 + 2 + 3 + \ldots + 36 = 666$.

111.   Let t_1 and t_2 represent the times for the two segments of the trip.

	Rate	Time	Distance
Chicago to Atlanta	45	t_1	$45t_1$
Atlanta to Miami	55	t_2	$55t_2$

Since Atlanta is halfway between Chicago and Miami, the distances are equal.

$$45t_1 = 55t_2 \quad \rightarrow \quad t_1 = \frac{55}{45}t_2 = \frac{11}{9}t_2$$

Computing the average speed:

$$\text{Avg Speed} = \frac{\text{Distance}}{\text{Time}} = \frac{45t_1 + 55t_2}{t_1 + t_2} = \frac{45\left(\frac{11}{9}t_2\right) + 55t_2}{\frac{11}{9}t_2 + t_2}$$

$$= \frac{55t_2 + 55t_2}{\frac{11t_2 + 9t_2}{9}} = \frac{110t_2}{\frac{20t_2}{9}} = \frac{990t_2}{20t_2} = \frac{99}{2} = 49.5 \text{ miles per hour}$$

The average speed for the trip from Chicago to Miami is 49.5 miles per hour.

113 – 115. Answers will vary.

Chapter 1

Equations and Inequalities

1.4   Radical Equations; Equations Quadratic in Form

1. $\sqrt{2t-1} = 1$

$$\left(\sqrt{2t-1}\right)^2 = 1^2$$

$$2t - 1 = 1 \rightarrow 2t = 2 \rightarrow t = 1$$

Check: $\sqrt{2(1)-1} = \sqrt{1} = 1$

The solution is $t = 1$.

3. $\sqrt{3t+4} = -6$

Since the principal square root is always a non-negative number, this equation has no real solution

5. $\sqrt[3]{1-2x} - 3 = 0$

$$\sqrt[3]{1-2x} = 3$$

$$\left(\sqrt[3]{1-2x}\right)^3 = 3^3$$

$$1 - 2x = 27 \rightarrow -2x = 26 \rightarrow x = -13$$

Check: $\sqrt[3]{1-2(-13)} - 3$

$$= \sqrt[3]{27} - 3 = 0$$

The solution is $x = -13$.

7. $x = 8\sqrt{x}$

$$(x)^2 = \left(8\sqrt{x}\right)^2$$

$$x^2 = 64x \rightarrow x^2 - 64x = 0$$

$$x(x-64) = 0 \rightarrow x = 0 \text{ or } x = 64$$

Check

$x = 0: \quad 0 = 8\sqrt{0} \rightarrow 0 = 0$

$x = 64: \quad 64 = 8\sqrt{64} \rightarrow 64 = (8)(8) = 64$

The solution set is $\{0, 64\}$.

9. $\sqrt{15-2x} = x$

$$\left(\sqrt{15-2x}\right)^2 = x^2$$

$$15 - 2x = x^2 \rightarrow x^2 + 2x - 15 = 0$$

$(x+5)(x-3) = 0 \rightarrow x = -5 \text{ or } x = 3$

Check -5: $\sqrt{15-2(-5)} = \sqrt{25}$

$$= 5 \neq -5$$

Check 3: $\sqrt{15-2(3)} = \sqrt{9} = 3 = 3$

The solution is $x = 3$.

11. $x = 2\sqrt{x-1}$

$$x^2 = \left(2\sqrt{x-1}\right)^2$$

$$x^2 = 4(x-1) \rightarrow x^2 = 4x - 4$$

$$x^2 - 4x + 4 = 0 \rightarrow (x-2)^2 = 0 \rightarrow x = 2$$

Check: $2 = 2\sqrt{2-1} \rightarrow 2 = 2$

The solution is $x = 2$.

13.
$$\sqrt{x^2 - x - 4} = x + 2$$
$$\left(\sqrt{x^2 - x - 4}\right)^2 = (x+2)^2$$
$$x^2 - x - 4 = x^2 + 4x + 4$$
$$-8 = 5x \rightarrow -\frac{8}{5} = x$$

Check

$$x = -\frac{8}{5} : \sqrt{\left(-\frac{8}{5}\right)^2 - \left(-\frac{8}{5}\right) - 4} = \left(-\frac{8}{5}\right) + 2$$

$$\sqrt{\frac{64}{25} + \frac{8}{5} - 4} = \frac{2}{5} \rightarrow \sqrt{\frac{64 + 40 - 100}{25}} = \frac{2}{5}$$

$$\sqrt{\frac{4}{25}} = \frac{2}{5} \rightarrow \frac{2}{5} = \frac{2}{5} \text{ , The solution is } x = -\frac{8}{5}.$$

15.
$$3 + \sqrt{3x+1} = x$$
$$\sqrt{3x+1} = x - 3$$
$$\left(\sqrt{3x+1}\right)^2 = (x-3)^2$$
$$3x + 1 = x^2 - 6x + 9 \rightarrow 0 = x^2 - 9x + 8$$
$$(x-1)(x-8) = 0 \rightarrow x = 1 \text{ or } x = 8$$

Check 1: $3 + \sqrt{3(1)+1}$
$$= 3 + \sqrt{4} = 5 \neq 1$$
Check 8: $3 + \sqrt{3(8)+1}$
$$= 3 + \sqrt{25} = 8 = 8$$
The solution is $x = 8$.

17.
$$\sqrt{2x+3} - \sqrt{x+1} = 1$$
$$\sqrt{2x+3} = 1 + \sqrt{x+1}$$
$$\left(\sqrt{2x+3}\right)^2 = \left(1 + \sqrt{x+1}\right)^2$$
$$2x + 3 = 1 + 2\sqrt{x+1} + x + 1$$
$$x + 1 = 2\sqrt{x+1}$$
$$(x+1)^2 = \left(2\sqrt{x+1}\right)^2$$
$$x^2 + 2x + 1 = 4(x+1)$$
$$x^2 + 2x + 1 = 4x + 4 \rightarrow x^2 - 2x - 3 = 0$$
$$(x+1)(x-3) = 0 \rightarrow x = -1 \text{ or } x = 3$$

Check -1: $\sqrt{2(-1)+3} - \sqrt{-1+1}$
$$= \sqrt{1} - \sqrt{0} = 1 - 0 = 1 = 1$$
Check 3: $\sqrt{2(3)+3} - \sqrt{3+1}$
$$= \sqrt{9} - \sqrt{4} = 3 - 2 = 1 = 1$$
The solution is $x = -1$ or $x = 3$.

19.
$$\sqrt{3x+1} - \sqrt{x-1} = 2$$
$$\sqrt{3x+1} = 2 + \sqrt{x-1}$$
$$\left(\sqrt{3x+1}\right)^2 = \left(2 + \sqrt{x-1}\right)^2$$
$$3x + 1 = 4 + 4\sqrt{x-1} + x - 1$$
$$2x - 2 = 4\sqrt{x-1}$$
$$(2x-2)^2 = \left(4\sqrt{x-1}\right)^2$$
$$4x^2 - 8x + 4 = 16(x-1)$$
$$x^2 - 2x + 1 = 4x - 4 \rightarrow x^2 - 6x + 5 = 0$$
$$(x-1)(x-5) = 0 \rightarrow x = 1 \text{ or } x = 5$$

Check 1: $\sqrt{3(1)+1} - \sqrt{1-1}$
$$= \sqrt{4} - \sqrt{0} = 2 - 0 = 2 = 2$$
Check 5: $\sqrt{3(5)+1} - \sqrt{5-1}$
$$= \sqrt{16} - \sqrt{4} = 4 - 2 = 2 = 2$$
The solution is $x = 1$ or $x = 5$.

21. $\sqrt{3-2\sqrt{x}} = \sqrt{x}$

$\left(\sqrt{3-2\sqrt{x}}\right)^2 = \left(\sqrt{x}\right)^2$

$3 - 2\sqrt{x} = x$

$-2\sqrt{x} = x - 3 \rightarrow \left(-2\sqrt{x}\right)^2 = (x-3)^2$

$4x = x^2 - 6x + 9 \rightarrow 0 = x^2 - 10x + 9$

$0 = (x-9)(x-1) \rightarrow x = 9$ or $x = 1$

Check

$x = 9$: $\sqrt{3-2\sqrt{9}} = \sqrt{9}$

$\sqrt{3-2(3)} = 3 \rightarrow \sqrt{-3} \neq 3$

Check

$x = 1$: $\sqrt{3-2\sqrt{1}} = \sqrt{1}$

$\sqrt{3-2(1)} = 1 \rightarrow \sqrt{1} = 1$

The solution is $x = 1$.

23. $(3x+1)^{1/2} = 4$

$\left((3x+1)^{1/2}\right)^2 = (4)^2$

$3x + 1 = 16 \rightarrow 3x = 15 \rightarrow x = 5$

Check

$x = 5$: $(3(5)+1)^{1/2} = 4$

$16^{1/2} = 4 \rightarrow 4 = 4$

The solution is $x = 5$.

25. $(5x-2)^{1/3} = 2$

$\left((5x-2)^{1/3}\right)^3 = (2)^3$

$5x - 2 = 8 \rightarrow 5x = 10 \rightarrow x = 2$

Check

$x = 2$: $(5(2)-2)^{1/3} = 2$

$8^{1/3} = 2 \rightarrow 2 = 2$

The solution is $x = 2$.

27. $(x^2+9)^{1/2} = 5$

$\left((x^2+9)^{1/2}\right)^2 = (5)^2$

$x^2 + 9 = 25 \rightarrow x^2 = 16$

$x = -4$ or $x = 4$

Check

$x = -4$: $\left((-4)^2 + 9\right)^{1/2} = 5$

$25^{1/2} = 5 \rightarrow 5 = 5$

$x = 4$: $\left((4)^2 + 9\right)^{1/2} = 5$

$25^{1/2} = 5 \rightarrow 5 = 5$

The solution set is $\{-4, 4\}$.

29. $x^{3/2} - 3x^{1/2} = 0$

$x^{3/2} = 3x^{1/2}$

$\left(x^{3/2}\right)^2 = \left(3x^{1/2}\right)^2$

$x^3 = 9x \rightarrow x^3 - 9x = 0$

$x(x^2 - 9) = 0 \rightarrow x = 0$ or $x = -3$ or $x = 3$

Check

$x = 0$: $0^{3/2} - 3\left(0^{1/2}\right) = 0$

$0 = 0$

$x = -3$: $(-3)^{3/2} - 3\left((-3)^{1/2}\right) = 0$

$\left(\sqrt{-3}\right)^3 - 3\left(\sqrt{-3}\right) \neq 0$

$x = 3$: $(3)^{3/2} - 3\left((3)^{1/2}\right) = 0$

$(3)^{3/2} - (3)^{3/2} = 0 \rightarrow 0 = 0$

The solution set is $\{0, 3\}$.

31.
$$x^4 - 5x^2 + 4 = 0$$
$$(x^2 - 4)(x^2 - 1) = 0$$

$x^2 - 4 = 0$ or $x^2 - 1 = 0$

$x = \pm 2$ or $x = \pm 1$

The solution set is $\{-2, -1, 1, 2\}$.

33.
$$3x^4 - 2x^2 - 1 = 0$$
$$(3x^2 + 1)(x^2 - 1) = 0$$

$3x^2 + 1 = 0$ or $x^2 - 1 = 0$

$3x^2 = -1$, which is impossible

or $x = \pm 1$

The solution set is $\{-1, 1\}$.

35.
$$x^6 + 7x^3 - 8 = 0$$
$$(x^3 + 8)(x^3 - 1) = 0$$

$x^3 + 8 = 0$ or $x^3 - 1 = 0$

$x^3 = -8 \rightarrow x = -2$

or $x^3 = 1 \rightarrow x = 1$

The solution set is $\{-2, 1\}$.

37.
$$(x + 2)^2 + 7(x + 2) + 12 = 0$$

let $p = x + 2 \rightarrow p^2 = (x + 2)^2$

$$p^2 + 7p + 12 = 0$$
$$(p + 3)(p + 4) = 0$$

$p + 3 = 0$ or $p + 4 = 0$

$p = -3 \rightarrow x + 2 = -3 \rightarrow x = -5$

or $p = -4 \rightarrow x + 2 = -4 \rightarrow x = -6$

The solution set is $\{-6, -5\}$.

39.
$$(3x + 4)^2 - 6(3x + 4) + 9 = 0$$

let $p = 3x + 4 \rightarrow p^2 = (3x + 4)^2$

$$p^2 - 6p + 9 = 0$$
$$(p - 3)(p - 3) = 0$$
$$p - 3 = 0$$

$p = 3 \rightarrow 3x + 4 = 3 \rightarrow x = -\dfrac{1}{3}$

The solution set is $\left\{-\dfrac{1}{3}\right\}$.

41.
$$2(s + 1)^2 - 5(s + 1) = 3$$

let $p = s + 1 \rightarrow p^2 = (s + 1)^2$

$$2p^2 - 5p = 3$$
$$2p^2 - 5p - 3 = 0$$
$$(2p + 1)(p - 3) = 0$$

$2p + 1 = 0$ or $p - 3 = 0$

$p = -\dfrac{1}{2} \rightarrow s + 1 = -\dfrac{1}{2} \rightarrow s = -\dfrac{3}{2}$

or $p = 3 \rightarrow s + 1 = 3 \rightarrow s = 2$

The solution set is $\left\{-\dfrac{3}{2}, 2\right\}$.

43. $x - 4x\sqrt{x} = 0$
$x = 4x\sqrt{x}$

$(x)^2 = \left(4x\sqrt{x}\right)^2$

$x = 16x^2 x \rightarrow x = 16x^3 \rightarrow 0 = 16x^3 - x$

$0 = x\left(16x^2 - 1\right) \rightarrow x = 0$

or $16x^2 - 1 = 0 \rightarrow x = \pm\dfrac{1}{4}$

Check

$x = 0: \quad 0 - 4(0)\sqrt{0} = 0$

$\qquad\qquad 0 = 0$

$x = -\dfrac{1}{4}: \quad \left(-\dfrac{1}{4}\right) - 4\left(-\dfrac{1}{4}\right)\sqrt{-\dfrac{1}{4}} \neq 0$

$x = \dfrac{1}{4}: \quad \left(\dfrac{1}{4}\right) - 4\left(\dfrac{1}{4}\right)\sqrt{\dfrac{1}{4}} = 0$

$\left(\dfrac{1}{4}\right) - 1\left(\dfrac{1}{2}\right) = 0 \rightarrow -\dfrac{1}{4} \neq 0$

The solution set is $\{0\}$.

45. $x + \sqrt{x} = 20$
let $p = \sqrt{x} \rightarrow p^2 = x$

$p^2 + p = 20$

$p^2 + p - 20 = 0 \rightarrow (p + 5)(p - 4) = 0$

$p + 5 = 0$ or $p - 4 = 0$

$p = -5 \rightarrow \sqrt{x} = -5 \rightarrow x = 25$

or $p = 4 \rightarrow \sqrt{x} = 4 \rightarrow x = 16$

Check

$x = 25: \quad 25 + \sqrt{25} = 20$

$\qquad\qquad 25 + 5 \neq 20$

$x = 16: \quad 16 + \sqrt{16} = 20$

$\qquad\qquad 16 + 4 = 20$

The solution set is $\{16\}$.

47. $t^{1/2} - 2t^{1/4} + 1 = 0$
let $p = t^{1/4} \rightarrow p^2 = t^{1/2}$

$p^2 - 2p + 1 = 0 \rightarrow (p - 1)(p - 1) = 0$

$p - 1 = 0 \rightarrow p = 1 \rightarrow t^{1/4} = 1 \rightarrow t = 1$

Check

$t = 1: \quad 1^{1/2} - 2(1)^{1/4} + 1 = 0$

$\qquad\qquad 1 - 2 + 1 = 0 \rightarrow 0 = 0$

The solution set is $\{1\}$.

49. $4x^{1/2} - 9x^{1/4} + 4 = 0$
$\quad$ let $p = x^{1/4} \rightarrow p^2 = x^{1/2}$

$4p^2 - 9p + 4 = 0$

$p = \dfrac{9 \pm \sqrt{81 - 64}}{8} = \dfrac{9 \pm \sqrt{17}}{8} \rightarrow x^{1/4} = \dfrac{9 \pm \sqrt{17}}{8} \rightarrow x = \left(\dfrac{9 \pm \sqrt{17}}{8}\right)^4$

Check

$x = \left(\dfrac{9 + \sqrt{17}}{8}\right)^4 : \quad 4\left(\left(\dfrac{9 + \sqrt{17}}{8}\right)^4\right)^{1/2} - 9\left(\left(\dfrac{9 + \sqrt{17}}{8}\right)^4\right)^{1/4} + 4 = 0$

$4\left(\dfrac{9 + \sqrt{17}}{8}\right)^2 - 9\left(\dfrac{9 + \sqrt{17}}{8}\right) + 4 = 0$

$4\dfrac{\left(9 + \sqrt{17}\right)^2}{64} - 9\left(\dfrac{9 + \sqrt{17}}{8}\right) + 4 = 0$

$$64\left(4\frac{\left(9+\sqrt{17}\right)^2}{64}-9\left(\frac{9+\sqrt{17}}{8}\right)+4\right)=(0)(64)$$

$$4\left(9+\sqrt{17}\right)^2-72\left(9+\sqrt{17}\right)+256=0$$

$$4\left(81+18\sqrt{17}+17\right)-72\left(9+\sqrt{17}\right)+256=0$$

$$324+72\sqrt{17}+68-648-72\sqrt{17}+256=0\rightarrow0=0$$

$$x=\left(\frac{9-\sqrt{17}}{8}\right)^4 : 4\left(\left(\frac{9-\sqrt{17}}{8}\right)^4\right)^{1/2}-9\left(\left(\frac{9-\sqrt{17}}{8}\right)^4\right)^{1/4}+4=0$$

$$4\left(\frac{9-\sqrt{17}}{8}\right)^2-9\left(\frac{9-\sqrt{17}}{8}\right)+4=0\rightarrow4\left(81-18\sqrt{17}+17\right)-72\left(9-\sqrt{17}\right)+256=0$$

$$324-72\sqrt{17}+68-648+72\sqrt{17}+256=0\rightarrow0=0$$

$$4\frac{\left(9-\sqrt{17}\right)^2}{64}-9\left(\frac{9-\sqrt{17}}{8}\right)+4=0\Bigg\}\rightarrow64\left(4\frac{\left(9-\sqrt{17}\right)^2}{64}-9\left(\frac{9-\sqrt{17}}{8}\right)+4\right)=(0)(64)$$

$$\rightarrow4\left(9-\sqrt{17}\right)^2-72\left(9-\sqrt{17}\right)+256=0\ \rightarrow0=0\ \therefore\text{ the solution set is }\left\{\frac{9\pm\sqrt{17}}{8}\right\}$$

51. $\sqrt[4]{5x^2-6}=x$

$\left(\sqrt[4]{5x^2-6}\right)^4=x^4$

$5x^2-6=x^4$

$0=x^4-5x^2+6$

$let\ p=x^2\rightarrow p^2=x^4$

$0=p^2-5p+6\rightarrow(p-3)(p-2)=0$

$p=3\rightarrow x^2=3\rightarrow x=\pm\sqrt{3}$

or $p=2\rightarrow x^2=2\rightarrow x=\pm\sqrt{2}$

Check

$x=-\sqrt{3}:\ \sqrt[4]{5\left(-\sqrt{3}\right)^2-6}=-\sqrt{3}$

$\sqrt[4]{15-6}=-\sqrt{3}\rightarrow\sqrt[4]{9}\neq-\sqrt{3}$

$x=\sqrt{3}:\ \sqrt[4]{5\left(\sqrt{3}\right)^2-6}=\sqrt{3}$

$\sqrt[4]{15-6}=\sqrt{3}\rightarrow\sqrt[4]{9}=\sqrt{3}\rightarrow\sqrt{3}=\sqrt{3}$

$x=-\sqrt{2}:\ \sqrt[4]{5\left(-\sqrt{2}\right)^2-6}=-\sqrt{2}$

$\sqrt[4]{10-6}=-\sqrt{2}\rightarrow\sqrt[4]{4}\neq-\sqrt{2}$

$x=\sqrt{2}:\ \sqrt[4]{5\left(\sqrt{2}\right)^2-6}=\sqrt{2}$

$\sqrt[4]{10-6}=\sqrt{2}$

$\sqrt[4]{4}=\sqrt{2}\rightarrow\sqrt{2}=\sqrt{2}$

The solution set is $\left\{\sqrt{2},\sqrt{3}\right\}$.

53. $x^2 + 3x + \sqrt{x^2 + 3x} = 6$

let $p = \sqrt{x^2 + 3x} \rightarrow p^2 = x^2 + 3x$

$p^2 + p = 6 \rightarrow p^2 + p - 6 = 0$

$(p + 3)(p - 2) = 0 \rightarrow p = -3 \text{ or } p = 2$

$\rightarrow \sqrt{x^2 + 3x} = -3$ which is impossible

since the principal square root is always

a non-negative number.

or

$\sqrt{x^2 + 3x} = 2 \rightarrow x^2 + 3x = 4$

$x^2 + 3x - 4 = 0 \rightarrow (x + 4)(x - 1) = 0$

$x = -4 \text{ or } x = 1$

Check

$x = -4: \; (-4)^2 + 3(-4) + \sqrt{(-4)^2 + 3(-4)} = 6$

$16 - 12 + \sqrt{16 - 12} = 6$

$16 - 12 + \sqrt{4} = 6 \rightarrow 6 = 6$

$x = 1: \; (1)^2 + 3(1) + \sqrt{(1)^2 + 3(1)} = 6$

$1 + 3 + \sqrt{1 + 3} = 6 \rightarrow 4 + \sqrt{4} = 6 \rightarrow 6 = 6$

The solution set is $\{-4, 1\}$.

55.

$$\frac{1}{(x+1)^2} = \frac{1}{x+1} + 2$$

let $p = \dfrac{1}{x+1} \rightarrow p^2 = \left(\dfrac{1}{x+1}\right)^2$

$p^2 = p + 2 \rightarrow p^2 - p - 2 = 0$

$(p + 1)(p - 2) = 0 \rightarrow p = -1 \text{ or } p = 2$

$p = -1 \rightarrow \dfrac{1}{x+1} = -1 \rightarrow 1 = -x - 1 \rightarrow x = -2$

or $\dfrac{1}{x+1} = 2 \rightarrow 1 = 2x + 2 \rightarrow x = -\dfrac{1}{2}$

Check

$x = -2: \; \dfrac{1}{(-2+1)^2} = \dfrac{1}{-2+1} + 2$

$1 = -1 + 2 \rightarrow 1 = 1$

$x = -\dfrac{1}{2}: \; \dfrac{1}{\left(-\dfrac{1}{2}+1\right)^2} = \dfrac{1}{-\dfrac{1}{2}+1} + 2$

$4 = 2 + 2 \rightarrow 4 = 4$

The solution set is $\left\{-2, -\dfrac{1}{2}\right\}$.

57. $3x^{-2} - 7x^{-1} - 6 = 0$

let $p = x^{-1} \rightarrow p^2 = x^{-2}$

$3p^2 - 7p - 6 = 0$

$(3p + 2)(p - 3) = 0$

$p = -\dfrac{2}{3} \text{ or } p = 3$

$p = -\dfrac{2}{3} \rightarrow x^{-1} = -\dfrac{2}{3} \rightarrow (x^{-1})^{-1}$

$= \left(-\dfrac{2}{3}\right)^{-1} \rightarrow x = -\dfrac{3}{2}$

or

$p = 3 \rightarrow x^{-1} = 3 \rightarrow (x^{-1})^{-1} = (3)^{-1} \rightarrow x = \dfrac{1}{3}$

Check

$x = -\dfrac{3}{2}: \; 3\left(-\dfrac{3}{2}\right)^{-2} - 7\left(-\dfrac{3}{2}\right)^{-1} - 6 = 0$

$3\left(\dfrac{4}{9}\right) - 7\left(-\dfrac{2}{3}\right) - 6 = 0$

$\dfrac{4}{3} + \dfrac{14}{3} - 6 = 0 \rightarrow 6 - 6 = 0 \rightarrow 0 = 0$

$x = \dfrac{1}{3}: \; 3\left(\dfrac{1}{3}\right)^{-2} - 7\left(\dfrac{1}{3}\right)^{-1} - 6 = 0$

$3(9) - 7(3) - 6 = 0$

$27 - 21 - 6 = 0 \rightarrow 6 - 6 = 0 \rightarrow 0 = 0$

The solution set is $\left\{-\dfrac{3}{2}, \dfrac{1}{3}\right\}$.

59. $2x^{2/3} - 5x^{1/3} - 3 = 0$

let $p = x^{1/3} \rightarrow p^2 = x^{2/3}$

$2p^2 - 5p - 3 = 0 \rightarrow (2p+1)(p-3) = 0$

$p = -\dfrac{1}{2}$ or $p = 3$

$p = -\dfrac{1}{2} \rightarrow x^{1/3} = -\dfrac{1}{2}$

$\rightarrow \left(x^{1/3}\right)^3 = \left(-\dfrac{1}{2}\right)^3 \rightarrow x = -\dfrac{1}{8}$

or

$p = 3 \rightarrow x^{1/3} = 3 \rightarrow \left(x^{1/3}\right)^3 = (3)^3$

$\rightarrow x = 27$

Check

$x = -\dfrac{1}{8}: \ 2\left(-\dfrac{1}{8}\right)^{2/3} - 5\left(-\dfrac{1}{8}\right)^{1/3} - 3 = 0$

$2\left(\dfrac{1}{4}\right) - 5\left(-\dfrac{1}{2}\right) - 3 = 0$

$\dfrac{1}{2} + \dfrac{5}{2} - 3 = 0 \rightarrow 3 - 3 = 0 \rightarrow 0 = 0$

$x = 27: \ 2(27)^{2/3} - 5(27)^{1/3} - 3 = 0$

$2(9) - 5(3) - 3 = 0$

$18 - 15 - 3 = 0 \rightarrow 3 - 3 = 0 \rightarrow 0 = 0$

The solution set is $\left\{-\dfrac{1}{8}, 27\right\}$.

61. $\left(\dfrac{v}{v+1}\right)^2 + \dfrac{2v}{v+1} = 8$

let $p = \dfrac{v}{v+1} \rightarrow p^2 = \left(\dfrac{v}{v+1}\right)^2$

$\left(\dfrac{v}{v+1}\right)^2 + \dfrac{2v}{v+1} = 8 \rightarrow \left(\dfrac{v}{v+1}\right)^2 + 2\left(\dfrac{v}{v+1}\right) = 8$

$p^2 + 2p = 8 \rightarrow p^2 + 2p - 8 = 0$

$(p+4)(p-2) = 0 \rightarrow p = -4$ or $p = 2$

$p = -4 \rightarrow \dfrac{v}{v+1} = -4$

$\rightarrow v = -4v - 4 \rightarrow v = -\dfrac{4}{5}$

or

$p = 2 \rightarrow \dfrac{v}{v+1} = 2 \rightarrow v = 2v + 2 \rightarrow v = -2$

Check

$v = -\dfrac{4}{5}: \ \left(\dfrac{-\dfrac{4}{5}}{-\dfrac{4}{5}+1}\right)^2 + \dfrac{2\left(-\dfrac{4}{5}\right)}{\left(-\dfrac{4}{5}\right)+1} = 8$

$\dfrac{\left(\dfrac{16}{25}\right)}{\left(\dfrac{1}{25}\right)} + \dfrac{\left(-\dfrac{8}{5}\right)}{\left(\dfrac{1}{5}\right)} = 8$

$16 - 8 = 8 \rightarrow 8 = 8$

$v = -2: \ \left(\dfrac{-2}{-2+1}\right)^2 + \dfrac{2(-2)}{(-2)+1} = 8$

$4 + 4 = 8 \rightarrow 8 = 8$

The solution set is $\left\{-\dfrac{4}{5}, -2\right\}$.

63. $x - 4x^{1/2} + 2 = 0$

    let $p = x^{1/2} \to p^2 = x^2$

    $p^2 - 4p + 2 = 0$

    $p = \dfrac{4 \pm \sqrt{16 - 8}}{2} = \dfrac{4 \pm \sqrt{8}}{2}$

    $p = \dfrac{4 + \sqrt{8}}{2} \to x^{1/2} = \dfrac{4 + \sqrt{8}}{2}$

    $\to \left(x^{1/2}\right)^2 = \left(\dfrac{4 + \sqrt{8}}{2}\right)^2 \to x = \left(\dfrac{4 + \sqrt{8}}{2}\right)^2$

    or

    $p = \dfrac{4 - \sqrt{8}}{2} \to x^{1/2} = \dfrac{4 - \sqrt{8}}{2}$

    $\to \left(x^{1/2}\right)^2 = \left(\dfrac{4 - \sqrt{8}}{2}\right)^2 \to x = \left(\dfrac{4 - \sqrt{8}}{2}\right)^2$

Check

$x = \left(\dfrac{4 + \sqrt{8}}{2}\right)^2 : \left(\dfrac{4 + \sqrt{8}}{2}\right)^2 - 4\left(\dfrac{4 + \sqrt{8}}{2}\right) + 2 = 0$

$\dfrac{16 + 8\sqrt{8} + 8}{4} - 4\left(\dfrac{4 + \sqrt{8}}{2}\right) + 2 = 0$

$4 + 2\sqrt{8} + 2 - 2\left(4 + \sqrt{8}\right) + 2 = 0$

$4 + 2\sqrt{8} + 2 - 8 - 2\sqrt{8} + 2 = 0$

$0 = 0$

$x = \left(\dfrac{4 - \sqrt{8}}{2}\right)^2 : \left(\dfrac{4 - \sqrt{8}}{2}\right)^2 - 4\left(\dfrac{4 - \sqrt{8}}{2}\right) + 2 = 0$

$\dfrac{16 - 8\sqrt{8} + 8}{4} - 4\left(\dfrac{4 - \sqrt{8}}{2}\right) + 2 = 0$

$4 - 2\sqrt{8} + 2 - 2\left(4 - \sqrt{8}\right) + 2 = 0$

$4 - 2\sqrt{8} + 2 - 8 + 2\sqrt{8} + 2 = 0 \to 0 = 0$

The solution set is

$\left\{\left(\dfrac{4 + \sqrt{8}}{2}\right)^2, \left(\dfrac{4 - \sqrt{8}}{2}\right)^2\right\} \to \{11.66, 0.34\}.$

65. $x^4 + \sqrt{3}x^2 - 3 = 0$

    let $p = x^2 \to p^2 = x^4$

    $p^2 + \sqrt{3}p - 3 = 0$

    $p = \dfrac{-\sqrt{3} \pm \sqrt{3 + 12}}{2} = \dfrac{-\sqrt{3} \pm \sqrt{15}}{2}$

    $p = \dfrac{-\sqrt{3} + \sqrt{15}}{2}$

    $\to x^2 = \dfrac{-\sqrt{3} + \sqrt{15}}{2} \to x = \pm\sqrt{\dfrac{-\sqrt{3} + \sqrt{15}}{2}}$

or

$p = \dfrac{-\sqrt{3} - \sqrt{15}}{2}$

$\to x^2 = \dfrac{-\sqrt{3} - \sqrt{15}}{2} \to$

$x = \pm\sqrt{\dfrac{-\sqrt{3} - \sqrt{15}}{2}}$

which is impossible since $\dfrac{-\sqrt{3} - \sqrt{15}}{2} < 0$

Check

$$x = \sqrt{\dfrac{-\sqrt{3}+\sqrt{15}}{2}}:$$

$$\left(\sqrt{\dfrac{-\sqrt{3}+\sqrt{15}}{2}}\right)^4 + \sqrt{3}\left(\sqrt{\dfrac{-\sqrt{3}+\sqrt{15}}{2}}\right)^2 - 3 = 0$$

$$\left(\dfrac{-\sqrt{3}+\sqrt{15}}{2}\right)^2 + \sqrt{3}\left(\dfrac{-\sqrt{3}+\sqrt{15}}{2}\right) - 3 = 0$$

$$\left(\dfrac{3-2\sqrt{3}\sqrt{15}+15}{4}\right) + \left(\dfrac{\sqrt{3}(-\sqrt{3})+\sqrt{3}\sqrt{15}}{2}\right) - 3 = 0$$

$$\left(\dfrac{18-2\sqrt{45}}{4}\right) + \left(\dfrac{-3+\sqrt{45}}{2}\right) - 3 = 0$$

$$\left(\dfrac{9-\sqrt{45}}{2}\right) + \left(\dfrac{-3+\sqrt{45}}{2}\right) - 3 = 0$$

$$\left(\dfrac{9-\sqrt{45}-3+\sqrt{45}}{2}\right) - 3 = 0$$

$$3 - 3 = 0 \rightarrow 0 = 0$$

$$x = -\sqrt{\dfrac{-\sqrt{3}+\sqrt{15}}{2}}:$$

$$\left(-\sqrt{\dfrac{-\sqrt{3}+\sqrt{15}}{2}}\right)^4 + \sqrt{3}\left(-\sqrt{\dfrac{-\sqrt{3}+\sqrt{15}}{2}}\right)^2 - 3 = 0$$

$$\left(\dfrac{-\sqrt{3}+\sqrt{15}}{2}\right)^2 + \sqrt{3}\left(\dfrac{-\sqrt{3}+\sqrt{15}}{2}\right) - 3 = 0$$

$$\left(\dfrac{3-2\sqrt{3}\sqrt{15}+15}{4}\right) + \left(\dfrac{\sqrt{3}(-\sqrt{3})+\sqrt{3}\sqrt{15}}{2}\right) - 3 = 0$$

$$\left(\dfrac{18-2\sqrt{45}}{4}\right) + \left(\dfrac{-3+\sqrt{45}}{2}\right) - 3 = 0$$

$$\left(\dfrac{9-\sqrt{45}}{2}\right) + \left(\dfrac{-3+\sqrt{45}}{2}\right) - 3 = 0$$

$$\left(\dfrac{9-\sqrt{45}-3+\sqrt{45}}{2}\right) - 3 = 0 \rightarrow 3 - 3 = 0 \rightarrow 0 = 0$$

The solution set is

$$\left\{\sqrt{\dfrac{-\sqrt{3}+\sqrt{15}}{2}}, -\sqrt{\dfrac{-\sqrt{3}+\sqrt{15}}{2}}\right\}$$

$$\rightarrow \{1.04, -1.04\}$$

67. $\pi(1+t)^2 = \pi + 1 + t$

let $p = 1 + t \rightarrow p^2 = (1+t)^2$

$$\pi p^2 = \pi + p \rightarrow \pi p^2 - p - \pi = 0$$

$$p = \dfrac{1 \pm \sqrt{1+4\pi^2}}{2\pi}$$

$$\rightarrow 1 + t = \dfrac{1 \pm \sqrt{1+4\pi^2}}{2\pi}$$

$$\rightarrow t = -1 + \dfrac{1 \pm \sqrt{1+4\pi^2}}{2\pi}$$

$$t = -1 + \dfrac{1 \pm \sqrt{1+4\pi^2}}{2\pi}$$

Check

$$t = -1 + \dfrac{1 + \sqrt{1+4\pi^2}}{2\pi}:$$

$$\pi\left(\dfrac{1+\sqrt{1+4\pi^2}}{2\pi}\right)^2 = \pi + \dfrac{1+\sqrt{1+4\pi^2}}{2\pi}$$

$$\pi\left(\dfrac{1+2\sqrt{1+4\pi^2}+1+4\pi^2}{4\pi^2}\right) = \pi + \dfrac{1+\sqrt{1+4\pi^2}}{2\pi}$$

$$\dfrac{2+2\sqrt{1+4\pi^2}+4\pi^2}{4\pi} = \dfrac{2\pi^2+1+\sqrt{1+4\pi^2}}{2\pi}$$

$$\dfrac{1+\sqrt{1+4\pi^2}+2\pi^2}{2\pi} = \dfrac{2\pi^2+1+\sqrt{1+4\pi^2}}{2\pi}$$

$$0 = 0$$

$t = -1 + \dfrac{1 - \sqrt{1 + 4\pi^2}}{2\pi}$:

$$\pi\left(\dfrac{1 - \sqrt{1 + 4\pi^2}}{2\pi}\right)^2 = \pi + \dfrac{1 - \sqrt{1 + 4\pi^2}}{2\pi}$$

$$\pi\left(\dfrac{1 - 2\sqrt{1 + 4\pi^2} + 1 + 4\pi^2}{4\pi^2}\right) = \pi + \dfrac{1 - \sqrt{1 + 4\pi^2}}{2\pi}$$

$$\dfrac{2 - 2\sqrt{1 + 4\pi^2} + 4\pi^2}{4\pi} = \dfrac{2\pi^2 + 1 - \sqrt{1 + 4\pi^2}}{2\pi}$$

$$\dfrac{1 - \sqrt{1 + 4\pi^2} + 2\pi^2}{2\pi} = \dfrac{2\pi^2 + 1 - \sqrt{1 + 4\pi^2}}{2\pi}$$

$0 = 0$

The solution set is

$$\left\{ -1 + \dfrac{1 + \sqrt{1 + 4\pi^2}}{2\pi}, -1 + \dfrac{1 - \sqrt{1 + 4\pi^2}}{2\pi} \right\}$$

$\rightarrow \{0.17, -1.85\}$

69. $k^2 - k = 12 \rightarrow k^2 - k - 12 = 0$
      $(k - 4)(k + 3) = 0$

   $k = 4$ or $k = -3$

   $\rightarrow \dfrac{x + 3}{x - 3} = 4$

   $\rightarrow x + 3 = 4x - 12 \rightarrow x = 15$

   or

   $\dfrac{x + 3}{x - 3} = -3$

   $\rightarrow x + 3 = -3x + 9 \rightarrow x = \dfrac{3}{2}$

and since neither of these x values causes
a denominator to equal zero, the solution

set is $\left\{\dfrac{3}{2}, 15\right\}$.

71.   Graph the equations and to find the x-
      coordinate of the points of intersection:

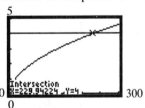

The distance to the water's surface is
approximately 229.94 feet.

73.   Answers will vary, one example is $x - \sqrt{x} - 2 = 0$

Equations and Inequalities

1.5   Solving Inequalities

1-65 odd

1. $[0, 2]$ $0 \le x \le 2$

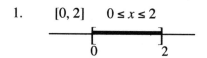

3. $(-1, 2)$ $-1 < x < 2$

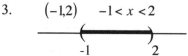

5. $[0, 3)$ $0 \le x < 3$

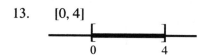

7.   (a) $6 < 8$
     (b) $-2 < 0$
     (c) $9 < 15$
     (d) $-6 > -10$

9.   (a) $7 > 0$
     (b) $-1 > -8$
     (c) $12 > -9$
     (d) $-8 < 6$

11.   (a) $2x + 4 < 5$
      (b) $2x - 4 < -3$
      (c) $6x + 3 < 6$
      (d) $-4x - 2 > -4$

13. $[0, 4]$

15. $[4, 6)$

17. $[4, \infty)$

19. $(-\infty, -4)$

21. $2 \le x \le 5$

23. $-3 < x < -2$

25. $x \ge 4$

27. $x < -3$

29.   If $x < 5$, then $x - 5 < 0$.

31.   If $x > -4$, then $x + 4 > 0$.

33.   If $x \ge -4$, then $3x \ge -12$.

35.   If $x > 6$, then $-2x < -12$.

37.   If $x \ge 5$, then $-4x \le -20$.

39.   If $2x > 6$, then $x > 3$.

41.   If $-\dfrac{1}{2}x \le 3$, then $x \ge -6$.

43. $x + 1 < 5$

$x + 1 - 1 < 5 - 1 \rightarrow x < 4$

$\{x \mid x < 4\}$ or $(-\infty, 4)$

45. $1 - 2x \leq 3$

$-2x \leq 2 \rightarrow x \geq -1$

$\{x \mid x \geq -1\}$ or $[-1, +\infty)$

47. $3x - 7 > 2$

$3x > 9 \rightarrow x > 3$

$\{x \mid x > 3\}$ or $(3, +\infty)$

49. $3x - 1 \geq 3 + x$

$2x \geq 4 \rightarrow x \geq 2$

$\{x \mid x \geq 2\}$ or $[2, +\infty)$

51. $-2(x + 3) < 8$
$-2x - 6 < 8$

$-2x < 14$

$x > -7$

$\{x \mid x > -7\}$ or $(-7, +\infty)$

53.

$4 - 3(1 - x) \leq 3$

$4 - 3 + 3x \leq 3$

$3x + 1 \leq 3$

$3x \leq 2$

$x \leq \dfrac{2}{3}$

$\left\{x \mid x \leq \dfrac{2}{3}\right\}$ or $\left(-\infty, \dfrac{2}{3}\right]$

55.

$\dfrac{1}{2}(x - 4) > x + 8$

$\dfrac{1}{2}x - 2 > x + 8$

$-\dfrac{1}{2}x > 10$

$x < -20$

$\{x \mid x < -20\}$ or $(-\infty, -20)$

57.

$\dfrac{x}{2} \geq 1 - \dfrac{x}{4}$

$2x \geq 4 - x$

$3x \geq 4$

$x \geq \dfrac{4}{3}$

$\left\{x \mid x \geq \dfrac{4}{3}\right\}$ or $\left[\dfrac{4}{3}, +\infty\right)$

59.

$$0 \le 2x - 6 \le 4$$
$$6 \le 2x \le 10$$
$$3 \le x \le 5$$
$$\{x \mid 3 \le x \le 5\} \text{ or } [3, 5]$$

61.

$$-5 \le 4 - 3x \le 2$$
$$-9 \le -3x \le -2$$
$$3 \ge x \ge \frac{2}{3}$$
$$\left\{x \,\middle|\, \frac{2}{3} \le x \le 3\right\} \text{ or } \left[\frac{2}{3}, 3\right]$$

63.

$$-3 < \frac{2x - 1}{4} < 0$$
$$-12 < 2x - 1 < 0$$
$$-11 < 2x < 1$$
$$\frac{-11}{2} < x < \frac{1}{2}$$
$$\left\{x \,\middle|\, \frac{-11}{2} < x < \frac{1}{2}\right\} \text{ or } \left(\frac{-11}{2}, \frac{1}{2}\right)$$

65.

$$1 < 1 - \frac{1}{2}x < 4$$
$$0 < -\frac{1}{2}x < 3$$
$$0 > x > -6$$
$$\{x \mid -6 < x < 0\} \text{ or } (-6, 0)$$

67.

$$(x + 2)(x - 3) > (x - 1)(x + 1)$$
$$x^2 - x - 6 > x^2 - 1$$
$$-x - 6 > -1$$
$$-x > 5$$
$$x < -5$$
$$\{x \mid x < -5\} \text{ or } (-\infty, -5)$$

69.

$$x(4x + 3) \le (2x + 1)^2$$
$$4x^2 + 3x \le 4x^2 + 4x + 1$$
$$3x \le 4x + 1$$
$$-x \le 1$$
$$x \ge -1$$
$$\{x \mid x \ge -1\} \text{ or } [-1, +\infty)$$

71.

$$\frac{1}{2} \le \frac{x + 1}{3} < \frac{3}{4}$$
$$6 \le 4x + 4 < 9$$
$$2 \le 4x < 5$$
$$\frac{1}{2} \le x < \frac{5}{4}$$
$$\left\{x \,\middle|\, \frac{1}{2} \le x < \frac{5}{4}\right\} \text{ or } \left[\frac{1}{2}, \frac{5}{4}\right)$$

73.

$$(4x + 2)^{-1} < 0$$
$$\frac{1}{4x + 2} < 0 \rightarrow 4x + 2 < 0$$
$$x < -\frac{1}{2}$$
$$\left\{x \,\middle|\, x < -\frac{1}{2}\right\} \text{ or } \left(-\infty, -\frac{1}{2}\right)$$

75.

$$0 < \frac{2}{x} < \frac{3}{5} \rightarrow 0 < \frac{2}{x} \quad \text{and} \quad \frac{2}{x} < \frac{3}{5}$$

$$0 < \frac{2}{x} \rightarrow x > 0 \quad \text{therefore} \quad \frac{2}{x} < \frac{3}{5} \rightarrow 10 < 3x \rightarrow \frac{10}{3} < x$$

$$\left\{ x \middle| \frac{10}{3} < x \right\} \text{ or } \left(\frac{10}{3}, +\infty \right)$$

10/3

77.

$$0 < (2x-4)^{-1} < \frac{1}{2} \rightarrow 0 < \frac{1}{2x-4} \quad \text{and} \quad \frac{1}{2x-4} < \frac{1}{2}$$

$$0 < \frac{1}{2x-4} \rightarrow 2x-4 > 0 \quad \text{therefore} \quad \frac{1}{2x-4} < \frac{1}{2} \rightarrow 2 < 2x-4 \rightarrow 3 < x$$

$$\left\{ x \middle| 3 < x \right\} \text{ or } (3, +\infty)$$

3

79.   If $-1 < x < 1$, then $3 < x+4 < 5 \rightarrow a = 3, b = 5$

81.   If $2 < x < 3$, then $-12 < -4x < -8 \rightarrow a = -12, b = -8$

83.   If $0 < x < 4$, then $0 < 2x < 8 \rightarrow 3 < 2x+3 < 11 \rightarrow a = 3, b = 11$

85.
If $-3 < x < 0$, then $1 < x+4 < 4$

$$\rightarrow 1 > \frac{1}{x+4} > \frac{1}{4} \rightarrow \frac{1}{4} < \frac{1}{x+4} < 1 \rightarrow a = \frac{1}{4}, b = 1$$

87.   If $6 < 3x < 12$, then $2 < x < 4 \rightarrow 4 < x^2 < 16 \rightarrow a = 4, b = 16$

89.   We need $3x + 6 \geq 0 \rightarrow 3x \geq -6 \rightarrow x \geq -2$, so the domain is $\{x | x \geq -2\}$.

91. $21 < \text{young adult's age} < 30$

93.   (a)   An average 25-year-old male can expect to live at least 48.4 more years.
$25 + 48.4 = 73.4$. Therefore, the average age of a 25-year-old male will be ≥ 73.4.

(b)   An average 25-year-old female can expect to live at least 54.7 more years.
$25 + 54.7 = 79.7$. Therefore, the average age of a 25-year-old female will be ≥ 79.7.

(c)   By the given information, a female can expect to live 6.3 years longer.

95. Let P represent the selling price and C represent the commission.
Calculating the commission:
$$C = 45{,}000 + 0.25(P - 900{,}000) = 45{,}000 + 0.25P - 225{,}000 = 0.25P - 180{,}000$$
Calculate the commission range, given the price range:
$$900{,}000 \le \qquad P \qquad \le 1{,}100{,}000$$
$$0.25(900{,}000) \le \quad 0.25P \quad \le 0.25(1{,}100{,}000)$$
$$225{,}000 \le \quad 0.25P \quad \le 275{,}000$$
$$225{,}000 - 180{,}000 \le 0.25P - 180{,}000 \le 275{,}000 - 180{,}000$$
$$45{,}000 \le \qquad C \qquad \le 95{,}000$$
The agent's commission ranges from \$45,000 to \$95,000, inclusive.
$$\frac{45{,}000}{900{,}000} = 0.05 = 5\% \quad \text{to} \quad \frac{95{,}000}{1{,}100{,}000} = 0.086 = 8.6\%, \text{ inclusive.}$$
As a percent of selling price, the commission ranges from 5% to 8.6%.

97. Let W represent the weekly wage and T represent the withholding tax.
Calculating the tax:
$$T = 69.90 + 0.28(W - 517) = 69.90 + 0.28W - 144.76 = 0.28W - 74.86$$
Calculating the withholding tax range, given the range of weekly wages:
$$525 \le \qquad W \quad \le 600$$
$$0.28(525) \le \quad 0.28W \quad \le 0.28(600)$$
$$147 \le \quad 0.28W \quad \le 168$$
$$147 - 74.86 \le 0.28W - 74.86 \le 168 - 74.86$$
$$72.14 \le \qquad T \qquad \le 93.14$$
The amount of withholding tax ranges from \$72.14 to \$93.14, inclusive.

99. Let K represent the monthly usage in kilowatt-hours.
Let C represent the monthly customer bill.
Calculating the bill:
$$C = 0.10494K + 9.36$$
Calculating the range of kilowatt-hours, given the range of bills:
$$80.24 \le \qquad C \qquad \le 271.80$$
$$80.24 \le 0.10494K + 9.36 \le 271.80$$
$$70.88 \le \quad 0.10494K \quad \le 262.44$$
$$675.43 \le \qquad K \qquad \le 2500.86$$
The range of usage in kilowatt-hours varied from 675.43 to 2500.86.

101. Let C represent the dealer's cost and M represent the markup over dealer's cost.
If the price is \$8800, then $8800 = C + MC = C(1 + M)$
Solving for C: $\quad C = \dfrac{8800}{1 + M}$
Calculating the range of dealer costs, given the range of markups:
$$0.12 \le \quad M \quad \le 0.18 \rightarrow 1.12 \le 1 + M \le 1.18$$
$$\frac{1}{1.12} \ge \frac{1}{1 + M} \ge \frac{1}{1.18} \rightarrow \frac{8800}{1.12} \ge \frac{8800}{1 + M} \ge \frac{8800}{1.18}$$
$$7857.14 \ge \quad C \quad \ge 7457.63$$
The dealer's cost ranged from \$7457.63 to \$7857.14, inclusive.

103. Let T represent the score on the last test and G represent the course grade.
Calculating the course grade and solving for the last test:
$$G = \frac{68 + 82 + 87 + 89 + T}{5} = \frac{326 + T}{5} \rightarrow T = 5G - 326$$
Calculating the range of scores on the last test, given the grade range:
$$80 \le \quad G \quad < 90$$
$$400 \le \quad 5G \quad < 450$$
$$74 \le 5G - 326 < 124$$
$$74 \le \quad T \quad < 124$$
The fifth test must be greater than or equal to 74.

105.   Since $a < b$

$$\frac{a}{2} < \frac{b}{2} \qquad\qquad \frac{a}{2} < \frac{b}{2}$$

$$\frac{a}{2} + \frac{a}{2} < \frac{a}{2} + \frac{b}{2} \qquad \frac{a}{2} + \frac{b}{2} < \frac{b}{2} + \frac{b}{2} \qquad \text{Thus, } a < \frac{a+b}{2} < b$$

$$a < \frac{a+b}{2} \qquad\qquad \frac{a+b}{2} < b$$

107.   If $0 < a < b$, then $0 < a^2 < ab$ and $0 < ab < b^2$
$$ab - a^2 > 0 \qquad\qquad b^2 - ab > 0$$
$$ab > a^2 > 0 \qquad\qquad b^2 > ab > 0$$
$$\left(\sqrt{ab}\right)^2 > a^2 \qquad\qquad b^2 > \left(\sqrt{ab}\right)^2$$
$$\sqrt{ab} > a \qquad\qquad b > \sqrt{ab}$$
Thus, $a < \sqrt{ab} < b$

109. For $0 < a < b$, $\dfrac{1}{h} = \dfrac{1}{2}\left(\dfrac{1}{a} + \dfrac{1}{b}\right)$

$$h \cdot \frac{1}{h} = \frac{1}{2}\left(\frac{b+a}{ab}\right) \cdot h \quad \rightarrow \quad 1 = \frac{1}{2}\left(\frac{b+a}{ab}\right) \cdot h \quad \rightarrow \quad \frac{2ab}{a+b} = h$$

$$h - a = \frac{2ab}{a+b} - a \qquad\qquad b - h = b - \frac{2ab}{a+b}$$

$$= \frac{2ab - a(a+b)}{a+b} \qquad\qquad = \frac{b(a+b) - 2ab}{a+b}$$

$$= \frac{2ab - a^2 - ab}{a+b} \qquad\qquad = \frac{ab + b^2 - 2ab}{a+b}$$

$$= \frac{ab - a^2}{a+b} \qquad\qquad = \frac{b^2 - ab}{a+b}$$

$$= \frac{a(b-a)}{a+b} > 0 \qquad\qquad = \frac{b(b-a)}{a+b} > 0$$

Therefore, $h > a$. $\qquad\qquad$ Therefore, $h < b$. $\qquad\qquad$ Thus, $a < h < b$.

111. Answers will vary.

Equations and Inequalities

1.6 Equations and Inequalities Involving Absolute Value   1-23 odd

1. $|2x| = 6$
   $2x = 6$ or $2x = -6$
   $x = 3$ or $\quad x = -3$
   The solution set is $\{-3, 3\}$.

3. $|2x + 3| = 5$
   $2x + 3 = 5$ or $2x + 3 = -5$
   $2x = 2$ or $\quad 2x = -8$
   $x = 1$ or $\quad x = -4$
   The solution set is $\{-4, 1\}$.

5. $|1 - 4t| + 8 = 13 \rightarrow |1 - 4t| = 5$
   $1 - 4t = 5$ or $1 - 4t = -5$
   $-4t = 4$ or $\quad -4t = -6$
   $t = -1$ or $\quad t = \dfrac{3}{2}$
   The solution set is $\left\{-1, \dfrac{3}{2}\right\}$.

7. $|-2x| = 8$
   $-2x = 8$ or $-2x = -8$
   $x = -4$ or $\quad x = 4$
   The solution set is $\{-4, 4\}$.

9. $|-2|x = 4$
   $2x = 4$
   $x = 2$
   The solution set is $\{2\}$.

11. $\dfrac{2}{3}|x| = 9$
    $|x| = \dfrac{27}{2} \rightarrow x = \dfrac{27}{2}$ or $x = -\dfrac{27}{2}$
    The solution set is $\left\{-\dfrac{27}{2}, \dfrac{27}{2}\right\}$.

13. $\left|\dfrac{x}{3} + \dfrac{2}{5}\right| = 2$
    $\dfrac{x}{3} + \dfrac{2}{5} = 2$ or $\dfrac{x}{3} + \dfrac{2}{5} = -2$
    $5x + 6 = 30$ or $5x + 6 = -30$
    $5x = 24$ or $\quad 5x = -36$
    $x = \dfrac{24}{5}$ or $\quad x = -\dfrac{36}{5}$
    The solution set is $\left\{-\dfrac{36}{5}, \dfrac{24}{5}\right\}$.

15. $|u - 2| = -\dfrac{1}{2}$
    impossible, since absolute value always yields a non-negative number.

17.

$$4 - |2x| = 3 \rightarrow -|2x| = -1$$
$$\rightarrow |2x| = 1$$

$$2x = 1 \quad \text{or} \quad 2x = -1$$

$$x = \frac{1}{2} \quad \text{or} \quad x = -\frac{1}{2}$$

The solution set is $\left\{-\frac{1}{2}, \frac{1}{2}\right\}$.

19. $|x^2 - 9| = 0$

$$x^2 - 9 = 0$$
$$x^2 = 9$$
$$x = \pm 3$$

The solution set is $\{-3, 3\}$.

21. $|x^2 - 2x| = 3$

$$x^2 - 2x = 3 \quad \text{or} \quad x^2 - 2x = -3$$
$$x^2 - 2x - 3 = 0 \quad \text{or} \quad x^2 - 2x + 3 = 0$$
$$(x - 3)(x + 1) = 0$$

or $\quad x = \dfrac{2 \pm \sqrt{4 - 12}}{2} = \dfrac{2 \pm \sqrt{-8}}{2}$

$$x = 3, x = -1 \quad \text{or} \quad \rightarrow \text{no real solution}$$

The solution set is $\{-1, 3\}$.

(23) $|x^2 + x - 1| = 1$

$$x^2 + x - 1 = 1 \quad \text{or} \quad x^2 + x - 1 = -1$$
$$x^2 + x - 2 = 0 \quad \text{or} \quad x^2 + x = 0$$
$$(x - 1)(x + 2) = 0 \quad \text{or} \quad x(x + 1) = 0$$
$$x = 1, x = -2 \quad \text{or} \quad x = 0, x = -1$$

The solution set is $\{-2, -1, 0, 1\}$.

25. $|2x| < 8$

$$-8 < 2x < 8$$
$$-4 < x < 4$$

$\{x \mid -4 < x < 4\}$ or $(-4, 4)$

27. $|3x| > 12$

$$3x < -12 \quad \text{or} \quad 3x > 12$$
$$x < -4 \quad \text{or} \quad x > 4$$

$\{x \mid x < -4 \text{ or } x > 4\}$ or

$$(-\infty, -4) \cup (4, +\infty)$$

29. $|x - 2| + 2 < 3$

$$|x - 2| < 1$$
$$-1 < x - 2 < 1$$
$$1 < x < 3$$

$\{x \mid 1 < x < 3\}$ or $(1, 3)$

31. $|3t - 2| \le 4$

$$-4 \le 3t - 2 \le 4$$
$$-2 \le 3t \le 6$$
$$\frac{-2}{3} \le t \le 2$$

$\left\{t \mid -\dfrac{2}{3} \le t \le 2\right\}$ or $\left[-\dfrac{2}{3}, 2\right]$

33. $|x-3| \geq 2$
$x - 3 \leq -2$ or $x - 3 \geq 2$
$x \leq 1$ or $x \geq 5$
$\{x \mid x \leq 1 \text{ or } x \geq 5\}$
or $(-\infty, 1] \cup [5, \infty)$

35. $|1 - 4x| - 7 < -2$
$|1 - 4x| < 5$
$-5 < 1 - 4x < 5$
$-6 < -4x < 4$
$-1 < x < \dfrac{3}{2}$
$\left\{x \mid -1 < x < \dfrac{3}{2}\right\}$ or $\left(-1, \dfrac{3}{2}\right)$

37. $|1 - 2x| > 3$
$1 - 2x < -3$ or $1 - 2x > 3$
$-2x < -4$ or $-2x > 2$
$x > 2$ or $x < -1$
$\{x \mid x < -1 \text{ or } x > 2\}$ or $(-\infty, -1) \cup (2, \infty)$

39. $|-4x| + |-5| \leq 1$
$|4x| + 5 \leq 1$
$|4x| \leq -4$
but this is impossible since absolute value always yields a non-negative number.

41. $|-2x| > |-3|$
$|2x| > 3$
$2x < -3$ or $2x > 3$
$x < -\dfrac{3}{2}$ or $x > \dfrac{3}{2}$
$\left\{x \mid x < -\dfrac{3}{2} \text{ or } x > \dfrac{3}{2}\right\}$
or $\left(-\infty, -\dfrac{3}{2}\right) \cup \left(\dfrac{3}{2}, +\infty\right)$

43. $-|2x - 1| \geq -3$
$|2x - 1| \leq 3$
$-3 \leq 2x - 1 \leq 3$
$-2 \leq 2x \leq 4$
$-1 \leq x \leq 2$
$\{x \mid -1 \leq x \leq 2\}$ or $[-1, 2]$

45.
$|x - 1| < 3 \rightarrow -3 < x - 1 < 3$
$\rightarrow -2 < x < 4$
$\rightarrow 2 < x + 4 < 8$
$\rightarrow a = 2, b = 8$

47.
$|x + 4| \leq 2 \rightarrow -2 \leq x + 4 \leq 2$
$\rightarrow -6 \leq x \leq -2$
$\rightarrow -12 \leq 2x \leq -4$
$\rightarrow -15 \leq 2x - 3 \leq -7$
$\rightarrow a = -15, b = -7$

49.

$$|x - 2| \leq 7 \rightarrow -7 \leq x - 2 \leq 7$$

$$\rightarrow -5 \leq x \leq 9$$

$$\rightarrow -15 \leq x - 10 \leq -1$$

$$\rightarrow -\frac{1}{15} \geq \frac{1}{x - 10} \geq -1$$

$$\rightarrow -1 \leq \frac{1}{x - 10} \leq -\frac{1}{15}$$

$$\rightarrow a = -1, b = -\frac{1}{15}$$

51.   If $b \neq 0$, prove $\left|\frac{a}{b}\right| = \frac{|a|}{|b|}$.

Case1: $\dfrac{a}{b} \geq 0 \rightarrow a \geq 0$ and $b > 0$ or $a \leq 0$ and $b < 0$.

if $a \geq 0$ and $b > 0$ then $|a| = a$ and $|b| = b$.

so, $\dfrac{a}{b} \geq 0 \rightarrow \left|\dfrac{a}{b}\right| = \dfrac{a}{b} = \dfrac{|a|}{|b|}$.

if $a \leq 0$ and $b < 0$ then $|a| = -a$ and $|b| = -b$.

so, $\dfrac{a}{b} \geq 0 \rightarrow \left|\dfrac{a}{b}\right| = \dfrac{a}{b} = \dfrac{-|a|}{-|b|} = \dfrac{|a|}{|b|}$.

Case2: $\dfrac{a}{b} < 0 \rightarrow a > 0$ and $b < 0$ or $a < 0$ and $b > 0$.

if $a > 0$ and $b < 0$ then $|a| = a$ and $|b| = -b$.

now, $\dfrac{a}{b} < 0 \rightarrow \left|\dfrac{a}{b}\right| = -\left(\dfrac{a}{b}\right) = -\left(\dfrac{a}{-b}\right) = \dfrac{a}{b}$.

if $a < 0$ and $b > 0$ then $|a| = -a$ and $|b| = b$.

now, $\dfrac{a}{b} < 0 \rightarrow \left|\dfrac{a}{b}\right| = -\left(\dfrac{a}{b}\right) = -\left(\dfrac{-a}{b}\right) = \dfrac{a}{b}$.

53. $|a + b|^2 = |a + b| \cdot |a + b|$

Case 1: $a + b \geq 0 \rightarrow |a + b| = a + b$

so $|a + b| \cdot |a + b| = (a + b)(a + b) = a^2 + 2ab + b^2$

$\leq |a|^2 + 2|a| \cdot |b| + |b|^2$ by problem 52

$= (|a| + |b|)^2$

$\therefore (|a + b|)^2 \leq (|a| + |b|)^2 \rightarrow |a + b| \leq |a| + |b|$

Case 2: $a + b < 0 \to |a + b| = -(a + b)$

so $|a + b| \cdot |a + b| = (-(a + b))(-(a + b))$

$= (a + b)(a + b) = a^2 + 2ab + b^2$

$\leq |a|^2 + 2|a| \cdot |b| + |b|^2$ by problem 52

$= (|a| + |b|)^2$

$\therefore (|a + b|)^2 \leq (|a| + |b|)^2 \to |a + b| \leq |a| + |b|$

55. x differs from 3 by less than $\dfrac{1}{2}$

$$|x - 3| < \frac{1}{2}$$

$$\frac{-1}{2} < x - 3 < \frac{7}{2}$$

$$\frac{5}{2} < x < \frac{7}{2}$$

$$\left\{ x \left| \frac{3}{2} < x < \frac{5}{2} \right. \right\}$$

57. x differs from -3 by more than 2

$$|x - (-3)| > 2$$

$$x + 3 < -2 \text{ or } x + 3 > 2$$

$$x < -5 \quad \text{or} \quad x > -1$$

$$\left\{ x | x < -5 \text{ or } x > -1 \right\}$$

59. A temperature x that differs from $98.6°$ F by at least $1.5°$

$$|x - 98.6°| \geq 1.5°$$

$$x - 98.6° \leq -1.5° \quad \text{or} \quad x - 98.6° \geq 1.5°$$

$$x \leq 97.1° \quad \text{or} \quad x \geq 100.1°$$

The temperatures that are considered unhealthy are those that are less than $97.1°$F or greater than $100.1°$F, inclusive.

61. given that $a > 0$

$$x^2 < a \to x^2 - a < 0$$

$$\left(x + \sqrt{a} \right)\left(x - \sqrt{a} \right) < 0$$

if $x < -\sqrt{a}$, then $x + \sqrt{a} < 0$ and $x - \sqrt{a} < -2\sqrt{a} < 0$

therefore $\left(x + \sqrt{a} \right)\left(x - \sqrt{a} \right) > 0$

if $-\sqrt{a} < x < \sqrt{a}$, then $0 < x + \sqrt{a} < 2\sqrt{a}$ and $-2\sqrt{a} < x - \sqrt{a} < 0$

therefore $\left(x + \sqrt{a} \right)\left(x - \sqrt{a} \right) < 0$

if $x > \sqrt{a}$, then $x + \sqrt{a} > 2\sqrt{a} > 0$ and $x - \sqrt{a} > 0$

therefore $\left(x + \sqrt{a} \right)\left(x - \sqrt{a} \right) > 0$

So the solution set for $x^2 < a$ is $\left\{ \text{real numbers } x | -\sqrt{a} < x < \sqrt{a} \right\}$

63.
$$\left\{ \text{real numbers } x | -1 < x < 1 \right\}$$

65.
$$\left\{ \text{real numbers } x | x \leq -3 \text{ or } x \geq 3 \right\}$$

67.

$$\{\text{real numbers } x \mid -4 \le x \le 4\}$$

69.

$$\{\text{real numbers } x \mid x < -2 \text{ or } x > 2\}$$

71.

$$\left| \, 3x - |2x+1| \, \right| = 4$$

$$\rightarrow 3x - |2x+1| = 4 \text{ or } 3x - |2x+1| = -4$$

$$3x - |2x+1| = 4 \rightarrow 3x - 4 = |2x+1|$$

$$\rightarrow 2x+1 = 3x-4 \; \rightarrow 2x+1 = 3x-4 \rightarrow 5 = x$$

$$\text{or } 2x+1 = -(3x-4) \rightarrow 2x+1 = -3x+4 \rightarrow 5x = 3 \rightarrow x = \frac{3}{5}$$

$$3x - |2x+1| = -4 \rightarrow 3x + 4 = |2x+1|$$

$$\rightarrow 2x+1 = 3x+4 \; \rightarrow 2x+1 = 3x+4 \rightarrow -3 = x$$

$$\text{or } 2x+1 = -(3x+4) \rightarrow 2x+1 = -3x-4 \rightarrow 5x = -5 \rightarrow x = -1$$

however, the only values that check in the original equation are $x = 5$ and $x = -1$.

73.   The absolute value of a real number is always greater than or equal to zero.

75.   if $x > 0$, then $|x| = x$, therefore $|x| > 0$.

if $x < 0$, then $|x| = -x$. So $x < 0 \rightarrow -x > 0 \rightarrow |x| > 0$.

Equations and Inequalities

1.R   Chapter Review

1. $2 - \dfrac{x}{3} = 8$

    $6 - x = 24 \rightarrow x = -18$

3. $-2(5 - 3x) + 8 = 4 + 5x$

    $-10 + 6x + 8 = 4 + 5x$

      $6x - 2 = 4 + 5x$

          $x = 6$

5. $\dfrac{3x}{4} - \dfrac{x}{3} = \dfrac{1}{12}$

    $9x - 4x = 1 \rightarrow 5x = 1 \rightarrow x = \dfrac{1}{5}$

7. $\dfrac{x}{x - 1} = \dfrac{6}{5}$

    $5x = 6x - 6 \rightarrow 6 = x$

and since $x = 6$ does not cause a denominator to equal zero, the solution set is $\{6\}$.

9. $x(1 - x) = 6$

$x - x^2 = 6 \rightarrow 0 = x^2 - x + 6$

    $0 = (x - 3)(x + 2) \rightarrow x = 3 \text{ or } x = -2$

11. $\dfrac{1}{2}\left(x - \dfrac{1}{3}\right) = \dfrac{3}{4} - \dfrac{x}{6}$

    $\dfrac{x}{2} - \dfrac{1}{6} = \dfrac{3}{4} - \dfrac{x}{6}$

    $6x - 2 = 9 - 2x \rightarrow 8x = 11 \rightarrow x = \dfrac{11}{8}$

13. $(x - 1)(2x + 3) = 3$

    $2x^2 + x - 3 = 3$

    $2x^2 + x - 6 = 0 \rightarrow (2x - 3)(x + 2) = 0$

          $x = \dfrac{3}{2} \text{ or } x = -2$

15. $2x + 3 = 4x^2$

    $0 = 4x^2 - 2x - 3$

    $x = \dfrac{2 \pm \sqrt{4 + 48}}{8} = \dfrac{2 \pm \sqrt{52}}{8}$

      $= \dfrac{2 \pm 2\sqrt{13}}{8} = \dfrac{1 \pm \sqrt{13}}{4}$

17. $\sqrt[3]{x^2 - 1} = 2$

    $\left(\sqrt[3]{x^2 - 1}\right)^3 = (2)^3$

      $x^2 - 1 = 8 \rightarrow x^2 = 9 \rightarrow x = \pm 3$

Check:

      $x = -3$ $x = 3$

$\sqrt[3]{(-3)^2 - 1} = 2$ $\sqrt[3]{(3)^2 - 1} = 2$

    $\sqrt[3]{9 - 1} = 2$ $\sqrt[3]{9 - 1} = 2$

       $\sqrt[3]{8} = 2$ $\sqrt[3]{8} = 2$

         $2 = 2$ $2 = 2$

so the solution set is $\{-3, 3\}$.

19. $x(x+1)+2=0$

$\qquad x^2+x+2=0$

$$x=\frac{-1\pm\sqrt{1-8}}{2}=\frac{-1\pm\sqrt{-7}}{2}$$

no real solutions

21. $x^4-5x^2+4=0$

$\qquad\left(x^2-4\right)\left(x^2-1\right)=0$

$\qquad x^2-4=0 \ \text{ or } \ x^2-1=0$

$\qquad x=\pm 2 \ \text{ or } \ x=\pm 1$

23. $\quad \sqrt{2x-3}+x=3$

$\qquad\qquad \sqrt{2x-3}=3-x$

$\qquad\qquad 2x-3=9-6x+x^2$

$\qquad x^2-8x+12=0$

$\qquad (x-2)(x-6)=0$

$\qquad\qquad\qquad x=2 \ \text{ or } \ x=6$

Check 2: $\sqrt{2(2)-3}+2=\sqrt{1}+2=3$

Check 6: $\sqrt{2(6)-3}+6=\sqrt{9}+6$

$\qquad\qquad\qquad =9\neq 3$

The solution is $x=2$.

25. $\quad x^{3/2}+5x^{1/2}=0$

$\qquad\qquad x^{3/2}=-5x^{1/2}$

$\qquad\left(x^{3/2}\right)^2=\left(-5x^{1/2}\right)^2$

$\qquad\qquad x^3=25x$

$\qquad x^3-25x=0$

$\qquad x\left(x^2-25\right)=0$

$\qquad x(x-5)(x+5)=0$

$\qquad\qquad\qquad x=0$

$\qquad\qquad x-5=0\rightarrow x=5$

$\qquad\qquad x+5=0\rightarrow x=-5$

Check $x=0$:

$0^{3/2}+5(0)^{1/2}=0$

$0+0=0$

$0=0$

Check $x=5$:

$5^{3/2}+5(5)^{1/2}=0$

$5^{3/2}+5^{3/2}=0$

$2\left(5^{3/2}\right)\neq 0$

Check $x=-5$:

$(-5)^{3/2}+5(-5)^{1/2}=0$

$\left(\sqrt{-5}\right)^3+5\sqrt{-5}=0$

but $\sqrt{-5}$ is undefined.

The solution set is $\{0\}$.

27.

$$\sqrt{x+1}+\sqrt{x-1}=\sqrt{2x+1}$$

$$\left(\sqrt{x+1}+\sqrt{x-1}\right)^2=\left(\sqrt{2x+1}\right)^2$$

$$x+1+2\sqrt{x+1}\sqrt{x-1}+x-1=2x+1$$

$$2x+2\sqrt{x+1}\sqrt{x-1}=2x+1$$

$$2\sqrt{x+1}\sqrt{x-1}=1\rightarrow\left(2\sqrt{x+1}\sqrt{x-1}\right)^2=(1)^2\rightarrow 4(x+1)(x-1)=1$$

$$4x^2-4=1\rightarrow 4x^2=5\rightarrow x^2=\frac{5}{4}\rightarrow x=\pm\frac{\sqrt{5}}{2}$$

Check :

$$x=\frac{\sqrt{5}}{2}\rightarrow\sqrt{\frac{\sqrt{5}}{2}+1}+\sqrt{\frac{\sqrt{5}}{2}-1}=\sqrt{2\left(\frac{\sqrt{5}}{2}\right)+1}$$

$$1.79890743995=1.79890743995$$

$$x=-\frac{\sqrt{5}}{2}\rightarrow\sqrt{-\frac{\sqrt{5}}{2}+1}+\sqrt{-\frac{\sqrt{5}}{2}-1}=\sqrt{2\left(-\frac{\sqrt{5}}{2}\right)+1}$$

impossible since $-\dfrac{\sqrt{5}}{2}-1<0$

The solution set is $\left\{\dfrac{\sqrt{5}}{2}\right\}$.

29. $2\sqrt[3]{x^2}-\sqrt[3]{x}=1$

$$2\sqrt[3]{x^2}-\sqrt[3]{x}-1=0\rightarrow 2x^{2/3}-x^{1/3}-1=0$$

$$p=x^{1/3}\rightarrow p^2=x^{2/3}$$

$$2p^2-p-1=0\rightarrow(2p+1)(p-1)=0$$

$$p=-\frac{1}{2}\quad\text{or}\quad p=1$$

$$p=-\frac{1}{2}\rightarrow x^{1/3}=-\frac{1}{2}$$

$$\rightarrow\left(x^{1/3}\right)^3=\left(-\frac{1}{2}\right)^3\rightarrow x=-\frac{1}{8}$$

$$p=1\rightarrow x^{1/3}=1$$

$$\rightarrow\left(x^{1/3}\right)^3=(1)^3\rightarrow x=1$$

the solution set is $\left\{-\dfrac{1}{8},1\right\}$

Check

$$x=-\frac{1}{8}:2\sqrt[3]{\left(-\frac{1}{8}\right)^2}-\sqrt[3]{-\frac{1}{8}}-1=0$$

$$2\left(\frac{1}{4}\right)-\left(-\frac{1}{2}\right)-1=0\rightarrow\frac{1}{2}+\frac{1}{2}-1=0\rightarrow 0=0$$

$$x=1:2\sqrt[3]{1^2}-\sqrt[3]{1}-1=0$$

$$2-1-1=0\rightarrow 2-2=0\rightarrow 0=0$$

31. $x^{-6} - 7x^{-3} - 8 = 0$

$$p = x^{-3} \to p^2 = x^{-6}$$

$$p^2 - 7p - 8 = 0 \to (p-8)(p+1) = 0$$

$$p = 8 \quad \text{or} \quad p = -1$$

$$p = 8 \to x^{-3} = 8 \to \left(x^{-3}\right)^{-1/3} = (8)^{-1/3} \to x = \frac{1}{2}$$

$$p = -1 \to x^{-3} = -1 \to \left(x^{-3}\right)^{-1/3} = (-1)^{-1/3} \to x = -1$$

Check :

$$x = \frac{1}{2} : \left(\frac{1}{2}\right)^{-6} - 7(p)^{-3} - 8 = 0 \to 64 - 56 - 8 = 0 \to 0 = 0 \qquad \text{the solution set is } \left\{\frac{1}{2}, -1\right\}$$

$$x = -1 : (-1)^{-6} - 7(-1)^{-3} - 8 = 0 \to 1 + 7 - 8 = 0 \to 0 = 0$$

33. $x^2 + m^2 = 2mx + (nx)^2$

$$x^2 + m^2 = 2mx + n^2 x^2 \to x^2 - n^2 x^2 - 2mx + m^2 = 0$$

$$\left(1 - n^2\right)x^2 - 2mx + m^2 = 0$$

$$x = \frac{2m \pm \sqrt{4m^2 - 4m^2\left(1 - n^2\right)}}{2\left(1 - n^2\right)} = \frac{2m \pm \sqrt{4m^2\left(1 - \left(1 - n^2\right)\right)}}{2\left(1 - n^2\right)}$$

$$= \frac{2m \pm 2m\sqrt{1 - \left(1 - n^2\right)}}{2\left(1 - n^2\right)} = \frac{m \pm m\sqrt{n^2}}{1 - n^2} = \frac{m \pm mn}{1 - n^2} = \frac{m\left(1 \pm n\right)}{1 - n^2}$$

$$x = \frac{m\left(1 + n\right)}{1 - n^2} = \frac{m\left(1 + n\right)}{\left(1 + n\right)\left(1 - n\right)} = \frac{m}{1 - n}$$

or   the solution set is $\left\{\dfrac{m}{1-n}, \dfrac{m}{1+n}\right\}$.

$$x = \frac{m\left(1 - n\right)}{1 - n^2} = \frac{m\left(1 - n\right)}{\left(1 + n\right)\left(1 - n\right)} = \frac{m}{1 + n}$$

35. $10a^2 x^2 - 2abx - 36b^2 = 0$

$$5a^2 x^2 - abx - 18b^2 = 0$$

$$\left(5ax + 9b\right)\left(ax - 2b\right) = 0 \qquad \text{the solution set is } \left\{-\frac{9b}{5a}, \frac{2b}{a}\right\}.$$

$$x = -\frac{9b}{5a} \quad \text{or} \quad x = \frac{2b}{a}$$

37. $\sqrt{x^2 + 3x + 7} - \sqrt{x^2 - 3x + 9} + 2 = 0$

$\sqrt{x^2 + 3x + 7} = \sqrt{x^2 - 3x + 9} - 2$

$\left(\sqrt{x^2 + 3x + 7}\right)^2 = \left(\sqrt{x^2 - 3x + 9} - 2\right)^2$

$x^2 + 3x + 7 = x^2 - 3x + 9 - 4\sqrt{x^2 - 3x + 9} + 4$

$6x - 6 = -4\sqrt{x^2 - 3x + 9}$

$\left(6(x-1)\right)^2 = \left(-4\sqrt{x^2 - 3x + 9}\right)^2$

$36\left(x^2 - 2x + 1\right) = 16\left(x^2 - 3x + 9\right)$

$36x^2 - 72x + 36 = 16x^2 - 48x + 144$

$20x^2 - 24x - 108 = 0 \rightarrow 5x^2 - 6x - 27 = 0$

$(5x + 9)(x - 3) = 0$

$x = -\dfrac{9}{5}$ or $x = 3$

Check $x = -\dfrac{9}{5}$:

$\sqrt{\left(-\dfrac{9}{5}\right)^2 + 3\left(-\dfrac{9}{5}\right) + 7} - \sqrt{\left(-\dfrac{9}{5}\right)^2 - 3\left(-\dfrac{9}{5}\right) + 9} + 2 = 0$

$\sqrt{\dfrac{81}{25} - \dfrac{27}{5} + 7} - \sqrt{\dfrac{81}{25} + \dfrac{27}{5} + 9} + 2 = 0$

$\sqrt{\dfrac{81 - 135 + 175}{25}} - \sqrt{\dfrac{81 + 135 + 225}{25}} + 2 = 0$

$\sqrt{\dfrac{121}{25}} - \sqrt{\dfrac{441}{25}} + 2 = 0$

$\dfrac{11}{5} - \dfrac{21}{5} + 2 = 0$

$0 = 0$

Check :

$x = 3 : \sqrt{(3)^2 + 3(3) + 7} - \sqrt{(3)^2 - 3(3) + 9} + 2 = 0$

$\sqrt{9 + 9 + 7} - \sqrt{9 - 9 + 9} + 2 = 0$ the solution set is $\left\{-\dfrac{9}{5}\right\}$.

$\sqrt{25} - \sqrt{9} + 2 = 0$

$2 + 2 = 0$

$4 \neq 0$

39. $|2x+3|=7$
$2x+3=7$ or $2x+3=-7$
$2x=4$ or $\quad 2x=-10$
$x=2$ or $\quad\quad x=-5$
The solution set is $\{-5, 2\}$.

41. $|2-3x|+2=9 \rightarrow |2-3x|=7$
$2-3x=7$ or $2-3x=-7$
$3x=-5$ or $\quad 3x=9$
$x=-\dfrac{5}{2}$ or $\quad\quad x=3$
The solution set is $\left\{-\dfrac{5}{2}, 3\right\}$

43. $\dfrac{2x-3}{5}+2 \le \dfrac{x}{2}$
$2(2x-3)+10(2) \le 5x$
$4x-6+20 \le 5x$
$14 \le x \rightarrow x \ge 14$
$\left\{x \mid x \ge 14\right\}$ or $[14, +\infty)$

45. $-9 \le \dfrac{2x+3}{-4} \le 7$
$36 \ge 2x+3 \ge -28$
$33 \ge \quad 2x \quad \ge -31$
$\dfrac{33}{2} \ge \quad x \quad \ge \dfrac{-31}{2}$
$\dfrac{-31}{2} \le \quad x \quad \le \dfrac{33}{2}$
$\left\{x \mid \dfrac{-31}{2} \le x \le \dfrac{33}{2}\right\}$ or $\left[\dfrac{-31}{2}, \dfrac{33}{2}\right]$

47. $6 > \dfrac{3-3x}{12} > 2$
$72 > 3-3x > 24$
$69 > -3x > 21$
$-23 < \quad x \quad < -7$
$\left\{x \mid -23 < x < -7\right\}$ or $(-23, -7)$

49. $|3x+4| < \dfrac{1}{2}$
$\dfrac{-1}{2} < 3x+4 < \dfrac{1}{2}$
$\dfrac{-9}{2} < \quad 3x \quad < \dfrac{-7}{2}$
$\dfrac{-3}{2} < \quad x \quad < \dfrac{-7}{6}$
$\left\{x \mid -\dfrac{3}{2} < x < -\dfrac{7}{6}\right\}$ or $\left(-\dfrac{3}{2}, -\dfrac{7}{6}\right)$

51. $|2x - 5| \geq 9$
$2x - 5 \leq -9$ or $2x - 5 \geq 9$
$2x \leq -4$ or $\quad 2x \geq 14$
$x \leq -2$ or $\quad\quad x \geq 7$
$\{x \mid x \leq -2 \text{ or } x \geq 7\}$
$\quad\quad$ or $(-\infty, -2] \cup [7, +\infty)$

53. $2 + |2 - 3x| \leq 4$
$|2 - 3x| \leq 2$
$-2 \leq 2 - 3x \leq 2$
$-4 \leq -3x \leq 0 \to \dfrac{4}{3} \geq x \geq 0$
$0 \leq x \leq \dfrac{4}{3}$
$\left\{ x \,\middle|\, 0 \leq x \leq \dfrac{4}{3} \right\}$ or $\left[0, \dfrac{4}{3} \right]$

55. $1 - |2 - 3x| < -4$
$-|2 - 3x| < -5 \to |2 - 3x| > 5$
$2 - 3x < -5$ or $2 - 3x > 5$
$7 < 3x$ or $\quad -3 > 3x$
$\dfrac{7}{3} < x$ or $\quad -1 > x$
$\to x < -1$ or $\quad x > \dfrac{7}{3}$
$\left\{ x \,\middle|\, x < -1 \text{ or } x > \dfrac{7}{3} \right\}$
$\quad\quad$ or $(-\infty, -1) \cup \left(\dfrac{7}{3}, +\infty \right)$

57. $\left(\dfrac{6}{2} \right)^2 = 9$

59. $\left(\dfrac{\left(-\dfrac{4}{3} \right)}{2} \right)^2 = \dfrac{4}{9}$

61. Using $s = vt$, we have
$t = 3$ and $v = 1100$. Finding the
distance s in feet:
$\quad\quad s = 1100(3) = 3300$
The storm is 3300 feet away.

63. Let s represent the distance the plane can travel.

	Rate	Time	Distance
With wind	250+30=280	$\dfrac{\left(\dfrac{s}{2} \right)}{280}$	$\dfrac{s}{2}$
Against wind	250–30=220	$\dfrac{\left(\dfrac{s}{2} \right)}{220}$	$\dfrac{s}{2}$

Since the total time is at most 5 hours, we have:

$$\dfrac{\left(\dfrac{s}{2} \right)}{280} + \dfrac{\left(\dfrac{s}{2} \right)}{220} \leq 5 \to \dfrac{s}{560} + \dfrac{s}{440} \leq 5$$

$$11s + 14s \leq 5(6160) \to 25s \leq 30800 \to s \leq 1232$$

The plane can travel at most 1232 miles or 616 miles one way and return 616 miles.

65.   Let t represent the time it takes the helicopter to reach the raft.

	Rate	Time	Distance
Raft	5	t	$5t$
Helicopter	90	t	$90t$

Since the total distance is 150 miles, we have:

$$5t + 90t = 150 \rightarrow 95t = 150 \rightarrow t = 1.58 \text{ hours} = 1 \text{ hour and } 35 \text{ minutes}$$

The helicopter will reach the raft in 1 hour and 35 minutes.

67.   Let t represent the time it takes Clarissa to complete the job by herself.

	Time to do job alone	Part of job done in one day	Time on Job	Part of total job done by each person
Clarissa	t	$\dfrac{1}{t}$	6	$\dfrac{6}{t}$
Shawna	$t+5$	$\dfrac{1}{t+5}$	6	$\dfrac{6}{t+5}$

Since the two people paint one house, we have:

$$\frac{6}{t} + \frac{6}{t+5} = 1 \rightarrow 6(t+5) + 6t = t(t+5) \rightarrow 6t + 30 + 6t = t^2 + 5t$$

$$t^2 - 7t - 30 = 0 \rightarrow (t-10)(t+3) = 0 \rightarrow t = 10 \text{ or } t = -3$$

It takes Clarissa 10 days to paint the house when working by herself.

69.

% acid	amount	amount of acid
40%	60	$(0.40)(60)$
15%	x	$(0.15)(x)$
25%	$60+x$	$(0.25)(60+x)$

$$(0.40)(60) + (0.15)(x) = (0.25)(60+x)$$

$$24 + .15x = 15 + .25x \rightarrow 9 = 0.1x \rightarrow x = 90$$

90 cubic centimeters of the 15% solution must be added, producing 150 cubic centimeters of the 25% solution.

71.

% salt	amount	Amount of salt
10%	64	$(0.10)(64)$
0%	x	$(0.00)(x)$
2%	$64+x$	$(0.02)(64+x)$

$$(0.10)(64) + (0.00)(x) = (0.02)(64+x)$$

$$6.4 = 1.28 + .02x$$

$$5.12 = 0.2x \rightarrow x = 256$$

256 ounces of water must be added.

73.   length of $\text{leg}_1 = x$, length of $\text{leg}_2 = 17 - x$, by the Pythagorean Theorem we have
$$x^2 + (17 - x)^2 = (13)^2$$
$$x^2 + x^2 - 34x + 289 = 169 \rightarrow 2x^2 - 34x + 120 = 0$$
$$x^2 - 17x + 60 = 0 \rightarrow (x - 12)(x - 5) = 0 \rightarrow x = 12 \ \text{ or } \ x = 5$$
the legs are 5 inches and 12 inches long.

75.   The effective speed of the train (i.e., relative to the man) is $30 - 4 = 26$ miles per hour. The
time is 5 seconds $= \dfrac{5}{60}$ minutes $= \dfrac{5}{3600}$ hours $= \dfrac{1}{720}$ hours.
$$s = vt = 26\left(\dfrac{1}{720}\right) = \dfrac{26}{720} \text{ miles } = \dfrac{26}{720} \cdot 5280 = 190.67 \text{ feet}$$
The freight train is 190.67 feet long.

77.   Let t represent the time it takes the smaller pump to fill the tank.

	Time to do job alone	Part of job done in one hour	Time on Job	Part of total job done by each pump
3hp Pump	12	$\dfrac{1}{12}$	$t + 4$	$\dfrac{t + 4}{12}$
8hp Pump	8	$\dfrac{1}{8}$	4	$\dfrac{4}{8}$

Since the two pumps fill one tank, we have:
$$\dfrac{t + 4}{12} + \dfrac{4}{8} = 1 \rightarrow \dfrac{t + 4}{12} = \dfrac{1}{2}$$
$$2t + 8 = 12 \rightarrow 2t = 4 \rightarrow t = 2$$
It takes the small pump a total of 2 more hours to fill the tank.

79.   Let x represent the number of passengers over 20.
Then $20 + x$ represents the total number of passengers.
$15 - 0.1x$ represents the fare for each passenger.
Solving the equation for total cost ($482.40), we have:
$$(20 + x)(15 - 0.1x) = 482.40$$
$$300 + 13x - 0.1x^2 = 482.40 \rightarrow -0.1x^2 + 13x - 182.40 = 0$$
$$x^2 - 130x + 1824 = 0 \rightarrow (x - 114)(x - 16) = 0 \rightarrow x = 114 \ \text{ or } \ x = 16$$
Since the capacity of the bus is 44, we discard the 114. The total number of passengers is
$20 + 16 = 36$, and the ticket price per passenger is $15 - 0.1(16) = \$13.40$.
So 36 people went on the trip; each person paid $13.40.

81.   Let r_S represent Scott's rate and let r_T represent Todd's rate.
The time for Scott to run 95 meters is the same as for Todd to run 100 meters.
$$\dfrac{95}{r_S} = \dfrac{100}{r_T}$$
$$r_S = 0.95 r_T$$
$$d_S = 0.95 d_T$$

If Todd starts from 5 meters behind the start:
$$d_T = 105$$
$$d_S = 0.95 d_T = 0.95(105) = 99.75$$

(a)   The race does not end in a tie.

(b)   Todd wins the race.

(c)   Todd wins by 0.25 meters.

(d)   To end in a tie:
$$100 = 0.95(100 + x)$$
$$100 = 95 + 0.95x$$
$$5 = 0.95x$$
$$x = 5.263 \text{ meters}$$

(e) $95 = 0.95(100)$ Therefore, the race ends in a tie.

Graphs

2.1 Rectangular Coordinates

1. (a) Quadrant II
   (b) Positive x-axis
   (c) Quadrant III
   (d) Quadrant I
   (e) Negative y-axis
   (f) Quadrant IV

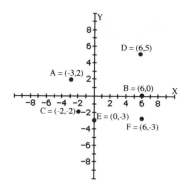

3. The points will be on a vertical line that is two units to the right of the y-axis.

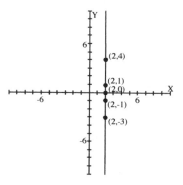

5. $d(P_1, P_2) = \sqrt{(2-0)^2 + (1-0)^2} = \sqrt{4+1} = \sqrt{5}$

7. $d(P_1, P_2) = \sqrt{(-2-1)^2 + (2-1)^2} = \sqrt{9+1} = \sqrt{10}$

9. $d(P_1, P_2) = \sqrt{(5-3)^2 + (4-(-4))^2} = \sqrt{2^2 + 8^2} = \sqrt{4+64} = \sqrt{68} = 2\sqrt{17}$

11. $d(P_1, P_2) = \sqrt{(6-(-3))^2 + (0-2)^2} = \sqrt{9^2 + (-2)^2} = \sqrt{81+4} = \sqrt{85}$

13. $d(P_1, P_2) = \sqrt{(6-4)^2 + (4-(-3))^2} = \sqrt{2^2 + 7^2} = \sqrt{4+49} = \sqrt{53}$

15. $d(P_1, P_2) = \sqrt{\left(2.3 - (-0.2)\right)^2 + \left(1.1 - 0.3\right)^2} = \sqrt{(2.5)^2 + (0.8)^2}$
$$= \sqrt{6.25 + 0.64} = \sqrt{6.89} \approx 2.625$$

17. $d(P_1, P_2) = \sqrt{(0 - a)^2 + (0 - b)^2} = \sqrt{a^2 + b^2}$

19. $A = (-2, 5),\ \ B = (1, 3),\ \ C = (-1, 0)$

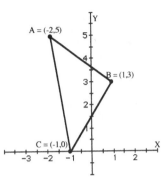

$d(A, B) = \sqrt{\left(1 - (-2)\right)^2 + (3 - 5)^2} = \sqrt{3^2 + (-2)^2}$
$$= \sqrt{9 + 4} = \sqrt{13}$$
$d(B, C) = \sqrt{(-1 - 1)^2 + (0 - 3)^2} = \sqrt{(-2)^2 + (-3)^2}$
$$= \sqrt{4 + 9} = \sqrt{13}$$
$d(A, C) = \sqrt{\left(-1 - (-2)\right)^2 + (0 - 5)^2} = \sqrt{1^2 + (-5)^2}$
$$= \sqrt{1 + 25} = \sqrt{26}$$

Verifying that $\triangle\, ABC$ is a right triangle by the Pythagorean Theorem:
$$\left[d(A,B)\right]^2 + \left[d(B,C)\right]^2 = \left[d(A,C)\right]^2 \rightarrow \left(\sqrt{13}\right)^2 + \left(\sqrt{13}\right)^2 = \left(\sqrt{26}\right)^2$$
$$13 + 13 = 26 \rightarrow 26 = 26$$

The area of a triangle is $A = \dfrac{1}{2} \cdot bh$. In this problem,
$$A = \tfrac{1}{2}\left[d(A,B)\right] \cdot \left[d(B,C)\right] = \frac{1}{2} \cdot \sqrt{13} \cdot \sqrt{13} = \frac{1}{2} \cdot 13 = \frac{13}{2} \text{ square units}$$

21. $A = (-5, 3),\ \ B = (6, 0),\ \ C = (5, 5)$

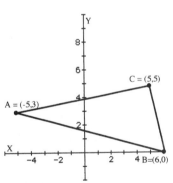

$d(A, B) = \sqrt{\left(6 - (-5)\right)^2 + (0 - 3)^2} = \sqrt{11^2 + (-3)^2}$
$$= \sqrt{121 + 9} = \sqrt{130}$$
$d(B, C) = \sqrt{(5 - 6)^2 + (5 - 0)^2} = \sqrt{(-1)^2 + 5^2}$
$$= \sqrt{1 + 25} = \sqrt{26}$$
$d(A, C) = \sqrt{\left(5 - (-5)\right)^2 + (5 - 3)^2} = \sqrt{10^2 + 2^2}$
$$= \sqrt{100 + 4} = \sqrt{104}$$

Verifying that $\triangle\, ABC$ is a right triangle by the Pythagorean Theorem:
$$\left[d(A,C)\right]^2 + \left[d(B,C)\right]^2 = \left[d(A,B)\right]^2 \rightarrow \left(\sqrt{104}\right)^2 + \left(\sqrt{26}\right)^2 = \left(\sqrt{130}\right)^2$$
$$104 + 26 = 130 \rightarrow 130 = 130$$

The area of a triangle is $A = \dfrac{1}{2} \cdot bh$. In this problem,
$$A = \frac{1}{2} \cdot \left[d(A,C)\right] \cdot \left[d(B,C)\right] = \frac{1}{2} \cdot \sqrt{104} \cdot \sqrt{26} = \frac{1}{2} \cdot \sqrt{2704} = \frac{1}{2} \cdot 52 = 26 \text{ square units}$$

23. $A = (4,-3),\ \ B = (0,-3),\ \ C = (4,2)$

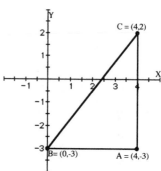

$$d(A,B) = \sqrt{(0-4)^2 + (-3-(-3))^2} = \sqrt{(-4)^2 + 0^2}$$
$$= \sqrt{16+0} = \sqrt{16} = 4$$
$$d(B,C) = \sqrt{(4-0)^2 + (2-(-3))^2} = \sqrt{4^2 + 5^2}$$
$$= \sqrt{16+25} = \sqrt{41}$$
$$d(A,C) = \sqrt{(4-4)^2 + (2-(-3))^2} = \sqrt{0^2 + 5^2}$$
$$= \sqrt{0+25} = \sqrt{25} = 5$$

Verifying that Δ ABC is a right triangle by the Pythagorean Theorem:
$$\left[d(A,B) \right]^2 + \left[d(A,C) \right]^2 = \left[d(B,C) \right]^2$$
$$4^2 + 5^2 = \left(\sqrt{41} \right)^2 \rightarrow 16 + 25 = 41 \rightarrow 41 = 41$$

The area of a triangle is $A = \dfrac{1}{2} \cdot bh$. In this problem,
$$A = \frac{1}{2} \left[d(A,B) \right] \cdot \left[d(A,C) \right] = \frac{1}{2} \cdot 4 \cdot 5 = 10 \text{ square units}$$

25. All points having an x-coordinate of 2 are of the form (2, y). Those which are 5 units from (–2, –1) are:
$$\sqrt{(2-(-2))^2 + (y-(-1))^2} = 5 \rightarrow \sqrt{4^2 + (y+1)^2} = 5$$
$$\text{Squaring both sides:}\ \ 4^2 + (y+1)^2 = 25$$
$$16 + y^2 + 2y + 1 = 25 \rightarrow y^2 + 2y - 8 = 0$$
$$(y+4)(y-2) = 0 \rightarrow y = -4\ \text{ or }\ y = 2$$
Therefore, the points are (2, –4) or (2, 2).

27. All points on the x-axis are of the form (x, 0). Those which are 5 units from (4, –3) are:
$$\sqrt{(x-4)^2 + (0-(-3))^2} = 5 \rightarrow \sqrt{(x-4)^2 + 3^2} = 5$$
$$\text{Squaring both sides:}\ \ (x-4)^2 + 9 = 25$$
$$x^2 - 8x + 16 + 9 = 25 \rightarrow x^2 - 8x = 0$$
$$x(x-8) = 0 \rightarrow x = 0\ \text{ or }\ x = 8$$
Therefore, the points are (0, 0) or (8, 0).

29. The coordinates of the midpoint are:
$$(x,y) = \left(\frac{x_1 + x_2}{2}, \frac{y_1 + y_2}{2} \right) = \left(\frac{5+3}{2}, \frac{-4+2}{2} \right) = \left(\frac{8}{2}, \frac{-2}{2} \right) = (4,-1)$$

31. The coordinates of the midpoint are:
$$(x,y) = \left(\frac{x_1 + x_2}{2}, \frac{y_1 + y_2}{2} \right) = \left(\frac{-3+6}{2}, \frac{2+0}{2} \right) = \left(\frac{3}{2}, \frac{2}{2} \right) = \left(\frac{3}{2}, 1 \right)$$

33. The coordinates of the midpoint are:

$$(x,y) = \left(\frac{x_1 + x_2}{2}, \frac{y_1 + y_2}{2}\right) = \left(\frac{4+6}{2}, \frac{-3+1}{2}\right) = \left(\frac{10}{2}, \frac{-2}{2}\right) = (5,-1)$$

35. The coordinates of the midpoint are:

$$(x,y) = \left(\frac{x_1 + x_2}{2}, \frac{y_1 + y_2}{2}\right) = \left(\frac{-0.2+2.3}{2}, \frac{0.3+1.1}{2}\right) = \left(\frac{2.1}{2}, \frac{1.4}{2}\right) = (1.05, 0.7)$$

37. The coordinates of the midpoint are:

$$(x,y) = \left(\frac{x_1 + x_2}{2}, \frac{y_1 + y_2}{2}\right) = \left(\frac{a+0}{2}, \frac{b+0}{2}\right) = \left(\frac{a}{2}, \frac{b}{2}\right)$$

39. The midpoint of AB is: $D = \left(\frac{0+0}{2}, \frac{0+6}{2}\right) = (0, 3)$

   The midpoint of AC is: $E = \left(\frac{0+4}{2}, \frac{0+4}{2}\right) = (2, 2)$

   The midpoint of BC is: $F = \left(\frac{0+4}{2}, \frac{6+4}{2}\right) = (2, 5)$

   $d(C,D) = \sqrt{(0-4)^2 + (3-4)^2} = \sqrt{(-4)^2 + (-1)^2} = \sqrt{16+1} = \sqrt{17}$

   $d(B,E) = \sqrt{(2-0)^2 + (2-6)^2} = \sqrt{2^2 + (-4)^2} = \sqrt{4+16} = \sqrt{20} = 2\sqrt{5}$

   $d(A,F) = \sqrt{(2-0)^2 + (5-0)^2} = \sqrt{2^2 + 5^2} = \sqrt{4+25} = \sqrt{29}$

41. $d(P_1, P_2) = \sqrt{(-4-2)^2 + (1-1)^2} = \sqrt{(-6)^2 + 0^2} = \sqrt{36} = 6$

   $d(P_2, P_3) = \sqrt{(-4-(-4))^2 + (-3-1)^2} = \sqrt{0^2 + (-4)^2} = \sqrt{16} = 4$

   $d(P_1, P_3) = \sqrt{(-4-2)^2 + (-3-1)^2} = \sqrt{(-6)^2 + (-4)^2} = \sqrt{36+16} = \sqrt{52} = 2\sqrt{13}$

   Since $\left[d(P_1,P_2)\right]^2 + \left[d(P_2,P_3)\right]^2 = \left[d(P_1,P_3)\right]^2$, the triangle is a right triangle.

43. $d(P_1, P_2) = \sqrt{(0-(-2))^2 + (7-(-1))^2} = \sqrt{2^2 + 8^2} = \sqrt{4+64} = \sqrt{68} = 2\sqrt{17}$

   $d(P_2, P_3) = \sqrt{(3-0)^2 + (2-7)^2} = \sqrt{3^2 + (-5)^2} = \sqrt{9+25} = \sqrt{34}$

   $d(P_1, P_3) = \sqrt{(3-(-2))^2 + (2-(-1))^2} = \sqrt{5^2 + 3^2} = \sqrt{25+9} = \sqrt{34}$

   Since $d(P_2, P_3) = d(P_1, P_3)$, the triangle is isosceles.

   Since $\left[d(P_1,P_3)\right]^2 + \left[d(P_2,P_3)\right]^2 = \left[d(P_1,P_2)\right]^2$, the triangle is also a right triangle.

   Therefore, the triangle is an isosceles right triangle.

45. $P_1 = (1,3),\ P_2 = (5,15)$

   $d(P_1,P_2) = \sqrt{(5-1)^2 + (15-3)^2} = \sqrt{4^2 + 12^2} = \sqrt{16+144} = \sqrt{160} = 4\sqrt{10}$

47. $P_1 = (-4,6),\ P_2 = (4,-8)$

   $d(P_1,P_2) = \sqrt{(4-(-4))^2 + (-8-6)^2} = \sqrt{8^2 + (-14)^2} = \sqrt{64+196} = \sqrt{260} = 2\sqrt{65}$

49. Plot the vertices of the square at
(0, 0), (0, s), (s, s), and (s, 0).

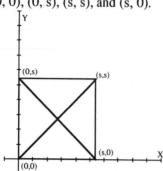

Find the midpoints of the diagonals.

$$M_1 = \left(\frac{0+s}{2}, \frac{0+s}{2}\right) = \left(\frac{s}{2}, \frac{s}{2}\right)$$

$$M_2 = \left(\frac{0+s}{2}, \frac{s+0}{2}\right) = \left(\frac{s}{2}, \frac{s}{2}\right)$$

Since the coordinates of the midpoints
are the same, the diagonals of a square
intersect at their midpoints.

51. Using the Pythagorean Theorem:

$$90^2 + 90^2 = d^2$$
$$8100 + 8100 = d^2$$
$$16200 = d^2$$
$$d = \sqrt{16200}$$
$$d = 90\sqrt{2} \approx 127.28 \text{ feet}$$

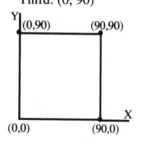

53. (a) First: (90, 0), Second: (90, 90)
        Third: (0, 90)

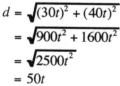

(b) Using the distance formula:

$$d = \sqrt{(310-90)^2 + (15-90)^2}$$
$$= \sqrt{220^2 + (-75)^2}$$
$$= \sqrt{54025} \approx 232.4 \text{ feet}$$

(c) Using the distance formula:

$$d = \sqrt{(300-0)^2 + (300-90)^2}$$
$$= \sqrt{300^2 + 210^2}$$
$$= \sqrt{134100} \approx 366.2 \text{ feet}$$

55. The Intrepid heading east moves a distance 30t after t
hours. The truck heading south moves a distance 40t
after t hours. Their distance apart after t hours is:

$$d = \sqrt{(30t)^2 + (40t)^2}$$
$$= \sqrt{900t^2 + 1600t^2}$$
$$= \sqrt{2500t^2}$$
$$= 50t$$

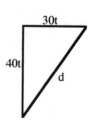

Graphs

2.2   Graphs of Equations

1.
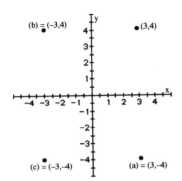

3.
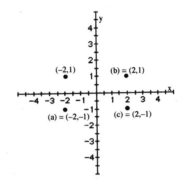

5.
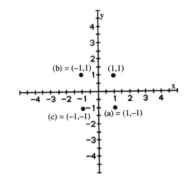

7.
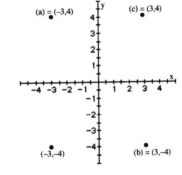

9.
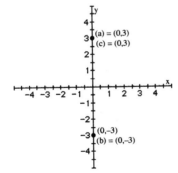

11.   (a) $(-1, 0), (1, 0)$ (b)   symmetric to the x-axis, y-axis and origin

13.   (a) $\left(-\dfrac{\pi}{2}, 0\right), \left(\dfrac{\pi}{2}, 0\right), (0, 1)$ (b)   symmetric to the y-axis

15. (a) $(0, 0)$ (b)   symmetric to the x-axis

17. (a) $(1, 0)$ (b)   not symmetric to x-axis, y-axis, or origin

19. (a) $(-1.5, 0), (1.5, 0), (0, -2)$ (b)   symmetric to the y-axis

21. (a)   none   (b)   symmetric to the origin

23. $y = x^4 - \sqrt{x}$

$$0 = 0^4 - \sqrt{0} \qquad\qquad 1 = 1^4 - \sqrt{1} \qquad\qquad 0 = (-1)^4 - \sqrt{-1}$$
$$0 = 0 \qquad\qquad\qquad 1 \neq 0 \qquad\qquad\qquad 0 \neq 1 - \sqrt{-1}$$

$(0, 0)$ is on the graph of the equation.

25. $y^2 = x^2 + 9$

$$3^2 = 0^2 + 9 \qquad\qquad 0^2 = 3^2 + 9 \qquad\qquad 0^2 = (-3)^2 + 9$$
$$9 = 9 \qquad\qquad\qquad 0 \neq 18 \qquad\qquad\qquad 0 \neq 18$$

$(0, 3)$ is on the graph of the equation.

27. $x^2 + y^2 = 4$

$$0^2 + 2^2 = 4 \qquad\qquad (-2)^2 + 2^2 = 4 \qquad\qquad \sqrt{2}^2 + \sqrt{2}^2 = 4$$
$$4 = 4 \qquad\qquad\qquad 8 \neq 4 \qquad\qquad\qquad 4 = 4$$

$(0, 2)$ and $\left(\sqrt{2}, \sqrt{2}\right)$ are on the graph of the equation.

29. $x^2 = y$

y - intercept: Let $x = 0$, then $y = 0$ $(0,0)$
x - intercept: Let $y = 0$, then $x = 0$ $(0,0)$

Test for symmetry:

x - axis: Replace y by $-y$ so $x^2 = -y$, which is not equivalent to $x^2 = y$.

y - axis: Replace x by $-x$ so $(-x)^2 = y$ or $x^2 = y$, which is equivalent to $x^2 = y$.

Origin: Replace x by $-x$ and y by $-y$ so $(-x)^2 = -y$ or $x^2 = -y$,

which is not equivalent to $x^2 = y$.

Therefore, the graph is symmetric with respect to the y - axis.

31. $y = 3x$

y - intercept: Let $x = 0$, then $y = 0$ $(0,0)$
x - intercept: Let $y = 0$, then $x = 0$ $(0,0)$

Test for symmetry:

x - axis: Replace y by $-y$ so $-y = 3x$, which is not equivalent to $y = 3x$.

y - axis: Replace x by $-x$ so $y = 3(-x)$ or $y = -3x$,

which is not equivalent to $y = 3x$.

Origin: Replace x by $-x$ and y by $-y$ so $-y = 3(-x)$ or $y = 3x$,

which is equivalent to $y = 3x$.

Therefore, the graph is symmetric with respect to the origin.

33. $x^2 + y - 9 = 0$

y-intercept: Let $x = 0$, then $y = 9$ $(0,9)$

x-intercept: Let $y = 0$, then $x = \pm 3$ $(-3,0),(3,0)$

     Test for symmetry:

      x-axis: Replace y by $-y$ so $x^2 + (-y) - 9 = 0$ or $x^2 - y - 9 = 0$,

           which is not equivalent to $x^2 + y - 9 = 0$.

      y-axis: Replace x by $-x$ so $(-x)^2 + y - 9 = 0$ or $x^2 + y - 9 = 0$,

           which is equivalent to $x^2 + y - 9 = 0$.

     Origin: Replace x by $-x$ and y by $-y$ so $(-x)^2 + (-y) - 9 = 0$ or $x^2 - y - 9 = 0$,

           which is not equivalent to $x^2 + y - 9 = 0$.

Therefore, the graph is symmetric with respect to the y-axis.

35. $9x^2 + 4y^2 = 36$

y-intercept: Let $x = 0$, then $y = \pm 3$ $(0,-3),(0,3)$

x-intercept: Let $y = 0$, then $x = \pm 2$ $(-2,0),(2,0)$

     Test for symmetry:

      x-axis: Replace y by $-y$ so $9x^2 + 4(-y)^2 = 36$ or $9x^2 + 4y^2 = 36$,

           which is equivalent to $9x^2 + 4y^2 = 36$.

      y-axis: Replace x by $-x$ so $9(-x)^2 + 4y^2 = 36$ or $9x^2 + 4y^2 = 36$,

           which is equivalent to $9x^2 + 4y^2 = 36$.

     Origin: Replace x by $-x$ and y by $-y$ so $9(-x)^2 + 4(-y)^2 = 36$ or $9x^2 + 4y^2 = 36$,

           which is equivalent to $9x^2 + 4y^2 = 36$.

Therefore, the graph is symmetric with respect to the x-axis, the y-axis and the origin.

37. $y = x^3 - 27$

     y-intercept: Let $x = 0$, then $y = 0^3 - 27$

                        $y = -27$ $(0,-27)$

     x-intercept: Let $y = 0$, then $0 = x^3 - 27$

                        $x^3 = 27 \rightarrow x = 3$ $(3,0)$

     Test for symmetry:

      x-axis: Replace y by $-y$ so $-y = x^3 - 27$, which is not

            equivalent to $y = x^3 - 27$.

      y-axis: Replace x by $-x$ so $y = (-x)^3 - 27$ or $y = -x^3 - 27$,

            which is not equivalent to $y = x^3 - 27$.

     Origin: Replace x by $-x$ and y by $-y$ so $-y = (-x)^3 - 27$ or

            $y = x^3 + 27$, which is not equivalent to $y = x^3 - 27$.

Therefore, the graph is not symmetric to the x-axis, the y-axis, or the origin.

39. $y = x^2 - 3x - 4$

    y - intercept: Let $x = 0$, then $y = 0^2 - 3(0) - 4$

$$y = -4 \qquad (0, -4)$$

    x - intercept: Let $y = 0$, then $0 = x^2 - 3x - 4$

$$(x - 4)(x + 1) = 0$$
$$x = 4 \quad x = -1 \quad (4, 0), (-1, 0)$$

Test for symmetry:

    x - axis: Replace y by $-y$ so $-y = x^2 - 3x - 4$, which is not

               equivalent to $y = x^2 - 3x - 4$.

    y - axis: Replace x by $-x$ so $y = (-x)^2 - 3(-x) - 4$ or $y = x^2 + 3x - 4$,

               which is not equivalent to $y = x^2 - 3x - 4$.

    Origin: Replace x by $-x$ and y by $-y$ so $-y = (-x)^2 - 3(-x) - 4$ or

               $y = -x^2 - 3x + 4$, which is not equivalent to $y = x^2 - 3x - 4$.

Therefore, the graph is not symmetric to the x-axis, the y-axis, or the origin.

41. $y = \dfrac{3x}{x^2 + 9}$

    y - intercept : Let $x = 0$, then $y = \dfrac{0}{0 + 9}$

$$y = 0 \qquad (0, 0)$$

    x - intercept : Let $y = 0$, then $0 = \dfrac{3x}{x^2 + 9}$

$$3x = 0 \rightarrow x = 0 \quad (0, 0)$$

Test for symmetry:

    x - axis: Replace y by $-y$ so $-y = \dfrac{3x}{x^2 + 9}$, which is not

               equivalent to $y = \dfrac{3x}{x^2 + 9}$.

    y - axis: Replace x by $-x$ so $y = \dfrac{3(-x)}{(-x)^2 + 9}$ or $y = \dfrac{-3x}{x^2 + 9}$,

               which is not equivalent to $y = \dfrac{3x}{x^2 + 9}$.

    Origin: Replace x by $-x$ and y by $-y$ so $-y = \dfrac{-3x}{(-x)^2 + 9}$ or

               $y = \dfrac{3x}{x^2 + 9}$, which is equivalent to $y = \dfrac{3x}{x^2 + 9}$.

Therefore, the graph is symmetric with respect to the origin.

43. $y = \dfrac{-x^3}{x^2 - 9}$

y - intercept : Let $x = 0$, then $y = \dfrac{0}{-9} = 0$

$(0,0)$

x - intercept : Let $y = 0$, then $0 = \dfrac{-x^3}{x^2 - 9} \rightarrow -x^3 = 0$

$x = 0$ $(0,0)$

Test for symmetry:

x - axis: Replace y by $-y$ so $-y = \dfrac{-x^3}{x^2 - 9}$, which is not

equivalent to $y = \dfrac{-x^3}{x^2 - 9}$.

y - axis: Replace x by $-x$ so $y = \dfrac{-(-x)^3}{(-x)^2 - 9}$ or $y = \dfrac{x^3}{x^2 - 9}$,

which is not equivalent to $y = \dfrac{-x^3}{x^2 - 9}$.

Origin :   Replace x by $-x$ and y by $-y$ so $-y = \dfrac{-(-x)^3}{(-x)^2 - 9}$ or

$-y = \dfrac{x^3}{x^2 - 9}$, which is equivalent to $y = \dfrac{-x^3}{x^2 - 9}$.

Therefore, the graph is symmetric with respect to the origin.

45. $y = x^3$

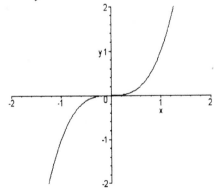

47. $y = \sqrt{x}$

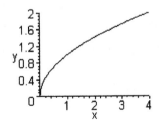

49. $y = 3x + 5$
$2 = 3a + 5$
$3a = -3 \rightarrow a = -1$

51. $2x + 3y = 6$
$2a + 3b = 6 \rightarrow b = 2 - \dfrac{2}{3}a$

53.   (a)

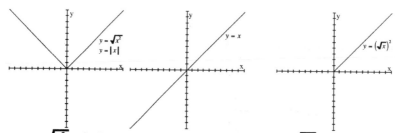

(b)   Since $\sqrt{x^2} = |x|$, then for all x, the graphs of $y = \sqrt{x^2}$ and $y = |x|$ are the same.

(c)   For $y = \left(\sqrt{x}\right)^2$, the domain of the variable x is $x \geq 0$; for $y = x$, the domain of the variable x is all real numbers. Thus, $\left(\sqrt{x}\right)^2 = x$ only for $x \geq 0$.

(d)   For $y = \sqrt{x^2}$, the range of the variable y is $y \geq 0$; for $y = x$, the range of the variable y is all real numbers. Also, $\sqrt{x^2} = x$ only if $x \geq 0$.

55.   If the equation has x-axis and y-axis symmetry, then we have the following:

x – axis symmetry means $(x, y) \leftrightarrow (x, -y)$

y – axis symmetry means $(x, y) \leftrightarrow (-x, y)$

$\therefore (x, -y) \leftrightarrow (-x, y)$

but the third statement is equivalent to origin symmetry.

If the equation has x-axis and origin symmetry, then we have the following:

x – axis symmetry means $(x, y) \leftrightarrow (x, -y)$

origin symmetry means $(x, y) \leftrightarrow (-x, -y)$

$\therefore (x, -y) \leftrightarrow (-x, -y)$

but the third statement is equivalent to y-axis symmetry.

If the equation has y-axis and origin symmetry, then we have the following:

y – axis symmetry means $(x, y) \leftrightarrow (-x, y)$

origin symmetry means $(x, y) \leftrightarrow (-x, -y)$

$\therefore (-x, y) \leftrightarrow (-x, -y)$

but the third statement is equivalent to x-axis symmetry.

Graphs

2.3 Lines

1. (a) Slope $= \dfrac{1-0}{2-0} = \dfrac{1}{2}$

    (b) If x increases by 2 units, y will increase by 1 unit.

3. (a) Slope $= \dfrac{1-2}{1-(-2)} = -\dfrac{1}{3}$

    (b) If x increases by 3 units, y will decrease by 1 unit.

5. $(x_1, y_1) \quad (x_2, y_2)$
    $(2,3) \quad (4,0)$

    Slope $= \dfrac{y_2 - y_1}{x_2 - x_1} = \dfrac{0-3}{4-2} = \dfrac{-3}{2}$

    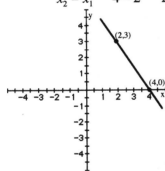

7. $(x_1, y_1) \quad (x_2, y_2)$
    $(-2,3) \quad (2,1)$

    Slope $= \dfrac{y_2 - y_1}{x_2 - x_1} = \dfrac{1-3}{2-(-2)} = \dfrac{-2}{4} = \dfrac{-1}{2}$

    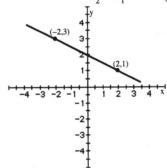

9. (x_1, y_1) (x_2, y_2)
    $(-3, -1)$ $(2, -1)$

    Slope $= \dfrac{y_2 - y_1}{x_2 - x_1} = \dfrac{-1 - (-1)}{2 - (-3)} = \dfrac{0}{5} = 0$

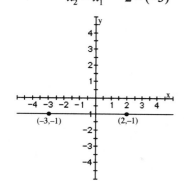

11. (x_1, y_1) (x_2, y_2)
     $(-1, 2)$ $(-1, -2)$

     Slope $= \dfrac{y_2 - y_1}{x_2 - x_1} = \dfrac{-2 - 2}{-1 - (-1)} = \dfrac{-4}{0}$

     Slope is undefined.

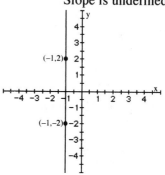

13.

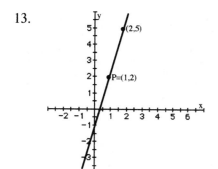

15.

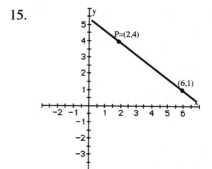

17

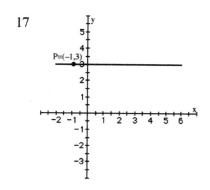

19.

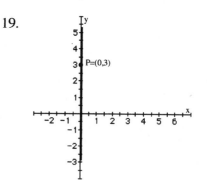

21. Slope $= 4 \rightarrow$ if x increases by 1, y increases by 4

original point $(1,2)$

Answers will vary. Three possible points are:
$x = 1 + 1 = 2$ and $y = 2 + 4 = 6$

$(2,6)$

$x = 2 + 1 = 3$ and $y = 6 + 4 = 10$

$(3,10)$

$x = 3 + 1 = 4$ and $y = 10 + 4 = 14$

$(4,14)$

23. Slope $= -\dfrac{3}{2} \rightarrow$ if x increases by 2, y decreases by 3

original point $(2,-4)$

Answers will vary. Three possible points are:
$x = 2 + 2 = 4$ and $y = -4 - 3 = -7$

$(4,-7)$

$x = 4 + 2 = 6$ and $y = -7 - 3 = -10$

$(6,-10)$

$x = 6 + 2 = 8$ and $y = -10 - 3 = -13$

$(8,-13)$

25. Slope $= -2 \rightarrow$ if x increases by 1, y decreases by 2

original point $(-2,-3)$

Answers will vary. Three possible points are:
$x = -2 + 1 = -1$ and $y = -3 - 2 = -5$

$(-1,-5)$

$x = -1 + 1 = 0$ and $y = -5 - 2 = -7$

$(0,-7)$

$x = 0 + 1 = 1$ and $y = -7 - 2 = -9$

$(1,-9)$

27. $(0,0)$ and $(2,1)$ are points on the line.

Slope $= \dfrac{1-0}{2-0} = \dfrac{1}{2}$

y - intercept is 0; using $y = mx + b$:

$y = \dfrac{1}{2}x + 0$

$2y = x$

$0 = x - 2y$

$x - 2y = 0$ or $y = \dfrac{1}{2}x$

29. $(-2,2)$ and $(1,1)$ are points on the line.

Slope $= \dfrac{1-2}{1-(-2)} = -\dfrac{1}{3}$

Using $y - y_1 = m(x - x_1)$

$y - 1 = -\dfrac{1}{3}(x-1) \rightarrow y - 1 = -\dfrac{1}{3}x + \dfrac{1}{3}$

$y = -\dfrac{1}{3}x + \dfrac{4}{3}$

$x + 3y = 4$ or $y = -\dfrac{1}{3}x + \dfrac{4}{3}$

31. Slope $= 3$; containing $(-2,3)$

$y - y_1 = m(x - x_1)$

$y - 3 = 3(x - (-2))$

$y - 3 = 3x + 6$

$y = 3x + 9$

$3x - y = -9$ or $y = 3x + 9$

33. Slope $= -\dfrac{2}{3}$; containing $(1,-1)$

$y - y_1 = m(x - x_1)$

$y - (-1) = \dfrac{-2}{3}(x-1) \rightarrow y + 1 = \dfrac{-2}{3}x + \dfrac{2}{3} \rightarrow y = \dfrac{-2}{3}x - \dfrac{1}{3}$

$2x + 3y = -1$ or $y = \dfrac{-2}{3}x - \dfrac{1}{3}$

35. Containing $(1,3)$ and $(-1,2)$

$$m = \frac{2-3}{-1-1} = \frac{-1}{-2} = \frac{1}{2}$$

$$y - y_1 = m(x - x_1)$$

$$y - 3 = \frac{1}{2}(x - 1)$$

$$y - 3 = \frac{1}{2}x - \frac{1}{2}$$

$$y = \frac{1}{2}x + \frac{5}{2}$$

$$x - 2y = -5 \text{ or } y = \frac{1}{2}x + \frac{5}{2}$$

37. Slope $= -3$; y-intercept $= 3$

$$y = mx + b$$

$$y = -3x + 3$$

$$3x + y = 3 \text{ or } y = -3x + 3$$

39. x-intercept $= 2$; y-intercept $= -1$

Points are $(2,0)$ and $(0,-1)$

$$m = \frac{-1-0}{0-2} = \frac{-1}{-2} = \frac{1}{2}$$

$$y = mx + b$$

$$y = \frac{1}{2}x - 1$$

$$x - 2y = 2 \text{ or } y = \frac{1}{2}x - 1$$

41. Slope undefined; passing through $(2,4)$

This is a vertical line.

$$x = 2$$

No slope intercept form.

43. $y = 2x + 3$

Slope $= 2$

y-intercept $= 3$

45. $\frac{1}{2}y = x - 1$

$$y = 2x - 2$$

Slope $= 2$

y-intercept $= -2$

47. $y = \dfrac{1}{2}x + 2$

Slope $= \dfrac{1}{2}$

y-intercept $= 2$

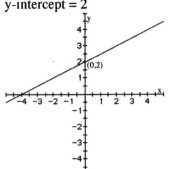

49. $x + 2y = 4$

$2y = -x + 4$

$y = -\dfrac{1}{2}x + 2$

Slope $= -\dfrac{1}{2}$

y-intercept $= 2$

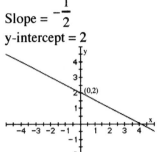

51. $2x - 3y = 6$

$-3y = -2x + 6$

$y = \dfrac{2}{3}x - 2$

Slope $= \dfrac{2}{3}$

y-intercept $= -2$

53. $x + y = 1$

$y = -x + 1$

Slope $= -1$

y-intercept $= 1$

55. $x = -4$
     Slope is undefined
     y-intercept - none

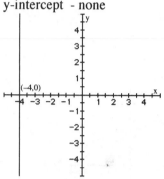

57. $y = 5$
     Slope = 0
     y-intercept = 5

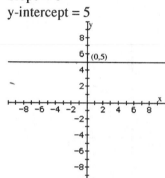

59. $y - x = 0$
     $y = x$
     Slope = 1
     y-intercept = 0

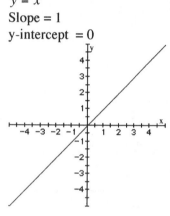

61. $2y - 3x = 0$
     $2y = 3x$

     $y = \dfrac{3}{2}x$

     Slope = $\dfrac{3}{2}$
     y-intercept = 0

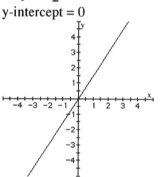

63. The equation of the x-axis is $y = 0$. (The slope is 0 and the y-intercept is 0.)

65. $(^\circ C, ^\circ F) = (0, 32);\quad (^\circ C, ^\circ F) = (100, 212)$

     slope $= \dfrac{212 - 32}{100 - 0} = \dfrac{180}{100} = \dfrac{9}{5}$

     $^\circ F - 32 = \dfrac{9}{5}(^\circ C - 0)$

     $^\circ F - 32 = \dfrac{9}{5}(^\circ C)$

     $^\circ C = \dfrac{5}{9}(^\circ F - 32)$

     If $^\circ F = 70$, then

     $^\circ C = \dfrac{5}{9}(70 - 32) = \dfrac{5}{9}(38)$

     $^\circ C \approx 21^\circ$

67. (a) Since there is only a profit of $0.50 per copy and the expense of $100 must be deducted, the profit is:
$$P = 0.50x - 100$$
     (b) $P = 0.50(1000) - 100$
          $= 500 - 100$
          $= \$400$
     (c) $P = 0.50(5000) - 100$
          $= 2500 - 100$
          $= \$2400$

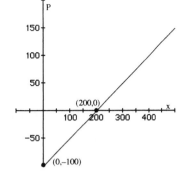

69. $C = 0.06543x + 5.65$
     For 300 kWh,
     $C = 0.06543(300) + 5.65$
     $= \$25.28$
     For 750 kWh,
     $C = 0.06543(750) + 5.65$
     $= \$54.72$

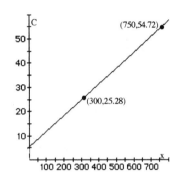

71. (b)   73. (d)

75. Slope = 1; y-intercept = 2   77. Slope $= -\dfrac{1}{3}$; y-intercept = 1

     $y = x + 2$ or $x - y = -2$ $y = -\dfrac{1}{3}x + 1$ or $x + 3y = 3$

79. (b), (c), (e) and (g)   81. Answers will vary.

83. Not every line has two distinct intercepts since a horizontal line might not touch the x-axis and a vertical line might not touch the y-axis.
     A line must have at least one intercept since a vertical line always crosses the x-axis, a horizontal line always crosses the y-axis and a non-vertical, non-horizontal line always crosses both axes.

85. Two lines with the same non-zero x-intercept and the same y-intercept must have the same slope and therefore must be represented by equivalent equations.

87. Two lines that have the same y-intercept but different slopes can only have the same x-intercept if the y-intercept is zero.

89. Answers will vary.

117

Graphs

2.4   Parallel and Perpendicular Lines; Circles

1. parallel line: slope $= 6$

    perpendicular line: slope $= -\dfrac{1}{6}$

3. parallel line: slope $= -\dfrac{1}{2}$

    perpendicular line: slope $= 2$

5. $2x - 4y + 5 = 0 \rightarrow y = \dfrac{1}{2}x + \dfrac{5}{4}$

    parallel line: slope $= \dfrac{1}{2}$

    perpendicular line: slope $= -2$

7. $3x + 5y - 10 = 0 \rightarrow y = -\dfrac{3}{5}x + 2$

    parallel line: slope $= -\dfrac{3}{5}$

    perpendicular line: slope $= \dfrac{5}{3}$

9. parallel line: slope is undefined

    perpendicular line: slope $= 0$

11. $y - y_1 = m(x - x_1), \ m = 2$

    $y - 3 = 2(x - 3)$

    $y - 3 = 2x - 6$

    $y = 2x - 3$

    $2x - y = 3$ or $y = 2x - 3$

13. $y - y_1 = m(x - x_1), \ m = -\dfrac{1}{2}$

    $y - 2 = \dfrac{-1}{2}(x - 1)$

    $y - 2 = \dfrac{-1}{2}x + \dfrac{1}{2}$

    $y = \dfrac{-1}{2}x + \dfrac{5}{2}$

    $x + 2y = 5$ or $y = \dfrac{-1}{2}x + \dfrac{5}{2}$

15. Parallel to $y = 2x$; Slope $= 2$

    Containing $(-1, 2)$

    $y - y_1 = m(x - x_1)$

    $y - 2 = 2(x - (-1))$

    $y - 2 = 2x + 2$

    $y = 2x + 4$

    $2x - y = -4$ or $y = 2x + 4$

17. Parallel to $2x - y = -2$; Slope $= 2$

    Containing $(0,0)$

    $y - y_1 = m(x - x_1)$

    $y - 0 = 2(x - 0)$

    $y = 2x$

    $2x - y = 0$ or $y = 2x$

19. Parallel to $x = 5$;

    Containing $(4,2)$

    This is a vertical line.

    $x = 4$

    No slope intercept form.

21. Perpendicular to $y = \dfrac{1}{2}x + 4$;
Slope of perpendicular $= -2$
Containing $(1,-2)$
$$y - y_1 = m(x - x_1)$$
$$y - (-2) = -2(x - 1)$$
$$y + 2 = -2x + 2$$
$$y = -2x$$
$$2x + y = 0 \ \text{ or } \ y = -2x$$

23. Perpendicular to $2x + y = 2$;
Containing $(-3,0)$
Slope of perpendicular $= \dfrac{1}{2}$
$$y - y_1 = m(x - x_1)$$
$$y - 0 = \dfrac{1}{2}(x - (-3))$$
$$y = \dfrac{1}{2}x + \dfrac{3}{2}$$
$$x - 2y = -3 \ \text{ or } \ y = \dfrac{1}{2}x + \dfrac{3}{2}$$

25. Perpendicular to $x = 8$;
Slope of perpendicular $= 0$
Containing $(3,4)$
$$y - y_1 = m(x - x_1)$$
$$y - 4 = 0(x - 3)$$
$$y - 4 = 0$$
$$y = 4$$
$$y = 4 \ \text{ or } \ y = 0x + 4$$

27. Center $= (2, 1)$
Radius $=$ distance from $(0,1)$ to $(2,1)$
$$= \sqrt{(2 - 0)^2 + (1 - 1)^2}$$
$$= \sqrt{4} = 2$$
$$(x - 2)^2 + (y - 1)^2 = 4$$

29. Center $=$ midpoint of $(1,2)$ and $(4,2)$
$$= \left(\dfrac{1 + 4}{2}, \dfrac{2 + 2}{2}\right) = \left(\dfrac{5}{2}, 2\right)$$
Radius $=$ distance from $\left(\dfrac{5}{2}, 2\right)$ to $(4,2)$
$$= \sqrt{\left(4 - \dfrac{5}{2}\right)^2 + (2 - 2)^2}$$
$$= \sqrt{\dfrac{9}{4}} = \dfrac{3}{2}$$
$$\left(x - \dfrac{5}{2}\right)^2 + (y - 2)^2 = \dfrac{9}{4}$$

31. $(x - h)^2 + (y - k)^2 = r^2$
$(x - 0)^2 + (y - 0)^2 = 2^2$
$$x^2 + y^2 = 4$$
General form:
$$x^2 + y^2 - 4 = 0$$

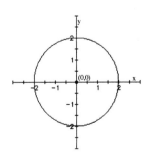

33. $(x-h)^2 + (y-k)^2 = r^2$
$(x-1)^2 + (y-(-1))^2 = 1^2$
$\qquad (x-1)^2 + (y+1)^2 = 1$
General form:
$x^2 - 2x + 1 + y^2 + 2y + 1 = 1$
$\qquad x^2 + y^2 - 2x + 2y + 1 = 0$

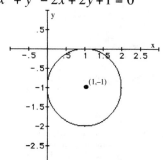

35. $(x-h)^2 + (y-k)^2 = r^2$
$(x-0)^2 + (y-2)^2 = 2^2$
$\qquad x^2 + (y-2)^2 = 4$
General form:
$x^2 + y^2 - 4y + 4 = 4$
$\qquad x^2 + y^2 - 4y = 0$

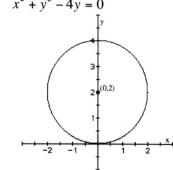

37. $(x-h)^2 + (y-k)^2 = r^2$
$(x-4)^2 + (y-(-3))^2 = 5^2$
$\qquad (x-4)^2 + (y+3)^2 = 25$
General form:
$x^2 - 8x + 16 + y^2 + 6y + 9 = 25$
$\qquad x^2 + y^2 - 8x + 6y = 0$

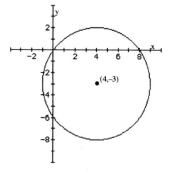

39. $x^2 + y^2 = 4$
$x^2 + y^2 = 2^2$
Center: $(0,0)$
Radius $= 2$

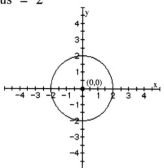

41. $2(x-3)^2 + 2y^2 = 8$
$\quad (x-3)^2 + y^2 = 4$
Center: $(3,0)$
Radius $= 2$

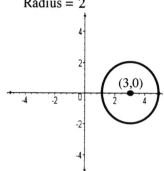

43. $x^2 + y^2 + 4x - 4y - 1 = 0$

$$x^2 + 4x + y^2 - 4y = 1$$

$$(x^2 + 4x + 4) + (y^2 - 4y + 4) = 1 + 4 + 4$$

$$(x + 2)^2 + (y - 2)^2 = 3^2$$

Center: $(-2, 2)$

Radius = 3

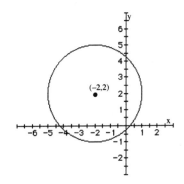

45. $x^2 + y^2 - x + 2y + 1 = 0$

$$x^2 - x + y^2 + 2y = -1$$

$$\left(x^2 - x + \frac{1}{4}\right) + (y^2 + 2y + 1) = -1 + \frac{1}{4} + 1$$

$$\left(x - \frac{1}{2}\right)^2 + (y + 1)^2 = \left(\frac{1}{2}\right)^2$$

Center: $\left(\frac{1}{2}, -1\right)$

Radius = $\frac{1}{2}$

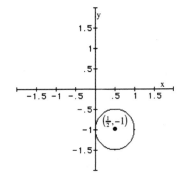

47. $2x^2 + 2y^2 - 12x + 8y - 24 = 0$

$$x^2 + y^2 - 6x + 4y = 12$$

$$x^2 - 6x + y^2 + 4y = 12$$

$$(x^2 - 6x + 9) + (y^2 + 4y + 4) = 12 + 9 + 4$$

$$(x - 3)^2 + (y + 2)^2 = 5^2$$

Center: $(3, -2)$

Radius = 5

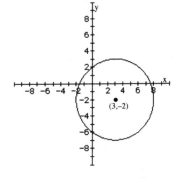

49.   Center at $(0,0)$; containing point $(-3, 2)$.

$$r = \sqrt{(-3 - 0)^2 + (2 - 0)^2} = \sqrt{9 + 4} = \sqrt{13}$$

Equation:

$$(x - 0)^2 + (y - 0)^2 = \left(\sqrt{13}\right)^2$$

$$x^2 + y^2 = 13$$

$$x^2 + y^2 - 13 = 0$$

51.   Center at $(2,3)$; tangent to the x-axis.

$$r = 3$$

Equation:

$$(x - 2)^2 + (y - 3)^2 = 3^2$$

$$x^2 - 4x + 4 + y^2 - 6y + 9 = 9$$

$$x^2 + y^2 - 4x - 6y + 4 = 0$$

53.   Endpoints of a diameter are $(1,4)$ and $(-3,2)$.
The center is at the midpoint of that diameter:

Center: $\left(\dfrac{1+(-3)}{2}, \dfrac{4+2}{2}\right) = (-1,3)$

Radius: $r = \sqrt{(1-(-1))^2 + (4-3)^2} = \sqrt{4+1} = \sqrt{5}$

Equation:

$$(x-(-1))^2 + (y-3)^2 = \left(\sqrt{5}\right)^2$$
$$x^2 + 2x + 1 + y^2 - 6y + 9 = 5$$
$$x^2 + y^2 + 2x - 6y + 5 = 0$$

55.   Consider the points $A(-2,5)$, $B(1,3)$ and $C(-1,0)$

slope of $\overline{AB} = \dfrac{3-5}{1-(-2)} = -\dfrac{2}{3}$; slope of $\overline{AC} = \dfrac{0-5}{-1-(-2)} = -\dfrac{5}{3}$; slope of $\overline{BC} = \dfrac{0-3}{-1-1} = \dfrac{3}{2}$

Therefore, $\triangle ABC$ has a right angle at vertex B since

slope $\overline{AB} = -\dfrac{2}{3}$ and slope $\overline{BC} = \dfrac{3}{2} \rightarrow \overline{AB} \perp \overline{BC}$

57.   Consider the points $A(-1,0)$, $B(2,3)$, $C(1,-2)$ and $D(4,1)$

slope of $\overline{AB} = \dfrac{3-0}{2-(-1)} = 1$; slope of $\overline{CD} = \dfrac{1-(-2)}{4-1} = 1$

slope of $\overline{AC} = \dfrac{-2-0}{1-(-1)} = -1$; slope of $\overline{BD} = \dfrac{1-3}{4-2} = -1$

Therefore, the quadrilateral $ACDB$ is a parallelogram since

slope $\overline{AB} = 1$ and slope $\overline{CD} = 1 \rightarrow \overline{AB}$ is parallel to $\overline{CD}$

slope $\overline{AC} = -1$ and slope $\overline{BD} = -1 \rightarrow \overline{AC}$ is parallel to $\overline{BD}$

Furthermore,

slope $\overline{AB} = 1$ and slope $\overline{BD} = -1 \rightarrow \overline{AB} \perp \overline{BD}$

slope $\overline{AC} = -1$ and slope $\overline{CD} = 1 \rightarrow \overline{AC} \perp \overline{CD}$

So the quadrilateral $ACDB$ is a rectangle.

59.   (c)   61.   (b)   62.   (a)

63. $(x+3)^2 + (y-1)^2 = 16$ 65. $(x-2)^2 + (y-2)^2 = 9$

67. (b), (c), (e) and (g)   69. (c)

71. Consider the diagram

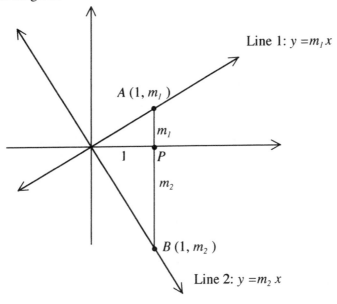

$$\text{length of } \overline{OA} = \sqrt{1 + m_1^{\,2}}$$
$$\text{length of } \overline{OB} = \sqrt{1 + m_2^{\,2}}$$
$$\text{length of } \overline{AB} = m_1 - m_2$$

Now consider the equation

$$\left(\sqrt{1 + m_1^{\,2}}\right)^2 + \left(\sqrt{1 + m_2^{\,2}}\right)^2 = \left(m_1 - m_2\right)^2$$

If this equation is valid, then $\triangle AOB$ is a right triangle with right angle at vertex O.

$$\left(\sqrt{1 + m_1^{\,2}}\right)^2 + \left(\sqrt{1 + m_2^{\,2}}\right)^2 = \left(m_1 - m_2\right)^2$$
$$1 + m_1^{\,2} + 1 + m_2^{\,2} = m_1^{\,2} - 2m_1 m_2 + m_2^{\,2}$$
$$2 + m_1^{\,2} + m_2^{\,2} = m_1^{\,2} - 2m_1 m_2 + m_2^{\,2}$$

but we are assuming that $m_1 m_2 = -1$, so we have

$$2 + m_1^{\,2} + m_2^{\,2} = m_1^{\,2} - 2(-1) + m_2^{\,2}$$
$$2 + m_1^{\,2} + m_2^{\,2} = m_1^{\,2} + 2 + m_2^{\,2}$$
$$0 = 0$$

Therefore, by the converse of the Pythagorean Theorem, $\triangle AOB$ is a right triangle with right angle at vertex O. Thus Line1 $\perp$ Line2.

73. (a) $x^2 + (mx + b)^2 = r^2$

$x^2 + m^2 x^2 + 2bmx + b^2 = r^2$

$(1 + m^2)x^2 + 2bmx + b^2 - r^2 = 0$

There is one solution if and only if the discriminant is zero.

$$(2bm)^2 - 4(1 + m^2)(b^2 - r^2) = 0$$

$$4b^2 m^2 - 4b^2 + 4r^2 - 4b^2 m^2 + 4m^2 r^2 = 0$$

$$-4b^2 + 4r^2 + 4m^2 r^2 = 0$$

$$-b^2 + r^2 + m^2 r^2 = 0$$

$$r^2(1 + m^2) = b^2$$

(b)   Using the quadratic formula, knowing that the discriminant is zero:

$$x = \frac{-2bm}{2(1 + m^2)} = \frac{-bm}{\dfrac{b^2}{r^2}} = \frac{-bmr^2}{b^2} = \frac{-mr^2}{b}$$

$$y = m\left(\frac{-mr^2}{b}\right) + b = \frac{-m^2 r^2}{b} + b = \frac{-m^2 r^2 + b^2}{b} = \frac{r^2}{b}$$

(c)   The slope of the tangent line is m.

The slope of the line joining the point of tangency and the center is:

$$\frac{\dfrac{r^2}{b} - 0}{\dfrac{-mr^2}{b} - 0} = \frac{r^2}{b} \cdot \frac{b}{-mr^2} = -\frac{1}{m}$$

75. $x^2 + y^2 - 4x + 6y + 4 = 0$

$(x^2 - 4x + 4) + (y^2 + 6y + 9) = -4 + 4 + 9$

$(x - 2)^2 + (y + 3)^2 = 9$

Center: $(2, -3)$

Slope from center to $\left(3, 2\sqrt{2} - 3\right)$ is $\dfrac{2\sqrt{2} - 3 - (-3)}{3 - 2} = \dfrac{2\sqrt{2}}{1} = 2\sqrt{2}$

Slope of the tangent line is: $\dfrac{-1}{2\sqrt{2}} = \dfrac{-\sqrt{2}}{4}$

Equation of the tangent line:

$$y - \left(2\sqrt{2} - 3\right) = \frac{-\sqrt{2}}{4}(x - 3) \rightarrow y - 2\sqrt{2} + 3 = \frac{-\sqrt{2}}{4}x + \frac{3\sqrt{2}}{4}$$

$$4y - 8\sqrt{2} + 12 = -\sqrt{2}x + 3\sqrt{2} \rightarrow \sqrt{2}x + 4y = 11\sqrt{2} - 12$$

77. Find the centers of the two circles:

$$x^2 + y^2 - 4x + 6y + 4 = 0$$

$(x^2 - 4x + 4) + (y^2 + 6y + 9) = -4 + 4 + 9$

$(x - 2)^2 + (y + 3)^2 = 9$ Center $(2, -3)$

$$x^2 + y^2 + 6x + 4y + 9 = 0$$

$(x^2 + 6x + 9) + (y^2 + 4y + 4) = -9 + 9 + 4$

$(x + 3)^2 + (y + 2)^2 = 4$ Center $(-3, -2)$

Find the slope of the line containing the centers:
$$m = \frac{-2-(-3)}{-3-2} = \frac{1}{-5}$$
Find the equation of the line containing the centers:
$$y + 3 = \frac{-1}{5}(x-2)$$
$$5y + 15 = -x + 2$$
$$x + 5y = -13$$

79. $2x - y = C$

Graph the lines:
$$2x - y = -2$$
$$2x - y = 0$$
$$2x - y = 4$$
All the lines have the same slope, 2.
The lines are parallel.

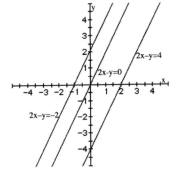

81. $y = 2$

Graphs

2.5 Scatter Diagrams; Linear Curve Fitting

1. Linear, $m > 0$

3. Linear, $m < 0$

5. Nonlinear

7. (a)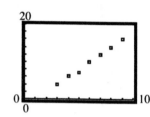

(b) Answers will vary. We select (4,6) and (8,14). The slope of the line containing these points is:
$$m = \frac{14-6}{8-4} = \frac{8}{4} = 2$$
The equation of the line is:
$$y - y_1 = m(x - x_1)$$
$$y - 6 = 2(x - 4)$$
$$y - 6 = 2x - 8$$
$$y = 2x - 2$$

(c)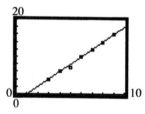

(d) Using the LINear REGresssion program, the line of best fit is:
$$y = 2.0357x - 2.3571$$

(e)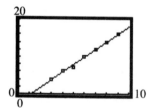

126

9. (a)

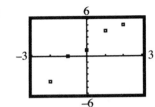

(b) Answers will vary. We select $(-2,-4)$ and $(1,4)$. The slope of the line containing these points is:

$$m = \frac{4-(-4)}{1-(-2)} = \frac{8}{3}$$

The equation of the line is:

$$y - y_1 = m(x - x_1)$$

$$y - (-4) = \frac{8}{3}(x - (-2))$$

$$y + 4 = \frac{8}{3}x + \frac{16}{3}$$

$$y = \frac{8}{3}x + \frac{4}{3}$$

(c)

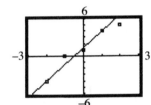

(d) Using the LINear REGresssion program, the line of best fit is:

$$y = 2.2x + 1.2$$

(e)

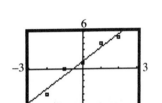

11. (a)

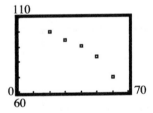

(b) Answers will vary. We select $(30,95)$ and $(60,70)$. The slope of the line containing these points is:

$$m = \frac{70-95}{60-30} = \frac{-25}{30} = \frac{-5}{6}$$

The equation of the line is:

$$y - y_1 = m(x - x_1)$$

$$y - 95 = \frac{-5}{6}(x - 30)$$

$$y - 95 = \frac{-5}{6}x + 25$$

$$y = \frac{-5}{6}x + 120$$

(c)

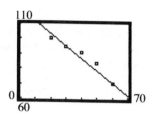

(d)   Using the LINear REGresssion program, the line of best fit is:
$$y = -0.72x + 116.6$$

(e)

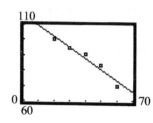

13.   (a)

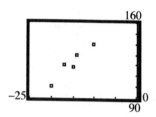

(b)   Answers will vary. We select $(-20, 100)$ and $(-15, 118)$. The slope of the line containing these points is:
$$m = \frac{118 - 100}{-15 - (-20)} = \frac{18}{5}$$
The equation of the line is:
$$y - y_1 = m(x - x_1)$$
$$y - 100 = \frac{18}{5}(x - (-20))$$
$$y - 100 = \frac{18}{5}x + 72$$
$$y = \frac{18}{5}x + 172$$

(c)

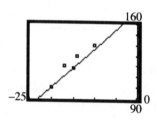

(d)   Using the LINear REGresssion program, the line of best fit is:
$$y = 3.8613x + 180.2920$$

(e)

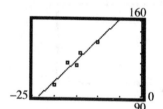

15. (a)

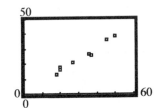

(b) using points $(20,16)$ and $(50,39)$,

$$slope = \frac{39-16}{50-20} = \frac{23}{30}$$

the point slope formula yields

$$C - 16 = \frac{23}{30}(I - 20)$$

$$C = \left(\frac{23}{30}\right)I - \frac{460}{30} + 16$$

$$C = 0.76I + 0.67$$

(c) As disposable income increases by $1, consumption increases by $0.76.

(d) $C = 0.77(42) + 0.67 = \$33.01$
A family with disposable income of $42,000 consumes about $33,010.

(e) $C = 0.7549I + 0.6266$

17. (a) (Data used in graphs is in thousands.)

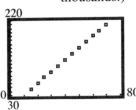

(b) $L = 2.9814I - 0.0761$

(c)

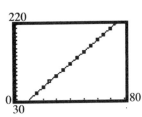

(d) As annual income increases by $1, the loan amount increases by $2.9814.

(e) $L = 2.9814(42) - 0.0761 = 125.143$
A person with an annual income of $42,000 would qualify for a loan of about $125,143.

19. (a)

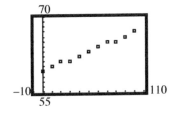

(b) $T = 0.0782h + 59.0909$

(c)

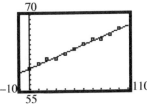

(d) As relative humidity increases by 1%, the apparent temperature increases by 0.0782°.

(e) $T = 0.0782(75) + 59.0909 = 64.96$
A relative humidity of 75% would give an apparent temperature of 65°.

21.   (a)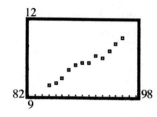

(b) $M = 0.1633x - 4.4691$

(c)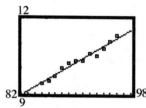

(d)   As the year increases by 1, the average miles per car (in thousands) increases by 0.1633.

(e) $M = 0.1633(97) - 4.4691 = 11.371$
In 1997, the average number of miles driven per car is 11,371.

Graphs

2.6 Variation

1. $y = kx$

   $2 = 10k \rightarrow k = \dfrac{1}{5}$

   $y = \dfrac{1}{5}x$

3. $A = kx^2$

   $4\pi = 4k \rightarrow k = \pi$

   $A = \pi x^2$

5. $F = \dfrac{k}{d^2}$

   $10 = \dfrac{k}{25} \rightarrow k = 250$

   $F = \dfrac{250}{d^2}$

7. $z = k(x^2 + y^2)$

   $5 = k(3^2 + 4^2) \rightarrow k = \dfrac{1}{5}$

   $z = \dfrac{1}{5}(x^2 + y^2)$

9. $M = \dfrac{kd^2}{\sqrt{x}}$

   $24 = \dfrac{k(4^2)}{\sqrt{9}} \rightarrow 24 = \dfrac{16k}{3} \rightarrow k = 4.5$

   $M = \dfrac{4.5(d^2)}{\sqrt{x}}$

11. $T^2 = \dfrac{ka^3}{d^2}$

    $2^2 = \dfrac{k(2^3)}{4^2} \rightarrow k = 8$

    $T^2 = \dfrac{8a^3}{d^2}$

13. $V = \dfrac{4}{3}\pi r^3$

15. $A = \dfrac{1}{2}bh$

17. $V = \pi r^2 h$

19. $F = \dfrac{(6.67 \times 10^{-11})mM}{d^2}$

21. $s = kt^2$

    $16 = k(1)^2 \rightarrow k = 16$

    in 3 seconds $s = (16)(9) = 144\ feet$

    $64 = 16t^2 \rightarrow t^2 = 4 \rightarrow t = \pm 2$

    so it takes 2 seconds to fall 64 feet.

23. $E = kw$

    $3 = k(20) \rightarrow k = \dfrac{3}{20}$

    when $w = 15$, $E = \left(\dfrac{3}{20}\right)(15) = 2.25$

25. $W = \dfrac{k}{d^2}$

$55 = \dfrac{k}{3960^2} \rightarrow k = 862488000$

when $d = 3965$,

$W = \dfrac{862488000}{3965^2} = 54.86$ pounds

27. $h = ksd^3$

$36 = k(75)(2)^3 \rightarrow k = 0.06$

when $h = 45$ and $s = 125$,

$45 = (0.06)(125)(d)^3$

$\rightarrow d = \sqrt[3]{\dfrac{45}{7.5}} \approx 0.84$ inches

29. $K = kmv^2$

$400 = k(25)(100)^2 \rightarrow k = 0.0016$

when $v = 150$,

$K = (0.0016)(25)(150)^2 = 900$ foot $-$ pounds

31. $S = \dfrac{kpd}{t}$

$100 = \dfrac{k(25)(5)}{(0.75)} \rightarrow k = 0.6$

when $p = 40, d = 8$ and $t = 0.50$

$S = \dfrac{(0.6)(40)(8)}{(0.50)} = 320$ pounds

33. $R = \dfrac{kl}{r^2}$

$10 = \dfrac{k(50)}{(0.006)^2} \rightarrow k = 7.2 \times 10^{-6}$

when $l = 100$ and $r = 0.007$,

$R = \dfrac{(7.2 \times 10^{-6})(100)}{(0.007)^2} = 14.69$ ohms

35. $v = \sqrt{g}\sqrt{r} = \sqrt{gr}$

37. $v = \sqrt{gr}$

$v = \sqrt{g(3960 + 140)} = \sqrt{(g)(4100)}$

$\approx \sqrt{(79036)(4100)} \approx 18001.32$ mph

39. The satellite travels the circumference of the circular orbit once in 1.5 hours.
We also know that

circumference of a circle $= 2\pi$ (radius)

distance $=$ (rate)(time)

$\therefore 2\pi r = vt \rightarrow v = \dfrac{2\pi r}{t} = \dfrac{2\pi r}{1.5} = \dfrac{4\pi}{3}r$

so $\quad v = \sqrt{gr} = \dfrac{4\pi}{3}r \rightarrow gr = \dfrac{16\pi^2}{9}r^2$

$0 = \dfrac{16\pi^2}{9}r^2 - gr \rightarrow r\left(\dfrac{16\pi^2}{9}r - g\right) = 0$

$\rightarrow r = 0$ or $\dfrac{16\pi^2}{9}r - g = 0 \rightarrow r = (g)\left(\dfrac{9}{16\pi^2}\right) \approx (79036)\left(\dfrac{9}{16\pi^2}\right) \approx 4504.51$

therefore the satellite is $4504.51 - 3960 = 544.51$ miles above Earth.

41. $F = \dfrac{mv^2}{r}$

43. $F = \dfrac{mv^2}{r}$

$$v = 120 + (0.10)(120) = 132 \text{ km/hr} = \dfrac{110}{3}\text{m/sec}$$

$$F = \dfrac{(150)\left(\dfrac{110}{3}\right)^2}{100} \approx 2016.67 \text{ newtons}$$

so the force is increased by $\dfrac{2016.67 - 1666.67}{1666.67} = \dfrac{350}{1666.67} \approx 0.21 = 21\%.$

45. $F = \dfrac{mv^2}{r}$

we compare $F = \dfrac{mv^2}{L}$ with $F = \dfrac{m(3v)^2}{L} = \dfrac{9mv^2}{L}$

therefore, the force needed is 9 times greater.

47 – 49.   Answers will vary.

Chapter 2

Graphs

2.R   Chapter Review

1. Intercepts: $(0,0)$
    Test for symmetry:
    x-axis: Replace y by $-y$ so $2x = 3(-y)^2$ or $2x = 3y^2$, which is
    equivalent to $2x = 3y^2$.

    y-axis: Replace x by $-x$ so $2(-x) = 3y^2$ or $-2x = 3y^2$,
    which is not equivalent to $2x = 3y^2$.

    Origin: Replace x by $-x$ and y by $-y$ so $2(-x) = 3(-y)^2$ or
    $-2x = 3y^2$, which is not equivalent to $2x = 3y^2$.
    Therefore, the graph is symmetric with respect to the x-axis.

3. Intercepts: $(0, 2)$, $(0, -2)$, $(4, 0)$, $(-4, 0)$
    Test for symmetry:
    x-axis: Replace y by $-y$ so $x^2 + 4(-y)^2 = 16$ or $x^2 + 4y^2 = 16$,
    which is equivalent to $x^2 + 4y^2 = 16$.

    y-axis: Replace x by $-x$ so $(-x)^2 + 4y^2 = 16$ or $x^2 + 4y^2 = 16$,
    which is equivalent to $x^2 + 4y^2 = 16$.

    Origin: Replace x by $-x$ and y by $-y$ so $(-x)^2 + 4(-y)^2 = 16$ or $x^2 + 4y^2 = 16$,
    which is equivalent to $x^2 + 4y^2 = 16$.
    Therefore, the graph is symmetric with respect to the x-axis, the y-axis and the
    origin.

5. Intercepts: $(0, 1)$
    Test for symmetry:
    x-axis: Replace y by $-y$ so $-y = x^4 + 2x^2 + 1$,
    which is not equivalent to $y = x^4 + 2x^2 + 1$.

    y-axis: Replace x by $-x$ so $y = (-x)^4 + 2(-x)^2 + 1$ or $y = x^4 + 2x^2 + 1$,
    which is equivalent to $y = x^4 + 2x^2 + 1$.

    Origin: Replace x by $-x$ and y by $-y$ so $-y = (-x)^4 + 2(-x)^2 + 1$ or $-y = x^4 + 2x^2 + 1$,
    which is not equivalent to $y = x^4 + 2x^2 + 1$.
    Therefore, the graph is symmetric with respect to the y-axis.

7.   Intercepts: $(0,0)$, $(0,-2)$, $(-1,0)$
Test for symmetry:

x - axis: Replace y by $-y$ so $x^2 + x + (-y)^2 + 2(-y) = 0$ or $x^2 + x + y^2 - 2y = 0$,
    which is not equivalent to $x^2 + x + y^2 + 2y = 0$.

y - axis: Replace x by $-x$ so $(-x)^2 + (-x) + y^2 + 2y = 0$ or $x^2 - x + y^2 + 2y = 0$,
    which is not equivalent to $x^2 + x + y^2 + 2y = 0$.

Origin :   Replace x by $-x$ and y by $-y$ so $(-x)^2 + (-x) + (-y)^2 + 2(-y) = 0$ or
    $x^2 - x + y^2 - 2y = 0$, which is not equivalent to
    $x^2 + x + y^2 + 2y = 0$.

Therefore, the graph is not symmetric to the x-axis, the y-axis, or the origin.

9.   Slope $= -2$; containing $(3,-1)$
$$y - y_1 = m(x - x_1)$$
$$y - (-1) = -2(x - 3)$$
$$y + 1 = -2x + 6$$
$$y = -2x + 5$$
$$2x + y = 5 \text{ or } y = -2x + 5$$

11.   Slope undefined; containing $(-3,4)$
This is a vertical line.
$$x = -3$$
    No slope intercept form.

13.   y-intercept $= -2$; containing $(5,-3)$
Points are $(5,-3)$ and $(0,-2)$
$$m = \frac{-2 - (-3)}{0 - 5} = \frac{1}{-5} = -\frac{1}{5}$$
$$y = mx + b$$
$$y = \frac{-1}{5}x - 2$$
$$x + 5y = -10 \text{ or } y = \frac{-1}{5}x - 2$$

15.   Parallel to $2x - 3y = -4$;
Slope $= \frac{2}{3}$; containing $(-5,3)$
$$y - y_1 = m(x - x_1)$$
$$y - 3 = \frac{2}{3}(x - (-5))$$
$$y - 3 = \frac{2}{3}x + \frac{10}{3}$$
$$y = \frac{2}{3}x + \frac{19}{3}$$
$$2x - 3y = -19 \text{ or } y = \frac{2}{3}x + \frac{19}{3}$$

17.   Perpendicular to $x + y = 2$;
Containing $(4,-3)$
Slope of perpendicular $= 1$
$$y - y_1 = m(x - x_1)$$
$$y - (-3) = 1(x - 4)$$
$$y + 3 = x - 4$$
$$y = x - 7$$
$$x - y = 7 \text{ or } y = x - 7$$

19. $4x - 5y = -20$
x-intercept $= -5$; y-intercept $= 4$

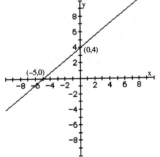

21. $\frac{1}{2}x - \frac{1}{3}y = -\frac{1}{6}$

x-intercept $= -\frac{1}{3}$; y-intercept $= \frac{1}{2}$

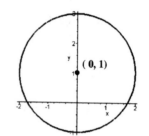

23. $\sqrt{2}x + \sqrt{3}y = \sqrt{6}$

x-intercept $= \sqrt{3}$; y-intercept $= \sqrt{2}$

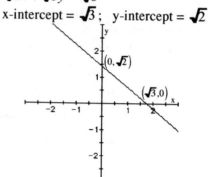

25. $x^2 + (y-1)^2 = 4$

Center: $(0,1)$
Radius $= 2$

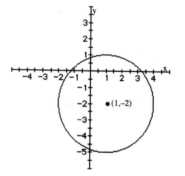

27. $x^2 + y^2 - 2x + 4y - 4 = 0$
$$x^2 - 2x + y^2 + 4y = 4$$
$$(x^2 - 2x + 1) + (y^2 + 4y + 4) = 4 + 1 + 4$$
$$(x-1)^2 + (y+2)^2 = 3^2$$
Center: $(1,-2)$ Radius $= 3$

29. $3x^2 + 3y^2 - 6x + 12y = 0$
$$x^2 + y^2 - 2x + 4y = 0$$
$$x^2 - 2x + y^2 + 4y = 0$$
$$(x^2 - 2x + 1) + (y^2 + 4y + 4) = 1 + 4$$
$$(x-1)^2 + (y+2)^2 = \left(\sqrt{5}\right)^2$$
Center: $(1,-2)$ Radius $= \sqrt{5}$

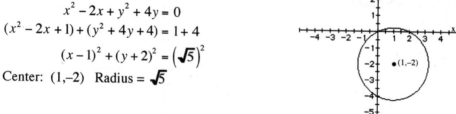

31. Given the points (7,4) and (–3,2).

Slope: $m = \dfrac{2-4}{-3-7} = \dfrac{-2}{-10} = \dfrac{1}{5}$

Distance: $d = \sqrt{(-3-7)^2 + (2-4)^2} = \sqrt{100+4} = \sqrt{104} = 2\sqrt{26}$

Midpoint: $\left(\dfrac{7+(-3)}{2}, \dfrac{4+2}{2}\right) = (2,3)$

33. Given the points $A = (-2, 0)$, $B = (-4, 4)$, $C = (8, 5)$.

(a) Find the distance between each pair of points.

$d_{A,B} = \sqrt{(-4-(-2))^2 + (4-0)^2} = \sqrt{4+16} = \sqrt{20} = 2\sqrt{5}$

$d_{B,C} = \sqrt{(8-(-4))^2 + (5-4)^2} = \sqrt{144+1} = \sqrt{145}$

$d_{A,C} = \sqrt{(8-(-2))^2 + (5-0)^2} = \sqrt{100+25} = \sqrt{125} = 5\sqrt{5}$

$\left(\sqrt{20}\right)^2 + \left(\sqrt{125}\right)^2 = \left(\sqrt{145}\right)^2 \rightarrow 20+125 = 145 \rightarrow 145 = 145$

The Pythagorean theorem is satisfied, so this is a right triangle.

(b) Find the slopes:

$m_{AB} = \dfrac{4-0}{-4-(-2)} = \dfrac{4}{-2} = -2; \quad m_{BC} = \dfrac{5-4}{8-(-4)} = \dfrac{1}{12}; \quad m_{AC} = \dfrac{5-0}{8-(-2)} = \dfrac{5}{10} = \dfrac{1}{2}$

$m_{AB} \cdot m_{AC} = -2 \cdot \dfrac{1}{2} = -1$

Since the product of the slopes is –1, the sides of the triangle are perpendicular and the triangle is a right triangle.

35. slope of $\overline{AB} = \dfrac{1-5}{6-2} = -1$; slope of $\overline{AC} = \dfrac{-1-5}{8-2} = -1$; slope of $\overline{BC} = \dfrac{-1-1}{8-6} = -1$

therefore the points are collinear.

37. $Area = A = kx^2, x = $ length of a side of the triangle

$A = \dfrac{\sqrt{3}}{4}, x = 1 \rightarrow \dfrac{\sqrt{3}}{4} = (k)(1) \rightarrow k = \dfrac{\sqrt{3}}{4}$

$A = 16 \rightarrow A = \left(\dfrac{\sqrt{3}}{4}\right)(x) = 16 \rightarrow x = \dfrac{48}{\sqrt{3}} = 16\sqrt{3} \text{ cm.}$

39. period (in days) $= T$, mean distance (in millon miles) from sun $= a$

$T^2 = ka^3$

$T = 365, a = 93 \rightarrow 365^2 = (k)(93)^3 \rightarrow k = \dfrac{365^2}{93^3} \approx 0.1656292013$

$T = 88 \rightarrow 88^2 = \left(\dfrac{365^2}{93^3}\right)(a)^3 \rightarrow a^3 = (88^2)\left(\dfrac{93^3}{365^2}\right)$

$\rightarrow a = \sqrt[3]{(88^2)\left(\dfrac{93^3}{365^2}\right)} \approx 36.025 \text{ million miles}$

41. (a)

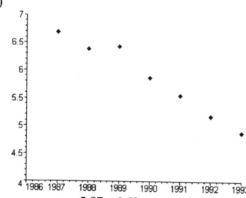

(b)   slope = $\dfrac{5.87 - 6.69}{1990 - 1987} = -0.27\overline{3}$

(c)   for each 1 year increase, the concentration decreases by $0.27\overline{3}$ ppm.

(d)   slope = $\dfrac{4.88 - 5.87}{1993 - 1990} = -0.33$

(e)   for each 1 year increase, the concentration decreases by 0.33 ppm.

(f) $y = 618.477 - 0.308x$

(g)   for each 1 year increase, the concentration decreases by 0.308 ppm.

(h)   Answers will vary.

(i)   As time passes, the average level of carbon monoxide is decreasing more rapidly.

43.   Answers will vary.

45.   Set the axes so that the field's maximum dimension is along the x-axis.

Let $2h = width$, $2k = height$, therefore the point farthest from the origin has coordinates $P(h, k)$. So the distance from the origin to point P is $r = \sqrt{h^2 + k^2}$ = the radius of the circle

Using 1 sprinkler arm:

If we place the sprinkler at the origin, we get a circle with equation $x^2 + y^2 = r^2$, where $r = \sqrt{h^2 + k^2}$. So how much water is wasted ? The area of the field = $A_F = 4hk$.

The area of the circular water pattern $A_C = \pi \cdot r^2 = \pi \cdot \left(\sqrt{h^2 + k^2}\right)^2 = \pi \cdot \left(h^2 + k^2\right)$.

Therefore the amount of water wasted = $A_C - A_F = \pi \cdot \left(h^2 + k^2\right) - 4hk$.

Using 2 sprinkler arms:

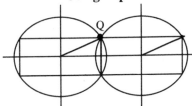

Place sprinkler 1 at $\frac{1}{4} \cdot (width)$ and sprinkler 2 at $\frac{3}{4} \cdot (width)$. Let the origin correspond to the center of the circle formed by sprinkler 1, the arm must be set so that the water will hit the point $Q\left(\frac{1}{2}h, k\right)$.

The distance from the origin to point Q is given by $r = \sqrt{\frac{1}{4}h^2 + k^2}$ = the radius of circle 1.

We need the same settings for sprinkler 2.

So the total area of the 2 circles = $2\pi \cdot r^2 = 2\pi\left(\sqrt{\frac{1}{4}h^2 + k^2}\right)^2 = 2\pi\left(\frac{1}{4}h^2 + k^2\right)$

Therefore the amount of water wasted = $A_C - A_F = 2\pi\left(\frac{1}{4}h^2 + k^2\right) - 4hk$.

In order to decide when to switch from Case 1 to Case 2, we want to determine when the waste in Case 2 is less than the waste in Case 1.

That is, we want to solve: $2\pi\left(\frac{1}{4}h^2 + k^2\right) - 4hk < \pi \cdot \left(h^2 + k^2\right) - 4hk$

$2\pi\left(\frac{1}{4}h^2 + k^2\right) - 4hk < \pi \cdot \left(h^2 + k^2\right) - 4hk \rightarrow \frac{\pi}{2}h^2 + 2\pi k^2 - 4hk < \pi h^2 + \pi k^2 - 4hk$

$\frac{\pi}{2}h^2 + 2\pi k^2 < \pi h^2 + \pi k^2 \rightarrow \frac{1}{2}h^2 + 2k^2 < h^2 + k^2 \rightarrow k^2 < \frac{1}{2}h^2 \rightarrow k < \sqrt{\frac{1}{2}} \cdot h$

So Case 2 is the better choice when the rectangle's dimensions obey the inequality $\frac{k}{h} < \frac{\sqrt{2}}{2}$.

Functions and Their Graphs

3.1 Functions

1. Function
   Domain: {Dad, Colleen, Kaleigh, Marissa}
   Range: {Jan. 8, Mar. 15, Sept. 17}

3. Not a function

5. ~~Function~~ *not a*
   ~~Domain: {2, -3, 4, 1}~~ *function*
   ~~Range: {6, 9, 10}~~

7. Function
   Domain: {1, 2, 3, 4}
   Range: {3}

9. Not a function

11. Function
    Domain: {-2, -1, 0, 1}
    Range: {4, 1, 0}

13. $f(x) = 3x^2 + 2x - 4$

   (a) $f(0) = 3(0)^2 + 2(0) - 4 = -4$

   (b) $f(1) = 3(1)^2 + 2(1) - 4 = 3 + 2 - 4 = 1$

   (c) $f(-1) = 3(-1)^2 + 2(-1) - 4 = 3 - 2 - 4 = -3$

   (d) $f(-x) = 3(-x)^2 + 2(-x) - 4 = 3x^2 - 2x - 4$

   (e) $-f(x) = -(3x^2 + 2x - 4) = -3x^2 - 2x + 4$

   (f) $f(x+1) = 3(x+1)^2 + 2(x+1) - 4 = 3(x^2 + 2x + 1) + 2x + 2 - 4$
        $= 3x^2 + 6x + 3 + 2x + 2 - 4 = 3x^2 + 8x + 1$

   (g) $f(2x) = 3(2x)^2 + 2(2x) - 4 = 12x^2 + 4x - 4$

   (h) $f(x+h) = 3(x+h)^2 + 2(x+h) - 4 = 3(x^2 + 2xh + h^2) + 2x + 2h - 4$
        $= 3x^2 + 6xh + 3h^2 + 2x + 2h - 4$

15. $f(x) = \dfrac{x}{x^2 + 1}$

(a) $f(0) = \dfrac{0}{0^2 + 1} = \dfrac{0}{1} = 0$

(b) $f(1) = \dfrac{1}{1^2 + 1} = \dfrac{1}{2}$

(c) $f(-1) = \dfrac{-1}{(-1)^2 + 1} = \dfrac{-1}{1+1} = -\dfrac{1}{2}$

(d) $f(-x) = \dfrac{-x}{(-x)^2 + 1} = \dfrac{-x}{x^2 + 1}$

(e) $-f(x) = -\dfrac{x}{x^2 + 1} = \dfrac{-x}{x^2 + 1}$

(f) $f(x+1) = \dfrac{x+1}{(x+1)^2 + 1} = \dfrac{x+1}{x^2 + 2x + 1 + 1} = \dfrac{x+1}{x^2 + 2x + 2}$

(g) $f(2x) = \dfrac{2x}{(2x)^2 + 1} = \dfrac{2x}{4x^2 + 1}$

(h) $f(x+h) = \dfrac{x+h}{(x+h)^2 + 1} = \dfrac{x+h}{x^2 + 2xh + h^2 + 1}$

17. $f(x) = |x| + 4$

(a) $f(0) = |0| + 4 = 0 + 4 = 4$

(b) $f(1) = |1| + 4 = 1 + 4 = 5$

(c) $f(-1) = |-1| + 4 = 1 + 4 = 5$

(d) $f(-x) = |-x| + 4 = |x| + 4$

(e) $-f(x) = -(|x| + 4) = -|x| - 4$

(f) $f(x+1) = |x+1| + 4$

(g) $f(2x) = |2x| + 4 = 2|x| + 4$

(h) $f(x+h) = |x+h| + 4$

19. $f(x) = \dfrac{2x + 1}{3x - 5}$

(a) $f(0) = \dfrac{2(0) + 1}{3(0) - 5} = \dfrac{0 + 1}{0 - 5} = -\dfrac{1}{5}$

(b) $f(1) = \dfrac{2(1) + 1}{3(1) - 5} = \dfrac{2 + 1}{3 - 5} = \dfrac{3}{-2} = -\dfrac{3}{2}$

(c) $f(-1) = \dfrac{2(-1) + 1}{3(-1) - 5} = \dfrac{-2 + 1}{-3 - 5} = \dfrac{-1}{-8} = \dfrac{1}{8}$

(d) $f(-x) = \dfrac{2(-x) + 1}{3(-x) - 5} = \dfrac{-2x + 1}{-3x - 5} = \dfrac{2x - 1}{3x + 5}$

(e) $-f(x) = -\dfrac{2x + 1}{3x - 5} = \dfrac{-2x - 1}{3x - 5}$

(f) $f(x+1) = \dfrac{2(x+1) + 1}{3(x+1) - 5} = \dfrac{2x + 2 + 1}{3x + 3 - 5} = \dfrac{2x + 3}{3x - 2}$

(g) $f(2x) = \dfrac{2(2x) + 1}{3(2x) - 5} = \dfrac{4x + 1}{6x - 5}$

(h) $f(x+h) = \dfrac{2(x+h) + 1}{3(x+h) - 5} = \dfrac{2x + 2h + 1}{3x + 3h - 5}$

21. Graph $y = x^2$. The graph passes the vertical line test. Thus, the equation represents a function.

23. Graph $y = \dfrac{1}{x}$. The graph passes the vertical line test. Thus, the equation represents a function.

25. $y^2 = 4 - x^2$
Solve for y: $y = \pm\sqrt{4 - x^2}$
For $x = 0, y = \pm 2$. Thus, $(0,2)$ and $(0,-2)$ are on the graph. This is not a function, since a distinct x corresponds to two different y's.

27. $x = y^2$
Solve for y: $y = \pm\sqrt{x}$
For $x = 1, y = \pm 1$. Thus, $(1,1)$ and $(1,-1)$ are on the graph. This is not a function, since a distinct x corresponds to two different y's.

29. Graph $y = 2x^2 - 3x + 4$. The graph passes the vertical line test. Thus, the equation represents a function.

31. $2x^2 + 3y^2 = 1$
Solve for y:

$$2x^2 + 3y^2 = 1 \rightarrow 3y^2 = 1 - 2x^2 \rightarrow y^2 = \frac{1 - 2x^2}{3}$$

$$y = \pm\sqrt{\frac{1 - 2x^2}{3}}$$

For $x = 0, y = \pm\sqrt{\dfrac{1}{3}}$. Thus, $\left(0, \sqrt{\dfrac{1}{3}}\right)$ and $\left(0, -\sqrt{\dfrac{1}{3}}\right)$ are on the graph. This is not a function, since a distinct x corresponds to two different y's.

33. $f(x) = -5x + 4$
Domain: {Real Numbers}

35. $f(x) = \dfrac{x}{x^2 + 1}$
Domain: {Real Numbers}

37. $g(x) = \dfrac{x}{x^2 - 16}$

$x^2 - 16 \neq 0$

$x^2 \neq 16 \rightarrow x \neq \pm 4$

Domain: $\{x \mid x \neq -4, x \neq 4\}$

39. $F(x) = \dfrac{x - 2}{x^3 + x}$

$x^3 + x \neq 0$

$x(x^2 + 1) \neq 0$

$x \neq 0, \quad x^2 \neq -1$

Domain: $\{x \mid x \neq 0\}$

41. $h(x) = \sqrt{3x - 12}$

$$3x - 12 \geq 0$$
$$3x \geq 12$$
$$x \geq 4$$
Domain: $\left\{x \mid x \geq 4\right\}$

43. $f(x) = \dfrac{4}{\sqrt{x - 9}}$

$$x - 9 > 0$$
$$x > 9$$
Domain: $\left\{x \mid x > 9\right\}$

45. $p(x) = \sqrt{\dfrac{2}{x - 1}}$

$$\dfrac{2}{x - 1} > 0 \quad \rightarrow \quad x - 1 > 0 \quad \rightarrow \quad x > 1$$
Domain: $\left\{x \mid x > 1\right\}$

47. (a) $f(0) = 3$ since $(0, 3)$ is on the graph.
        $f(-6) = -3$ since $(-6, -3)$ is on the graph.
     (b) $f(6) = 0$ since $(6, 0)$ is on the graph.
        $f(11) = 1$ since $(11, 1)$ is on the graph.
     (c) $f(3)$ is positive since $f(3) \approx 3.7$.
     (d) $f(-4)$ is negative since $f(-4) = -1$.
     (e) $f(x) = 0$ when $x = -3$, $x = 6$, and $x = 10$.
     (f) $f(x) > 0$ when $-3 < x < 6$, and $10 < x \leq 11$.
     (g) The domain of f is $\left\{x \mid -6 \leq x \leq 11\right\}$ or $[-6, 11]$
     (h) The range of f is $\left\{y \mid -3 \leq y \leq 4\right\}$ or $[-3, 4]$
     (i) The x-intercepts are $(-3, 0)$, $(6, 0)$, and $(11, 0)$.
     (j) The y-intercept is $(0, 3)$.
     (k) The line $y = \dfrac{1}{2}$ intersects the graph 3 times.
     (l) The line $x = 5$ intersects the graph 1 times.
     (m) $f(x) = 3$ when $x = 0$ and $x = 4$.
     (n) $f(x) = -2$ when $x = -5$ and $x = 8$.

49. Not a function since vertical lines will intersect the graph in more than one point.

51. Function   (a) Domain: $\left\{x \mid -\pi \leq x \leq \pi\right\}$;   Range: $\left\{y \mid -1 \leq y \leq 1\right\}$
                (b) $\left(-\dfrac{\pi}{2}, 0\right)$, $\left(\dfrac{\pi}{2}, 0\right)$, $(0, 1)$ (c) y-axis

53. Not a function since vertical lines will intersect the graph in more than one point.

55. Function   (a) Domain: $\left\{x \mid x > 0\right\}$;   Range: $\left\{y \mid y \in \text{Real Numbers}\right\}$
                (b) $(1, 0)$
                (c) No symmetry to the x-axis, y-axis, or origin.

57. Function   (a)   Domain: $\{x|x \in \text{Real Numbers}\}$;   Range: $\{y|y \le 2\}$
                (b) $(-3,0), (3,0), (0,2)$
                (c)   y-axis

59. Function   (a)   Domain: $\{x|x \in \text{Real Numbers}\}$;   Range: $\{y|y \ge -3\}$
                (b) $(1,0), (3,0), (0,9)$
                (c)   No symmetry to the x-axis, y-axis, or origin.

61. $f(x) = 2x^2 - x - 1$

(a) $f(-1) = 2(-1)^2 - (-1) - 1 = 2$ $(-1,2)$ is on the graph of f.

(b) $f(-2) = 2(-2)^2 - (-2) - 1 = 9$ $(-2,9)$ is on the graph of f.

(c)   Solve for x:
$$-1 = 2x^2 - x - 1 \rightarrow 0 = 2x^2 - x$$
$$0 = x(2x - 1) \rightarrow x = 0, x = \frac{1}{2}$$
$(0, -1)$ and $\left(\frac{1}{2}, -1\right)$ are points on the graph of f.

(d)   The domain of f is: $\{x|x \text{ is any real number}\}$.

(e)   x-intercepts:
$$f(x) = 0 \rightarrow 2x^2 - x - 1 = 0 \rightarrow (2x+1)(x-1) = 0$$
$$\rightarrow x = -\frac{1}{2}, x = 1 \rightarrow \left(-\frac{1}{2}, 0\right) \text{ and } (1,0)$$

(f)   y-intercept: $f(0) = 2(0)^2 - 0 - 1 = 0 \rightarrow (0,0)$

63. $f(x) = \dfrac{x+2}{x-6}$

(a) $f(3) = \dfrac{3+2}{3-6} = \dfrac{5}{-3} \ne 14$ $(3,14)$ is not on the graph of f.

(b) $f(4) = \dfrac{4+2}{4-6} = \dfrac{6}{-2} = -3$ $(4,-3)$ is the point on the graph of f.

(c)   Solve for x:
$$2 = \frac{x+2}{x-6}$$
$$2x - 12 = x + 2 \qquad\qquad (14, 2) \text{ is a point on the graph of } f.$$
$$x = 14$$

(d)   The domain of f is $\{x|x \ne 6\}$.

(e)   x-intercepts:
$$f(x) = 0$$
$$\frac{x+2}{x-6} = 0 \rightarrow x + 2 = 0$$
$$\rightarrow x = -2 \rightarrow (-2,0)$$

(f)   y-intercept: $f(0) = \dfrac{0+2}{0-6} = -\dfrac{1}{3} \rightarrow \left(0, -\dfrac{1}{3}\right)$

65. $f(x) = \dfrac{2x^2}{x^4 + 1}$

(a) $f(-1) = \dfrac{2(-1)^2}{(-1)^4 + 1} = \dfrac{2}{2} = 1$ $(-1,1)$ is a point on the graph of f.

(b) $f(2) = \dfrac{2(2)^2}{(2)^4 + 1} = \dfrac{8}{17}$ $\left(2, \dfrac{8}{17}\right)$ is a point on the graph of f.

(c) Solve for x:

$$1 = \dfrac{2x^2}{x^4 + 1}$$

$$x^4 + 1 = 2x^2$$

$$x^4 - 2x^2 + 1 = 0 \qquad (1,1) \text{ and } (-1,1) \text{ are points on the graph of } f.$$

$$(x^2 - 1)^2 = 0$$

$$x^2 - 1 = 0 \to x = \pm 1$$

(d) The domain of f is $\{\text{Real Numbers}\}$.

(e) x-intercepts:

$$f(x) = 0$$

$$\dfrac{2x^2}{x^4 + 1} = 0 \to 2x^2 = 0 \to x = 0 \to (0,0)$$

(f) y-intercept: $f(0) = \dfrac{2x^2}{x^4 + 1} = \dfrac{0}{0 + 1} = 0 \to (0,0)$

67. Solving for A:

$f(x) = 2x^3 + Ax^2 + 4x - 5$ and $f(2) = 5$

$f(2) = 2(2)^3 + A(2)^2 + 4(2) - 5$

$5 = 16 + 4A + 8 - 5 \to 5 = 4A + 19$

$-14 = 4A \to A = -\dfrac{7}{2}$

69. Solving for A:

$f(x) = \dfrac{3x + 8}{2x - A}$ and $f(0) = 2$

$f(0) = \dfrac{3(0) + 8}{2(0) - A}$

$2 = \dfrac{8}{-A}$

$-2A = 8$

$A = -4$

71. Solving for A:

$f(x) = \dfrac{2x - A}{x - 3}$ and $f(4) = 0$

$f(4) = \dfrac{2(4) - A}{4 - 3}$

$0 = \dfrac{8 - A}{1}$

$0 = 8 - A$

$A = 8$

f is undefined when $x = 3$.

73. (a) III   (b) IV   (c) I   (d) V   (e) II

75.

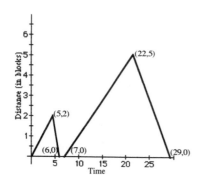

77. (a) Two times
    (b) Kevin's distance from home increased steadily at a rate of 1.5 miles per hour.
    (c) Kevin's distance from home did not change.
    (d) Kevin's distance from home decreased steadily at a rate of 10 miles per hour.
    (e) Kevin stayed at home for 0.2 hours.
    (f) Kevin's distance from home increased rapidly at the beginning and then tapered off to a very slow change in distance from home.
    (g) Kevin's distance from home did not change.
    (h) Kevin's distance from home decreased rapidly at the beginning of the interval and then tapered off as he got closer to home.
    (i) The furthest distance Kevin is from home is 3 miles.

79. (a) $H(1) = 20 - 4.9(1)^2 = 20 - 4.9 = 15.1$ meters
    $H(1.1) = 20 - 4.9(1.1)^2 = 20 - 4.9(1.21) = 20 - 5.929 = 14.071$ meters
    $H(1.2) = 20 - 4.9(1.2)^2 = 20 - 4.9(1.44) = 20 - 7.056 = 12.944$ meters
    $H(1.3) = 20 - 4.9(1.3)^2 = 20 - 4.9(1.69) = 20 - 8.281 = 11.719$ meters

    (b)
$H(x) = 15$	$H(x) = 10$	$H(x) = 5$
$15 = 20 - 4.9x^2$	$10 = 20 - 4.9x^2$	$5 = 20 - 4.9x^2$
$-5 = -4.9x^2$	$-10 = -4.9x^2$	$-15 = -4.9x^2$
$x^2 = 1.0204$	$x^2 = 2.0408$	$x^2 = 3.0612$
$x = 1.01$ seconds	$x = 1.43$ seconds	$x = 1.75$ seconds

    (c) $H(x) = 0$
    $0 = 20 - 4.9x^2$
    $-20 = -4.9x^2 \rightarrow x^2 = 4.0816 \rightarrow x = 2.02$ seconds

81. $h(x) = \dfrac{-32x^2}{130^2} + x$

    (a) $h(100) = \dfrac{-32(100)^2}{130^2} + 100 = \dfrac{-320000}{16900} + 100 = -18.93 + 100 = 81.07$ feet

    (b) $h(300) = \dfrac{-32(300)^2}{130^2} + 300 = \dfrac{-2880000}{16900} + 300 = -170.41 + 300 = 129.59$ feet

    (c) $h(500) = \dfrac{-32(500)^2}{130^2} + 500 = \dfrac{-8000000}{16900} + 500 = -473.37 + 500 = 26.63$ feet

(d)   Solve $h(x) = \dfrac{-32x^2}{130^2} + x = 0$

$$x\left(\dfrac{-32x}{130^2} + 1\right) = 0 \rightarrow x = 0 \ \text{ or } \ \dfrac{-32x}{130^2} + 1 = 0 \rightarrow 1 = \dfrac{32x}{130^2} \rightarrow x = \dfrac{130^2}{32} = 528.125 \text{ feet}$$

83. $C(x) = 100 + \dfrac{x}{10} + \dfrac{36000}{x}$

(a) $C(500) = 100 + \dfrac{500}{10} + \dfrac{36000}{500} = 100 + 50 + 72 = \$222$

(b) $C(450) = 100 + \dfrac{450}{10} + \dfrac{36000}{450} = 100 + 45 + 80 = \$225$

(c) $C(600) = 100 + \dfrac{600}{10} + \dfrac{36000}{600} = 100 + 60 + 60 = \$220$

(d) $C(400) = 100 + \dfrac{400}{10} + \dfrac{36000}{400} = 100 + 40 + 90 = \$230$

(e)   Graphing:

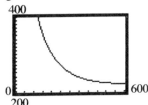

(f)   As x varies from 400 to 600 mph, the cost decreases from \$230 to \$220.

85.   Let x represent the length of the rectangle.

Then $\dfrac{x}{2}$ represents the width of the rectangle, since the length is twice the width.

The function for the area is: $A(x) = x \cdot \dfrac{x}{2} = \dfrac{x^2}{2} = \dfrac{1}{2}x^2$

87.   Let x represent the number of hours worked.
The function for the gross salary is: $G(x) = 10x$

89.   (a)   The relation is not a function
because 23 is paired with both 56
and 53.

(b)
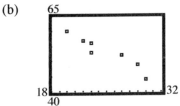

(c)   Using the points (20,60) and
(30, 44) we get

$D = -1.6p + 92$

91.   (a)   The relation is a function. Each time
value is paired with exactly one
distance value.

(b)
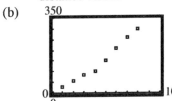

(c)   Using the points (0,0) and
(8, 300) we get
$s = 37.5t$

(d) As the price of the jeans increases by \$1, the demand for the jeans decreases by 1.6.

(e) $D(p) = -1.6p + 92$

(f) Domain: $\{p | p > 0\}$

(g) $D(28) = -1.6(28) + 92$

$= 47.2 \approx 47$

Demand is about 47 pairs.

(h) $D = -1.3355p + 86.1974$

(d) As the time increases by 1 hour, the distances increases by 37.5 miles.

(e) $s(t) = 37.5t$

(f) Domain: $\{t | t \geq 0\}$

(g) $s(11) = 37.5(11)$

$= 412.5$ miles

(h) $s = 37.7833t - 19.1333$

93. (a) $h(x) = 2x$

$h(a+b) = 2(a+b) = 2a + 2b = h(a) + h(b);$ $h(x) = 2x$ has the property.

(b) $g(x) = x^2$

$g(a+b) = (a+b)^2 = a^2 + 2ab + b^2 \neq a^2 + b^2 = h(a) + h(b)$

$g(x) = x^2$ does not have the property.

(c) $F(x) = 5x - 2$

$F(a+b) = 5(a+b) - 2 = 5a + 5b - 2 \neq 5a - 2 + 5b - 2 = h(a) + h(b)$

$F(x) = 5x - 2$ does not have the property.

(d) $G(x) = \dfrac{1}{x}$

$G(a+b) = \dfrac{1}{a+b} \neq \dfrac{1}{a} + \dfrac{1}{b} = h(a) + h(b)$

$G(x) = \dfrac{1}{x}$ does not have the property.

95. No, $x = -1$ is not in the domain of g, but it is in the domain of f.

97. A function may have any number of x-intercepts; it can have only one y-intercept.

99. The only such function is $f(x) = 0$.

Functions and Their Graphs

3.2   Properties of Functions

1.   Yes

3.   No   It only increases on (5, 10).

5. f is increasing on the intervals: (–8, –2), (0, 2), (5, 10).

7.   Yes. The local maximum at $x = 2$ is 10.

9. f has local maxima at $x = -2$ and $x = 2$. The local maxima are 6 and 10, respectively.

11. (a)   Intercepts: (–2,0), (2,0), and (0,3).
     (b)   Domain: $\left\{x \mid -4 \le x \le 4\right\}$; Range: $\left\{y \mid 0 \le y \le 3\right\}$.
     (c)   Interval notation: Increasing: (–2, 0) and (2, 4); Decreasing: (–4, –2) and (0, 2).
           Inequality notation: Increasing: $-2 < x < 0$ and $2 < x < 4$
                                  Decreasing: $-4 < x < -2$ and $0 < x < 2$
     (d)   Since the graph is symmetric to the y-axis, the function is <u>even</u>.

13. (a)   Intercepts: (0,1).
     (b)   Domain: { Real Numbers }; Range: $\left\{y \mid y > 0\right\}$.
     (c)   Interval notation: Increasing: $(-\infty,+\infty)$; Decreasing: never.
           Inequality notation: Increasing: $-\infty < x < +\infty$
                                 Decreasing: never
     (d)   Since the graph is not symmetric to the y-axis or the origin, the function is <u>neither</u> even nor odd.

15. (a) Intercepts: $(-\pi, 0)$, $(0,0)$, and $(\pi, 0)$.

(b) Domain: $\{x | -\pi \le x \le \pi\}$; Range: $\{y | -1 \le y \le 1\}$.

(c) Interval notation: Increasing: $\left(-\dfrac{\pi}{2}, \dfrac{\pi}{2}\right)$; Decreasing: $\left(-\pi, -\dfrac{\pi}{2}\right)$ and $\left(\dfrac{\pi}{2}, \pi\right)$.

Inequality notation: Increasing: $-\dfrac{\pi}{2} < x < \dfrac{\pi}{2}$

Decreasing: $-\pi < x < -\dfrac{\pi}{2}$ and $\dfrac{\pi}{2} < x < \pi$

(d) Since the graph is symmetric to the origin, the function is <u>odd</u>.

17. (a) Intercepts: $\left(0, \dfrac{1}{2}\right), \left(\dfrac{1}{3}, 0\right)$, and $\left(\dfrac{5}{2}, 0\right)$.

(b) Domain: $\{x | -3 \le x \le 3\}$; Range: $\{y | -1 \le y \le 2\}$.

(c) Interval notation: Increasing: $(2, 3)$; Decreasing: $(-1, 1)$;
     Constant: $(-3, -1)$ and $(1, 2)$.
     Inequality notation: Increasing: $2 < x < 3$; Decreasing: $-1 < x < 1$;
     Constant: $-3 < x < -1$ and $1 < x < 2$.

(d) Since the graph is not symmetric to the y-axis or the origin, the function is <u>neither</u> even nor odd.

19. (a) Intercepts: $(0, 2), (-2, 0)$, and $(2, 0)$.

(b) Domain: $\{x | -4 \le x \le 4\}$; Range: $\{y | 0 \le y \le 2\}$.

(c) Interval notation: Increasing: $(-2, 0)$ and $(2, 4)$;
     Decreasing: $(-4, -2)$ and $(0, 2)$.
     Inequality notation: Increasing: $-2 < x < 0$ and $2 < x < 4$;
     Decreasing: $-4 < x < -2$ and $0 < x < 2$.

(d) Since the graph is symmetric to the y-axis, the function is <u>even</u>.

21. (a) f has a local maximum of 3 at $x = 0$.

(b) f has a local minimum of 0 at both $x = -2$ and $x = 2$.

23. (a) f has a local maximum of 1 at $x = \dfrac{\pi}{2}$.

(b) f has a local minimum of -1 at $x = -\dfrac{\pi}{2}$.

25. $f(x) = 5x$

(a) $\dfrac{f(x) - f(1)}{x - 1} = \dfrac{5x - 5}{x - 1}$

(b) $= \dfrac{5(x - 1)}{x - 1} = 5$

$\dfrac{f(2) - f(1)}{2 - 1} = \dfrac{10 - 5}{2 - 1} = \dfrac{5}{1} = 5$

(c) Slope = 5; Containing $(1, 5)$:

$y - 5 = 5(x - 1)$

$y - 5 = 5x - 5$

$y = 5x$

27. $f(x) = 1 - 3x$

(a) $\dfrac{f(x) - f(1)}{x - 1} = \dfrac{1 - 3x - (-2)}{x - 1}$

$= \dfrac{-3x + 3}{x - 1} = \dfrac{-3(x - 1)}{x - 1} = -3$

(b) $\dfrac{f(2) - f(1)}{2 - 1} = \dfrac{1 - 3(2) - (-2)}{2 - 1}$

$= \dfrac{-3}{1} = -3$

(c) Slope = -3; Containing $(1, -2)$:

$y - (-2) = -3(x - 1)$

$y + 2 = -3x + 3 \rightarrow y = -3x + 1$

29. $f(x) = x^2 - 2x$

(a) $\dfrac{f(x) - f(1)}{x - 1} = \dfrac{x^2 - 2x - (-1)}{x - 1}$

$= \dfrac{x^2 - 2x + 1}{x - 1} = \dfrac{(x - 1)^2}{x - 1} = x - 1$

(b) $\dfrac{f(2) - f(1)}{2 - 1} = \dfrac{2^2 - 2(2) - (-1)}{2 - 1} = \dfrac{1}{1} = 1$

Slope = 1; Containing $(1, -1)$:

(c) $y - (-1) = 1(x - 1)$

$y + 1 = 1x - 1 \rightarrow y = x - 2$

31. $f(x) = x^3 - x$

(a) $\dfrac{f(x) - f(1)}{x - 1} = \dfrac{x^3 - x - 0}{x - 1} = \dfrac{x^3 - x}{x - 1}$

$= \dfrac{x(x - 1)(x + 1)}{x - 1} = x^2 + x$

(b) $\dfrac{f(2) - f(1)}{2 - 1} = \dfrac{2^3 - 2 - 0}{2 - 1} = \dfrac{6}{1} = 6$

(c) Slope = 6; Containing $(1, 0)$:

$y - 0 = 6(x - 1)$

$y = 6x - 6$

33. $f(x) = \dfrac{2}{x + 1}$

(a) $\dfrac{f(x) - f(1)}{x - 1} = \dfrac{\left(\dfrac{2}{x + 1} - 1\right)}{x - 1} = \dfrac{\left(\dfrac{2 - x - 1}{x + 1}\right)}{x - 1}$

$= \dfrac{1 - x}{(x - 1)(x + 1)} = \dfrac{-1}{x + 1}$

(b) $\dfrac{f(2) - f(1)}{2 - 1} = \dfrac{\left(\dfrac{2}{2 + 1} - 1\right)}{2 - 1}$

(c) $= \dfrac{\left(-\dfrac{1}{3}\right)}{1} = -\dfrac{1}{3}$

Slope = $-\dfrac{1}{3}$; Containing $(1, 1)$:

$y - 1 = -\dfrac{1}{3}(x - 1)$

$y - 1 = -\dfrac{1}{3}x + \dfrac{1}{3} \rightarrow y = -\dfrac{1}{3}x + \dfrac{4}{3}$

35. $f(x) = \sqrt{x}$

(a) $\dfrac{f(x) - f(1)}{x - 1} = \dfrac{\left(\dfrac{1}{x^2} - 1\right)}{x - 1} = \dfrac{\left(\dfrac{1 - x^2}{x^2}\right)}{x - 1}$

$= \dfrac{(1 - x)(1 + x)}{x^2(x - 1)} = \dfrac{-x - 1}{x^2}$

(b) $\dfrac{f(2) - f(1)}{2 - 1} = \dfrac{\left(\dfrac{1}{2^2} - 1\right)}{2 - 1} = \dfrac{\left(-\dfrac{3}{4}\right)}{1} = -\dfrac{3}{4}$

(c) Slope = $-\dfrac{3}{4}$; Containing $(1, 1)$:

$y - 1 = -\dfrac{3}{4}(x - 1)$

$y - 1 = -\dfrac{3}{4}x + \dfrac{3}{4} \rightarrow y = -\dfrac{3}{4}x + \dfrac{7}{4}$

37. $f(x) = 4x^3$

$\qquad f(-x) = 4(-x)^3 = -4x^3$

$\quad f$ is odd.

39. $g(x) = -3x^2 - 5$

$\qquad g(-x) = -3(-x)^2 - 5 = -3x^2 - 5$

$\quad g$ is even.

41. $F(x) = \sqrt[3]{x}$

$\qquad F(-x) = \sqrt[3]{-x} = -\sqrt[3]{x}$

$\quad F$ is odd.

43. $f(x) = x + |x|$

$\qquad f(-x) = -x + |-x| = -x + |x|$

$\quad f$ is neither even nor odd.

45. $g(x) = \dfrac{1}{x^2}$

$g(-x) = \dfrac{1}{(-x)^2} = \dfrac{1}{x^2}$, g is even.

47. $h(x) = \dfrac{-x^3}{3x^2 - 9}$

$h(-x) = \dfrac{-(-x)^3}{3(-x)^2 - 9} = \dfrac{x^3}{3x^2 - 9}$, h is odd.

49. $\quad f(x) = 2x + 5$

$m_{\text{sec}} = \dfrac{f(x+h) - f(x)}{h} = \dfrac{2(x+h) + 5 - 2x - 5}{h} = \dfrac{2h}{h} = 2$

50. $\quad f(x) = -3x + 2$

$m_{\text{sec}} = \dfrac{f(x+h) - f(x)}{h} = \dfrac{-3(x+h) + 2 - (-3x + 2)}{h} = \dfrac{-3h}{h} = -3$

51. $\quad f(x) = x^2 + 2x$

$m_{\text{sec}} = \dfrac{f(x+h) - f(x)}{h} = \dfrac{(x+h)^2 + 2(x+h) - (x^2 + 2x)}{h}$

$\qquad = \dfrac{x^2 + 2xh + h^2 + 2x + 2h - x^2 - 2x}{h} = \dfrac{2xh + h^2 + 2h}{h} = 2x + h + 2$

53. $\quad f(x) = 2x^2 - 3x + 1$

$m_{\text{sec}} = \dfrac{f(x+h) - f(x)}{h} = \dfrac{2(x+h)^2 - 3(x+h) + 1 - (2x^2 - 3x + 1)}{h}$

$\qquad = \dfrac{2(x^2 + 2xh + h^2) - 3x - 3h + 1 - 2x^2 + 3x - 1}{h}$

$\qquad = \dfrac{2x^2 + 4xh + 2h^2 - 3x - 3h + 1 - 2x^2 + 3x - 1}{h} = \dfrac{4xh + 2h^2 - 3h}{h} = 4x + 2h - 3$

55. $\quad f(x) = \dfrac{1}{x}$

$m_{\text{sec}} = \dfrac{f(x+h) - f(x)}{h} = \dfrac{\left(\dfrac{1}{x+h} - \dfrac{1}{x} \right)}{h}$

$\qquad = \dfrac{\left(\dfrac{x - (x+h)}{(x+h)x} \right)}{h} = \left(\dfrac{x - x - h}{(x+h)x} \right)\left(\dfrac{1}{h} \right) = \left(\dfrac{-h}{(x+h)x} \right)\left(\dfrac{1}{h} \right) = \dfrac{-1}{(x+h)x}$

57. (a), (b), (e)

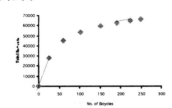

(c)   Average rate of change $= \dfrac{28000 - 0}{25 - 0} = \dfrac{28000}{25} = 1120$

(d)   For each additional bicycle sold between 0 and 25, the total revenue increases by $1120.

(f)   Average rate of change $= \dfrac{64835 - 62360}{223 - 190} = \dfrac{2475}{33} = 75$

(g)   For each additional bicycle sold between 190 and 223, the total revenue increases by $75.

59. (a), (b), (e)

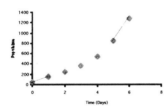

(c)   Average rate of change $= \dfrac{153 - 50}{1 - 0} = \dfrac{103}{1} = 103$

(d)   The population is increasing at a rate of 103 per day between day 0 and day 1.

(f)   Average rate of change $= \dfrac{1280 - 839}{6 - 5} = \dfrac{441}{1} = 441$

(g)   The population is increasing at a rate of 441 per day between day 5 and day 6.

(h)   As time passes, the average rate of change of the population is increasing.

61.   One at most because if f is increasing it could only cross the x-axis at most one time. It could not "turn" and cross it again or it would start to decrease.

Chapter 3

Functions and Their Graphs

3.3   Library of Functions; Piecewise-Defined Functions

1.   C   3.   E   5.   B   7.   F

9.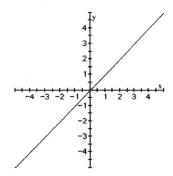

11.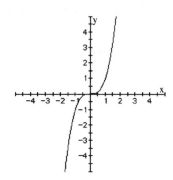

13.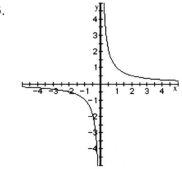

15.   (a) $f(-2) = (-2)^2 = 4$

     (b) $f(0) = 2$

     (c) $f(2) = 2(2) + 1 = 5$

17.   (a) $f(1.2) = \operatorname{int}(2(1.2)) = \operatorname{int}(2.4) = 2$

     (b) $f(1.6) = \operatorname{int}(2(1.6)) = \operatorname{int}(3.2) = 3$

     (c) $f(-1.8) = \operatorname{int}(2(-1.8)) = \operatorname{int}(-3.6) = -4$

19. $f(x) = \begin{cases} 2x & \text{if } x \neq 0 \\ 1 & \text{if } x = 0 \end{cases}$

    (a)   Domain: {Real Numbers}

    (b)   x-intercept: none

          y-intercept: (0,1)

(c)

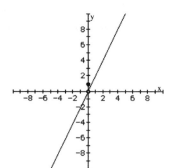

(d)   Range: $\left\{ y \,\middle|\, y \neq 0 \right\}$

21. $f(x) = \begin{cases} -2x + 3 & \text{if } x < 1 \\ 3x - 2 & \text{if } x \geq 1 \end{cases}$

   (a) Domain: {Real Numbers}

   (b) x-intercept: none

        y-intercept: (0,3)

   (c)

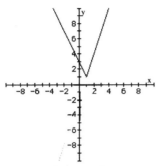

   (d) Range: $\{y \mid y \geq 1\}$

23. $f(x) = \begin{cases} x + 3 & \text{if } -2 \leq x < 1 \\ 5 & \text{if } x = 1 \\ -x + 2 & \text{if } x > 1 \end{cases}$

   (a) Domain: $\{x \mid x \geq -2\}$

   (b) x-intercept: (2, 0)

        y-intercept: (0, 3)

   (c)

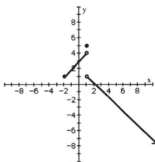

   (d) Range: $\{y \mid y < 4\} \cup \{5\}$

25. $f(x) = \begin{cases} 1 + x & \text{if } x < 0 \\ x^2 & \text{if } x \geq 0 \end{cases}$

   (a) Domain: {Real Numbers}

   (b) x-intercept: (−1,0), (0,0)

        y-intercept: (0,0)

   (c)

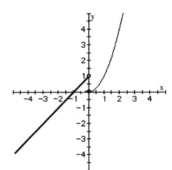

   (d) Range: {Real Numbers}

27. $f(x) = \begin{cases} |x| & \text{if } -2 \leq x < 0 \\ 1 & \text{if } x = 0 \\ x^3 & \text{if } x > 0 \end{cases}$

   (a) Domain: $\{x \mid x \geq -2\}$

   (b) x-intercept: none

        y-intercept: (0, 1)

   (c)

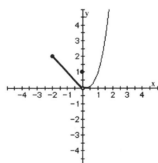

   (d) Range: $\{y \mid y > 0\}$

29. $h(x) = 2\,\text{int}(x)$
    (a)   Domain: {Real Numbers}
    (b)   x-intercept: all ordered pairs
          $(x,0)$ when $0 \le x < 1$.
        y-intercept: $(0,0)$
    (c)

31. $f(x) = \begin{cases} -x & \text{if } -1 \le x \le 0 \\ \dfrac{1}{2}x & \text{if } 0 < x \le 2 \end{cases}$

33. $f(x) = \begin{cases} -x & \text{if } x \le 0 \\ -x+2 & \text{if } 0 < x \le 2 \end{cases}$

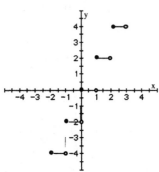

    (d)   Range: {Even Integers}

35.   (a)   Charge for 50 therms: $C = 9.45 + 0.36375(50) + 0.3128(50) = \$43.28$
     (b)   Charge for 500 therms:
          $C = 9.45 + 0.36375(50) + 0.11445(450) + 0.3128(500) = \$235.54$
     (c)   The monthly charge function:

$$C = \begin{cases} 9.45 + 0.36375x + 0.3128x & \text{for } 0 \le x \le 50 \\ 9.45 + 0.36375(50) + 0.11445(x-50) + 0.3128x & \text{for } x > 50 \end{cases}$$

$$= \begin{cases} 9.45 + 0.67655x & \text{for } 0 \le x \le 50 \\ 9.45 + 18.1875 + 0.11445x - 5.7225 + 0.3128x & \text{for } x > 50 \end{cases}$$

$$= \begin{cases} 9.45 + 0.67655x & \text{for } 0 \le x \le 50 \\ 21.915 + 0.42725x & \text{for } x > 50 \end{cases}$$

     (d)

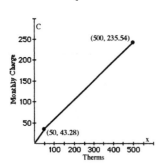

37.   (a) $W = 10°C$
     (b) $W = 33 - \dfrac{(10.45 + 10\sqrt{5} - 5)(33 - 10)}{22.04} = 3.98°C$
     (c) $W = 33 - \dfrac{(10.45 + 10\sqrt{15} - 15)(33 - 10)}{22.04} = -2.67°C$
     (d) $W = 33 - 1.5958(33 - 10) = -3.7°C$

(e)   When $0 \leq v < 1.79$, the wind speed is so small that there is no effect on the temperature.

(f)   For each drop of $1°$ in temperature, the wind chill factor drops approximately $1.6°C$. When the wind speed exceeds 20, there is a constant drop in temperature.

39.   Each graph is that of $y = x^2$, but shifted vertically. If $y = x^2 + k$, $k > 0$, the shift is up k units; if $y = x^2 + k$, $k < 0$, the shift is down $|k|$ units. The graph of $y = x^2 - 4$ is the same as the graph of $y = x^2$, but shifted down 4 units. The graph of $y = x^2 + 5$ is the graph of $y = x^2$, but shifted up 5 units.

41.   Each graph is that of $y = |x|$, but either compressed or stretched. If $y = k|x|$ and $k > 1$, the graph is stretched; if $y = k|x|$ and $0 < k < 1$, the graph is compressed. The graph of $y = \frac{1}{4}|x|$ is the same as the graph of $y = |x|$, but compressed. The graph of $y = 5|x|$ is the same as the graph of $y = |x|$, but stretched.

43.   The graph of $y = \sqrt{-x}$ is the reflection about the y-axis of the graph of $y = \sqrt{x}$. The same type of reflection occurs when graphing $y = 2x + 1$ and $y = 2(-x) + 1$. The conclusion is that the graph of $y = f(-x)$ is the reflection about the y-axis of the graph of $y = f(x)$.

45.   For the graph of $y = x^n$, n a positive even integer, as n increases, the graph of the function is narrower for $|x| > 1$ and flatter for $|x| < 1$.

47. $f(x) = \begin{cases} 1 & \text{if } x \text{ is rational} \\ 0 & \text{if } x \text{ is irrational} \end{cases}$ Domain = { all real numbers}   Range = $\{0,1\}$

y-intercept: $x = 0 \rightarrow x$ is rational $\rightarrow y = 1$, so the y-intercept is $(0, 1)$.
x-intercept: $y = 0 \rightarrow x$ is irrational, so the graph has infinitely many x-intercepts, namely, there is an x-intercept at each irrational value for x.
$f(-x) = 1 = f(x)$ when x is rational; $f(-x) = 0 = f(x)$ when x is irrational
$\therefore f$ is even.
The graph of f consists of 2 infinite clusters of distinct points, extending horizontally in both directions.
One cluster is located 1 unit above the x-axis, and the other is located along the x-axis.

Functions and Their Graphs

3.4 Graphing Techniques: Transformations

1. B   3. H   5. I   7. L   9. F

11. G   13. $y = (x - 4)^3$ 15. $y = x^3 + 4$ 17. $y = -x^3$ 19. $y = 4x^3$

21. (1) $y = \sqrt{x} + 2$

    (2) $y = -\left(\sqrt{x} + 2\right)$

    (3) $y = -\left(\sqrt{-x} + 2\right)$

23. (1) $y = -\sqrt{x}$

    (2) $y = -\sqrt{x} + 2$

    (3) $y = -\sqrt{x + 3} + 2$

25. C

27. C

29. $f(x) = x^2 - 1$

Using the graph of $y = x^2$, vertically shift downward 1 unit.

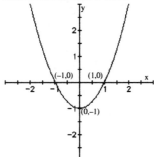

31. $g(x) = x^3 + 1$

Using the graph of $y = x^3$, vertically shift upward 1 unit.

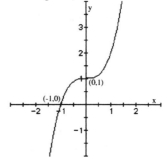

33. $h(x) = \sqrt{x - 2}$

Using the graph of $y = \sqrt{x}$, horizontally shift to the right 2 units.

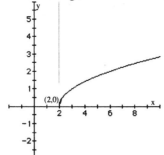

35. $f(x) = (x - 1)^3 + 2$

Using the graph of $y = x^3$, horizontally shift to the right 1 unit, then vertically shift up 2 units.

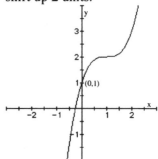

37. $g(x) = 4\sqrt{x}$

Using the graph of $y = \sqrt{x}$, vertically stretch by a factor of 4.

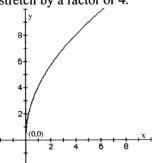

39. $h(x) = \dfrac{1}{2x}$

Using the graph of $y = \dfrac{1}{x}$, vertically compress by a factor of $\dfrac{1}{2}$.

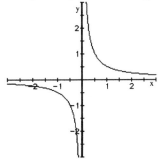

41. $f(x) = -|x|$

Reflect the graph of $y = |x|$, about the x-axis.

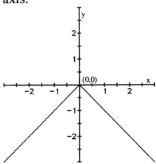

43. $g(x) = |-x|$

Reflect the graph of $y = |x|$, about the y-axis.

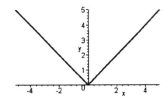

45. $h(x) = -x^3 + 2$

Reflect the graph of $y = x^3$ on the x-axis, vertically shift upward 2 units.

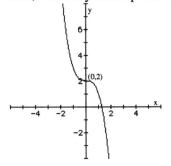

47. $f(x) = 2(x+1)^2 - 3$

Using the graph of $y = x^2$, horizontally shift to the left 1 unit, vertically stretch by a factor of 2, and vertically shift downward 3 units.

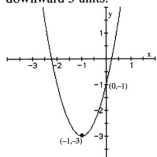

49. $g(x) = \sqrt{x-2} + 1$

Using the graph of $y = \sqrt{x}$, horizontally shift to the right 2 units and vertically shift upward 1 unit.

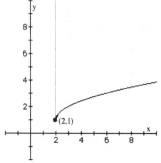

51. $h(x) = \sqrt{-x} - 2$

Reflect the graph of $y = \sqrt{x}$, about the y-axis and vertically shift downward 2 units.

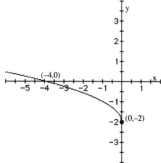

53. $f(x) = -(x+1)^3 - 1$

Using the graph of $y = x^3$, horizontally shift to the left 1 units, reflect the graph on the x-axis, and vertically shift downward 1 unit.

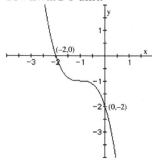

55. $g(x) = 2|1 - x| = 2|x - 1|$

Using the graph of $y = |x|$, horizontally shift to the right 1 unit, and vertically stretch by a factor or 2.

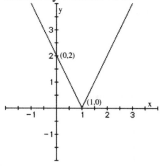

57. $h(x) = 2\,\text{int}(x - 1)$

Using the graph of $y = \text{int}(x)$, horizontally shift to the right 1 unit, and vertically stretch by a factor of 2.

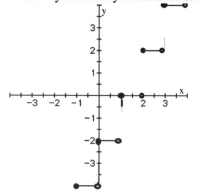

59.   (a) $F(x) = f(x) + 3$
Shift up 3 units.

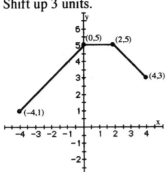

(b) $G(x) = f(x+2)$
Shift left 2 units.

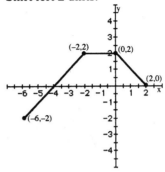

(c) $P(x) = -f(x)$
Reflect about the x-axis.

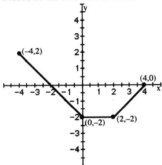

(d) $H(x) = f(x+1) - 2$
Shift left 1 unit and shift down 2 units.

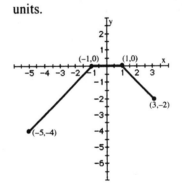

(e) $Q(x) = \frac{1}{2} f(x)$
Compress vertically by a factor of $\frac{1}{2}$.

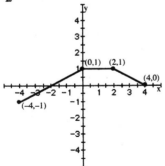

(f) $g(x) = f(-x)$
Reflect about y-axis.

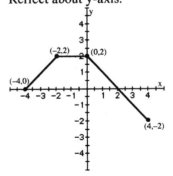

(g) $h(x) = f(2x)$
Compress horizontally by a factor
of $\dfrac{1}{2}$.

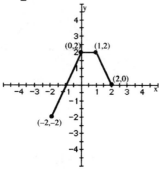

61.   (a) $F(x) = f(x) + 3$
Shift up 3 units.

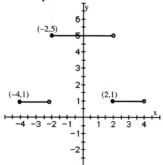

(b) $G(x) = f(x + 2)$
Shift left 2 units.

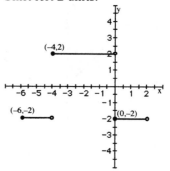

(c) $P(x) = -f(x)$
Reflect about the x-axis.

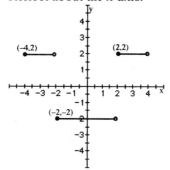

(d) $H(x) = f(x + 1) - 2$
Shift left 1 unit and shift down 2
units.

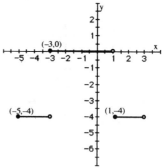

(e) $Q(x) = \frac{1}{2}f(x)$

Compress vertically by a factor of $\frac{1}{2}$.

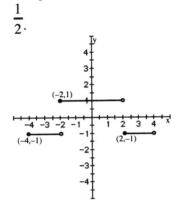

(f) $g(x) = f(-x)$

Reflect about y-axis.

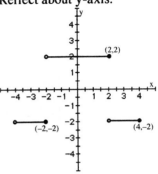

(g) $h(x) = f(2x)$

Compress horizontally by a factor of $\frac{1}{2}$.

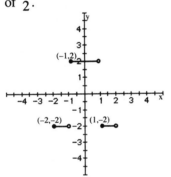

63. (a) $F(x) = f(x) + 3$

Shift up 3 units.

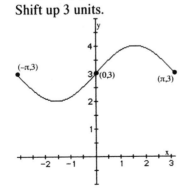

(b) $G(x) = f(x + 2)$

Shift left 2 units.

(c) $P(x) = -f(x)$
Reflect about the x-axis.

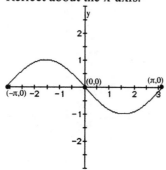

(d) $H(x) = f(x+1) - 2$
Shift left 1 unit and shift down 2 units.

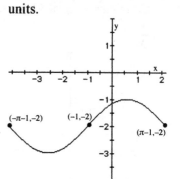

(e) $Q(x) = \dfrac{1}{2} f(x)$

Compress vertically by a factor of $\dfrac{1}{2}$.

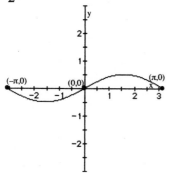

(f) $g(x) = f(-x)$
Reflect about y-axis.

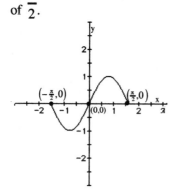

(g) $h(x) = f(2x)$
Compress horizontally by a factor of $\dfrac{1}{2}$.

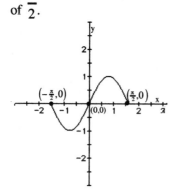

65. (a) $y = |x + 1|$

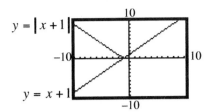

$y = x + 1$

(b) $y = |4 - x^2|$

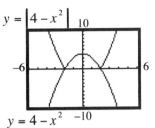

$y = 4 - x^2$

(c) $y = |x^3 + x|$

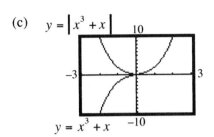

$y = x^3 + x$

(d)   Any part of the graph of $y = f(x)$ that lies below the x-axis is reflected about the x-axis to obtain the graph of $y = |f(x)|$.

67. (a) $y = |f(x)|$

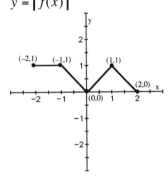

(b) $y = f(|x|)$

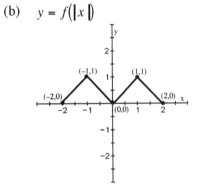

69. $f(x) = x^2 + 2x$
      $f(x) = (x^2 + 2x + 1) - 1$
      $f(x) = (x + 1)^2 - 1$
      Using $f(x) = x^2$, shift left 1 unit and shift down 1 unit.

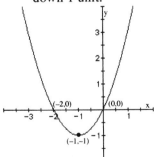

71. $f(x) = x^2 - 8x + 1$
      $f(x) = (x^2 - 8x + 16) + 1 - 16$
      $f(x) = (x - 4)^2 - 15$
      Using $f(x) = x^2$, shift right 4 units and shift down 15 units.

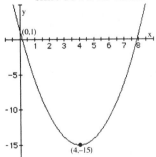

73. $f(x) = x^2 + x + 1$

$$f(x) = \left(x^2 + x + \frac{1}{4}\right) + 1 - \frac{1}{4}$$

$$f(x) = \left(x + \frac{1}{2}\right)^2 + \frac{3}{4}$$

Using $f(x) = x^2$, shift left $\frac{1}{2}$ unit and shift up $\frac{3}{4}$ unit.

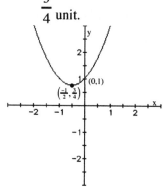

75. $y = (x - c)^2$

If $c = 0$, $y = x^2$.

If $c = 3$, $y = (x - 3)^2$; shift right 3 units.

If $c = -2$, $y = (x + 2)^2$; shift left 2 units.

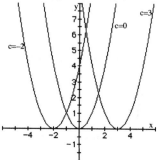

77. $F = \frac{9}{5}C + 32$

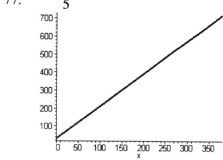

$F = \frac{9}{5}(K - 273) + 32$

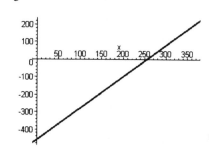

Shift the graph 273 units to the right.

79. (a)

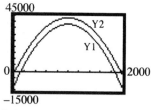

(b) Select the 10% tax since the profits are higher.

(c) The graph of Y1 is obtained by shifting the graph of $p(x)$ vertically down 10,000. The graph of Y2 is obtained by multiplying the y-coordinate of the graph of $p(x)$ by 0.9. Thus, Y2 is the graph of $p(x)$ vertically compressed by a factor of 0.9.

(d) Select the 10% tax since the graph of $Y1 = 0.9p(x) \geq Y2 = -0.05x^2 + 100x - 6800$ for all x in the domain.

Chapter 3

Functions and Their Graphs

3.5 Operations on Functions; Composite Functions

1. $f(x) = 3x + 4$ $g(x) = 2x - 3$
   (a) $(f + g)(x) = 3x + 4 + 2x - 3 = 5x + 1$ The domain is all real numbers.
   (b) $(f - g)(x) = (3x + 4) - (2x - 3) = 3x + 4 - 2x + 3 = x + 7$
       The domain is all real numbers.
   (c) $(f \cdot g)(x) = (3x + 4)(2x - 3) = 6x^2 - 9x + 8x - 12 = 6x^2 - x - 12$
       The domain is all real numbers.
   (d) $\left(\dfrac{f}{g}\right)(x) = \dfrac{3x + 4}{2x - 3}$ The domain is all real numbers except $\dfrac{3}{2}$.

3. $f(x) = x - 1$ $g(x) = 2x^2$
   (a) $(f + g)(x) = x - 1 + 2x^2 = 2x^2 + x - 1$ The domain is all real numbers.
   (b) $(f - g)(x) = (x - 1) - (2x^2) = x - 1 - 2x^2 = -2x^2 + x - 1$
       The domain is all real numbers.
   (c) $(f \cdot g)(x) = (x - 1)(2x^2) = 2x^3 - 2x^2$ The domain is all real numbers.
   (d) $\left(\dfrac{f}{g}\right)(x) = \dfrac{x - 1}{2x^2}$ The domain is all real numbers except 0.

5. $f(x) = \sqrt{x}$ $g(x) = 3x - 5$
   (a) $(f + g)(x) = \sqrt{x} + 3x - 5$ The domain is $\{x \mid x \geq 0\}$.
   (b) $(f - g)(x) = \sqrt{x} - (3x - 5) = \sqrt{x} - 3x + 5$ The domain is $\{x \mid x \geq 0\}$.
   (c) $(f \cdot g)(x) = \sqrt{x}(3x - 5) = 3x\sqrt{x} - 5\sqrt{x}$ The domain is $\{x \mid x \geq 0\}$.
   (d) $\left(\dfrac{f}{g}\right)(x) = \dfrac{\sqrt{x}}{3x - 5}$ The domain is $\left\{x \mid x \geq 0 \text{ and } x \neq \dfrac{5}{3}\right\}$.

7. $f(x) = 1 + \dfrac{1}{x}$ $g(x) = \dfrac{1}{x}$

(a) $(f + g)(x) = 1 + \dfrac{1}{x} + \dfrac{1}{x} = 1 + \dfrac{2}{x}$ The domain is $\{x \mid x \neq 0\}$.

(b) $(f - g)(x) = 1 + \dfrac{1}{x} - \dfrac{1}{x} = 1$ The domain is $\{x \mid x \neq 0\}$.

(c) $(f \cdot g)(x) = \left(1 + \dfrac{1}{x}\right)\dfrac{1}{x} = \dfrac{1}{x} + \dfrac{1}{x^2}$ The domain is $\{x \mid x \neq 0\}$.

(d) $\left(\dfrac{f}{g}\right)(x) = \dfrac{\left(1 + \dfrac{1}{x}\right)}{\left(\dfrac{1}{x}\right)} = \dfrac{\left(\dfrac{x+1}{x}\right)}{\left(\dfrac{1}{x}\right)} = \dfrac{x+1}{x} \cdot \dfrac{x}{1} = x + 1$ The domain is $\{x \mid x \neq 0\}$.

9. $f(x) = \dfrac{2x+3}{3x-2}$ $g(x) = \dfrac{4x}{3x-2}$

(a) $(f + g)(x) = \dfrac{2x+3}{3x-2} + \dfrac{4x}{3x-2} = \dfrac{2x+3+4x}{3x-2} = \dfrac{6x+3}{3x-2}$

The domain is $\left\{x \mid x \neq \dfrac{2}{3}\right\}$.

(b) $(f - g)(x) = \dfrac{2x+3}{3x-2} - \dfrac{4x}{3x-2} = \dfrac{2x+3-4x}{3x-2} = \dfrac{-2x+3}{3x-2}$

The domain is $\left\{x \mid x \neq \dfrac{2}{3}\right\}$.

(c) $(f \cdot g)(x) = \left(\dfrac{2x+3}{3x-2}\right)\left(\dfrac{4x}{3x-2}\right) = \dfrac{8x^2+12x}{(3x-2)^2}$

The domain is $\left\{x \mid x \neq \dfrac{2}{3}\right\}$.

(d) $\left(\dfrac{f}{g}\right)(x) = \dfrac{\left(\dfrac{2x+3}{3x-2}\right)}{\left(\dfrac{4x}{3x-2}\right)} = \dfrac{2x+3}{3x-2} \cdot \dfrac{3x-2}{4x} = \dfrac{2x+3}{4x}$

The domain is $\left\{x \mid x \neq \dfrac{2}{3} \text{ and } x \neq 0\right\}$.

11. $f(x) = 3x + 1$ $(f + g)(x) = 6 - \dfrac{1}{2}x$

$6 - \dfrac{1}{2}x = 3x + 1 + g(x) \rightarrow 5 - \dfrac{7}{2}x = g(x) \rightarrow g(x) = 5 - \dfrac{7}{2}x$

13. $f(x) = 2x$ $g(x) = 3x^2 + 1$

(a) $(f \circ g)(4) = f(g(4)) = f\left(3(4)^2 + 1\right) = f(49) = 2(49) = 98$

(b) $(g \circ f)(2) = g(f(2)) = g(2 \cdot 2) = g(4) = 3(4)^2 + 1 = 48 + 1 = 49$

(c) $(f \circ f)(1) = f(f(1)) = f(2(1)) = f(2) = 2(2) = 4$

(d) $(g \circ g)(0) = g(g(0)) = g\left(3(0)^2 + 1\right) = g(1) = 3(1)^2 + 1 = 4$

15. $f(x) = 4x^2 - 3$ $g(x) = 3 - \dfrac{1}{2}x^2$

(a) $(f \circ g)(4) = f(g(4)) = f\left(3 - \dfrac{1}{2} \cdot (4)^2\right) = f(-5) = 4(-5)^2 - 3 = 97$

(b) $(g \circ f)(2) = g(f(2)) = g(4(2)^2 - 3) = g(13) = 3 - \dfrac{1}{2}(13)^2 = 3 - \dfrac{169}{2} = -\dfrac{163}{2}$

(c) $(f \circ f)(1) = f(f(1)) = f(4(1)^2 - 3) = f(1) = 4(1)^2 - 3 = 1$

(d) $(g \circ g)(0) = g(g(0)) = g\left(3 - \dfrac{1}{2}(0)^2\right) = g(3) = 3 - \dfrac{1}{2}(3)^2 = 3 - \dfrac{9}{2} = -\dfrac{3}{2}$

17. $f(x) = \sqrt{x}$ $g(x) = 2x$

(a) $(f \circ g)(4) = f(g(4)) = f(2(4)) = f(8) = \sqrt{8} = 2\sqrt{2}$

(b) $(g \circ f)(2) = g(f(2)) = g\left(\sqrt{2}\right) = 2\sqrt{2}$

(c) $(f \circ f)(1) = f(f(1)) = f\left(\sqrt{1}\right) = f(1) = \sqrt{1} = 1$

(d) $(g \circ g)(0) = g(g(0)) = g(2(0)) = g(0) = 2(0) = 0$

19. $f(x) = |x|$ $g(x) = \dfrac{1}{x^2 + 1}$

(a) $(f \circ g)(4) = f(g(4)) = f\left(\dfrac{1}{4^2 + 1}\right) = f\left(\dfrac{1}{17}\right) = \left|\dfrac{1}{17}\right| = \dfrac{1}{17}$

(b) $(g \circ f)(2) = g(f(2)) = g(|2|) = g(2) = \dfrac{1}{2^2 + 1} = \dfrac{1}{5}$

(c) $(f \circ f)(1) = f(f(1)) = f(|1|) = f(1) = |1| = 1$

(d) $(g \circ g)(0) = g(g(0)) = g\left(\dfrac{1}{0^2 + 1}\right) = g(1) = \dfrac{1}{1^2 + 1} = \dfrac{1}{2}$

21. $f(x) = \dfrac{3}{x + 1}$ $g(x) = \sqrt{x}$

(a) $(f \circ g)(4) = f(g(4)) = f\left(\sqrt{4}\right) = f(2) = \dfrac{3}{2 + 1} = \dfrac{3}{3} = 1$

(b) $(g \circ f)(2) = g(f(2)) = g\left(\dfrac{3}{2 + 1}\right) = g\left(\dfrac{3}{3}\right) = \sqrt{1} = 1$

(c) $(f \circ f)(1) = f(f(1)) = f\left(\dfrac{3}{1 + 1}\right) = f\left(\dfrac{3}{2}\right) = \dfrac{3}{\left(\left(\dfrac{3}{2}\right) + 1\right)} = \dfrac{3}{\left(\dfrac{5}{2}\right)} = \dfrac{6}{5}$

(d) $(g \circ g)(0) = g(g(0)) = g\left(\sqrt{0}\right) = g(0) = \sqrt{0} = 0$

23. The domain of g is $\{x \mid x \neq 0\}$. The domain of f is $\{x \mid x \neq 1\}$.

Thus, $g(x) \neq 1$, so we solve:

$g(x) = 1$

$\dfrac{2}{x} = 1$ Thus, $x \neq 2$; so the domain of $f \circ g$ is $\{x \mid x \neq 0, x \neq 2\}$.

$x = 2$

25. The domain of g is $\{x \mid x \neq 0\}$. The domain of f is $\{x \mid x \neq 1\}$.
Thus, $g(x) \neq 1$, so we solve:
$$g(x) = 1 \rightarrow \frac{-4}{x} = 1 \rightarrow x = -4$$
Thus, $x \neq -4$; so the domain of $f \circ g$ is $\{x \mid x \neq -4, x \neq 0\}$.

27. The domain of g is $\{\text{Real Numbers}\}$. The domain of f is $\{x \mid x \geq 0\}$.
Thus, $g(x) \geq 0$, so we solve:
$$g(x) \geq 0 \rightarrow 2x + 3 \geq 0 \rightarrow x \geq -\frac{3}{2}$$
Thus, the domain of $f \circ g$ is $\left\{x \mid x \geq -\frac{3}{2}\right\}$.

29. The domain of g is $\{x \mid x \geq 1\}$. The domain of f is $\{\text{Real Numbers}\}$.
Thus, the domain of $f \circ g$ is $\{x \mid x \geq 1\}$.

31. $f(x) = 2x + 3 \qquad g(x) = 3x$
The domain of f is all real numbers. The domain of g is all real numbers.
(a) $(f \circ g)(x) = f(g(x)) = f(3x) = 2(3x) + 3 = 6x + 3$ Domain: All real numbers.
(b) $(g \circ f)(x) = g(f(x)) = g(2x + 3) = 3(2x + 3) = 6x + 9$
      Domain: All real numbers.
(c) $(f \circ f)(x) = f(f(x)) = f(2x + 3) = 2(2x + 3) + 3 = 4x + 6 + 3 = 4x + 9$
      Domain: All real numbers.
(d) $(g \circ g)(x) = g(g(x)) = g(3x) = 3(3x) = 9x$ Domain: All real numbers.

33. $f(x) = 3x + 1 \qquad g(x) = x^2$
The domain of f is all real numbers. The domain of g is all real numbers.
(a) $(f \circ g)(x) = f(g(x)) = f(x^2) = 3x^2 + 1$ Domain: All real numbers.
(b) $(g \circ f)(x) = g(f(x)) = g(3x + 1) = (3x + 1)^2 = 9x^2 + 6x + 1$
      Domain: All real numbers.
(c) $(f \circ f)(x) = f(f(x)) = f(3x + 1) = 3(3x + 1) + 1 = 9x + 3 + 1 = 9x + 4$
      Domain: All real numbers.
(d) $(g \circ g)(x) = g(g(x)) = g(x^2) = (x^2)^2 = x^4$ Domain: All real numbers.

35. $f(x) = x^2 \qquad g(x) = x^2 + 4$
The domain of f is all real numbers. The domain of g is all real numbers.
(a) $(f \circ g)(x) = f(g(x)) = f(x^2 + 4) = (x^2 + 4)^2 = x^4 + 8x^2 + 16$
      Domain: All real numbers.
(b) $(g \circ f)(x) = g(f(x)) = g(x^2) = (x^2)^2 + 4 = x^4 + 4$ Domain: All real numbers.
(c) $(f \circ f)(x) = f(f(x)) = f(x^2) = (x^2)^2 = x^4$ Domain: All real numbers.
(d) $(g \circ g)(x) = g(g(x)) = g(x^2 + 4) = (x^2 + 4)^2 + 4 = x^4 + 8x^2 + 16 + 4$
      $= x^4 + 8x^2 + 20$ Domain: All real numbers.

37. $f(x) = \dfrac{3}{x-1}$ 　 $g(x) = \dfrac{2}{x}$ 　 The domain of f is $\{x \mid x \neq 1\}$.

The domain of g is $\{x \mid x \neq 0\}$.

(a) $(f \circ g)(x) = f(g(x)) = f\left(\dfrac{2}{x}\right) = \dfrac{3}{\left(\dfrac{2}{x} - 1\right)} = \dfrac{3}{\left(\dfrac{2-x}{x}\right)} = \dfrac{3x}{2-x}$

Domain of $f \circ g$ is $\{x \mid x \neq 0, \, x \neq 2\}$.

(b) $(g \circ f)(x) = g(f(x)) = g\left(\dfrac{3}{x-1}\right) = \dfrac{2}{\left(\dfrac{3}{x-1}\right)} = \dfrac{2(x-1)}{3}$

Domain of $g \circ f$ is $\{x \mid x \neq 1\}$

(c) $(f \circ f)(x) = f(f(x)) = f\left(\dfrac{3}{x-1}\right) = \dfrac{3}{\left(\dfrac{3}{x-1} - 1\right)} = \dfrac{3}{\left(\dfrac{3-(x-1)}{x-1}\right)} = \dfrac{3(x-1)}{4-x}$

Domain of $f \circ f$ is $\{x \mid x \neq 1, \, x \neq 4\}$.

(d) $(g \circ g)(x) = g(g(x)) = g\left(\dfrac{2}{x}\right) = \dfrac{2}{\left(\dfrac{2}{x}\right)} = \dfrac{2x}{2} = x$ 　 Domain of $g \circ g$ is $\{x \mid x \neq 0\}$.

39. $f(x) = \dfrac{x}{x-1}$ 　 $g(x) = -\dfrac{4}{x}$

The domain of f is $\{x \mid x \neq 1\}$. The domain of g is $\{x \mid x \neq 0\}$.

(a) $(f \circ g)(x) = f(g(x)) = f\left(-\dfrac{4}{x}\right) = \dfrac{\left(-\dfrac{4}{x}\right)}{\left(-\dfrac{4}{x} - 1\right)} = \dfrac{\left(-\dfrac{4}{x}\right)}{\left(\dfrac{-4-x}{x}\right)} = \dfrac{-4}{-4-x}$

Domain of $f \circ g$ is $\{x \mid x \neq -4, \, x \neq 0\}$.

(b) $(g \circ f)(x) = g(f(x)) = g\left(\dfrac{x}{x-1}\right) = -\dfrac{4}{\left(\dfrac{x}{x-1}\right)} = \dfrac{-4(x-1)}{x}$

Domain of $g \circ f$ is $\{x \mid x \neq 0, \, x \neq 1\}$.

(c) $(f \circ f)(x) = f(f(x)) = f\left(\dfrac{x}{x-1}\right) = \dfrac{\left(\dfrac{x}{x-1}\right)}{\left(\dfrac{x}{x-1} - 1\right)} = \dfrac{\left(\dfrac{x}{x-1}\right)}{\left(\dfrac{x-(x-1)}{x-1}\right)} = \dfrac{x}{1} = x$

Domain of $f \circ f$ is $\{x \mid x \neq 1\}$.

(d) $(g \circ g)(x) = g(g(x)) = g\left(-\dfrac{4}{x}\right) = -\dfrac{4}{\left(-\dfrac{4}{x}\right)} = \dfrac{-4x}{-4} = x$

Domain of $g \circ g$ is $\{x \mid x \neq 0\}$.

41. $f(x) = \sqrt{x}$ $g(x) = 2x + 3$
The domain of f is $\{x \mid x \geq 0\}$. The domain of g is {Real Numbers}.

(a) $(f \circ g)(x) = f(g(x)) = f(2x + 3) = \sqrt{2x + 3}$ Domain of $f \circ g$ is $\left\{ x \mid x \geq -\dfrac{3}{2} \right\}$.

(b) $(g \circ f)(x) = g(f(x)) = g(\sqrt{x}) = 2\sqrt{x} + 3$ Domain of $g \circ f$ is $\{x \mid x \geq 0\}$.

(c) $(f \circ f)(x) = f(f(x)) = f(\sqrt{x}) = \sqrt{\sqrt{x}} = x^{1/4} = \sqrt[4]{x}$
Domain of $f \circ f$ is $\{x \mid x \geq 0\}$.

(d) $(g \circ g)(x) = g(g(x)) = g(2x + 3) = 2(2x + 3) + 3 = 4x + 6 + 3 = 4x + 9$
Domain of $g \circ g$ is {Real Numbers}.

43. $f(x) = x^2 + 1$ $g(x) = \sqrt{x - 1}$
The domain of f is {Real Numbers}. The domain of g is $\{x \mid x \geq 1\}$.

(a) $(f \circ g)(x) = f(g(x)) = f(\sqrt{x - 1}) = (\sqrt{x - 1})^2 + 1 = x - 1 + 1 = x$
Domain of $f \circ g$ is $\{x \mid x \geq 1\}$.

(b) $(g \circ f)(x) = g(f(x)) = g(x^2 + 1) = \sqrt{x^2 + 1 - 1} = \sqrt{x^2} = |x|$
Domain of $g \circ f$ {Real Numbers}.

(c) $(f \circ f)(x) = f(f(x)) = f(x^2 + 1) = (x^2 + 1)^2 + 1 = x^4 + 2x^2 + 1 + 1 = x^4 + 2x^2 + 2$
Domain of $f \circ f$ is {Real Numbers}.

(d)   Domain of $g \circ g$ is $\{x \mid x \geq 2\}$.
$(g \circ g)(x) = g(g(x)) = g(\sqrt{x - 1}) = \sqrt{\sqrt{x - 1} - 1}$

45. $f(x) = ax + b$ $g(x) = cx + d$ The domain of f is {Real Numbers}.
The domain of g is {Real Numbers}.

(a) $(f \circ g)(x) = f(g(x)) = f(cx + d) = a(cx + d) + b = acx + ad + b$
Domain of $f \circ g$ is {Real Numbers}.

(b) $(g \circ f)(x) = g(f(x)) = g(ax + b) = c(ax + b) + d = acx + bc + d$
Domain of $g \circ f$ is {Real Numbers}.

(c) $(f \circ f)(x) = f(f(x)) = f(ax + b) = a(ax + b) + b = a^2x + ab + b$
Domain of $f \circ f$ is {Real Numbers}.

(d) $(g \circ g)(x) = g(g(x)) = g(cx + d) = c(cx + d) + d = c^2x + cd + d$
Domain of $g \circ g$ is {Real Numbers}.

47. $(f \circ g)(x) = f(g(x)) = f\left(\dfrac{1}{2}x\right) = 2\left(\dfrac{1}{2}x\right) = x$

$(g \circ f)(x) = g(f(x)) = g(2x) = \dfrac{1}{2}(2x) = x$

49. $(f \circ g)(x) = f(g(x)) = f(\sqrt[3]{x}) = (\sqrt[3]{x})^3 = x$
$(g \circ f)(x) = g(f(x)) = g(x^3) = \sqrt[3]{x^3} = x$

51. $(f \circ g)(x) = f(g(x)) = f\left(\frac{1}{2}(x+6)\right) = 2\left(\frac{1}{2}(x+6)\right) - 6 = x + 6 - 6 = x$

$(g \circ f)(x) = g(f(x)) = g(2x - 6) = \frac{1}{2}((2x - 6) + 6) = \frac{1}{2}(2x) = x$

53. $(f \circ g)(x) = f(g(x)) = f\left(\frac{1}{a}(x - b)\right) = a\left(\frac{1}{a}(x - b)\right) + b = x - b + b = x$

$(g \circ f)(x) = g(f(x)) = g(ax + b) = \frac{1}{a}((ax + b) - b) = \frac{1}{a}(ax) = x$

55. $H(x) = (2x + 3)^4$ $\qquad f(x) = x^4, \quad g(x) = 2x + 3$

57. $H(x) = \sqrt{x^2 + 1}$ $\qquad f(x) = \sqrt{x}, \quad g(x) = x^2 + 1$

59. $H(x) = |2x + 1|$ $\qquad f(x) = |x|, \quad g(x) = 2x + 1$

61. $f(x) = 2x^3 - 3x^2 + 4x - 1 \qquad g(x) = 2$
$(f \circ g)(x) = f(g(x)) = f(2) = 2(2)^3 - 3(2)^2 + 4(2) - 1 = 16 - 12 + 8 - 1 = 11$
$(g \circ f)(x) = g(f(x)) = g(2x^3 - 3x^2 + 4x - 1) = 2$

63. $f(x) = 2x^2 + 5 \qquad g(x) = 3x + a$
$(f \circ g)(x) = f(g(x)) = f(3x + a) = 2(3x + a)^2 + 5$
When $x = 0, (f \circ g)(0) = 23$
Solving:

$$2(3 \cdot 0 + a)^2 + 5 = 23 \rightarrow 2a^2 + 5 = 23 \rightarrow 2a^2 = 18 \rightarrow a^2 = 9 \rightarrow a = -3 \text{ or } 3$$

65. $S(r) = 4\pi r^2 \qquad r(t) = \frac{2}{3}t^3, \ t \geq 0$

$S(r(t)) = S\left(\frac{2}{3}t^3\right) = 4\pi\left(\frac{2}{3}t^3\right)^2 = 4\pi\left(\frac{4}{9}t^6\right) = \frac{16}{9}\pi t^6$

67. $N(t) = 100t - 5t^2, \ 0 \leq t \leq 10 \qquad C(N) = 15000 + 8000 N$
$C(N(t)) = C(100t - 5t^2) = 15000 + 8000(100t - 5t^2)$
$\qquad = 15,000 + 800,000t - 40,000t^2$

69. $p = -\frac{1}{4}x + 100 \qquad 0 \leq x \leq 400$

$\frac{1}{4}x = 100 - p \rightarrow x = 4(100 - p)$

$C = \frac{\sqrt{x}}{25} + 600 = \frac{\sqrt{4(100 - p)}}{25} + 600 = \frac{2\sqrt{100 - p}}{25} + 600$

71. $V = \pi r^2 h \qquad h = 2r \qquad \rightarrow V(r) = \pi r^2 (2r) = 2\pi r^3$

73. Given that f and g are odd functions, we know that
$f(-x) = -f(x)$ and $g(-x) = -g(x)$ for all x in the domain of f and g respectively.
The composite function $f \circ g = f(g(x))$ has the following property:
$f(g(-x)) = f(-g(x))$ since g is odd
$= -f(g(x))$ since f is odd, $\therefore f \circ g$ is odd

Functions and Their Graphs

3.6   Mathematical Models; Constructing Functions

1.   If $V = \pi r^2 h$ and $h = 2r$, then $V(r) = \pi r^2(2r) = 2\pi r^3$.

3.   (a)   If $p = -\frac{1}{6}x + 100$ and $R = x\,p$, then $R(x) = x\left(-\frac{1}{6}x + 100\right) = -\frac{1}{6}x^2 + 100x$.

   (b) $R(200) = -\frac{1}{6}(200)^2 + 100(200) = \$13,333$

   (c)   Graphing:

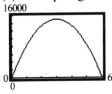

   (d) 300; \$15,000   (e) $p = -\frac{1}{6}(300) + 100 = -50 + 100 = \$50$

5.   (a)   If $x = -5p + 100$ and $R = x\,p$, then $p = \frac{100 - x}{5}$ and

$$R(x) = x\left(\frac{100 - x}{5}\right) = -\frac{1}{5}x^2 + 20x.$$

   (b) $R(15) = -\frac{1}{5}(15)^2 + 20(15) = \$255$

   (c)   Graphing:

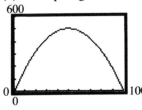

   (d) 50; \$500   (e) $p = \frac{100 - 50}{5} = \frac{50}{5} = \$10$

7. (a) Let x be the width of the rectangle and let y be the length of the rectangle.
        Then, the perimeter is: $P = 2y + 2x = 400$.
        Solving for y: $y = \dfrac{400 - 2x}{2} = 200 - x$.
        The area function is: $A(x) = y(x) = (200 - x)x = -x^2 + 200x$.
    (b) The domain is: $\{x \mid 0 < x < 200\}$
    (c) Graphing:

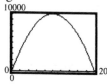

The area is largest when $x = 100$ yards.

9. (a) The distance d from P to the origin is $d = \sqrt{x^2 + y^2}$. Since P is a point on the graph
        of $y = x^2 - 8$, we have: $d(x) = \sqrt{x^2 + (x^2 - 8)^2} = \sqrt{x^4 - 15x^2 + 64}$
    (b) $d(0) = \sqrt{0^4 - 15(0)^2 + 64} = \sqrt{64} = 8$
    (c) $d(1) = \sqrt{(1)^4 - 15(1)^2 + 64} = \sqrt{1 - 15 + 64} = \sqrt{50} = 5\sqrt{2} \approx 7.07$
    (d) Graphing:

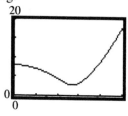

(e) d is smallest when x is 2.74.

11. (a) The distance d from P to the point $(1, 0)$ is $d = \sqrt{(x-1)^2 + y^2}$. Since P is a point on
        the graph of $y = \sqrt{x}$, we have:
        $$d(x) = \sqrt{(x-1)^2 + \left(\sqrt{x}\right)^2} = \sqrt{x^2 - x + 1}$$
    (b) Graphing:

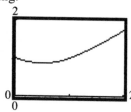

(c) d is smallest when x is 0.50.

13. By definition, a triangle has area $A = \dfrac{1}{2}bh, b =$ base, $h =$ height. Because a vertex of the
    triangle is at the origin, we know that $b = x$ and $h = y$. Expressing the area of the triangle
    as a function of x, we have: $A(x) = \dfrac{1}{2}xy = \dfrac{1}{2}x\left(x^3\right) = \dfrac{1}{2}x^4$.

15. (a) $A(x) = xy = x(16 - x^2) = -x^3 + 16x$

(b) Domain: $\{x \mid 0 < x < 4\}$

(c) Graphing: The area is largest when x is approximately 2.31.

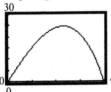

17. (a) $A(x) = (2x)(2y) = 4x(4 - x^2)^{1/2}$

(b) $p(x) = 2(2x) + 2(2y) = 4x + 4(4 - x^2)^{1/2}$

(c) Graphing:

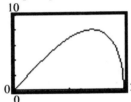

The area is largest when x is approximately 1.41.

(d) Graphing:

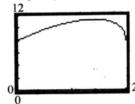

The perimeter is largest when x is approximately 1.41.

19. (a) $C =$ circumference, $A =$ area, $r =$ radius, $x =$ side of square

$C = 2\pi r = 10 - 4x \quad \rightarrow \quad r = \dfrac{5 - 2x}{\pi}$

$A(x) = x^2 + \pi r^2 = x^2 + \pi\left(\dfrac{5 - 2x}{\pi}\right)^2 = x^2 + \dfrac{25 - 20x + 4x^2}{\pi}$

(b) Since the lengths must be positive, we have:
$10 - 4x > 0 \quad$ and $x > 0$

$-4x > -10 \rightarrow x < 2.5$ and $x > 0$

Domain: $\{x \mid 0 < x < 2.5\}$

(c) Graphing: The area is smallest when x is approximately 1.40 meters.

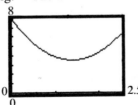

21. (a) Since the wire of length x is bent into a circle, the circumference is x.
Therefore, $C(x) = x$.

(b) Since $C = x = 2\pi r$, $r = \dfrac{x}{2\pi}$.

$A(x) = \pi r^2 = \pi\left(\dfrac{x}{2\pi}\right)^2 = \dfrac{x^2}{4\pi}$.

23. (a) A = area, r = radius;   diameter = $2r$ (b) p = perimeter

         $A(r) = (2r)(r) = 2r^2$ $p(r) = 2(2r) + 2r = 6r$

25.   Area of the equilateral triangle $= \dfrac{1}{2}x \cdot \dfrac{\sqrt{3}}{2}x = \dfrac{\sqrt{3}}{4}x^2$

     Area of $\dfrac{1}{3}$ of the equilateral triangle $= \dfrac{1}{2}x\sqrt{r^2 - \left(\dfrac{x}{2}\right)^2} = \dfrac{1}{2}x\sqrt{r^2 - \dfrac{x^2}{4}} = \dfrac{1}{3} \cdot \dfrac{\sqrt{3}}{4}x^2$

     Solving for r^2:

$$\dfrac{1}{2}x\sqrt{r^2 - \dfrac{x^2}{4}} = \dfrac{1}{3} \cdot \dfrac{\sqrt{3}}{4}x^2$$

$$\sqrt{r^2 - \dfrac{x^2}{4}} = \dfrac{2}{x} \cdot \dfrac{\sqrt{3}}{12}x^2 \rightarrow \sqrt{r^2 - \dfrac{x^2}{4}} = \dfrac{\sqrt{3}}{6}x \rightarrow r^2 - \dfrac{x^2}{4} = \dfrac{3}{36}x^2 \rightarrow r^2 = \dfrac{x^2}{3}$$

     Area inside the circle, but outside the triangle:

$$A(x) = \pi r^2 - \dfrac{\sqrt{3}}{4}x^2 = \pi\dfrac{x^2}{3} - \dfrac{\sqrt{3}}{4}x^2 = \left(\dfrac{\pi}{3} - \dfrac{\sqrt{3}}{4}\right)x^2$$

27. $C = \begin{cases} 95 & \text{if } x = 7 \\ 119 & \text{if } 7 < x \le 8 \\ 143 & \text{if } 8 < x \le 9 \\ 167 & \text{if } 9 < x \le 10 \\ 190 & \text{if } 10 < x \le 14 \end{cases}$

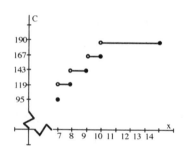

29.

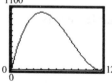

                                       $d^2 = d_1^{\ 2} + d_2^{\ 2}$

                                       $d^2 = (30t)^2 + (40t)^2$

                                       $d(t) = \sqrt{900t^2 + 1600t^2}$

                                       $d(t) = \sqrt{2500t^2} = 50t$

31. (a)   length $= 24 - 2x$

          width $= 24 - 2x$

          height $= x$

          $V(x) = x(24 - 2x)(24 - 2x) = x(24 - 2x)^2$

   (b) $V(3) = 3(24 - 2(3))^2 = 3(18)^2 = 3(324) = 972$ cu. in.

   (c) $V(10) = 3(24 - 2(10))^2 = 3(4)^2 = 3(16) = 48$ cu. in.

   (d)

The volume is largest when $x = 4$ inches.

33. r = radius of cylinder, h = height of cylinder, V = volume of cylinder

$$r^2 + \left(\frac{h}{2}\right)^2 = R^2 \rightarrow r^2 + \frac{h^2}{4} = R^2$$

$$r^2 = R^2 - \frac{h^2}{4} \rightarrow r^2 = \frac{4R^2 - h^2}{4}$$

$$V = \pi r^2 h \longrightarrow V(h) = \pi\left(\frac{4R^2 - h^2}{4}\right)h = \frac{\pi}{4}\left(4R^2 h - h^3\right)$$

35.   (a)   The total cost of installing the cable along the road is $10x$. If cable is installed x miles along the road, there are $5 - x$ miles left from the road to the house and where the cable ends.

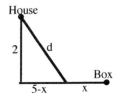

$$d = \sqrt{(5-x)^2 + 2^2} = \sqrt{25 - 10x + x^2 + 4}$$
$$= \sqrt{x^2 - 10x + 29}$$

The total cost of installing the cable is:
$$C(x) = 10x + 14\sqrt{x^2 - 10x + 29}$$
Domain: $\left\{x \mid 0 < x < 5\right\}$

(b) $C(1) = 10(1) + 14\sqrt{1^2 - 10(1) + 29} = 10 + 14\sqrt{20} \approx 10 + 62.61 = \$72.61$

(c) $C(3) = 10(3) + 14\sqrt{3^2 - 10(3) + 29} = 30 + 14\sqrt{8} \approx 30 + 39.60 = \$69.60$

(d)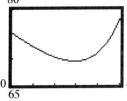

X	Y1
1.5	71.436
2	70.478
2.5	69.822
3	69.598
3.5	70
4	71.305
	73.862

X=4.5

The table indicates that $x = 3$ results in the least cost.

(e)   Using MINIMUM, the graph indicates that $x = 2.96$ results in the least cost.

37.   Consider the diagram shown below.

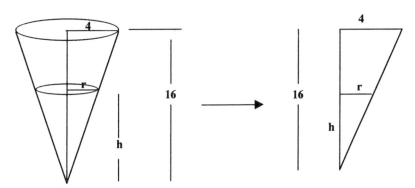

We can extract a pair of similar triangles from the diagram.
Since the smaller triangle is similar to the larger triangle, we have the proportion

$$\frac{r}{h} = \frac{4}{16} \rightarrow \frac{r}{h} = \frac{1}{4} \rightarrow r = \frac{1}{4}h$$

Substituting into the volume formula for the conical portion of water,

$$V = \frac{1}{3}\pi r^2 h = \frac{1}{3}\pi\left(\frac{1}{4}h\right)^2 h = \frac{1}{48}\pi h^3, \text{ so we have the volume function } V(h) = \frac{1}{48}\pi h^3.$$

Functions and Their Graphs

3.R Chapter Review

1. $f(4) = -5$ gives the ordered pair $(4,-5)$. $f(0) = 3$ gives $(0,3)$.

   Finding the slope: $m = \dfrac{3-(-5)}{0-4} = \dfrac{8}{-4} = -2$

   Using slope-intercept form: $f(x) = -2x + 3$

3. $f(x) = \dfrac{Ax+5}{6x-2}$ and $f(1) = 4$

   Solving:
   $$\frac{A(1)+5}{6(1)-2} = 4$$
   $$\frac{A+5}{4} = 4$$
   $$A + 5 = 16$$
   $$A = 11$$

5. (b), (c), and (d) pass the vertical line test and therefore are functions.

7. $f(x) = \dfrac{3x}{x^2-4}$

   (a) $f(-x) = \dfrac{3(-x)}{(-x)^2-4} = \dfrac{-3x}{x^2-4}$

   (b) $-f(x) = -\left(\dfrac{3x}{x^2-4}\right) = \dfrac{-3x}{x^2-4}$

   (c) $f(x+2) = \dfrac{3(x+2)}{(x+2)^2-4} = \dfrac{3x+6}{x^2+4x+4-4} = \dfrac{3x+6}{x^2+4x}$

   (d) $f(x-2) = \dfrac{3(x-2)}{(x-2)^2-4} = \dfrac{3x-6}{x^2-4x+4-4} = \dfrac{3x-6}{x^2-4x}$

   (e) $f(2x) = \dfrac{3(2x)}{(2x)^2-4} = \dfrac{6x}{4x^2-4} = \dfrac{3x}{2x^2-2}$

9. $f(x) = \sqrt{x^2 - 4}$

(a) $f(-x) = \sqrt{(-x)^2 - 4} = \sqrt{x^2 - 4}$

(b) $-f(x) = -\sqrt{x^2 - 4}$

(c) $f(x+2) = \sqrt{(x+2)^2 - 4} = \sqrt{x^2 + 4x + 4 - 4} = \sqrt{x^2 + 4x}$

(d) $f(x-2) = \sqrt{(x-2)^2 - 4} = \sqrt{x^2 - 4x + 4 - 4} = \sqrt{x^2 - 4x}$

(e) $f(2x) = \sqrt{(2x)^2 - 4} = \sqrt{4x^2 - 4} = 2\sqrt{x^2 - 1}$

11. $f(x) = \dfrac{x^2 - 4}{x^2}$

(a) $f(-x) = \dfrac{(-x)^2 - 4}{(-x)^2} = \dfrac{x^2 - 4}{x^2}$

(b) $-f(x) = -\left(\dfrac{x^2 - 4}{x^2}\right) = \dfrac{4 - x^2}{x^2}$

(c) $f(x+2) = \dfrac{(x+2)^2 - 4}{(x+2)^2} = \dfrac{x^2 + 4x + 4 - 4}{x^2 + 4x + 4} = \dfrac{x^2 + 4x}{x^2 + 4x + 4}$

(d) $f(x-2) = \dfrac{(x-2)^2 - 4}{(x-2)^2} = \dfrac{x^2 - 4x + 4 - 4}{x^2 - 4x + 4} = \dfrac{x^2 - 4x}{x^2 - 4x + 4}$

(e) $f(2x) = \dfrac{(2x)^2 - 4}{(2x)^2} = \dfrac{4x^2 - 4}{4x^2} = \dfrac{x^2 - 1}{x^2}$

13. $f(x) = \dfrac{x}{x^2 - 9}$

The denominator cannot be zero:
$$x^2 - 9 \neq 0$$
$$(x+3)(x-3) \neq 0 \rightarrow x \neq -3 \text{ or } 3$$
Domain: $\left\{x \mid x \neq -3,\ x \neq 3\right\}$

15. $f(x) = \sqrt{2 - x}$

The radicand must be positive:
$$2 - x \geq 0 \rightarrow x \leq 2$$
Domain: $\left\{x \mid x \leq 2\right\}$ or $(-\infty, 2]$

17. $f(x) = \dfrac{\sqrt{x}}{|x|}$

The radicand must be positive and the
denominator cannot be zero: $x > 0$
Domain: $\left\{x \mid x > 0\right\}$ or $(0, +\infty)$

19. $f(x) = \dfrac{x}{x^2 + 2x - 3}$

The denominator cannot be zero:
$$x^2 + 2x - 3 \neq 0$$
$$(x+3)(x-1) \neq 0$$
$$x \neq -3 \text{ or } 1$$
Domain: $\left\{x \mid x \neq -3,\ x \neq 1\right\}$

21. $f(x) = \begin{cases} 3x-2 & \text{if } x \le 1 \\ x+1 & \text{if } x > 1 \end{cases}$

    (a)   Domain: {Real Numbers}

    (b)   x-intercept: $\left(\dfrac{2}{3},0\right)$

            y-intercept: $(0,-2)$

    (c)

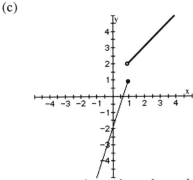

    (d)   Range: $\{y > 2\} \cup \{y \le 1\}$

23. $f(x) = \begin{cases} x & \text{if } -4 \le x < 0 \\ 1 & \text{if } x = 0 \\ 3x & \text{if } x > 0 \end{cases}$

    (a)   Domain: $\{x \mid x \ge -4\}$

    (b)   x-intercept: none

            y-intercept: $(0, 1)$

    (c)

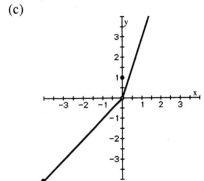

    (d)   Range: $\{y \mid y \ge -4, y \ne 0\}$

25. $f(x) = 2 - 5x$

$$\frac{f(x) - f(2)}{x-2} = \frac{2-5x-(-8)}{x-2} = \frac{-5x+10}{x-2} = \frac{-5(x-2)}{x-2} = -5$$

27. $f(x) = 3x - 4x^2$

$$\frac{f(x) - f(2)}{x-2} = \frac{3x-4x^2-(-10)}{x-2} = \frac{-4x^2+3x+10}{x-2}$$

$$= \frac{-(4x^2-3x-10)}{x-2} = \frac{-(4x+5)(x-2)}{x-2} = -4x-5$$

29. $f(x) = x^3 - 4x$

$$f(-x) = (-x)^3 - 4(-x) = -x^3 + 4x = -\left(x^3 - 4x\right) = -f(x)$$

f is odd.

31. $h(x) = \dfrac{1}{x^4} + \dfrac{1}{x^2} + 1$

$$h(-x) = \frac{1}{(-x)^4} + \frac{1}{(-x)^2} + 1 = \frac{1}{x^4} + \frac{1}{x^2} + 1 = h(x) \qquad h \text{ is even.}$$

33. $G(x) = 1 - x + x^3$

$$G(-x) = 1 - (-x) + (-x)^3 = 1 + x - x^3 \ne -G(x) \ne G(x)$$

G is neither even nor odd.

35. $f(x) = \dfrac{x}{1+x^2}$

$$f(-x) = \frac{-x}{1+(-x)^2} = \frac{-x}{1+x^2} = -f(x) \qquad\qquad f \text{ is odd.}$$

37. $F(x) = |x| - 4$

Using the graph of $y = |x|$, vertically shift the graph downward 4 units.

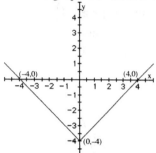

Intercepts: $(-4,0), (4,0), (0,-4)$
Domain: {Real Numbers}
Range: $\{y | y \geq -4\}$

39. $g(x) = -2|x|$

Reflect the graph of $y = |x|$ about the x-axis and vertically stretch the graph by a factor of 2.

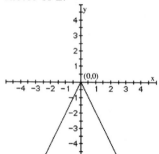

Intercepts: $(0,0)$
Domain: {Real Numbers}
Range: $\{y | y \leq 0\}$

41. $h(x) = \sqrt{x - 1}$

Using the graph of $y = \sqrt{x}$, horizontally shift the graph to the right 1 unit.
Intercepts: $(1,0)$
Domain: $\{x | x \geq 1\}$
Range: $\{y | y \geq 0\}$

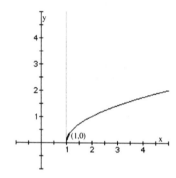

43. $f(x) = \sqrt{1 - x} = \sqrt{-1(x - 1)}$

Reflect the graph of $y = \sqrt{x}$ about the y-axis and horizontally shift the graph to the right 1 unit..

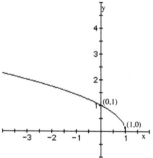

Intercepts: $(1,0), (0,1)$
Domain: $\{x | x \leq 1\}$
Range: $\{y | y \geq 0\}$

45. $h(x) = (x - 1)^2 + 2$

Using the graph of $y = x^2$, horizontally shift the graph to the right 1 unit and vertically shift the graph up 2 units.

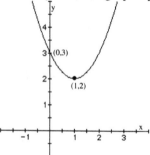

Intercepts: $(0,3)$
Domain: {Real Numbers}
Range: $\{y | y \geq 2\}$

47. $g(x) = 3(x-1)^3 + 1$

Using the graph of $y = x^3$, horizontally shift the graph to the right 1 unit, vertically stretch the graph by a factor of 3, and vertically shift the graph up 1 unit.

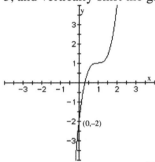

Intercepts: $(0,-2)$, $\left(1 - \dfrac{\sqrt[3]{3}}{3}, 0\right)$

Domain: {Real Numbers}
Range: {Real Numbers}

49. $f(x) = 3x - 5 \qquad g(x) = 1 - 2x^2$
   (a) $(f \circ g)(2) = f(g(2)) = f\left(1 - 2(2)^2\right) = f(-7) = 3(-7) - 5 = -26$
   (b) $(g \circ f)(-2) = g(f(-2)) = g(3(-2) - 5) = g(-11) = 1 - 2(-11)^2 = -241$
   (c) $(f \circ f)(4) = f(f(4)) = f(3(4) - 5) = f(7) = 3(7) - 5 = 16$
   (d) $(g \circ g)(-1) = g(g(-1)) = g\left(1 - 2(-1)^2\right) = g(-1) = 1 - 2(-1)^2 = -1$

51. $f(x) = \sqrt{x+2} \qquad g(x) = 2x^2 + 1$
   (a) $(f \circ g)(2) = f(g(2)) = f\left(2(2)^2 + 1\right) = f(9) = \sqrt{9+2} = \sqrt{11}$
   (b) $(g \circ f)(-2) = g(f(-2)) = g\left(\sqrt{-2+2}\right) = g(0) = 2(0)^2 + 1 = 1$
   (c) $(f \circ f)(4) = f(f(4)) = f\left(\sqrt{4+2}\right) = f\left(\sqrt{6}\right) = \sqrt{\sqrt{6}+2}$
   (d) $(g \circ g)(-1) = g(g(-1)) = g\left(2(-1)^2 + 1\right) = g(3) = 2(3)^2 + 1 = 19$

53. $f(x) = \dfrac{1}{x^2 + 4} \qquad g(x) = 3x - 2$
   (a) $(f \circ g)(2) = f(g(2)) = f(3(2) - 2) = f(4) = \dfrac{1}{4^2 + 4} = \dfrac{1}{20}$
   (b) $(g \circ f)(-2) = g(f(-2)) = g\left(\dfrac{1}{(-2)^2 + 4}\right) = g\left(\dfrac{1}{8}\right) = 3\left(\dfrac{1}{8}\right) - 2 = \dfrac{-13}{8}$
   (c) $(f \circ f)(4) = f(f(4)) = f\left(\dfrac{1}{4^2 + 4}\right) = f\left(\dfrac{1}{20}\right) = \dfrac{1}{\left(\dfrac{1}{20}\right)^2 + 4} = \dfrac{1}{\left(\dfrac{1601}{400}\right)} = \dfrac{400}{1601}$
   (d) $(g \circ g)(-1) = g(g(-1)) = g(3(-1) - 2) = g(-5) = 3(-5) - 2 = -17$

55. $f(x) = 2 - x$ $g(x) = 3x + 1$
The domain of f is all real numbers. The domain of g is all real numbers.
(a) $(f \circ g)(x) = f(g(x)) = f(3x + 1) = 2 - (3x + 1) = 2 - 3x - 1 = 1 - 3x$
    Domain: All real numbers.
(b) $(g \circ f)(x) = g(f(x)) = g(2 - x) = 3(2 - x) + 1 = 6 - 3x + 1 = 7 - 3x$
    Domain: All real numbers.
(c) $(f \circ f)(x) = f(f(x)) = f(2 - x) = 2 - (2 - x) = 2 - 2 + x = x$
    Domain: All real numbers.
(d) $(g \circ g)(x) = g(g(x)) = g(3x + 1) = 3(3x + 1) + 1 = 9x + 3 + 1 = 9x + 4$
    Domain: All real numbers.

57. $f(x) = 3x^2 + x + 1$ $g(x) = |3x|$
The domain of f is all real numbers. The domain of g is all real numbers.
(a) $(f \circ g)(x) = f(g(x)) = f(|3x|) = 3(|3x|)^2 + (|3x|) + 1 = 27x^2 + 3|x| + 1$
    Domain: All real numbers.
(b) $(g \circ f)(x) = g(f(x)) = g(3x^2 + x + 1) = |3(3x^2 + x + 1)| = |9x^2 + 3x + 3|$
    Domain: All real numbers.
(c) $(f \circ f)(x) = f(f(x)) = f(3x^2 + x + 1) = 3(3x^2 + x + 1)^2 + (3x^2 + x + 1) + 1$
    $= 3(9x^4 + 6x^3 + 7x^2 + 2x + 1) + 3x^2 + x + 1 + 1$
    $= 27x^4 + 18x^3 + 24x^2 + 7x + 5$
    Domain: All real numbers.
(d) $(g \circ g)(x) = g(g(x)) = g(|3x|) = |3|3x|| = 9|x|$ Domain: All real numbers.

59. $f(x) = \dfrac{x+1}{x-1}$ $g(x) = \dfrac{1}{x}$
The domain of f is $\{x | x \neq 1\}$. The domain of g is $\{x | x \neq 0\}$.

(a) $(f \circ g)(x) = f(g(x)) = f\left(\dfrac{1}{x}\right) = \dfrac{\left(\dfrac{1}{x} + 1\right)}{\left(\dfrac{1}{x} - 1\right)} = \dfrac{\left(\dfrac{1+x}{x}\right)}{\left(\dfrac{1-x}{x}\right)} = \dfrac{1+x}{1-x}$
    Domain of $f \circ g$ is $\{x | x \neq 0, x \neq 1\}$.

(b) $(g \circ f)(x) = g(f(x)) = g\left(\dfrac{x+1}{x-1}\right) = \dfrac{1}{\left(\dfrac{x+1}{x-1}\right)} = \dfrac{x-1}{x+1}$
    Domain of $g \circ f$ is $\{x | x \neq -1, x \neq 1\}$.

(c) $(f \circ f)(x) = f(f(x)) = f\left(\dfrac{x+1}{x-1}\right) = \dfrac{\left(\dfrac{x+1}{x-1} + 1\right)}{\left(\dfrac{x+1}{x-1} - 1\right)} = \dfrac{\left(\dfrac{x+1+x-1}{x-1}\right)}{\left(\dfrac{x+1-(x-1)}{x-1}\right)} = \dfrac{2x}{2} = x$
    Domain of $f \circ f$ is $\{x | x \neq 1\}$.

(d) $(g \circ g)(x) = g(g(x)) = g\left(\dfrac{1}{x}\right) = \dfrac{1}{\left(\dfrac{1}{x}\right)} = x$ Domain of $g \circ g$ is $\{x \mid x \neq 0\}$.

61. (a) $y = f(-x)$
      Reflect about the y-axis.

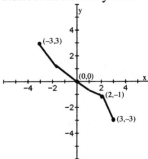

(b) $y = -f(x)$
      Reflect about the x-axis.

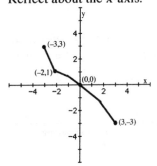

(c) $y = f(x + 2)$
      Horizontally shift left 2 units.

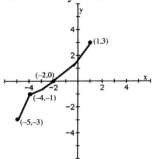

(d) $y = f(x) + 2$
      Vertically shift up 2 units.

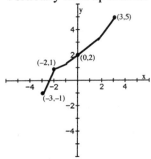

(e) $y = 2f(x)$
      Vertical stretch by a factor of 2.

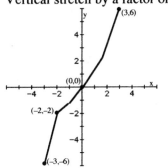

(f) $y = f(3x)$
      Horizontal compression by $\dfrac{1}{3}$.

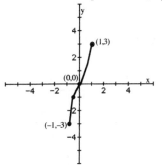

63.   we have the points $(h_1, T_1) = (0, 30)$ and $(h_2, T_2) = (10000, 5)$

$$slope = \frac{\Delta T}{\Delta h} = \frac{5 - 30}{10000 - 0} = \frac{-25}{10000} = -0.0025$$

using the point-slope formula yields

$$T - T_1 = m(h - h_1) \rightarrow T - 30 = -0.0025(h - 0)$$

$$T - 30 = -0.0025h \rightarrow T = -0.0025h + 30 \therefore T(h) = -0.0025h + 30$$

65. $S = kxd^3$, $x = $ width; $d = $ depth

in the diagram, depth = diameter of the log = 6

$$S(x) = kx(6)^3 = 216kx \qquad\qquad \text{domain is } \{x \mid 0 \le x \le 6\}$$

67. (a)   (b)

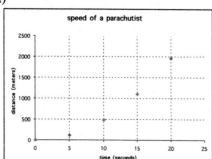   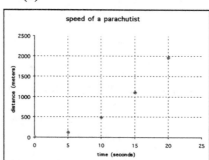

(c)   average rate of change $= \dfrac{112.5 - 0}{5 - 0} = \dfrac{112.5}{5} = 22.5$ feet per second

(d)   for each 1 second increase in time, the distance fallen increases by 22.5 feet

(e)

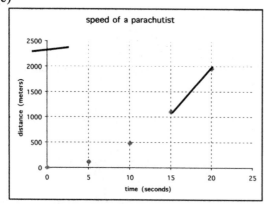

(f)   average rate of change $= \dfrac{1960 - 1102.5}{20 - 15} = \dfrac{857.5}{5} = 171.5$ feet per second

(g)   for each 1 second increase in time, the distance fallen increases by 171.5 feet

(h)   the average rate of change of distance is increasing as time passes

69. (a) We are given that the volume = 500 cubic feet, so we have

$$V = \pi r^2 h = 100 \rightarrow h = \frac{500}{\pi r^2}$$

Total Cost = cost of top + cost of bottom + cost of body

$$= 2(\text{cost of top}) + \text{cost of body}$$

$$= 2(\text{area of top})(\text{cost per area of top}) + (\text{area of body})(\text{cost per area of body})$$

$$= 2(\pi r^2)(.06) + (2\pi rh)(.04) = 0.12\pi r^2 + .08\pi rh = .12\pi r^2 + .08\pi r\left(\frac{500}{\pi r^2}\right)$$

$$= .12\pi r^2 + \frac{40}{r}, \quad \therefore C(r) = .12\pi r^2 + \frac{40}{r}$$

(b) $C(4) = .12\pi(4)^2 + \frac{40}{4} = 1.92\pi + 10 \approx 16.03$ dollars

(c) $C(8) = .12\pi(8)^2 + \frac{40}{8} = 7.68\pi + 5 \approx 29.13$ dollars

(d)

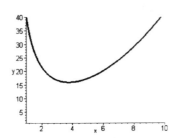

The minimum value occurs at $r \approx 3.79 \rightarrow C(3.79) \approx \$15.97$

71. $S = 4\pi r^2 \rightarrow r = \sqrt{\frac{S}{4\pi}}$ $V(S) = \frac{4}{3}\pi r^3 = \frac{4\pi}{3}\left(\sqrt{\frac{S}{4\pi}}\right)^3 = \frac{4\pi}{3} \cdot \frac{S}{4\pi}\sqrt{\frac{S}{4\pi}} = \frac{S}{6}\sqrt{\frac{S}{\pi}}$

$V(2S) = \frac{2S}{6}\sqrt{\frac{2S}{\pi}} = 2\sqrt{2}\left(\frac{S}{6}\sqrt{\frac{S}{\pi}}\right)$ The volume is $2\sqrt{2}$ times as large.

Polynomial and Rational Functions

4.1 Quadratic Functions and Models

1. D   3. A   5. B   7. E

9. $f(x) = \frac{1}{4}x^2$

Using the function $y = x^2$, compress vertically by a factor of $\frac{1}{4}$.

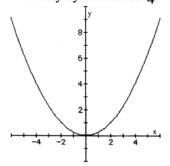

11. $f(x) = \frac{1}{4}x^2 - 2$

Using the function $y = x^2$, compress vertically by a factor of $\frac{1}{4}$, and shift downward 2 units.

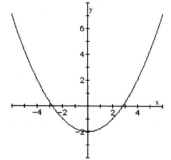

13. $f(x) = \frac{1}{4}x^2 + 2$

Using the function $y = x^2$, compress vertically by a factor of $\frac{1}{4}$, and shift upward 2 units.

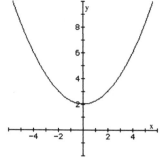

15. $f(x) = \frac{1}{4}x^2 + 1$

Using the function $y = x^2$, compress vertically by a factor of $\frac{1}{4}$, and shift upward 1 unit.

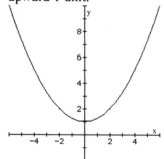

17. $f(x) = x^2 + 4x + 2$

Completing the square:

$f(x) = (x^2 + 4x + 4) + 2 - 4$

$= (x + 2)^2 - 2$

Using the function $y = x^2$, shift the graph to the left 2 units, and shift downward 2 units.

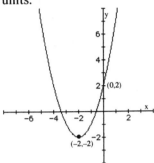

19. $f(x) = 2x^2 - 4x + 1$

Completing the square:

$f(x) = 2(x^2 - 2x + 1) + 1 - 2$

$= 2(x - 1)^2 - 1$

Using the function $y = x^2$, shift the graph to the right 1 unit, stretch the graph vertically by a factor of 2, and shift downward 1 unit.

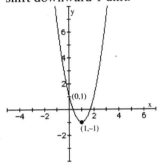

21. $f(x) = -x^2 - 2x$

Completing the square:

$f(x) = -(x^2 + 2x + 1) + 1$

$= -(x + 1)^2 + 1$

Using the function $y = x^2$, shift the graph to the left 1 unit, reflect the graph on the x-axis, and shift upward 1 unit.

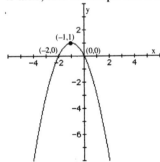

23. $f(x) = \dfrac{1}{2}x^2 + x - 1$

Completing the square:

$f(x) = \dfrac{1}{2}(x^2 + 2x + 1) - 1 - \dfrac{1}{2}$

$= \dfrac{1}{2}(x + 1)^2 - \dfrac{3}{2}$

Using the function $y = x^2$, shift the graph to the left 1 unit, compress the graph vertically by a factor of $\dfrac{1}{2}$, and shift downward $\dfrac{3}{2}$ units.

25. $f(x) = -x^2 - 6x$

$a = -1, b = -6, c = 0$. Since $a = -1 < 0$, the graph opens down.

The x-coordinate of the vertex is $x = \dfrac{-b}{2a} = \dfrac{-(-6)}{2(-1)} = \dfrac{6}{-2} = -3$.

The y-coordinate of the vertex is $f\left(\dfrac{-b}{2a}\right) = f(-3) = -(-3)^2 - 6(-3) = -9 + 18 = 9$.

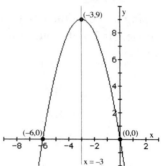

Thus, the vertex is $(-3, 9)$.
The axis of symmetry is the line $x = -3$.
The discriminant is:
$$b^2 - 4ac = (-6)^2 - 4(-1)(0) = 36 > 0,$$
so the graph has two x-intercepts.
The x-intercepts are found by solving:
$$-x^2 - 6x = 0$$
$$-x(x + 6) = 0$$
$$x = 0 \text{ or } x = -6$$
The x-intercepts are –6 and 0.
The y-intercept is $f(0) = 0$.

27. $f(x) = 2x^2 - 8x$

$a = 2, b = -8, c = 0$. Since $a = 2 > 0$, the graph opens up.

The x-coordinate of the vertex is $x = \dfrac{-b}{2a} = \dfrac{-(-8)}{2(2)} = \dfrac{8}{4} = 2$.

The y-coordinate of the vertex is $f\left(\dfrac{-b}{2a}\right) = f(2) = 2(2)^2 - 8(2) = 8 - 16 = -8$.

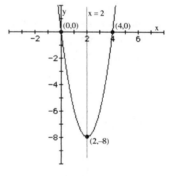

Thus, the vertex is $(2, -8)$.
The axis of symmetry is the line $x = 2$.
The discriminant is:
$$b^2 - 4ac = (-8)^2 - 4(2)(0) = 64 > 0,$$
so the graph has two x-intercepts.
The x-intercepts are found by solving:
$$2x^2 - 8x = 0$$
$$2x(x - 4) = 0$$
$$x = 0 \text{ or } x = 4$$
The x-intercepts are 0 and 4.
The y-intercept is $f(0) = 0$.

29. $f(x) = x^2 + 2x - 8$

$a = 1, b = 2, c = -8$. Since $a = 1 > 0$, the graph opens up.

The x-coordinate of the vertex is $x = \dfrac{-b}{2a} = \dfrac{-2}{2(1)} = \dfrac{-2}{2} = -1$.

The y-coordinate of the vertex is $f\left(\dfrac{-b}{2a}\right) = f(-1) = (-1)^2 + 2(-1) - 8 = 1 - 2 - 8 = -9$.

Thus, the vertex is $(-1, -9)$.
The axis of symmetry is the line $x = -1$.
The discriminant is:
$$b^2 - 4ac = 2^2 - 4(1)(-8) = 4 + 32 = 36 > 0,$$
so the graph has two x-intercepts.
The x-intercepts are found by solving:
$$x^2 + 2x - 8 = 0$$
$$(x + 4)(x - 2) = 0$$
$$x = -4 \text{ or } x = 2$$
The x-intercepts are -4 and 2.
The y-intercept is $f(0) = -8$.

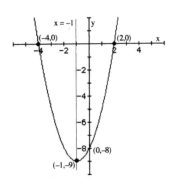

31. $f(x) = x^2 + 2x + 1$
$a = 1, b = 2, c = 1.$ Since $a = 1 > 0$, the graph opens up.

The x-coordinate of the vertex is $x = \dfrac{-b}{2a} = \dfrac{-2}{2(1)} = \dfrac{-2}{2} = -1$.

The y-coordinate of the vertex is $f\left(\dfrac{-b}{2a}\right) = f(-1) = (-1)^2 + 2(-1) + 1 = 1 - 2 + 1 = 0$.

Thus, the vertex is $(-1, 0)$.
The axis of symmetry is the line $x = -1$.
The discriminant is:
$$b^2 - 4ac = 2^2 - 4(1)(1) = 4 - 4 = 0,$$
so the graph has one x-intercept.
The x-intercept is found by solving:
$$x^2 + 2x + 1 = 0$$
$$(x + 1)^2 = 0$$
$$x = -1$$
The x-intercept is -1.
The y-intercept is $f(0) = 1$.

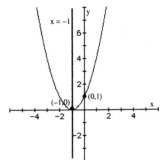

33. $f(x) = 2x^2 - x + 2$
$a = 2, b = -1, c = 2.$ Since $a = 2 > 0$, the graph opens up.

The x-coordinate of the vertex is $x = \dfrac{-b}{2a} = \dfrac{-(-1)}{2(2)} = \dfrac{1}{4}$.

The y-coordinate of the vertex is $f\left(\dfrac{-b}{2a}\right) = f\left(\dfrac{1}{4}\right) = 2\left(\dfrac{1}{4}\right)^2 - \dfrac{1}{4} + 2 = \dfrac{1}{8} - \dfrac{1}{4} + 2 = \dfrac{15}{8}$.

Thus, the vertex is $\left(\dfrac{1}{4}, \dfrac{15}{8}\right)$.

The axis of symmetry is the line $x = \dfrac{1}{4}$.

The discriminant is:
$$b^2 - 4ac = (-1)^2 - 4(2)(2) = 1 - 16 = -15,$$
so the graph has no x-intercepts.
The y-intercept is $f(0) = 2$.

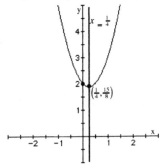

35. $f(x) = -2x^2 + 2x - 3$

$a = -2, b = 2, c = -3.$ Since $a = -2 < 0$, the graph opens down.

The x-coordinate of the vertex is $x = \dfrac{-b}{2a} = \dfrac{-(2)}{2(-2)} = \dfrac{-2}{-4} = \dfrac{1}{2}$. The y-coordinate of the

vertex is $f\left(\dfrac{-b}{2a}\right) = f\left(\dfrac{1}{2}\right) = -2\left(\dfrac{1}{2}\right)^2 + 2\left(\dfrac{1}{2}\right) - 3 = -\dfrac{1}{2} + 1 - 3 = -\dfrac{5}{2}.$

Thus, the vertex is $\left(\dfrac{1}{2}, \dfrac{-5}{2}\right)$.

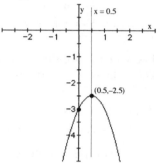

The axis of symmetry is the line $x = \dfrac{1}{2}$.

The discriminant is:

$b^2 - 4ac = 2^2 - 4(-2)(-3) = 4 - 24 = -20,$

so the graph has no x-intercepts.

The y-intercept is $f(0) = -3$.

37. $f(x) = 3x^2 + 6x + 2$

$a = 3, b = 6, c = 2.$ Since $a = 3 > 0$, the graph opens up.

The x-coordinate of the vertex is $x = \dfrac{-b}{2a} = \dfrac{-6}{2(3)} = \dfrac{-6}{6} = -1$. The y-coordinate of the

vertex is $f\left(\dfrac{-b}{2a}\right) = f(-1) = 3(-1)^2 + 6(-1) + 2 = 3 - 6 + 2 = -1.$

Thus, the vertex is $(-1, -1)$.

The axis of symmetry is the line $x = -1$.

The discriminant is:

$b^2 - 4ac = 6^2 - 4(3)(2) = 36 - 24 = 12,$

so the graph has two x-intercepts.

The x-intercepts are found by solving:

$x = \dfrac{-b \pm \sqrt{b^2 - 4ac}}{2a} = \dfrac{-6 \pm \sqrt{12}}{2(3)}$

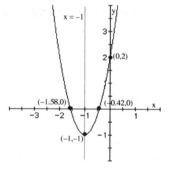

$= \dfrac{-6 \pm 2\sqrt{3}}{6} = \dfrac{-3 \pm \sqrt{3}}{3} \approx \dfrac{-3 \pm 1.732}{3}$

The x-intercepts are approximately -0.42 and -1.58.

The y-intercept is $f(0) = 2$.

39. $f(x) = -4x^2 - 6x + 2$

$a = -4, b = -6, c = 2.$ Since $a = -4 < 0$, the graph opens down.

The x-coordinate of the vertex is $x = \dfrac{-b}{2a} = \dfrac{-(-6)}{2(-4)} = \dfrac{6}{-8} = -\dfrac{3}{4}$. The y-coordinate of the

vertex is $f\left(\dfrac{-b}{2a}\right) = f\left(-\dfrac{3}{4}\right) = -4\left(-\dfrac{3}{4}\right)^2 - 6\left(-\dfrac{3}{4}\right) + 2 = -\dfrac{9}{4} + \dfrac{9}{2} + 2 = \dfrac{17}{4}.$

Thus, the vertex is $\left(-\dfrac{3}{4}, \dfrac{17}{4}\right)$.

The axis of symmetry is the line $x = -\dfrac{3}{4}$.

The discriminant is:

$$b^2 - 4ac = (-6)^2 - 4(-4)(2) = 36 + 32 = 68,$$

so the graph has two x-intercepts.
The x-intercepts are found by solving:

$$x = \frac{-b \pm \sqrt{b^2 - 4ac}}{2a} = \frac{-(-6) \pm \sqrt{68}}{2(-4)}$$

$$= \frac{6 \pm 2\sqrt{17}}{-8} = \frac{-3 \pm \sqrt{17}}{4} \approx \frac{-3 \pm 4.123}{4}$$

The x-intercepts are approximately -1.78 and 0.28.
The y-intercept is $f(0) = 2$.

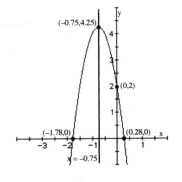

41. $f(x) = 2x^2 + 12x$, $a = 2, b = 12, c = 0$. Since $a = 2 > 0$, the graph opens up, so
the vertex is a minimum point. The minimum occurs at
$x = \dfrac{-b}{2a} = \dfrac{-12}{2(2)} = \dfrac{-12}{4} = -3$. The minimum value is
$f\left(\dfrac{-b}{2a}\right) = f(-3) = 2(-3)^2 + 12(-3) = 18 - 36 = -18$.

43. $f(x) = 2x^2 + 12x - 3$, $a = 2, b = 12, c = -3$. Since $a = 2 > 0$, the graph opens up,
so the vertex is a minimum point. The minimum occurs at
$x = \dfrac{-b}{2a} = \dfrac{-12}{2(2)} = \dfrac{-12}{4} = -3$. The minimum value is
$f\left(\dfrac{-b}{2a}\right) = f(-3) = 2(-3)^2 + 12(-3) - 3 = 18 - 36 - 3 = -21$.

45. $f(x) = -x^2 + 10x - 4$
$a = -1, b = 10, c = -4$. Since $a = -1 < 0$, the graph opens down, so the vertex is a
maximum point. The maximum occurs at $x = \dfrac{-b}{2a} = \dfrac{-10}{2(-1)} = \dfrac{-10}{-2} = 5$. The maximum
value is $f\left(\dfrac{-b}{2a}\right) = f(5) = -(5)^2 + 10(5) - 4 = -25 + 50 - 4 = 21$.

47. $f(x) = -3x^2 + 12x + 1$
$a = -3, b = 12, c = 1$. Since $a = -3 < 0$, the graph opens down, so the vertex is a
maximum point. The maximum occurs at $x = \dfrac{-b}{2a} = \dfrac{-12}{2(-3)} = \dfrac{-12}{-6} = 2$. The maximum
value is $f\left(\dfrac{-b}{2a}\right) = f(2) = -3(2)^2 + 12(2) + 1 = -12 + 24 + 1 = 13$.

49.   (a) $f(x) = 1(x - (-3))(x - 1) = 1(x + 3)(x - 1) = 1(x^2 + 2x - 3) = x^2 + 2x - 3$

           $f(x) = 2(x - (-3))(x - 1) = 2(x + 3)(x - 1) = 2(x^2 + 2x - 3) = 2x^2 + 4x - 6$

           $f(x) = -2(x - (-3))(x - 1) = -2(x + 3)(x - 1)$

$$= -2(x^2 + 2x - 3) = -2x^2 - 4x + 6$$

           $f(x) = 5(x - (-3))(x - 1) = 5(x + 3)(x - 1) = 5(x^2 + 2x - 3) = 5x^2 + 10x - 15$

   (b)   The value of a multiplies the value of the y-intercept by the value of a. The values of the x-intercepts are not changed.

   (c)   The axis of symmetry is unaffected by the value of a.

   (d)   The y-coordinate of the vertex is multiplied by the value of a.

   (e)   The x-coordinate of the vertex is the midpoint of the x-intercepts.

51. $R(p) = -4p^2 + 4000p$

     $a = -4,\ b = 4000,\ c = 0$. Since $a = -4 < 0$, the graph is a parabola that opens down, so the vertex is a maximum point. The maximum occurs at

$$p = \frac{-b}{2a} = \frac{-4000}{2(-4)} = \frac{-4000}{-8} = 500.$$

$$R(500) = -4(500)^2 + 4000(500) = -1000000 + 2000000 = 1{,}000{,}000.$$

     Thus, the unit price should be \$500 for maximum revenue. The maximum revenue is \$1,000,000.

53.   (a) $R(x) = x\left(-\dfrac{1}{6}x + 100\right) = -\dfrac{1}{6}x^2 + 100x$.

   (b) $R(200) = \dfrac{-1}{6}(200)^2 + 100(200) = \dfrac{-20000}{3} + 20000 = \dfrac{40000}{3} \approx \$13{,}333$

   (c) $x = \dfrac{-b}{2a} = \dfrac{-100}{2\left(-\dfrac{1}{6}\right)} = \dfrac{-100}{\left(-\dfrac{1}{3}\right)} = \dfrac{300}{1} = 300$

$$R(300) = -\frac{1}{6}(300)^2 + 100(300) = -15000 + 30000 = \$15{,}000$$

   (d) $p = -\dfrac{1}{6}(300) + 100 = -50 + 100 = \$50$

55.   (a)   If $x = -5p + 100$, then $p = \dfrac{100 - x}{5}$. $R(x) = x\left(\dfrac{100 - x}{5}\right) = -\dfrac{1}{5}x^2 + 20x$

   (b) $R(15) = -\dfrac{1}{5}(15)^2 + 20(15) = -45 + 300 = \$255$

   (c) $x = \dfrac{-b}{2a} = \dfrac{-20}{2\left(-\dfrac{1}{5}\right)} = \dfrac{-20}{\left(-\dfrac{2}{5}\right)} = \dfrac{100}{2} = 50$

$$R(50) = -\frac{1}{5}(50)^2 + 20(50) = -500 + 1000 = \$500$$

   (d) $p = \dfrac{100 - 50}{5} = \dfrac{50}{5} = \$10$

57. (a)   Let x = width and y = length of the rectangular area.
$$P = 2x + 2y = 400 \rightarrow y = \frac{400 - 2x}{2} = 200 - x$$
Then $A(x) = (200 - x)x = 200x - x^2 = -x^2 + 200x$

(b) $x = \frac{-b}{2a} = \frac{-200}{2(-1)} = \frac{-200}{-2} = 100$ yards

(c) $A(100) = -100^2 + 200(100) = -10000 + 20000 = 10,000$ sq yds.

59. (a)   Let x = width and y = length of the rectangular area.
$$2x + y = 4000 \quad \rightarrow \quad y = 4000 - 2x$$
Then $A(x) = (4000 - 2x)x = 4000x - 2x^2 = -2x^2 + 4000x$

(b) $x = \frac{-b}{2a} = \frac{-4000}{2(-2)} = \frac{-4000}{-4} = 1000$

(c) $A(1000) = -2(1000)^2 + 4000(1000) = -2000000 + 4000000 = 2,000,000$
The largest area that can be enclosed is 2,000,000 square meters.

61. (a) $a = -\dfrac{32}{2500}, b = 1, c = 200.$ The maximum height occurs when
$$x = \frac{-b}{2a} = \frac{-1}{2\left(-\dfrac{32}{2500}\right)} = \frac{2500}{64} = 39.0625 \text{ feet from base of the cliff.}$$

(b)   The maximum height is
$$h(39.0625) = \frac{-32(39.0625)^2}{2500} + 39.0625 + 200 = 219.53 \text{ feet.}$$

(c)   Solving when $h(x) = 0$:
$$-\frac{32}{2500}x^2 + x + 200 = 0 \rightarrow x = \frac{-1 \pm \sqrt{1^2 - 4\left(-\dfrac{32}{2500}\right)(200)}}{2\left(-\dfrac{32}{2500}\right)} = \frac{-1 \pm \sqrt{11.24}}{-0.0256}$$

$$x \approx -91.90 \text{ or } x \approx 170.02$$
Since the distance cannot be negative, the projectile strikes the water 170.02 feet from the base of the cliff.

(d)   Graphing:

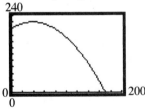

(e)   Solving when $h(x) = 100$:

$$-\frac{32}{2500}x^2 + x + 200 = 100$$

$$-\frac{32}{2500}x^2 + x + 100 = 0$$

$$x = \frac{-1 \pm \sqrt{1^2 - 4\left(-\frac{32}{2500}\right)(100)}}{2\left(-\frac{32}{2500}\right)} = \frac{-1 \pm \sqrt{6.12}}{-0.0256}; \quad x \approx -57.57 \text{ or } x \approx 135.70$$

Since the distance cannot be negative, the projectile is 100 feet above the water 135.70 feet from the base of the cliff.

63.   Locate the origin at the point where the cable touches the road. Then the equation of the parabola is of the form: $y = ax^2$, where $a > 0$. Since the point $(200, 75)$ is on the parabola, we can find the constant a:

$$75 = a(200)^2 \quad \rightarrow \quad a = \frac{75}{200^2} = 0.001875$$

When $x = 100$, we have:
$$y = 0.001875(100)^2 = 18.75 \text{ meters}.$$

65.   Let $x =$ the depth of the gutter and $y =$ the width of the gutter.
Then $A = xy$ is the cross-sectional area of the gutter.
Since the aluminum sheets for the gutter are 12 inches wide, we have
$$2x + y = 12 \text{ or } y = 12 - 2x.$$
The area is to be maximized, so: $A = xy = x(12 - 2x) = -2x^2 + 12x$.
This equation is a parabola opening down; thus, it has a maximum when
$$x = \frac{-b}{2a} = \frac{-12}{2(-2)} = \frac{-12}{-4} = 3.$$

Thus, a depth of 3 inches produces a maximum cross-sectional area.

67.   Let $x =$ the width of the rectangle or the diameter of the semicircle.
Let $y =$ the length of the rectangle.

The perimeter of each semicircle is $\frac{\pi x}{2}$.

The perimeter of the track is given by: $\frac{\pi x}{2} + \frac{\pi x}{2} + y + y = 1500$.

Solving for x:
$$\frac{\pi x}{2} + \frac{\pi x}{2} + y + y = 1500$$
$$\pi x + 2y = 1500$$
$$\pi x = 1500 - 2y$$
$$x = \frac{1500 - 2y}{\pi}$$

The area of the rectangle is: $A = xy = \left(\frac{1500 - 2y}{\pi}\right)y = \frac{-2}{\pi}y^2 + \frac{1500}{\pi}y$

This equation is a parabola opening down; thus, it has a maximum when

$$y = \frac{-b}{2a} = \frac{\dfrac{-1500}{\pi}}{2\left(\dfrac{-2}{\pi}\right)} = \frac{-1500}{-4} = 375. \quad \text{Thus, } x = \frac{1500 - 2(375)}{\pi} = \frac{750}{\pi} \approx 238.73.$$

The dimensions for the rectangle with maximum area are $\dfrac{750}{\pi} \approx 238.73$ meters by 375 meters.

Problems 69 – 73. The equations for the curves that are graphed on the screens use many more decimal places in order to get the desired accuracy.

69. (a)   Graphing: The data appear to be quadratic with $a < 0$.

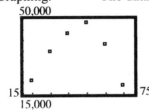

   (b) $I(x) = -42.6x^2 + 3806x - 38526$

$$x = \frac{-b}{2a} = \frac{-3806}{2(-42.6)} = 44.695$$

   An individual will earn the most income at an age of 44.7 years.

   (c)   The maximum income will be:

$$I(44.7) = -42.6(44.7)^2 + 3805(44.7) - 38526 = \$46,438.87$$

   (d) and (e)   Graphing the quadratic function of best fit:

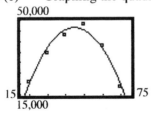

71. (a)   Graphing: The data appears to be quadratic with $a > 0$.

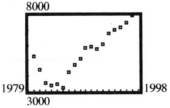

   (b)   Note: The coefficients given in the text are incorrect. The correct function is:

$$I(x) = 17.199x^2 - 68147.78x + 67507955$$

$$x = \frac{-b}{2a} = \frac{-(-68147.78)}{2(17.199)} \approx 1981.16 \qquad \text{Imports were lowest in 1981.}$$

    (c)   The predicted number of barrels imported in 1998 (using the equation to many more decimal places) is: $I(1998) \approx 3165$ thousand barrels

    (d) and (e)   Graphing the quadratic function of best fit:

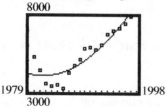

73. (a)   Graphing: The data appears to be quadratic with $a < 0$.

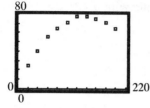

    (b) $h(x) = -0.0037x^2 + 1.03x + 5.7$

$$x = \frac{-b}{2a} = \frac{-1.03}{2(-0.0037)} \approx 139.19 \text{ feet}$$

The ball travels about 139 feet before reaching its maximum height.

    (c)   The maximum height will be: (using the equation to many more decimal places)

$$h(139) = -0.0037(139)^2 + 1.03(139) + 5.7 \approx 77.38 \text{ feet}$$

    (d) and (e)   Graphing the quadratic function of best fit:

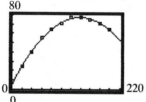

75. We have:

$$a(-h)^2 + b(-h) + c = ah^2 - bh + c = y_0$$
$$a(0)^2 + b(0) + c = c = y_1$$
$$a(h)^2 + b(h) + c = ah^2 + bh + c = y_2$$

Equating the two equations for the area, we have:

$$y_0 + 4y_1 + y_2 = ah^2 - bh + c + 4c + ah^2 + bh + c = 2ah^2 + 6c$$

Therefore, Area $= \frac{h}{3}\left(2ah^2 + 6c\right) = \frac{h}{3}\left(y_0 + 4y_1 + y_2\right).$

77. $f(x) = 2x^2 + 8, \quad h = 2$

Area $= \frac{2}{3}\left(2(2)(2)^2 + 6(8)\right) = \frac{2}{3}(16 + 48) = \frac{2}{3}(64) = \frac{128}{3}$

79. $f(x) = -x^2 + x + 4, \quad h = 1$

$\qquad$ Area $= \frac{1}{3}\left(2(-1)(1)^2 + 6(4)\right) = \frac{1}{3}(-2 + 24) = \frac{1}{3}(22) = \frac{22}{3}$

81.   If x is even, then ax^2 and bx are even. When two even numbers are added to an odd number the result is odd. Thus, $f(x)$ is odd.

$\qquad$ If x is odd, then ax^2 and bx are odd. The sum of three odd numbers results in an odd number. Thus, $f(x)$ is odd.

83. $\qquad f(x) = x^2 + 2x - 3; \qquad f(x) = x^2 + 2x + 1; \qquad f(x) = x^2 + 2x$

$\qquad$ each member of this family will be a parabola with the following characteristics:

- opens upwards since $a > 0$
- vertex occurs at $\quad x = \dfrac{-b}{2a} = \dfrac{-2}{2(1)} = -1$
- there is at least one x-intercept since $b^2 - 4ac \geq 0$

Polynomial and Rational Functions

4.2 Polynomial Functions

1. $f(x) = 4x + x^3$ is a polynomial function of degree 3.

3. $g(x) = \dfrac{1-x^2}{2} = \dfrac{1}{2} - \dfrac{1}{2}x^2$ is a polynomial function of degree 2.

5. $f(x) = 1 - \dfrac{1}{x} = 1 - x^{-1}$ is not a polynomial function because it contains a negative exponent.

7. $g(x) = x^{3/2} - x^2 + 2$ is not a polynomial function because it contains a fractional exponent.

9. $F(x) = 5x^4 - \pi x^3 + \dfrac{1}{2}$ is a polynomial function of degree 4.

11. $G(x) = 2(x-1)^2(x^2+1)$ is a polynomial function of degree 4.

13. $f(x) = (x+1)^4$
Using the graph of $y = x^4$, shift the graph horizontally, 1 unit to the left.

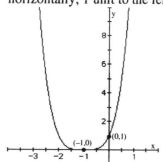

15. $f(x) = x^5 - 3$
Using the graph of $y = x^5$, shift the graph vertically, 3 units down.

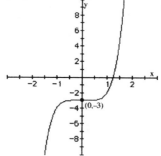

17. $f(x) = \dfrac{1}{2}x^4$

Using the graph of $y = x^4$, compress the graph vertically by a factor of $\dfrac{1}{2}$.

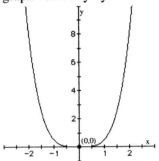

19. $f(x) = -x^5$

Using the graph of $y = x^5$, reflect the graph about the x-axis.

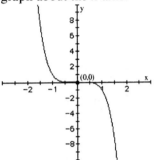

21. $f(x) = (x-1)^5 + 2$

Using the graph of $y = x^5$, shift the graph horizontally, 1 unit to the right, and shift vertically 2 units up.

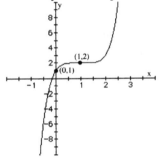

23. $f(x) = 2(x+1)^4 + 1$

Using the graph of $y = x^4$, shift the graph horizontally, 1 unit to the left, stretch vertically by a factor of 2, and shift vertically 1 unit up.

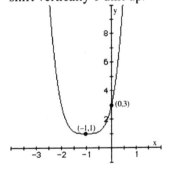

25. $f(x) = 4 - (x - 2)^5 = -(x - 2)^5 + 4$
Using the grah of $y = x^5$, shift the graph horizontally, 2 units to the right, reflect about the x-axis, and shift vertically 4 units up.

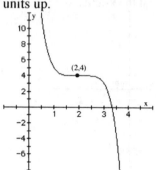

27. $f(x) = a(x - (-1))(x - 1)(x - 3)$
For $a = 1$: $f(x) = (x + 1)(x - 1)(x - 3)$
$f(x) = (x^2 - 1)(x - 3) = x^3 - 3x^2 - x + 3$

29. $f(x) = a(x - (-3))(x - 0)(x - 4)$
For $a = 1$: $f(x) = (x + 3)(x)(x - 4)$
$$f(x) = (x^2 + 3x)(x - 4)$$
$$= x^3 - 4x^2 + 3x^2 - 12x$$
$$= x^3 - x^2 - 12x$$

31. $f(x) = a(x - (-4))(x - (-1))(x - 2)(x - 3)$
For $a = 1$: $f(x) = (x + 4)(x + 1)(x - 2)(x - 3)$
$$f(x) = (x^2 + 5x + 4)(x^2 - 5x + 6)$$
$$f(x) = x^4 - 5x^3 + 6x^2 + 5x^3 - 25x^2 + 30x + 4x^2 - 20x + 24$$
$$f(x) = x^4 - 15x^2 + 10x + 24$$

33. The real zeros of $f(x) = 3(x - 7)(x + 3)^2$ are: 7, with multiplicity one; and –3, with multiplicity two. The graph crosses the x-axis at 7 and touches it at –3.
The function resembles $y = 3x^3$ for large values of $|x|$.

35. The real zeros of $f(x) = 4(x^2 + 1)(x - 2)^3$ are: 2, with multiplicity three. $x^2 + 1 = 0$ has no real solution. The graph crosses the x-axis at 2.
The function resembles $y = 4x^5$ for large values of $|x|$.

37. The real zeros of $f(x) = -2\left(x + \frac{1}{2}\right)^2 (x^2 + 4)^2$ are: $-\frac{1}{2}$, with multiplicity two. $x^2 + 4 = 0$ has no real solution. The graph touches the x-axis at $\frac{-1}{2}$.
The function resembles $y = 2x^6$ for large values of $|x|$.

39. The real zeros of $f(x) = (x - 5)^3 (x + 4)^2$ are: 5, with multiplicity three; and –4, with multiplicity two. The graph crosses the x-axis at 5 and touches it at –4.
The function resembles $y = x^5$ for large values of $|x|$.

41. $f(x) = 3(x^2 + 8)(x^2 + 9)^2$ has no real zeros. $x^2 + 8 = 0$ and $x^2 + 9 = 0$ have no real solutions. The graph neither touches nor crosses the x-axis. The function resembles $y = 3x^6$ for large values of $|x|$.

43.   The real zeros of $f(x) = -2x^2(x^2 - 2)$ are: $-\sqrt{2}$ and $\sqrt{2}$ with multiplicity one; and 0, with multiplicity two. The graph touches the x-axis at $-\sqrt{2}$ and $\sqrt{2}$ and crosses the x-axis at 2.The function resembles $y = -2x^4$ for large values of $|x|$.

45. $f(x) = (x - 1)^2$
   (a)   x-intercept: 1; y-intercept: 1
   (b)   touches x-axis at x = 1
   (c) $y = x^2$
   (d)   1
   (e)

interval	$x < 1$	$x > 1$
test number	-1	2
Value of f	$f(-1) = 4$	$f(2) = 1$
Above or below x-axis	above	above
Point on graph	(-1,4)	(2,1)

   f is above the x-axis for
       $(-\infty, 1) \cup (1, \infty)$
   (f)

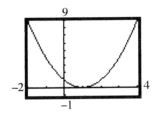

47. $f(x) = x^2(x - 3)$
   (a)   x-intercepts: 0, 3; y-intercept: 0
   (b)   touches x-axis at x = 0 ; crosses x-axis at x = 3
   (c) $y = x^3$ (d) 2
   (e)

interval	$x < 0$	$0 < x < 3$	$x > 3$
Test number	-1	2	4
Value of f	$f(-1) = -4$	$f(2) = -4$	$f(4) = 16$
Above or below x-axis	below	below	above
Point on graph	(-1,-4)	(2,-4)	(4,16)

   f is below the x-axis for $(-\infty, 0) \cup (0, 3)$; f is above the x-axis for $(3, \infty)$
   (f)

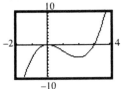

49. $f(x) = 6x^3(x+4)$
   (a)   x-intercepts: –4, 0; y-intercept: 0
   (b)   crosses x-axis at x = –4 and x = 0
   (c) $y = 6x^4$ (d)   3
   (e)

interval	$x < -4$	$-4 < x < 0$	$x > 0$
Test number	-5	-2	1
Value of f	$f(-5) = 750$	$f(-2) = -96$	$f(1) = 30$
Above or below x-axis	above	below	above
Point on graph	(-5,750)	(-2,-96)	(1,30)

   f is above the x-axis for $(-\infty, -4) \cup (0, \infty)$; f is below the x-axis for $(-4, 0)$
   (f)

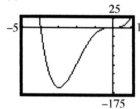

51. $f(x) = -4x^2(x+2)$
   (a)   x-intercepts: 0, - 2; y-intercept: 0
   (b)   crosses x-axis at x = - 2 ; touches x-axis at x = 0
   (c) $y = -4x^3$ (d)   2
   (e)

interval	$x < -2$	$-2 < x < 0$	$x > 0$
Test number	-3	-1	1
Value of f	$f(-3) = 36$	$f(-1) = -4$	$f(1) = -12$
Above or below x-axis	above	below	below
Point on graph	(-3,36)	(-1,-4)	(1,-12)

   f is above the x-axis for $(-\infty, -2)$
   f is below the x-axis for $(-2, 0) \cup (0, \infty)$
   (f)

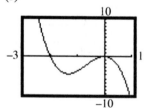

53. $f(x) = x(x-2)(x+4)$

   (a)   x-intercepts: 0, - 4, 2; y-intercept: 0
   (b)   crosses x-axis at x = 0, x = - 4 and x = 2
   (c) $y = x^3$ (d)   2
   (e)

interval	$x < -4$	$-4 < x < 0$	$0 < x < 2$	$x > 2$
Test number	-5	-2	1	3
Value of f	$f(-5) = -35$	$f(-2) = 16$	$f(1) = -5$	$f(3) = 21$
Above or below x-axis	below	above	below	above
Point on graph	(-5,-35)	(-2,16)	(1,-5)	(3,21)

   f is above the x-axis for $(-4,0) \cup (2,\infty)$; f is below the x-axis for $(-\infty,-4) \cup (0,2)$

   (f)

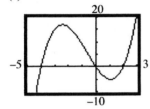

55. $f(x) = 4x - x^3 = x(4 - x^2) = x(2+x)(2-x)$

   (a)   x-intercepts: 0, - 2, 2; y-intercept: 0
   (b)   crosses x-axis at x = 0, x = - 2 and x = 2
   (c) $y = -x^3$ (d)   2
   (e)

interval	$x < -2$	$-2 < x < 0$	$0 < x < 2$	$x > 2$
Test number	-3	-1	1	3
Value of f	$f(-3) = 15$	$f(-1) = -3$	$f(1) = 3$	$f(3) = -15$
Above or below x-axis	above	below	above	below
Point on graph	(-3,15)	(-1,-3)	(1,3)	(3,-15)

   f is above the x-axis for $(-\infty,-2) \cup (0,2)$; f is below the x-axis for $(-2,0) \cup (2,\infty)$

   (f)

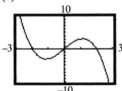

57. $f(x) = x^2(x - 2)(x + 2)$

(a)   x-intercepts: 0, - 2, 2; y-intercept: 0

(b)   crosses x-axis at x = - 2 and x = 2; touches x-axis at x = 0

(c) $y = x^4$ (d)   3

(e)

interval	$x < -2$	$-2 < x < 0$	$0 < x < 2$	$x > 2$
Test number	-3	-1	1	3
Value of f	$f(-3) = 45$	$f(-1) = -3$	$f(1) = -3$	$f(3) = 45$
Above or below x-axis	above	below	below	above
Point on graph	(-3,45)	(-1,-3)	(1,-3)	(3,45)

f is above the x-axis for $(-\infty,-2) \cup (2,\infty)$; f is below the x-axis for $(-2,0) \cup (0,2)$

(f)

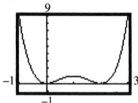

59. $f(x) = x^2(x - 2)^2$

(a)   x-intercepts: 0, 2; y-intercept: 0

(b)   touches x-axis at x = 0 and x = 2

(c) $y = x^4$ (d)   3

(e)

interval	$x < 0$	$0 < x < 2$	$x > 2$
Test number	-1	1	3
Value of f	$f(-1) = 9$	$f(1) = 1$	$f(1) = 9$
Above or below x-axis	above	above	above
Point on graph	(-1,9)	(1,1)	(1,9)

f is above the x-axis for $(-\infty,0) \cup (0,2) \cup (2,\infty)$

(f)

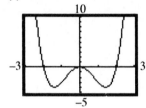

61. $f(x) = x^2(x-3)(x+1)$

(a)   x-intercepts: 0, - 1, 3; y-intercept: 0

(b)   crosses x-axis at x = - 1 and x = 3; touches x-axis at x = 0

(c) $y = x^4$ (d)   3

(e)

interval	$x < -1$	$-1 < x < 0$	$0 < x < 3$	$x > 3$
Test number	-2	-0.5	2	4
Value of f	$f(-2) = 20$	$f(-0.5) = -0.4375$	$f(2) = -12$	$f(4) = 80$
Above or below x-axis	above	below	below	above
Point on graph	(-2,20)	(-0.5,-0.4375)	(2,-12)	(4,80)

f is above the x-axis for $(-\infty,-1) \cup (3,\infty)$; f is below the x-axis for $(-1,0) \cup (0,3)$

(f)

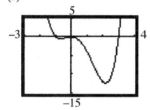

63. $f(x) = (x+2)^2(x-4)^2$

(a)   x-intercepts: - 2, 4; y-intercept: 64

(b)   touches x-axis at x = - 2 and x = 4

(c) $y = x^4$ (d)   3

(e)

interval	$x < -2$	$-2 < x < 4$	$x > 4$
Test number	-3	0	5
Value of f	$f(-3) = 49$	$f(0) = 64$	$f(5) = 49$
Above or below x-axis	above	above	above
Point on graph	(-3,49)	(0,64)	(5,49)

f is above the x-axis for $(-\infty,-2) \cup (-2,4) \cup (4,\infty)$

(f)

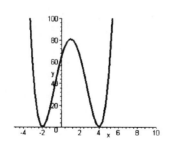

65. $f(x) = x^2(x-2)(x^2+3)$
   (a)   x-intercepts: 0, 2; y-intercept: 0
   (b)   crosses x-axis at x = 2 ; touches x-axis at x = 0
   (c) $y = x^5$ (d)   4
   (e)

interval	$x < 0$	$0 < x < 2$	$x > 2$
Test number	-1	1	3
Value of f	$f(-1) = -12$	$f(1) = -4$	$f(3) = 108$
Above or below x-axis	below	below	above
Point on graph	(-1,-12)	(1,-4)	(3,108)

   f is above the x-axis for $(2,\infty)$; f is below the x-axis for $(-\infty,0)\cup(0,2)$
   (f)

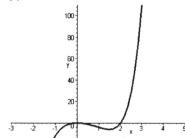

67. $f(x) = -x^2(x^2-1)(x+1) = -x^2(x-1)(x+1)(x+1) = -x^2(x-1)(x+1)^2$
   (a)   x-intercepts: 0, - 1, 1; y-intercept: 0
   (b)   crosses x-axis at x = 1; touches x-axis at x = 0 and x = - 1
   (c) $y = -x^5$ (d)   4
   (e)

interval	$x < -1$	$-1 < x < 0$	$0 < x < 1$	$x > 1$
Test number	-2	-0.5	0.5	2
Value of f	$f(-2) = 12$	$f(-0.5) = 0.09375$	$f(0.5) = 0.28125$	$f(2) = -36$
Above or below x-axis	above	above	above	below
Point on graph	(-3,360)	(-0.5,0.09375)	(0.5,0.28125)	(2,-36)

   f is above the x-axis for $(-\infty,-1)\cup(-1,0)\cup(0,1)$
   f is below the x-axis for $(1,\infty)$
   (f)

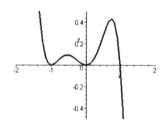

69.   c,e and f

71. c and e

73.
$$f(x) = x^3 + 0.2x^2 - 1.5876x - 0.31752$$

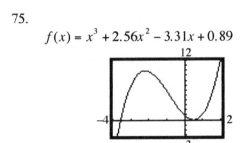

x-intercepts: –1.26, –0.2, 1.26

turning points: (–0.80, 0.57);
(0.66, –0.99)

75.
$$f(x) = x^3 + 2.56x^2 - 3.31x + 0.89$$

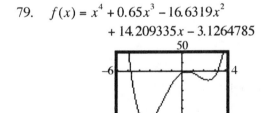

x-intercepts: –3.56, 0.50

turning points: (–2.21, 9.91);
(0.50, 0)

77. $f(x) = x^4 - 2.5x^2 + 0.5625$

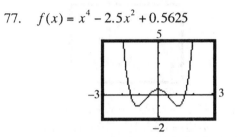

x-intercepts: –1.50, –0.50, 0.50, 1.50

turning points: (0, 0.5625);
(–1.12, –1);
(1.12, –1)

79. $f(x) = x^4 + 0.65x^3 - 16.6319x^2$
$+ 14.209335x - 3.1264785$

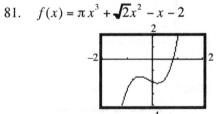

x-intercepts: –4.78, 0.45, 3.23

turning points: (0.45, 0)
(–3.32, –135.92);
(2.38, –22.67)

81. $f(x) = \pi x^3 + \sqrt{2}x^2 - x - 2$

x-intercept: 0.84
turning points: (–0.51, –1.54);
(0.21, –2.12)

83. $f(x) = 2x^4 - \pi x^3 + \sqrt{5}x - 4$

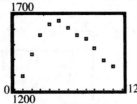

x-intercepts: –1.07, 1.62
turning point: (–0.42, –4.64)

85. $f(x) = -2x^5 - \sqrt{2}x^2 - x - \sqrt{2}$

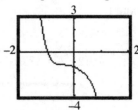

x-intercept: –0.98
no turning points

87. (a)   Graphing: The graph may be a cubic relation.

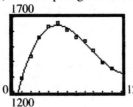

(b) $M(x) = 1.52x^3 - 39.81x^2 + 282.29x + 1035.5$
$M(8) = 1.52(8)^3 - 39.81(8)^2 + 282.29(8) + 1035.5 = 1580.22$
According to the function there would be approximately 1,580,220 motor vehicle
thefts in 1994.

(c) and (d)   Graphing the cubic function of best fit:

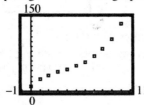

(e) answers will vary

89. (a)   Graphing: The graph may be a cubic relation.

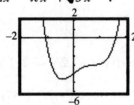

(b)   Average rate of change $= \dfrac{50 - 43}{5 - 4} = \dfrac{7}{1} = 7$

(c)   Average rate of change $= \dfrac{105 - 85}{9 - 8} = \dfrac{20}{1} = 20$

(d) $C(x) = 0.2x^3 - 2.3x^2 + 14.3x + 10.2$
$C(11) = 0.2(11)^3 - 2.3(11)^2 + 14.3(11) + 10.2 \approx 155.4$
The cost of manufacturing 11 Cavaliers in 1 hour would be approximately $155,400.

(e) and (f)   Graphing the cubic function of best fit:

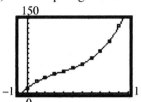

(g)   The y-intercept would indicate the fixed costs before any cars are made.

91.   The graph of a polynomial function will always have a y-intercept since the domain of every polynomial function is the set of real numbers. Therefore $f(0)$ will always produce a y-coordinate on the graph.
A polynomial function might have no x-intercepts. For example $f(x) = x^2 + 1$ has no x-intercepts since the equation $x^2 + 1 = 0$ has no real solutions.

93.   Answers will vary, one such polynomial is $f(x) = x^2(x+1)(4-x)(x-2)^2$

95. $f(x) = \dfrac{1}{x}$ is piecewise smooth and not continuous; $g(x) = |x|$ is continuous but not smooth.

Chapter 4

Polynomial and Rational Functions

4.3 Rational Functions I

1. In $R(x) = \dfrac{4x}{x-3}$, the denominator, $q(x) = x - 3$, has a zero at 3. Thus, the domain of $R(x)$ is all real numbers except 3.

3. In $H(x) = \dfrac{-4x^2}{(x-2)(x+4)}$, the denominator, $q(x) = (x-2)(x+4)$, has zeros at 2 and -4. Thus, the domain of $H(x)$ is all real numbers except 2 and -4.

5. In $F(x) = \dfrac{3x(x-1)}{2x^2 - 5x - 3}$, the denominator, $q(x) = 2x^2 - 5x - 3 = (2x+1)(x-3)$, has zeros at $-\dfrac{1}{2}$ and 3. Thus, the domain of $F(x)$ is all real numbers except $-\dfrac{1}{2}$ and 3.

7. In $R(x) = \dfrac{x}{x^3 - 8}$, the denominator, $q(x) = x^3 - 8 = (x-2)(x^2 + 2x + 4)$, has a zero at 2. ($x^2 + 2x + 4$ has no real zeros.) Thus, the domain of $R(x)$ is all real numbers except 2.

9. In $H(x) = \dfrac{3x^2 + x}{x^2 + 4}$, the denominator, $q(x) = x^2 + 4$, has no real zeros. Thus, the domain of $H(x)$ is all real numbers

11. In $R(x) = \dfrac{3(x^2 - x - 6)}{4(x^2 - 9)}$, the denominator, $q(x) = 4(x^2 - 9) = 4(x-3)(x+3)$, has zeros at 3 and -3. Thus, the domain of $R(x)$ is all real numbers except 3 and -3.

13. (a) Domain: $\{x \mid x \neq 2\}$; Range: $\{y \mid y \neq 1\}$
    (b) Intercept: $(0, 0)$ (c) Horizontal Asymptote: $y = 1$
    (d) Vertical Asymptote: $x = 2$ (e) Oblique Asymptote: none

15. (a) Domain: $\{x \mid x \neq 0\}$; Range: all real numbers
    (b) Intercepts: $(-1, 0), (1, 0)$ (c) Horizontal Asymptote: none
    (d) Vertical Asymptote: $x = 0$ (e) Oblique Asymptote: $y = 2x$

17. (a) Domain: $\{x \mid x \neq -2, x \neq 2\}$; Range: $\{y \mid y \leq 0 \text{ or } y > 1\}$
    (b) Intercept: $(0, 0)$ (c) Horizontal Asymptote: $y = 1$
    (d) Vertical Asymptotes: $x = -2, x = 2$ (e)   Oblique Asymptote: none

19. $F(x) = 2 + \dfrac{1}{x}$

Using the function, $y = \dfrac{1}{x}$, shift the graph vertically 2 units to up.

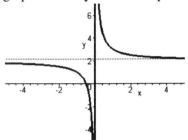

21. $R(x) = \dfrac{1}{(x-1)^2}$

Using the function, $y = \dfrac{1}{x^2}$, shift the graph horizontally 1 unit to the right.

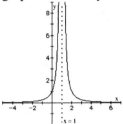

23. $H(x) = \dfrac{-2}{x+1}$

Using the function $y = \dfrac{1}{x}$, shift the graph horizontally 1 unit to the left, reflect about the x-axis, and stretch vertically by a factor of 2.

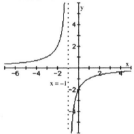

25. $R(x) = \dfrac{-1}{x^2 + 4x + 4} = \dfrac{-1}{(x+2)^2}$

Using the function $y = \dfrac{1}{x^2}$, shift the graph horizontally 2 units to the left, then reflect across the x-axis

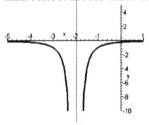

27. $G(x) = 1 + \dfrac{2}{(x-3)^2} = \dfrac{2}{(x-3)^2} + 1$

Using the function $y = \dfrac{1}{x^2}$, shift the graph 3 units right, stretch vertically by a factor of 2, and shift vertically 1 unit up.

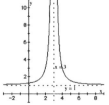

29. $R(x) = \dfrac{x^2 - 4}{x^2} = 1 - \dfrac{4}{x^2}$

Using the function $y = \dfrac{1}{x^2}$, reflect about the x-axis, stretch vertically by a factor of 4 and shift vertically 1 unit up.

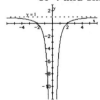

31. $R(x) = \dfrac{3x}{x+4}$

The degree of the numerator, $p(x) = 3x$, is $n = 1$. The degree of the denominator, $q(x) = x+4$, is $m = 1$. Since $n = m$, the line $y = \dfrac{3}{1} = 3$ is a horizontal asymptote. The denominator is zero at $x = -4$, so $x = -4$ is a vertical asymptote.

33. $H(x) = \dfrac{x^4 + 2x^2 + 1}{x^2 - x + 1}$

The degree of the numerator, $p(x) = x^4 + 2x^2 + 1$, is $n = 4$. The degree of the denominator, $q(x) = x^2 - x + 1$, is $m = 2$. Since $n > m+1$, there is no horizontal asymptote or oblique asymptote. The denominator has no real zeros, so there is no vertical asymptote.

35. $T(x) = \dfrac{x^3}{x^4 - 1}$

The degree of the numerator, $p(x) = x^3$, is $n = 3$. The degree of the denominator, $q(x) = x^4 - 1$ is $m = 4$. Since $n < m$, the line $y = 0$ is a horizontal asymptote. The denominator is zero at $x = -1$ and $x = 1$, so $x = -1$ and $x = 1$ are vertical asymptotes.

37. $Q(x) = \dfrac{5 - x^2}{3x^4}$

The degree of the numerator, $p(x) = 5 - x^2$, is $n = 2$. The degree of the denominator, $q(x) = 3x^4$ is $m = 4$. Since $n < m$, the line $y = 0$ is a horizontal asymptote. The denominator is zero at $x = 0$, so $x = 0$ is a vertical asymptote.

39. $R(x) = \dfrac{3x^4 + 4}{x^3 + 3x}$

The degree of the numerator, $p(x) = 3x^4 + 4$, is $n = 4$. The degree of the denominator, $q(x) = x^3 + 3x$ is $m = 3$. Since $n = m+1$, there is an oblique asymptote.
Dividing:

$$\begin{array}{r} 3x \\ x^3 + 3x \overline{\smash{\big)}\, 3x^4 + 0x^3 + 0x^2 + 0x + 4} \\ \underline{3x^4 + 9x^2 } \\ -9x^2 + 0x + 4 \end{array} \qquad R(x) = 3x + \dfrac{-9x^2 + 4}{x^3 + 3x}$$

Thus, the oblique asymptote is $y = 3x$.
The denominator is zero at $x = 0$, so $x = 0$ is a vertical asymptote.

41. $G(x) = \dfrac{x^3 - 1}{x - x^2}, \; x \neq 1$

The degree of the numerator, $p(x) = x^3 - 1$, is $n = 3$. The degree of the denominator, $q(x) = x - x^2$ is $m = 2$. Since $n = m+1$, there is an oblique asymptote.

Dividing:

$$
\begin{array}{r}
-x-1 \\
-x^2+x\overline{\smash{\big)}\,x^3+0x^2+0x-1} \\
\underline{x^3-\ x^2} \\
x^2+0x \\
\underline{x^2-\ x} \\
x-1
\end{array}
$$

$G(x) = -x-1+\dfrac{x-1}{x-x^2} = -x-1-\dfrac{1}{x},\ x \neq 1$

Thus, the oblique asymptote is $y = -x-1$.

$G(x)$ must be in lowest terms to find the vertical asymptote:

$$G(x) = \frac{x^3-1}{x-x^2} = \frac{(x-1)(x^2+x+1)}{-x(x-1)} = \frac{x^2+x+1}{-x}$$

The denominator is zero at $x = 0$, so $x = 0$ is a vertical asymptotes.

43. $g(h) = \dfrac{3.99 \times 10^{14}}{\left(6.374 \times 10^6 + h\right)^2}$

(a) $g(0) = \dfrac{3.99 \times 10^{14}}{\left(6.374 \times 10^6 + 0\right)^2} \approx 9.821\ m/s^2$

(b) $g(443) = \dfrac{3.99 \times 10^{14}}{\left(6.374 \times 10^6 + 443\right)^2} \approx 9.8195\ m/s^2$

(c) $g(8448) = \dfrac{3.99 \times 10^{14}}{\left(6.374 \times 10^6 + 8448\right)^2} \approx 9.795\ m/s^2$

(d) $g(h) = \dfrac{3.99 \times 10^{14}}{\left(6.374 \times 10^6 + h\right)^2} \approx \dfrac{3.99 \times 10^{14}}{h^2} \to 0$ as $h \to \infty$

$\therefore y = 0$ is the horizontal asymptote.

(e)

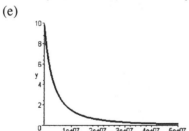

(f) $g(h) = \dfrac{3.99 \times 10^{14}}{\left(6.374 \times 10^6 + h\right)^2} = 0$, to solve this equation would require that

$3.99 \times 10^{14} = 0$, which is impossible. Therefore, there is no height above sea level at which $g = 0$. In other words, there is no point in the entire universe that is unaffected by the Earth's gravity!

217

45.   A rational function $R(x) = \dfrac{p(x)}{q(x)}$ has a vertical asymptote at x = c in each of these cases:

Case 1: $R(c) = \dfrac{nonzero}{zero}$

That is, whenever x = c yields a zero in the denominator of the function formula. And the denominator will equal zero only if it contains the factor $(x-c)^n$, for some $n > 0$.

Case 2: $R(c) = \dfrac{(x-c)^m}{(x-c)^n}$, where $n > 0$, $m > 0$ and $n > m$.

That is, whenever x = c yields a zero in the numerator and denominator of the function formula such that the multiplicity is greater in the denominator.

47.   No, $R(x) = \dfrac{p(x)}{q(x)}$ has an oblique asymptote only when the degree of $p(x)$ is exceeds the degree of $q(x)$ by exactly 1.

Moreover, $R(x) = \dfrac{p(x)}{q(x)}$ has a horizontal asymptote only when the degree of $p(x)$ is less than or equal to the degree of $q(x)$.

These conditions are mutually exclusive.

Chapter 4

Polynomial and Rational Functions

4.4 Rational Functions II: Analyzing Graphs

In problems 1-37, we will use the terminology: $R(x) = \dfrac{p(x)}{q(x)}$, *where the degree of* $p(x) = n$ *and the degree of* $q(x) = m$. *The graphs in Step 6 are in dot mode.*

1. $R(x) = \dfrac{x+1}{x(x+4)}$ $p(x) = x+1$; $q(x) = x(x+4) = x^2 + 4x$; $n = 1$; $m = 2$

   Step 1: Domain: $\{x \mid x \ne -4, x \ne 0\}$
   Step 2: (a)   The x-intercept is the zero of $p(x)$: -1
   　　　　 (b)   There is no y-intercept; $R(0)$ is not defined, since $q(0) = 0$.
   Step 3: $R(-x) = \dfrac{-x+1}{-x(-x+4)} = \dfrac{-x+1}{x^2-4x}$; this is neither $R(x)$ nor $-R(x)$, so there is no symmetry.
   Step 4: The vertical asymptotes are the zeros of $q(x)$: $x = -4$ and $x = 0$
   Step 5: Since $n < m$, the line $y = 0$ is the horizontal asymptote.
   　　　　 $R(x)$ intersects $y = 0$ at $(-1, 0)$.
   Step 6: Graphing:　　　　　　　　　　Step 7:　Graphing by hand:

   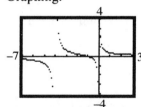　　　　　　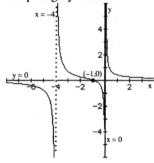

3. $R(x) = \dfrac{3x+3}{2x+4}$ $p(x) = 3x+3$; $q(x) = 2x+4$; $n = 1$; $m = 1$

   Step 1: Domain: $\{x \mid x \ne -2\}$
   Step 2: (a)   The x-intercept is the zero of $p(x)$: -1
   　　　　 (b)   The y-intercept is $R(0) = \dfrac{3(0)+3}{2(0)+4} = \dfrac{3}{4}$.
   Step 3: $R(-x) = \dfrac{3(-x)+3}{2(-x)+4} = \dfrac{-3x+3}{-2x+4} = \dfrac{3x-3}{2x-4}$; this is neither $R(x)$ nor $-R(x)$, so there is no symmetry.

Step 4:   The vertical asymptote is the zero of $q(x)$: $x = -2$

Step 5:   Since $n = m$, the line $y = \dfrac{3}{2}$ is the horizontal asymptote.

$R(x)$ does not intersect $y = \dfrac{3}{2}$.

Step 6:   Graphing: Step 7:   Graphing by hand:

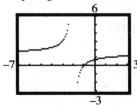   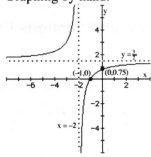

5. $R(x) = \dfrac{3}{x^2 - 4}$ $p(x) = 3$; $q(x) = x^2 - 4$; $n = 0$; $m = 2$

Step 1:   Domain: $\left\{x \,\middle|\, x \neq -2, x \neq 2\right\}$

Step 2:   (a)   There is no x-intercept.

(b)   The y-intercept is $R(0) = \dfrac{3}{0^2 - 4} = \dfrac{3}{-4} = \dfrac{-3}{4}$.

Step 3: $R(-x) = \dfrac{3}{(-x)^2 - 4} = \dfrac{3}{x^2 - 4} = R(x)$; $R(x)$ is symmetric to the y-axis.

Step 4:   The vertical asymptotes are the zeros of $q(x)$: $x = -2$ and $x = 2$

Step 5:   Since $n < m$, the line $y = 0$ is the horizontal asymptote.

$R(x)$ does not intersect $y = 0$.

Step 6:   Graphing: Step 7:   Graphing by hand:

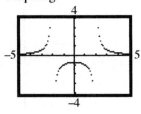   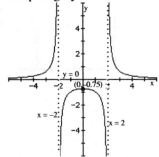

7. $P(x) = \dfrac{x^4 + x^2 + 1}{x^2 - 1}$ $p(x) = x^4 + x^2 + 1$; $q(x) = x^2 - 1$; $n = 4$; $m = 2$

Step 1:   Domain: $\left\{x \,\middle|\, x \neq -1, x \neq 1\right\}$

Step 2:   (a)   There is no x-intercept.

(b)   The y-intercept is $P(0) = \dfrac{0^4 + 0^2 + 1}{0^2 - 1} = \dfrac{1}{-1} = -1$.

Step 3: $P(-x) = \dfrac{(-x)^4 + (-x)^2 + 1}{(-x)^2 - 1} = \dfrac{x^4 + x^2 + 1}{x^2 - 1} = P(x)$; $P(x)$ is symmetric to the y-axis.

Step 4:   The vertical asymptotes are the zeros of $q(x)$: $x = -1$ and $x = 1$

Step 5:   Since $n > m + 1$, there is no horizontal asymptote and no oblique asymptote.

Step 6: Graphing:

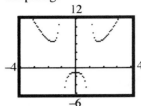

Step 7:   Graphing by hand:

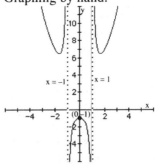

9. $H(x) = \dfrac{x^3 - 1}{x^2 - 9}$ $p(x) = x^3 - 1;\ q(x) = x^2 - 9;\ n = 3;\ m = 2$

Step 1:   Domain: $\left\{ x \mid x \neq -3,\, x \neq 3 \right\}$

Step 2:   (a)   The x-intercept is the zero of $p(x)$: 1.

(b)   The y-intercept is $H(0) = \dfrac{0^3 - 1}{0^2 - 9} = \dfrac{-1}{-9} = \dfrac{1}{9}$.

Step 3: $H(-x) = \dfrac{(-x)^3 - 1}{(-x)^2 - 9} = \dfrac{-x^3 - 1}{x^2 - 9}$; this is neither $H(x)$ nor $-H(x)$, so there is no symmetry.

Step 4:   The vertical asymptotes are the zeros of $q(x)$: $x = -3$ and $x = 3$

Step 5:   Since $n = m + 1$, there is an oblique asymptote. Dividing:

$$\begin{array}{r} x \\ x^2 - 9 \overline{)\,x^3 + 0x^2 + 0x - 1\,} \\ \underline{x^3 \qquad\ \ -9x\ \ } \\ 9x - 1 \end{array} \qquad H(x) = x + \dfrac{9x - 1}{x^2 - 9}$$

The oblique asymptote is $y = x$.

Solve to find intersection points:

$$\dfrac{x^3 - 1}{x^2 - 9} = x \ \rightarrow\ x^3 - 1 = x^3 - 9x$$

$$-1 = -9x \rightarrow x = \dfrac{1}{9}$$

The oblique asymptote intersects $H(x)$ at $\left(\dfrac{1}{9}, \dfrac{1}{9} \right)$.

Step 6: Graphing:

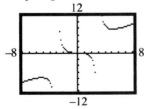

Step 7:   Graphing by hand:

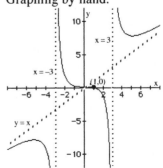

11. $R(x) = \dfrac{x^2}{x^2 + x - 6} = \dfrac{x^2}{(x+3)(x-2)}$ $p(x) = x^2$; $q(x) = x^2 + x - 6$; $n = 2$; $m = 2$

Step 1: Domain: $\{x \mid x \ne -3, x \ne 2\}$

Step 2: (a) The x-intercept is the zero of $p(x)$: 0

(b) The y-intercept is $R(0) = \dfrac{0^2}{0^2 + 0 - 6} = \dfrac{0}{-6} = 0$.

Step 3: $R(-x) = \dfrac{(-x)^2}{(-x)^2 + (-x) - 6} = \dfrac{x^2}{x^2 - x - 6}$; this is neither $R(x)$ nor $-R(x)$, so there is no symmetry.

Step 4: The vertical asymptotes are the zeros of $q(x)$: $x = -3$ and $x = 2$

Step 5: Since $n = m$, the line $y = 1$ is the horizontal asymptote.

$R(x)$ intersects $y = 1$ at $(6, 1)$, since:

$$\frac{x^2}{x^2 + x - 6} = 1 \rightarrow x^2 = x^2 + x - 6 \rightarrow 0 = x - 6 \rightarrow x = 6$$

Step 6: Graphing:

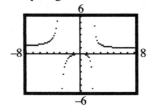

Step 7: Graphing by hand:

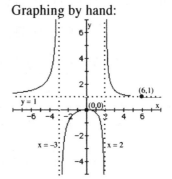

13. $G(x) = \dfrac{x}{x^2 - 4} = \dfrac{x}{(x+2)(x-2)}$ $p(x) = x$; $q(x) = x^2 - 4$; $n = 1$; $m = 2$

Step 1: Domain: $\{x \mid x \ne -2, x \ne 2\}$

Step 2: (a) The x-intercept is the zero of $p(x)$: 0

(b) The y-intercept is $G(0) = \dfrac{0}{0^2 - 4} = \dfrac{0}{-4} = 0$.

Step 3: $G(-x) = \dfrac{-x}{(-x)^2 - 4} = \dfrac{-x}{x^2 - 4} = -G(x)$; $G(x)$ is symmetric to the origin.

Step 4: The vertical asymptotes are the zeros of $q(x)$: $x = -2$ and $x = 2$

Step 5: Since $n < m$, the line $y = 0$ is the horizontal asymptote.

$G(x)$ intersects $y = 0$ at $(0, 0)$.

Step 6:   Graphing:

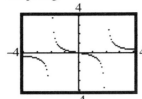

Step 7:   Graphing by hand:

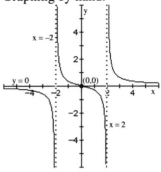

15. $R(x) = \dfrac{3}{(x-1)(x^2-4)} = \dfrac{3}{(x-1)(x+2)(x-2)}$ $p(x) = 3;\ q(x) = (x-1)(x^2-4);$
$n = 0;\ m = 3$

Step 1:   Domain: $\{x \mid x \neq -2,\ x \neq 1,\ x \neq 2\}$

Step 2:   (a)   There is no x-intercept.

(b)   The y-intercept is $R(0) = \dfrac{3}{(0-1)(0^2-4)} = \dfrac{3}{4}$.

Step 3: $R(-x) = \dfrac{3}{(-x-1)\big((-x)^2-4\big)} = \dfrac{3}{(-x-1)(x^2-4)}$; this is neither $R(x)$ nor $-R(x)$,

so there is no symmetry.

Step 4:   The vertical asymptotes are the zeros of $q(x)$: $x = -2$, $x = 1$, and $x = 2$

Step 5:   Since $n < m$, the line $y = 0$ is the horizontal asymptote.
$R(x)$ does not intersect $y = 0$.

Step 6:   Graphing:

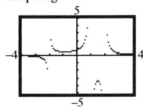

Step 7:   Graphing by hand:

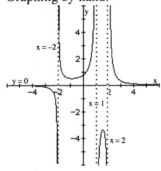

17. $H(x) = \dfrac{4(x^2-1)}{x^4-16} = \dfrac{4(x-1)(x+1)}{(x^2+4)(x+2)(x-2)}$ $p(x) = 4(x^2-1);\ q(x) = x^4-16;$
$n = 2;\ m = 4$

Step 1:   Domain: $\{x \mid x \neq -2,\ x \neq 2\}$

Step 2:   (a)   The x-intercepts are the zeros of $p(x)$: -1 and 1

(b)   The y-intercept is $H(0) = \dfrac{4(0^2-1)}{0^4-16} = \dfrac{-4}{-16} = \dfrac{1}{4}$.

Step 3: $H(-x) = \dfrac{4\big((-x)^2-1\big)}{(-x)^4-16} = \dfrac{4(x^2-1)}{x^4-16} = H(x);\ H(x)$ is symmetric to the y-axis.

Step 4:   The vertical asymptotes are the zeros of $q(x)$: $x = -2$, and $x = 2$

Step 5:   Since $n < m$, the line $y = 0$ is the horizontal asymptote.

$H(x)$ intersects $y = 0$ at $(-1, 0)$ and $(1, 0)$.

Step 6:   Graphing: Step 7:   Graphing by hand:

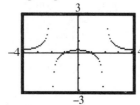   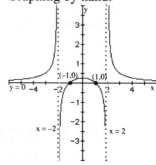

19. $F(x) = \dfrac{x^2 - 3x - 4}{x + 2} = \dfrac{(x + 1)(x - 4)}{x + 2}$ $p(x) = x^2 - 3x - 4$; $q(x) = x + 2$; $n = 2$; $m = 1$

Step 1:   Domain: $\{x \mid x \neq -2\}$

Step 2:   (a)   The x-intercepts are the zeros of $p(x)$: -1 and 4.

(b)   The y-intercept is $F(0) = \dfrac{0^2 - 3(0) - 4}{0 + 2} = \dfrac{-4}{2} = -2$.

Step 3: $F(-x) = \dfrac{(-x)^2 - 3(-x) - 4}{-x + 2} = \dfrac{x^2 + 3x - 4}{-x + 2}$; this is neither $F(x)$ nor $-F(x)$, so

there is no symmetry.

Step 4:   The vertical asymptote is the zero of $q(x)$: $x = -2$

Step 5:   Since $n = m + 1$, there is an oblique asymptote. Dividing:

$$
\begin{array}{r}
x - 5 \\
x + 2 \overline{) x^2 - 3x - 4} \\
\underline{x^2 + 2x } \\
-5x - 4 \\
\underline{-5x - 10} \\
6
\end{array}
\qquad F(x) = x - 5 + \dfrac{6}{x + 2}
$$

The oblique asymptote is $y = x - 5$.

Solve to find intersection points:

$$\dfrac{x^2 - 3x - 4}{x + 2} = x - 5 \rightarrow x^2 - 3x - 4 = x^2 - 3x - 10 \rightarrow -4 = -10$$

Since there is no solution, the oblique asymptote does not intersect $F(x)$.

Step 6:   Graphing:

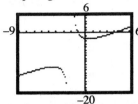

Step 7:   Graphing by hand:

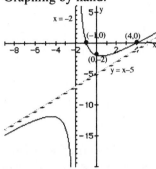

21. $R(x) = \dfrac{x^2 + x - 12}{x - 4} = \dfrac{(x+4)(x-3)}{x-4}$ $p(x) = x^2 + x - 12;\ q(x) = x - 4;\ n = 2;\ m = 1$

Step 1:   Domain: $\{x \mid x \neq 4\}$

Step 2:   (a)   The x-intercepts are the zeros of $p(x)$: -4 and 3.

        (b)   The y-intercept is $R(0) = \dfrac{0^2 + 0 - 12}{0 - 4} = \dfrac{-12}{-4} = 3$.

Step 3: $R(-x) = \dfrac{(-x)^2 + (-x) - 12}{-x - 4} = \dfrac{x^2 - x - 12}{-x - 4}$; this is neither $R(x)$ nor $-R(x)$, so there is no symmetry.

Step 4:   The vertical asymptote is the zero of $q(x)$: $x = 4$

Step 5:   Since $n = m + 1$, there is an oblique asymptote. Dividing:

$$
\begin{array}{r}
x + 5 \\
x - 4 \overline{)\, x^2 + \ x - 12} \\
\underline{x^2 - 4x} \\
5x - \ 12 \\
\underline{5x - 20} \\
8
\end{array}
\qquad R(x) = x + 5 + \dfrac{8}{x - 4}
$$

The oblique asymptote is $y = x + 5$.

Solve to find intersection points:

$$\dfrac{x^2 + x - 12}{x - 4} = x + 5$$

$$x^2 + x - 12 = x^2 + x - 20$$

$$-12 = -20$$

Since there is no solution, the oblique asymptote does not intersect $R(x)$.

Step 6:   Graphing:

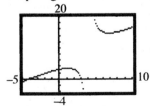

Step 7:   Graphing by hand:

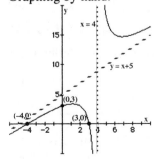

23. $F(x) = \dfrac{x^2 + x - 12}{x + 2} = \dfrac{(x+4)(x-3)}{x+2}$ $p(x) = x^2 + x - 12;\ q(x) = x + 2;\ n = 2;\ m = 1$

Step 1:   Domain: $\{x \mid x \neq -2\}$

Step 2:   (a)   The x-intercepts are the zeros of $p(x)$: -4 and 3.

(b)   The y-intercept is $F(0) = \dfrac{0^2 + 0 - 12}{0 + 2} = \dfrac{-12}{2} = -6$.

Step 3: $F(-x) = \dfrac{(-x)^2 + (-x) - 12}{-x + 2} = \dfrac{x^2 - x - 12}{-x + 2}$; this is neither $F(x)$ nor $-F(x)$, so there is no symmetry.

Step 4:   The vertical asymptote is the zero of $q(x)$: $x = -2$

Step 5:   Since $n = m + 1$, there is an oblique asymptote. Dividing:

$$\begin{array}{r} x - 1 \\ x + 2 \overline{)x^2 + \ x - 12} \\ \underline{x^2 + 2x} \\ -x - 12 \\ \underline{-x - 2} \\ -10 \end{array} \qquad F(x) = x - 1 + \dfrac{-10}{x + 2}$$

The oblique asymptote is $y = x - 1$.

Solve to find intersection points:

$$\dfrac{x^2 + x - 12}{x + 2} = x - 1 \to x^2 + x - 12 = x^2 + x - 2 \to -12 = -2$$

Since there is no solution, the oblique asymptote does not intersect $F(x)$.

Step 6:   Graphing:

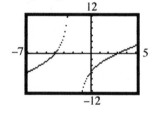

Step 7:   Graphing by hand:

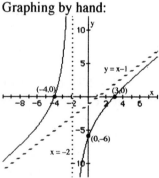

25. $R(x) = \dfrac{x(x-1)^2}{(x+3)^3}$ $p(x) = x(x-1)^2;\ q(x) = (x+3)^3;\ n = 3;\ m = 3$

Step 1:   Domain: $\{x \mid x \neq -3\}$

Step 2:   (a)   The x-intercepts are the zeros of $p(x)$: 0 and 1

(b)   The y-intercept is $R(0) = \dfrac{0(0-1)^2}{(0+3)^3} = \dfrac{0}{27} = 0$.

Step 3: $R(-x) = \dfrac{-x(-x-1)^2}{(-x+3)^3}$; this is neither $R(x)$ nor $-R(x)$, so there is no symmetry.

Step 4:   The vertical asymptote is the zero of $q(x)$: $x = -3$

Step 5:   Since $n = m$, the line $y = 1$ is the horizontal asymptote.

Solve to find intersection points:

$$\frac{x(x-1)^2}{(x+3)^3} = 1 \rightarrow x^3 - 2x^2 + x = x^3 + 9x^2 + 27x + 27$$

$$0 = 11x^2 + 26x + 27$$

Since there is no real solution, $R(x)$ does not intersect $y = 1$.

Step 6:   Graphing:

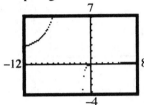

Step 7:   Graphing by hand:

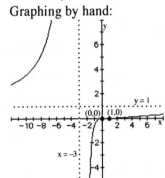

27. $R(x) = \dfrac{x^2 + x - 12}{x^2 - x - 6} = \dfrac{(x+4)(x-3)}{(x-3)(x+2)} = \dfrac{x+4}{x+2}$ $p(x) = x^2 + x - 12;\ q(x) = x^2 - x - 6;$

$n = 2;\ m = 2$

Step 1:   Domain: $\left\{x \mid x \neq -2, x \neq 3\right\}$

Step 2:   (a)   The x-intercept is the zero of $p(x)$: -4 (3 is not a zero because reduced form must be used to find the zeros.)

(b)   The y-intercept is $R(0) = \dfrac{0^2 + 0 - 12}{0^2 - 0 - 6} = \dfrac{-12}{-6} = 2$.

Step 3: $R(-x) = \dfrac{(-x)^2 + (-x) - 12}{(-x)^2 - (-x) - 6} = \dfrac{x^2 - x - 12}{x^2 + x - 6}$; this is neither $R(x)$ nor $-R(x)$, so there is no symmetry.

Step 4:   The vertical asymptote is the zero of $q(x)$: $x = -2$ ($x = 3$ is not a vertical asymptote because reduced form must be used to find the them.)

Step 5:   Since $n = m$, the line $y = 1$ is the horizontal asymptote.

$R(x)$ does not intersect $y = 1$ because $R(x)$ is not defined at $x = 3$.

$$\frac{x^2 + x - 12}{x^2 - x - 6} = 1 \rightarrow x^2 + x - 12 = x^2 - x - 6$$

$$2x = 6 \rightarrow x = 3$$

Step 6:   Graphing:

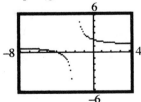

Step 7:   Graphing by hand:

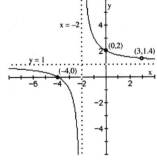

29.　$R(x) = \dfrac{6x^2 - 7x - 3}{2x^2 - 7x + 6} = \dfrac{(3x+1)(2x-3)}{(2x-3)(x-2)} = \dfrac{3x+1}{x-2}$　$p(x) = 6x^2 - 7x - 3;$

$q(x) = 2x^2 - 7x + 6;$　$n = 2;$　$m = 2$

Step 1:　Domain: $\left\{x \,\middle|\, x \neq \dfrac{3}{2},\, x \neq 2\right\}$

Step 2:　(a)　The x-intercept is the zero of $p(x)$: $-\dfrac{1}{3}$　($\dfrac{3}{2}$ is not a zero because reduced

form must be used to find the zeros.)

(b)　The y-intercept is $R(0) = \dfrac{6(0)^2 - 7(0) - 3}{2(0)^2 - 7(0) + 6} = \dfrac{-3}{6} = \dfrac{-1}{2}$.

Step 3:　$R(-x) = \dfrac{6(-x)^2 - 7(-x) - 3}{2(-x)^2 - 7(-x) + 6} = \dfrac{6x^2 + 7x - 3}{2x^2 + 7x + 6}$; this is neither $R(x)$ nor $-R(x)$, so

there is no symmetry.

Step 4:　The vertical asymptote is the zero of $q(x)$: $x = 2$　($x = \dfrac{3}{2}$ is not a vertical

asymptote because reduced form must be used to find the them.)

Step 5:　Since $n = m$, the line $y = 3$ is the horizontal asymptote.

$R(x)$ does not intersect $y = 3$ because $R(x)$ is not defined at $x = \dfrac{3}{2}$.

$$\dfrac{6x^2 - 7x - 3}{2x^2 - 7x + 6} = 3$$

$$6x^2 - 7x - 3 = 6x^2 - 21x + 18$$

$$14x = 21$$

$$x = \dfrac{3}{2}$$

Step 6:　Graphing:

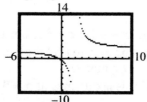

Step 7:　Graphing by hand:

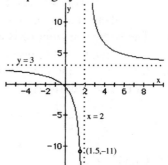

31.　$R(x) = \dfrac{x^2 + 5x + 6}{x + 3} = \dfrac{(x+2)(x+3)}{x+3} = x + 2$　$p(x) = x^2 + 5x + 6;$　$q(x) = x + 3;$

$n = 2;$　$m = 1$

Step 1:　Domain: $\left\{x \,\middle|\, x \neq -3\right\}$

Step 2:　(a)　The x-intercept is the zero of $p(x)$: -2　(-3 is not a zero because reduced

form must be used to find the zeros.)

(b)　The y-intercept is $R(0) = \dfrac{0^2 + 5(0) + 6}{0 + 3} = \dfrac{6}{3} = 2$.

Step 3: $R(-x) = \dfrac{(-x)^2 + 5(-x) + 6}{-x + 3} = \dfrac{x^2 - 5x + 6}{-x + 3}$; this is neither $R(x)$ nor $-R(x)$, so there is no symmetry.

Step 4:   There are no vertical asymptotes. ($x = -3$ is not a vertical asymptote because reduced form must be used to find the them.)

Step 5:   Since $n = m + 1$ there is a oblique asymptote. The line $y = x + 2$ is the oblique asymptote.

The oblique asymptote does not intersect $R(x)$.

Step 6:   Graphing:

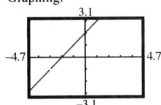

Step 7:   Graphing by hand:

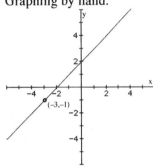

33. $f(x) = x + \dfrac{1}{x} = \dfrac{x^2 + 1}{x}$ $p(x) = x^2 + 1$; $q(x) = x$; $n = 2$; $m = 1$

Step 1:   Domain: $\{x \mid x \neq 0\}$

Step 2:   (a)   There are no x-intercepts.

         (b)   There is no y-intercept because 0 is not in the domain.

Step 3: $f(-x) = \dfrac{(-x)^2 + 1}{-x} = \dfrac{x^2 + 1}{-x} = -f(x)$; The graph of $f(x)$ is symmetric to the origin.

Step 4:   The vertical asymptote is the zero of $q(x)$: $x = 0$

Step 5:   Since $n = m + 1$, there is an oblique asymptote. Dividing:

$$\begin{array}{r} x \\ x \overline{) x^2 + 1} \\ \underline{x^2} \\ 1 \end{array}$$

$f(x) = x + \dfrac{1}{x}$

The oblique asymptote is $y = x$.

Solve to find intersection points:

$$\dfrac{x^2 + 1}{x} = x \rightarrow x^2 + 1 = x^2 \rightarrow 1 = 0$$

Since there is no solution, the oblique asymptote does not intersect $f(x)$.

Step 6: Graphing: Step 7:   Graphing by hand:

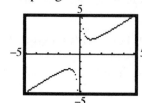

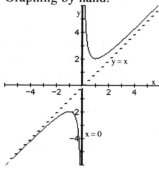

35. $f(x) = x^2 + \dfrac{1}{x} = \dfrac{x^3+1}{x}$ $p(x) = x^3 + 1;$ $q(x) = x;$ $n = 3;$ $m = 1$

Step 1: Domain: $\{x \mid x \neq 0\}$

Step 2: (a)   The x-intercept is the zero of $p(x)$: -1

(b)   There is no y-intercept because 0 is not in the domain.

Step 3: $f(-x) = \dfrac{(-x)^3 + 1}{-x} = \dfrac{-x^3 + 1}{-x}$; this is neither $f(x)$ nor $-f(x)$, so there is no symmetry.

Step 4: The vertical asymptote is the zero of $q(x)$: $x = 0$

Step 5: Since $n > m + 1$, there is no horizontal or oblique asymptote.

Step 6: Graphing: Step 7:   Graphing by hand:

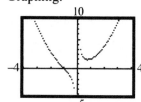

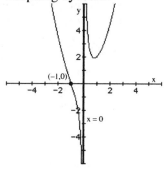

37. $f(x) = x + \dfrac{1}{x^3} = \dfrac{x^4+1}{x^3}$ $p(x) = x^4 + 1;$ $q(x) = x^3;$ $n = 4;$ $m = 3$

Step 1: Domain: $\{x \mid x \neq 0\}$

Step 2: (a)   There are no x-intercepts.

(b)   There is no y-intercept because 0 is not in the domain.

Step 3: $f(-x) = \dfrac{(-x)^4 + 1}{(-x)^3} = \dfrac{x^4 + 1}{-x^3} = -f(x)$; The graph of $f(x)$ is symmetric to the origin.

Step 4: The vertical asymptote is the zero of $q(x)$: $x = 0$

Step 5: Since $n = m + 1$, there is an oblique asymptote. Dividing:

$$f(x) = x + \dfrac{1}{x^3}$$

The oblique asymptote is $y = x$.

Solve to find intersection points:

$$\frac{x^4+1}{x^3} = x \rightarrow x^4 + 1 = x^4 \rightarrow 1 = 0$$

Since there is no solution, the oblique asymptote does not intersect $f(x)$.

Step 6:   Graphing: Step 7:   Graphing by hand:

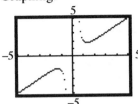   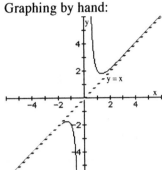

39. $f(x) = \dfrac{x^2}{x^2 - 4}$ 41. $f(x) = \dfrac{(x-1)^3(x-3)}{(x+1)^2(x-2)^2}$

43.   (a) $C(t) = \dfrac{t}{2t^2 + 1} \approx \dfrac{t}{2t^2} = \dfrac{1}{2t} \rightarrow 0$ as $t \rightarrow \pm\infty$

therefore the horizontal asymptote is $y = 0$.

The concentration of the drug decreases to 0 as time increases.

(b)   Graphing:

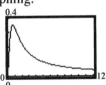

(c)   Using MAXIMUM, the concentration is highest when $t = 0.71$ hours.

45.   (a)   The average cost function is: $\overline{C}(x) = \dfrac{0.2x^3 - 2.3x^2 + 14.3x + 10.2}{x}$

(b) $\overline{C}(6) = \dfrac{0.2(6)^3 - 2.3(6)^2 + 14.3(6) + 10.2}{6} = \dfrac{56.4}{6} = 9.4$

The average cost of producing 6 Cavaliers per hour is $9400.

(c) $\overline{C}(9) = \dfrac{0.2(9)^3 - 2.3(9)^2 + 14.3(9) + 10.2}{9} = \dfrac{98.4}{9} = 10.933$

The average cost of producing 9 Cavaliers per hour is $10,933.

(d)   Graphing:

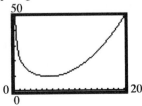

   (e)   Using MINIMUM, the number of Cavaliers that should be produced per hour to minimize cost is 6.38.

   (f)   The minimum average cost is $9,366.

47.   (a)   The surface area is the sum of the areas of the six sides.
$$S = xy + xy + xy + xy + x^2 + x^2 = 4xy + 2x^2$$
The volume is $x \cdot x \cdot y = x^2 y = 10{,}000 \quad \rightarrow \quad y = \dfrac{10000}{x^2}$

Thus, $S(x) = 4x\left(\dfrac{10000}{x^2}\right) + 2x^2 = 2x^2 + \dfrac{40000}{x} = \dfrac{2x^3 + 40000}{x}$

   (b)   Graphing:

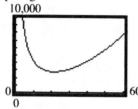

   (c)   The minimum surface area (amount of cardboard) is 2,785 square inches.

   (d)   The surface area is a minimum when $x = 21.544$.
$$y = \dfrac{10000}{21.544^2} = 21.545$$
The dimensions of the box are: 21.544 in. by 21.544 in. by 21.545 in.

49.   (a) $500 = \pi r^2 h \quad \rightarrow \quad h = \dfrac{500}{\pi r^2}$

$$C(r) = 6(2\pi r^2) + 4(2\pi rh) = 12\pi r^2 + 8\pi r\left(\dfrac{500}{\pi r^2}\right) = 12\pi r^2 + \dfrac{4000}{r}$$

   (b)   Graphing:

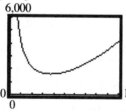

          The cost is least for $r = 3.76$ cm.

51.

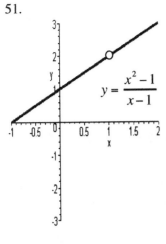

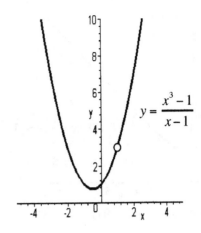

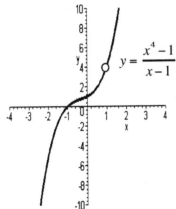

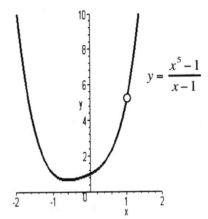

x = 1 is not a vertical asymptote because of the following behavior:

$$y = \frac{x^2 - 1}{x - 1} = \frac{(x+1)(x-1)}{x-1} = x + 1 \text{ when } x \neq 1$$

$$y = \frac{x^3 - 1}{x - 1} = \frac{(x-1)(x^2 + x + 1)}{x-1} = x^2 + x + 1 \text{ when } x \neq 1$$

$$y = \frac{x^4 - 1}{x - 1} = \frac{(x^2 + 1)(x^2 - 1)}{x-1} = \frac{(x^2 + 1)(x-1)(x+1)}{x-1} = x^3 + x^2 + x + 1 \text{ when } x \neq 1$$

$$y = \frac{x^5 - 1}{x - 1} = \frac{(x^4 + x^3 + x^2 + x + 1)(x-1)}{x-1} = x^4 + x^3 + x^2 + x + 1 \text{ when } x \neq 1$$

In general, the graph of $y = \dfrac{x^n - 1}{x - 1}, n \geq 1$ an integer will have a "hole" with coordinates $(1, n)$.

53.

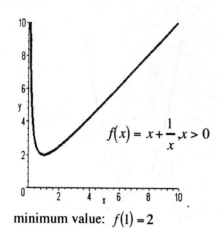

$$f(x) = x + \frac{1}{x}, x > 0$$

minimum value: $f(1) = 2$

55.

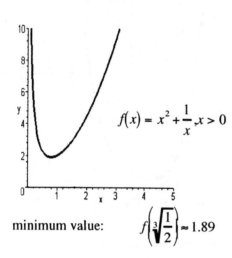

$$f(x) = x^2 + \frac{1}{x}, x > 0$$

minimum value: $f\left(\sqrt[3]{\frac{1}{2}}\right) \approx 1.89$

57.

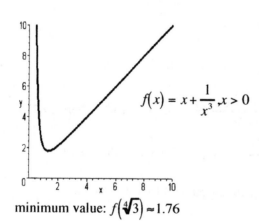

$$f(x) = x + \frac{1}{x^3}, x > 0$$

minimum value: $f\left(\sqrt[4]{3}\right) \approx 1.76$

59.   Answers will vary.

61.   Answers will vary, one example is $R(x) = \dfrac{2(x-3)(x+2)^2}{(x-1)^3}$

Chapter 4

Polynomial and Rational Functions

4.5 Polynomial and Rational Inequalities

1. $(x-5)(x+2) < 0$ $\qquad f(x) = (x-5)(x+2)$
    $x = 5, x = -2$ are the zeros.

Interval	Test Number	$f(x)$	Positive/Negative
$-\infty < x < -2$	-3	8	Positive
$-2 < x < 5$	0	-10	Negative
$5 < x < \infty$	6	8	Positive

The solution set is $\left\{ x \mid -2 < x < 5 \right\}$

3. $x^2 - 4x \geq 0$ $\qquad\qquad f(x) = x^2 - 4x$
    $x(x-4) \geq 0$
    $x = 0, x = 4$ are the zeros.

Interval	Test Number	$f(x)$	Positive/Negative
$-\infty < x < 0$	-1	5	Positive
$0 < x < 4$	1	-3	Negative
$4 < x < \infty$	5	5	Positive

The solution set is $\left\{ x \mid x \leq 0 \text{ or } x \geq 4 \right\}$.

5. $x^2 - 9 < 0$ $\qquad\qquad f(x) = x^2 - 9$
    $(x+3)(x-3) < 0;$ $\qquad x = -3, x = 3$ are the zeros.

Interval	Test Number	$f(x)$	Positive/Negative
$-\infty < x < -3$	-4	7	Positive
$-3 < x < 3$	0	-9	Negative
$3 < x < \infty$	4	7	Positive

The solution set is $\left\{ x \mid -3 < x < 3 \right\}$.

7. $x^2 + x \geq 2$ $\qquad f(x) = x^2 + x - 2$
    $x^2 + x - 2 \geq 0 \rightarrow (x+2)(x-1) \geq 0$
    $\qquad\qquad\qquad x = -2, x = 1$ are the zeros.

Interval	Test Number	$f(x)$	Positive/Negative
$-\infty < x < -2$	-5	18	Positive
$-2 < x < 1$	0	-2	Negative
	4	18	Positive
$1 < x < \infty$			

The solution set is $\left\{ x \mid x \leq -2 \text{ or } x \geq 1 \right\}$.

9. $2x^2 \le 5x + 3$ $f(x) = 2x^2 - 5x - 3$

$$2x^2 - 5x - 3 \le 0 \to (2x + 1)(x - 3) \le 0$$

$x = -\dfrac{1}{2}, x = 3$ are the zeros.

Interval	Test Number	$f(x)$	Positive/Negative
$-\infty < x < -1/2$	-1	4	Positive
$-1/2 < x < 3$	0	-3	Negative
$3 < x < \infty$	4	9	Positive

The solution set is $\left\{ x \middle| -\dfrac{1}{2} \le x \le 3 \right\}$.

11. $x(x - 7) > 8$ $f(x) = x^2 - 7x - 8$

$$x^2 - 7x > 8 \to x^2 - 7x - 8 > 0 \to (x + 1)(x - 8) > 0$$

$x = -1, x = 8$ are the zeros.

Interval	Test Number	$f(x)$	Positive/Negative
$-\infty < x < -1$	-2	10	Positive
$-1 < x < 8$	0	-8	Negative
$8 < x < \infty$	9	10	Positive

The solution set is $\left\{ x \middle| x < -1 \text{ or } x > 8 \right\}$.

13. $4x^2 + 9 < 6x$ $f(x) = 4x^2 - 6x + 9$

$$4x^2 - 6x + 9 < 0$$

$$b^2 - 4ac = (-6)^2 - 4(4)(9) = 36 - 144 = -108$$

Since the discriminant is negative, there are no real zeros.
There is only one interval, the entire number line; choose any value and test.
For $x = 0$, $4x^2 - 6x + 9 = 9 > 0$. Thus, there are no real zeros.

15. $6(x^2 - 1) > 5x$ $f(x) = 6x^2 - 5x - 6$

$$6x^2 - 6 > 5x \to 6x^2 - 5x - 6 > 0 \to (3x + 2)(2x - 3) > 0$$

$x = -\dfrac{2}{3}, x = \dfrac{3}{2}$ are the zeros.

Interval	Test Number	$f(x)$	Positive/Negative
$-\infty < x < -2/3$	-1	5	Positive
$-2/3 < x < 3/2$	0	-6	Negative
$3/2 < x < \infty$	2	8	Positive

The solution set is $\left\{ x \middle| x < -\dfrac{2}{3} \text{ or } x > \dfrac{3}{2} \right\}$.

17. $(x-1)(x^2+x+4) \ge 0$ $f(x) = (x-1)(x^2+x+4)$

$x = 1$ is the zero. $x^2+x+4 = 0$ has no real zeros.

Interval	Test Number	$f(x)$	Positive/Negative
$-\infty < x < 1$	0	-4	Negative
$1 < x < \infty$	2	10	Positive

The solution set is $\{x \mid x \ge 1\}$.

19. $(x-1)(x-2)(x-3) \le 0$ $f(x) = (x-1)(x-2)(x-3)$

$x = 1$, $x = 2$, $x = 3$ are the zeros.

Interval	Test Number	$f(x)$	Positive/Negative
$-\infty < x < 1$	0	-6	Negative
$1 < x < 2$	1.5	0.375	Positive
$2 < x < 3$	2.5	-0.375	Negative
$3 < x < \infty$	4	6	Positive

The solution set is $\{x \mid x \le 1 \text{ or } 2 \le x \le 3\}$.

21. $x^3 - 2x^2 - 3x > 0$ $f(x) = x^3 - 2x^2 - 3x$

$x(x^2 - 2x - 3) > 0 \rightarrow x(x+1)(x-3) > 0$

$x = -1$, $x = 0$, $x = 3$ are the zeros.

Interval	Test Number	$f(x)$	Positive/Negative
$-\infty < x < -1$	-2	-10	Negative
$-1 < x < 0$	-0.5	0.875	Positive
$0 < x < 3$	1	-4	Negative
$3 < x < \infty$	4	20	Positive

The solution set is $\{x \mid -1 < x < 0 \text{ or } x > 3\}$.

23. $x^4 > x^2$ $f(x) = x^4 - x^2$

$x^4 - x^2 > 0 \rightarrow x^2(x^2 - 1) > 0 \rightarrow x^2(x+1)(x-1) > 0$

$x = -1$, $x = 0$, $x = 1$ are the zeros.

Interval	Test Number	$f(x)$	Positive/Negative
$-\infty < x < -1$	-2	12	Positive
$-1 < x < 0$	-0.5	-0.1875	Negative
$0 < x < 1$	0.5	-0.1875	Negative
$1 < x < \infty$	2	12	Positive

The solution set is $\{x \mid x < -1 \text{ or } x > 1\}$.

25. $x^3 \ge 4x^2$ $f(x) = x^3 - 4x^2$

$x^3 - 4x^2 \ge 0 \rightarrow x^2(x-4) \ge 0$

$x = 0$, $x = 4$ are the zeros.

Interval	Test Number	$f(x)$	Positive/Negative
$-\infty < x < 0$	-1	-3	Negative
$0 < x < 4$	0.5	-0.875	Negative
$4 < x < \infty$	5	25	Positive

The solution set is $\{x \mid x \ge 4\}$.

27. $x^4 > 1$ $f(x) = x^4 - 1$

$x^4 - 1 > 0 \rightarrow (x^2 + 1)(x^2 - 1) > 0 \rightarrow (x^2 + 1)(x + 1)(x - 1) > 0$

$x = -1$, $x = 1$ are the zeros.

Interval	Test Number	$f(x)$	Positive/Negative
$-\infty < x < -1$	-2	15	Positive
$-1 < x < 1$	0	-1	Negative
$1 < x < \infty$	2	15	Positive

The solution set is $\left\{ x \mid x < -1 \text{ or } x > 1 \right\}$.

29. $\dfrac{x+1}{x-1} > 0$ $f(x) = \dfrac{x+1}{x-1}$

The zeros and values where the expression is undefined are $x = -1$, and $x = 1$.

Interval	Test Number	$f(x)$	Positive/Negative
$-\infty < x < -1$	-2	1/3	Positive
$-1 < x < 1$	0	-1	Negative
$1 < x < \infty$	2	3	Positive

The solution set is $\left\{ x \mid x < -1 \text{ or } x > 1 \right\}$.

31. $\dfrac{(x-1)(x+1)}{x} < 0$ $f(x) = \dfrac{(x-1)(x+1)}{x}$

The zeros and values where the expression is undefined are $x = -1$, $x = 0$, and $x = 1$.

Interval	Test Number	$f(x)$	Positive/Negative
$-\infty < x < -1$	-2	-1.5	Negative
$-1 < x < 0$	-0.5	1.5	Positive
$0 < x < 1$	0.5	-1.5	Negative
$1 < x < \infty$	2	1.5	Positive

The solution set is $\left\{ x \mid x < -1 \text{ or } 0 < x < 1 \right\}$.

33. $\dfrac{(x-2)^2}{x^2 - 1} \geq 0$ $f(x) = \dfrac{(x-2)^2}{x^2 - 1}$

$\dfrac{(x-2)^2}{(x+1)(x-1)} \geq 0$

The zeros and values where the expression is undefined are $x = -1$, $x = 1$, and $x = 2$.

Interval	Test Number	$f(x)$	Positive/Negative
$-\infty < x < -1$	-2	16/3	Positive
$-1 < x < 1$	0	-4	Negative
$1 < x < 2$	1.5	0.2	Positive
$2 < x < \infty$	3	0.125	Positive

The solution set is $\left\{ x \mid x < -1 \text{ or } x > 1 \right\}$.

35. $6x - 5 < \dfrac{6}{x}$ $f(x) = 6x - 5 - \dfrac{6}{x}$

$6x - 5 - \dfrac{6}{x} < 0 \rightarrow \dfrac{6x^2 - 5x - 6}{x} < 0 \rightarrow \dfrac{(2x - 3)(3x + 2)}{x} < 0$

The zeros and values where the expression is undefined are $x = \frac{-2}{3}$, $x = 0$, and $x = \frac{3}{2}$.

Interval	Test Number	$f(x)$	Positive/Negative
$-\infty < x < -2/3$	-1	-5	Negative
$-2/3 < x < 0$	-0.5	4	Positive
$0 < x < 3/2$	1	-5	Negative
$3/2 < x < \infty$	2	4	Positive

The solution set is $\left\{ x \mid x < \frac{-2}{3} \text{ or } 0 < x < \frac{3}{2} \right\}$.

37. $\dfrac{x+4}{x-2} \le 1$ $f(x) = \dfrac{x+4}{x-2} - 1$

$\dfrac{x+4}{x-2} - 1 \le 0 \rightarrow \dfrac{x+4-(x-2)}{x-2} \le 0 \rightarrow \dfrac{6}{x-2} \le 0$

The value where the expression is undefined is $x = 2$.

Interval	Test Number	$f(x)$	Positive/Negative
$-\infty < x < 2$	0	-3	Negative
$2 < x < \infty$	3	6	Positive

The solution set is $\left\{ x \mid x < 2 \right\}$.

39. $\dfrac{3x-5}{x+2} \le 2$ $f(x) = \dfrac{3x-5}{x+2} - 2$

$\dfrac{3x-5}{x+2} - 2 \le 0 \rightarrow \dfrac{3x-5-2(x+2)}{x+2} \le 0 \rightarrow \dfrac{x-9}{x+2} \le 0$

The zeros and values where the expression is undefined are $x = -2$, and $x = 9$.

Interval	Test Number	$f(x)$	Positive/Negative
$-\infty < x < -2$	-3	12	Positive
$-2 < x < 9$	0	-4.5	Negative
$9 < x < \infty$	10	$1/12$	Positive

The solution set is $\left\{ x \mid -2 < x \le 9 \right\}$.

41. $\dfrac{1}{x-2} < \dfrac{2}{3x-9}$ $f(x) = \dfrac{1}{x+2} - \dfrac{2}{3x-9}$

$\dfrac{1}{x-2} - \dfrac{2}{3x-9} < 0 \rightarrow \dfrac{3x-9-2(x-2)}{(x-2)(3x-9)} < 0 \rightarrow \dfrac{x-5}{(x-2)(3x-9)} < 0$

The zeros and values where the expression is undefined are $x = 2$, $x = 3$, and $x = 5$.

Interval	Test Number	$f(x)$	Positive/Negative
$-\infty < x < 2$	0	$-5/18$	Negative
$2 < x < 3$	2.5	$10/3$	Positive
$3 < x < 5$	4	$-1/6$	Negative
$5 < x < \infty$	6	$1/36$	Positive

The solution set is $\left\{ x \mid x < 2 \text{ or } 3 < x < 5 \right\}$.

43.

$$\frac{2x+5}{x+1} > \frac{x+1}{x-1} \qquad\qquad f(x) = \frac{2x+5}{x+1} - \frac{x+1}{x-1}$$

$$\frac{2x+5}{x+1} - \frac{x+1}{x-1} > 0 \rightarrow \frac{(2x+5)(x-1)-(x+1)(x+1)}{(x+1)(x-1)} > 0$$

$$\frac{2x^2+3x-5-\left(x^2+2x+1\right)}{(x+1)(x-1)} > 0 \rightarrow \frac{x^2+x-6}{(x+1)(x-1)} > 0 \rightarrow \frac{(x+3)(x-2)}{(x+1)(x-1)} > 0$$

The zeros and values where the expression is undefined are $x = -3, x = -1, x = 1, x = 2$.

Interval	Test Number	$f(x)$	Positive/Negative
$-\infty < x < -3$	-4	2/5	Positive
$-3 < x < -1$	-2	$-4/3$	Negative
$-1 < x < 1$	0	6	Positive
$1 < x < 2$	1.5	$-9/5$	Negative
$2 < x < \infty$	3	3/4	Positive

The solution set is $\left\{ x \mid x < -3, \ -1 < x < 1, \ x > 2 \right\}$.

45.

$$\frac{x^2(3+x)(x+4)}{(x+5)(x-1)} \geq 0 \qquad\qquad f(x) = \frac{x^2(3+x)(x+4)}{(x+5)(x-1)}$$

The zeros and values where the expression is undefined are
$x = -5, x = -4, x = -3, x = 0$ and $x = 1$.

Interval	Test Number	$f(x)$	Positive/Negative
$-\infty < x < -5$	-6	216/7	Positive
$-5 < x < -4$	-4.5	$-243/44$	Negative
$-4 < x < -3$	-3.5	49/108	Positive
$-3 < x < 0$	-1	$-3/4$	Negative
$0 < x < 1$	0.5	$-63/44$	Negative
$1 < x < \infty$	2	120/7	Positive

The solution set is

47. Let x be the positive number. Then

$$x^3 > 4x^2 \rightarrow x^3 - 4x^2 > 0 \rightarrow x^2(x-4) > 0$$

The zeros are $x = 0$ and $x = 4$. $f(x) = x^3 - 4x^2$

Interval	Test Number	$f(x)$	Positive/Negative
$-\infty < x < 0$	-1	-5	Negative
$0 < x < 4$	1	-3	Negative
$4 < x < \infty$	5	25	Positive

The solution set is $\left\{ x \mid x > 4 \right\}$. All real numbers larger than 4 satisfy the condition.

49. The domain of the expression includes all values for which

$$x^2 - 16 \geq 0 \rightarrow (x+4)(x-4) \geq 0$$

The zeros are $x = -4$ and $x = 4$. $f(x) = x^2 - 16$

Interval	Test Number	$f(x)$	Positive/Negative
$-\infty < x < -4$	-5	9	Positive
$-4 < x < 4$	0	-16	Negative
$4 < x < \infty$	5	9	Positive

The domain is $\left\{ x \mid x \leq -4 \text{ or } x \geq 4 \right\}$

51. The domain of the expression includes all values for which
$$\frac{x-2}{x+4} \geq 0$$
The zeros and values where the expression is undefined are $x = -4$ and $x = 2$.
$$f(x) = \frac{x-2}{x+4}$$

Interval	Test Number	$f(x)$	Positive/Negative
$-\infty < x < -4$	-5	7	Positive
$-4 < x < 2$	0	$-1/2$	Negative
$2 < x < \infty$	3	$1/7$	Positive

The domain is $\left\{ x \mid x < -4 \text{ or } x \geq 2 \right\}$.

53. Find the values of t for which
$$80t - 16t^2 > 96$$

$-16t^2 + 80t - 96 > 0 \rightarrow 16t^2 - 80t + 96 < 0 \rightarrow 16(t^2 - 5t + 6) < 0 \rightarrow 16(t-2)(t-3) < 0$

The zeros are $t = 2$ and $t = 3$. $s(t) = 16t^2 - 80t + 96$

Interval	Test Number	$s(t)$	Positive/Negative
$-\infty < t < 2$	1	32	Positive
$2 < t < 3$	2.5	-4	Negative
$3 < t < \infty$	4	32	Positive

The solution set is $\left\{ t \mid 2 < t < 3 \right\}$. The ball is more than 96 feet above the ground for times between 2 and 3 seconds.

55. Profit = Revenue – Cost
The zeros are approximately $x = 7.75$ and $x = 32.25$.
$$f(x) = x^2 - 40x + 250$$

Interval	Test Number	$f(x)$	Positive/Negative
$0 < x < 7.75$	7	19	Positive
$7.75 < x < 32.25$	10	-50	Negative
$32.25 < x < \infty$	40	250	Positive

The profit is at least \$50 when at least 8 and no more than 32 watches are sold.

57. The equation $x^2 + kx + 1 = 0$ has no real solutions whenever the discriminant is less than zero.
Solving $b^2 - 4ac = k^2 - 4 < 0 \rightarrow (k+4)(k-4) < 0$
The zeros are $k = -4$ and $k = 4$.
$$f(k) = k^2 - 4$$

Interval	Test Number	$f(x)$	Positive/Negative
$-\infty < k < -4$	-5	21	Positive
$-4 < k < 4$	0	-4	Negative
	5	21	Positive
$4 < k < \infty$			

Therefore the equation $x^2 + kx + 1 = 0$ has no real solutions whenever $-4 < k < 4$.

59. Answers will vary, for example,
$x^2 < 0$ has no real solution $x^2 \leq 0$ has exactly one real solution.

Polynomial and Rational Functions

4.R Chapter Review

1. $f(x) = (x-2)^2 + 2 = x^2 - 4x + 4 + 2 = x^2 - 4x + 6$

   $a = 1, b = -4, c = 6.$ Since $a = 1 > 0,$ the graph opens up.

   The x-coordinate of the vertex is $x = \dfrac{-b}{2a} = \dfrac{-(-4)}{2(1)} = \dfrac{4}{2} = 2.$

   The y-coordinate of the vertex is $f\!\left(\dfrac{-b}{2a}\right) = f(2) = (2)^2 - 4(2) + 6 = 2.$

   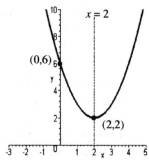

   Thus, the vertex is $(2, 2)$.
   The axis of symmetry is the line $x = 2.$
   The discriminant is:
   $$b^2 - 4ac = (-4)^2 - 4(1)(6) = -8 < 0,$$
   so the graph has no x-intercepts.
   The y-intercept is $f(0) = 6.$

3. $f(x) = \dfrac{1}{4}x^2 - 16$

   $a = \dfrac{1}{4}, b = 0, c = -16.$ Since $a = \dfrac{1}{4} > 0,$ the graph opens up.

   The x-coordinate of the vertex is
   $$x = \frac{-b}{2a} = \frac{-0}{2\left(\dfrac{1}{4}\right)} = \frac{0}{\left(\dfrac{1}{2}\right)} = 0$$

   The y-coordinate of the vertex is $f\!\left(\dfrac{-b}{2a}\right) = f(0) = \dfrac{1}{4}(0)^2 - 16 = -16.$

Thus, the vertex is $(0, -16)$.
The axis of symmetry is the line $x = 0$.
The discriminant is:

$$b^2 - 4ac = (0)^2 - 4\left(\frac{1}{4}\right)(-16) = 16 > 0,$$

so the graph has two x-intercepts.
The x-intercepts are found by solving:

$$\frac{1}{4}x^2 - 16 = 0$$

$$x^2 - 64 = 0 \rightarrow x^2 = 64 \rightarrow x = 8 \text{ or } x = -8$$

The x-intercepts are -8 and 8.
The y-intercept is $f(0) = -16$.

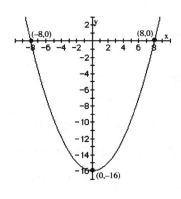

5. $f(x) = -4x^2 + 4x$
$a = -4, b = 4, c = 0$. Since $a = -4 < 0$, the graph opens down.
The x-coordinate of the vertex is $x = \dfrac{-b}{2a} = \dfrac{-4}{2(-4)} = \dfrac{-4}{-8} = \dfrac{1}{2}$.

The y-coordinate of the vertex is $f\left(\dfrac{-b}{2a}\right) = f\left(\dfrac{1}{2}\right) = -4\left(\dfrac{1}{2}\right)^2 + 4\left(\dfrac{1}{2}\right) = -1 + 2 = 1$.

Thus, the vertex is $\left(\dfrac{1}{2}, 1\right)$.

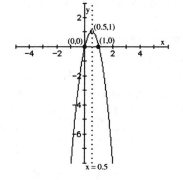

The axis of symmetry is the line $x = \dfrac{1}{2}$.
The discriminant is:

$$b^2 - 4ac = 4^2 - 4(-4)(0) = 16 > 0,$$

so the graph has two x-intercepts.
The x-intercepts are found by solving:
$-4x^2 + 4x = 0 \rightarrow -4x(x-1) = 0 \rightarrow x = 0 \text{ or } x = 1$
The x-intercepts are 0 and 1.
The y-intercept is $f(0) = -4(0)^2 + 4(0) = 0$.

7. $f(x) = \dfrac{9}{2}x^2 + 3x + 1$

$a = \dfrac{9}{2}, b = 3, c = 1$. Since $a = \dfrac{9}{2} > 0$, the graph opens up.

The x-coordinate of the vertex is $x = \dfrac{-b}{2a} = \dfrac{-3}{2\left(\dfrac{9}{2}\right)} = \dfrac{-3}{9} = -\dfrac{1}{3}$.

The y-coordinate of the vertex is $f\left(\dfrac{-b}{2a}\right) = f\left(-\dfrac{1}{3}\right) = \dfrac{9}{2}\left(-\dfrac{1}{3}\right)^2 + 3\left(-\dfrac{1}{3}\right) + 1 = \dfrac{1}{2} - 1 + 1 = \dfrac{1}{2}$.

Thus, the vertex is $\left(-\dfrac{1}{3}, \dfrac{1}{2}\right)$.

The axis of symmetry is the line $x = -\dfrac{1}{3}$.

The discriminant is:
$$b^2 - 4ac = 3^2 - 4\left(\dfrac{9}{2}\right)(1) = 9 - 18 = -9 < 0,$$

so the graph has no x-intercepts.

The y-intercept is $f(0) = \dfrac{9}{2}(0)^2 + 3(0) + 1 = 1$.

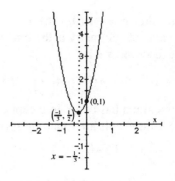

9. $f(x) = 3x^2 + 4x - 1$

$a = 3, b = 4, c = -1$. Since $a = 3 > 0$, the graph opens up.

The x-coordinate of the vertex is $x = \dfrac{-b}{2a} = \dfrac{-4}{2(3)} = \dfrac{-4}{6} = -\dfrac{2}{3}$.

The y-coordinate of the vertex is $f\left(\dfrac{-b}{2a}\right) = f\left(-\dfrac{2}{3}\right) = 3\left(-\dfrac{2}{3}\right)^2 + 4\left(-\dfrac{2}{3}\right) - 1 = \dfrac{4}{3} - \dfrac{8}{3} - 1 = -\dfrac{7}{3}$.

Thus, the vertex is $\left(-\dfrac{2}{3}, -\dfrac{7}{3}\right)$.

The axis of symmetry is the line $x = -\dfrac{2}{3}$.

The discriminant is:
$$b^2 - 4ac = (4)^2 - 4(3)(-1) = 16 + 12 = 28 > 0,$$

so the graph has two x-intercepts.

The x-intercepts are found by solving:
$$x = \dfrac{-b \pm \sqrt{b^2 - 4ac}}{2a} = \dfrac{-4 \pm \sqrt{28}}{2(3)}$$
$$= \dfrac{-4 \pm 2\sqrt{7}}{6} = \dfrac{-2 \pm \sqrt{7}}{3} \approx \dfrac{-2 \pm 2.646}{3}$$

The x-intercepts are approximately 0.22 and -1.55.

The y-intercept is $f(0) = 3(0)^2 + 4(0) - 1 = -1$.

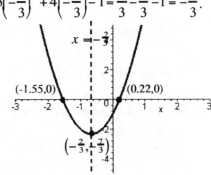

11. $f(x) = (x+2)^3$

Using the graph of $y = x^3$, shift the graph horizontally, 2 units to the left.

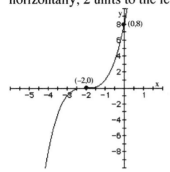

13. $f(x) = -(x-1)^4$

Using the graph of $y = x^4$, shift the graph horizontally, 1 unit right, and reflect about the x-axis.

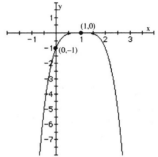

15. $f(x) = (x-1)^4 + 2$

Using the graph of $y = x^4$, shift the graph horizontally, 1 unit to the right, and shift vertically 2 units up.

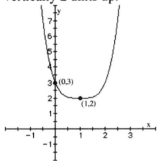

17. $f(x) = 3x^2 - 6x + 4$

$a = 3, b = -6, c = 4$. Since $a = 3 > 0$, the graph opens up, so the vertex is a minimum point. The minimum occurs at $x = \dfrac{-b}{2a} = \dfrac{-(-6)}{2(3)} = \dfrac{6}{6} = 1$. The minimum value is

$f\left(\dfrac{-b}{2a}\right) = f(1) = 3(1)^2 - 6(1) + 4 = 3 - 6 + 4 = 1$.

19. $f(x) = -x^2 + 8x - 4$

$a = -1, b = 8, c = -4$. Since $a = -1 < 0$, the graph opens down, so the vertex is a maximum point. The maximum occurs at $x = \dfrac{-b}{2a} = \dfrac{-8}{2(-1)} = \dfrac{-8}{-2} = 4$. The maximum

value is $f\left(\dfrac{-b}{2a}\right) = f(4) = -(4)^2 + 8(4) - 4 = -16 + 32 - 4 = 12$.

21. $f(x) = -3x^2 + 12x + 4$

$a = -3, b = 12, c = 4.$ Since $a = -3 < 0$, the graph opens down, so the vertex is a maximum point. The maximum occurs at $x = \dfrac{-b}{2a} = \dfrac{-12}{2(-3)} = \dfrac{-12}{-6} = 2$. The maximum value is $f\left(\dfrac{-b}{2a}\right) = f(2) = -3(2)^2 + 12(2) + 4 = -12 + 24 + 4 = 16.$

23. $f(x) = x(x + 2)(x + 4)$

(a) x-intercepts: –4, –2, 0;
     y-intercept: 0
(b) crosses x axis at x = –4, –2, 0
(c) $y = x^3$ (d)   2
(e)

	$x < -4$	$-4 < x < -2$	$-2 < x < 0$	$x > 0$
Sign of f	-	+	-	+
Above or below x-axis	below	above	below	above

Graph of f is above the x-axis for $(-4,-2) \cup (0,\infty)$
Graph of f is below the x-axis for $(-\infty,-4) \cup (-2,0)$

(f)

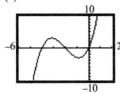

25. $f(x) = (x - 2)^2(x + 4)$
(a) x-intercepts: - 4, 2; y-intercept: 16
(b) crosses x axis at x = - 4 and touches the x axis at x = 2
(c) $y = x^3$ (d)   2
(e)

	$x < -4$	$-4 < x < 2$	$2 < x$
Sign of f	-	+	+
Above or below x-axis	below	above	above

Graph of f is above the x-axis for $(-4,-2) \cup (2,\infty)$
Graph of f is below the x-axis for $(-\infty,-4)$

(f)

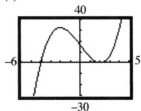

27. $f(x) = -2x^3 + 4x^2 = -2x^2(x - 2)$

   (a)   x-intercepts: 0, 2; y-intercept: 0
   (b)   crosses x axis at x = 2 and touches the x axis at x = 0
   (c) $y = -2x^3$ (d)   2
   (e)

	$x < 0$	$0 < x < 2$	$2 < x$
Sign of f	+	+	-
Above or below x-axis	above	above	below

   Graph of f is above the x-axis for $(-\infty, 0) \cup (0, 2)$

   Graph of f is below the x-axis for $(2, \infty)$

   (f)

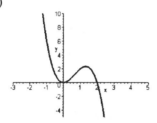

29. $f(x) = (x - 1)^2(x + 3)(x + 1)$

   (a)   x-intercepts: - 3, - 1, 1; y-intercept: 3
   (b)   crosses x axis at x = - 3, - 1 and touches x-axis at x = 1
   (c) $y = x^4$ (d)   3
   (e)

	$x < -3$	$-3 < x < -1$	$-1 < x < 1$	$1 < x$
Sign of f	+	-	+	+
Above or below x-axis	above	below	above	above

   Graph of f is above the x-axis for $(-\infty, -3) \cup (-1, 1) \cup (1, \infty)$

   Graph of f is below the x-axis for $(-3, -1)$

   (f)

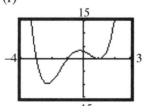

31. $R(x) = \dfrac{2x - 6}{x}$ $p(x) = 2x - 6;\ q(x) = x;\ n = 1;\ m = 1$

   Step 1:   Domain: $\{x \mid x \neq 0\}$

   Step 2:   (a)   The x-intercept is the zero of $p(x)$: 3
   　　　　　(b)   There is no y-intercept because 0 is not in the domain.

   Step 3: $R(-x) = \dfrac{2(-x) - 6}{-x} = \dfrac{-2x - 6}{-x} = \dfrac{2x + 6}{x}$; this is neither $R(x)$ nor $-R(x)$, so there

   　　　　　is no symmetry.

Step 4:   The vertical asymptote is the zero of $q(x)$: $x = 0$
Step 5:   Since $n = m$, the line $y = 2$ is the horizontal asymptote.
          $R(x)$ does not intersect $y = 2$.

Step 6:   Graphing: Step 7:   Graphing by hand:

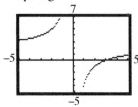   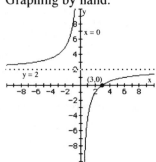

33. $H(x) = \dfrac{x+2}{x(x-2)}$ $p(x) = x + 2;$ $q(x) = x(x-2) = x^2 - 2x;$ $n = 1;$ $m = 2$

Step 1:   Domain: $\{x \mid x \neq 0,\ x \neq 2\}$
Step 2:   (a)   The x-intercept is the zero of $p(x)$: -2
          (b)   There is no y-intercept because 0 is not in the domain.
Step 3: $H(-x) = \dfrac{-x+2}{-x(-x-2)} = \dfrac{-x+2}{x^2+2x}$; this is neither $H(x)$ nor $-H(x)$, so there is no
          symmetry.
Step 4:   The vertical asymptotes are the zeros of $q(x)$: $x = 0$ and $x = 2$
Step 5:   Since $n < m$, the line $y = 0$ is the horizontal asymptote.
          $R(x)$ intersects $y = 0$ at $(-2, 0)$.
Step 6:   Graphing: Step 7:   Graphing by hand:

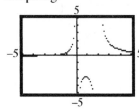   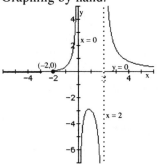

35. $R(x) = \dfrac{x^2+x-6}{x^2-x-6} = \dfrac{(x+3)(x-2)}{(x-3)(x+2)}$ $p(x) = x^2 + x - 6;$ $q(x) = x^2 - x - 6;$
          $n = 2;$ $m = 2$

Step 1:   Domain: $\{x \mid x \neq -2,\ x \neq 3\}$
Step 2:   (a)   The x-intercepts are the zeros of $p(x)$: -3 and 2
          (b)   The y-intercept is $R(0) = \dfrac{0^2+0-6}{0^2-0-6} = \dfrac{-6}{-6} = 1$.
Step 3: $R(-x) = \dfrac{(-x)^2+(-x)-6}{(-x)^2-(-x)-6} = \dfrac{x^2-x-6}{x^2+x-6}$; this is neither $R(x)$ nor $-R(x)$, so there
          is no symmetry.

Step 4:   The vertical asymptotes are the zeros of $q(x)$: $x = -2$ and $x = 3$

Step 5:   Since $n = m$, the line $y = 1$ is the horizontal asymptote.

$R(x)$ intersects $y = 1$ at $(0, 1)$, since:

$$\frac{x^2 + x - 6}{x^2 - x - 6} = 1$$

$$x^2 + x - 6 = x^2 - x - 6$$

$$2x = 0$$

$$x = 0$$

Step 6:   Graphing:

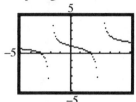

Step 7:   Graphing by hand:

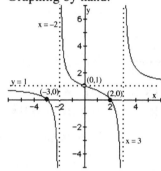

37. $F(x) = \dfrac{x^3}{x^2 - 4}$ $p(x) = x^3$; $q(x) = x^2 - 4$; $n = 3$; $m = 2$

Step 1:   Domain: $\left\{x \mid x \neq -2,\ x \neq 2\right\}$

Step 2:   (a)   The x-intercept is the zero of $p(x)$: 0.

(b)   The y-intercept is $F(0) = \dfrac{0^3}{0^2 - 4} = \dfrac{0}{-4} = 0$.

Step 3: $F(-x) = \dfrac{(-x)^3}{(-x)^2 - 4} = \dfrac{-x^3}{x^2 - 4} = -F(x)$; $F(x)$ is symmetric to the origin.

Step 4:   The vertical asymptotes are the zeros of $q(x)$: $x = -2$ and $x = 2$

Step 5:   Since $n = m + 1$, there is an oblique asymptote. Dividing:

$$\begin{array}{r} x \\ x^2 - 4 \overline{) x^3 + 0x^2 + 0x + 0} \\ \underline{x^3 - 4x } \\ 4x \end{array}$$

$$F(x) = x + \frac{4x}{x^2 - 4}$$

The oblique asymptote is $y = x$.

Solve to find intersection points:

$$\frac{x^3}{x^2 - 4} = x \rightarrow x^3 = x^3 - 4x \rightarrow 0 = -4x \rightarrow x = 0$$

The oblique asymptote intersects $F(x)$ at $(0, 0)$.

249

Step 6: Graphing: Step 7:   Graphing by hand:

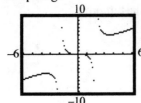

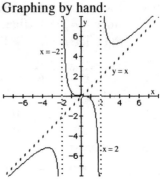

39. $R(x) = \dfrac{2x^4}{(x-1)^2}$ $p(x) = 2x^4$; $q(x) = (x-1)^2$; $n = 4$; $m = 2$

Step 1:   Domain: $\{x \mid x \neq 1\}$

Step 2:   (a)   The x-intercept is the zero of $p(x)$: 0

         (b)   The y-intercept is $R(0) = \dfrac{2(0)^4}{(0-1)^2} = \dfrac{0}{1} = 0$.

Step 3: $R(-x) = \dfrac{2(-x)^4}{(-x-1)^2} = \dfrac{2x^4}{(x+1)^2}$; this is neither $R(x)$ nor $-R(x)$, so there is no symmetry.

Step 4:   The vertical asymptote is the zero of $q(x)$: $x = 1$

Step 5:   Since $n > m+1$, there is no horizontal asymptote and no oblique asymptote.

Step 6:   Graphing: Step 7:   Graphing by hand:

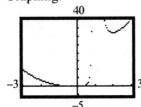

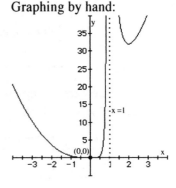

41. $G(x) = \dfrac{x^2 - 4}{x^2 - x - 2} = \dfrac{(x+2)(x-2)}{(x-2)(x+1)} = \dfrac{x+2}{x+1}$ $p(x) = x^2 - 4$; $q(x) = x^2 - x - 2$;

                                              $n = 2$; $m = 2$

Step 1:   Domain: $\{x \mid x \neq -1,\ x \neq 2\}$

Step 2:   (a)   The x-intercept is the zero of $p(x)$: -2 (2 is not a zero because reduced form must be used to find the zeros.)

         (b)   The y-intercept is $G(0) = \dfrac{0^2 - 4}{0^2 - 0 - 2} = \dfrac{-4}{-2} = 2$.

Step 3: $G(-x) = \dfrac{(-x)^2 - 4}{(-x)^2 - (-x) - 2} = \dfrac{x^2 - 4}{x^2 + x - 2}$; this is neither $G(x)$ nor $-G(x)$, so there is no symmetry.

Step 4:   The vertical asymptote is the zero of $q(x)$: $x = -1$ ($x = 2$ is not a vertical
           asymptote because reduced form must be used to find the them.)

Step 5:   Since $n = m$, the line $y = 1$ is the horizontal asymptote.

           $G(x)$ does not intersect $y = 1$ because $G(x)$ is not defined at $x = 2$.

$$\frac{x^2 - 4}{x^2 - x - 2} = 1 \rightarrow x^2 - 4 = x^2 - x - 2 \rightarrow -2 = -x \rightarrow x = 2$$

Step 6:   Graphing: Step 7:   Graphing by hand:

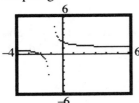

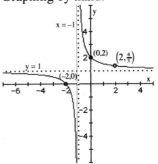

43. $2x^2 + 5x - 12 < 0$ $f(x) = 2x^2 + 5x - 12$

           $(x + 4)(2x - 3) < 0$

           $x = -4, x = \dfrac{3}{2}$ are the zeros.

Interval	Test Number	$f(x)$	Positive/Negative
$-\infty < x < -4$	-5	13	Positive
$-4 < x < 3/2$	0	-12	Negative
$3/2 < x < \infty$	2	6	Positive

The solution set is $\left\{ x \middle| -4 < x < \dfrac{3}{2} \right\}$.

45. $\dfrac{6}{x + 3} \geq 1$ $f(x) = \dfrac{6}{x + 3} - 1$

$$\frac{6}{x + 3} - 1 \geq 0 \rightarrow \frac{6 - 1(x + 3)}{x + 3} \geq 0 \rightarrow \frac{-x + 3}{x + 3} \geq 0$$

The zeros and values where the expression is undefined are $x = -3$, and $x = 3$.

Interval	Test Number	$f(x)$	Positive/Negative
$-\infty < x < -3$	-4	-7	Negative
$-3 < x < 3$	0	1	Positive
$3 < x < \infty$	4	$-1/7$	Negative

The solution set is $\left\{ x \middle| -3 < x \leq 3 \right\}$.

47. $\dfrac{2x - 6}{1 - x} < 2$ $f(x) = \dfrac{2x - 6}{1 - x} - 2$

$$\frac{2x - 6}{1 - x} - 2 < 0 \rightarrow \frac{2x - 6 - 2(1 - x)}{1 - x} < 0 \rightarrow \frac{4x - 8}{1 - x} < 0$$

The zeros and values where the expression is undefined are $x = 1$, and $x = 2$.

Interval	Test Number	$f(x)$	Positive/Negative
$-\infty < x < 1$	0	-8	Negative
$1 < x < 2$	1.5	4	Positive
$2 < x < \infty$	3	-2	Negative

The solution set is $\left\{ x \mid x < 1 \text{ or } x > 2 \right\}$.

49. $\dfrac{(x-2)(x-1)}{x-3} > 0$ $f(x) = \dfrac{(x-2)(x-1)}{x-3}$

The zeros and values where the expression is undefined are $x = 1$, $x = 2$, and $x = 3$.

Interval	Test Number	$f(x)$	Positive/Negative
$-\infty < x < 1$	0	$-2/3$	Negative
$1 < x < 2$	1.5	$1/6$	Positive
$2 < x < 3$	2.5	$-3/2$	Negative
$3 < x < \infty$	4	6	Positive

The solution set is $\left\{ x \mid 1 < x < 2 \text{ or } x > 3 \right\}$.

51. $\dfrac{x^2 - 8x + 12}{x^2 - 16} > 0$ $f(x) = \dfrac{x^2 - 8x + 12}{x^2 - 16}$

$\dfrac{(x-2)(x-6)}{(x+4)(x-4)} > 0$

The zeros and values where the expression is undefined are $x = -4$, $x = 2$, $x = 4$, $x = 6$.

Interval	Test Number	$f(x)$	Positive/Negative
$-\infty < x < -4$	-5	$77/9$	Positive
$-4 < x < 2$	0	$-3/4$	Negative
$2 < x < 4$	3	$3/7$	Positive
$4 < x < 6$	5	$-1/3$	Negative
$6 < x < \infty$	7	$5/33$	Positive

The solution set is $\left\{ x \mid x < -4, \, 2 < x < 4, \, x > 6 \right\}$.

53.

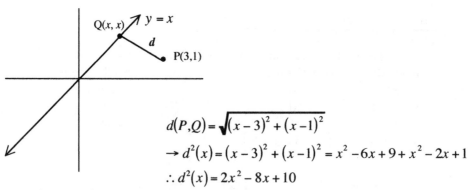

$$d(P,Q) = \sqrt{(x-3)^2 + (x-1)^2}$$
$$\rightarrow d^2(x) = (x-3)^2 + (x-1)^2 = x^2 - 6x + 9 + x^2 - 2x + 1$$
$$\therefore d^2(x) = 2x^2 - 8x + 10$$

Since $d^2(x) = 2x^2 - 8x + 10$ is a quadratic function with $a = 2 > 0$, the vertex corresponds to the minimum value for the function.

The vertex occurs at $x = -\dfrac{b}{2a} = -\dfrac{-8}{2(2)} = 2$. Therefore the point Q on the line $y = x$ will be closest to the point $P = (3,1)$ when $Q = (2,2)$.

55. Since there are 200 feet of border, we know that $2x + 2y = 200$.
The area is to be maximized, so $A = x \cdot y$.
Solving the perimeter formula for y:
$$2x + 2y = 200 \rightarrow 2y = 200 - 2x \rightarrow y = 100 - x$$
The area function is: $A(x) = x(100 - x) = -x^2 + 100x$
The maximum value occurs at the vertex:
$$x = \frac{-b}{2a} = \frac{-100}{2(-1)} = \frac{-100}{-2} = 50$$
The pond should be 50 feet by 50 feet for maximum area.

57. Consider the diagram

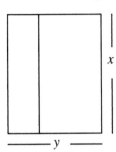

Total amount of fence $= 3x + 2y = 10000$

$$\therefore y = \frac{10000 - 3x}{2} = 5000 - \frac{3}{2}x$$

Total enclosed area $= (x)(y) = (x)\left(5000 - \frac{3}{2}x\right)$

$$\therefore A(x) = 5000x - \frac{3}{2}x^2 = -\frac{3}{2}x^2 + 5000x \text{ is a quadratic function with } a = -\frac{3}{2} < 0.$$

So the vertex corresponds to the maximum value for this function.
The vertex occurs when
$$x = -\frac{b}{2a} = -\frac{5000}{2\left(-\frac{3}{2}\right)} = \frac{5000}{3} \rightarrow \text{the maximum area is } A\left(\frac{5000}{3}\right) = -\frac{3}{2}\left(\frac{5000}{3}\right)^2 + 5000\left(\frac{5000}{3}\right)$$

$$= -\frac{3}{2}\left(\frac{25000000}{9}\right) + \frac{25000000}{3} = -\frac{12500000}{3} + \frac{25000000}{3}$$

$$= \frac{12500000}{3} \approx 4166666.67 \text{ square meters}$$

59. Consider the diagram

d = diameter of the semicircles = width of the rectangle
x = length of the rectangle
$\therefore$ outside dimension length $= 2x + 2(\text{circumference of a semicircle})$

$$= 2x + \text{circumference of a circle} = 2x + \pi d = 100 \rightarrow x = \frac{100 - \pi d}{2} = 50 - \frac{1}{2}\pi d$$

Total enclosed area = (area of the rectangle) + 2(area of a semicircle)
                    = (area of the rectangle) + area of a circle

$$= (x)(d) + \pi r^2 = (x)(d) + \pi\left(\frac{d}{2}\right)^2 = \left(50 - \frac{1}{2}\pi d\right)(d) + \pi\left(\frac{d}{2}\right)^2$$

$$= 50d - \frac{1}{2}\pi d^2 + \frac{1}{4}\pi d^2 = 50d - \frac{1}{4}\pi d^2 = -\frac{1}{4}\pi d^2 + 50d$$

$\therefore A(d) = -\frac{1}{4}\pi d^2 + 50d$ is a quadratic function with $a = -\frac{1}{4}\pi < 0$. Therefore the vertex corresponds to the maximum value for the function.

The vertex occurs when $x = -\dfrac{b}{2a} = -\dfrac{50}{2\left(-\dfrac{1}{4}\pi\right)} = \dfrac{100}{\pi}$

$\rightarrow$ the maximum area is $A\left(\dfrac{100}{\pi}\right) = -\dfrac{1}{4}\pi\left(\dfrac{100}{\pi}\right)^2 + 50\left(\dfrac{100}{\pi}\right) \approx 795.78$ square meters

61. (a) Graphing:

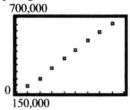

$A(t) = -212t^3 + 2429t^2 + 59569t + 130003$

(b) $A(11) = -212(11)^3 + 2429(11)^2 + 59569(11) + 130003 = 796999$ cases

(c) and (d)   Graphing the cubic function of best fit:

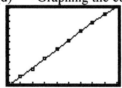

(e) answers will vary

63. Answers will vary, one example is $p(x) = -5(x^2 + 1)(x + 1)^3\left(x - \dfrac{3}{5}\right)$

65. (a) The degree is even.   (b)   The leading coefficient is positive.
    (c) The function is even - it is symmetric to the y-axis.
    (d) x^2 is a factor because the curve touches the x-axis at the origin.
    (e) The minimum degree is 8.
    (f) Answers will vary, 5 possibilities are:

$$p_1(x) = x^2(x + 3)(x + 2)(x + 1)(x - 1)(x - 2)(x - 3)$$
$$p_2(x) = x^4(x + 3)(x + 2)(x + 1)(x - 1)(x - 2)(x - 3)$$
$$p_3(x) = x^6(x + 3)(x + 2)(x + 1)(x - 1)(x - 2)(x - 3)$$
$$p_4(x) = x^8(x + 3)(x + 2)(x + 1)(x - 1)(x - 2)(x - 3)$$
$$p_5(x) = x^{10}(x + 3)(x + 2)(x + 1)(x - 1)(x - 2)(x - 3)$$

Chapter 5

The Zeros of a Polynomial Function

5.1   Synthetic Division

1.   Use synthetic division:

$$2\overline{)\begin{array}{rrrr} 1 & -1 & 2 & 4 \\ & 2 & 2 & 8 \\ \hline 1 & 1 & 4 & 12 \end{array}}$$

Quotient: $x^2 + x + 4$ Remainder: 12

3.   Use synthetic division:

$$3\overline{)\begin{array}{rrrr} 3 & 2 & -1 & 3 \\ & 9 & 33 & 96 \\ \hline 3 & 11 & 32 & 99 \end{array}}$$

Quotient: $3x^2 + 11x + 32$ Remainder: 99

5.   Use synthetic division:

$$-3\overline{)\begin{array}{rrrrrr} 1 & 0 & -4 & 0 & 1 & 0 \\ & -3 & 9 & -15 & 45 & -138 \\ \hline 1 & -3 & 5 & -15 & 46 & -138 \end{array}}$$

Quotient : $x^4 - 3x^3 + 5x^2 - 15x + 46$; Remainder : -138

7.   Use synthetic division:

$$1\overline{)\begin{array}{rrrrrrr} 4 & 0 & -3 & 0 & 1 & 0 & 5 \\ & 4 & 4 & 1 & 1 & 2 & 2 \\ \hline 4 & 4 & 1 & 1 & 2 & 2 & 7 \end{array}}$$

Quotient : $4x^5 + 4x^4 + x^3 + x^2 + 2x + 2$; Remainder : 7

9.   Use synthetic division:

$$-1.1\overline{)\begin{array}{rrrr} 0.1 & 0 & 0.2 & 0 \\ & -0.11 & 0.121 & -0.3531 \\ \hline 0.1 & -0.11 & 0.321 & -0.3531 \end{array}}$$

Quotient: $0.1x^2 - 0.11x + 0.321$ Remainder: -0.3531

11. Use synthetic division:

$$1\overline{)1 \quad 0 \quad 0 \quad 0 \quad -1}$$
$$ \quad 1 \quad 1 \quad 1 \quad 1$$
$$\overline{1 \quad 1 \quad 1 \quad 1 \quad 1 \quad 0}$$

Quotient: $x^4 + x^3 + x^2 + x + 1$ Remainder: 0

13. Use synthetic division:

$$2\overline{)4 \quad -3 \quad -8 \quad 4}$$
$$ \quad 8 \quad 10 \quad 4$$
$$\overline{4 \quad 5 \quad 2 \quad 8}$$

Remainder $= 8 \ne 0$; therefore $x - 2$ is not a factor of $f(x)$.

15. Use synthetic division:

$$2\overline{)3 \quad -6 \quad 0 \quad -5 \quad 10}$$
$$ \quad 6 \quad 0 \quad 0 \quad -10$$
$$\overline{3 \quad 0 \quad 0 \quad -5 \quad 0}$$

Remainder $= 0$; therefore $x - 2$ is a factor of $f(x)$.

17. Use synthetic division:

$$-3\overline{)3 \quad 0 \quad 0 \quad 82 \quad 0 \quad 0 \quad 27}$$
$$ \quad -9 \quad 27 \quad -81 \quad -3 \quad 9 \quad -27$$
$$\overline{3 \quad -9 \quad 27 \quad 1 \quad -3 \quad 9 \quad 0}$$

Remainder $= 0$; therefore $x + 3$ is a factor of $f(x)$.

19. Use synthetic division:

$$-4\overline{)4 \quad 0 \quad -64 \quad 0 \quad 1 \quad 0 \quad -15}$$
$$ \quad -16 \quad 64 \quad 0 \quad 0 \quad -4 \quad 16$$
$$\overline{4 \quad -16 \quad 0 \quad 0 \quad 1 \quad -4 \quad 1}$$

Remainder $= 1 \ne 0$; therefore $x + 3$ is not a factor of $f(x)$.

21. Use synthetic division:

$$\tfrac{1}{2}\overline{)2 \quad -1 \quad 0 \quad 2 \quad -1}$$
$$\phantom{\tfrac{1}{2})2} \quad 1 \quad 0 \quad 0 \quad 1$$
$$\overline{2 \quad 0 \quad 0 \quad 2 \quad 0}$$

Remainder $= 0$; therefore $x - \dfrac{1}{2}$ is a factor of $f(x)$.

23.   Use synthetic division:

$$-2\overline{)\begin{array}{rrrr} 1 & -2 & 3 & 5 \\ & -2 & 8 & -22 \\ \hline 1 & -4 & 11 & -17 \end{array}}$$

$$\frac{x^3 - 2x^2 + 3x + 5}{x + 2} = x^2 - 4x + 11 + \frac{-17}{x + 2}$$

$$a + b + c + d = 1 - 4 + 11 - 17 = -9$$

The Zeros of a Polynomial Function

5.2   The Real Zeros of a Polynomial Function

1. $f(x) = 4x^3 - 3x^2 - 8x + 4;\quad c = 2$
$f(2) = 4(2)^3 - 3(2)^2 - 8(2) + 4 = 32 - 12 - 16 + 4 = 8 \neq 0$
Thus, 2 is not a zero of f ∴ $x - 2$ is not a factor of f.

3. $f(x) = 3x^4 - 6x^3 - 5x + 10;\quad c = 2$
$f(2) = 3(2)^4 - 6(2)^3 - 5(2) + 10 = 48 - 48 - 10 + 10 = 0$
Thus, 2 is a zero of f ∴ $x - 2$ is a factor of f.

5. $f(x) = 3x^6 + 82x^3 + 27;\quad c = -3$
$f(-3) = 3(-3)^6 + 82(-3)^3 + 27 = 2187 - 2214 - 27 = 0$
Thus, –3 is a zero of f ∴ $x + 3$ is a factor of f.
Use synthetic division to find the factors.

$-3)$	3	0	0	82	0	0	27
		-9	27	-81	-3	9	-27
	3	-9	27	1	-3	9	0

The factored form is: $f(x) = (x + 3)\left(3x^5 - 9x^4 + 27x^3 + x^2 - 3x + 9\right).$

7. $f(x) = 4x^6 - 64x^4 + x^2 - 15;\quad c = -4$
Use synthetic division to determine whether -4 is a zero.

$-4)$	4	0	-64	0	1	0	-15
		-16	64	0	0	-4	16
	4	-16	0	0	1	-4	1

Thus, -4 is not a zero of f ∴ $x + 4$ is not a factor of f.

9. $f(x) = 2x^4 - x^3 + 2x - 1; \quad c = \dfrac{1}{2}$

$f\left(\dfrac{1}{2}\right) = 2\left(\dfrac{1}{2}\right)^4 - \left(\dfrac{1}{2}\right)^3 + 2\left(\dfrac{1}{2}\right) - 1 = \dfrac{1}{8} - \dfrac{1}{8} + 1 - 1 = 0$

Thus, $\dfrac{1}{2}$ is a zero of f $\therefore$ $x - \dfrac{1}{2}$ is a factor of f.

Factoring:

$$f(x) = 2x^4 - x^3 + 2x - 1 = 2x^3\left(x - \dfrac{1}{2}\right) + 2\left(x - \dfrac{1}{2}\right) = \left(x - \dfrac{1}{2}\right)(2x^3 + 2)$$

$$= 2\left(x - \dfrac{1}{2}\right)(x^3 + 1) = 2\left(x - \dfrac{1}{2}\right)(x + 1)(x^2 - x + 1)$$

11. $f(x) = -4x^7 + x^3 - x^2 + 2$

The maximum number of zeros is the degree of the polynomial which is 7.
Examining $f(x) = -4x^7 + x^3 - x^2 + 2$, there are 3 variations in sign; thus, there are 3 or 1 positive real zeros.
Examining $f(-x) = -4(-x)^7 + (-x)^3 - (-x)^2 + 2 = 4x^7 - x^3 - x^2 + 2$, there are 2 variations in sign; thus, there are 2 or 0 negative real zeros.

13. $f(x) = 2x^6 - 3x^2 - x + 1$

The maximum number of zeros is the degree of the polynomial which is 6.
Examining $f(x) = 2x^6 - 3x^2 - x + 1$, there are 2 variations in sign; thus, there are 2 or 0 positive real zeros.
Examining $f(-x) = 2(-x)^6 - 3(-x)^2 - (-x) + 1 = 2x^6 - 3x^2 + x + 1$, there are 2 variations in sign; thus, there are 2 or 0 negative real zeros.

15. $f(x) = 3x^3 - 2x^2 + x + 2$

The maximum number of zeros is the degree of the polynomial which is 3.
Examining $f(x) = 3x^3 - 2x^2 + x + 2$, there are 2 variations in sign; thus, there are 2 or 0 positive real zeros.
Examining $f(-x) = 3(-x)^3 - 2(-x)^2 + (-x) + 2 = -3x^3 - 2x^2 - x + 2$, there is 1 variation in sign; thus, there is 1 negative real zero.

17. $f(x) = -x^4 + x^2 - 1$

The maximum number of zeros is the degree of the polynomial which is 4.
Examining $f(x) = -x^4 + x^2 - 1$, there are 2 variations in sign; thus, there are 2 or 0 positive real zeros.
Examining $f(-x) = -(-x)^4 + (-x)^2 - 1 = -x^4 + x^2 - 1$, there are 2 variations in sign; thus, there are 2 or 0 negative real zeros.

19. $f(x) = x^5 + x^4 + x^2 + x + 1$

The maximum number of zeros is the degree of the polynomial which is 5.
Examining $f(x) = x^5 + x^4 + x^2 + x + 1$, there are no variations in sign; thus, there are 0 positive real zeros.

Examining $f(-x) = (-x)^5 + (-x)^4 + (-x)^2 + (-x) + 1 = -x^5 + x^4 + x^2 - x + 1$, there are 3 variations in sign; thus, there are 3 or 1 negative real zeros.

21. $f(x) = x^6 - 1$

The maximum number of zeros is the degree of the polynomial which is 6.

Examining $f(x) = x^6 - 1$, there is 1 variation in sign; thus, there is 1 positive real zero.

Examining $f(-x) = (-x)^6 - 1 = x^6 - 1$, there is 1 variation in sign; thus, there is 1 negative real zero.

23. $f(x) = 3x^4 - 3x^3 + x^2 - x + 1$

p must be a factor of 1: $p = \pm 1$

q must be a factor of 3: $q = \pm 1, \pm 3$

The possible rational zeros are: $\dfrac{p}{q} = \pm 1, \pm \dfrac{1}{3}$

25. $f(x) = x^5 - 6x^2 + 9x - 3$

p must be a factor of -3: $p = \pm 1, \pm 3$

q must be a factor of 1: $q = \pm 1$

The possible rational zeros are: $\dfrac{p}{q} = \pm 1, \pm 3$

27. $f(x) = -4x^3 - x^2 + x + 2$

p must be a factor of 2: $p = \pm 1, \pm 2$

q must be a factor of -4: $q = \pm 1, \pm 2, \pm 4$

The possible rational zeros are: $\dfrac{p}{q} = \pm 1, \pm 2, \pm \dfrac{1}{2}, \pm \dfrac{1}{4}$

29. $f(x) = 6x^4 - x^2 + 9$

p must be a factor of 9: $p = \pm 1, \pm 3, \pm 9$

q must be a factor of 6: $q = \pm 1, \pm 2, \pm 3, \pm 6$

The possible rational zeros are: $\dfrac{p}{q} = \pm 1, \pm \dfrac{1}{2}, \pm \dfrac{1}{3}, \pm \dfrac{1}{6}, \pm 3, \pm \dfrac{3}{2}, \pm 9, \pm \dfrac{9}{2}$

31. $f(x) = 2x^5 - x^3 + 2x^2 + 12$

p must be a factor of 12: $p = \pm 1, \pm 2, \pm 3, \pm 4, \pm 6, \pm 12$

q must be a factor of 2: $q = \pm 1, \pm 2$

The possible rational zeros are: $\dfrac{p}{q} = \pm 1, \pm 2, \pm 4, \pm \dfrac{1}{2}, \pm 3, \pm \dfrac{3}{2}, \pm 6, \pm 12$

33. $f(x) = 6x^4 + 2x^3 - x^2 + 20$

p must be a factor of 20: $p = \pm 1, \pm 2, \pm 4, \pm 5, \pm 10, \pm 20$

q must be a factor of 6: $q = \pm 1, \pm 2, \pm 3, \pm 6$

The possible rational zeros are:

$$\dfrac{p}{q} = \pm 1, \pm 2, \pm \dfrac{1}{2}, \pm \dfrac{1}{3}, \pm \dfrac{2}{3}, \pm \dfrac{1}{6}, \pm 4, \pm \dfrac{4}{3}, \pm 5, \pm \dfrac{5}{2}, \pm \dfrac{5}{3}, \pm \dfrac{5}{6}, \pm 10, \pm \dfrac{10}{3}, \pm 20, \pm \dfrac{20}{3}$$

35. $f(x) = x^3 + 2x^2 - 5x - 6$

Step 1: $f(x)$ has at most 3 real zeros.

Step 2:   By Descartes Rule of Signs, there is 1 positive real zero.
Also because $f(-x) = (-x)^3 + 2(-x)^2 - 5(-x) - 6 = -x^3 + 2x^2 + 5x - 6$, there are 2 or 0 negative real zeros.

Step 3:   Possible rational zeros:

$$p = \pm 1, \pm 2, \pm 3, \pm 6; \quad q = \pm 1; \quad \frac{p}{q} = \pm 1, \pm 2, \pm 3, \pm 6$$

Step 4:   Using synthetic division:

$$
\begin{array}{r}
-3{\overline{)}}1 \quad 2 \quad -5 \quad -6 \\
\underline{-3 \quad\;\; 3 \quad\;\; 6} \\
1 \;\; -1 \;\; -2 \quad\;\; 0
\end{array}
$$

Since the remainder is 0, $x - (-3) = x + 3$ is a factor. The other factor is the quotient: $x^2 - x - 2$.

Thus, $f(x) = (x + 3)(x^2 - x - 2) = (x + 3)(x + 1)(x - 2)$.

The zeros are –3, –1, and 2.

37. $f(x) = 2x^3 - x^2 + 2x - 1; \; f(-x) = 2(-x)^3 - (-x)^2 + 2(-x) - 1 = -2x^3 - x^2 - 2x - 1$

Step 1: $f(x)$ has at most 3 real zeros.

Step 2:   By Descartes Rule of Signs, there are 3 or 1 positive real zeros;
thus, there are no negative real zeros.

Step 3:   Possible rational zeros:

$$p = \pm 1 \quad q = \pm 1, \pm 2; \quad \frac{p}{q} = \pm 1, \pm \frac{1}{2}$$

Step 4:   Using synthetic division:

$$
\begin{array}{r}
-1{\overline{)}}2 \quad -1 \quad 2 \quad -1 \\
\underline{-2 \quad\;\; 3 \quad -5} \\
2 \;\; -3 \;\; 5 \;\; \{-6\} \rightarrow
\end{array}
$$

$x + 1$ is **not** a factor

So we try $x - 1$

$$
\begin{array}{r}
1{\overline{)}}2 \quad -1 \quad 2 \quad -1 \\
\underline{2 \quad\;\; 1 \quad\;\; 3} \\
2 \;\; 1 \;\; 3 \;\; \{2\} \rightarrow
\end{array}
$$

$x - 1$ is **not** a factor

Let's try $x - \dfrac{1}{2}$

$$
\begin{array}{r}
\tfrac{1}{2}{\overline{)}}2 \quad -1 \quad 2 \quad -1 \\
\underline{1 \quad\;\; 0 \quad\;\; 1} \\
2 \;\; 0 \;\; 2 \;\; 0 \rightarrow
\end{array}
$$

$x - \dfrac{1}{2}$ **is** a factor ∴ the quotient is $2x^2 + 2$.

Thus, $f(x) = 2x^3 - x^2 + 2x - 1 = \left(x - \dfrac{1}{2}\right)(2x^2 + 2)$.

Since $2x^2 + 2 = 0$ has no real solutions, $x = \dfrac{1}{2}$ is the only real zero.

39. $f(x) = x^4 + x^2 - 2$

Step 1: $f(x)$ has at most 4 real zeros.

Step 2: By Descartes Rule of Signs, this is one positive real zero.
$f(-x) = (-x)^4 + (-x)^2 - 2 = x^4 + x^2 - 2$; thus, there is 1 negative real zero.

Step 3: Possible rational zeros:
$$p = \pm 1, \pm 2; \quad q = \pm 1; \quad \frac{p}{q} = \pm 1, \pm 2$$

Step 4: Using synthetic division:

$$-1\overline{)\begin{array}{ccccc} 1 & 0 & 1 & 0 & 2 \\ & -1 & 1 & -2 & 2 \\ \hline 1 & -1 & 2 & -2 & 0 \end{array}} \rightarrow$$

Since the remainder is 0, $x - (-1) = x + 1$ is a factor. The other factor is the quotient: $x^3 - x^2 + 2x - 2$.

Thus, $f(x) = (x+1)(x^3 - x^2 + 2x - 2)$. We can factor $x^3 - x^2 + 2x - 2$ by grouping terms: $x^3 - x^2 + 2x - 2 = x^2(x-1) + 2(x-1) = (x-1)(x^2 + 2)$

Thus, $f(x) = (x+1)(x-1)(x^2 + 2)$. Since $x^2 + 2 = 0$ has no real solutions, we have two real zeros for f, namely -1 and 1.

41. $f(x) = 4x^4 + 7x^2 - 2$

Step 1: $f(x)$ has at most 4 real zeros.

Step 2: By Descartes Rule of Signs, there is 1 positive real zero.
$f(-x) = 4(-x)^4 + 7(-x)^2 - 2 = 4x^4 + 7x^2 - 2$; thus, there is one negative real zero.

Step 3: Possible rational zeros: $p = \pm 1, \pm 2; \quad q = \pm 1, \pm 2, \pm 4$
$$\frac{p}{q} = \pm 1, \pm \frac{1}{2}, \pm \frac{1}{4} \pm 2$$

We can factor f as follows:
$$f(x) = 4x^4 + 7x^2 - 2 = (4x^2 - 1)(x^2 + 2) = (2x+1)(2x-1)(x^2 + 2).$$

Thus, we have two real zeros, $-\frac{1}{2}$ and $\frac{1}{2}$.

43. $f(x) = x^4 + x^3 - 3x^2 - x + 2$

Step 1: $f(x)$ has at most 4 real zeros.

Step 2: By Descartes Rule of Signs, there are 2 or 0 positive real zeros.
$f(-x) = (-x)^4 + (-x)^3 - 3(-x)^2 - (-x) + 2 = x^4 - x^3 - 3x^2 + x + 2$; thus, there are 2 or 0 negative real zeros.

Step 3: Possible rational zeros:
$$p = \pm 1, \pm 2; \quad q = \pm 1; \quad \frac{p}{q} = \pm 1, \pm 2$$

Step 4: Using synthetic division:

$$-2\overline{)\begin{array}{ccccc} 1 & 1 & -3 & -1 & 2 \\ & -2 & 2 & 2 & -2 \\ \hline 1 & -1 & -1 & 1 & 0 \end{array}} \qquad -1\overline{)\begin{array}{cccc} 1 & -1 & -1 & 1 \\ & -1 & 2 & -1 \\ \hline 1 & -2 & 1 & 0 \end{array}}$$

Since the remainder is 0, $x + 2$ and $x + 1$ are factors. The other factor is the
quotient: $x^2 - 2x + 1$.

Thus, $f(x) = (x + 2)(x + 1)(x - 1)^2$.

The zeros are -2, -1, and 1 (multiplicity 2).

45. $f(x) = 4x^5 - 8x^4 - x + 2$

Step 1: $f(x)$ has at most 5 real zeros.

Step 2: By Descartes Rule of Signs, there are 2 or 0 positive real zeros.
$f(-x) = 4(-x)^5 - 8(-x)^4 - (-x) + 2 = -4x^5 - 8x^4 + x + 2$;
thus, there is 1 negative real zero.

Step 3: Possible rational zeros:
$$p = \pm 1, \pm 2; \quad q = \pm 1, \pm 2, \pm 4; \quad \frac{p}{q} = \pm 1, \pm 2, \pm \frac{1}{2}, \pm \frac{1}{4}$$

Step 4: Using synthetic division:

$$\begin{array}{r|rrrrr} 2 & 4 & -8 & 0 & 0 & -1 & 2 \\ & & 8 & 0 & 0 & 0 & -2 \\ \hline & 4 & 0 & 0 & 0 & -1 & 0 \end{array}$$

Since the remainder is 0, $x - 2$ is a factor. The other factor is the quotient:
$4x^4 - 1$.

Factoring,
$$f(x) = (x - 2)\left(4x^4 - 1\right) = (x - 2)(2x^2 - 1)(2x^2 + 1)$$
$$= (x - 2)\left(\sqrt{2}x - 1\right)\left(\sqrt{2}x + 1\right)\left(2x^2 + 1\right)$$

The zeros are $\dfrac{-\sqrt{2}}{2}, \dfrac{\sqrt{2}}{2}$, and 2 or $-0.71, -0.71$, and 2.

47. $x^4 - x^3 + 2x^2 - 4x - 8 = 0$

The solutions of the equation are the zeros of $f(x) = x^4 - x^3 + 2x^2 - 4x - 8$.

Step 1: $f(x)$ has at most 4 real zeros.

Step 2: By Descartes Rule of Signs, there are 3 or 1 positive real zeros.
$f(-x) = (-x)^4 - (-x)^3 + 2(-x)^2 - 4(-x) - 8 = x^4 + x^3 + 2x^2 + 4x - 8$;
thus, there is 1 negative real zero.

Step 3: Possible rational zeros:
$$p = \pm 1, \pm 2, \pm 4, \pm 8; \quad q = \pm 1; \quad \frac{p}{q} = \pm 1, \pm 2, \pm 4, \pm 8$$

Step 4: Using synthetic division:

$$\begin{array}{r|rrrrr} -1 & 1 & -1 & 2 & -4 & -8 \\ & & -1 & 2 & -4 & 8 \\ \hline & 1 & -2 & 4 & -8 & 0 \end{array} \qquad \begin{array}{r|rrrr} 2 & 1 & -2 & 4 & -8 \\ & & 2 & 0 & 8 \\ \hline & 1 & 0 & 4 & 0 \end{array}$$

Since the remainder is 0, $x + 1$ and $x - 2$ are factors. The other factor is the
quotient: $x^2 + 4$.

The zeros are -1 and 2. ($x^2 + 4 = 0$ has no real solutions.)

49. $3x^3 + 4x^2 - 7x + 2 = 0$

The solutions of the equation are the zeros of $f(x) = 3x^3 + 4x^2 - 7x + 2$.

Step 1: $f(x)$ has at most 3 real zeros.

Step 2: By Descartes Rule of Signs, there are 2 or 0 positive real zeros.
$f(-x) = 3(-x)^3 + 4(-x)^2 - 7(-x) + 2 = -3x^3 + 4x^2 + 7x + 2$;
thus, there is 1 negative real zero.

Step 3: Possible rational zeros:

$$p = \pm 1, \pm 2; \quad q = \pm 1, \pm 3; \quad \frac{p}{q} = \pm 1, \pm 2, \pm \frac{1}{3}, \pm \frac{2}{3}$$

Step 4: Using synthetic division:

$$\frac{2}{3} \overline{\big)3 \quad 4 \quad -7 \quad 2}$$
$$\underline{\quad\quad 2 \quad 4 \quad -2}$$
$$3 \quad 6 \quad -3 \quad 0$$

Since the remainder is 0, $x - \dfrac{2}{3}$ is a factor. The other factor is the quotient:
$3x^2 + 6x - 3$.

$$f(x) = \left(x - \frac{2}{3}\right)(3x^2 + 6x - 3) = 3\left(x - \frac{2}{3}\right)(x^2 + 2x - 1)$$

Using the quadratic formula to solve $x^2 + 2x - 1 = 0$:

$$x = \frac{-2 \pm \sqrt{4 - 4(1)(-1)}}{2(1)} = \frac{-2 \pm \sqrt{8}}{2} = \frac{-2 \pm 2\sqrt{2}}{2} = -1 \pm \sqrt{2}$$

The zeros are $\dfrac{2}{3}, -1 + \sqrt{2}$, and $-1 - \sqrt{2}$ or 0.67, 0.41, and –2.41.

51. $3x^3 - x^2 - 15x + 5 = 0$

Solving by factoring:

$$x^2(3x-1) - 5(3x-1) = 0 \rightarrow (3x-1)(x^2 - 5) = 0 \rightarrow (3x-1)\left(x - \sqrt{5}\right)\left(x + \sqrt{5}\right) = 0$$

The solutions of the equation are $\dfrac{1}{3}, \sqrt{5}$, and $-\sqrt{5}$ or 0.33, 2.24, and –2.24.

53. $x^4 + 4x^3 + 2x^2 - x + 6 = 0$

The solutions of the equation are the zeros of $f(x) = x^4 + 4x^3 + 2x^2 - x + 6$.

Step 1: $f(x)$ has at most 4 real zeros.

Step 2: By Descartes Rule of Signs, there are 2 or 0 positive real zeros.
$f(-x) = (-x)^4 + 4(-x)^3 + 2(-x)^2 - (-x) + 6 = x^4 - 4x^3 + 2x^2 + x + 6$;
thus, there are 2 or 0 negative real zeros.

Step 3: Possible rational zeros:

$$p = \pm 1, \pm 2, \pm 3, \pm 6; \quad q = \pm 1; \quad \frac{p}{q} = \pm 1, \pm 2, \pm 3, \pm 6$$

Step 4: Using synthetic division:

$$-3\overline{\big)1 \quad 4 \quad 2 \quad -1 \quad 6} \qquad\qquad -2\overline{\big)1 \quad 1 \quad -1 \quad 2}$$
$$\underline{\quad\quad -3 \quad -3 \quad 3 \quad -6} \qquad\qquad\qquad \underline{\quad\quad -2 \quad 2 \quad -2}$$
$$1 \quad 1 \quad -1 \quad 2 \quad 0 \qquad\qquad\qquad 1 \quad -1 \quad 1 \quad 0$$

Since the remainder is 0, $x + 3$ and $x + 2$ are factors. The other factor is the quotient: $x^2 - x + 1$.

The zeros are -3 and -2. ($x^2 - x + 1 = 0$ has no real solutions.)

55. $x^3 - \dfrac{2}{3}x^2 + \dfrac{8}{3}x + 1 = 0$

The solutions of the equation are the zeros of $f(x) = x^3 - \dfrac{2}{3}x^2 + \dfrac{8}{3}x + 1$.

Step 1: $f(x)$ has at most 3 real zeros.

Step 2: By Descartes Rule of Signs, there are 2 or 0 positive real zeros.

$$f(-x) = (-x)^3 - \frac{2}{3}(-x)^2 + \frac{8}{3}(-x) + 1 = -x^3 - \frac{2}{3}x^2 - \frac{8}{3}x + 1;$$

thus, there is 1 negative real zero.

Step 3: Use the equivalent equation $3x^3 - 2x^2 + 8x + 3 = 0$ to find the possible rational zeros:

$$p = \pm 1, \pm 3; \quad q = \pm 1, \pm 3; \quad \frac{p}{q} = \pm 1, \pm 3, \pm \frac{1}{3}$$

Step 4: Using synthetic division:

$$
-\frac{1}{3}\overline{\left) 1 \quad -\frac{2}{3} \quad \frac{8}{3} \quad 1 \right.}
$$

$$
\begin{array}{cccc}
 & -\dfrac{1}{3} & \dfrac{1}{3} & -1 \\
\hline
1 & -1 & 3 & 0
\end{array}
$$

Since the remainder is 0, $x + \dfrac{1}{3}$ is a factor. The other factor is the quotient: $x^2 - x + 3$.

The real zero is $-\dfrac{1}{3}$. ($x^2 - x + 3 = 0$ has no real solutions.)

57. $2x^4 - 19x^3 + 57x^2 - 64x + 20 = 0$

The solutions of the equation are the zeros of $f(x) = 2x^4 - 19x^3 + 57x^2 - 64x + 20.$

Step 1: $f(x)$ has at most 4 real zeros.

Step 2: By Descartes Rule of Signs, there are 4, 2 or 0 positive real zeros.

$$f(-x) = 2(-x)^4 - 19(-x)^3 + 57(-x)^2 - 64(-x) + 20$$

$$= 2x^4 + 19x^3 + 57x^2 + 64x + 20$$

thus, there are no negative real zeros.

Step 3: To find the possible rational zeros:

$$p = \pm 1, \pm 2, \pm 4, \pm 5, \pm 10, \pm 20; \quad q = \pm 1, \pm 2;$$

$$\frac{p}{q} = \pm 1, \pm \frac{1}{2}, \pm 2, \pm 4, \pm 5, \pm \frac{5}{2}, \pm 10, \pm 20$$

Step 4: Using synthetic division:

$$\begin{array}{r} 1)\overline{\,2 \quad -19 \quad 57 \quad -64 \quad 20\,} \\ 2 \quad -17 \quad 40 \quad -24 \\ \hline 2 \quad -17 \quad 40 \quad -24 \quad \{-4\} \end{array}$$

$$\begin{array}{r} \frac{1}{2})\overline{\,2 \quad -19 \quad 57 \quad -64 \quad \quad 20\,} \\ 1 \quad -9 \quad \quad 24 \quad -20 \\ \hline 2 \quad -18 \quad 48 \quad -40 \quad \quad 0 \end{array}$$

Thus, $x - \dfrac{1}{2}$ is a factor.

So :

$$f(x) = 2x^4 - 19x^3 + 57x^2 - 64x + 20 = \left(x - \frac{1}{2}\right)\left(2x^3 - 18x^2 + 48x - 40\right)$$

$$= 2\left(x - \frac{1}{2}\right)\left(x^3 - 9x^2 + 24x - 20\right)$$

Now try x = 2 as a solution to the equation $x^3 - 9x^2 + 24x - 20 = 0$.

$$\begin{array}{r} 2)\overline{\,1 \quad -9 \quad 24 \quad -20\,} \\ 2 \quad -14 \quad 20 \\ \hline 1 \quad -7 \quad 10 \quad \quad 0 \end{array}$$

Thus, $x^3 - 9x^2 + 24x - 20 = (x-2)(x^2 - 7x + 10) = (x-2)(x-2)(x-5)$

So we have

$$f(x) = 2x^4 - 19x^3 + 57x^2 - 64x + 20 = 2\left(x - \frac{1}{2}\right)(x-2)^2(x-5)$$.

Therefore, f has real zeros $\dfrac{1}{2}, 2, 5$, and 2 is a zero of multiplicity 2.

59. $f(x) = x^3 + 2x^2 + 5x - 6 = (x+3)(x+1)(x-2)$.

x-intercepts: $-3, -1, 2$;   y-intercept: -6;   crosses x axis at $x = -3, -1, 2$

	$x < -3$	$-3 < x < -1$	$-1 < x < 2$	$x > 2$
Sign of f	$-$	$+$	$-$	$+$
Above or below x-axis	below	above	below	above

Graph of f is above the x-axis for $(-3, -1) \cup (2, \infty)$

Graph of f is below the x-axis for $(-\infty, -3) \cup (-1, -2)$

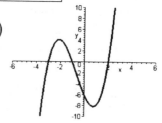

61. $f(x) = 2x^3 - x^2 + 2x - 1 = \left(x - \dfrac{1}{2}\right)\left(2x^2 + 2\right).$

x-intercepts: $\dfrac{1}{2}$;   y-intercept: -1;   crosses x axis at x = $\dfrac{1}{2}$

	$x < \dfrac{1}{2}$	$x > \dfrac{1}{2}$
Sign of f	-	+
Above or below x-axis	below	above

Graph of f is above the x-axis for $\left(\dfrac{1}{2}, \infty\right)$

Graph of f is below the x-axis for $\left(-\infty, \dfrac{1}{2}\right)$

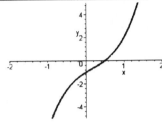

63. $f(x) = x^4 + x^2 - 2 = (x + 1)(x - 1)(x^2 + 2).$

x-intercepts: −1, 1;   y-intercept: -2;   crosses x axis at x = −1, 1

	$x < -1$	$-1 < x < 1$	$x > 1$
Sign of f	+	-	+
Above or below x-axis	above	below	above

Graph of f is above the x-axis for $(-\infty, -1) \cup (1, \infty)$

Graph of f is below the x-axis for $(-1, -1)$

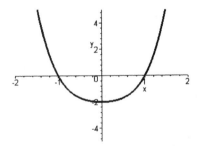

65. $f(x) = 4x^4 + 7x^2 - 2 = (2x + 1)(2x - 1)(x^2 + 2).$

x-intercepts: $-\dfrac{1}{2}, \dfrac{1}{2}$;   y-intercept: -2;   crosses x axis at x = $-\dfrac{1}{2}, \dfrac{1}{2}$

	$x < -\dfrac{1}{2}$	$-\dfrac{1}{2} < x < \dfrac{1}{2}$	$x > \dfrac{1}{2}$
Sign of f	+	-	+
Above or below x-axis	above	below	above

Graph of f is above the x-axis for $\left(-\infty,-\dfrac{1}{2}\right)\cup\left(\dfrac{1}{2},\infty\right)$

Graph of f is below the x-axis for $\left(-\dfrac{1}{2},\dfrac{1}{2}\right)$

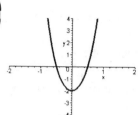

67. $f(x) = x^4 + x^3 - 3x^2 - x + 2 = (x+2)(x+1)(x-1)^2$.

     x-intercepts: –2, –1, 1;   y-intercept: 2

     crosses x axis at x = –2, –1;   touches x axis at x = 1

	$x<-2$	$-2<x<-1$	$-1<x<1$	$x>1$
Sign of f	+	-	+	+
Above or below x-axis	above	below	above	above

     Graph of f is above the x-axis for $(-\infty,-2)\cup(-1,1)\cup(1,\infty)$

     Graph of f is below the x-axis for $(-2,-1)$

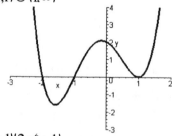

69. $f(x) = 4x^5 - 8x^4 - x + 2 = (x-2)(\sqrt{2}x - 1)(\sqrt{2}x + 1)(2x^2 + 1)$

     x-intercepts: $-\dfrac{1}{\sqrt{2}},\dfrac{1}{\sqrt{2}},2$;   y-intercept: 2

     crosses x axis at x = $-\dfrac{1}{\sqrt{2}},\dfrac{1}{\sqrt{2}},2$

	$x<-\dfrac{1}{\sqrt{2}}$	$-\dfrac{1}{\sqrt{2}}<x<\dfrac{1}{\sqrt{2}}$	$\dfrac{1}{\sqrt{2}}<x<2$	$x>2$
Sign of f	-	+	-	+
Above or below x-axis	below	above	below	above

     Graph of f is above the x-axis for $\left(-\dfrac{1}{\sqrt{2}},\dfrac{1}{\sqrt{2}}\right)\cup(2,\infty)$

     Graph of f is below the x-axis for $\left(-\infty,-\dfrac{1}{\sqrt{2}}\right)\cup\left(\dfrac{1}{\sqrt{2}},2\right)$

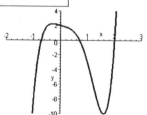

71. $f(x) = x^4 - 3x^2 - 4$
$a_3 = 0, a_2 = -3, a_1 = 0, a_0 = -4$

$Max\{1, |-4| + |0| + |-3| + |0|\} = Max\{1, 4 + 0 + 3 + 0\} = Max\{1, 7\} = 7$

$1 + Max\{|-4|, |0|, |-3|, |0|\} = 1 + Max\{4, 0, 3, 0\} = 1 + 4 = 5$
The smaller of the two numbers is 5. Thus, every zero of f lies between -5 and 5.

73. $f(x) = x^4 + x^3 - x - 1$
$a_3 = 1, a_2 = 0, a_1 = -1, a_0 = -1$

$Max\{1, |-1| + |-1| + |0| + |1|\} = Max\{1, 1 + 1 + 0 + 1\} = Max\{1, 3\} = 3$

$1 + Max\{|-1|, |-1|, |0|, |1|\} = 1 + Max\{1, 1, 0, 1\} = 1 + 1 = 2$
The smaller of the two numbers is 2. Thus, every zero of f lies between -2 and 2.

75. $f(x) = 3x^4 + 3x^3 - x^2 - 12x - 12 = 3\left(x^4 + x^3 - \frac{1}{3}x^2 - 4x - 4\right)$

Note: The leading coefficient must be 1.

$a_3 = 1, a_2 = -\frac{1}{3}, a_1 = -4, a_0 = -4$

$Max\left\{1, |-4| + |-4| + \left|-\frac{1}{3}\right| + |1|\right\} = Max\left\{1, 4 + 4 + \frac{1}{3} + 1\right\} = Max\left\{1, \frac{28}{3}\right\} = \frac{28}{3}$

$1 + Max\left\{|-4|, |-4|, \left|-\frac{1}{3}\right|, |1|\right\} = 1 + Max\left\{4, 4, \frac{1}{3}, 1\right\} = 1 + 4 = 5$
The smaller of the two numbers is 5. Thus, every zero of f lies between -5 and 5.

77. $f(x) = 4x^5 - x^4 + 2x^3 - 2x^2 + x - 1 = 4\left(x^5 - \frac{1}{4}x^4 + \frac{1}{2}x^3 - \frac{1}{2}x^2 + \frac{1}{4}x - \frac{1}{4}\right)$

Note: The leading coefficient must be 1. $a_4 = -\frac{1}{4}, a_3 = \frac{1}{2}, a_2 = -\frac{1}{2}, a_1 = \frac{1}{4}, a_0 = -\frac{1}{4}$

$Max\left\{1, \left|-\frac{1}{4}\right| + \left|\frac{1}{4}\right| + \left|-\frac{1}{2}\right| + \left|\frac{1}{2}\right| + \left|-\frac{1}{4}\right|\right\} = Max\left\{1, \frac{1}{4} + \frac{1}{4} + \frac{1}{2} + \frac{1}{2} + \frac{1}{4}\right\} = Max\left\{1, \frac{7}{4}\right\} = \frac{7}{4}$

$1 + Max\left\{\left|-\frac{1}{4}\right|, \left|\frac{1}{4}\right|, \left|-\frac{1}{2}\right|, \left|\frac{1}{2}\right|, \left|-\frac{1}{4}\right|\right\} = 1 + Max\left\{\frac{1}{4}, \frac{1}{4}, \frac{1}{2}, \frac{1}{2}, \frac{1}{4}\right\} = 1 + \frac{1}{2} = \frac{3}{2}$

The smaller of the two numbers is $\frac{3}{2}$. Thus, every zero of f lies between $-\frac{3}{2}$ and $\frac{3}{2}$.

79. $f(x) = 8x^4 - 2x^2 + 5x - 1$; $[0, 1]$
$f(0) = -1 < 0$ and $f(1) = 10 > 0$
Since one is positive and one is negative, there is a zero in the interval.

81. $f(x) = 2x^3 + 6x^2 - 8x + 2$; $[-5, -4]$
$f(-5) = -58 < 0$ and $f(-4) = 2 > 0$
Since one is positive and one is negative, there is a zero in the interval.

83. $f(x) = x^5 - x^4 + 7x^3 - 7x^2 - 18x + 18;$ $[1.4, 1.5]$
    $f(1.4) = -0.1754 < 0$ and $f(1.5) = 1.4063 > 0$
    Since one is positive and one is negative,
    there is a zero in the interval.

85. $8x^4 - 2x^2 + 5x - 1 = 0;$ $0 \le r \le 1$

    Consider the function $f(x) = 8x^4 - 2x^2 + 5x - 1$
    Subdivide the interval [0,1] into 10 equal subintervals:

    [0,0.1]; [0.1,0.2]; [0.2,0.3]; [0.3,0.4]; [0.4,0.5]; [0.5,0.6]; [0.6,0.7]; [0.7,0.8];
    [0.8,0.9]; [0.9,1]

    $f(0) = -1; f(0.1) = -0.5192$
    $f(0.1) = -0.5192; f(0.2) = -0.0672$
    $f(0.2) = -0.0672; f(0.3) = 0.3848$ so f has a real zero on the interval [0.2,0.3].
    Subdivide the interval [0.2,0.3] into 10 equal subintervals:

    [0.2,0.21]; [0.21,0.22]; [0.22,0.23]; [0.23,0.24]; [0.24,0.25]; [0.25,0.26];[0.26,0.27];
    [0.27,0.28]; [0.28,0.29]; [0.29,0.3]

    $f(0.2) = -0.0672; f(0.21) = -0.02264$
    $f(0.21) = -0.02264; f(0.22) = 0.0219$ so f has a real zero on the interval
                                                  [0.21,0.22], therefore $r = 0.21$, correct
                                                  to 2 decimal places.

87. $2x^3 + 6x^2 - 8x + 2 = 0;$ $-5 \le r \le -4$

    Consider the function $f(x) = 2x^3 + 6x^2 - 8x + 2$
    Subdivide the interval [-5,-4] into 10 equal subintervals:

    [-5,-4.9]; [-4.9,-4.8]; [-4.8,-4.7]; [-4.7,-4.6]; [-4.6,-4.5]; [-4.5,-4.4]; [-4.4,-4.3];
    [-4.3,-4.2]; [-4.2,-4.1]; [-4.1,-4]

    $f(-5) = -58; f(-4.9) = -50.038$
    $f(-4.9) = -50.038; f(-4.8) = -42.544$
    $f(-4.8) = -42.544; f(-4.7) = -35.506$
    $f(-4.7) = -35.506; f(-4.6) = -28.912$
    $f(-4.6) = -28.912; f(-4.5) = -22.75$
    $f(-4.5) = -22.75; f(-4.4) = -17$
    $f(-4.4) = -17; f(-4.3) = -11.674$
    $f(-4.3) = -11.674; f(-4.2) = -6.736$
    $f(-4.2) = -6.736; f(-4.1) = -2.182$
    $f(-4.1) = -2.182; f(-4) = 2$ so f has a real zero on the interval [-4.1,-4].
    Subdivide the interval [-4.1,-4] into 10 equal subintervals:

[-4.1,-4.09]; [-4.09,-4.08]; [-4.08,-4.07]; [-4.07,-4.06]; [-4.06,-4.05]; [-4.05,-4.04];
[-4.04,-4.03]; [-4.03,-4.02]; [-4.02,-4.01]; [-4.01,-4]

$f(-4.1) = -2.182; f(-4.09) = -1.7473$
$f(-4.09) = -1.7473; f(-4.08) = -1.3162$
$f(-4.08) = -1.3162; f(-4.07) = -0.8889$
$f(-4.07) = -0.8889; f(-4.06) = -0.4652$
$f(-4.06) = -0.4652; f(-4.05) = -0.0452$
$f(-4.05) = -0.4652; f(-4.04) = 0.3711$ so f has a real zero on the interval [-4.05,-4.04], therefore $r = -4.05$, correct to 2 decimal places.

89. $f(x) = x^3 + x^2 + x - 4$

$f(1) = -1; f(2) = 10$ so f has a real zero on the interval [1,2],

Subdivide the interval [1,2] into 10 equal subintervals:

[1,1.1]; [1.1,1.2]; [1.2,1.3]; [1.3,1.4]; [1.4,1.5]; [1.5,1.6]; [1.6,1.7]; [1.7,1.8];
[1.8,1.9]; [1.9,2]

$f(1) = -1; f(1.1) = -0.359$
$f(1.1) = -0.359; f(1.2) = 0.368$ so f has a real zero on the interval [1.1,1.2].
Subdivide the interval [1,1.2] into 10 equal subintervals:

[1,1.11]; [1.11,1.12]; [1.12,1.13]; [1.13,1.14]; [1.14,1.15]; [1.15,1.16];[1.16,1.17];
[1.17,1.18]; [1.18,1.19]; [1.19,1.2]

$f(1) = -1; f(1.11) = -0.2903$ so f has a real zero on the interval
$f(1.11) = -0.2903; f(1.12) = -0.2207$ [1.15,1.16], therefore $r = 1.15$, correct
$f(1.12) = -0.2207; f(1.13) = -0.1502$ to 2 decimal places.
$f(1.13) = -0.1502; f(1.14) = -0.0789$
$f(1.14) = -0.0789; f(1.15) = -0.0066$
$f(1.15) = -0.0066; f(1.16) = 0.0665$

91. $f(x) = 2x^4 - 3x^3 - 4x^2 - 8$
$f(2) = -16; f(3) = 37$ so f has a real zero on the interval [2,3],
Subdivide the interval [2,3] into 10 equal subintervals:

[2,2.1]; [2.1,2.2]; [2.2,2.3]; [2.3,2.4]; [2.4,2.5]; [2.5,2.6]; [2.6,2.7]; [2.7,2.8];
[2.8,2.9]; [2.9,3]

$f(2) = -16; f(2.1) = -14.5268$

$f(2.1) = -14.5268; f(2.2) = -12.4528$

$f(2.2) = -12.4528; f(2.3) = -9.6928$

$f(2.3) = -9.6928; f(2.4) = -6.1568$

$f(2.4) = -6.1568; f(2.5) = -1.75$

$f(2.5) = -1.75; f(2.6) = 3.6272$ so f has a real zero on the interval [2.5,2.6].

Subdivide the interval [2.5,2.6] into 10 equal subintervals:

[2.5,2.51]; [2.51,2.52]; [2.52,2.53]; [2.53,2.54]; [2.54,2.55]; [2.55,2.56];[2.56,2.57];
[2.57,2.58]; [2.58,2.59]; [2.59,2.6]

$f(2.5) = -1.75; f(2.51) = -1.2576$

$f(2.51) = -1.2576; f(2.52) = -0.7555$

$f(2.52) = -0.7555; f(2.53) = -0.2434$

$f(2.53) = -0.2434; f(2.54) = 0.2787$

so f has a real zero on the interval [2.53,2.54], therefore $r = 2.53$, correct to 2 decimal places.

93. $x - 2$ is a factor of $f(x) = x^3 - kx^2 + kx + 2$ only if the remainder that results when $f(x)$ is divided by $x - 2$ is 0. Dividing, we have:

$$2\overline{)1 \quad -k \quad\quad k \quad\quad 2}$$
$$\underline{2 \quad -2k+4 \quad -2k+8}$$
$$1 \quad -k+2 \quad -k+4 \quad -2k+10$$

Set the remainder equal to zero and solve: $-2k + 10 = 0 \rightarrow -2k = -10 \rightarrow k = 5$

95.   By the Remainder Theorem we know that the remainder from synthetic division by c is equal to $f(c)$. Thus the easiest way to find the remainder is to evaluate:
$f(1) = 2(1)^{20} - 8(1)^{10} + 1 - 2 = 2 - 8 + 1 - 2 = -7$. The remainder is –7.

97.   We want to prove that $x - c$ is a factor of $x^n - c^n$, for any positive integer n. By the Factor Theorem, $x - c$ will be a factor of $f(x)$ provided $f(c) = 0$. Here, $f(x) = x^n - c^n$, so that $f(c) = c^n - c^n = 0$. Therefore, $x - c$ is a factor of $x^n - c^n$.

99. $x^3 - 8x^2 + 16x - 3 = 0$ has solution $x = 3$, so $x - 3$ is a factor of
$f(x) = x^3 - 8x^2 + 16x - 3$.

Using synthetic division

$$3\overline{)1 \quad -8 \quad 16 \quad -3}$$
$$\underline{3 \quad -15 \quad\quad 3}$$
$$1 \quad -5 \quad 1 \quad\quad 0$$

$\therefore f(x) = x^3 - 8x^2 + 16x - 3 = (x - 3)(x^2 - 5x + 1)$.

Solving $x^2 - 5x + 1 = 0$ $x = \dfrac{5 \pm \sqrt{25 - 4}}{2} = \dfrac{5 \pm \sqrt{21}}{2}$

The sum of these two roots is $\dfrac{5 + \sqrt{21}}{2} + \dfrac{5 - \sqrt{21}}{2} = \dfrac{10}{2} = 5$.

101. $f(x) = 2x^3 + 3x^2 - 6x + 7$
    By the Rational Zero Theorem, the only possible rational zeros are:
    $$\frac{p}{q} = \pm 1, \pm 7, \pm \frac{1}{2}, \pm \frac{7}{2}$$ Since $\frac{1}{3}$ is not in the list of possible rational zeros, it is not a zero of $f(x)$.

103. $f(x) = 2x^6 - 5x^4 + x^3 - x + 1$
    By the Rational Zero Theorem, the only possible rational zeros are:
    $$\frac{p}{q} = \pm 1, \pm \frac{1}{2}$$ Since $\frac{3}{5}$ is not in the list of possible rational zeros, it is not a zero of $f(x)$.

105. Let x be the length of a side of the original cube.
    After removing the 1 inch slice, one dimension will be $x - 1$.
    The volume of the new solid will be:
    $$(x-1) \cdot x \cdot x = 294 \rightarrow x^3 - x^2 = 294 \rightarrow x^3 - x^2 - 294 = 0$$
    By Descartes Rule of Signs, we know that there is one positive real solution.
    The possible rational zeros are:
    $$p = \pm 1, \pm 2, \pm 3, \pm 6, \pm 7, \pm 14, \pm 21, \pm 42, \pm 49, \pm 98, \pm 147, \pm 294; \quad q = \pm 1$$
    The rational zeros are the same as the values for p.
    Using synthetic division:

    $$7 \overline{)\begin{array}{cccc} 1 & -1 & 0 & -294 \\ & 7 & 42 & 294 \\ \hline 1 & 6 & 42 & 0 \end{array}}$$

    7 is a zero, so the length of the original edge of the cube was 7 inches.

107. $f(x) = x^n + a_{n-1}x^{n-1} + a_{n-2}x^{n-2} + ... + a_1 x + a_0$; where $a_{n-1}, a_{n-2}, ... a_1, a_0$ are integers

    If r is a real zero of f, then r is either rational or irrational. We know that the rational roots of f must be of the form $\frac{p}{q}$ where p is a divisor of a_0 and q is a divisor of 1. This means that $q = \pm 1$. So if r is rational, then $r = \frac{p}{q} = \pm p$. Therefore, r is an integer or r is irrational.

109. (a) $f(x) = 8x^4 - 2x^2 + 5x - 1$ $0 \le r \le 1$
At Step 0 we have the interval $[0,1]$.
$f(0) = -1; \quad f(1) = 10$
Let m = the midpoint of the interval being considered.
So $m_0 = 0.5$

n	m_{n-1}	$f(m_{n-1})$	New interval
1	0.5	$f(0.5) = 1.5 > 0$	$[0, 0.5]$
2	0.25	$f(0.25) = 0.15625 > 0$	$[0, 0.25]$
3	0.125	$f(0.125) = -0.4043 < 0$	$[0.125, 0.25]$
4	0.1875	$f(0.1875) = -0.1229 < 0$	$[0.1875, 0.25]$
5	0.21875	$f(0.21875) = 0.0164 > 0$	$[0.1875, 0.21875]$
6	0.203125	$f(0.203125) = -0.0533 < 0$	$[0.203125, 0.21875]$
7	0.2109375	$f(0.2109375) = -0.0185 < 0$	$[0.2109375, 0.21875]$
8	0.21484375		

Since the midpoint value at Step 8 agrees with the midpoint value at Step 7 to two decimal places, $r = 0.21$, correct to 2 decimal places.

(b) $f(x) = x^4 + 8x^3 - x^2 + 2;$ $-1 \le r \le 0$
At Step 0 we have the interval $[-1, 0]$.
$f(-1) = -6; \quad f(0) = 2$
Let m = the midpoint of the interval being considered.
So $m_0 = -0.5$

n	m_{n-1}	$f(m_{n-1})$	New interval
1	- 0.5	$f(-0.5) = 0.8125 > 0$	$[-1, -0.5]$
2	- 0.75	$f(-0.75) = -1.6211 < 0$	$[-0.75, -0.5]$
3	-0.625	$f(-0.625) = -0.1912 < 0$	$[-0.625, -0.5]$
4	-0.5625	$f(-0.5625) = 0.3599 > 0$	$[-0.625, -0.5625]$
5	-0.59375	$f(-0.59375) = 0.0972 > 0$	$[-0.625, -0.59375]$
6	-0.609375	$f(-0.609375) = -0.04372 < 0$	$[-0.609375, -0.59375]$
7	-0.6015625		

Since the midpoint value at Step 7 agrees with the midpoint value at Step 6 to two decimal places, $r = -0.60$, correct to 2 decimal places.

(c) $f(x) = 2x^3 + 6x^2 - 8x + 2; \quad -5 \le r \le -4$

At Step 0 we have the interval [-5,-4].

$f(-5) = -58; \quad f(-4) = 2$

Let m = the midpoint of the interval being considered.

So $m_0 = -4.5$

n	m_{n-1}	$f(m_{n-1})$	New interval
1	- 4.5	$f(-4.5) = -22.75 < 0$	[-4.5,- 4]
2	- 4.25	$f(-4.25) = -9.1562 < 0$	[-4.25,- 4]
3	-4.125	$f(-4.125) = -3.2852 < 0$	[-4.125,-4]
4	-4.0625	$f(-4.0625) = -0.5708 < 0$	[-4.0625,-4]
5	-4.03125	$f(-4.03125) = 0.7324 > 0$	[-4.0625, -4.03125]
6	-4.046875	$f(-4.046875) = 0.0852 > 0$	[-4.0625, -4.046875]
7	-4.0546875	$f(-4.0546875) = -0.2417 < 0$	[-4.0546875, -4.046875]
8	-4.05078125		

Since the midpoint value at Step 8 agrees with the midpoint value at Step 7 to two decimal places, $r = -4.05$, correct to 2 decimal places.

(d) $f(x) = 3x^3 - 10x + 9; \quad -3 \le r \le -2$

At Step 0 we have the interval [-3,-2].

$f(-3) = -42; \quad f(-2) = 5$

Let m = the midpoint of the interval being considered.

So $m_0 = -2.5$

n	m_{n-1}	$f(m_{n-1})$	New interval
1	- 2.5	$f(-2.5) = -12.875 < 0$	[-2.5,- 2]
2	- 2.25	$f(-2.25) = -2.6719 < 0$	[-2.25,- 2]
3	-2.125	$f(-2.125) = 1.4629 > 0$	[-2.25,- 2.125]
4	-2.1875	$f(-2.1875) = -0.5276 < 0$	[-2.1875,- 2.125]
5	-2.15625	$f(-2.15625) = 0.4866 > 0$	[-2.1875,-2.15625]
6	-2.171875	$f(-2.171875) = -0.0157 < 0$	[-2.171875,-2.15625]
7	-2.1640625	$f(-2.1640625) = 0.2366 > 0$	[-2.171875,- 2.1640625]
8	-2.16796875		

Since the midpoint value at Step 8 agrees with the midpoint value at Step 7 to two decimal places, $r = -2.16$, correct to 2 decimal places.

(e) $f(x) = x^3 + x^2 + x - 4;$ $1 \le r \le 2$

At Step 0 we have the interval [1,2].

$f(1) = -1;$ $f(2) = 10$

Let m = the midpoint of the interval being considered.

So $m_0 = 1.5$

n	m_{n-1}	$f(m_{n-1})$	New interval
1	1.5	$f(1.5) = 3.125 > 0$	[1,1.5]
2	1.25	$f(1.25) = 0.7656 > 0$	[1,1.25]
3	1.125	$f(1.125) = -0.1855 < 0$	[1.125,1.25]
4	1.1875	$f(1.1875) = 0.2722 > 0$	[1.125,1.1875]
5	1.15625	$f(1.15625) = 0.0390 > 0$	[1.125,1.15625]
6	1.140625	$f(1.140625) = -0.0744 < 0$	[1.140625,1.15625]
7	1.1484375		

Since the midpoint value at Step 7 agrees with the midpoint value at Step 6 to two decimal places, $r = 1.14$, correct to 2 decimal places.

(f) $f(x) = 2x^4 + x^2 - 1;$ $0 \le r \le 1$

At Step 0 we have the interval [0,1].

$f(0) = -1;$ $f(1) = 2$

Let m = the midpoint of the interval being considered.

So $m_0 = 0.5$

n	m_{n-1}	$f(m_{n-1})$	New interval
1	0.5	$f(0.5) = -0.625 < 0$	[0.5,1]
2	0.75	$f(0.75) = 0.1593 > 0$	[0.5,0.75]
3	0.625	$f(0.625) = -0.3042 < 0$	[0.625,0.75]
4	0.6875	$f(0.6875) = -0.0805 < 0$	[0.6875,0.75]
5	0.71875	$f(0.71875) = 0.0504 > 0$	[0.6875,0.71875]
6	0.703125	$f(0.703125) = -0.0168 < 0$	[0.703125,0.71875]
7	0.7109375	$f(0.7109375) = 0.0164 > 0$	[0.703125, 0.7109375]
8	0.70703125	$f(0.70703125) = -0.0032 < 0$	[0.70703125, 0.7109375]
9	0.708984375		

Since the midpoint value at Step 9 agrees with the midpoint value at Step 8 to two decimal places, $r = 0.70$, correct to 2 decimal places.

(g) $f(x) = 2x^4 - 3x^3 - 4x^2 - 8;$ $2 \le r \le 3$

At Step 0 we have the interval [2,3]

$f(2) = -16;$ $f(3) = 37$

Let m = the midpoint of the interval being considered.

So $m_0 = 2.5$

n	m_{n-1}	$f(m_{n-1})$	New interval
1	2.5	$f(2.5) = -1.75 < 0$	[2.5,3]
2	2.75	$f(2.75) = 13.7422 > 0$	[2.5,2.75]
3	2.625	$f(2.625) = 5.1352 > 0$	[2.5,2.625]
4	2.5625	$f(2.5625) = 1.4905 > 0$	[2.5,2.5625]
5	2.53125	$f(2.53125) = -0.1787 < 0$	[2.53125,2.5625]
6	2.546875	$f(2.546875) = 0.6435 > 0$	[2.53125, 2.546875]
7	2.5390625	$f(2.5390625) = 0.2293 > 0$	[2.53125, 2.5390625]
8	2.53515625		

Since the midpoint value at Step 8 agrees with the midpoint value at Step 7 to two decimal places, $r = 2.53$, correct to 2 decimal places.

(h) $f(x) = 3x^3 - 2x^2 - 20;$ $2 \le r \le 3$

At Step 0 we have the interval [2,3].

$f(2) = -4;$ $f(3) = 43$

Let m = the midpoint of the interval being considered.

So $m_0 = 2.5$

n	m_{n-1}	$f(m_{n-1})$	New interval
1	2.5	$f(2.5) = 14.375 > 0$	[2,2.5]
2	2.25	$f(2.25) = 4.0469 > 0$	[2,2.25]
3	2.125	$f(2.125) = -0.2441 < 0$	[2.125,2.25]
4	2.1875	$f(2.1875) = 1.8323 > 0$	[2.125,2.1875]
5	2.15625	$f(2.15625) = 0.7771 > 0$	[2.125,2.15625]
6	2.140625	$f(2.140625) = 0.2622 > 0$	[2.125, 2.140625]
7	2.1328125	$f(2.1328125) = 0.0080 > 0$	[2.125, 2.1328125]
8	2.1315625		

Since the midpoint value at Step 8 agrees with the midpoint value at Step 7 to two decimal places, $r = 2.13$, correct to 2 decimal places.

Chapter 5

The Zeros of a Polynomial Function

5.3 Complex Numbers; Quadratic Equations with a Negative Discriminant

1. $(2 - 3i) + (6 + 8i) = (2 + 6) + (-3 + 8)i = 8 + 5i$

3. $(-3 + 2i) - (4 - 4i) = (-3 - 4) + (2 - (-4))i = -7 + 6i$

5. $(2 - 5i) - (8 + 6i) = (2 - 8) + (-5 - 6)i = -6 - 11i$

7. $3(2 - 6i) = 6 - 18i$ 9. $2i(2 - 3i) = 4i - 6i^2 = 4i - 6(-1) = 6 + 4i$

11. $(3 - 4i)(2 + i) = 6 + 3i - 8i - 4i^2 = 6 - 5i - 4(-1) = 10 - 5i$

13. $(-6 + i)(-6 - i) = 36 + 6i - 6i - i^2 = 36 - (-1) = 37$

15. $\dfrac{10}{3 - 4i} = \dfrac{10}{3 - 4i} \cdot \dfrac{3 + 4i}{3 + 4i} = \dfrac{30 + 40i}{9 + 12i - 12i - 16i^2} = \dfrac{30 + 40i}{9 - 16(-1)} = \dfrac{30 + 40i}{25}$

$= \dfrac{30}{25} + \dfrac{40}{25}i = \dfrac{6}{5} + \dfrac{8}{5}i$

17. $\dfrac{2 + i}{i} = \dfrac{2 + i}{i} \cdot \dfrac{-i}{-i} = \dfrac{-2i - i^2}{-i^2} = \dfrac{-2i - (-1)}{-(-1)} = \dfrac{1 - 2i}{1} = 1 - 2i$

19. $\dfrac{6 - i}{1 + i} = \dfrac{6 - i}{1 + i} \cdot \dfrac{1 - i}{1 - i} = \dfrac{6 - 6i - i + i^2}{1 - i + i - i^2} = \dfrac{6 - 7i + (-1)}{1 - (-1)} = \dfrac{5 - 7i}{2} = \dfrac{5}{2} - \dfrac{7}{2}i$

21. $\left(\dfrac{1}{2} + \dfrac{\sqrt{3}}{2}i\right)^2 = \dfrac{1}{4} + 2\left(\dfrac{1}{2}\right)\left(\dfrac{\sqrt{3}}{2}i\right) + \dfrac{3}{4}i^2 = \dfrac{1}{4} + \dfrac{\sqrt{3}}{2}i + \dfrac{3}{4}(-1) = -\dfrac{1}{2} + \dfrac{\sqrt{3}}{2}i$

23. $(1 + i)^2 = 1 + 2i + i^2 = 1 + 2i + (-1) = 2i$

25. $i^{23} = i^{22+1} = i^{22} \cdot i = \left(i^2\right)^{11} \cdot i = (-1)^{11}i = -i$

27. $i^{-15} = \dfrac{1}{i^{15}} = \dfrac{1}{i^{14+1}} = \dfrac{1}{i^{14} \cdot i} = \dfrac{1}{\left(i^2\right)^7 \cdot i} = \dfrac{1}{(-1)^7 i} = \dfrac{1}{-i} = \dfrac{1}{-i} \cdot \dfrac{i}{i} = \dfrac{i}{-i^2} = \dfrac{i}{-(-1)} = i$

29. $i^6 - 5 = (i^2)^3 - 5 = (-1)^3 - 5 = -1 - 5 = -6$

31. $6i^3 - 4i^5 = i^3(6 - 4i^2) = i^2 \cdot i(6 - 4(-1)) = -1 \cdot i(10) = -10i$

33. $(1 + i)^3 = (1 + i)(1 + i)(1 + i) = (1 + 2i + i^2)(1 + i) = (1 + 2i - 1)(1 + i) = 2i(1 + i)$
     $= 2i + 2i^2 = 2i + 2(-1) = -2 + 2i$

35. $i^7(1 + i^2) = i^7(1 + (-1)) = i^7(0) = 0$

37. $i^6 + i^4 + i^2 + 1 = (i^2)^3 + (i^2)^2 + i^2 + 1 = (-1)^3 + (-1)^2 + (-1) + 1 = -1 + 1 - 1 + 1 = 0$

39. $\sqrt{-4} = 2i$ 41. $\sqrt{-25} = 5i$

43. $\sqrt{(3 + 4i)(4i - 3)} = \sqrt{12i - 9 + 16i^2 - 12i} = \sqrt{-9 + 16(-1)} = \sqrt{-25} = 5i$

45. $x^2 + 4 = 0$
     $a = 1, b = 0, c = 4,\quad b^2 - 4ac = 0^2 - 4(1)(4) = -16$

     $x = \dfrac{-0 \pm \sqrt{-16}}{2(1)} = \dfrac{\pm 4i}{2} = \pm 2i \;\rightarrow\;$ The solution set is $\{\pm 2i\}$.

47. $x^2 - 16 = 0$
     $a = 1, b = 0, c = -16,\quad b^2 - 4ac = 0^2 - 4(1)(-16) = 64$

     $x = \dfrac{-0 \pm \sqrt{64}}{2(1)} = \dfrac{\pm 8}{2} = \pm 4 \;\rightarrow\;$ The solution set is $\{\pm 4\}$.

49. $x^2 - 6x + 13 = 0$
     $a = 1, b = -6, c = 13,\quad b^2 - 4ac = (-6)^2 - 4(1)(13) = 36 - 52 = -16$

     $x = \dfrac{-(-6) \pm \sqrt{-16}}{2(1)} = \dfrac{6 \pm 4i}{2} = 3 \pm 2i \;\rightarrow\;$ The solution set is $\{3 - 2i, 3 + 2i\}$.

51. $x^2 - 6x + 10 = 0$
     $a = 1, b = -6, c = 10,\quad b^2 - 4ac = (-6)^2 - 4(1)(10) = 36 - 40 = -4$

     $x = \dfrac{-(-6) \pm \sqrt{-4}}{2(1)} = \dfrac{6 \pm 2i}{2} = 3 \pm i$
     The solution set is $\{3 - i, 3 + i\}$.

53. $8x^2 - 4x + 1 = 0$
     $a = 8, b = -4, c = 1,\quad b^2 - 4ac = (-4)^2 - 4(8)(1) = 16 - 32 = -16$

     $x = \dfrac{-(-4) \pm \sqrt{-16}}{2(8)} = \dfrac{4 \pm 4i}{16} = \dfrac{1}{4} \pm \dfrac{1}{4}i$

     The solution set is $\left\{ \dfrac{1}{4} - \dfrac{1}{4}i, \dfrac{1}{4} + \dfrac{1}{4}i \right\}$.

55. $5x^2 + 1 = 2x \rightarrow 5x^2 - 2x + 1 = 0$

$a = 5, b = -2, c = 1,\quad b^2 - 4ac = (-2)^2 - 4(5)(1) = 4 - 20 = -16$

$x = \dfrac{-(-2) \pm \sqrt{-16}}{2(5)} = \dfrac{2 \pm 4i}{10} = \dfrac{1}{5} \pm \dfrac{2}{5}i$

The solution set is $\left\{ \dfrac{1}{5} - \dfrac{2}{5}i,\ \dfrac{1}{5} + \dfrac{2}{5}i \right\}$.

57. $x^2 + x + 1 = 0$

$a = 1, b = 1, c = 1,\quad b^2 - 4ac = 1^2 - 4(1)(1) = 1 - 4 = -3$

$x = \dfrac{-1 \pm \sqrt{-3}}{2(1)} = \dfrac{-1 \pm \sqrt{3}\,i}{2} = \dfrac{-1}{2} \pm \dfrac{\sqrt{3}}{2}i$

The solution set is $\left\{ \dfrac{-1}{2} - \dfrac{\sqrt{3}}{2}i,\ \dfrac{-1}{2} + \dfrac{\sqrt{3}}{2}i \right\}$.

59. $x^3 - 8 = 0$

$(x - 2)(x^2 + 2x + 4) = 0$

$x - 2 = 0 \rightarrow x = 2$

$x^2 + 2x + 4 = 0$

$a = 1, b = 2, c = 4,\quad b^2 - 4ac = 2^2 - 4(1)(4) = 4 - 16 = -12$

$x = \dfrac{-2 \pm \sqrt{-12}}{2(1)} = \dfrac{-2 \pm 2\sqrt{3}\,i}{2} = -1 \pm \sqrt{3}i$

The solution set is $\left\{ 2,\ -1 - \sqrt{3}i,\ -1 + \sqrt{3}i \right\}$.

61. $x^4 = 16 \rightarrow x^4 - 16 = 0$

$(x^2 - 4)(x^2 + 4) = 0 \rightarrow (x - 2)(x + 2)(x^2 + 4) = 0$

$x - 2 = 0 \rightarrow x = 2$

$x + 2 = 0 \rightarrow x = -2$

$x^2 + 4 = 0 \rightarrow x = \pm 2i$

The solution set is $\left\{ -2,\ 2,\ -2i,\ 2i \right\}$.

63. $x^4 + 13x^2 + 36 = 0$

$(x^2 + 9)(x^2 + 4) = 0$

$x^2 + 9 = 0 \rightarrow x = \pm 3i$

$x^2 + 4 = 0 \rightarrow x = \pm 2i$

The solution set is $\left\{ -3i,\ 3i,\ -2i,\ 2i \right\}$.

65. $3x^2 - 3x + 4 = 0$

$a = 3, b = -3, c = 4,\quad b^2 - 4ac = (-3)^2 - 4(3)(4) = 9 - 48 = -39$

The equation has two complex conjugate solutions.

67. $2x^2 + 3x - 4 = 0$

$a = 2, b = 3, c = -4, \quad b^2 - 4ac = 3^2 - 4(2)(-4) = 9 + 32 = 41$

The equation has two unequal real solutions.

69. $9x^2 - 12x + 4 = 0$

$a = 9, b = -12, c = 4, \quad b^2 - 4ac = (-12)^2 - 4(9)(4) = 144 - 144 = 0$

The equation has a repeated real solution.

71. The other solution is the conjugate of $2 + 3i$, or $2 - 3i$.

73. $z + \bar{z} = 3 - 4i + \overline{3 - 4i} = 3 - 4i + 3 + 4i = 6$

75. $z \cdot \bar{z} = (3 - 4i)(\overline{3 - 4i}) = (3 - 4i)(3 + 4i) = 9 + 12i - 12i - 16i^2 = 9 - 16(-1) = 25$

77. $z + \bar{z} = a + bi + \overline{a + bi} = a + bi + a - bi = 2a$

$z - \bar{z} = a + bi - (\overline{a + bi}) = a + bi - (a - bi) = a + bi - a + bi = 2bi$

79. $\overline{z + w} = \overline{(a + bi) + (c + di)} = \overline{(a + c) + (b + d)i} = (a + c) - (b + d)i$

$\qquad\qquad = (a - bi) + (c - di) = \overline{a + bi} + \overline{c + di} = \bar{z} + \bar{w}$

81. Answers will vary.

Chapter 5

The Zeros of a Polynomial Function

5.4   Complex Zeros; Fundamental Theorem of Algebra

1. Since complex zeros appear in conjugate pairs, $4 + i$, the conjugate of $4 - i$, is the remaining zero of f.

3. Since complex zeros appear in conjugate pairs, $-i$, the conjugate of i, and $1 - i$, the conjugate of $1 + i$, are the remaining zeros of f.

5. Since complex zeros appear in conjugate pairs, $-i$, the conjugate of i, and $-2i$, the conjugate of $2i$, are the remaining zeros of f.

7. Since complex zeros appear in conjugate pairs, $-i$, the conjugate of i, is the remaining zero of f.

9. Since complex zeros appear in conjugate pairs, $2 - i$, the conjugate of $2 + i$, and $-3 + i$, the conjugate of $-3 - i$, are the remaining zeros of f.

11. Since $3 + 2i$ is a zero, its conjugate $3 - 2i$ is also a zero of f. Finding the function:
$$f(x) = (x-4)(x-4)(x-(3+2i))(x-(3-2i)) = \left(x^2 - 8x + 16\right)((x-3) - 2i)((x-3) + 2i)$$
$$= \left(x^2 - 8x + 16\right)\left(x^2 - 6x + 9 - 4i^2\right) = \left(x^2 - 8x + 16\right)\left(x^2 - 6x + 13\right)$$
$$= x^4 - 6x^3 + 13x^2 - 8x^3 + 48x^2 - 104x + 16x^2 - 96x + 208$$
$$= x^4 - 14x^3 + 77x^2 - 200x + 208$$

13. Since $-i$ is a zero, its conjugate i is also a zero, and since $1 + i$ is a zero, its conjugate $1 - i$ is also a zero of f. Finding the function:
$$f(x) = (x-2)(x+i)(x-i)(x-(1+i))(x-(1-i))$$
$$= (x-2)\left(x^2 - i^2\right)((x-1) - i)((x-1) + i) = (x-2)\left(x^2 + 1\right)\left(x^2 - 2x + 1 - i^2\right)$$
$$= \left(x^3 - 2x^2 + x - 2\right)\left(x^2 - 2x + 2\right)$$
$$= x^5 - 2x^4 + 2x^3 - 2x^4 + 4x^3 - 4x^2 + x^3 - 2x^2 + 2x - 2x^2 + 4x - 4$$
$$= x^5 - 4x^4 + 7x^3 - 8x^2 + 6x - 4$$

15. Since $-i$ is a zero, its conjugate i is also a zero of f. Finding the function:
$$f(x) = (x-3)(x-3)(x+i)(x-i) = \left(x^2 - 6x + 9\right)\left(x^2 - i^2\right)$$
$$= \left(x^2 - 6x + 9\right)\left(x^2 + 1\right) = x^4 + x^2 - 6x^3 - 6x + 9x^2 + 9 = x^4 - 6x^3 + 10x^2 - 6x + 9$$

17. Since $2i$ is a zero, its conjugate $-2i$ is also a zero of f. $x - 2i$ and $x + 2i$ are factors of f.
Thus, $(x - 2i)(x + 2i) = x^2 + 4$ is a factor of f. Using division to find the other factor:

$$
\begin{array}{r}
x - 4 \\
x^2 + 4 \overline{\smash{)}\, x^3 - 4x^2 + 4x - 16} \\
\underline{x^3 \qquad\;\; + 4x} \\
-4x^2 \qquad - 16 \\
\underline{-4x^2 \qquad - 16}
\end{array}
$$

$x - 4$ is a factor and the remaining zero is 4. The zeros of f are $4, 2i, -2i$.

19. Since $-2i$ is a zero, its conjugate $2i$ is also a zero of f. $x - 2i$ and $x + 2i$ are factors of f.
Thus, $(x - 2i)(x + 2i) = x^2 + 4$ is a factor of f. Using division to find the other factor:

$$
\begin{array}{r}
2x^2 + 5x - 3 \\
x^2 + 4 \overline{\smash{)}\, 2x^4 + 5x^3 + 5x^2 + 20x - 12} \\
\underline{2x^4 \qquad\quad + 8x^2} \\
5x^3 - 3x^2 + 20x \\
\underline{5x^3 \qquad\quad + 20x} \\
-3x^2 \qquad - 12 \\
\underline{-3x^2 \qquad - 12}
\end{array}
$$

$2x^2 + 5x - 3 = (2x - 1)(x + 3)$ are factors and the remaining zeros are $\dfrac{1}{2}$ and -3. The

zeros of f are $2i, -2i, -3, \dfrac{1}{2}$.

21. Since $3 - 2i$ is a zero, its conjugate $3 + 2i$ is also a zero of h. $x - (3 - 2i)$ and $x - (3 + 2i)$
are factors of h. Thus,
$(x - (3 - 2i))(x - (3 + 2i)) = ((x - 3) + 2i)((x - 3) - 2i) = x^2 - 6x + 9 - 4i^2 = x^2 - 6x + 13$ is
a factor of h. Using division to find the other factor:

$$
\begin{array}{r}
x^2 - 3x - 10 \\
x^2 - 6x + 13 \overline{\smash{)}\, x^4 - 9x^3 + 21x^2 + 21x - 130} \\
\underline{x^4 - 6x^3 + 13x^2} \\
-3x^3 + 8x^2 + 21x \\
\underline{-3x^3 + 18x^2 - 39x} \\
-10x^2 + 60x - 130 \\
\underline{-10x^2 + 60x - 130}
\end{array}
$$

$x^2 - 3x - 10 = (x + 2)(x - 5)$ are factors and the remaining zeros are –2 and 5. The zeros of
h are $3 - 2i, 3 + 2i, -2, 5$.

23.   Since $-4i$ is a zero, its conjugate $4i$ is also a zero of h. $x - 4i$ and $x + 4i$ are factors of h. Thus, $(x - 4i)(x + 4i) = x^2 + 16$ is a factor of h.   Using division to find the other factor:

$$
\require{enclose}
\begin{array}{r}
3x^3 + 2x^2 - 33x - 22 \\
x^2 + 16 \enclose{longdiv}{3x^5 + 2x^4 + 15x^3 + 10x^2 - 528x - 352} \\
\underline{3x^5 + 48x^3} \\
2x^4 - 33x^3 + 10x^2 \\
\underline{2x^4 + 32x^2} \\
-33x^3 - 22x^2 - 528x \\
\underline{-33x^3 - 528x} \\
-22x^2 - 352 \\
\underline{-22x^2 - 352}
\end{array}
$$

$3x^3 + 2x^2 - 33x - 22 = x^2(3x + 2) - 11(3x + 2) = (3x + 2)(x^2 - 11)$

$= (3x + 2)(x - \sqrt{11})(x + \sqrt{11})$ are factors and the remaining zeros are $-\dfrac{2}{3}, \sqrt{11},$ and $-\sqrt{11}$.

The zeros of h are $4i, -4i, -\sqrt{11}, \sqrt{11}, -\dfrac{2}{3}$.

25. $f(x) = x^3 - 1 = (x - 1)(x^2 + x + 1)$ The zeros of $x^2 + x + 1 = 0$ are:

$$x = \frac{-1 \pm \sqrt{1^2 - 4(1)(1)}}{2(1)} = \frac{-1 \pm \sqrt{-3}}{2} = -\frac{1}{2} + \frac{\sqrt{3}}{2}i \text{ or } -\frac{1}{2} - \frac{\sqrt{3}}{2}i$$

The zeros are: $1, -\dfrac{1}{2} + \dfrac{\sqrt{3}}{2}i, -\dfrac{1}{2} - \dfrac{\sqrt{3}}{2}i$.

27. $f(x) = x^3 - 8x^2 + 25x - 26$

    Step 1: $f(x)$ has 3 complex zeros.

    Step 2:   By Descartes Rule of Signs, there are 3 or 1 positive real zeros.

               $f(-x) = (-x)^3 - 8(-x)^2 + 25(-x) - 26 = -x^3 - 8x^2 - 25x - 26$; thus, there are no negative real zeros.

    Step 3:   Possible rational zeros:

$$p = \pm 1, \pm 2, \pm 13, \pm 26; \quad q = \pm 1; \quad \frac{p}{q} = \pm 1, \pm 2, \pm 13, \pm 26$$

    Step 4:   Using synthetic division:

$$
\begin{array}{r|rrrr}
2 & 1 & -8 & 25 & -26 \\
  &   & 2 & -12 & 26 \\
\hline
  & 1 & -6 & 13 & 0
\end{array}
$$

         Since the remainder is 0, $x - 2$ is a factor.   The other factor is the quotient:

         $x^2 - 6x + 13$.

         Using the quadratic formula to find the zeros of $x^2 - 6x + 13 = 0$:

$$x = \frac{-(-6) \pm \sqrt{(-6)^2 - 4(1)(13)}}{2(1)} = \frac{6 \pm \sqrt{-16}}{2} = \frac{6 \pm 4i}{2} = 3 \pm 2i.$$

         The complex zeros are $2, \; 3 - 2i, \; 3 + 2i$.

29. $f(x) = x^4 + 5x^2 + 4 = \left(x^2 + 4\right)\left(x^2 + 1\right) = (x + 2i)(x - 2i)(x + i)(x - i)$
      The zeros are: $-2i,\ -i,\ i,\ 2i$.

31. $f(x) = x^4 + 2x^3 + 22x^2 + 50x - 75$
      Step 1: $f(x)$ has 4 complex zeros.
      Step 2:   By Descartes Rule of Signs, there is 1 positive real zero.
      $$f(-x) = (-x)^4 + 2(-x)^3 + 22(-x)^2 + 50(-x) - 75$$
      $$= x^4 - 2x^3 + 22x^2 - 50x - 75$$
      thus, there are 3 or 1 negative real zeros.
      Step 3:   Possible rational zeros:
      $$p = \pm 1,\ \pm 3,\ \pm 5,\ \pm 15,\ \pm 25,\ \pm 75;\quad q = \pm 1;$$
      $$\frac{p}{q} = \pm 1,\ \pm 3,\ \pm 5,\ \pm 15,\ \pm 25,\ \pm 75$$
      Step 4:   Using synthetic division:

$$
\begin{array}{r|rrrrr}
-3 & 1 & 2 & 22 & 50 & -75 \\
   &   & -3 & 3 & -75 & 75 \\
\hline
   & 1 & -1 & 25 & -25 & 0
\end{array}
$$

   Since the remainder is 0, $x + 3$ is a factor. The other factor is the quotient:
   $$x^3 - x^2 + 25x - 25 = x^2(x - 1) + 25(x - 1) = (x - 1)\left(x^2 + 25\right)$$
   $$= (x - 1)(x + 5i)(x - 5i)$$
   The complex zeros are $-3,\ 1,\ -5i,\ 5i$.

33. $f(x) = 3x^4 - x^3 - 9x^2 + 159x - 52$
      Step 1: $f(x)$ has 4 complex zeros.
      Step 2:   By Descartes Rule of Signs, there are 3 or 1 positive real zeros.
      $$f(-x) = 3(-x)^4 - (-x)^3 - 9(-x)^2 + 159(-x) - 52$$
      $$= 3x^4 + x^3 - 9x^2 - 159x - 52$$
      thus, there is 1 negative real zero.
      Step 3:   Possible rational zeros:

   $$p = \pm 1,\ \pm 2,\ \pm 4,\ \pm 13,\ \pm 26,\ \pm 52;\quad q = \pm 1,\ \pm 3;$$
   $$\frac{p}{q} = \pm 1,\ \pm 2,\ \pm 4,\ \pm 13,\ \pm 26,\ \pm 52,\ \pm \frac{1}{3},\ \pm \frac{2}{3},\ \pm \frac{4}{3},\ \pm \frac{13}{3},\ \pm \frac{26}{3},\ \pm \frac{52}{3}$$
   Step 4:   Using synthetic division:

$$
\begin{array}{r|rrrrr}
-4 & 3 & -1 & -9 & 159 & -52 \\
   &   & -12 & 52 & -172 & 52 \\
\hline
   & 3 & -13 & 43 & -13 & 0
\end{array}
\qquad
\begin{array}{r|rrrr}
\frac{1}{3} & 3 & -13 & 43 & -13 \\
            &   & 1 & -4 & 13 \\
\hline
            & 3 & -12 & 39 & 0
\end{array}
$$

   Since the remainder is 0, $x + 4$ and $x - \dfrac{1}{3}$ are factors. The other factor is the
   quotient: $3x^2 - 12x + 39 = 3\left(x^2 - 4x + 13\right)$.

Using the quadratic formula to find the zeros of $x^2 - 4x + 13 = 0$:

$$x = \frac{-(-4) \pm \sqrt{(-4)^2 - 4(1)(13)}}{2(1)} = \frac{4 \pm \sqrt{-36}}{2} = \frac{4 \pm 6i}{2} = 2 \pm 3i.$$

The complex zeros are $-4, \dfrac{1}{3}, 2 - 3i, 2 + 3i$.

35. If the coefficients are real numbers and $2 + i$ is a zero, then $2 - i$ would also be a zero. This would then require a polynomial of degree 4.

37. If the coefficients are real numbers, then complex zeros must appear in conjugate pairs. We have a conjugate pair and one real zero. Thus, there is only one remaining zero and it must be real because a complex zero would require a pair and the polynomial would then have to be of degree 5.

Chapter 5

The Zeros of a Polynomial Function

5.R   Chapter Review

1.
$$1)\overline{8 \quad -3 \quad 1 \quad 4}$$
$$\underline{\quad \quad 8 \quad 5 \quad 6}$$
$$8 \quad 5 \quad 6 \quad 10$$

$$\therefore 8x^3 - 3x^2 + x + 4 = (x-1)(8x^2 + 5x + 6) + \frac{10}{x-1}$$

$$q(x) = 8x^2 + 5x + 6; \qquad R = \frac{10}{x-1}$$

3.
$$-2)\overline{1 \quad -2 \quad 0 \quad 1 \quad -1}$$
$$\underline{\quad \quad -2 \quad 8 \quad -16 \quad 30}$$
$$1 \quad -4 \quad 8 \quad -15 \quad 29$$

$$\therefore x^4 - 2x^3 + x - 1 = (x+2)(x^3 - 4x^2 + 8x - 15) + \frac{29}{x+2}$$

$$q(x) = x^3 - 4x^2 + 8x - 15; \qquad R = \frac{29}{x+2}$$

5. $f(x) = 12x^6 - 8x^4 + 1$ at $x = 4$

$$4)\overline{12 \quad 0 \quad -8 \quad 0 \quad 0 \quad 0 \quad 1}$$
$$\underline{\quad \quad 48 \quad 192 \quad 736 \quad 2944 \quad 11776 \quad 47104}$$
$$12 \quad 48 \quad 184 \quad 736 \quad 2944 \quad 11776 \quad 47105$$

$$f(4) = 47105$$

7. $f(x) = 12x^8 - x^7 + 8x^4 - 2x^3 + x + 3$
Examining $f(x)$, there are 4 variations in sign; thus, there are 4 or 2 or 0 positive real zeros.
Examining $f(-x) = 12(-x)^8 - (-x)^7 + 8(-x)^4 - 2(-x)^3 + (-x) + 3$
$= 12x^8 + x^7 + 8x^4 + 2x^3 - x + 3$, there are 2 variations in sign; thus, there are 2 or 0 negative real zeros.

287

9. $f(x) = 12x^8 - x^7 + 6x^4 - x^3 + x - 3$

p must be a factor of -3: $p = \pm 1, \pm 3$

q must be a factor of 12: $q = \pm 1, \pm 2, \pm 3, \pm 4, \pm 6, \pm 12$

The possible rational zeros are: $\dfrac{p}{q} = \pm 1, \pm 3, \pm \dfrac{1}{2}, \pm \dfrac{3}{2}, \pm \dfrac{1}{3}, \pm \dfrac{1}{4}, \pm \dfrac{3}{4}, \pm \dfrac{1}{6}, \pm \dfrac{1}{12}$

11. $f(x) = x^3 - 3x^2 - 6x + 8$

Step 1: $f(x)$ has at most 3 real zeros.

Step 2: By Descartes Rule of Signs, there are 2 or 0 positive real zeros.
Also because $f(-x) = (-x)^3 - 3(-x)^2 - 6(-x) + 8 = -x^3 - 3x^2 + 6x + 8$, there is 1 negative real zero.

Step 3: Possible rational zeros:

$$p = \pm 1, \pm 2, \pm 4, \pm 8; \quad q = \pm 1; \quad \frac{p}{q} = \pm 1, \pm 2, \pm 4, \pm 8$$

Step 4: Using the Bounds on Zeros Theorem:
$$a_2 = -3, \quad a_1 = -6, \quad a_0 = 8$$
$$\text{Max}\left\{1, |8| + |-6| + |-3|\right\} = \text{Max}\left\{1, 17\right\} = 17$$
$$1 + \text{Max}\left\{|8|, |-6|, |-3|\right\} = 1 + 8 = 9$$

The smaller of the two numbers is 9. Thus, every zero of f lies between -9 and 9.

Step 5: Using synthetic division:

$$
\begin{array}{r|rrrr}
-2 & 1 & -3 & -6 & 8 \\
   &   & -2 & 10 & -8 \\
\hline
   & 1 & -5 & 4 & 0
\end{array}
$$

Since the remainder is 0, $x - (-2) = x + 2$ is a factor. The other factor is the quotient: $x^2 - 5x + 4$.

Thus, $f(x) = (x + 2)\left(x^2 - 5x + 4\right) = (x + 2)(x - 1)(x - 4)$.

The zeros are -2, 1, and 4.

13. $f(x) = 4x^3 + 4x^2 - 7x + 2$

Step 1: $f(x)$ has at most 3 real zeros.

Step 2: By Descartes Rule of Signs, there are 2 or 0 positive real zeros.
$f(-x) = 4(-x)^3 + 4(-x)^2 - 7(-x) + 2 = -4x^3 + 4x^2 + 7x + 2$; thus, there is 1 negative real zero.

Step 3: Possible rational zeros:

$$p = \pm 1, \pm 2; \quad q = \pm 1, \pm 2, \pm 4; \quad \frac{p}{q} = \pm 1, \pm 2, \pm \frac{1}{2}, \pm \frac{1}{4}$$

Step 4: Using the Bounds on Zeros Theorem:
$$f(x) = 4\left(x^3 + x^2 - \frac{7}{4}x + \frac{1}{2}\right) \rightarrow a_2 = 1, \quad a_1 = -\frac{7}{4}, \quad a_0 = \frac{1}{2}$$

$$\text{Max}\left\{1, \left|\frac{1}{2}\right| + \left|-\frac{7}{4}\right| + |1|\right\} = \text{Max}\left\{1, \frac{13}{4}\right\} = \frac{13}{4} = 3.25$$

$$1 + \text{Max}\left\{\left|\frac{1}{2}\right|, \left|-\frac{7}{4}\right|, |1|\right\} = 1 + \frac{7}{4} = \frac{11}{4} = 2.75$$

The smaller of the two numbers is 2.75. Thus, every zero of f lies between -2.75 and 2.75.

Step 5: Using synthetic division:

$$-2{\overline{\smash{\big)}\,4 \quad\ \ 4 \quad -7 \quad\ \ 2}}$$
$$\underline{\qquad\ -8 \quad\ \ 8 \quad -2}$$
$$4 \quad -4 \quad\ \ 1 \quad\ \ 0$$

Since the remainder is 0, $x-(-2) = x+2$ is a factor. The other factor is the quotient: $4x^2 - 4x + 1$. Thus,

$$f(x) = (x+2)\left(4x^2 - 4x + 1\right) = (x+2)(2x-1)(2x-1).$$

The zeros are –2 and $\dfrac{1}{2}$ (multiplicity 2).

15. $f(x) = x^4 - 4x^3 + 9x^2 - 20x + 20$

Step 1: $f(x)$ has at most 4 real zeros.

Step 2: By Descartes Rule of Signs, there are 4 or 2 or 0 positive real zeros.

$$f(-x) = (-x)^4 - 4(-x)^3 + 9(-x)^2 - 20(-x) + 20$$

$$= x^4 + 4x^3 + 9x^2 + 20x + 20;$$

thus, there are no negative real zeros.

Step 3: Possible rational zeros:

$$p = \pm1, \pm2, \pm4, \pm5, \pm10, \pm20; \quad q = \pm1;$$

$$\frac{p}{q} = \pm1, \pm2, \pm4, \pm5, \pm10, \pm20$$

Step 4: Using the Bounds on Zeros Theorem:

$$a_3 = -4, \quad a_2 = 9, \quad a_1 = -20, \quad a_0 = 20$$

$$\text{Max}\,\{1, |20| + |-20| + |9| + |-4|\} = \text{Max}\,\{1, 53\} = 53$$

$$1 + \text{Max}\,\{|20|, |-20|, |9|, |-4|\} = 1 + 20 = 21$$

The smaller of the two numbers is 21. Thus, every zero of f lies between –21 and 21.

Step 5: Using synthetic division:

$$2{\overline{\smash{\big)}\,1 \quad -4 \quad\ \ 9 \quad -20 \quad\ \ 20}} \qquad\qquad 2{\overline{\smash{\big)}\,1 \quad -2 \quad\ 5 \quad -10}}$$
$$\underline{\qquad\ \ 2 \quad -4 \quad\ \ 10 \quad -20} \qquad\qquad\qquad \underline{\ \ 2 \quad\ \ 0 \quad\ \ 10}$$
$$1 \quad -2 \quad\ \ 5 \quad -10 \quad\ \ 0 \qquad\qquad\quad 1 \quad\ \ 0 \quad\ 5 \quad\ \ 0$$

Since the remainder is 0, $x-2$ is a factor twice. The other factor is the quotient: $x^2 + 5$.

Thus, $f(x) = (x-2)(x-2)\left(x^2 + 5\right) = (x-2)^2\left(x^2 + 5\right)$.

The zero is 2 (multiplicity 2). ($x^2 + 5 = 0$ has no real solutions.)

17. $2x^4 + 2x^3 - 11x^2 + x - 6 = 0$

The solutions of the equation are the zeros of $f(x) = 2x^4 + 2x^3 - 11x^2 + x - 6$.

Step 1: $f(x)$ has at most 4 real zeros.

Step 2: By Descartes Rule of Signs, there are 3 or 1 positive real zeros.

$$f(-x) = 2(-x)^4 + 2(-x)^3 - 11(-x)^2 + (-x) - 6 = 2x^4 - 2x^3 - 11x^2 - x - 6;$$

thus, there is 1 negative real zero.

Step 3: Possible rational zeros:

$$p = \pm1, \pm2, \pm3, \pm6; \quad q = \pm1, \pm2; \quad \frac{p}{q} = \pm1, \pm2, \pm3, \pm6, \pm\frac{1}{2}, \pm\frac{3}{2}$$

Step 4:   Using the Bounds on Zeros Theorem:

$$f(x) = 2\left(x^4 + x^3 - \frac{11}{2}x^2 + \frac{1}{2}x - 3\right) \rightarrow a_3 = 1, \ a_2 = -\frac{11}{2}, \ a_1 = \frac{1}{2}, \ a_0 = -3$$

$$\text{Max}\left\{1, |-3| + \left|\frac{1}{2}\right| + \left|-\frac{11}{2}\right| + |1|\right\} = \text{Max}\{1, 10\} = 10$$

$$1 + \text{Max}\left\{|-3|, \left|\frac{1}{2}\right|, \left|-\frac{11}{2}\right|, |1|\right\} = 1 + \frac{11}{2} = \frac{13}{2} = 6.5$$

The smaller of the two numbers is 6.5. Thus, every zero of f lies between –6.5 and 6.5.

Step 5:   Using synthetic division:

$$
\begin{array}{r|rrrrr}
-3 & 2 & 2 & -11 & 1 & -6 \\
   &   & -6 & 12 & -3 & 6 \\
\hline
   & 2 & -4 & 1 & -2 & 0
\end{array}
\qquad
\begin{array}{r|rrrr}
2 & 2 & -4 & 1 & -2 \\
  &   & 4 & 0 & 2 \\
\hline
  & 2 & 0 & 1 & 0
\end{array}
$$

Since the remainder is 0, $x + 3$ and $x - 2$ are factors. The other factor is the quotient: $2x^2 + 1$. The zeros are –3 and 2. ($2x^2 + 1 = 0$ has no real solutions.)

19. $2x^4 + 7x^3 + x^2 - 7x - 3 = 0$

The solutions of the equation are the zeros of $f(x) = 2x^4 + 7x^3 + x^2 - 7x - 3$.

Step 1: $f(x)$ has at most 4 real zeros.

Step 2:   By Descartes Rule of Signs, there is 1 positive real zero.
$f(-x) = 2(-x)^4 + 7(-x)^3 + (-x)^2 - 7(-x) - 3 = 2x^4 - 7x^3 + x^2 + 7x - 3$;
thus, there are 3 or 1 negative real zeros.

Step 3:   Possible rational zeros:

$$p = \pm 1, \pm 3; \quad q = \pm 1, \pm 2; \quad \frac{p}{q} = \pm 1, \pm 3, \pm\frac{1}{2}, \pm\frac{3}{2}$$

Step 4:   Using the Bounds on Zeros Theorem:

$$f(x) = 2\left(x^4 + \frac{7}{2}x^3 + \frac{1}{2}x^2 - \frac{7}{2}x - \frac{3}{2}\right) \rightarrow a_3 = \frac{7}{2}, \ a_2 = \frac{1}{2}, \ a_1 = -\frac{7}{2}, \ a_0 = -\frac{3}{2}$$

$$\text{Max}\left\{1, \left|-\frac{3}{2}\right| + \left|-\frac{7}{2}\right| + \left|\frac{1}{2}\right| + \left|\frac{7}{2}\right|\right\} = \text{Max}\{1, 9\} = 9$$

$$1 + \text{Max}\left\{\left|-\frac{3}{2}\right|, \left|-\frac{7}{2}\right|, \left|\frac{1}{2}\right|, \left|\frac{7}{2}\right|\right\} = 1 + \frac{7}{2} = \frac{9}{2} = 4.5$$

The smaller of the two numbers is 4.5. Thus, every zero of f lies between –4.5 and 4.5.

Step 5:   Using synthetic division:

$$
\begin{array}{r|rrrrr}
-3 & 2 & 7 & 1 & -7 & -3 \\
   &   & -6 & -3 & 6 & 3 \\
\hline
   & 2 & 1 & -2 & -1 & 0
\end{array}
\qquad
\begin{array}{r|rrrr}
-1 & 2 & 1 & -2 & -1 \\
   &   & -2 & 1 & 1 \\
\hline
   & 2 & -1 & -1 & 0
\end{array}
$$

Since the remainder is 0, $x + 3$ and $x + 1$ are factors. The other factor is the quotient: $2x^2 - x - 1$.

Thus, $f(x) = (x + 3)(x + 1)\left(2x^2 - x - 1\right) = (x + 3)(x + 1)(2x + 1)(x - 1)$.

The zeros are $-3, -1, -\frac{1}{2}$, and 1.

21. $f(x) = x^3 - 3x^2 - 6x + 8$.

Step 1: $f(x)$ has at most 3 real zeros.

Step 2:   By Descartes Rule of Signs, there are 2 or no positive real zeros.

$$f(-x) = (-x)^3 - 3(-x)^2 - 6(-x) + 8 = -x^3 - 3x^2 + 6x + 8;$$

thus, there is 1 negative real zero.

Step 3:   Possible rational zeros:
$$p = \pm 1, \pm 2, \pm 4, \pm 8; \quad q = \pm 1;$$

$$\frac{p}{q} = \pm 1, \pm 2, \pm 4, \pm 8$$

Step 4:   Using synthetic division:

$$
\begin{array}{r|rrrr}
-1 & 1 & -3 & -6 & 8 \\
   &   & -1 & 4 & 2 \\
\hline
   & 1 & -4 & -2 & \{10\}
\end{array}
$$
$\rightarrow x + 1$ is not a factor

$$
\begin{array}{r|rrrr}
1 & 1 & -3 & -6 & 8 \\
  &   & 1 & -2 & -8 \\
\hline
  & 1 & -2 & -8 & 0
\end{array}
$$
$\rightarrow x - 1$ is a factor

Thus, $f(x) = (x - 1)(x^2 - 2x - 8) = (x - 1)(x - 4)(x + 2)$.

The zeros are 1, 4, and - 2.

23. $f(x) = 4x^3 + 4x^2 - 7x + 2$.

Step 1: $f(x)$ has at most 3 real zeros.

Step 2:   By Descartes Rule of Signs, there are 2 or no positive real zeros.

$$f(-x) = 4(-x)^3 + 4(-x)^2 - 7(-x) + 2 = -4x^3 + 4x^2 + 7x + 2;$$

thus, there is 1 negative real zero.

Step 3:   Possible rational zeros:
$$p = \pm 1, \pm 2; \quad q = \pm 1, \pm 2, \pm 4;$$

$$\frac{p}{q} = \pm 1, \pm \frac{1}{2}, \pm \frac{1}{4}, \pm 2$$

Step 4:   Using synthetic division:

$$
\begin{array}{r|rrrr}
-1 & 4 & 4 & -7 & 2 \\
   &   & -4 & 0 & 7 \\
\hline
   & 4 & 0 & -7 & \{9\}
\end{array}
$$
$\rightarrow x + 1$ is not a factor

$$
\begin{array}{r|rrrr}
1 & 4 & 4 & -7 & 2 \\
  &   & 4 & 8 & 1 \\
\hline
  & 4 & 8 & 1 & \{3\}
\end{array}
$$
$\rightarrow x - 1$ is not a factor

$$
\begin{array}{r}
-2{\overline{\smash{\big)}\,4 \quad\; 4 \quad -7 \quad\; 2}} \\
-8 \quad\; 8 \quad -2 \\
\hline
4 \quad\; -4 \quad\; 1 \quad\; 0
\end{array}
\qquad \rightarrow x+2 \text{ is a factor}
$$

Thus, $f(x) = (x+2)\left(4x^2 - 4x + 1\right) = (x+2)(4x-2)\left(x - \dfrac{1}{2}\right) = 4(x+2)\left(x - \dfrac{1}{2}\right)^2$.

The zeros are -2, and $\dfrac{1}{2}$ (with multiplicity 2).

25. $f(x) = x^4 - 4x^3 + 9x^2 - 20x + 20$.

Step 1: $f(x)$ has at most 4 real zeros.

Step 2: By Descartes Rule of Signs, there are 4, 2 or no positive real zeros.

$f(-x) = (-x)^4 - 4(-x)^3 + 9(-x)^2 - 20(-x) + 20 = x^4 + 4x^3 + 9x^2 + 20x + 20;$
thus, there are no negative real zeros.

Step 3: Possible rational zeros:

$$p = \pm 1, \pm 2, \pm 4, \pm 5, \pm 10, \pm 20; \quad q = \pm 1;$$

$$\frac{p}{q} = \pm 1, \pm 2, \pm 4, \pm 5, \pm 10, \pm 20$$

Step 4: Using synthetic division:

$$
\begin{array}{r}
1{\overline{\smash{\big)}\,1 \quad -4 \quad\; 9 \quad -20 \quad\; 20}} \\
1 \quad -3 \quad\; 6 \quad -14 \\
\hline
1 \quad -3 \quad\; 6 \quad -14 \quad \{6\}
\end{array}
\qquad \rightarrow x - 1 \text{ is not a factor}
$$

$$
\begin{array}{r}
2{\overline{\smash{\big)}\,1 \quad -4 \quad\; 9 \quad -20 \quad\; 20}} \\
2 \quad -4 \quad\; 10 \quad -20 \\
\hline
2 \quad -2 \quad\; 5 \quad -10 \quad\; 0
\end{array}
\qquad \rightarrow x - 2 \text{ is a factor}
$$

Thus, $f(x) = (x-2)\left(x^3 - 2x^2 + 5x - 10\right)$. We can factor $x^3 - 2x^2 + 5x - 10$ by grouping

$$x^3 - 2x^2 + 5x - 10 = x^2(x-2) + 5(x-2) = (x-2)(x^2 + 5)$$

$$= (x-2)\left(x + \sqrt{5}i\right)\left(x - \sqrt{5}i\right) \rightarrow f(x) = (x-2)^2\left(x + \sqrt{5}i\right)\left(x - \sqrt{5}i\right)$$

The zeros are 2 (multiplicity 2), $\sqrt{5}i$, and $-\sqrt{5}i$.

27. $f(x) = 2x^4 + 2x^3 - 11x^2 + x - 6$.

Step 1: $f(x)$ has at most 4 real zeros.

Step 2: By Descartes Rule of Signs, there are 3 or 1 positive real zeros.

$f(-x) = 2(-x)^4 + 2(-x)^3 - 11(-x)^2 + (-x) - 6 = 2x^4 - 2x^3 - 11x^2 - x - 6;$
thus, there is 1 negative real zero.

Step 3:   Possible rational zeros:
$$p = \pm 1, \pm 2, \pm 3, \pm 6; \quad q = \pm 1, \pm 2;$$
$$\frac{p}{q} = \pm 1, \pm \frac{1}{2}, \pm 2, \pm 3, \pm \frac{3}{2} \pm 6$$

Step 4:   Using synthetic division:

$$-1\overline{)2 \quad 2 \; -11 \quad 1 \quad -6}$$
$$\underline{\quad\quad -2 \quad 0 \quad 11 \; -12}$$
$$2 \quad 0 \; -11 \quad 12 \; \{-18\}$$
$\rightarrow x+1$ is not a factor

$$1\overline{)2 \quad 2 \; -11 \quad 1 \quad -6}$$
$$\underline{\quad\quad 2 \quad 4 \; -7 \; -6}$$
$$2 \quad 4 \; -7 \; -6 \; \{-12\}$$
$\rightarrow x-1$ is not a factor

$$-2\overline{)2 \quad 2 \; -11 \quad 1 \quad -6}$$
$$\underline{\quad\quad -4 \quad 4 \quad 14 \; -30}$$
$$2 \; -2 \; -7 \quad 15 \; \{-36\}$$
$\rightarrow x+2$ is not a factor

$$2\overline{)2 \quad 2 \; -11 \quad 1 \quad -6}$$
$$\underline{\quad\quad 4 \quad 12 \quad 2 \quad 6}$$
$$2 \quad 6 \quad 1 \quad 3 \quad 0$$
$\rightarrow x-2$ is a factor

Thus, $f(x) = (x-2)(2x^3 + 6x^2 + x + 3)$.

We can factor $2x^3 + 6x^2 + x + 3$ by grouping
$$2x^3 + 6x^2 + x + 3 = 2x^2(x+3) + (x+3) = (x+3)(2x^2 + 1)$$
$$= (x+3)(\sqrt{2}x + i)(\sqrt{2}x - i) \rightarrow f(x) = (x-2)(x+3)(\sqrt{2}x + i)(\sqrt{2}x - i)$$

The zeros are 2, -3, $-\dfrac{\sqrt{2}}{2}i$, and $\dfrac{\sqrt{2}}{2}i$.

29. $f(x) = 2x^4 + 7x^3 + x^2 - 7x - 3$.

Step 1: $f(x)$ has at most 4 real zeros.

Step 2:   By Descartes Rule of Signs, there is 1 positive real zero.
$$f(-x) = 2(-x)^4 + 7(-x)^3 + (-x)^2 - 7(-x) - 3 = 2x^4 - 7x^3 + x^2 + 7x - 3;$$
thus, there are 3 or 1 negative real zeros.

Step 3:   Possible rational zeros:
$$p = \pm 1, \pm 3; \quad q = \pm 1, \pm 2;$$
$$\frac{p}{q} = \pm 1, \pm \frac{1}{2}, \pm 3, \pm \frac{3}{2}$$

Step 4:   Using synthetic division:

$$\begin{array}{r|rrrrr} 1) & 2 & 7 & 1 & -7 & -3 \\ & & 2 & 9 & 10 & 3 \\ \hline & 2 & 9 & 10 & 3 & 0 \end{array}$$ $\to x-1$ is a factor

Thus, $f(x) = (x-1)(2x^3 + 9x^2 + 10x + 3)$.

Note: $g(x) = 2x^3 + 9x^2 + 10x + 3$ has the same possible rational roots as f. However, since we have already found the only positive real zero for f, so we only need to look at the possible negative zeros, $\dfrac{p}{q} = -1, -\dfrac{1}{2}, -3, -\dfrac{3}{2}$.

$$\begin{array}{r|rrrr} -1) & 2 & 9 & 10 & 3 \\ & & -2 & -7 & -3 \\ \hline & 2 & 7 & 3 & 0 \end{array}$$ $\to x+1$ is a factor

$$2x^3 + 9x^2 + 10x + 3 = (x+1)(2x^2 + 7x + 3)$$
$$= (x+1)(2x+1)(x+3) \to f(x) = (x-1)(x+1)(2x+1)(x+3)$$

The zeros are 1, -1, $-\dfrac{1}{2}$, and -3.

31. $f(x) = x^3 - x^2 - 4x + 2$
$a_2 = -1, \quad a_1 = -4, \quad a_0 = 2$
Max $\left\{1, |2| + |-4| + |-1|\right\}$ = Max $\left\{1, 7\right\}$ = 7
$1 +$ Max $\left\{|2|, |-4|, |-1|\right\} = 1 + 4 = 5$
The smaller of the two numbers is 5, $\therefore$ every zero of f lies between -5 and 5.

33. $f(x) = 2x^3 - 7x^2 - 10x + 35 = 2\left(x^3 - \dfrac{7}{2}x^2 - 5x + \dfrac{35}{2}\right)$

$a_2 = -\dfrac{7}{2}, \quad a_1 = -5, \quad a_0 = \dfrac{35}{2}$

Max $\left\{1, \left|\dfrac{35}{2}\right| + |-5| + \left|-\dfrac{7}{2}\right|\right\}$ = Max $\left\{1, 26\right\}$ = 26

$1 +$ Max $\left\{\left|\dfrac{35}{2}\right|, |-5|, \left|-\dfrac{7}{2}\right|\right\} = 1 + \dfrac{35}{2} = \dfrac{37}{2} = 18.5$

The smaller of the two numbers is 18.5, $\therefore$ every zero of f lies between -18.5 and 18.5.

35. $f(x) = 3x^3 - x - 1; \quad [0, 1]$
$f(0) = -1 < 0$ and $f(1) = 1 > 0$
Since one is positive and one is negative, there is a zero in the interval.

37. $f(x) = 8x^4 - 4x^3 - 2x - 1; \quad [0, 1]$
$f(0) = -1 < 0$ and $f(1) = 1 > 0$
Since one is positive and one is negative, there is a zero in the interval.

39. $f(x) = x^3 - x - 2$

$f(1) = -2; \ f(2) = 4,$ so by the Intermediate Value Theorem, f has a zero on the
interval [1,2].

Subdivide the interval [1,2] into 10 equal subintervals:

[1,1.1]; [1.1,1.2]; [1.2,1.3]; [1.3,1.4]; [1.4,1.5]; [1.5,1.6]; [1.6,1.7]; [1.7,1.8];
[1.8,1.9]; [1.9,2]

$f(1) = -2; f(1.1) = -1.769$
$f(1.1) = -1.769; f(1.2) = -1.472$
$f(1.2) = -1.472; f(1.3) = -1.103$
$f(1.3) = -1.103; f(1.4) = -0.656$
$f(1.4) = -0.656; f(1.5) = -0.125$
$f(1.5) = -0.125; f(1.6) = 0.496$ so f has a real zero on the interval [1.5,1.6].

Subdivide the interval [1.5,1.6] into 10 equal subintervals:

[1.5,1.51]; [1.51,1.52]; [1.52,1.53]; [1.53,1.54]; [1.54,1.55]; [1.55,1.56];[1.56,1.57];
[1.57,1.58]; [1.58,1.59]; [1.59,1.6]

$f(1.5) = -0.125; f(1.51) = -0.0670$
$f(1.51) = -0.0670; f(1.52) = -0.0082$
$f(1.52) = -0.0082; f(1.53) = 0.0516$ so f has a real zero on the interval
[1.52,1.53], therefore $r = 1.52$,
correct to 2 decimal places.

41. $f(x) = 8x^4 - 4x^3 - 2x - 1$

$f(0) = -1; \ f(1) = 1,$ so by the Intermediate Value Theorem, f has a zero on the
interval [0,1].

Subdivide the interval [0,1] into 10 equal subintervals:

[0,0.1]; [0.1,0.2]; [0.2,0.3]; [0.3,0.4]; [0.4,0.5]; [0.5,0.6]; [0.6,0.7]; [0.7,0.8];
[0.8,0.9]; [0.9,1]

$f(0) = -1; f(0.1) = -1.2032$
$f(0.1) = -1.2032; f(0.2) = -1.4192$
$f(0.2) = -1.4192; f(0.3) = -1.6432$
$f(0.3) = -1.6432; f(0.4) = -1.8512$
$f(0.4) = -1.8512; f(0.5) = -2$
$f(0.5) = -2; f(0.6) = -2.0272$
$f(0.6) = -2.0272; f(0.7) = -1.8512$
$f(0.7) = -1.8512; f(0.8) = -1.3712$
$f(0.8) = -1.3712; f(0.9) = -0.4672$
$f(0.9) = -0.4672; f(1) = 1$ so f has a real zero on the interval [0.9,1].

Subdivide the interval [0.9,1] into 10 equal subintervals:

[0.9,0.91]; [0.91,0.92]; [0.92,0.93]; [0.93,0.94]; [0.94,0.95]; [0.95,0.96];[0.96,0.97]; [0.97,0.98]; [0.98,0.99]; [0.99,1]

$f(0.9) = -0.4672; f(0.91) = -0.3483$
$f(0.91) = -0.3483; f(0.92) = -0.2236$
$f(0.92) = -0.2236; f(0.93) = -0.0930$
$f(0.93) = -0.0930; f(0.94) = 0.0437$

so f has a real zero on the interval [0.93,0.94], therefore $r = 0.93$, correct to 2 decimal places.

43. $(6 + 3i) - (2 - 4i) = (6 - 2) + (3 - (-4))i = 4 + 7i$

45. $4(3 - i) + 3(-5 + 2i) = 12 - 4i - 15 + 6i = -3 + 2i$

47. $\dfrac{3}{3+i} = \dfrac{3}{3+i} \cdot \dfrac{3-i}{3-i} = \dfrac{9-3i}{9-3i+3i-i^2} = \dfrac{9-3i}{10} = \dfrac{9}{10} - \dfrac{3}{10}i$

49. $i^{50} = i^{48} \cdot i^2 = (i^4)^{12} \cdot i^2 = 1^{12}(-1) = -1$

51. $(2 + 3i)^3 = (2 + 3i)^2(2 + 3i) = (4 + 12i + 9i^2)(2 + 3i) = (-5 + 12i)(2 + 3i)$
     $= -10 - 15i + 24i + 36i^2 = -46 + 9i$

53. Since complex zeros appear in conjugate pairs, $4 - i$, the conjugate of $4 + i$, is the remaining zero of f.

55. Since complex zeros appear in conjugate pairs, $-i$, the conjugate of i, and $1 - i$, the conjugate of $1 + i$, are the remaining zeros of f.

57. $x^2 + x + 1 = 0$
     $a = 1, b = 1, c = 1,\quad b^2 - 4ac = 1^2 - 4(1)(1) = 1 - 4 = -3$
     $x = \dfrac{-1 \pm \sqrt{-3}}{2(1)} = \dfrac{-1 \pm \sqrt{3}i}{2} = \dfrac{-1}{2} \pm \dfrac{\sqrt{3}}{2}i \rightarrow$ The solution set is $\left\{ \dfrac{-1}{2} - \dfrac{\sqrt{3}}{2}i, \dfrac{-1}{2} + \dfrac{\sqrt{3}}{2}i \right\}.$

59. $2x^2 + x - 2 = 0$
     $a = 2, b = 1, c = -2,\quad b^2 - 4ac = 1^2 - 4(2)(-2) = 1 + 16 = 17$
     $x = \dfrac{-1 \pm \sqrt{17}}{2(2)} = \dfrac{-1 \pm \sqrt{17}}{4} \rightarrow$ The solution set is $\left\{ \dfrac{-1 - \sqrt{17}}{4}, \dfrac{-1 + \sqrt{17}}{4} \right\}.$

61. $x^2 + 3 = x$
     $x^2 - x + 3 = 0$
     $a = 1, b = -1, c = 3,\quad b^2 - 4ac = (-1)^2 - 4(1)(3) = 1 - 12 = -11$
     $x = \dfrac{-(-1) \pm \sqrt{-11}}{2(1)} = \dfrac{1 \pm \sqrt{11}i}{2} = \dfrac{1}{2} \pm \dfrac{\sqrt{11}}{2}i \rightarrow$ The solution set is $\left\{ \dfrac{1}{2} - \dfrac{\sqrt{11}}{2}i, \dfrac{1}{2} + \dfrac{\sqrt{11}}{2}i \right\}.$

63. $x(1-x) = 6$

$-x^2 + x - 6 = 0$

$a = -1, b = 1, c = -6, \quad b^2 - 4ac = 1^2 - 4(-1)(-6) = 1 - 24 = -23$

$x = \dfrac{-1 \pm \sqrt{-23}}{2(-1)} = \dfrac{-1 \pm \sqrt{23}\,i}{-2} = \dfrac{1}{2} \pm \dfrac{\sqrt{23}}{2}i \rightarrow$ The solution set is $\left\{ \dfrac{1}{2} - \dfrac{\sqrt{23}}{2}i, \ \dfrac{1}{2} + \dfrac{\sqrt{23}}{2}i \right\}$.

65. $x^4 + 2x^2 - 8 = 0$

$\left(x^2 + 4\right)\left(x^2 - 2\right) = 0 \rightarrow x^2 + 4 = 0 \ \text{ or } \ x^2 - 2 = 0$

$x^2 = -4 \ \rightarrow x = \pm 2i$

$x^2 = 2 \rightarrow x = \pm\sqrt{2}$

The solution set is $\left\{ -2i, \ 2i, \ -\sqrt{2}, \ \sqrt{2} \right\}$.

67. $x^3 - x^2 - 8x + 12 = 0$

The solutions of the equation are the zeros of the function $f(x) = x^3 - x^2 - 8x + 12$.

Step 1: $f(x)$ has 3 complex zeros.

Step 2:   By Descartes Rule of Signs, there are 2 or 0 positive real zeros.
$f(-x) = (-x)^3 - (-x)^2 - 8(-x) + 12 = -x^3 - x^2 + 8x + 12$; thus, there is 1 negative real zero.

Step 3:   Possible rational zeros:

$p = \pm 1, \pm 2, \pm 3, \pm 4, \pm 6, \pm 12; \quad q = \pm 1; \quad \dfrac{p}{q} = \pm 1, \pm 2, \pm 3, \pm 4, \pm 6, \pm 12$

Step 4:   Using synthetic division:

$$\begin{array}{r|rrrr} 2 & 1 & -1 & -8 & 12 \\ & & 2 & 2 & -12 \\ \hline & 1 & 1 & -6 & 0 \end{array}$$

Since the remainder is 0, $x - 2$ is a factor. The other factor is the quotient:
$x^2 + x - 6 = (x + 3)(x - 2)$.

The complex zeros are $-3, 2$ (multiplicity 2).

69. $3x^4 - 4x^3 + 4x^2 - 4x + 1 = 0$

The solutions of the equation are the zeros of the function $f(x) = 3x^4 - 4x^3 + 4x^2 - 4x + 1$

Step 1: $f(x)$ has 4 complex zeros.

Step 2:   By Descartes Rule of Signs, there are 4 or 2 or 0 positive real zeros.
$f(-x) = 3(-x)^4 - 4(-x)^3 + 4(-x)^2 - 4(-x) + 1 = 3x^4 + 4x^3 + 4x^2 + 4x + 1;$
thus, there are no negative real zeros.

Step 3:   Possible rational zeros:

$p = \pm 1; \quad q = \pm 1, \pm 3; \quad \dfrac{p}{q} = \pm 1, \pm \dfrac{1}{3}$

Step 4:   Using synthetic division:

$$\begin{array}{r|rrrrr} 1 & 3 & -4 & 4 & -4 & 1 \\ & & 3 & -1 & 3 & -1 \\ \hline & 3 & -1 & 3 & -1 & 0 \end{array} \qquad \begin{array}{r|rrrr} \frac{1}{3} & 3 & -1 & 3 & -1 \\ & & 1 & 0 & 1 \\ \hline & 3 & 0 & 3 & 0 \end{array}$$

Since the remainder is 0, $x - 1$ and $x - \dfrac{1}{3}$ are factors. The other factor is the quotient: $3x^2 + 3 = 3\left(x^2 + 1\right)$.

Solving $x^2 + 1 = 0 \rightarrow x^2 = -1 \rightarrow x = \pm i$

The complex zeros are $1,\ \dfrac{1}{3},\ -i,\ i$.

Chapter 6

Exponential and Logarithmic Functions

6.1   One-to-One Functions; Inverse Functions

1.   (a)   Domain   Range   (b)   Inverse is a function.

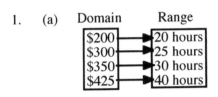

3.   (a)   Domain   Range   (b)   Inverse is not a function since $200
                                                       corresponds to two elements in the
                                                       range.

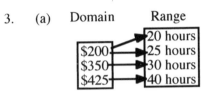

5.   (a) $\{(6,2), (6,-3), (9,4), (10,1)\}$ (b)   Inverse is not a function since 6
                                                       corresponds to 2 and -3.

7.   (a) $\{(0,0), (1,1), (16,2), (81,3)\}$ (b)   Inverse is a function.

9.   Every horizontal line intersects the graph of f at exactly one point. One-to-One.

11.   There are horizontal lines that intersect the graph of f at more than one point.
      Not One-to-One.

13.   Every horizontal line intersects the graph of f at exactly one point. One-to-One.

15. Graphing the inverse:

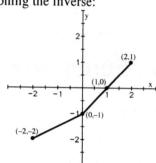

17.   Graphing the inverse:

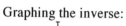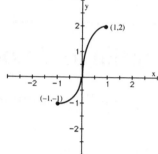

19. Graphing the inverse:

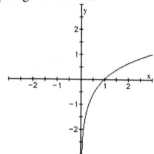

21. $f(x) = 3x + 4,$ $g(x) = \dfrac{1}{3}(x - 4)$

$f(g(x)) = f\left(\dfrac{1}{3}(x-4)\right) = 3\left(\dfrac{1}{3}(x-4)\right) + 4 = (x-4) + 4 = x$

$g(f(x)) = g(3x+4) = \dfrac{1}{3}\left((3x+4) - 4\right) = \dfrac{1}{3}(3x) = x$

23. $f(x) = 4x - 8,$ $g(x) = \dfrac{x}{4} + 2$

$f(g(x)) = f\left(\dfrac{x}{4} + 2\right) = 4\left(\dfrac{x}{4} + 2\right) - 8 = (x + 8) - 8 = x$

$g(f(x)) = g(4x - 8) = \dfrac{4x - 8}{4} + 2 = x - 2 + 2 = x$

25. $f(x) = x^3 - 8,$ $g(x) = \sqrt[3]{x + 8}$

$f(g(x)) = f\left(\sqrt[3]{x+8}\right) = \left(\sqrt[3]{x+8}\right)^3 - 8 = (x+8) - 8 = x$

$g(f(x)) = g(x^3 - 8) = \sqrt[3]{(x^3 - 8) + 8} = \sqrt[3]{x^3} = x$

27. $f(x) = \dfrac{1}{x}, \qquad g(x) = \dfrac{1}{x}$ $\qquad\qquad f(g(x)) = f\left(\dfrac{1}{x}\right) = \dfrac{1}{\frac{1}{x}} = x$

$\qquad\qquad\qquad\qquad\qquad\qquad\qquad\qquad g(f(x)) = g\left(\dfrac{1}{x}\right) = \dfrac{1}{\frac{1}{x}} = x$

29. $f(x) = \dfrac{2x+3}{x+4}, \qquad g(x) = \dfrac{4x-3}{2-x}$

$\qquad f(g(x)) = f\left(\dfrac{4x-3}{2-x}\right) = \dfrac{2\left(\frac{4x-3}{2-x}\right)+3}{\left(\frac{4x-3}{2-x}\right)+4} = \dfrac{\frac{8x-6+6-3x}{2-x}}{\frac{4x-3+8-4x}{2-x}} = \dfrac{\frac{5x}{2-x}}{\frac{5}{2-x}}$

$\qquad\qquad = \dfrac{5x}{2-x} \cdot \dfrac{2-x}{5} = x$

$\qquad g(f(x)) = g\left(\dfrac{2x+3}{x+4}\right) = \dfrac{4\left(\frac{2x+3}{x+4}\right)-3}{2-\left(\frac{2x+3}{x+4}\right)} = \dfrac{\frac{8x+12-3x-12}{x+4}}{\frac{2x+8-2x-3}{x+4}} = \dfrac{\frac{5x}{x+4}}{\frac{5}{x+4}}$

$\qquad\qquad = \dfrac{5x}{x+4} \cdot \dfrac{x+4}{5} = x$

31. $f(x) = 3x$

$\quad y = 3x$

$\quad x = 3y \quad$ Inverse

$\quad y = \dfrac{x}{3} \rightarrow f^{-1}(x) = \dfrac{x}{3}$

Verify: $f\left(f^{-1}(x)\right) = f\left(\dfrac{x}{3}\right) = 3\left(\dfrac{x}{3}\right) = x$

$\qquad\qquad f^{-1}\left(f(x)\right) = f^{-1}(3x) = \dfrac{3x}{3} = x$

Domain of f = range of $f^{-1} = (-\infty, \infty)$
Range of f = domain of $f^{-1} = (-\infty, \infty)$

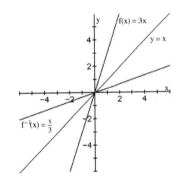

33. $f(x) = 4x + 2$

$\quad y = 4x + 2$

$\quad x = 4y + 2 \quad$ Inverse

$\quad 4y = x - 2 \rightarrow y = \dfrac{x-2}{4} \rightarrow f^{-1}(x) = \dfrac{x-2}{4}$

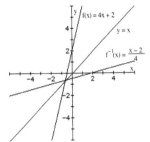

Verify: $f\left(f^{-1}(x)\right) = f\left(\dfrac{x-2}{4}\right) = 4\left(\dfrac{x-2}{4}\right) + 2 = x - 2 + 2 = x$

$\qquad\qquad f^{-1}\left(f(x)\right) = f^{-1}(4x+2) = \dfrac{(4x+2)-2}{4} = \dfrac{4x}{4} = x$

Domain of f = range of $f^{-1} = (-\infty, \infty)$
Range of f = domain of $f^{-1} = (-\infty, \infty)$

35.　$f(x) = x^3 - 1$

　　$y = x^3 - 1$

　　$x = y^3 - 1$　Inverse

　　$y^3 = x + 1 \rightarrow y = \sqrt[3]{x+1} \rightarrow f^{-1}(x) = \sqrt[3]{x+1}$

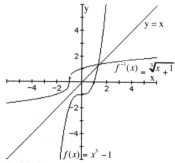

Verify:　$f\left(f^{-1}(x)\right) = f\left(\sqrt[3]{x+1}\right) = \left(\sqrt[3]{x+1}\right)^3 - 1 = x + 1 - 1 = x$

　　$f^{-1}(f(x)) = f^{-1}(x^3 - 1) = \sqrt[3]{(x^3 - 1) + 1} = \sqrt[3]{x^3} = x$

Domain of f = range of $f^{-1} = (-\infty, \infty)$

Range of f = domain of $f^{-1} = (-\infty, \infty)$

37.　$f(x) = x^2 + 4, \; x \geq 0$

　　$y = x^2 + 4 \; x \geq 0$

　　$x = y^2 + 4 \; y \geq 0$　Inverse

　　$y^2 = x - 4 \; y \geq 0$

　　$y = \sqrt{x-4} \rightarrow f^{-1}(x) = \sqrt{x-4}$

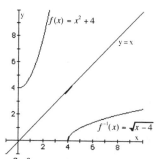

Verify:

$f\left(f^{-1}(x)\right) = f\left(\sqrt{x-4}\right) =$

$\left(\sqrt{x-4}\right)^2 + 4 = x - 4 + 4 = x$

　$f^{-1}(f(x)) = f^{-1}(x^2 + 4) = \sqrt{(x^2 + 4) - 4}$

　$= \sqrt{x^2} = |x| = x, \, x \geq 0$

Domain of f =
range of $f^{-1} = [0, \infty)$

Range of f =
domain of $f^{-1} = [4, \infty)$

39.　$f(x) = \dfrac{4}{x}$

　　$y = \dfrac{4}{x}$

　　$x = \dfrac{4}{y}$　Inverse

　　$xy = 4 \rightarrow y = \dfrac{4}{x} \rightarrow f^{-1}(x) = \dfrac{4}{x}$

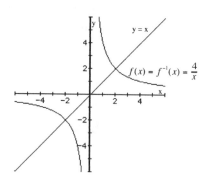

Verify:　$f\left(f^{-1}(x)\right) = f\left(\dfrac{4}{x}\right) = \dfrac{4}{\left(\dfrac{4}{x}\right)} = 4 \cdot \dfrac{x}{4} = x$

　　$f^{-1}(f(x)) = f^{-1}\left(\dfrac{4}{x}\right) = \dfrac{4}{\left(\dfrac{4}{x}\right)} = 4 \cdot \dfrac{x}{4} = x$

Domain of f = range of f^{-1} = all real numbers except 0
Range of f = domain of f^{-1} = all real numbers except 0

41. $f(x) = \dfrac{1}{x-2}$

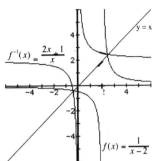

$$y = \dfrac{1}{x-2} \rightarrow x = \dfrac{1}{y-2} \quad \text{Inverse}$$

$$x(y-2) = 1 \rightarrow xy - 2x = 1 \rightarrow xy = 2x + 1$$

$$y = \dfrac{2x+1}{x} \rightarrow f^{-1}(x) = \dfrac{2x+1}{x}$$

Verify: $f\left(f^{-1}(x)\right) = f\left(\dfrac{2x+1}{x}\right) = \dfrac{1}{\left(\dfrac{2x+1}{x} - 2\right)} = \dfrac{1}{\left(\dfrac{2x+1-2x}{x}\right)} = \dfrac{1}{\left(\dfrac{1}{x}\right)} = x$

$$f^{-1}(f(x)) = f^{-1}\left(\dfrac{1}{x-2}\right) = \dfrac{2\left(\dfrac{1}{x-2}\right)+1}{\left(\dfrac{1}{x-2}\right)} = \dfrac{\left(\dfrac{2+x-2}{x-2}\right)}{\left(\dfrac{1}{x-2}\right)} = \dfrac{x}{x-2} \cdot \dfrac{x-2}{1} = x$$

Domain of f = range of f^{-1} = all real numbers except 2
Range of f = domain of f^{-1} = all real numbers except 0

43. $f(x) = \dfrac{2}{3+x}$

$$y = \dfrac{2}{3+x}$$

$$x = \dfrac{2}{3+y} \quad \text{Inverse}$$

Domain of f =
range of f^{-1} = all real numbers except -3

Range of f =
domain of f^{-1} = all real numbers except 0

$$x(3+y) = 2$$

$$3x + xy = 2 \rightarrow xy = 2 - 3x$$

$$y = \dfrac{2-3x}{x} \rightarrow f^{-1}(x) = \dfrac{2-3x}{x}$$

Verify: $f\left(f^{-1}(x)\right) = f\left(\dfrac{2-3x}{x}\right) = \dfrac{2}{3+\left(\dfrac{2-3x}{x}\right)} = \dfrac{2}{\left(\dfrac{3x+2-3x}{x}\right)} = \dfrac{2}{\left(\dfrac{2}{x}\right)} = 2 \cdot \dfrac{x}{2} = x$

$$f^{-1}(f(x)) = f^{-1}\left(\dfrac{2}{3+x}\right) = \dfrac{2-3\left(\dfrac{2}{3+x}\right)}{\left(\dfrac{2}{3+x}\right)} = \dfrac{\left(\dfrac{6+2x-6}{3+x}\right)}{\left(\dfrac{2}{3+x}\right)} = \dfrac{2x}{3+x} \cdot \dfrac{3+x}{2} = x$$

45. $f(x) = \dfrac{3x}{x+2}$

$y = \dfrac{3x}{x+2}$

$x = \dfrac{3y}{y+2}$ Inverse

$x(y+2) = 3y$

$xy + 2x = 3y$

$2x = 3y - xy$

$2x = y(3-x)$

$\dfrac{2x}{3-x} = y \rightarrow f^{-1}(x) = \dfrac{2x}{3-x}$

Domain of f =
range of f^{-1} = all real numbers except -2

Range of f =
domain of f^{-1} = all real numbers except 3

Verify: $f(f^{-1}(x)) = f\left(\dfrac{2x}{3-x}\right) = \dfrac{3\left(\dfrac{2x}{3-x}\right)}{\left(\dfrac{2x}{3-x}\right)+2} = \dfrac{\left(\dfrac{6x}{3-x}\right)}{\left(\dfrac{2x+2(3-x)}{3-x}\right)} = \dfrac{\left(\dfrac{6x}{3-x}\right)}{\left(\dfrac{2x+6-2x}{3-x}\right)}$

$= \dfrac{\left(\dfrac{6x}{3-x}\right)}{\left(\dfrac{6}{3-x}\right)} = \left(\dfrac{6x}{3-x}\right)\cdot\left(\dfrac{3-x}{6}\right) = x$

$f^{-1}(f(x)) = f^{-1}\left(\dfrac{3x}{x+2}\right) = \dfrac{2\left(\dfrac{3x}{x+2}\right)}{3-\left(\dfrac{3x}{x+2}\right)} = \dfrac{\left(\dfrac{6x}{x+2}\right)}{\left(\dfrac{3(x+2)-3x}{x+2}\right)} = \dfrac{\left(\dfrac{6x}{x+2}\right)}{\left(\dfrac{3x+6-3x}{x+2}\right)}$

$= \dfrac{\left(\dfrac{6x}{x+2}\right)}{\left(\dfrac{6}{x+2}\right)} = \left(\dfrac{6x}{x+2}\right)\cdot\left(\dfrac{x+2}{6}\right) = x$

47. $f(x) = \dfrac{2x}{3x-1}$ Domain of f =

$\qquad y = \dfrac{2x}{3x-1}$ range of f^{-1} = all real numbers except $\dfrac{1}{3}$

$\qquad x = \dfrac{2y}{3y-1}$ Inverse   Range of f =

$\qquad x(3y-1) = 2y$ domain of f^{-1} = all real numbers except $\dfrac{2}{3}$

$\qquad 3xy - x = 2y$

$\qquad 3xy - 2y = x$

$\qquad y(3x-2) = x \rightarrow y = \dfrac{x}{3x-2}$

$\qquad f^{-1}(x) = \dfrac{x}{3x-2}$

Verify:

$$f\left(f^{-1}(x)\right) = f\left(\dfrac{x}{3x-2}\right) = \dfrac{2\left(\dfrac{x}{3x-2}\right)}{3\left(\dfrac{x}{3x-2}\right) - 1} = \dfrac{\left(\dfrac{2x}{3x-2}\right)}{\left(\dfrac{3x-1(3x-2)}{3x-2}\right)} = \dfrac{\left(\dfrac{2x}{3x-2}\right)}{\left(\dfrac{3x-3x+2}{3x-2}\right)} = \dfrac{2x}{3x-2} \cdot \dfrac{3x-2}{2} = x$$

$$f^{-1}\left(f(x)\right) = f^{-1}\left(\dfrac{2x}{3x-1}\right) = \dfrac{\left(\dfrac{2x}{3x-1}\right)}{3\left(\dfrac{2x}{3x-1}\right) - 2} = \dfrac{\left(\dfrac{2x}{3x-1}\right)}{\left(\dfrac{6x-2(3x-1)}{3x-1}\right)} = \dfrac{\left(\dfrac{2x}{3x-1}\right)}{\left(\dfrac{6x-6x+2}{3x-1}\right)} = \dfrac{2x}{3x-1} \cdot \dfrac{3x-1}{2} = x$$

49. $f(x) = \dfrac{3x+4}{2x-3}$ Domain of f =

$\qquad y = \dfrac{3x+4}{2x-3}$ range of f^{-1} = all real numbers except $\dfrac{3}{2}$

$\qquad x = \dfrac{3y+4}{2y-3}$ Inverse

$\qquad x(2y-3) = 3y+4$ Range of f =

$\qquad 2xy - 3x = 3y+4$ domain of f^{-1} = all real numbers except $\dfrac{3}{2}$

$\qquad 2xy - 3y = 3x+4$

$\qquad y(2x-3) = 3x+4$

$\qquad y = \dfrac{3x+4}{2x-3}$

$\qquad f^{-1}(x) = \dfrac{3x+4}{2x-3}$

$$f\left(f^{-1}(x)\right) = f\left(\dfrac{3x+4}{2x-3}\right) = \dfrac{3\left(\dfrac{3x+4}{2x-3}\right) + 4}{2\left(\dfrac{3x+4}{2x-3}\right) - 3} = \dfrac{\left(\dfrac{9x+12+8x-12}{2x-3}\right)}{\left(\dfrac{6x+8-6x+9}{2x-3}\right)} = \dfrac{\left(\dfrac{17x}{2x-3}\right)}{\left(\dfrac{17}{2x-3}\right)}$$

Verify:

$$= \dfrac{17x}{2x-3} \cdot \dfrac{2x-3}{17} = x$$

$$f^{-1}(f(x)) = f^{-1}\left(\frac{3x+4}{2x-3}\right) = \frac{3\left(\frac{3x+4}{2x-3}\right)+4}{2\left(\frac{3x+4}{2x-3}\right)-3} = \frac{\left(\frac{9x+12+8x-12}{2x-3}\right)}{\left(\frac{6x+8-6x+9}{2x-3}\right)} = \frac{\left(\frac{17x}{2x-3}\right)}{\left(\frac{17}{2x-3}\right)}$$

$$= \frac{17x}{2x-3} \cdot \frac{2x-3}{17} = x$$

51. $f(x) = \dfrac{2x+3}{x+2}$ Domain of f =
          range of f^{-1} = all real numbers except –2

$y = \dfrac{2x+3}{x+2}$

$x = \dfrac{2y+3}{y+2}$ Inverse   Range of f =
          domain of f^{-1} = all real numbers except 2

$x(y+2) = 2y+3$

$xy + 2x = 2y + 3$

$xy - 2y = -2x + 3$

$y(x-2) = -2x+3$

$y = \dfrac{-2x+3}{x-2}$

$f^{-1}(x) = \dfrac{-2x+3}{x-2}$

Verify:

$$f\left(f^{-1}(x)\right) = f\left(\frac{-2x+3}{x-2}\right) = \frac{2\left(\frac{-2x+3}{x-2}\right)+3}{\left(\frac{-2x+3}{x-2}\right)+2} = \frac{\left(\frac{-4x+6+3x-6}{x-2}\right)}{\left(\frac{-2x+3+2x-4}{x-2}\right)} = \frac{\left(\frac{-x}{x-2}\right)}{\left(\frac{-1}{x-2}\right)}$$

$$= \frac{-x}{x-2} \cdot \frac{x-2}{-1} = x$$

$$f^{-1}(f(x)) = f^{-1}\left(\frac{2x+3}{x+2}\right) = \frac{-2\left(\frac{2x+3}{x+2}\right)+3}{\left(\frac{2x+3}{x+2}\right)-2} = \frac{\left(\frac{-4x-6+3x+6}{x+2}\right)}{\left(\frac{2x+3-2x-4}{x+2}\right)} = \frac{\left(\frac{-x}{x+2}\right)}{\left(\frac{-1}{x+2}\right)}$$

$$= \frac{-x}{x+2} \cdot \frac{x+2}{-1} = x$$

53. $f(x) = \dfrac{x^2-4}{2x^2}, x > 0$

$y = \dfrac{x^2-4}{2x^2}, x > 0$

$x = \dfrac{y^2-4}{2y^2}, y > 0$ Inverse

$2xy^2 = y^2 - 4, y > 0$

$2xy^2 - y^2 = -4, y > 0$

$y^2(2x - 1) = -4, y > 0$

$y^2 = \dfrac{-4}{2x-1} \rightarrow y = \sqrt{\dfrac{-4}{2x-1}}$

$f^{-1}(x) = \sqrt{\dfrac{-4}{2x-1}}, x > 0$

Domain of $f =$
range of $f^{-1} = (0, \infty)$

Range of $f =$
domain of $= f^{-1} = \left(0, \dfrac{1}{2}\right)$

Verify:

$f\left(f^{-1}(x)\right) = f\left(\sqrt{\dfrac{-4}{2x-1}}\right) = \dfrac{\left(\sqrt{\dfrac{-4}{2x-1}}\right)^2 - 4}{2\left(\sqrt{\dfrac{-4}{2x-1}}\right)^2} = \dfrac{\left(\dfrac{-4}{2x-1}-4\right)}{2\left(\dfrac{-4}{2x-1}\right)} = \dfrac{\left(\dfrac{-4-4(2x-1)}{2x-1}\right)}{\left(\dfrac{-8}{2x-1}\right)} = \dfrac{\left(\dfrac{-4-8x+4}{2x-1}\right)}{\left(\dfrac{-8}{2x-1}\right)}$

$= \dfrac{\left(\dfrac{-8x}{2x-1}\right)}{\left(\dfrac{-8}{2x-1}\right)} = \left(\dfrac{-8x}{2x-1}\right) \cdot \left(\dfrac{2x-1}{-8}\right) = x$

$f^{-1}\left(f(x)\right) = f^{-1}\left(\dfrac{x^2-4}{2x^2}\right) = \sqrt{\dfrac{-4}{2\left(\dfrac{x^2-4}{2x^2}\right)-1}} = \sqrt{\dfrac{-4}{\left(\dfrac{x^2-4}{x^2}\right)-1}} = \sqrt{\dfrac{-4}{\left(\dfrac{x^2-4-x^2}{x^2}\right)}} = \sqrt{\dfrac{-4}{\left(\dfrac{-4}{x^2}\right)}}$

$= \sqrt{\dfrac{-4}{1} \cdot \dfrac{x^2}{-4}} = \sqrt{x^2} = |x| = x$ when $x > 0$

55. $f(x) = mx + b, \quad m \neq 0$

$y = mx + b$

$x = my + b$ Inverse

$x - b = my$

$y = \dfrac{x-b}{m}$

$f^{-1}(x) = \dfrac{x-b}{m}, \quad m \neq 0$

57. f^{-1} lies in quadrant I. Whenever (a,b) is on f, then (b,a) is on f^{-1}. Since both coordinates of (a,b) are positive, both coordinates of (b,a) are positive and it is in quadrant I.

59. $f(x) = |x|, x \ge 0$ is one-to-one. Thus, $f(x) = x, x \ge 0$ and $f^{-1}(x) = x, x \ge 0$.

61. $f(x) = \dfrac{9}{5}x + 32 \qquad g(x) = \dfrac{5}{9}(x - 32)$

$f(g(x)) = f\left(\dfrac{5}{9}(x - 32)\right) = \dfrac{9}{5}\left[\dfrac{5}{9}(x - 32)\right] + 32 = x - 32 + 32 = x$

$g(f(x)) = g\left(\dfrac{9}{5}x + 32\right) = \dfrac{5}{9}\left(\dfrac{9}{5}x + 32 - 32\right) = \dfrac{5}{9}\left(\dfrac{9}{5}x\right) = x$

63. $T(l) = 2\pi\sqrt{\dfrac{l}{g}}, \quad g \approx 32.2$

$T = 2\pi\sqrt{\dfrac{l}{g}} \quad \rightarrow \quad \dfrac{T}{2\pi} = \sqrt{\dfrac{l}{g}}$

$\rightarrow \quad \dfrac{T^2}{4\pi^2} = \dfrac{l}{g} \quad \rightarrow \quad l = \dfrac{gT^2}{4\pi^2}$

$l(T) = \dfrac{gT^2}{4\pi^2}$

65. An even function cannot be one-to-one. When a function is even, $f(-x) = f(x)$. Thus, both x and $-x$ produce the same y value.

67. If the graph of a function and its inverse intersect, they must intersect at a point on the line $y = x$. However, the graphs do not have to intersect.

69. Answers will vary.

Chapter 6

Exponential and Logarithmic Functions

6.2 Exponential Functions

1. (a) $3^{2.2} = 11.212$ (b) $3^{2.23} = 11.587$ (c) $3^{2.236} = 11.664$ (d) $3^{\sqrt{5}} = 11.665$

3. (a) $2^{3.14} = 8.815$ (b) $2^{3.141} = 8.821$ (c) $2^{3.1415} = 8.824$ (d) $2^{\pi} = 8.825$

5. (a) $3.1^{2.7} = 21.217$ (b) $3.14^{2.71} = 22.217$
   (c) $3.141^{2.718} = 22.440$ (d) $\pi^{e} = 22.459$

7. $e^{1.2} = 3.320$

9. $e^{-0.85} = 0.427$

11. B   13. D   15. A   17. E

19. $f(x) = 2^{x} + 1$
    Using the graph of $y = 2^{x}$, shift the graph up 1 unit.
    Domain: $(-\infty, \infty)$
    Range: $(1, \infty)$
    Horizontal Asymptote: $y = 1$

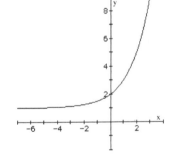

21. $f(x) = 3^{-x} - 2$
    Using the graph of $y = 3^{x}$, reflect the graph about the y-axis, and shift down 2 units.
    Domain: $(-\infty, \infty)$
    Range: $(-2, \infty)$
    Horizontal Asymptote: $y = -2$

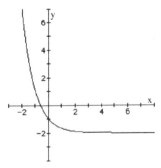

23. $f(x) = 2 + 3(4^x)$

Using the graph of $y = 4^x$, stretch the
graph vertically by a factor of 3, and shift
up 2 units.
Domain: $(-\infty, \infty)$
Range: $(2, \infty)$
Horizontal Asymptote: $y = 2$

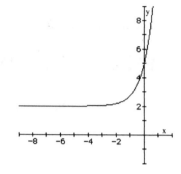

25. $f(x) = 2 + 3^{x/2}$

Using the graph of $y = 3^x$, stretch the
graph horizontally by a factor of 2, and
shift up 2 units.
Domain: $(-\infty, \infty)$
Range: $(2, \infty)$
Horizontal Asymptote: $y = 2$

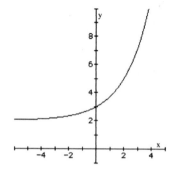

27. $f(x) = e^{-x}$

Using the graph of $y = e^x$, reflect the
graph about the y-axis.
Domain: $(-\infty, \infty)$
Range: $(0, \infty)$
Horizontal Asymptote: $y = 0$

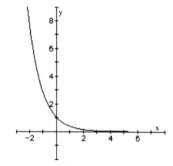

29. $f(x) = e^{x+2}$

Using the graph of $y = e^x$, shift the graph
2 units to the left.
Domain: $(-\infty, \infty)$
Range: $(0, \infty)$
Horizontal Asymptote: $y = 0$

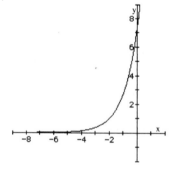

31. $f(x) = 5 - e^{-x}$

Using the graph of $y = e^x$, reflect the graph about the y-axis, reflect about the x-axis, and shift up 5 units.

Domain: $(-\infty, \infty)$

Range: $(-\infty, 5)$

Horizontal Asymptote: $y = 5$

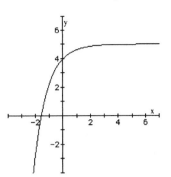

33. $f(x) = 2 - e^{-x/2}$

Using the graph of $y = e^x$, reflect the graph about the y-axis, stretch horizontally by a factor of 2, reflect about the x-axis, and shift up 2 units.

Domain: $(-\infty, \infty)$

Range: $(-\infty, 2)$

Horizontal Asymptote: $y = 2$

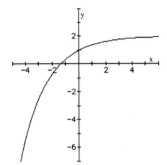

35. $2^{2x+1} = 4$

$2^{2x+1} = 2^2$

$2x + 1 = 2 \rightarrow 2x = 1 \rightarrow x = \dfrac{1}{2}$

The solution is $\left\{\dfrac{1}{2}\right\}$.

37. $3^{x^3} = 9^x$

$3^{x^3} = \left(3^2\right)^x$

$3^{x^3} = 3^{2x}$

$x^3 = 2x \rightarrow x^3 - 2x = 0 \rightarrow x(x^2 - 2) = 0$

$x = 0$ or $x^2 = 2$

$x = 0$ or $x = \pm\sqrt{2}$

The solution is $\left\{-\sqrt{2},\ 0,\ \sqrt{2}\right\}$.

39. $8^{x^2 - 2x} = \dfrac{1}{2}$

$\left(2^3\right)^{x^2 - 2x} = 2^{-1}$

$2^{3x^2 - 6x} = 2^{-1}$

$3x^2 - 6x = -1 \rightarrow 3x^2 - 6x + 1 = 0$

$x = \dfrac{-(-6) \pm \sqrt{(-6)^2 - 4(3)(1)}}{2(3)}$

$= \dfrac{6 \pm \sqrt{24}}{6} = \dfrac{6 \pm 2\sqrt{6}}{6} = \dfrac{3 \pm \sqrt{6}}{3}$

The solution is $\left\{\dfrac{3 - \sqrt{6}}{3},\ \dfrac{3 + \sqrt{6}}{3}\right\}$.

41. $2^x \cdot 8^{-x} = 4^x$

$2^x \cdot \left(2^3\right)^{-x} = \left(2^2\right)^x$

$2^x \cdot 2^{-3x} = 2^{2x}$

$2^{-2x} = 2^{2x}$

$-2x = 2x \rightarrow -4x = 0 \rightarrow x = 0$

The solution is $\{0\}$.

43. $\left(\dfrac{1}{5}\right)^{2-x} = 25$

$\left(5^{-1}\right)^{2-x} = 5^2$

$5^{x-2} = 5^2$

$x - 2 = 2 \rightarrow x = 4$
The solution is {4}.

45. $4^x = 8$

$\left(2^2\right)^x = 2^3$

$2^{2x} = 2^3$

$2x = 3 \rightarrow x = \dfrac{3}{2}$

The solution is $\left\{\dfrac{3}{2}\right\}$.

47. $e^{x^2} = e^{3x} \cdot \dfrac{1}{e^2}$

$e^{x^2} = e^{3x-2}$

$x^2 = 3x - 2$

$x^2 - 3x + 2 = 0$

$(x-1)(x-2) = 0 \rightarrow x = 1$ or $x = 2$
The solution is {1, 2}.

49. $4^x = 7$

$\left(4^x\right)^{-2} = 7^{-2} \quad \rightarrow \quad 4^{-2x} = \dfrac{1}{7^2} = \dfrac{1}{49}$

51. $3^{-x} = 2$

$\left(3^{-x}\right)^{-2} = 2^{-2} \quad \rightarrow \quad 3^{2x} = \dfrac{1}{2^2} = \dfrac{1}{4}$

53. $f(x) = \begin{cases} e^{-x} & \text{if } x < 0 \\ e^x & \text{if } x \geq 0 \end{cases}$

domain $= (-\infty, \infty)$
range $= [1, \infty)$
y-intercept (0, 1)

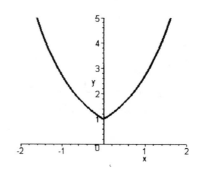

55. $f(x) = \begin{cases} -e^x & \text{if } x < 0 \\ -e^{-x} & \text{if } x \geq 0 \end{cases}$

domain $= (-\infty, \infty)$
range $= [-1, 0)$
y-intercept (0, - 1)
horizontal asymptote $y = 0$

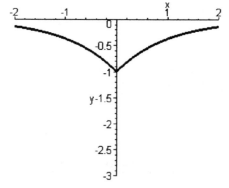

57. $p = 100e^{-0.03n}$

(a) $p = 100e^{-0.03(10)} = 100e^{-.03} \approx 100(0.741) = 74.1\%$ of light

(b) $p = 100e^{-0.03(25)} = 100e^{-.75} \approx 100(0.472) = 47.2\%$ of light

59. $w(d) = 50e^{-0.004\,d}$

   (a) $w(30) = 50e^{-0.004(30)} = 50e^{-0.12} \approx 50(0.887) = 44.35$ watts

   (b) $w(365) = 50e^{-0.004(365)} = 50e^{-1.46} \approx 50(0.232) = 11.61$ watts

61. $D(h) = 5e^{-0.4\,h}$

   $D(1) = 5e^{-0.4(1)} = 5e^{-0.4} \approx 5(0.670) = 3.35$ milligrams

   $D(6) = 5e^{-0.4(6)} = 5e^{-2.4} \approx 5(0.091) = 0.45$ milligrams

63. $F(t) = 1 - e^{-0.1t}$

   (a) $F(10) = 1 - e^{-0.1(10)} = 1 - e^{-1} \approx 1 - 0.368 = 0.632 = 63.2\%$

   (b) $F(40) = 1 - e^{-0.1(40)} = 1 - e^{-4} \approx 1 - 0.018 = 0.982 = 98.2\%$

   (c) as $t \to +\infty$, $F(t) = 1 - e^{-0.1t} \to 1 - 0 = 1$

   (d) Graphing the function:

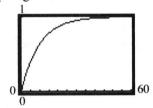

   (e) $F(7) \approx 50$, so 7 minutes are needed for the probability to reach 50%.

65. $P(x) = \dfrac{20^x e^{-20}}{x!}$

   (a) $P(15) = \dfrac{20^{15} e^{-20}}{15!} \approx 0.0516 = 5.16\%$ The probability that 15 cars will arrive between
   5:00 p.m. and 6:00 p.m. is 5.16%.

   (b) $P(20) = \dfrac{20^{20} e^{-20}}{20!} \approx 0.0888 = 8.88\%$ The probability that 20 cars will arrive between
   5:00 p.m. and 6:00 p.m. is 8.88%.

67. $R = 10^{\left(\frac{2345}{T} - \frac{2345}{D} + 2\right)}$

   (a) $R = 10^{\left(\frac{2345}{283} - \frac{2345}{278} + 2\right)} \approx 10^{1.851} \approx 70.96\%$

   (b) $R = 10^{\left(\frac{2345}{293} - \frac{2345}{288} + 2\right)} \approx 10^{1.861} \approx 72.61\%$

   (c) $R = 10^{\left(\frac{2345}{x} - \frac{2345}{x} + 2\right)} = 10^2 = 100\%$

69. $I = \dfrac{E}{R}\left[1 - e^{-\left(\frac{R}{L}\right)t}\right]$

   (a) $I = \dfrac{120}{10}\left[1 - e^{-\left(\frac{10}{5}\right)0.3}\right] = 12\left[1 - e^{-0.6}\right] \approx 5.414$ amperes after 0.3 second

   $I = \dfrac{120}{10}\left[1 - e^{-\left(\frac{10}{5}\right)0.5}\right] = 12\left[1 - e^{-1}\right] \approx 7.585$ amperes after 0.5 second

$$I = \frac{120}{10}\left[1 - e^{-\left(\frac{10}{5}\right)1}\right] = 12\left[1 - e^{-2}\right] \approx 10.376 \text{ amperes after 1 second}$$

(b)   As $t \to \infty$, $e^{-\left(\frac{10}{5}\right)t} \to 0$. Therefore, the maximum current is 12 amperes.

(c)   Graphing the function:

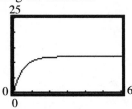

(d) $I = \dfrac{120}{5}\left[1 - e^{-\left(\frac{5}{10}\right)0.3}\right] = 24\left[1 - e^{-0.15}\right] \approx 3.343$ amperes after 0.3 second

$$I = \frac{120}{5}\left[1 - e^{-\left(\frac{5}{10}\right)0.5}\right] = 24\left[1 - e^{-0.25}\right] \approx 5.309 \text{ amperes after 0.5 second}$$

$$I = \frac{120}{5}\left[1 - e^{-\left(\frac{5}{10}\right)1}\right] = 24\left[1 - e^{-0.5}\right] \approx 9.443 \text{ amperes after 1 second}$$

(e)   As $t \to \infty$, $e^{-\left(\frac{5}{10}\right)t} \to 0$. Therefore, the maximum current is 24 amperes.

(f)   Graphing the function:

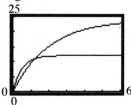

71. $2 + \dfrac{1}{2!} + \dfrac{1}{3!} + \dfrac{1}{4!} + \ldots + \dfrac{1}{n!}$

    $n = 4; \quad 2 + \dfrac{1}{2!} + \dfrac{1}{3!} + \dfrac{1}{4!} = 2.7083$

    $n = 6; \quad 2 + \dfrac{1}{2!} + \dfrac{1}{3!} + \dfrac{1}{4!} + \dfrac{1}{5!} + \dfrac{1}{6!} = 2.7181$

    $n = 8; \quad 2 + \dfrac{1}{2!} + \dfrac{1}{3!} + \dfrac{1}{4!} + \dfrac{1}{5!} + \dfrac{1}{6!} + \dfrac{1}{7!} + \dfrac{1}{8!} = 2.7182788$

    $n = 10; \quad 2 + \dfrac{1}{2!} + \dfrac{1}{3!} + \dfrac{1}{4!} + \dfrac{1}{5!} + \dfrac{1}{6!} + \dfrac{1}{7!} + \dfrac{1}{8!} + \dfrac{1}{9!} + \dfrac{1}{10!} = 2.7182818$

    $e = 2.718281828$

73. $f(x) = a^x$

    $\dfrac{f(x+h) - f(x)}{h} = \dfrac{a^{x+h} - a^x}{h} = \dfrac{a^x a^h - a^x}{h} = \dfrac{a^x\left(a^h - 1\right)}{h} = a^x\left(\dfrac{a^h - 1}{h}\right)$

75. $f(x) = a^x$

$f(-x) = a^{-x} = \dfrac{1}{a^x} = \dfrac{1}{f(x)}$

77. (a) $y = \dfrac{6}{1 + e^{-(5.085 - 0.1156(100))}} \approx 0.0092$ O - rings

(b) $y = \dfrac{6}{1 + e^{-(5.085 - 0.1156(60))}} \approx 0.8145$ O - rings

(c) $y = \dfrac{6}{1 + e^{-(5.085 - 0.1156(30))}} \approx 5.0063$ O - rings

(d)   Graphing:

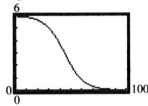

At 58°F, there would be 1 leaky O-ring.
At 44°F, there would be 3 leaky O-rings.
At 30°F, there would be 5 leaky O-rings.

79. We can use the function $f(t) = f(0)e^{kt}$
the number of bacteria doubles
every minute means

$f(1) = 2f(0)$

$f(0)e^{k\,(1)} = 2f(0)$

$e^k = 2$

the container is full after
60 minutes means

$f(60) = 4$

$f(0)e^{k(60)} = 4$

$f(0)\left(e^k\right)^{(60)} = 4$

$f(0)(2)^{(60)} = 4$

$\rightarrow f(0) = \dfrac{4}{2^{60}} = \dfrac{2^2}{2^{60}} = \dfrac{1}{2^{58}}$

We want to find t so that $f(t) = 2$.

$f(t) = f(0)e^{kt} = 2$

$f(0)\left(e^k\right)^t = 2 \rightarrow f(0)(2)^t = 2$

$\left(\dfrac{1}{2^{58}}\right)(2)^t = 2 \rightarrow 2^t = 2 \cdot 2^{58} = 2^{59} \rightarrow t = 59$ minutes

81. Answers will vary.

Chapter 6

Exponential and Logarithmic Functions

6.3 Logarithmic Functions

1. $9 = 3^2$ is equivalent to $2 = \log_3 9$

3. $a^2 = 1.6$ is equivalent to $2 = \log_a 1.6$

5. $1.1^2 = M$ is equivalent to $2 = \log_{1.1} M$

7. $2^x = 7.2$ is equivalent to $x = \log_2 7.2$

9. $x^{\sqrt{2}} = \pi$ is equivalent to $\sqrt{2} = \log_x \pi$

11. $e^x = 8$ is equivalent to $x = \ln 8$

13. $\log_2 8 = 3$ is equivalent to $2^3 = 8$

15. $\log_a 3 = 6$ is equivalent to $a^6 = 3$

17. $\log_3 2 = x$ is equivalent to $3^x = 2$

19. $\log_2 M = 1.3$ is equivalent to $2^{1.3} = M$

21. $\log_{\sqrt{2}} \pi = x$ is equivalent to $\left(\sqrt{2}\right)^x = \pi$

23. $\ln 4 = x$ is equivalent to $e^x = 4$

25. $\log_2 1 = 0$ since $2^0 = 1$

27. $\log_5 25 = 2$ since $5^2 = 25$

29. $\log_{\frac{1}{2}} 16 = -4$ since $\left(\dfrac{1}{2}\right)^{-4} = 2^4 = 16$

31. $\log_{10} \sqrt{10} = \dfrac{1}{2}$ since $10^{1/2} = \sqrt{10}$

33. $\log_{\sqrt{2}} 4 = 4$ since $\left(\sqrt{2}\right)^4 = 4$

35. $\ln \sqrt{e} = \dfrac{1}{2}$ since $e^{1/2} = \sqrt{e}$

37. The domain of $f(x) = \ln(x - 3)$ is:
$$x - 3 > 0 \rightarrow x > 3$$
$$\{x \mid x > 3\}$$

39. The domain of $F(x) = \log_2 x^2$ is:
$$x^2 > 0$$
$$\{x \mid x \neq 0\}$$

41. The domain of $h(x) = \log_{\frac{1}{2}}\left(x^2 - 2x + 1\right)$ is:
$$x^2 - 2x + 1 > 0 \rightarrow (x - 1)^2 > 0$$
$$\{x \mid x \neq 1\}$$

43. The domain of $f(x) = \ln\left(\dfrac{1}{x + 1}\right)$ is:
$$\dfrac{1}{x + 1} > 0 \rightarrow x + 1 > 0$$
$$x > -1$$
$$\{x \mid x > -1\}$$

45. The domain of $g(x) = \log_5\left(\dfrac{x+1}{x}\right)$ requires that $\dfrac{x+1}{x} > 0$.

The expression is zero or undefined when $x = -1$ or $x = 0$.

$$f(x) = \frac{x+1}{x}$$

Interval	Test Number		Positive/Negative
$-\infty < x < -1$	-2	$1/2$	Positive
$-1 < x < 0$	-0.5	-1	Negative
$0 < x < \infty$	1	2	Positive

The domain is $\{x \mid x < -1 \text{ or } x > 0\}$

47. $\ln\dfrac{5}{3} \approx 0.511$

49. $\dfrac{\ln(10/3)}{0.04} \approx 30.099$

51. For $f(x) = \log_a x$, find a so that $f(2) = \log_a 2 = 2$ or $a^2 = 2$ or $a = \sqrt{2}$.
(The base a must be positive by definition.)

53. B   55. D   57. A   59. E

61. $f(x) = \ln(x+4)$
Using the graph of $y = \ln x$, shift the
graph 4 units to the left.
Domain: $(-4, \infty)$
Range: $(-\infty, \infty)$
Vertical Asymptote: $x = -4$

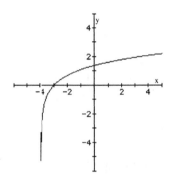

63. $f(x) = \ln(-x)$
Using the graph of $y = \ln x$, reflect the
graph about the y-axis.
Domain: $(-\infty, 0)$
Range: $(-\infty, \infty)$
Vertical Asymptote: $x = 0$

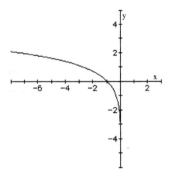

317

65. $g(x) = \ln(2x)$
Using the graph of $y = \ln x$, compress the
graph horizontally by a factor of $\dfrac{1}{2}$.
Domain: $(0, \infty)$
Range: $(-\infty, \infty)$
Vertical Asymptote: $x = 0$

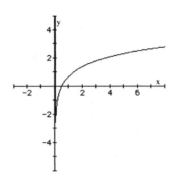

67. $f(x) = 3\ln x$
Using the graph of $y = \ln x$, stretch the
graph vertically by a factor of 3.
Domain: $(0, \infty)$
Range: $(-\infty, \infty)$
Vertical Asymptote: $x = 0$

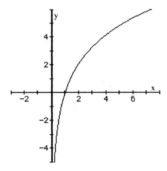

69. $g(x) = \ln(3 - x) = \ln(-(x - 3))$
Using the graph of $y = \ln x$, reflect the
graph about the y-axis, and shift 3 units to
the right.
Domain: $(-\infty, 3)$
Range: $(-\infty, \infty)$
Vertical Asymptote: $x = 3$

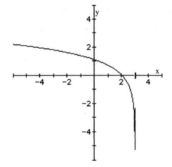

71. $f(x) = -\ln(x - 1)$
Using the graph of $y = \ln x$, shift the
graph 1 unit to the right, and reflect about
the x-axis.
Domain: $(1, \infty)$
Range: $(-\infty, \infty)$
Vertical Asymptote: $x = 1$

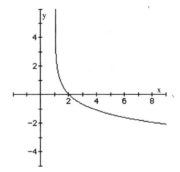

73. $\log_3 x = 2$
$x = 3^2 \rightarrow x = 9$

75. $\log_2(2x + 1) = 3$
$2x + 1 = 2^3 \rightarrow 2x + 1 = 8$
$2x = 7 \rightarrow x = \dfrac{7}{2}$

77. $\log_x 4 = 2$

$x^2 = 4$

$x = 2$ $(x \neq -2$, base is positive$)$

79. $\ln e^x = 5$

$e^x = e^5 \rightarrow x = 5$

81. $\log_4 64 = x$

$4^x = 64 \rightarrow 4^x = 4^3 \rightarrow x = 3$

83. $\log_3 243 = 2x + 1$

$3^{2x+1} = 243$

$3^{2x+1} = 3^5$

$2x + 1 = 5 \rightarrow 2x = 4 \rightarrow x = 2$

85. $e^{3x} = 10$

$3x = \ln 10 \rightarrow x = \dfrac{\ln 10}{3}$

87. $e^{2x+5} = 8$

$2x + 5 = \ln 8$

$2x = -5 + \ln 8 \rightarrow x = \dfrac{-5 + \ln 8}{2}$

89. $\log_3\left(x^2 + 1\right) = 2$

$x^2 + 1 = 3^2$

$x^2 + 1 = 9 \rightarrow x^2 = 8$

$x = \pm\sqrt{8} = \pm 2\sqrt{2}$

91. $\log_2 8^x = -3$

$8^x = 2^{-3}$

$8^x = \dfrac{1}{8} \rightarrow 8^x = 8^{-1} \rightarrow x = -1$

93. $f(x) = \begin{cases} \ln(-x) & \text{if } x < 0 \\ \ln x & \text{if } x > 0 \end{cases}$

Domain: $(-\infty, 0) \cup (0, \infty)$

Range: $(-\infty, \infty)$

x-intercept: $(-1, 0), (1, 0)$

vertical asymptote: $x = 0$

95. $f(x) = \begin{cases} -\ln x & \text{if } 0 < x < 1 \\ \ln x & \text{if } x \geq 1 \end{cases}$

Domain: $(0, \infty)$
Range: $[0, \infty)$
x-intercept: $(1, 0)$
vertical asymptote: $x = 0$

97. $P = 100e^{-0.1\,n}$

(a)
$50 = 100e^{-0.1\,n}$
$0.5 = e^{-0.1n}$
$\ln 0.5 = -0.1n$
$n = \dfrac{\ln 0.5}{-0.1}$
$n \approx 6.93$
7 panes of glass are needed.

(b)
$25 = 100e^{-0.1n}$
$0.25 = e^{-0.1\,n}$
$\ln 0.25 = -0.1n$
$n = \dfrac{\ln 0.25}{-0.1}$
$n \approx 13.86$
14 panes of glass are needed.

99. $w = 50e^{-0.004\,d}$

(a)
$30 = 50e^{-0.004\,d}$
$0.6 = e^{-0.004\,d}$
$\ln 0.6 = -0.004d$
$d = \dfrac{\ln 0.6}{-0.004}$
$d \approx 127.7$
Approximately 128 days.

(b)
$5 = 50e^{-0.004\,d}$
$0.1 = e^{-0.004\,d}$
$\ln 0.1 = -0.004d$
$d = \dfrac{\ln 0.1}{-0.004}$
$d \approx 575.6$
Approximately 576 days.

101. $F(t) = 1 - e^{-0.1\,t}$

(a)
$0.5 = 1 - e^{-0.1t}$
$-0.5 = -e^{-0.1\,t}$
$0.5 = e^{-0.1\,t}$
$\ln 0.5 = -0.1t$
$t = \dfrac{\ln 0.5}{-0.1}$
$n \approx 6.93$
Approximately 7 minutes.

(b)
$0.8 = 1 - e^{-0.1t}$
$-0.2 = -e^{-0.1t}$
$0.2 = e^{-0.1t}$
$\ln 0.2 = -0.1t$
$t = \dfrac{\ln 0.2}{-0.1}$
$n \approx 16.09$
Approximately 16 minutes.

(c) It is impossible for the probability to reach 100% because $e^{-0.1t}$ will never equal zero.

103. $D = 5e^{-0.4h}$

$\quad\quad 2 = 5e^{-0.4h}$

$\quad\; 0.4 = e^{-0.4h}$

$\quad \ln 0.4 = -0.4h$

$\quad\quad h = \dfrac{\ln 0.4}{-0.4}$

$\quad\quad h \approx 2.29$ hours

105. $I = \dfrac{E}{R}\left[1 - e^{-\left(\frac{R}{L}\right)t}\right]$

0.5 ampere:

$\quad 0.5 = \dfrac{12}{10}\left[1 - e^{-\left(\frac{10}{5}\right)t}\right]$

$\quad 0.4167 = 1 - e^{-2t}$

$\quad e^{-2t} = 0.5833$

$\quad -2t = \ln 0.5833$

$\quad\quad t = \dfrac{\ln 0.5833}{-2}$

$\quad\quad t = 0.2695$ seconds

1.0 ampere:

$\quad 1.0 = \dfrac{12}{10}\left[1 - e^{-\left(\frac{10}{5}\right)t}\right]$

$\quad 0.8333 = 1 - e^{-2t}$

$\quad e^{-2t} = 0.1667$

$\quad -2t = \ln 0.1667$

$\quad\quad t = \dfrac{\ln 0.1667}{-2}$

$\quad\quad t = 0.8958$ seconds

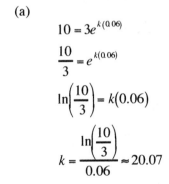

107. $R = 3e^{kx}$

(a)

$\quad 10 = 3e^{k(0.06)}$

$\quad \dfrac{10}{3} = e^{k(0.06)}$

$\quad \ln\left(\dfrac{10}{3}\right) = k(0.06)$

$\quad k = \dfrac{\ln\left(\dfrac{10}{3}\right)}{0.06} \approx 20.07$

(b)

$\quad R = 3e^{(20.07)(0.17)}$

$\quad R = 3e^{3.4119} \approx 90.97\%$

(c)

$\quad 100 = 3e^{(20.07)x}$

$\quad \dfrac{100}{3} = e^{(20.07)x}$

$\quad \ln\left(\dfrac{100}{3}\right) = (20.07)x$

$\quad x = \dfrac{\ln\left(\dfrac{100}{3}\right)}{(20.07)} \approx 0.1747$

(d)

$\quad 15 = 3e^{(20.07)(x)}$

$\quad 5 = e^{(20.07)(x)}$

$\quad \ln(5) = (20.07)(x)$

$\quad x = \dfrac{\ln(5)}{20.07} \approx 0.080$

(e)   Answers will vary.

109.   New $= \text{Old}\left(e^{Rt}\right)$

Age	Depreciation rate	Age	Depreciation rate
1	$38000 = 36600e^{R\,(1)}$ $\dfrac{38000}{36600} = e^{R}$ $\ln\left(\dfrac{38000}{36600}\right) = R$ $\rightarrow R \approx 0.03754 = 3.8\%$	2	$38000 = 32400e^{R\,(2)}$ $\dfrac{38000}{32400} = e^{2R}$ $\ln\left(\dfrac{38000}{32400}\right) = 2R$ $\dfrac{\ln\left(\dfrac{38000}{32400}\right)}{2} = R$ $\rightarrow R \approx 0.07971 = 8\%$

Age	Depreciation rate	Age	Depreciation rate
3	$38000 = 28750e^{R\,(3)}$ $\dfrac{38000}{28750} = e^{3R}$ $\ln\left(\dfrac{38000}{28750}\right) = 3R$ $\dfrac{\ln\left(\dfrac{38000}{28750}\right)}{3} = R$ $\rightarrow R \approx 0.0930 = 9.3\%$	4	$38000 = 25400e^{R\,(4)}$ $\dfrac{38000}{25400} = e^{4R}$ $\ln\left(\dfrac{38000}{25400}\right) = 4R$ $\dfrac{\ln\left(\dfrac{38000}{24500}\right)}{4} = R$ $\rightarrow R \approx 0.1007 = 10.1\%$

Age	Depreciation rate
5	$38000 = 21200e^{R\,(5)}$ $\dfrac{38000}{21200} = e^{5R}$ $\ln\left(\dfrac{38000}{21200}\right) = 5R$ $\dfrac{\ln\left(\dfrac{38000}{21200}\right)}{5} = R \rightarrow R \approx 0.1167 = 11.7\%$

Chapter 6

Exponential and Logarithmic Functions

6.4 Properties of Logarithms; Exponential and Logarithmic Models

1. $\log_3 3^{71} = 71$

3. $\ln e^{-4} = -4$

5. $2^{\log_2 7} = 7$

7. $\log_8 2 + \log_8 4 = \log_8(4 \cdot 2) = \log_8(8) = 1$

9. $\log_6 18 - \log_6 3 = \log_6\left(\dfrac{18}{3}\right) = \log_6(6) = 1$

11. $\log_2 6 \cdot \log_6 4$

$$= \log_6\left(4^{\log_2 6}\right) = \log_6\left(\left(2^2\right)^{\log_2 6}\right) = \log_6\left((2)^{2\log_2 6}\right) = \log_6\left((2)^{\log_2 6^2}\right) = \log_6\left(6^2\right) = 2$$

13. $3^{\log_3 5 - \log_3 4} = 3^{\log_3\left(\frac{5}{4}\right)} = \dfrac{5}{4}$

15. $e^{\log_{e^2} 16}$

    Simplify the exponent:

    $$\text{Let} \quad a = \log_{e^2} 16 \rightarrow \left(e^2\right)^a = 16$$

    $$e^{2a} = 16 = 4^2$$

    $$e^a = 4 \rightarrow a = \ln 4$$

    $$\text{Thus,} \quad e^{\log_{e^2} 16} = e^{\ln 4} = 4$$

17. $\ln 6 = \ln(3 \cdot 2) = \ln 3 + \ln 2 = b + a$

19. $\ln 1.5 = \ln\dfrac{3}{2} = \ln 3 - \ln 2 = b - a$

21. $\ln 8 = \ln 2^3 = 3 \cdot \ln 2 = 3a$

23. $\ln\sqrt[5]{6} = \ln 6^{1/5} = \dfrac{1}{5} \cdot \ln 6 = \dfrac{1}{5} \cdot \ln(2 \cdot 3) = \dfrac{1}{5} \cdot (\ln 2 + \ln 3) = \dfrac{1}{5} \cdot (a + b)$

25. $\log_a\left(u^2 v^3\right) = \log_a u^2 + \log_a v^3 = 2\log_a u + 3\log_a v$

27. $\log\dfrac{1}{M^3} = \log M^{-3} = -3\log M$

29. $\log_5\sqrt{\dfrac{a^3}{b}} = \log_5\left(\dfrac{a^3}{b}\right)^{1/2} = \log_5\dfrac{a^{3/2}}{b^{1/2}} = \log_5 a^{3/2} - \log_5 b^{1/2} = \dfrac{3}{2}\log_5 a - \dfrac{1}{2}\log_5 b$

31. $\ln\left(x^2\sqrt{1-x}\right) = \ln x^2 + \ln\sqrt{1-x} = \ln x^2 + \ln(1-x)^{1/2} = 2\ln x + \dfrac{1}{2}\ln(1-x)$

33. $\log_2\left(\dfrac{x^3}{x-3}\right) = \log_2 x^3 - \log_2(x-3) = 3\log_2 x - \log_2(x-3)$

35. $\log\left[\dfrac{x(x+2)}{(x+3)^2}\right] = \log x(x+2) - \log(x+3)^2 = \log x + \log(x+2) - 2\log(x+3)$

37. $\ln\left[\dfrac{x^2-x-2}{(x+4)^2}\right]^{1/3} = \dfrac{1}{3}\ln\left[\dfrac{(x-2)(x+1)}{(x+4)^2}\right] = \dfrac{1}{3}\left[\ln(x-2)(x+1) - \ln(x+4)^2\right]$

$= \dfrac{1}{3}\left[\ln(x-2) + \ln(x+1) - 2\ln(x+4)\right] = \dfrac{1}{3}\ln(x-2) + \dfrac{1}{3}\ln(x+1) - \dfrac{2}{3}\ln(x+4)$

39. $\ln\dfrac{5x\sqrt{1-3x}}{(x-4)^3} = \ln 5x\sqrt{1-3x} - \ln(x-4)^3 = \ln 5 + \ln x + \ln\sqrt{1-3x} - 3\ln(x-4)$

$= \ln 5 + \ln x + \ln(1-3x)^{1/2} - 3\ln(x-4) = \ln 5 + \ln x + \dfrac{1}{2}\ln(1-3x) - 3\ln(x-4)$

41. $3\log_5 u + 4\log_5 v = \log_5 u^3 + \log_5 v^4 = \log_5(u^3 v^4)$

43. $\log_{\frac{1}{2}}\sqrt{x} - \log_{\frac{1}{2}} x^3 = \log_{\frac{1}{2}}\left(\dfrac{\sqrt{x}}{x^3}\right) = \log_{\frac{1}{2}}\left(\dfrac{x^{1/2}}{x^3}\right) = \log_{\frac{1}{2}} x^{-5/2} = -\dfrac{5}{2}\log_{\frac{1}{2}} x$

45. $\ln\dfrac{x}{x-1} + \ln\dfrac{x+1}{x} - \ln\left(x^2-1\right) = \ln\left[\dfrac{x}{x-1}\cdot\dfrac{x+1}{x}\right] - \ln\left(x^2-1\right) = \ln\left[\dfrac{x+1}{x-1} \div \left(x^2-1\right)\right]$

$= \ln\left[\dfrac{x+1}{(x-1)(x-1)(x+1)}\right] = \ln\dfrac{1}{(x-1)^2} = \ln(x-1)^{-2} = -2\ln(x-1)$

47. $8\log_2\sqrt{3x-2} - \log_2\dfrac{4}{x} + \log_2 4 = \log_2\left(\sqrt{3x-2}\right)^8 - \left(\log_2 4 - \log_2 x\right) + \log_2 4$

$= \log_2(3x-2)^4 - \log_2 4 + \log_2 x + \log_2 4 = \log_2\left[x(3x-2)^4\right]$

49. $2\log_a 5x^3 - \dfrac{1}{2}\log_a(2x+3) = \log_a\left(5x^3\right)^2 - \log_a(2x-3)^{1/2} = \log_a\left[\dfrac{25x^6}{(2x-3)^{1/2}}\right]$

51. $\log_3 21 = \dfrac{\log 21}{\log 3} \approx \dfrac{1.32222}{0.47712} = 2.771$

53. $\log_{\frac{1}{3}} 71 = \dfrac{\log 71}{\log\left(\dfrac{1}{3}\right)} = \dfrac{\log 71}{-\log 3} \approx \dfrac{1.85126}{-0.47712} = -3.880$

55. $\log_{\sqrt{2}} 7 = \dfrac{\log 7}{\log\sqrt{2}} = \dfrac{\log 7}{\log 2^{1/2}} = \dfrac{\log 7}{\dfrac{1}{2}\log 2} \approx \dfrac{0.84510}{0.5(0.30103)} = 5.615$

57. $\log_{\pi} e = \dfrac{\ln e}{\ln \pi} \approx \dfrac{1}{1.14473} = 0.874$

59. $\log_2 3 \cdot \log_3 4 \cdot \log_4 5 \cdot \log_5 6 \cdot \log_6 7 \cdot \log_7 8$

$= \dfrac{\log 3}{\log 2} \cdot \dfrac{\log 4}{\log 3} \cdot \dfrac{\log 5}{\log 4} \cdot \dfrac{\log 6}{\log 5} \cdot \dfrac{\log 7}{\log 6} \cdot \dfrac{\log 8}{\log 7} = \dfrac{\log 8}{\log 2} = \dfrac{\log 2^3}{\log 2} = \dfrac{3\log 2}{\log 2} = 3$

61. $\log_2 3 \cdot \log_3 4 \cdot \ldots \cdot \log_n (n+1) \cdot \log_{n+1} 2$

$= \dfrac{\log 3}{\log 2} \cdot \dfrac{\log 4}{\log 3} \cdot \ldots \cdot \dfrac{\log(n+1)}{\log n} \cdot \dfrac{\log 2}{\log(n+1)} = \dfrac{\log 2}{\log 2} = 1$

63. $y = \log_4 x = \dfrac{\ln x}{\ln 4}$ or $y = \dfrac{\log x}{\log 4}$

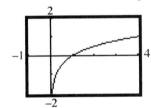

65. $y = \log_2(x+2) = \dfrac{\ln(x+2)}{\ln 2}$

or $y = \dfrac{\log(x+2)}{\log 2}$

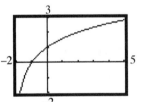

67. $y = \log_{x-1}(x+1) = \dfrac{\ln(x+1)}{\ln(x-1)}$

or $y = \dfrac{\log(x+1)}{\log(x-1)}$

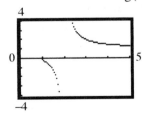

69. $\ln y = \ln x + \ln C$

$\ln y = \ln(xC)$

$y = Cx$

71. $\ln y = \ln x + \ln(x+1) + \ln C$

$\ln y = \ln(x(x+1)C)$

$y = Cx(x+1)$

73. $\ln y = 3x + \ln C$

$\ln y = \ln e^{3x} + \ln C$

$\ln y = \ln(Ce^{3x})$

$y = Ce^{3x}$

75. $\ln(y-3) = -4x + \ln C$

$\ln(y-3) = \ln e^{-4x} + \ln C$

$\ln(y-3) = \ln\left(Ce^{-4x}\right)$

$y - 3 = Ce^{-4x} \rightarrow y = Ce^{-4x} + 3$

77. $3\ln y = \frac{1}{2}\ln(2x+1) - \frac{1}{3}\ln(x+4) + \ln C$

$\ln y^3 = \ln(2x+1)^{1/2} - \ln(x+4)^{1/3} + \ln C$

$\ln y^3 = \ln\left[\frac{C(2x+1)^{1/2}}{(x+4)^{1/3}}\right] \rightarrow y^3 = \frac{C(2x+1)^{1/2}}{(x+4)^{1/3}} \rightarrow y = \left[\frac{C(2x+1)^{1/2}}{(x+4)^{\frac{1}{3}}}\right]^{1/3} \rightarrow y = \frac{\sqrt[3]{C}(2x+1)^{1/6}}{(x+4)^{1/9}}$

79. Verifying:

$$\log_a\left(x + \sqrt{x^2-1}\right) + \log_a\left(x - \sqrt{x^2-1}\right) = \log_a\left[\left(x + \sqrt{x^2-1}\right)\left(x - \sqrt{x^2-1}\right)\right]$$
$$= \log_a\left[x^2 - \left(x^2-1\right)\right] = \log_a\left[x^2 - x^2 + 1\right] = \log_a 1 = 0$$

81. Verifying:

$$2x + \ln\left(1 + e^{-2x}\right) = \ln e^{2x} + \ln\left(1 + e^{-2x}\right) = \ln\left(e^{2x}\left(1 + e^{-2x}\right)\right) = \ln\left(e^{2x} + e^0\right) = \ln\left(e^{2x} + 1\right)$$

83. $f(x) = \log_a x$

$$x = a^{f(x)} \rightarrow x^{-1} = a^{-f(x)} = \left(a^{-1}\right)^{f(x)} = \left(\frac{1}{a}\right)^{f(x)}$$

$$\log_{\frac{1}{a}} x^{-1} = f(x) \rightarrow -\log_{\frac{1}{a}} x = f(x) \rightarrow -f(x) = \log_{\frac{1}{a}} x$$

85. $f(x) = \log_a x$

$$a^{f(x)} = x \rightarrow \frac{1}{a^{f(x)}} = \frac{1}{x} \rightarrow a^{-f(x)} = \frac{1}{x} \rightarrow -f(x) = \log_a \frac{1}{x} = f\left(\frac{1}{x}\right)$$

87. If $A = \log_a M$ and $B = \log_a N$, then $a^A = M$ and $a^B = N$.

$$\log_a\left(\frac{M}{N}\right) = \log_a\left(\frac{a^A}{a^B}\right) = \log_a a^{A-B} = A - B = \log_a M - \log_a N$$

89. (a)   Graphing:

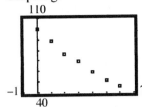

$A = 100e^{-0.1278(50)}$

(d) ≈ 0.1678 grams
(e) and (f) Graphing:

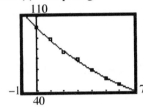

(b) $y = 100(0.88)^x$
$0.88 = e^{\ln(0.88)}$
$\rightarrow y = 100\left(e^{\ln(0.88)}\right)^x = 100e^{\ln(0.88)x}$

$A = A_0 e^{-0.1278t}, A_0 = 100$

(c)

$100e^{-0.1278t} = 50$

$e^{-0.1278t} = \dfrac{50}{100}$

$e^{-0.1278t} = 0.5$

$\ln\left(e^{-0.1278t}\right) = \ln(0.5)$

$-0.1278t = \ln(0.5)$

$t = \dfrac{\ln(0.5)}{-0.1278} \approx 5.42$ weeks

91. (a)   Graphing:

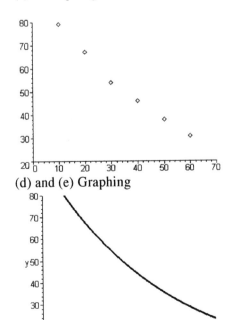

(d) and (e) Graphing

(b) $y = 96(0.98)^x$
$0.98 = e^{\ln(0.98)}$
$\rightarrow y = 96\left(e^{\ln(0.98)}\right)^x = 96e^{\ln(0.98)x}$

$A = A_0 e^{-0.0202t}, A_0 = 96$

(c)

$96e^{-0.0202t} = 60$

$e^{-0.0202t} = \dfrac{60}{96}$

$\ln(e^{-0.0202t}) = \ln\left(\dfrac{60}{96}\right)$

$-0.0202t = \ln\left(\dfrac{60}{96}\right)$

$t = \dfrac{\ln\left(\dfrac{60}{96}\right)}{-0.0202} \approx 23$ shoes

327

93. (a)   Graphing:

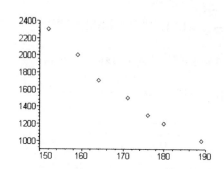

(c) and (d) Graphing:

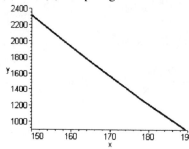

(b)

$$y = 32741 - 6071 \cdot \ln x$$

$$1650 = 32741 - 6071 \cdot \ln x$$

$$-31091 = -6071 \cdot \ln x$$

$$\frac{-31091}{-6071} = \ln x$$

$$\frac{31091}{6071} = \ln x$$

$$e^{\left(\frac{31091}{6071}\right)} = e^{\ln x} = x$$

$$x \approx 168 \quad \text{computers}$$

Exponential and Logarithmic Functions

6.5   Logarithmic and Exponential Equations

1. $\log_4(x+2) = \log_4 8$
     $x + 2 = 8 \rightarrow x = 6$

3. $\dfrac{1}{2}\log_3 x = 2\log_3 2$
     $\log_3 x^{1/2} = \log_3 2^2$
     $x^{1/2} = 4 \rightarrow x = 16$

5. $2\log_5 x = 3\log_5 4$
     $\log_5 x^2 = \log_5 4^3$
     $x^2 = 64$
     $x = \pm 8$
     Since $\log_5(-8)$ is undefined, the
     only solution is $x = 8$.

7. $3\log_2(x-1) + \log_2 4 = 5$
     $\log_2(x-1)^3 + \log_2 4 = 5$
     $\log_2 4(x-1)^3 = 5$
     $4(x-1)^3 = 2^5$
     $(x-1)^3 = \dfrac{32}{4} \rightarrow (x-1)^3 = 8$
     $x - 1 = 2 \rightarrow x = 3$

9. $\log x + \log(x+15) = 2$
     $\log x(x+15) = 2 \rightarrow x(x+15) = 10^2$
     $x^2 + 15x - 100 = 0 \rightarrow (x+20)(x-5) = 0 \rightarrow x = -20 \text{ or } x = 5$
     Since $\log(-20)$ is undefined, the only solution is $x = 5$.

11. $\ln x + \ln(x+2) = 4$
     $\ln x(x+2) = 4$
     $x(x+2) = e^4 \rightarrow x^2 + 2x - e^4 = 0$
     $$x = \frac{-2 \pm \sqrt{2^2 - 4(1)(-e^4)}}{2(1)} = \frac{-2 \pm \sqrt{4 + 4e^4}}{2}$$
     $$= \frac{-2 \pm 2\sqrt{1 + e^4}}{2} = -1 \pm \sqrt{1 + e^4}$$
     Since $\ln\left(-1 - \sqrt{1+e^4}\right)$ is undefined, the only solution is $x = -1 + \sqrt{1+e^4} \approx 6.456$.

13. $2^{2x} + 2^x - 12 = 0$

$\left(2^x\right)^2 + 2^x - 12 = 0$

$\left(2^x - 3\right)\left(2^x + 4\right) = 0$

$\quad 2^x - 3 = 0 \qquad \text{or } 2^x + 4 = 0$

$\qquad 2^x = 3 \qquad \text{or} \qquad 2^x = -4$

$\qquad x = \log_2 3 \qquad \text{No solution}$

$\qquad x \approx 1.585$

15. $3^{2x} + 3^{x+1} - 4 = 0$

$\left(3^x\right)^2 + 3 \cdot 3^x - 4 = 0$

$\left(3^x - 1\right)\left(3^x + 4\right) = 0$

$\quad 3^x - 1 = 0 \quad \text{or } 3^x + 4 = 0$

$\qquad 3^x = 1 \quad \text{or} \qquad 3^x = -4$

$\qquad x = 0 \qquad \qquad \text{No solution}$

17. $2^x = 10$

$\log\left(2^x\right) = \log 10$

$x \log 2 = 1$

$x = \dfrac{1}{\log 2} \approx 3.322$

19. $8^{-x} = 1.2$

$\log\left(8^{-x}\right) = \log 1.2$

$-x \log 8 = \log 1.2$

$x = \dfrac{\log 1.2}{-\log 8} \approx -0.088$

21. $3^{1-2x} = 4^x$

$\log\left(3^{1-2x}\right) = \log\left(4^x\right)$

$(1 - 2x)\log 3 = x \log 4$

$\log 3 - 2x \log 3 = x \log 4 \rightarrow \log 3 = x \log 4 + 2x \log 3 \rightarrow \log 3 = x(\log 4 + 2\log 3)$

$x = \dfrac{\log 3}{\log 4 + 2\log 3} \approx 0.307$

23. $\left(\dfrac{3}{5}\right)^x = 7^{1-x}$

$\log\left(\left(\dfrac{3}{5}\right)^x\right) = \log\left(7^{1-x}\right)$

$x \log\left(\dfrac{3}{5}\right) = (1 - x)\log 7 \rightarrow x(\log 3 - \log 5) = \log 7 - x \log 7$

$x \log 3 - x \log 5 + x \log 7 = \log 7 \rightarrow x(\log 3 - \log 5 + \log 7) = \log 7$

$x = \dfrac{\log 7}{\log 3 - \log 5 + \log 7} \approx 1.356$

25.
$$1.2^x = (0.5)^{-x}$$
$$\log 1.2^x = \log(0.5)^{-x}$$
$$x \log 1.2 = -x \log 0.5$$
$$x \log 1.2 + x \log 0.5 = 0$$
$$x(\log 1.2 + \log 0.5) = 0$$
$$x = 0$$

27.
$$\pi^{1-x} = e^x$$
$$\ln \pi^{1-x} = \ln e^x$$
$$(1-x)\ln \pi = x$$
$$\ln \pi - x \ln \pi = x$$
$$\ln \pi = x + x \ln \pi$$
$$\ln \pi = x(1 + \ln \pi)$$
$$x = \frac{\ln \pi}{1 + \ln \pi} \approx 0.534$$

29. $5(2^{3x}) = 8$
$$2^{3x} = \frac{8}{5}$$
$$\log 2^{3x} = \log\left(\frac{8}{5}\right) \rightarrow 3x \log 2 = \log 8 - \log 5 \rightarrow x = \frac{\log 8 - \log 5}{3 \log 2} \approx 0.226$$

31. $\log_a(x-1) - \log_a(x+6) = \log_a(x-2) - \log_a(x+3)$

$$\log_a\left(\frac{x-1}{x+6}\right) = \log_a\left(\frac{x-2}{x+3}\right) \rightarrow a^{\left(\log_a\left(\frac{x-1}{x+6}\right)\right)} = a^{\left(\log_a\left(\frac{x-2}{x+3}\right)\right)}$$

so

$$\frac{x-1}{x+6} = \frac{x-2}{x+3} \rightarrow (x-1)(x+3) = (x-2)(x+6)$$

$$x^2 + 2x - 3 = x^2 + 4x - 12 \rightarrow 2x - 3 = 4x - 12 \rightarrow 9 = 2x \rightarrow x = \frac{9}{2}$$

Since each of the original logarithms is defined for $x = \frac{9}{2}$, the solution is $x = \frac{9}{2}$.

33. $\log_{\frac{1}{3}}(x^2 + x) - \log_{\frac{1}{3}}(x^2 - x) = -1$

$$\log_{\frac{1}{3}}\left(\frac{x^2 + x}{x^2 - x}\right) = -1$$

$$\frac{x^2 + x}{x^2 - x} = \left(\frac{1}{3}\right)^{-1}$$

$$\frac{x(x+1)}{x(x-1)} = 3 \rightarrow x + 1 = 3(x-1)$$

$$x + 1 = 3x - 3 \rightarrow -2x = -4 \rightarrow x = 2$$

35.
$$\log_2(x+1) - \log_4 x = 1$$
$$\log_2(x+1) - \frac{\log_2 x}{\log_2 4} = 1$$
$$\log_2(x+1) - \frac{\log_2 x}{2} = 1$$
$$2 \log_2(x+1) - \log_2 x = 2$$
$$\log_2(x+1)^2 - \log_2 x = 2$$
$$\log_2 \frac{(x+1)^2}{x} = 2$$
$$\frac{(x+1)^2}{x} = 2^2$$
$$x^2 + 2x + 1 = 4x$$
$$x^2 - 2x + 1 = 0$$
$$(x-1)^2 = 0$$
$$x - 1 = 0$$
$$x = 1$$

37.
$$\log_{16} x + \log_4 x + \log_2 x = 7$$
$$\frac{\log_2 x}{\log_2 16} + \frac{\log_2 x}{\log_2 4} + \log_2 x = 7$$
$$\frac{\log_2 x}{4} + \frac{\log_2 x}{2} + \log_2 x = 7$$
$$\log_2 x + 2\log_2 x + 4\log_2 x = 28$$
$$7\log_2 x = 28$$
$$\log_2 x = 4$$
$$x = 2^4 = 16$$

39.
$$\left(\sqrt[3]{2}\right)^{2-x} = 2^{x^2}$$
$$\left(2^{1/3}\right)^{2-x} = 2^{x^2}$$
$$2^{\frac{1}{3}(2-x)} = 2^{x^2}$$
$$\frac{1}{3}(2-x) = x^2 \rightarrow 2 - x = 3x^2$$
$$3x^2 + x - 2 = 0 \rightarrow (3x-2)(x+1) = 0$$
$$x = \frac{2}{3} \text{ or } x = -1$$

41.
$$\frac{e^x + e^{-x}}{2} = 1$$
$$e^x + e^{-x} = 2$$
$$e^x\left(e^x + e^{-x}\right) = 2e^x \rightarrow e^{2x} + 1 = 2e^x$$
$$(e^x)^2 - 2e^x + 1 = 0 \rightarrow \left(e^x - 1\right)^2 = 0 \rightarrow e^x - 1 = 0 \rightarrow e^x = 1 \rightarrow x = 0$$

43.
$$\frac{e^x - e^{-x}}{2} = 2$$
$$e^x - e^{-x} = 4 \rightarrow e^x\left(e^x - e^{-x}\right) = 4e^x \rightarrow e^{2x} - 1 = 4e^x \rightarrow (e^x)^2 - 4e^x - 1 = 0$$
$$e^x = \frac{-(-4) \pm \sqrt{(-4)^2 - 4(1)(-1)}}{2(1)} = \frac{4 \pm \sqrt{20}}{2} = \frac{4 \pm 2\sqrt{5}}{2} = 2 \pm \sqrt{5}$$
$$x = \ln\left(2 + \sqrt{5}\right)$$
$\ln\left(2 - \sqrt{5}\right)$ is undefined; it is not a solution.

45. Using INTERSECT to solve:
$$y_1 = \ln(x) / \ln(5) + \ln(x) / \ln(3)$$
$$y_2 = 1$$

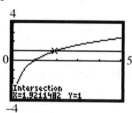

The solution is 1.92.

47. Using INTERSECT to solve:
$$y_1 = \ln(x+1) / \ln(5) - \ln(x-2) / \ln(4)$$
$$y_2 = 1$$

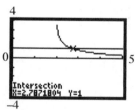

The solution is 2.79.

49.   Using INTERSECT to solve:
       $y_1 = e^x; \; y_2 = -x$

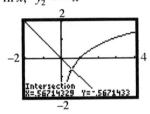

The solution is –0.57.

51.   Using INTERSECT to solve:
       $y_1 = e^x; \; y_2 = x^2$

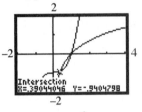

The solution is –0.70.

53.   Using INTERSECT to solve:
       $y_1 = \ln x; \; y_2 = -x$

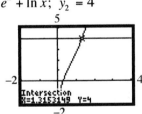

The solution is 0.57.

55.   Using INTERSECT to solve:
       $y_1 = \ln x; \; y_2 = x^3 - 1$

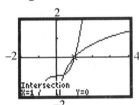

The solutions are 0.39, 1.00.

57.   Using INTERSECT to solve:
       $y_1 = e^x + \ln x; \; y_2 = 4$

The solution is 1.32.

59.   Using INTERSECT to solve:
       $y_1 = e^{-x}; \; y_2 = \ln x$

The solution is 1.31.

Chapter 6

Exponential and Logarithmic Functions

6.6   Compound Interest

1. $P = \$100,\ r = 0.04,\ n = 4,\ t = 2$
$$A = P\left[1 + \frac{r}{n}\right]^{nt} = 100\left[1 + \frac{0.04}{4}\right]^{(4)(2)} = \$108.29$$

3. $P = \$500,\ r = 0.08,\ n = 4,\ t = 2.5$
$$A = P\left[1 + \frac{r}{n}\right]^{nt} = 500\left[1 + \frac{0.08}{4}\right]^{(4)(2.5)} = \$609.50$$

5. $P = \$600,\ r = 0.05,\ n = 365,\ t = 3$
$$A = P\left[1 + \frac{r}{n}\right]^{nt} = 600\left[1 + \frac{0.05}{365}\right]^{(365)(3)} = \$697.09$$

7. $P = \$10,\ r = 0.11,\ t = 2$
$$A = Pe^{rt} = 10e^{(0.11)(2)} = \$12.46$$

9. $P = \$100,\ r = 0.10,\ t = 2.25$
$$A = Pe^{rt} = 100e^{(0.10)(2.25)} = \$125.23$$

11. $A = \$100,\ r = 0.06,\ n = 12,\ t = 2$
$$P = A\left[1 + \frac{r}{n}\right]^{-nt} = 100\left[1 + \frac{0.06}{12}\right]^{(-12)(2)} = \$88.72$$

13. $A = \$1000,\ r = 0.06,\ n = 365,\ t = 2.5$
$$P = A\left[1 + \frac{r}{n}\right]^{-nt} = 1000\left[1 + \frac{0.06}{365}\right]^{(-365)(2.5)} = \$860.72$$

15. $A = \$600,\ r = 0.04,\ n = 4,\ t = 2$
$$P = A\left[1 + \frac{r}{n}\right]^{-nt} = 600\left[1 + \frac{0.04}{4}\right]^{(-4)(2)} = \$554.09$$

17. $A = \$80,\ r = 0.09,\ t = 3.25$
$$P = Ae^{-rt} = 80e^{(-0.09)(3.25)} = \$59.71$$

19. $A = \$400,\ r = 0.10,\ t = 1$
$$P = Ae^{-rt} = 400e^{(-0.10)(1)} = \$361.93$$

21. $r_e = \left[1 + \dfrac{r}{n}\right]^n - 1 = \left[1 + \dfrac{0.0525}{4}\right]^4 - 1 = 1.0535 - 1 = 0.0535 = 5.35\%$

23. $2P = P(1 + r)^3$

$2 = (1 + r)^3 \rightarrow \sqrt[3]{2} = 1 + r \rightarrow r = \sqrt[3]{2} - 1 \approx 1.26 - 1 = 0.26 = 26\%$

25. 6% compounded quarterly:

$$A = 10,000\left[1 + \dfrac{0.06}{4}\right]^{(4)(1)} = \$10,613.64$$

$6\frac{1}{4}\%$ compounded annually:

$$A = 10,000[1 + 0.0625]^1 = \$10,625$$

$6\frac{1}{4}\%$ compounded annually yields the larger amount.

27. 9% compounded monthly:

$$A = 10,000\left[1 + \dfrac{0.09}{12}\right]^{(12)(1)} = \$10,938.07$$

8.8% compounded daily:

$$A = 10,000\left[1 + \dfrac{0.088}{365}\right]^{365} = \$10,919.77$$

9% compounded monthly yields the larger amount.

29. Compounded monthly:

$$2P = P\left[1 + \dfrac{0.08}{12}\right]^{12t}$$
$$2 = (1.00667)^{12t}$$
$$\ln 2 = 12t \ln(1.00667)$$
$$t = \dfrac{\ln 2}{12 \ln(1.00667)} \approx 8.69 \text{ years}$$

Compounded continuously:

$$2P = Pe^{0.08t}$$
$$2 = e^{0.08t}$$
$$\ln 2 = 0.08t$$
$$t = \dfrac{\ln 2}{0.08} \approx 8.66 \text{ years}$$

31. Compounded monthly:

$$150 = 100\left[1 + \dfrac{0.08}{12}\right]^{12t}$$
$$1.5 = (1.00667)^{12t}$$
$$\ln 1.5 = 12t \ln(1.00667)$$
$$t = \dfrac{\ln 1.5}{12 \ln(1.00667)} \approx 5.083 \text{ years}$$

Compounded continuously:

$$150 = 100e^{0.08t}$$
$$1.5 = e^{0.08t}$$
$$\ln 1.5 = 0.08t$$
$$t = \dfrac{\ln 1.5}{0.08} \approx 5.068 \text{ years}$$

33. $25,000 = 10,000e^{0.06t}$
$$2.5 = e^{0.06t}$$
$$\ln 2.5 = 0.06t$$
$$t = \dfrac{\ln 2.5}{0.06} \approx 15.27 \text{ years}$$

35. $A = 90,000(1 + 0.03)^5 = \$104,335$

37. $P = 15,000e^{(-0.05)(3)} = \$12,910.62$

39. $A = 1500(1 + 0.15)^5 = 1500(1.15)^5 = \$3017$

41. $850,000 = 650,000(1 + r)^3$

$\quad\quad 1.3077 = (1 + r)^3$

$\quad\quad \sqrt[3]{1.3077} = 1 + r \rightarrow r = \sqrt[3]{1.3077} - 1 \approx 0.0935 = 9.35\%$

43.   5.6% compounded continuously:

$\quad\quad A = 1000e^{(0.056)(1)} = \$1057.60$

$\quad\quad$ Jim does not have enough money to buy the computer.

$\quad\quad$ 5.9% compounded monthly:

$\quad\quad A = 1000\left[1 + \dfrac{0.059}{12}\right]^{12} = \$1060.62$

The second bank offers the better deal.

45.   Will - 9% compounded semiannually:

$\quad\quad A = 2000\left[1 + \dfrac{0.09}{2}\right]^{(2)(20)} = \$11,632.73$

Henry - 8.5% compounded continuously:

$\quad\quad A = 2000e^{(0.085)(20)} = \$10,947.89$

Will has more money after 20 years.

47. $P = 50,000; \ t = 5$

$\quad$ (a)   Simple interest at 12% per annum:

$\quad\quad\quad A = 50,000 + 50,000(0.12)(5) = \$80,000$

$\quad$ (b)   11.5% compounded monthly:

$\quad\quad\quad A = 50,000\left[1 + \dfrac{0.115}{12}\right]^{(12)(5)} = \$88,613.59$

$\quad$ (c)   11.25% compounded continuously:

$\quad\quad\quad A = 50,000e^{(0.1125)(5)} = \$87,752.73$

$\quad\quad$ Subtract \$50,000 from each to get the amount of interest:

$\quad\quad\quad$ (a)   \$30,000

$\quad\quad\quad$ (b)   \$38,613.59

$\quad\quad\quad$ (c)   \$37.752.73

Option (a) results in the least interest.

49.   (a) $A = \$10,000, \ r = 0.10, \ n = 12, \ t = 20$ (compounded monthly)

$\quad\quad\quad P = 10,000\left[1 + \dfrac{0.10}{12}\right]^{(-12)(20)} = \$1364.62$

$\quad$ (b) $A = \$10,000, \ r = 0.10, \ t = 20$ (compounded continuously)

$\quad\quad\quad P = 10,000e^{(-0.10)(20)} = \$1353.35$

51. $A = \$10,000, \ r = 0.08, \ n = 1, \ t = 10$ (compounded annually)

$\quad\quad\quad P = 10,000\left[1 + \dfrac{0.08}{1}\right]^{(-1)(10)} = \$4631.93$

53. (a) $y = \dfrac{\ln 2}{1 \cdot \ln\left(1 + \dfrac{0.12}{1}\right)} = \dfrac{\ln 2}{\ln 1.12} \approx 6.12 \text{ years}$

   (b) $y = \dfrac{\ln 3}{4 \cdot \ln\left(1 + \dfrac{0.06}{4}\right)} = \dfrac{\ln 3}{4 \ln 1.015} \approx 18.45 \text{ years}$

   (c) $mP = P\left[1 + \dfrac{r}{n}\right]^{nt}$

   $m = \left[1 + \dfrac{r}{n}\right]^{nt} \quad \rightarrow \quad \ln m = nt \cdot \ln\left[1 + \dfrac{r}{n}\right] \quad \rightarrow \quad t = \dfrac{\ln m}{n \cdot \ln\left[1 + \dfrac{r}{n}\right]}$

55. Answers will vary.   57. Answers will vary.

Chapter 6

Exponential and Logarithmic Functions

6.7   Growth and Decay; Newton's Law; Logistic Models

1. $P(t) = 500e^{0.02t}$

Find t when $P = 1000$:

$$1000 = 500e^{0.02t}$$
$$2 = e^{0.02t}$$
$$\ln 2 = 0.02t$$
$$t = \frac{\ln 2}{0.02} \approx 34.7 \text{ days}$$

Find t when $P = 2000$:

$$2000 = 500e^{0.02t}$$
$$4 = e^{0.02t}$$
$$\ln 4 = 0.02t$$
$$t = \frac{\ln 4}{0.02} \approx 69.3 \text{ days}$$

3. Find t when $A(t) = \frac{1}{2}A_0$:

$$\frac{1}{2}A_0 = A_0 e^{-0.0244t}$$
$$\frac{1}{2} = e^{-0.0244t}$$
$$\ln\left(\frac{1}{2}\right) = -0.0244t$$
$$t = \frac{\ln\left(\frac{1}{2}\right)}{-0.0244} \approx 28.4 \text{ years}$$

5. Use $N(t) = N_0 e^{kt}$ and solve for k:

$$1800 = 1000e^{k(1)}$$
$$1.8 = e^k$$
$$k = \ln 1.8 \approx 0.5878$$

When $t = 3$:

$$N(3) = 1000e^{0.5878(3)} = 5832 \text{ mosquitos}$$

Find t when $N(t) = 10,000$:

$$10,000 = 1000e^{0.5878t}$$
$$10 = e^{0.5878t}$$
$$\ln 10 = 0.5878t$$
$$t = \frac{\ln 10}{0.5878} \approx 3.9 \text{ days}$$

7. Use $P(t) = P_0 e^{kt}$ and solve for k:

$$2P_0 = P_0 e^{k(1.5)}$$

$$2 = e^{1.5k} \rightarrow \ln 2 = 1.5k \rightarrow k = \frac{\ln 2}{1.5} \approx 0.4621$$

When $t = 2$:

$$P(2) = 10,000e^{0.4621(2)} = 25,199 \text{ is the population 2 years from now.}$$

9. Use $A = A_0 e^{kt}$ and solve for k:

$$\frac{1}{2}A_0 = A_0 e^{k(1690)} \rightarrow \frac{1}{2} = e^{1690k}$$

$$\ln\left(\frac{1}{2}\right) = 1690k \rightarrow k = \frac{\ln 0.5}{1690} \approx -0.00041$$

When $A_0 = 10$ and $t = 50$:

$$A = 10e^{-0.00041\,(50)} = 9.797 \text{ grams}$$

11. Use $A = A_0 e^{kt}$ and solve for k:

$$\frac{1}{2}A_0 = A_0 e^{k(5600)}$$

$$\frac{1}{2} = e^{5600\,k}$$

$$\ln\left(\frac{1}{2}\right) = 5600k \rightarrow k = \frac{\ln 0.5}{5600} \approx -0.000124$$

Solve for t when $A = 0.3A_0$:

$$0.3A_0 = A_0 e^{-0.000124\,t}$$

$$0.3 = e^{-0.000124\,t}$$

$$\ln 0.3 = -0.000124t$$

$$t = \frac{\ln 0.3}{-0.000124}$$

$$\approx 9709 \text{ years ago}$$

13. (a) Using $u = T + (u_0 - T)e^{kt}$ where $t = 5$,
    $T = 70$, $u_0 = 450$, $u = 300$:

$$300 = 70 + (450 - 70)e^{k(5)}$$

$$230 = 380e^{5k}$$

$$0.6053 = e^{5k}$$

$$5k = \ln 0.6053$$

$$k = \frac{\ln 0.6053}{5} \approx -0.1004$$

$T = 70$, $u_0 = 450$, $u = 135$:

$$135 = 70 + (450 - 70)e^{-0.1004\,t}$$

$$65 = 380e^{-0.1004\,t}$$

$$0.17105 = e^{-0.1004\,t}$$

$$-0.1004\,t = \ln 0.17105$$

$$t = \frac{\ln 0.17105}{-0.1004} \approx 17.6 \text{ minutes}$$

The pizza will be cool enough to eat at 5:18 p.m.

(b) $T = 70$, $u_0 = 450$, $u = 160$:

$$160 = 70 + (450 - 70)e^{-0.1004\,t}$$

$$90 = 380e^{-0.1004\,t}$$

$$\frac{90}{380} = e^{-0.1004\,t}$$

$$\ln\left(\frac{90}{380}\right) = \ln e^{-0.1004\,t} = -0.1004\,t$$

$$t = \frac{\ln\left(\dfrac{90}{380}\right)}{-0.1004} \approx 14.35 \text{ minutes}$$

The pizza will be 160°F after about 14.3 minutes.

(c) As time passes the temperature gets closer to 70°F.

15. Using $u = T + (u_0 - T)e^{kt}$ where $t = 3$,
$T = 35$, $u_0 = 8$, $u = 15$:
$$15 = 35 + (8 - 35)e^{k(3)} \rightarrow -20 = -27e^{3k} \rightarrow 0.74074 = e^{3k}$$
$$3k = \ln 0.74074 \rightarrow k = \frac{\ln 0.74074}{3} \approx -0.100035$$
At $t = 5$:
$$u = 35 + (8 - 35)e^{-0.100035\,(5)} = 18.63°C$$
At $t = 10$:
$$u = 35 + (8 - 35)e^{-0.100035\,(10)} = 25.1°C$$

17. Use $A = A_0 e^{kt}$ and solve for k:
$$15 = 25e^{k(10)}$$
$$0.6 = e^{10k} \rightarrow \ln 0.6 = 10k \rightarrow k = \frac{\ln 0.6}{10} \approx -0.0511$$
When $A_0 = 25$ and $t = 24$:
$$A = 25e^{-0.0511\,(24)} = 7.33 \text{ kilograms}$$
Find t when $A = \frac{1}{2}A_0$:
$$0.5 = 25\,e^{-0.0511\,t}$$
$$0.02 = e^{-0.0511\,t} \rightarrow \ln 0.02 = -0.0511t \rightarrow t = \frac{\ln 0.02}{-0.0511} \approx 76.6 \text{ hours}$$

19. Use $A = A_0 e^{kt}$ and solve for k:
$$\frac{1}{2}A_0 = A_0 e^{k(8)}$$
$$0.5 = e^{8k} \rightarrow \ln 0.5 = 8k$$
$$k = \frac{\ln 0.5}{8} \approx -0.0866$$

Find t when $A = 0.1A_0$:
$$0.1A_0 = A_0 e^{-0.0866\,t}$$
$$0.1 = e^{-0.0866\,t} \rightarrow \ln 0.1 = -0.0866t$$
$$t = \frac{\ln 0.1}{-0.0866} \approx 26.6 \text{ days}$$

The farmers need to wait about 27 days before using the hay.

21. (a) $P(0) = \dfrac{0.9}{1 + 6e^{-0.32(0)}} = \dfrac{0.9}{1 + 6 \cdot 1} = \dfrac{0.9}{7} = 0.1286$

(b) The maximum proportion is the carrying capacity, 0.9.

(c)
$$0.8 = \frac{0.9}{1 + 6e^{-0.32\,t}}$$
$$0.8\left(1 + 6e^{-0.32t}\right) = 0.9 \rightarrow 1 + 6e^{-0.32t} = 1.125 \rightarrow 6e^{-0.32t} = 0.125$$
$$e^{-0.32t} = 0.020833 \rightarrow -0.32t = \ln(0.020833)$$
$$t = \frac{\ln(0.020833)}{-0.32} \approx 12.1$$

80% of households will own VCR's in 1996 (t = 12).

23. (a)   As $t \to \infty$, $e^{-0.439\,t} \to 0$. Thus, $P(t) \to 1000$. The carrying capacity is 1000.

   (b) $P(0) = \dfrac{1000}{1 + 32.33e^{-0.439\,(0)}} = \dfrac{1000}{33.33} = 30$

   (c) $800 = \dfrac{1000}{1 + 32.33e^{-0.439\,t}}$

   $800\left(1 + 32.33e^{-0.439\,t}\right) = 1000 \to 1 + 32.33e^{-0.439\,t} = 1.25$

   $32.33e^{-0.439\,t} = 0.25 \to e^{-0.439\,t} = 0.007733$

   $-0.439t = \ln(0.007733) \to t = \dfrac{\ln(0.007733)}{-0.439} \approx 11.076 \text{ hours}$

Chapter 6

Exponential and Logarithmic Functions

6.8   Logarithmic Scales

1. $L(10^{-5}) = 10\log\dfrac{10^{-5}}{10^{-12}} = 10\log 10^7 = 10\cdot 7 = 70$ decibels

3. $L(0.15) = 10\log\dfrac{1.5\times 10^{-1}}{10^{-12}} = 10\log\left(1.5\times 10^{11}\right)$

   $= 10\left(\log\left(1.5\right) + \log\left(10^{11}\right)\right) = 10\left(\log\left(1.5\right) + 11\right) \approx 111.76$ decibels

5. $L(x) = 10\log\left(\dfrac{x}{10^{-12}}\right) = 130$ decibels

   $10\log\left(\dfrac{x}{10^{-12}}\right) = 130 \rightarrow \log\left(\dfrac{x}{10^{-12}}\right) = 13$

   $\log\left(x\cdot 10^{12}\right) = 13 \rightarrow \log(x) + \log\left(10^{12}\right) = 13$

   $\log(x) + 12 = 13 \rightarrow \log(x) = 1 \rightarrow 10^{\log(x)} = 10^1$

   $x = 10^1 = 10$ watts per square meter

7. $M(10) = \log\dfrac{10}{10^{-3}} = \log 10^4 = 4$

9.   Mexico City:

$$\log(x \cdot 10^3) = 8.1$$

$$\log(x) + \log(10^3) = 8.1$$

$$\log(x) + 3 = 8.1$$

$$\log(x) = 5.1$$

$$10^{\log(x)} = 10^{5.1}$$

$$x = 10^{5.1} \approx 125892.54$$

San Francisco: $M(x) = \log\dfrac{x}{10^{-3}} = 6.9$

$$\log(x \cdot 10^3) = 6.9$$

$$\log(x) + \log(10^3) = 6.9$$

$$\log(x) + 3 = 6.9$$

$$\log(x) = 3.9$$

$$10^{\log(x)} = 10^{3.9}$$

$$x = 10^{3.9} \approx 7943.28$$

11.   Delta Center

$$L(x_1) = 10\log\left(\frac{x_1}{10^{-12}}\right) = 110 \ \text{decibels}$$

$$10\log\left(\frac{x_1}{10^{-12}}\right) = 110$$

$$\log(x_1 \cdot 10^{12}) = 11$$

$$\log(x_1) + \log(10^{12}) = 11$$

$$\log(x_1) + 12 = 11$$

$$\log(x_1) = -1$$

$$10^{\log(x_1)} = 10^{-1}$$

$$x_1 = 10^{-1} = 0.1$$

NBA guidelines

$$L(x_2) = 10\log\left(\frac{x_2}{10^{-12}}\right) = 95 \ \text{decibels}$$

$$10\log\left(\frac{x_2}{10^{-12}}\right) = 95$$

$$\log(x_2 \cdot 10^{12}) = 9.5$$

$$\log(x_2) + \log(10^{12}) = 9.5$$

$$\log(x_2) + 12 = 9.5$$

$$\log(x_2) = -2.5$$

$$10^{\log(x_2)} = 10^{-2.5}$$

$$x_2 = 10^{-2.5} \approx 0.0032$$

Therefore $\dfrac{x_1}{x_2} = \dfrac{0.1}{0.0032} = 31.25$, which means that the crowd noise was approximately 31 times louder than NBA guidelines allow.

Chapter 6

Exponential and Logarithmic Functions

6.R   Chapter Review

1. $f(x) = \dfrac{2x+3}{5x-2}$

$y = \dfrac{2x+3}{5x-2}$

$x = \dfrac{2y+3}{5y-2}$ Inverse

$x(5y-2) = 2y+3$

$5xy - 2x = 2y + 3$

$5xy - 2y = 2x + 3$

$y(5x-2) = 2x+3$

$y = \dfrac{2x+3}{5x-2} \rightarrow f^{-1}(x) = \dfrac{2x+3}{5x-2}$

Domain of f =

range of f^{-1} = all real numbers except $\dfrac{2}{5}$

Range of f =

domain of f^{-1} = all real numbers except $\dfrac{2}{5}$

3. $f(x) = \dfrac{1}{x-1}$

$y = \dfrac{1}{x-1}$

$x = \dfrac{1}{y-1}$ Inverse

$x(y-1) = 1$

$xy - x = 1$

$xy = x + 1$

$y = \dfrac{x+1}{x} \rightarrow f^{-1}(x) = \dfrac{x+1}{x}$

Domain of f =
range of f^{-1} = all real numbers except 1

Range of f =
domain of f^{-1} = all real numbers except 0

5. $f(x) = \dfrac{3}{x^{1/3}}$

$y = \dfrac{3}{x^{1/3}}$

$x = \dfrac{3}{y^{1/3}}$ Inverse

$xy^{1/3} = 3 \rightarrow y^{1/3} = \dfrac{3}{x}$

$y = \dfrac{27}{x^3} \rightarrow f^{-1}(x) = \dfrac{27}{x^3}$

Domain of $f =$
  range of $f^{-1} =$ all real numbers except 0

Range of $f =$
  domain of $f^{-1} =$ all real numbers except 0

7. $\log_2\left(\dfrac{1}{8}\right) = \log_2 2^{-3} = -3\log_2 2 = -3$

9. $\ln e^{\sqrt{2}} = \sqrt{2}$

11. $2^{\log_2 0.4} = 0.4$

13. $\log_3\left(\dfrac{uv^2}{w}\right) = \log_3 uv^2 - \log_3 w = \log_3 u + \log_3 v^2 - \log_3 w = \log_3 u + 2\log_3 v - \log_3 w$

15. $\log\left(x^2\sqrt{x^3+1}\right) = \log x^2 + \log\left(x^3+1\right)^{1/2} = 2\log x + \dfrac{1}{2}\log\left(x^3+1\right)$

17. $\ln\left(\dfrac{x\sqrt[3]{x^2+1}}{x-3}\right) = \ln\left(x\sqrt[3]{x^2+1}\right) - \ln(x-3) = \ln x + \ln\left(x^2+1\right)^{1/3} - \ln(x-3)$

$= \ln x + \dfrac{1}{3}\ln\left(x^2+1\right) - \ln(x-3)$

19. $3\log_4 x^2 + \dfrac{1}{2}\log_4\sqrt{x} = \log_4\left(x^2\right)^3 + \log_4\left(x^{1/2}\right)^{1/2} = \log_4 x^6 + \log_4 x^{1/4} = \log_4 x^6 \cdot x^{1/4}$

$= \log_4 x^{25/4} = \dfrac{25}{4}\log_4 x$

21. $\ln\left(\dfrac{x-1}{x}\right) + \ln\left(\dfrac{x}{x+1}\right) - \ln\left(x^2-1\right) = \ln\left(\dfrac{x-1}{x} \cdot \dfrac{x}{x+1}\right) - \ln\left(x^2-1\right) = \ln\left[\dfrac{\left(\dfrac{x-1}{x+1}\right)}{x^2-1}\right]$

$= \ln\left(\dfrac{x-1}{x+1} \cdot \dfrac{1}{(x-1)(x+1)}\right) = \ln\dfrac{1}{(x+1)^2} = \ln(x+1)^{-2} = -2\ln(x+1)$

23. $2\log 2 + 3\log x - \dfrac{1}{2}\big[\log(x+3) + \log(x-2)\big] = \log 2^2 + \log x^3 - \dfrac{1}{2}\log\big[(x+3)(x-2)\big]$

$$= \log 4x^3 - \log\big((x+3)(x-2)\big)^{1/2} = \log\left[\dfrac{4x^3}{\big[(x+3)(x-2)\big]^{1/2}}\right]$$

25. $\log_4 19 = \dfrac{\log 19}{\log 4} \approx 2.124$

27. $\ln y = 2x^2 + \ln C$
     $\ln y = \ln e^{2x^2} + \ln C$
     $\ln y = \ln\big(Ce^{2x^2}\big) \rightarrow y = Ce^{2x^2}$

29. $\ln(y-3) + \ln(y+3) = x + C$
     $\ln(y-3)(y+3) = x + C$
     $(y-3)(y+3) = e^{x+C}$
     $y^2 - 9 = e^{x+C}$
     $y^2 = 9 + e^{x+C}$
     $y = \sqrt{9 + e^{x+C}}$

31. $e^{y+C} = x^2 + 4$
     $\ln e^{y+C} = \ln(x^2 + 4)$
     $y + C = \ln(x^2 + 4)$
     $y = \ln(x^2 + 4) - C$

33. $f(x) = 2^{x-3}$
     Using the graph of $y = 2^x$, shift the graph
     3 units to the right.
     Domain: $(-\infty, \infty)$
     Range: $(0, \infty)$
     Horizontal Asymptote: $y = 0$

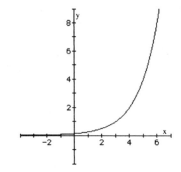

35. $f(x) = \dfrac{1}{2} \cdot 3^{-x}$
     Using the graph of $y = 3^x$, reflect the
     graph about the y-axis, and shrink

     vertically by a factor of $\dfrac{1}{2}$.
     Domain: $(-\infty, \infty)$
     Range: $(0, \infty)$
     Horizontal Asymptote: $y = 0$

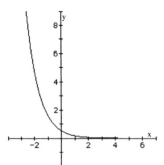

37. $f(x) = 1 - e^x$
Using the graph of $y = e^x$, reflect about
the x-axis, and shift up 1 unit.
Domain: $(-\infty, \infty)$
Range: $(-\infty, 1)$
Horizontal Asymptote: $y = 1$

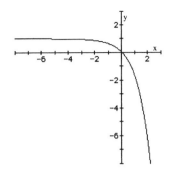

39. $f(x) = 3 + \ln x$
Using the graph of $y = \ln x$, shift the
graph up 3 units.
Domain: $(0, \infty)$
Range: $(-\infty, \infty)$
Vertical Asymptote: $x = 0$

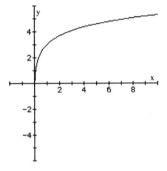

41. $f(x) = 3 - e^{-x}$
Using the graph of $y = e^x$, reflect the
graph about the y-axis, reflect about the
x-axis, and shift up 3 units.
Domain: $(-\infty, \infty)$
Range: $(-\infty, 3)$
Horizontal Asymptote: $y = 3$

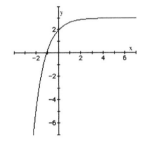

43. $4^{1-2x} = 2$
$\left(2^2\right)^{1-2x} = 2$
$2^{2-4x} = 2^1$
$2 - 4x = 1 \rightarrow -4x = -1 \rightarrow x = \dfrac{1}{4}$

45. $3^{x^2+x} = \sqrt{3}$
$3^{x^2+x} = 3^{1/2}$
$x^2 + x = \dfrac{1}{2} \rightarrow 2x^2 + 2x - 1 = 0 \rightarrow x = \dfrac{-2 \pm \sqrt{4 - 4(2)(-1)}}{2(2)} = \dfrac{-2 \pm \sqrt{12}}{4} = \dfrac{-2 \pm 2\sqrt{3}}{4} = \dfrac{-1 \pm \sqrt{3}}{2}$
$x = \dfrac{-1 - \sqrt{3}}{2}$ or $x = \dfrac{-1 + \sqrt{3}}{2}$

47. $\log_x 64 = -3$

$x^{-3} = 64$

$\left(x^{-3}\right)^{-1/3} = 64^{-1/3} \rightarrow x = \dfrac{1}{\sqrt[3]{64}} = \dfrac{1}{4}$

49.
$$5^x = 3^{x+2}$$
$$\log\left(5^x\right) = \log\left(3^{x+2}\right)$$
$$x \log 5 = (x+2)\log 3$$
$$x \log 5 = x \log 3 + 2\log 3$$
$$x \log 5 - x \log 3 = 2\log 3$$
$$x(\log 5 - \log 3) = 2\log 3$$
$$x = \frac{2\log 3}{\log 5 - \log 3}$$
$$x \approx 4.301$$

51. $9^{2x} = 27^{3x-4}$

$\left(3^2\right)^{2x} = \left(3^3\right)^{3x-4}$

$3^{4x} = 3^{9x-12}$

$4x = 9x - 12 \rightarrow -5x = -12 \rightarrow x = \dfrac{12}{5}$

53. $\log_3 \sqrt{x-2} = 2$

$\sqrt{x-2} = 3^2$

$x - 2 = 9^2 \rightarrow x - 2 = 81 \rightarrow x = 83$

55. $8 = 4^{x^2} \cdot 2^{5x}$

$2^3 = \left(2^2\right)^{x^2} \cdot 2^{5x}$

$2^3 = 2^{2x^2 + 5x}$

$3 = 2x^2 + 5x \rightarrow 0 = 2x^2 + 5x - 3$

$0 = (2x-1)(x+3) \rightarrow x = \dfrac{1}{2}$ or $x = -3$

57. $\log_6(x+3) + \log_6(x+4) = 1$

$\log_6(x+3)(x+4) = 1$

$(x+3)(x+4) = 6^1$

$x^2 + 7x + 12 = 6$

$x^2 + 7x + 6 = 0$

$(x+6)(x+1) = 0$

$x = -6$ or $x = -1$

The logarithms are undefined when
$x = -6$, so $x = -1$ is the only solution.

59. $e^{1-x} = 5$

$1 - x = \ln 5$

$-x = -1 + \ln 5$

$x = 1 - \ln 5 \approx -0.609$

61.
$$2^{3x} = 3^{2x+1}$$
$$\ln 2^{3x} = \ln 3^{2x+1}$$
$$3x \ln 2 = (2x+1)\ln 3$$
$$3x \ln 2 = 2x \ln 3 + \ln 3$$
$$3x \ln 2 - 2x \ln 3 = \ln 3$$
$$x(3\ln 2 - 2\ln 3) = \ln 3$$
$$x = \frac{\ln 3}{3\ln 2 - 2\ln 3}$$
$$x \approx -9.327$$

63. $h(300) = (30(0) + 8000)\log\left(\dfrac{760}{300}\right) = 8000\log 2.53333 = 3229.5$ meters

65. $h(x) = 10000$

$$10000 = (30(-100) + 8000) \log\left(\frac{760}{x}\right)$$

$$10000 = (5000) \log\left(\frac{760}{x}\right)$$

$$2 = \log\left(\frac{760}{x}\right)$$

$$10^2 = 10^{\log\left(\frac{760}{x}\right)}$$

$$100 = \frac{760}{x} \rightarrow x = \frac{760}{100} = 7.6 \text{ mm}$$

67. $P = 25e^{0.1d}$

(a) $P = 25e^{0.1(4)}$
$= 25e^{0.4}$
$= 37.3$ watts

(b) $50 = 25e^{0.1d}$
$2 = e^{0.1d}$
$\ln 2 = 0.1d$
$d = \dfrac{\ln 2}{0.1} = 6.9$ decibels

69. (a) $P = 90 - 80\left(\dfrac{3}{4}\right)^5 \approx 71.02\%$

(b) $P = 90 - 80\left(\dfrac{3}{4}\right)^{10} \approx 85.5\%$

(c) as $t \rightarrow \infty,\ P = 90 - 80\left(\dfrac{3}{4}\right)^t \rightarrow 90 - 0 = 90\%$

(d) $40 = 90 - 80\left(\dfrac{3}{4}\right)^t \rightarrow -50 = -80\left(\dfrac{3}{4}\right)^t \rightarrow \dfrac{5}{8} = \left(\dfrac{3}{4}\right)^t \rightarrow \ln\left(\dfrac{5}{8}\right) = \ln\left(\dfrac{3}{4}\right)^t$

$\rightarrow \ln\left(\dfrac{5}{8}\right) = t \cdot \ln\left(\dfrac{3}{4}\right) \rightarrow t = \dfrac{\ln\left(\dfrac{5}{8}\right)}{\ln\left(\dfrac{3}{4}\right)} \approx 1.63$ months

(e) $70 = 90 - 80\left(\dfrac{3}{4}\right)^t$

$-20 = -80\left(\dfrac{3}{4}\right)^t \rightarrow 0.25 = \left(\dfrac{3}{4}\right)^t \rightarrow \ln(0.25) = \ln\left(\dfrac{3}{4}\right)^t$

$\rightarrow \ln(0.25) = t \cdot \ln\left(\dfrac{3}{4}\right) \rightarrow t = \dfrac{\ln(0.25)}{\ln\left(\dfrac{3}{4}\right)} \approx 4.82$ months

71. (a) $n = \dfrac{\log 10000 - \log 90000}{\log(1 - 0.20)} = 9.85$ years

     (b) $n = \dfrac{\log 0.5i - \log i}{\log(1 - 0.15)} = \dfrac{\log \frac{0.5i}{i}}{\log 0.85} = \dfrac{\log 0.5}{\log 0.85} = 4.27$ years

73. $P = A\left(1 + \dfrac{r}{n}\right)^{-nt} = 85000\left(1 + \dfrac{0.04}{2}\right)^{-2(18)} = \$41,668.97$

75. $L\left(10^{-4}\right) = 10\log\left(\dfrac{10^{-4}}{10^{-12}}\right) = 10\log\left(10^8\right) = 10 \cdot 8 = 80$ decibels

77. $A = A_0 e^{kt}$

     $\dfrac{1}{2}A_0 = A_0 e^{k(5600)}$

     $0.5 = e^{5600\,k} \rightarrow \ln 0.5 = 5600k \rightarrow k = \dfrac{\ln 0.5}{5600} \approx -0.000124$

     $0.05A_0 = A_0 e^{-0.000124\,t}$

     $0.05 = e^{-0.000124\,t} \rightarrow \ln 0.05 = -0.000124\,t \rightarrow t = \dfrac{\ln 0.05}{-0.000124} \approx 24,159$ years ago

79. (a) Graphing:

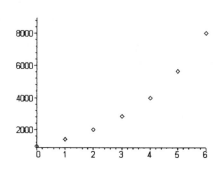

(b) $y = 1000\left(\sqrt{2}\right)^x$

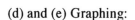
$\sqrt{2} = e^{\ln \sqrt{2}}$

$\rightarrow y = 1000\left(e^{\ln \sqrt{2}}\right)^x = 1000 e^{(\ln \sqrt{2})x}$

$N = N_0 e^{0.3466t}, N_0 = 1000, k = 0.3466$

(c) $N = 1000e^{0.3466(7)} \approx 11314$ bacteria

(d) and (e) Graphing:

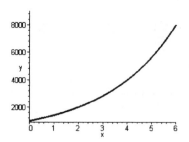

81. $P = P_0 e^{kt} = 5,840,445,216\,e^{0.0133(3)} = 6,078,190,457$

83. (a) $P(0) = \dfrac{0.8}{1 + 1.67e^{-0.16(0)}} = \dfrac{0.8}{1 + 1.67} = 0.2996$

     (b)   0.8

     (c)   Graphing:

     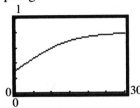

     (d)   Using INTERSECT we have:

     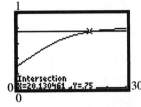

     75% use Windows 98 in 2018.

The Conics

7.2   The Parabola

1.   B   3.   E   5.   H   7.   C

9.   The focus is (4, 0) and the vertex is (0, 0). Both lie
on the horizontal line $y = 0$. $a = 4$ and since (4, 0)
is to the right of (0, 0), the parabola opens to the
right. The equation of the parabola is:

$$y^2 = 4ax$$
$$y^2 = 4 \cdot 4 \cdot x$$
$$y^2 = 16x$$

Letting $x = 4$, we find $y^2 = 64$ or $y = \pm 8$.
The points (4, 8) and (4, –8) define the latus rectum.

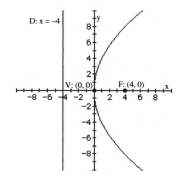

11.   The focus is (0, –3) and the vertex is (0, 0). Both lie
on the vertical line $x = 0$. $a = 3$ and since (0, –3) is
below (0, 0), the parabola opens down. The
equation of the parabola is:

$$x^2 = -4ay$$
$$x^2 = -4 \cdot 3 \cdot y$$
$$x^2 = -12y$$

Letting $y = -3$, we find $x^2 = 36$ or $x = \pm 6$.
The points (6, 3) and (6, –3) define the latus rectum.

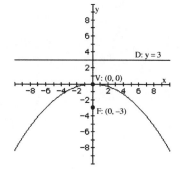

13.   The focus is (–2, 0) and the directrix is $x = 2$. The
vertex is (0, 0). $a = 2$ and since (–2, 0) is to the left
of (0, 0), the parabola opens to the left. The
equation of the parabola is:

$$y^2 = -4ax$$
$$y^2 = -4 \cdot 2 \cdot x$$
$$y^2 = -8x$$

Letting $x = -2$, we find $y^2 = 16$ or $y = \pm 4$. The
points (–2, 4) and (–2, –4) define the latus rectum.

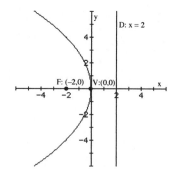

15. The directrix is $y = -\dfrac{1}{2}$ and the vertex is (0, 0). The focus is $\left(0,\dfrac{1}{2}\right)$. $a = \dfrac{1}{2}$ and since $\left(0,\dfrac{1}{2}\right)$ is above (0, 0), the parabola opens up. The equation of the parabola is:

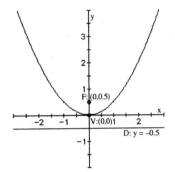

$$x^2 = 4ay$$

$$x^2 = 4 \cdot \dfrac{1}{2} \cdot y \rightarrow x^2 = 2y$$

Letting $y = \dfrac{1}{2}$, we find $x^2 = 1$ or $x = \pm 1$.

The points $\left(1,\dfrac{1}{2}\right)$ and $\left(-1,\dfrac{1}{2}\right)$ define the latus rectum.

17. The focus is (2, –5) and the vertex is (2, –3). Both lie on the vertical line $x = 2$. $a = 2$ and since (2, –5) is below (2, –3), the parabola opens down. The equation of the parabola is:

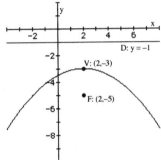

$$(x - h)^2 = -4a(y - k)$$
$$(x - 2)^2 = -4 \cdot 2 \cdot (y - (-3))$$
$$(x - 2)^2 = -8(y + 3)$$

Letting $y = -5$, we find $(x - 2)^2 = 16$ or $x - 2 = \pm 4$. So, $x = 6$ or $x = -2$. The points (6, –5) and (–2, –5) define the latus rectum.

19. Vertex: (0,0). Since the axis of symmetry is vertical, the parabola opens up or down. Since (2, 3) is above (0, 0), the parabola opens up. The equation has the form $x^2 = 4ay$. Substitute the coordinates of (2, 3) into the equation to find a:

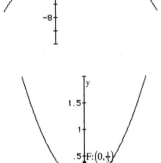

$$2^2 = 4a \cdot 3$$

$$4 = 12a \rightarrow a = \dfrac{1}{3}$$

The equation of the parabola is: $x^2 = \dfrac{4}{3}y$. The focus is $\left(0,\dfrac{1}{3}\right)$. Letting $y = \dfrac{1}{3}$, we find $x^2 = \dfrac{4}{9}$ or $x = \pm\dfrac{2}{3}$. The points $\left(\dfrac{2}{3},\dfrac{1}{3}\right)$ and $\left(-\dfrac{2}{3},\dfrac{1}{3}\right)$ define the latus rectum.

21. The directrix is $y = 2$ and the focus is $(-3, 4)$. This is a vertical case, so the vertex is $(-3, 3)$. $a = 1$ and since $(-3, 4)$ is above $y = 2$, the parabola opens up. The equation of the parabola is:

$$(x - h)^2 = 4a(y - k)$$
$$(x - (-3))^2 = 4 \cdot 1 \cdot (y - 3)$$
$$(x + 3)^2 = 4(y - 3)$$

Letting $y = 4$, we find $(x + 3)^2 = 4$ or $x + 3 = \pm 2$. So, $x = -1$ or $x = -5$. The points $(-1, 4)$ and $(-5, 4)$ define the latus rectum.

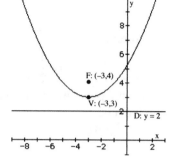

23. The directrix is $x = 1$ and the focus is $(-3, -2)$. This is a horizontal case, so the vertex is $(-1, -2)$. $a = 2$ and since $(-3, -2)$ is to the left of $x = 1$, the parabola opens to the left. The equation of the parabola is:

$$(y - k)^2 = -4a(x - h)$$
$$(y - (-2))^2 = -4 \cdot 2 \cdot (x - (-1))$$
$$(y + 2)^2 = -8(x + 1)$$

Letting $x = -3$, we find $(y + 2)^2 = 16$ or $y + 2 = \pm 4$. So, $y = 2$ or $y = -6$. The points $(-3, 2)$ and $(-3, -6)$ define the latus rectum.

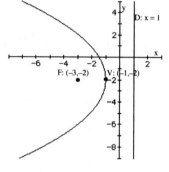

25. The equation $x^2 = 4y$ is in the form $x^2 = 4ay$ where $4a = 4$ or $a = 1$. Thus, we have:

    Vertex: $(0, 0)$
    Focus: $(0, 1)$
    Directrix: $y = -1$

To graph, enter: $y_1 = x^2 / 4$

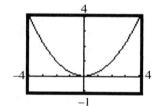

27. The equation $y^2 = -16x$ is in the form $y^2 = -4ax$ where $-4a = -16$ or $a = 4$. Thus, we have:

    Vertex: $(0, 0)$
    Focus: $(-4, 0)$
    Directrix: $x = 4$

To graph, enter: $y_1 = \sqrt{-16x}$; $y_2 = -\sqrt{-16x}$

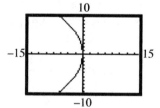

29. The equation $(y - 2)^2 = 8(x + 1)$ is in the form $(y - k)^2 = 4a(x - h)$ where $4a = 8$ or $a = 2$, $h = -1$, and $k = 2$. Thus, we have:

    Vertex: $(-1, 2)$
    Focus: $(1, 2)$
    Directrix: $x = -3$

To graph, enter:

$$y_1 = 2 + \sqrt{8(x + 1)}; \quad y_2 = 2 - \sqrt{8(x + 1)}$$

354

31. The equation $(x-3)^2 = -(y+1)$ is in the form

$(x-h)^2 = -4a(y-k)$ where $-4a = -1$ or $a = \dfrac{1}{4}$,

$h = 3$, and $k = -1$. Thus, we have:

    Vertex: $(3, -1)$

    Focus: $\left(3, -\dfrac{5}{4}\right)$

    Directrix: $y = -\dfrac{3}{4}$

To graph, enter: $y_1 = -1 - (x-3)^2$

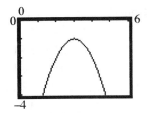

33. The equation $(y+3)^2 = 8(x-2)$ is in the form
$(y-k)^2 = 4a(x-h)$ where $4a = 8$ or $a = 2$,
$h = 2$, and $k = -3$. Thus, we have:

    Vertex: $(2, -3)$

    Focus: $(4, -3)$

    Directrix: $x = 0$

To graph, enter:

    $y_1 = -3 + \sqrt{8(x-2)}$; $y_2 = -3 - \sqrt{8(x-2)}$

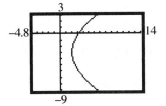

35. Complete the square to put in standard form:

$$y^2 - 4y + 4x + 4 = 0$$
$$y^2 - 4y + 4 = -4x$$
$$(y-2)^2 = -4x$$

The equation is in the form $(y-k)^2 = -4a(x-h)$
where $-4a = -4$ or $a = 1$, $h = 0$, and $k = 2$. Thus,
we have:

    Vertex: $(0, 2)$

    Focus: $(-1, 2)$

    Directrix: $x = 1$

To graph, enter: $y_1 = 2 + \sqrt{-4x}$; $y_2 = 2 - \sqrt{-4x}$

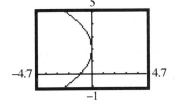

37. Complete the square to put in standard form:

$$x^2 + 8x = 4y - 8$$
$$x^2 + 8x + 16 = 4y - 8 + 16$$
$$(x+4)^2 = 4(y+2)$$

The equation is in the form $(x-h)^2 = 4a(y-k)$
where $4a = 4$ or $a = 1$, $h = -4$, and $k = -2$. Thus,
we have:

    Vertex: $(-4, -2)$

    Focus: $(-4, -1)$

    Directrix: $y = -3$

To graph, enter: $y_1 = -2 + (x+4)^2 / 4$

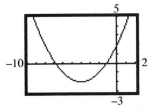

39. Complete the square to put in standard form:

$$y^2 + 2y - x = 0$$
$$y^2 + 2y + 1 = x + 1$$
$$(y + 1)^2 = x + 1$$

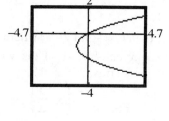

The equation is in the form $(y - k)^2 = 4a(x - h)$

where $4a = 1$ or $a = \dfrac{1}{4}$, $h = -1$, and $k = -1$. Thus, we have:

Vertex: $(-1, -1)$

Focus: $\left(-\dfrac{3}{4}, -1\right)$

Directrix: $x = -\dfrac{5}{4}$

To graph, enter: $y_1 = -1 + \sqrt{x + 1}$; $y_2 = -1 - \sqrt{x + 1}$

41. Complete the square to put in standard form:

$$x^2 - 4x = y + 4$$
$$x^2 - 4x + 4 = y + 4 + 4$$
$$(x - 2)^2 = y + 8$$

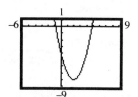

The equation is in the form $(x - h)^2 = 4a(y - k)$ where $4a = 1$ or $a = \dfrac{1}{4}$, $h = 2$, and $k = -8$.

Thus, we have:

Vertex: $(2, -8)$

Focus: $\left(2, -\dfrac{31}{4}\right)$

Directrix: $y = -\dfrac{33}{4}$ To graph, enter: $y_1 = -8 + (x - 2)^2$

43. $(y - 1)^2 = c(x - 0)$

$(y - 1)^2 = cx$

$(2 - 1)^2 = c(1) \rightarrow 1 = c$

$(y - 1)^2 = x$

45. $(y - 1)^2 = c(x - 2)$

$(0 - 1)^2 = c(1 - 2)$

$1 = -c \rightarrow c = -1$

$(y - 1)^2 = -(x - 2)$

47. $(x - 0)^2 = c(y - 1)$

$(2 - 0)^2 = c(2 - 1) \rightarrow 4 = c$

$x^2 = 4(y - 1)$

49. $(y - 0)^2 = c(x - (-2))$

$y^2 = c(x + 2)$

$1^2 = c(0 + 2) \rightarrow 1 = 2c \rightarrow c = \dfrac{1}{2}$

$y^2 = \dfrac{1}{2}(x + 2)$

51. Set up the problem so that the vertex of the parabola is at (0, 0) and it opens up. Then the equation of the parabola has the form: $x^2 = 4ay$. Since the parabola is 10 feet across and feet deep, the points (5, 4) and (–5, 4) are on the parabola.
Substitute and solve for a:
$$5^2 = 4a(4) \rightarrow 25 = 16a \rightarrow a = \frac{25}{16}$$
a is the distance from the vertex to the focus. Thus, the receiver (located at the focus) is $\frac{25}{16} = 1.5625$ feet, or 18.75 inches from the base of the dish, along the axis of the parabola.

53. Set up the problem so that the vertex of the parabola is at (0, 0) and it opens up. Then the equation of the parabola has the form: $x^2 = 4ay$. Since the parabola is 4 inches across and 1 inch deep, the points (2, 1) and (–2, 1) are on the parabola.
Substitute and solve for a:
$$2^2 = 4a(1) \quad \rightarrow \quad 4 = 4a \quad \rightarrow \quad a = 1$$
a is the distance from the vertex to the focus. Thus, the bulb (located at the focus) should be 1 inch, from the vertex.

55. Set up the problem so that the vertex of the parabola is at (0, 0) and it opens up. Then the equation of the parabola has the form: $x^2 = cy$.
The point (300, 80) is a point on the parabola.
Solve for c and find the equation:
$$300^2 = c(80) \rightarrow c = 1125$$
$$x^2 = 1125y$$

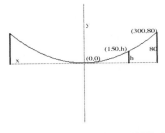

Since the height of the cable, 150 feet from the center, is to be found, the point (150, h) is a point on the parabola. Solve for h:
$$150^2 = 1125h \rightarrow 22500 = 1125h \rightarrow h = 20$$
The height of the cable, 150 feet from the center, is 20 feet.

57. Set up the problem so that the vertex of the parabola is at (0, 0) and it opens up. Then the equation of the parabola has the form: $x^2 = 4ay$. a is the distance from the vertex to the focus (where the source is located), so $a = 2$. Since the opening is 5 feet across, there is a point (2.5, y) on the parabola. Solve for y:
$$x^2 = 8y \rightarrow 2.5^2 = 8y \rightarrow 6.25 = 8y \rightarrow y = 0.78125 \text{ feet}$$
The depth of the searchlight should be 0.78125 feet.

59. Set up the problem so that the vertex of the parabola is at (0, 0) and it opens up. Then the equation of the parabola has the form: $x^2 = 4ay$. Since the parabola is 20 feet across and 6 feet deep, the points (10, 6) and (–10, 6) are on the parabola.
Substitute and solve for a:
$$10^2 = 4a(6) \rightarrow 100 = 24a \rightarrow a \approx 4.17 \text{ feet}$$
The heat source will be concentrated 4.17 feet from the base, along the axis of symmetry.

61. Set up the problem so that the vertex of the parabola is at $(0, 0)$ and it opens down. Then the equation of the parabola has the form: $x^2 = cy$.

    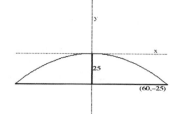

    The point $(60, -25)$ is a point on the parabola.
    Solve for c and find the equation:
    $$60^2 = c(-25) \rightarrow c = -144$$
    $$x^2 = -144y$$
    To find the height of the bridge, 10 feet from the center, the point $(10, y)$ is a point on the parabola. Solve for y:
    $$10^2 = -144y \rightarrow 100 = -144y \rightarrow y = -0.69$$
    The height of the bridge, 10 feet from the center, is $25 - 0.69 = 24.31$ feet.
    To find the height of the bridge, 30 feet from the center, the point $(30, y)$ is a point on the parabola. Solve for y:
    $$30^2 = -144y \rightarrow 900 = -144y \rightarrow y = -6.25$$
    The height of the bridge, 30 feet from the center, is $25 - 6.25 = 18.75$ feet.
    To find the height of the bridge, 50 feet from the center, the point $(50, y)$ is a point on the parabola. Solve for y:
    $$50^2 = -144y \rightarrow 2500 = -144y \rightarrow y = -17.36$$
    The height of the bridge, 50 feet from the center, is $25 - 17.36 = 7.64$ feet.

63. $Ax^2 + Ey = 0 \quad A \neq 0, \ E \neq 0$
    $$Ax^2 = -Ey \rightarrow x^2 = \frac{-E}{A}y$$
    This is the equation of a parabola with vertex at $(0, 0)$ and axis of symmetry being the y-axis. The focus is $\left(0, \frac{-E}{4A}\right)$. The directrix is $y = \frac{E}{4A}$.

65. $Ax^2 + Dx + Ey + F = 0 \quad A \neq 0$
    (a) If $E \neq 0$, then:
    $$Ax^2 + Dx = -Ey - F \rightarrow A\left(x^2 + \frac{D}{A}x + \frac{D^2}{4A^2}\right) = -Ey - F + \frac{D^2}{4A}$$
    $$\left(x + \frac{D}{2A}\right)^2 = \frac{1}{A}\left(-Ey - F + \frac{D^2}{4A}\right) \rightarrow \left(x + \frac{D}{2A}\right)^2 = \frac{-E}{A}\left(y + \frac{F}{E} - \frac{D^2}{4AE}\right)$$
    $$\left(x + \frac{D}{2A}\right)^2 = \frac{-E}{A}\left(y - \frac{D^2 - 4AF}{4AE}\right)$$
    This is the equation of a parabola whose vertex is $\left(\frac{-D}{2A}, \frac{D^2 - 4AF}{4AE}\right)$.

    (b) If $E = 0$, then
    $$Ax^2 + Dx + F = 0 \rightarrow x = \frac{-D \pm \sqrt{D^2 - 4AF}}{2A}$$
    If $D^2 - 4AF = 0$, then $x = \frac{-D}{2A}$ is a vertical line.

(c)   If $E = 0$, then

$$Ax^2 + Dx + F = 0 \rightarrow x = \frac{-D \pm \sqrt{D^2 - 4AF}}{2A}$$

If $D^2 - 4AF > 0$,

then $x = \dfrac{-D + \sqrt{D^2 - 4AF}}{2A}$ or $x = \dfrac{-D - \sqrt{D^2 - 4AF}}{2A}$ are two vertical lines.

(d)   If $E = 0$, then

$$Ax^2 + Dx + F = 0 \rightarrow x = \frac{-D \pm \sqrt{D^2 - 4AF}}{2A}$$

If $D^2 - 4AF < 0$, there is no real solution. The graph contains no points.

The Conics
7.3 The Ellipse

1. C   3. B

5. $\dfrac{x^2}{25} + \dfrac{y^2}{4} = 1$

The center of the ellipse is at the origin.
$a = 5,\; b = 2$. The vertices are (5, 0) and (–5, 0).
Find the value of c:
$$c^2 = a^2 - b^2 = 25 - 4 = 21 \rightarrow c = \sqrt{21}$$
The foci are $\left(\sqrt{21}, 0\right)$ and $\left(-\sqrt{21}, 0\right)$.
To graph, enter:
$$y_1 = 2\sqrt{(1 - x^2/25)};\; y_1 = -2\sqrt{(1 - x^2/25)}$$

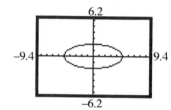

7. $\dfrac{x^2}{9} + \dfrac{y^2}{25} = 1$

The center of the ellipse is at the origin.
$a = 5,\; b = 3$. The vertices are (0, 5) and (0, –5).
Find the value of c:
$$c^2 = a^2 - b^2 = 25 - 9 = 16 \rightarrow c = 4$$
The foci are (0, 4) and (0, –4).
To graph, enter:
$$y_1 = 5\sqrt{(1 - x^2/9)};\; y_1 = -5\sqrt{(1 - x^2/9)}$$

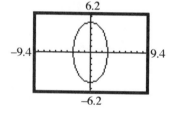

9. $4x^2 + y^2 = 16$

Divide by 16 to put in standard form:
$$\frac{4x^2}{16} + \frac{y^2}{16} = \frac{16}{16} \quad \rightarrow \quad \frac{x^2}{4} + \frac{y^2}{16} = 1$$
The center of the ellipse is at the origin.
$a = 4,\; b = 2$. The vertices are (0, 4) and (0, –4).
Find the value of c:
$$c^2 = a^2 - b^2 = 16 - 4 = 12$$
$$c = \sqrt{12} = 2\sqrt{3}$$
The foci are $\left(0, 2\sqrt{3}\right)$ and $\left(0, -2\sqrt{3}\right)$.
To graph, enter:
$$y_1 = \sqrt{(16 - 4x^2)};\; y_1 = -\sqrt{(16 - 4x^2)}$$

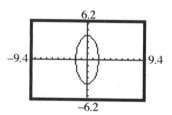

11. $4y^2 + x^2 = 8$
 Divide by 8 to put in standard form:
 $$\frac{4y^2}{8} + \frac{x^2}{8} = \frac{8}{8} \quad \rightarrow \quad \frac{x^2}{8} + \frac{y^2}{2} = 1$$
 The center of the ellipse is at the origin.
 $a = \sqrt{8} = 2\sqrt{2}, \; b = \sqrt{2}$. The vertices are
 $\left(2\sqrt{2}, 0\right)$ and $\left(-2\sqrt{2}, 0\right)$. Find the value of c:
 $$c^2 = a^2 - b^2 = 8 - 2 = 6$$
 $$c = \sqrt{6}$$
 The foci are $\left(\sqrt{6}, 0\right)$ and $\left(-\sqrt{6}, 0\right)$.
 To graph, enter:
 $y_1 = \sqrt{(2 - x^2 / 4)}; \; y_1 = -\sqrt{(2 - x^2 / 4)}$

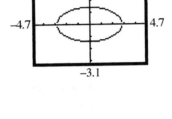

13. $x^2 + y^2 = 16$
 This is the equation of a circle whose center is at
 (0, 0) and radius = 4.
 To graph, enter: $y_1 = \sqrt{(16 - x^2)}; \; y_1 = -\sqrt{(16 - x^2)}$

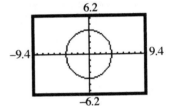

15. Center: $(0, 0)$; Focus: $(3, 0)$; Vertex: $(5, 0)$;
 Major axis is the x-axis; $a = 5$; $c = 3$. Find b:
 $$b^2 = a^2 - c^2 = 25 - 9 = 16$$
 $$b = 4$$
 Write the equation: $\dfrac{x^2}{25} + \dfrac{y^2}{16} = 1$

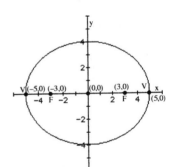

17. Center: $(0, 0)$; Focus: $(0, -4)$; Vertex: $(0, 5)$;
 Major axis is the y-axis; $a = 5$; $c = 4$. Find b:
 $$b^2 = a^2 - c^2 = 25 - 16 = 9$$
 $$b = 3$$
 Write the equation: $\dfrac{x^2}{9} + \dfrac{y^2}{25} = 1$

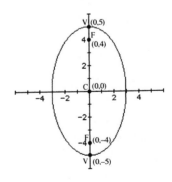

Chapter 7   The Conics

19. Foci: $(\pm 2, 0)$; Length of major axis is 6.
Center: $(0, 0)$; Major axis is the x-axis;
$a = 3$; $c = 2$. Find b:
$$b^2 = a^2 - c^2 = 9 - 4 = 5$$
$$b = \sqrt{5}$$
Write the equation: $\dfrac{x^2}{9} + \dfrac{y^2}{5} = 1$

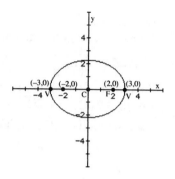

21. Foci: $(0, \pm 3)$; x-intercepts are ± 2. Center: $(0, 0)$;
Major axis is the y-axis; $c = 3$; $b = 2$. Find a:
$$a^2 = b^2 + c^2 = 4 + 9 = 13$$
$$a = \sqrt{13}$$
Write the equation: $\dfrac{x^2}{4} + \dfrac{y^2}{13} = 1$

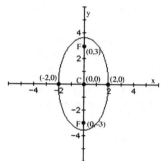

23. Center: $(0, 0)$; Vertex: $(0, 4)$; $b = 1$; Major axis is
the y-axis; $a = 4$; $b = 1$.

Write the equation: $\dfrac{x^2}{1} + \dfrac{y^2}{16} = 1$

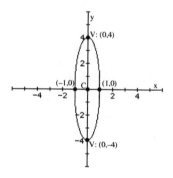

25. $\dfrac{(x+1)^2}{4} + \dfrac{(y-1)^2}{1} = 1$ 27. $\dfrac{(x-1)^2}{1} + \dfrac{y^2}{4} = 1$

29. The equation $\dfrac{(x-3)^2}{4} + \dfrac{(y+1)^2}{9} = 1$ is in the form $\dfrac{(x-h)^2}{b^2} + \dfrac{(y-k)^2}{a^2} = 1$ (major axis
parallel to the y-axis) where $a = 3$, $b = 2$, $h = 3$, and $k = -1$. Solving for c:
$$c^2 = a^2 - b^2 = 9 - 4 = 5$$
$$c = \sqrt{5}$$
Thus, we have:
    Center: $(3, -1)$
    Foci: $\left(3, -1 + \sqrt{5}\right)$, $\left(3, -1 - \sqrt{5}\right)$
    Vertices: $(3, 2), (3, -4)$
To graph, enter: $y_1 = -1 + 3\sqrt{1 - (x-3)^2/4}$;
    $y_2 = -1 - 3\sqrt{1 - (x-3)^2/4}$

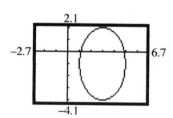

31. Divide by 16 to put the equation in standard form:
$$(x+5)^2 + 4(y-4)^2 = 16$$
$$\frac{(x+5)^2}{16} + \frac{4(y-4)^2}{16} = \frac{16}{16}$$
$$\frac{(x+5)^2}{16} + \frac{(y-4)^2}{4} = 1$$

The equation is in the form $\frac{(x-h)^2}{a^2} + \frac{(y-k)^2}{b^2} = 1$ (major axis parallel to the x-axis) where $a = 4$, $b = 2$, $h = -5$, and $k = 4$. Solving for c:
$$c^2 = a^2 - b^2 = 16 - 4 = 12$$
$$c = \sqrt{12} = 2\sqrt{3}$$

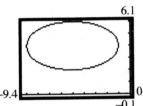

Thus, we have:

   Center: $(-5, 4)$

   Foci: $\left(-5 - 2\sqrt{3}, 4\right)$, $\left(-5 + 2\sqrt{3}, 4\right)$

   Vertices: $(-9, 4)$, $(-1, 4)$

To graph, enter: $y_1 = 4 + 2\sqrt{1 - (x+5)^2 / 16}$;
$$y_2 = 4 - 2\sqrt{1 - (x+5)^2 / 16}$$

33. Complete the square to put the equation in standard form:
$$x^2 + 4x + 4y^2 - 8y + 4 = 0$$
$$(x^2 + 4x + 4) + 4(y^2 - 2y + 1) = -4 + 4 + 4$$
$$(x+2)^2 + 4(y-1)^2 = 4$$
$$\frac{(x+2)^2}{4} + \frac{4(y-1)^2}{4} = \frac{4}{4}$$
$$\frac{(x+2)^2}{4} + \frac{(y-1)^2}{1} = 1$$

The equation is in the form $\frac{(x-h)^2}{a^2} + \frac{(y-k)^2}{b^2} = 1$ (major axis parallel to the x-axis) where $a = 2$, $b = 1$, $h = -2$, and $k = 1$. Solving for c:
$$c^2 = a^2 - b^2 = 4 - 1 = 3$$
$$c = \sqrt{3}$$

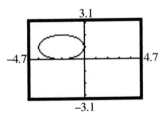

Thus, we have:

   Center: $(-2, 1)$

   Foci: $\left(-2 - \sqrt{3}, 1\right)$, $\left(-2 + \sqrt{3}, 1\right)$

   Vertices: $(-4, 1)$, $(0, 1)$

To graph, enter: $y_1 = 1 + \sqrt{1 - (x+2)^2 / 4}$;
$$y_2 = 1 - \sqrt{1 - (x+2)^2 / 4}$$

35. Complete the square to put the equation in standard form:

$$2x^2 + 3y^2 - 8x + 6y + 5 = 0$$
$$2(x^2 - 4x) + 3(y^2 + 2y) = -5$$
$$2(x^2 - 4x + 4) + 3(y^2 + 2y + 1) = -5 + 8 + 3$$
$$2(x - 2)^2 + 3(y + 1)^2 = 6$$
$$\frac{2(x - 2)^2}{6} + \frac{3(y + 1)^2}{6} = \frac{6}{6}$$
$$\frac{(x - 2)^2}{3} + \frac{(y + 1)^2}{2} = 1$$

The equation is in the form $\dfrac{(x - h)^2}{a^2} + \dfrac{(y - k)^2}{b^2} = 1$ (major axis parallel to the x-axis) where $a = \sqrt{3}$, $b = \sqrt{2}$, $h = 2$, and $k = -1$. Solving for c:
$$c^2 = a^2 - b^2 = 3 - 2 = 1 \quad \rightarrow \quad c = 1$$

Thus, we have:

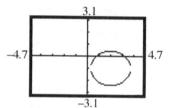

    Center: (2, -1)
    Foci: (1, -1), (3, -1)
    Vertices: $\left(2 - \sqrt{3}, -1\right)$, $\left(2 + \sqrt{3}, -1\right)$

To graph, enter: $y_1 = -1 + \sqrt{2 - 2(x - 2)^2 / 3}$;
$$y_2 = -1 - \sqrt{2 - 2(x - 2)^2 / 3}$$

37. Complete the square to put the equation in standard form:

$$9x^2 + 4y^2 - 18x + 16y - 11 = 0$$
$$9(x^2 - 2x) + 4(y^2 + 4y) = 11$$
$$9(x^2 - 2x + 1) + 4(y^2 + 4y + 4) = 11 + 9 + 16$$
$$9(x - 1)^2 + 4(y + 2)^2 = 36$$
$$\frac{9(x - 1)^2}{36} + \frac{4(y + 2)^2}{36} = \frac{36}{36}$$
$$\frac{(x - 1)^2}{4} + \frac{(y + 2)^2}{9} = 1$$

The equation is in the form $\dfrac{(x - h)^2}{b^2} + \dfrac{(y - k)^2}{a^2} = 1$ (major axis parallel to the y-axis) where $a = 3$, $b = 2$, $h = 1$, and $k = -2$. Solving for c:
$$c^2 = a^2 - b^2 = 9 - 4 = 5$$
$$c = \sqrt{5}$$

Thus, we have:

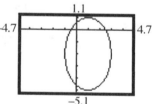

    Center: (1, -2)
    Foci: $\left(1, -2 + \sqrt{5}\right)$, $\left(1, -2 - \sqrt{5}\right)$
    Vertices: (1, 1), (1, -5)

To graph, enter: $y_1 = -2 + 3\sqrt{1 - (x - 1)^2 / 4}$;
$$y_2 = -2 - 3\sqrt{1 - (x - 1)^2 / 4}$$

39. Complete the square to put the equation in standard form:

$$4x^2 + y^2 + 4y = 0$$

$$4x^2 + y^2 + 4y + 4 = 4 \rightarrow 4x^2 + (y+2)^2 = 4$$

$$\frac{4x^2}{4} + \frac{(y+2)^2}{4} = \frac{4}{4} \rightarrow \frac{x^2}{1} + \frac{(y+2)^2}{4} = 1$$

The equation is in the form $\dfrac{(x-h)^2}{b^2} + \dfrac{(y-k)^2}{a^2} = 1$ (major axis parallel to the y-axis) where

$a = 2$, $b = 1$, $h = 0$, and $k = -2$. Solving for c:

$$c^2 = a^2 - b^2 = 4 - 1 = 3 \quad \rightarrow \quad c = \sqrt{3}$$

Thus, we have:

Center: $(0, -2)$

Foci: $\left(0, -2+\sqrt{3}\right)$, $\left(0, -2-\sqrt{3}\right)$

Vertices: $(0, 0)$, $(0, -4)$

To graph, enter: $y_1 = -2 + 2\sqrt{1-x^2}$;

$$y_2 = -2 - 2\sqrt{1-x^2}$$

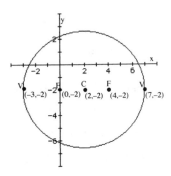

41. Center: $(2, -2)$; Vertex: $(7, -2)$; Focus: $(4, -2)$;
Major axis parallel to the x-axis; $a = 5$; $c = 2$.
Find b:

$$b^2 = a^2 - c^2 = 25 - 4 = 21 \rightarrow b = \sqrt{21}$$

Write the equation: $\dfrac{(x-2)^2}{25} + \dfrac{(y+2)^2}{21} = 1$

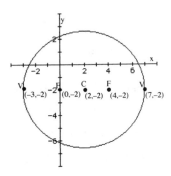

43. Vertices: $(4, 3)$, $(4, 9)$; Focus: $(4, 8)$;
Center: $(4, 6)$; Major axis parallel to the y-axis;
$a = 3$; $c = 2$. Find b:

$$b^2 = a^2 - c^2 = 9 - 4 = 5 \rightarrow b = \sqrt{5}$$

Write the equation: $\dfrac{(x-4)^2}{5} + \dfrac{(y-6)^2}{9} = 1$

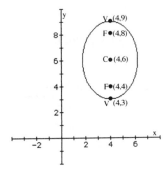

45. Foci: (5, 1), (–1, 1); length of the major axis = 8;
     Center (2, 1); Major axis parallel to the x-axis;
     $a = 4$; $c = 3$.   Find b:

$$b^2 = a^2 - c^2 = 16 - 9 = 7 \rightarrow b = \sqrt{7}$$

Write the equation: $\dfrac{(x-2)^2}{16} + \dfrac{(y-1)^2}{7} = 1$

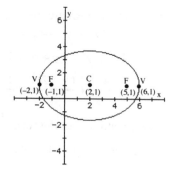

47. Center: (1, 2); Focus: (4, 2); contains the point
     (1, 3); Major axis parallel to the x-axis; $c = 3$.

The equation has the form: $\dfrac{(x-1)^2}{a^2} + \dfrac{(y-2)^2}{b^2} = 1$

Since the point (1, 3) is on the curve:

$$\frac{0}{a^2} + \frac{1}{b^2} = 1 \ \rightarrow \ \frac{1}{b^2} = 1 \ \rightarrow \ b^2 = 1 \ \rightarrow \ b = 1$$

Find a:

$$a^2 = b^2 + c^2 = 1 + 9 = 10 \ \rightarrow \ a = \sqrt{10}$$

Write the equation: $\dfrac{(x-1)^2}{10} + \dfrac{(y-2)^2}{1} = 1$

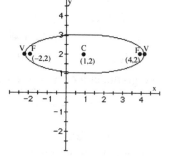

49. Center: (1, 2); Vertex: (4, 2); contains the point
     (1, 3); Major axis parallel to the x-axis; $a = 3$.

The equation has the form: $\dfrac{(x-1)^2}{a^2} + \dfrac{(y-2)^2}{b^2} = 1$

Since the point (1, 3) is on the curve:

$$\frac{0}{9} + \frac{1}{b^2} = 1 \ \rightarrow \ \frac{1}{b^2} = 1 \ \rightarrow \ b^2 = 1 \ \rightarrow \ b = 1$$

Write the equation: $\dfrac{(x-1)^2}{9} + \dfrac{(y-2)^2}{1} = 1$

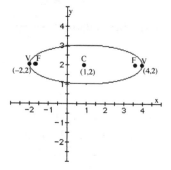

51. Rewrite the equation:

$$y = \sqrt{16 - 4x^2}$$
$$y^2 = 16 - 4x^2, \quad y \geq 0$$
$$4x^2 + y^2 = 16, \qquad y \geq 0$$
$$\frac{x^2}{4} + \frac{y^2}{16} = 1, \qquad y \geq 0$$

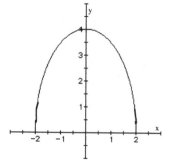

53.   Rewrite the equation:
$$y = -\sqrt{64 - 16x^2}$$
$$y^2 = 64 - 16x^2, \quad y \le 0$$
$$16x^2 + y^2 = 64, \quad\quad y \le 0$$
$$\frac{x^2}{4} + \frac{y^2}{64} = 1, \quad\quad y \le 0$$

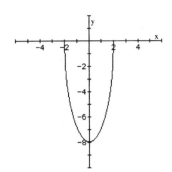

55.   The center of the ellipse is $(0, 0)$. The length of the major axis is 20, so $a = 10$. The length of half the minor axis is 6, so $b = 6$. The ellipse is situated with its major axis on the x-axis.

The equation is: $\frac{x^2}{100} + \frac{y^2}{36} = 1$.

57.   Assume that the half ellipse formed by the gallery is centered at $(0, 0)$. Since the hall is 100 feet long, $2a = 100$ or $a = 50$. The distance from the center to the foci is 25 feet, so $c = 25$. Find the height of the gallery which is b:
$$b^2 = a^2 - c^2 = 2500 - 625 = 1875 \ \rightarrow \ b = \sqrt{1875} \approx 43.3$$
The ceiling will be 43.3 feet high in the center.

59.   Place the semielliptical arch so that the x-axis coincides with the water and the y-axis passes through the center of the arch. Since the bridge has a span of 120 feet, the length of the major axis is 120, or $2a = 120$ or $a = 60$. The maximum height of the bridge is 25 feet, so $b = 25$. The equation is: $\frac{x^2}{3600} + \frac{y^2}{625} = 1$.

The height 10 feet from the center:
$$\frac{10^2}{3600} + \frac{y^2}{625} = 1 \rightarrow \frac{y^2}{625} = 1 - \frac{100}{3600} \rightarrow y^2 = 625 \cdot \frac{3500}{3600} \rightarrow y \approx 24.65 \text{ feet}$$
The height 30 feet from the center:
$$\frac{30^2}{3600} + \frac{y^2}{625} = 1 \rightarrow \frac{y^2}{625} = 1 - \frac{900}{3600} \rightarrow y^2 = 625 \cdot \frac{2700}{3600} \rightarrow y \approx 21.65 \text{ feet}$$
The height 50 feet from the center:
$$\frac{50^2}{3600} + \frac{y^2}{625} = 1 \rightarrow \frac{y^2}{625} = 1 - \frac{2500}{3600} \rightarrow y^2 = 625 \cdot \frac{1100}{3600} \rightarrow y \approx 13.82 \text{ feet}$$

61.   Place the semielliptical arch so that the x-axis coincides with the major axis and the y-axis passes through the center of the arch. Since the ellipse is 40 feet wide, the length of the major axis is 40, or $2a = 40$ or $a = 20$. The height is 15 feet at the center, so $b = 15$. The equation is: $\frac{x^2}{400} + \frac{y^2}{225} = 1$.

The height 10 feet either side of the center:
$$\frac{10^2}{400} + \frac{y^2}{225} = 1 \rightarrow \frac{y^2}{225} = 1 - \frac{100}{400} \rightarrow y^2 = 225 \cdot \frac{3}{4} \rightarrow y \approx 12.99 \text{ feet}$$
The height 20 feet either side of the center:
$$\frac{20^2}{400} + \frac{y^2}{225} = 1 \rightarrow \frac{y^2}{225} = 1 - \frac{400}{400} \rightarrow y^2 = 225 \cdot 0 \rightarrow y \approx 0 \text{ feet}$$

63. Since the mean distance is 93 million miles, a = 93 million. The length of the major axis is 186 million. The perihelion is 186 million – 94.5 million = 91.5 million miles. The distance from the center of the ellipse to the sun (focus) is 93 million – 91.5 million = 1.5 million miles; therefore, c = 1.5 million. Find b:

$$b^2 = a^2 - c^2 = \left(93 \times 10^6\right)^2 - \left(1.5 \times 10^6\right)^2 = 8.64675 \times 10^{15} \;\rightarrow\; b = 92.99 \times 10^6$$

The equation of the orbit is: $\dfrac{x^2}{\left(93 \times 10^6\right)^2} + \dfrac{y^2}{\left(92.99 \times 10^6\right)^2} = 1$.

65. The mean distance is 507 million – 23.2 million = 483.8 million miles.
The perihelion is 483.8 million – 23.2 million = 460.6 million miles.
Since $a = 483.8 \times 10^6$ and $c = 23.2 \times 10^6$, we can find b:

$$b^2 = a^2 - c^2 = \left(483.8 \times 10^6\right)^2 - \left(23.2 \times 10^6\right)^2 = 2.335242 \times 10^{17} \;\rightarrow\; b = 483.2 \times 10^6$$

The equation of the orbit of Jupiter is: $\dfrac{x^2}{\left(483.8 \times 10^6\right)^2} + \dfrac{y^2}{\left(483.2 \times 10^6\right)^2} = 1$.

67. If the x-axis is placed along the 100 foot length and the y-axis is placed along the 50 foot

length, the equation for the ellipse is: $\dfrac{x^2}{50^2} + \dfrac{y^2}{25^2} = 1$.

Find y when x = 40:

$$\frac{40^2}{50^2} + \frac{y^2}{25^2} = 1 \rightarrow \frac{y^2}{625} = 1 - \frac{1600}{2500} \rightarrow y^2 = 625 \cdot \frac{9}{25} \rightarrow y \approx 15 \text{ feet}$$

The width 10 feet from the side is 30 feet.

69. (a) Put the equation in standard ellipse form:
$$Ax^2 + Cy^2 + F = 0 \qquad A \neq 0, C \neq 0, F \neq 0$$
$$Ax^2 + Cy^2 = -F$$
$$\frac{Ax^2}{-F} + \frac{Cy^2}{-F} = 1$$
$$\frac{x^2}{(-F/A)} + \frac{y^2}{(-F/C)} = 1 \qquad \text{where } -F/A \text{ and } -F/C \text{ are positive}$$

This is the equation of an ellipse with center at (0, 0).
  (b) If $A = C$, the equation becomes:
$$Ax^2 + Ay^2 = -F \;\rightarrow\; x^2 + y^2 = \frac{-F}{A}$$

This is the equation of a circle with center at (0, 0) and radius of $\sqrt{\dfrac{-F}{A}}$.

71. Answers will vary.

The Conics
7.4   The Hyperbola

1.   B   3.   A

5.   Center: $(0, 0)$; Focus: $(3, 0)$; Vertex: $(1, 0)$;
     Transverse axis is the x-axis; $a = 1$; $c = 3$. Find b:
$$b^2 = c^2 - a^2 = 9 - 1 = 8$$
$$b = \sqrt{8} = 2\sqrt{2}$$
     Write the equation: $\dfrac{x^2}{1} - \dfrac{y^2}{8} = 1$
     To graph, enter: $y_1 = \sqrt{8(x^2 - 1)}$; $y_2 = -\sqrt{8(x^2 - 1)}$

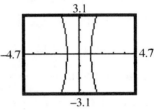

7.   Center: $(0, 0)$; Focus: $(0, -6)$; Vertex: $(0, 4)$
     Transverse axis is the y-axis; $a = 4$; $c = 6$. Find b:
$$b^2 = c^2 - a^2 = 36 - 16 = 20$$
$$b = \sqrt{20} = 2\sqrt{5}$$
     Write the equation: $\dfrac{y^2}{16} - \dfrac{x^2}{20} = 1$
     To graph, enter:
$$y_1 = 4\sqrt{1 + x^2 / 20}\,; \; y_2 = -4\sqrt{1 + x^2 / 20}$$

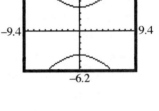

9.   Foci: $(-5, 0), (5, 0)$; Vertex: $(3, 0)$ Center: $(0, 0)$;
     Transverse axis is the x-axis; $a = 3$; $c = 5$. Find b:
$$b^2 = c^2 - a^2 = 25 - 9 = 16 \; \rightarrow \; b = 4$$
     Write the equation: $\dfrac{x^2}{9} - \dfrac{y^2}{16} = 1$
     To graph, enter:
$$y_1 = 4\sqrt{x^2 / 9 - 1}\,; \; y_2 = -4\sqrt{x^2 / 9 - 1}$$

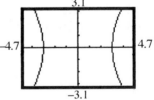

11. Vertices: $(0, -6), (0, 6)$; Asymptote: $y = 2x$;
     Center: $(0, 0)$; Transverse axis is the y-axis;
     $a = 6$. Find b using the slope of the asymptote:
$$\frac{a}{b} = \frac{6}{b} = 2 \; \rightarrow \; 2b = 6 \; \rightarrow \; b = 3$$
     Write the equation: $\dfrac{y^2}{36} - \dfrac{x^2}{9} = 1$
     To graph, enter:
$$y_1 = 6\sqrt{1 + x^2 / 9}\,; \; y_2 = -6\sqrt{1 + x^2 / 9}$$

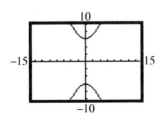

13. Foci: $(-4, 0)$, $(4, 0)$; Asymptote: $y = -x$;
     Center: $(0, 0)$; Transverse axis is the x-axis; $c = 4$.
     Using the slope of the asymptote:

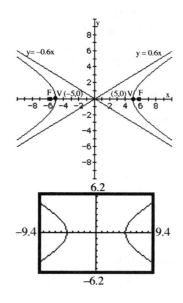

$$-\frac{b}{a} = -1 \;\rightarrow\; -b = -a \;\rightarrow\; b = a$$

Find b:

$$b^2 = c^2 - a^2$$

$$a^2 + b^2 = c^2 \qquad (c = 4)$$

$$b^2 + b^2 = 16 \rightarrow 2b^2 = 16$$

$$b^2 = 8 \;\rightarrow\; b = \sqrt{8} = 2\sqrt{2}$$

$$a = \sqrt{8} = 2\sqrt{2} \qquad (a = b)$$

Write the equation: $\dfrac{x^2}{8} - \dfrac{y^2}{8} = 1$

To graph, enter: $y_1 = \sqrt{x^2 - 8}$; $y_2 = -\sqrt{x^2 - 8}$

15. $\dfrac{x^2}{25} - \dfrac{y^2}{9} = 1$

The center of the hyperbola is at $(0, 0)$.
$a = 5$, $b = 3$. The vertices are $(5, 0)$ and $(-5, 0)$.
Find the value of c:

$$c^2 = a^2 + b^2 = 25 + 9 = 34 \rightarrow c = \sqrt{34}$$

The foci are $\left(\sqrt{34}, 0\right)$ and $\left(-\sqrt{34}, 0\right)$.

The transverse axis is $y = 0$.

The asymptotes are $y = \dfrac{3}{5}x$ and $y = -\dfrac{3}{5}x$.

To graph, enter:

$$y_1 = 3\sqrt{(x^2 / 25 - 1)};\;\; y_2 = -3\sqrt{(x^2 / 25 - 1)}$$

17. $4x^2 - y^2 = 16$

Divide both sides by 16 to put in standard form:

$$\frac{4x^2}{16} - \frac{y^2}{16} = \frac{16}{16} \rightarrow \frac{x^2}{4} - \frac{y^2}{16} = 1$$

The center of the hyperbola is at (0, 0).

$a = 2, \ b = 4$. The vertices are (2, 0) and (–2, 0).

Find the value of c:

$$c^2 = a^2 + b^2 = 4 + 16 = 20$$

$$c = \sqrt{20} = 2\sqrt{5}$$

The foci are $\left(2\sqrt{5}, 0\right)$ and $\left(-2\sqrt{5}, 0\right)$.

The transverse axis is $y = 0$.

The asymptotes are $y = 2x$ and $y = -2x$.

To graph, enter:

$$y_1 = 4\sqrt{(x^2/4 - 1)}; \ \ y_2 = -4\sqrt{(x^2/4 - 1)}$$

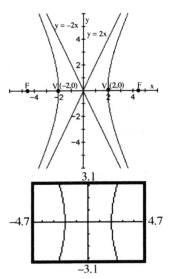

19. $y^2 - 9x^2 = 9$

Divide both sides by 9 to put in standard form:

$$\frac{y^2}{9} - \frac{9x^2}{9} = \frac{9}{9}$$

$$\frac{y^2}{9} - \frac{x^2}{1} = 1$$

The center of the hyperbola is at (0, 0).

$a = 3, \ b = 1$. The vertices are (0, 3) and (0, –3).

Find the value of c:

$$c^2 = a^2 + b^2 = 9 + 1 = 10$$

$$c = \sqrt{10}$$

The foci are $\left(0, \sqrt{10}\right)$ and $\left(0, -\sqrt{10}\right)$.

The transverse axis is $x = 0$.

The asymptotes are $y = 3x$ and $y = -3x$.

To graph, enter:

$$y_1 = \sqrt{(9x^2 + 9)}; \ \ y_2 = -\sqrt{(9x^2 + 9)}$$

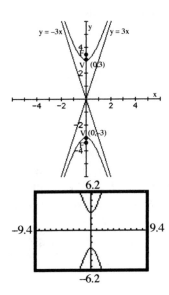

21. $y^2 - x^2 = 25$

Divide both sides by 25 to put in standard form:

$$\frac{y^2}{25} - \frac{x^2}{25} = 1$$

The center of the hyperbola is at $(0, 0)$.

$a = 5,\ b = 5$. The vertices are $(0, 5)$ and $(0, -5)$.

Find the value of c:

$$c^2 = a^2 + b^2 = 25 + 25 = 50$$

$$c = \sqrt{50} = 5\sqrt{2}$$

The foci are $\left(0, 5\sqrt{2}\right)$ and $\left(0, -5\sqrt{2}\right)$.

The transverse axis is $x = 0$.

The asymptotes are $y = x$ and $y = -x$.

To graph, enter:

$$y_1 = \sqrt{(x^2 + 25)};\ \ y_2 = -\sqrt{(x^2 + 25)}$$

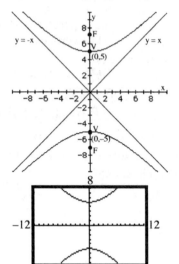

23. $x^2 - y^2 = 1$

25. $\dfrac{y^2}{36} - \dfrac{x^2}{9} = 1$

27. Center: $(4, -1)$; Focus: $(7, -1)$; Vertex: $(6, -1)$;

Transverse axis is parallel to the x-axis;

$a = 2;\ c = 3$. Find b:

$$b^2 = c^2 - a^2 = 9 - 4 = 5$$

$$b = \sqrt{5}$$

Write the equation: $\dfrac{(x-4)^2}{4} - \dfrac{(y+1)^2}{5} = 1$

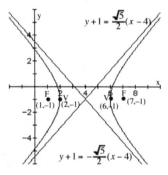

29. Center: $(-3, -4)$; Focus: $(-3, -8)$;

Vertex: $(-3, -2)$; Transverse axis is parallel to the y-axis; $a = 2;\ c = 4$. Find b:

$$b^2 = c^2 - a^2 = 16 - 4 = 12$$

$$b = \sqrt{12} = 2\sqrt{3}$$

Write the equation: $\dfrac{(y+4)^2}{4} - \dfrac{(x+3)^2}{12} = 1$

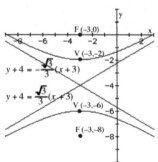

31. Foci: $(3, 7), (7, 7)$; Vertex: $(6, 7)$; Center: $(5, 7)$;
Transverse axis is parallel to the x-axis;
$a = 1$; $c = 2$. Find b:
$$b^2 = c^2 - a^2 = 4 - 1 = 3 \rightarrow b = \sqrt{3}$$
Write the equation: $\dfrac{(x-5)^2}{1} - \dfrac{(y-7)^2}{3} = 1$

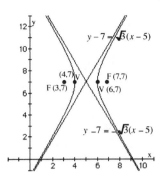

33. Vertices: $(-1, -1), (3, -1)$; Center: $(1, -1)$;
Transverse axis is parallel to the x-axis; $a = 2$.
Asymptote: $\dfrac{x-1}{2} = \dfrac{y+1}{3}$ Using the slope of the
asymptote:
$$\frac{b}{a} = \frac{b}{2} = \frac{3}{2} \rightarrow b = 3$$
Write the equation: $\dfrac{(x-1)^2}{4} - \dfrac{(y+1)^2}{9} = 1$

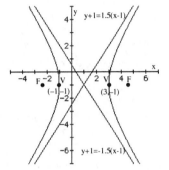

35. $\dfrac{(x-2)^2}{4} - \dfrac{(y+3)^2}{9} = 1$

The center of the hyperbola is at $(2, -3)$.
$a = 2,\ b = 3$. The vertices are $(0, -3)$ and $(4, -3)$.
Find the value of c:
$$c^2 = a^2 + b^2 = 4 + 9 = 13 \rightarrow c = \sqrt{13}$$
Foci: $\left(2 - \sqrt{13}, -3\right)$ and $\left(2 + \sqrt{13}, -3\right)$.
Transverse axis: $y = -3$.

Asymptotes: $y + 3 = \dfrac{3}{2}(x-2),\ y + 3 = -\dfrac{3}{2}(x-2)$.

To graph, enter: $y_1 = -3 + 3\sqrt{((x-2)^2 / 4 - 1)}$;
$$y_2 = -3 - 3\sqrt{((x-2)^2 / 4 - 1)}$$

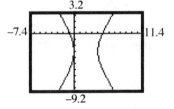

37. $(y-2)^2 - 4(x+2)^2 = 4$

Divide both sides by 4 to put in standard form:

$$\frac{(y-2)^2}{4} - \frac{(x+2)^2}{1} = 1$$

The center of the hyperbola is at $(-2, 2)$.
$a = 2, \ b = 1$. The vertices are $(-2, 4)$ and $(-2, 0)$.
Find the value of c:

$$c^2 = a^2 + b^2 = 4 + 1 = 5 \rightarrow c = \sqrt{5}$$

Foci: $\left(-2, 2 - \sqrt{5}\right)$ and $\left(-2, 2 + \sqrt{5}\right)$.

Transverse axis: $x = -2$.
Asymptotes: $y - 2 = 2(x+2), \ y - 2 = -2(x+2)$.
To graph, enter: $y_1 = 2 + 2\sqrt{((x+2)^2 + 1)};$

$$y_2 = 2 - 2\sqrt{((x+2)^2 + 1)}$$

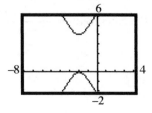

39. $(x+1)^2 - (y+2)^2 = 4$

Divide both sides by 4 to put in standard form:

$$\frac{(x+1)^2}{4} - \frac{(y+2)^2}{4} = 1$$

The center of the hyperbola is at $(-1, -2)$.
$a = 2, \ b = 2$. The vertices are $(-3, -2)$ and $(1, -2)$.
Find the value of c:

$$c^2 = a^2 + b^2 = 4 + 4 = 8$$

$$c = \sqrt{8} = 2\sqrt{2}$$

Foci: $\left(-1 - 2\sqrt{2}, -2\right)$ and $\left(-1 + 2\sqrt{2}, -2\right)$.

Transverse axis: $y = -2$.
Asymptotes: $y + 2 = x + 1, \ y + 2 = -(x + 1)$.
To graph, enter: $y_1 = -2 + 2\sqrt{((x+1)^2/4 - 1)};$

$$y_2 = -2 - 2\sqrt{((x+1)^2/4 - 1)}$$

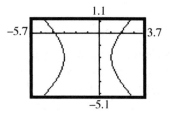

41.   Complete the square to put in standard form:

$$x^2 - y^2 - 2x - 2y - 1 = 0$$

$$(x^2 - 2x + 1) - (y^2 + 2y + 1) = 1 + 1 - 1 \rightarrow (x-1)^2 - (y+1)^2 = 1$$

The center of the hyperbola is at $(1, -1)$.
$a = 1, \ b = 1$. The vertices are $(0, -1)$ and $(2, -1)$.
Find the value of c:

$$c^2 = a^2 + b^2 = 1 + 1 = 2$$

$$c = \sqrt{2}$$

Foci: $\left(1 - \sqrt{2}, -1\right)$ and $\left(1 + \sqrt{2}, -1\right)$.

Transverse axis: $y = -1$.
Asymptotes: $y + 1 = x - 1, \ y + 1 = -(x - 1)$.
To graph, enter: $y_1 = -1 + \sqrt{((x-1)^2 - 1)};$

$$y_2 = -1 - \sqrt{((x-1)^2 - 1)}$$

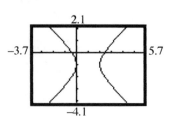

43. Complete the square to put in standard form:

$$y^2 - 4x^2 - 4y - 8x - 4 = 0$$

$$(y^2 - 4y + 4) - 4(x^2 + 2x + 1) = 4 + 4 - 4$$

$$(y-2)^2 - 4(x+1)^2 = 4 \to \frac{(y-2)^2}{4} - \frac{(x+1)^2}{1} = 1$$

The center of the hyperbola is at $(-1, 2)$.
$a = 2$, $b = 1$. The vertices are $(-1, 4)$ and $(-1, 0)$.
Find the value of c:

$$c^2 = a^2 + b^2 = 4 + 1 = 5 \to c = \sqrt{5}$$

Foci: $\left(-1, 2 - \sqrt{5}\right)$ and $\left(-1, 2 + \sqrt{5}\right)$.

Transverse axis: $x = -1$.
Asymptotes: $y - 2 = 2(x+1)$, $y - 2 = -2(x+1)$.

To graph, enter: $y_1 = 2 + 2\sqrt{((x+1)^2 + 1)}$;

$$y_2 = 2 - 2\sqrt{((x+1)^2 + 1)}$$

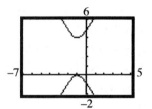

45. Complete the square to put in standard form:

$$4x^2 - y^2 - 24x - 4y + 16 = 0$$

$$4(x^2 - 6x + 9) - (y^2 + 4y + 4) = -16 + 36 - 4$$

$$4(x-3)^2 - (y+2)^2 = 16 \to \frac{(x-3)^2}{4} - \frac{(y+2)^2}{16} = 1$$

The center of the hyperbola is at $(3, -2)$.
$a = 2$, $b = 4$. The vertices are $(1, -2)$ and $(5, -2)$.
Find the value of c:

$$c^2 = a^2 + b^2 = 4 + 16 = 20$$

$$c = \sqrt{20} = 2\sqrt{5}$$

Foci: $\left(3 - 2\sqrt{5}, -2\right)$ and $\left(3 + 2\sqrt{5}, -2\right)$.

Transverse axis: $y = -2$.
Asymptotes: $y + 2 = 2(x-3)$, $y + 2 = -2(x-3)$.

To graph, enter: $y_1 = -2 + 4\sqrt{((x-3)^2 / 4 - 1)}$;

$$y_2 = -2 - 4\sqrt{((x-3)^2 / 4 - 1)}$$

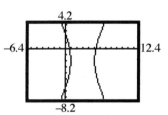

47. Complete the square to put in standard form:

$$y^2 - 4x^2 - 16x - 2y - 19 = 0$$

$$(y^2 - 2y + 1) - 4(x^2 + 4x + 4) = 19 + 1 - 16$$

$$(y-1)^2 - 4(x+2)^2 = 4 \rightarrow \frac{(y-1)^2}{4} - \frac{(x+2)^2}{1} = 1$$

The center of the hyperbola is at $(-2, 1)$.
$a = 2$, $b = 1$. The vertices are $(-2, 3)$ and $(-2, -1)$.
Find the value of c:

$$c^2 = a^2 + b^2 = 4 + 1 = 5 \rightarrow c = \sqrt{5}$$

Foci: $\left(-2, 1 - \sqrt{5}\right)$ and $\left(-2, 1 + \sqrt{5}\right)$.

Transverse axis: $x = -2$.

Asymptotes: $y - 1 = 2(x+2)$, $y - 1 = -2(x+2)$.

To graph, enter: $y_1 = 1 + 2\sqrt{((x+2)^2 + 1)}$;

$$y_2 = 1 - 2\sqrt{((x+2)^2 + 1)}$$

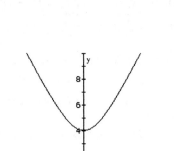

49. Rewrite the equation:

$$y = \sqrt{16 + 4x^2}$$
$$y^2 = 16 + 4x^2, \qquad y \ge 0$$
$$y^2 - 4x^2 = 16, \qquad y \ge 0$$
$$\frac{y^2}{16} - \frac{x^2}{4} = 1, \qquad y \ge 0$$

51. Rewrite the equation:

$$y = -\sqrt{-25 + x^2}$$
$$y^2 = -25 + x^2, \qquad y \le 0$$
$$x^2 - y^2 = 25, \qquad y \le 0$$
$$\frac{x^2}{25} - \frac{y^2}{25} = 1, \qquad y \le 0$$

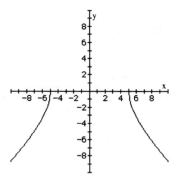

53. (a) Set up a coordinate system so that the two stations lie on the x-axis and the origin is midway between them. The ship lies on a hyperbola whose foci are the locations of the two stations. Since the time difference is 0.00038 seconds and the speed of the signal is 186,000 miles per second, the difference in the distances of the ships from each station is:

distance = (186,000)(0.00038) = 70.68 miles

The difference of the distances from the ship to each station, 70.68, equals $2a$, so $a = 35.34$ and the vertex of the corresponding hyperbola is at (35.34, 0). Since the focus is at (100, 0), following this hyperbola, the ship would reach shore 64.66 miles from the master station.

(b) The ship should follow a hyperbola with a vertex at (80, 0). For this hyperbola, $a = 80$, so the constant difference of the distances from the ship to each station is 160. The time difference the ship should look for is:

$$\text{time} = \frac{160}{186,000} = 0.00086 \text{ seconds}$$

(c) Find the equation of the hyperbola with vertex at (80, 0) and a focus at (100, 0). The form of the equation of the hyperbola is:

$$\frac{x^2}{a^2} - \frac{y^2}{b^2} = 1 \quad \text{where } a = 80.$$

Since $c = 100$ and $b^2 = c^2 - a^2 \;\rightarrow\; b^2 = 100^2 - 80^2 = 3600$.

The equation of the hyperbola is: $\dfrac{x^2}{6400} - \dfrac{y^2}{3600} = 1$.

Since the ship is 50 miles off shore, we have $y = 50$. Solve the equation for x:

$$\frac{x^2}{6400} - \frac{50^2}{3600} = 1 \;\rightarrow\; \frac{x^2}{6400} = 1 + \frac{2500}{3600} = \frac{61}{36} \;\rightarrow\; x^2 = 6400 \cdot \frac{61}{36}$$

$$x \approx 104 \text{ miles}$$

The ship's location is (104, 50).

55. (a) Set up a rectangular coordinate system so that the two devices lie on the x-axis and the origin is midway between them. The devices serve as foci to the hyperbola so $c = \dfrac{2000}{2} = 1000$. Since the explosion occurs 200 feet from point B, the vertex of the hyperbola is (800, 0); therefore, $a = 800$. Finding b:

$$b^2 = c^2 - a^2 \;\rightarrow\; b^2 = 1000^2 - 800^2 = 360000 \;\rightarrow\; b = 600$$

The equation of the hyperbola is:

$$\frac{x^2}{800^2} - \frac{y^2}{600^2} = 1$$

If $x = 1000$, find y:

$$\frac{1000^2}{800^2} - \frac{y^2}{600^2} = 1 \;\rightarrow\; \frac{y^2}{600^2} = \frac{1000^2}{800^2} - 1 = \frac{600^2}{800^2} \;\rightarrow\; y^2 = 600^2 \cdot \frac{600^2}{800^2}$$

$$y = 450 \text{ feet}$$

The second detonation should take place 450 feet north of point B.

377

57. If the eccentricity is close to 1, then $c \approx a$ and $b \approx 0$. When b is close to 0, the hyperbola is very narrow, because the slopes of the asymptotes are close to 0.

If the eccentricity is very large, then c is much larger than a and b is very large. The result is a hyperbola that is very wide.

59. $\dfrac{x^2}{4} - y^2 = 1 \quad (a = 2,\ b = 1)$

is a hyperbola with horizontal transverse axis,

centered at (0, 0) and has asymptotes: $y = \pm \dfrac{1}{2}x$

$y^2 - \dfrac{x^2}{4} = 1 \quad (a = 1,\ b = 2)$

is a hyperbola with vertical transverse axis, centered

at (0, 0) and has asymptotes: $y = \pm \dfrac{1}{2}x$

Since the two hyperbolas have the same asymptotes, they are conjugate.

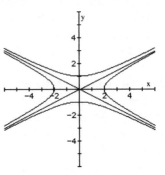

61. Put the equation in standard hyperbola form:

$$Ax^2 + Cy^2 + F = 0 \qquad A \neq 0,\ C \neq 0,\ F \neq 0$$

$$Ax^2 + Cy^2 = -F$$

$$\frac{Ax^2}{-F} + \frac{Cy^2}{-F} = 1$$

$$\frac{x^2}{-F/A} + \frac{y^2}{-F/C} = 1$$

Since $-F/A$ and $-F/C$ have opposite signs, this is a hyperbola with center at (0, 0).

The Conics
7.R   Chapter Review

1. $y^2 = -16x$
    This is a parabola.
    $a = 4$
    Vertex: $(0, 0)$;   Focus: $(-4, 0)$;   Directrix: $x = 4$

3. $\dfrac{x^2}{25} - y^2 = 1$
    This is a hyperbola.
    $a = 5,\ b = 1$. Find the value of c:
    $c^2 = a^2 + b^2 = 25 + 1 = 26 \ \rightarrow \ c = \sqrt{26}$
    Center: $(0, 0)$;   Vertices: $(5, 0), (-5, 0)$;   Foci: $\left(\sqrt{26},0\right), \left(-\sqrt{26},0\right)$
    Asymptotes: $y = \dfrac{1}{5}x;\ \ y = -\dfrac{1}{5}x$

5. $\dfrac{y^2}{25} + \dfrac{x^2}{16} = 1$
    This is an ellipse.
    $a = 5,\ b = 4$. Find the value of c:
    $c^2 = a^2 - b^2 = 25 - 16 = 9 \ \rightarrow \ c = 3$
    Center: $(0, 0)$;   Vertices: $(0, 5), (0, -5)$;   Foci: $(0, 3), (0, -3)$

7. $x^2 + 4y = 4$
    This is a parabola.
    Write in standard form:
    $x^2 = -4y + 4 \rightarrow x^2 = -4(y - 1)$
    $a = 1$
    Vertex: $(0, 1)$;   Focus: $(0, 0)$;   Directrix: $y = 2$

9. $4x^2 - y^2 = 8$
    This is a hyperbola.
    Write in standard form:
    $\dfrac{x^2}{2} - \dfrac{y^2}{8} = 1$
    $a = \sqrt{2},\ b = \sqrt{8} = 2\sqrt{2}$. Find the value of c:
    $c^2 = a^2 + b^2 = 2 + 8 = 10 \ \rightarrow \ c = \sqrt{10}$
    Center: $(0, 0)$;   Vertices: $\left(-\sqrt{2}, 0\right), \left(\sqrt{2}, 0\right)$; Foci: $\left(-\sqrt{10},0\right), \left(\sqrt{10},0\right)$
    Asymptotes: $y = 2x;\ \ y = -2x$

11. $x^2 - 4x = 2y$

This is a parabola.

Write in standard form:

$$x^2 - 4x + 4 = 2y + 4 \rightarrow (x-2)^2 = 2(y+2)$$

$a = \dfrac{1}{2}$

Vertex: $(2, -2)$;   Focus: $\left(2, -\dfrac{3}{2}\right)$;   Directrix: $y = -\dfrac{5}{2}$

13. $y^2 - 4y - 4x^2 + 8x = 4$

This is a hyperbola.

Write in standard form:

$$(y^2 - 4y + 4) - 4(x^2 - 2x + 1) = 4 + 4 - 4$$

$$(y-2)^2 - 4(x-1)^2 = 4 \rightarrow \frac{(y-2)^2}{4} - \frac{(x-1)^2}{1} = 1$$

$a = 2$, $b = 1$. Find the value of c:

$$c^2 = a^2 + b^2 = 4 + 1 = 5 \;\; \rightarrow \;\; c = \sqrt{5}$$

Center: $(1, 2)$;   Vertices: $(1, 0)$, $(1, 4)$;   Foci: $\left(1, 2 - \sqrt{5}\right)$, $\left(1, 2 + \sqrt{5}\right)$

Asymptotes: $y - 2 = 2(x-1)$; $y - 2 = -2(x-1)$

15. $4x^2 + 9y^2 - 16x - 18y = 11$

This is an ellipse.

Write in standard form:

$$4x^2 + 9y^2 - 16x - 18y = 11$$

$$4(x^2 - 4x + 4) + 9(y^2 - 2y + 1) = 11 + 16 + 9$$

$$4(x-2)^2 + 9(y-1)^2 = 36 \rightarrow \frac{(x-2)^2}{9} + \frac{(y-1)^2}{4} = 1$$

$a = 3$, $b = 2$. Find the value of c:

$$c^2 = a^2 - b^2 = 9 - 4 = 5 \;\; \rightarrow \;\; c = \sqrt{5}$$

Center: $(2, 1)$;   Vertices: $(-1, 1)$, $(5, 1)$;   Foci: $\left(2 - \sqrt{5}, 1\right)$, $\left(2 + \sqrt{5}, 1\right)$

17. $4x^2 - 16x + 16y + 32 = 0$

This is a parabola.

Write in standard form:

$$4(x^2 - 4x + 4) = -16y - 32 + 16$$

$$4(x-2)^2 = -16(y+1) \rightarrow (x-2)^2 = -4(y+1)$$

$a = 1$

Vertex: $(2, -1)$;   Focus: $(2, -2)$;   Directrix: $y = 0$

19. $9x^2 + 4y^2 - 18x + 8y = 23$
This is an ellipse.
Write in standard form:
$$9(x^2 - 2x + 1) + 4(y^2 + 2y + 1) = 23 + 9 + 4$$
$$9(x-1)^2 + 4(y+1)^2 = 36 \rightarrow \frac{(x-1)^2}{4} + \frac{(y+1)^2}{9} = 1$$
$a = 3, \ b = 2$. Find the value of c: $c^2 = a^2 - b^2 = 9 - 4 = 5 \ \rightarrow \ c = \sqrt{5}$
Center: $(1, -1)$;   Vertices: $(1, -4), (1, 2)$;   Foci: $\left(1, -1-\sqrt{5}\right), \left(1, -1+\sqrt{5}\right)$

21. Parabola: The focus is $(-2, 0)$ and the directrix is
$x = 2$. The vertex is $(0, 0)$. $a = 2$ and since $(-2, 0)$
is to the left of $(0, 0)$, the parabola opens to the left.
The equation of the parabola is:
$$y^2 = -4ax$$
$$y^2 = -4 \cdot 2 \cdot x$$
$$y^2 = -8x$$

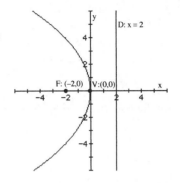

23. Hyperbola: Center: $(0, 0)$; Focus: $(0, 4)$;
Vertex: $(0, -2)$; Transverse axis is the y-axis;
$a = 2; \ c = 4$. Find b:
$$b^2 = c^2 - a^2 = 16 - 4 = 12$$
$$b = \sqrt{12} = 2\sqrt{3}$$
Write the equation: $\dfrac{y^2}{4} - \dfrac{x^2}{12} = 1$

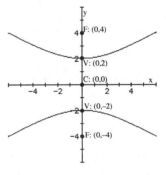

25. Ellipse: Foci: $(-3, 0), (3, 0)$; Vertex: $(4, 0)$;
Center: $(0, 0)$; Major axis is the x-axis;
$a = 4; \ c = 3$. Find b:
$$b^2 = a^2 - c^2 = 16 - 9 = 7$$
$$b = \sqrt{7}$$
Write the equation: $\dfrac{x^2}{16} + \dfrac{y^2}{7} = 1$

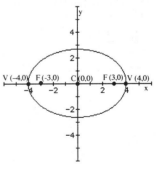

27. Parabola: The focus is (2, –4) and the vertex is
(2, –3). Both lie on the vertical line $x = 2$. $a = 1$
and since (2, –4) is below (2, –3), the parabola
opens down. The equation of the parabola is:
$$(x - h)^2 = -4a(y - k)$$
$$(x - 2)^2 = -4 \cdot 1 \cdot (y - (-3))$$
$$(x - 2)^2 = -4(y + 3)$$

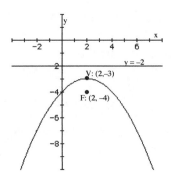

29. Hyperbola: Center: (–2, –3); Focus: (–4, –3);
Vertex: (–3, –3); Transverse axis is parallel to the
x-axis; $a = 1$; $c = 2$. Find b:
$$b^2 = c^2 - a^2 = 4 - 1 = 3$$
$$b = \sqrt{3}$$
Write the equation: $\dfrac{(x + 2)^2}{1} - \dfrac{(y + 3)^2}{3} = 1$

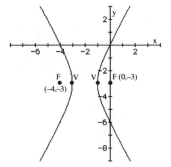

31. Ellipse: Foci: (–4, 2), (–4, 8); Vertex: (–4, 10);
Center: (–4, 5); Major axis is parallel to the y-axis;
$a = 5$; $c = 3$. Find b:
$$b^2 = a^2 - c^2 = 25 - 9 = 16$$
$$b = 4$$
Write the equation: $\dfrac{(x + 4)^2}{16} + \dfrac{(y - 5)^2}{25} = 1$

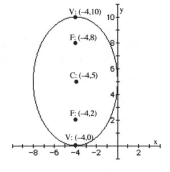

33. Hyperbola: Center: (–1, 2); $a = 3$; $c = 4$;
Transverse axis parallel to the x-axis; Find b:
$$b^2 = c^2 - a^2 = 16 - 9 = 7$$
$$b = \sqrt{7}$$
Write the equation: $\dfrac{(x + 1)^2}{9} - \dfrac{(y - 2)^2}{7} = 1$

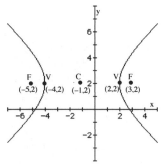

35. Hyperbola: Vertices: $(0, 1), (6, 1)$;

Asymptote: $3y + 2x - 9 = 0$; Center: $(3, 1)$;

Transverse axis is parallel to the x-axis; $a = 3$; The

slope of the asymptote is $-\dfrac{2}{3}$; Find b:

$$\dfrac{-b}{a} = \dfrac{-b}{3} = -\dfrac{2}{3} \;\rightarrow\; -3b = -6 \;\rightarrow\; b = 2$$

Write the equation: $\dfrac{(x-3)^2}{9} - \dfrac{(y-1)^2}{4} = 1$

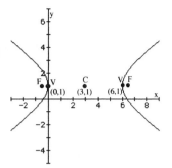

37. Write the equation in standard form:

$$4x^2 + 9y^2 = 36 \;\rightarrow\; \dfrac{x^2}{9} + \dfrac{y^2}{4} = 1$$

The center of the ellipse is $(0, 0)$. The major axis is the x-axis.

$a = 3;\ b = 2;\ c^2 = a^2 - b^2 = 9 - 4 = 5 \;\rightarrow\; c = \sqrt{5}$.

For the ellipse:

    Vertices: $(-3, 0), (3, 0)$

    Foci: $\left(-\sqrt{5}, 0\right), \left(\sqrt{5}, 0\right)$

For the hyperbola:

    Foci: $(-3, 0), (3, 0)$

    Vertices: $\left(-\sqrt{5}, 0\right), \left(\sqrt{5}, 0\right)$

    Center: $(0, 0)$

    $a = \sqrt{5};\ c = 3;\ b^2 = c^2 - a^2 = 9 - 5 = 4 \;\rightarrow\; b = 2$

The equation of the hyperbola is:

$$\dfrac{x^2}{5} - \dfrac{y^2}{4} = 1$$

39. Let (x, y) be any point in the collection of points.

The distance from (x, y) to $(3, 0) = \sqrt{(x-3)^2 + y^2}$.

The distance from (x, y) to the line $x = \dfrac{16}{3}$ is $\left| x - \dfrac{16}{3} \right|$.

Relating the distances, we have:

$$\sqrt{(x-3)^2 + y^2} = \dfrac{3}{4}\left| x - \dfrac{16}{3} \right|$$

$$(x-3)^2 + y^2 = \dfrac{9}{16}\left(x - \dfrac{16}{3} \right)^2$$

$$x^2 - 6x + 9 + y^2 = \dfrac{9}{16}\left(x^2 - \dfrac{32}{3}x + \dfrac{256}{9} \right)$$

$$16x^2 - 96x + 144 + 16y^2 = 9x^2 - 96x + 256 \rightarrow 7x^2 + 16y^2 = 112$$

$$\dfrac{7x^2}{112} + \dfrac{16y^2}{112} = 1 \rightarrow \dfrac{x^2}{16} + \dfrac{y^2}{7} = 1$$

The set of points is an ellipse.

41. Locate the parabola so that the vertex is at (0, 0) and opens up. It then has the equation: $x^2 = 4ay$. Since the light source is located at the focus and is 1 foot from the base, $a = 1$. The diameter is 2, so the point (1, y) is located on the parabola. Solve for y:

$$1^2 = 4(1)y \rightarrow 1 = 4y \rightarrow y = 0.25 \text{ feet}$$

The mirror should be 0.25 feet deep or 3 inches deep.

43. Place the semielliptical arch so that the x-axis coincides with the water and the y-axis passes through the center of the arch. Since the bridge has a span of 60 feet, the length of the major axis is 60, or $2a = 60$ or $a = 30$. The maximum height of the bridge is 20 feet, so $b = 20$. The equation is: $\dfrac{x^2}{900} + \dfrac{y^2}{400} = 1$.

The height 5 feet from the center:

$$\frac{5^2}{900} + \frac{y^2}{400} = 1 \rightarrow \frac{y^2}{400} = 1 - \frac{25}{900} \rightarrow y^2 = 400 \cdot \frac{875}{900} \rightarrow y \approx 19.72 \text{ feet}$$

The height 10 feet from the center:

$$\frac{10^2}{900} + \frac{y^2}{400} = 1 \rightarrow \frac{y^2}{400} = 1 - \frac{100}{900} \rightarrow y^2 = 400 \cdot \frac{800}{900} \rightarrow y \approx 18.86 \text{ feet}$$

The height 20 feet from the center:

$$\frac{20^2}{900} + \frac{y^2}{400} = 1 \rightarrow \frac{y^2}{400} = 1 - \frac{400}{900} \rightarrow y^2 = 400 \cdot \frac{500}{900} \rightarrow y \approx 14.91 \text{ feet}$$

45. (a) Set up a coordinate system so that the two stations lie on the x-axis and the origin is midway between them. The ship lies on a hyperbola whose foci are the locations of the two stations. Since the time difference is 0.00032 seconds and the speed of the signal is 186,000 miles per second, the difference in the distances of the ships from each station is:

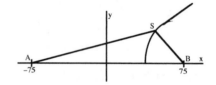

distance = (186,000)(0.00032) = 59.52 miles

The difference of the distances from the ship to each station, 59.52, equals $2a$, so $a = 29.76$ and the vertex of the corresponding hyperbola is at (29.76, 0). Since the focus is at (75, 0), following this hyperbola, the ship would reach shore 45.24 miles from the master station.

(b) The ship should follow a hyperbola with a vertex at (60, 0). For this hyperbola, $a = 60$, so the constant difference of the distances from the ship to each station is 120. The time difference the ship should look for is:

$$\text{time} = \frac{120}{186,000} = 0.000645 \text{ seconds}$$

(c) Find the equation of the hyperbola with vertex at (60, 0) and a focus at (75, 0). The form of the equation of the hyperbola is:

$$\frac{x^2}{a^2} - \frac{y^2}{b^2} = 1 \quad \text{where } a = 60.$$

Since $c = 75$ and $b^2 = c^2 - a^2 \rightarrow b^2 = 75^2 - 60^2 = 2025$.

The equation of the hyperbola is: $\dfrac{x^2}{3600} - \dfrac{y^2}{2025} = 1$.

Since the ship is 20 miles off shore, we have $y = 20$. Solve the equation for x:

$$\frac{x^2}{3600} - \frac{20^2}{2025} = 1 \;\rightarrow\; \frac{x^2}{3600} = 1 + \frac{400}{2025} = \frac{97}{81} \;\rightarrow\; x^2 = 3600 \cdot \frac{97}{81}$$

$$x \approx 66 \text{ miles}$$

The ship's location is $(66, 20)$.

47.   Answers will vary.

Chapter 8

Systems of Equations and Inequalities

8.1 Systems of Linear Equations: Two Equations Containing Two Variables

1. Substituting the values of the variables:
$$\begin{cases} 2x - y = 5 & \rightarrow \quad 2(2) - (-1) = 4 + 1 = 5 \\ 5x + 2y = 8 & \rightarrow \quad 5(2) + 2(-1) = 10 - 2 = 8 \end{cases}$$
Each equation is satisfied, so $x = 2$, $y = -1$ is a solution to the system of equations.

3. Substituting the values of the variables:
$$\begin{cases} 3x - 4y = 4 & \rightarrow \quad 3(2) - 4\left(\dfrac{1}{2}\right) = 6 - 2 = 4 \\ \dfrac{1}{2}x - 3y = -\dfrac{1}{2} & \rightarrow \quad \dfrac{1}{2}(2) - 3\left(\dfrac{1}{2}\right) = 1 - \dfrac{3}{2} = -\dfrac{1}{2} \end{cases}$$
Each equation is satisfied, so $x = 2, y = \dfrac{1}{2}$ is a solution to the system of equations.

5. Substituting the values of the variables:
$$\begin{cases} x^2 - y^2 = 3 & \rightarrow \quad 2^2 - 1^2 = 4 - 1 = 3 \\ xy = 2 & \rightarrow \quad (2)(1) = 2 \end{cases}$$
Each equation is satisfied, so $x = 2, y = 1$ is a solution to the system of equations.

7. Substituting the values of the variables:
$$\begin{cases} \dfrac{x}{1+x} + 3y = 6 & \rightarrow \quad \dfrac{0}{1+0} + 3(2) = 0 + 6 = 6 \\ x + 9y^2 = 36 & \rightarrow \quad 0 + 9(2)^2 = 0 + 9 \cdot 4 = 36 \end{cases}$$
Each equation is satisfied, so $x = 0, y = 2$ is a solution to the system.

9. Solve the first equation for y, substitute into the second equation and solve:
$$\begin{cases} x + y = 8 & \rightarrow \quad y = 8 - x \\ x - y = 4 \end{cases}$$
$$x - (8 - x) = 4 \rightarrow x - 8 + x = 4$$
$$2x = 12 \rightarrow x = 6$$
Since $x = 6$, $y = 8 - 6 = 2$
The solution of the system is $x = 6$, $y = 2$.

11. Multiply each side of the first equation by 3 and add the equations:

$$\begin{cases} 5x - y = 13 \\ 2x + 3y = 12 \end{cases} \xrightarrow{3} \begin{array}{l} 15x - 3y = 39 \\ 2x + 3y = 12 \end{array}$$

$$\begin{array}{rl} 17x & = 51 \\ x & = 3 \end{array}$$

Substitute and solve for y:

$$5(3) - y = 13 \to 15 - y = 13 \to -y = -2 \to y = 2$$

The solution of the system is $x = 3,\ y = 2$.

13. Solve the first equation for x and substitute into the second equation:

$$\begin{cases} 3x = 24 \quad \to \quad x = 8 \\ x + 2y = 0 \end{cases}$$

$$8 + 2y = 0 \to 2y = -8 \to y = -4$$

The solution of the system is $x = 8,\ y = -4$.

15. Multiply each side of the first equation by 2 and each side of the second equation by 3 to eliminate y:

$$\begin{cases} 3x - 6y = 2 \\ 5x + 4y = 1 \end{cases} \begin{array}{l} \xrightarrow{2} \quad 6x - 12y = 4 \\ \xrightarrow{3} \quad 15x + 12y = 3 \end{array}$$

$$\begin{array}{rl} 21x & = 7 \\ x & = \dfrac{1}{3} \end{array}$$

Substitute and solve for y:

$$3\left(\frac{1}{3}\right) - 6y = 2 \to 1 - 6y = 2 \to -6y = 1 \to y = -\frac{1}{6}$$

The solution of the system is $x = \dfrac{1}{3},\ y = -\dfrac{1}{6}$.

17. Solve the first equation for y, substitute into the second equation and solve:

$$\begin{cases} 2x + y = 1 \quad \to \quad y = 1 - 2x \\ 4x + 2y = 3 \end{cases}$$

$$4x + 2(1 - 2x) = 3 \to 4x + 2 - 4x = 3 \to 0x = 1$$

This has no solution, so the system is inconsistent.

19. Solve the first equation for y, substitute into the second equation and solve:

$$\begin{cases} 2x - y = 0 \quad \to \quad 2x = y \\ 3x + 2y = 7 \end{cases}$$

$$3x + 2(2x) = 7 \to 3x + 4x = 7 \to 7x = 7 \to x = 1$$

Since $x = 1,\ y = 2(1) = 2$ The solution of the system is $x = 1,\ y = 2$.

21. Solve the first equation for x, substitute into the second equation and solve:

$$\begin{cases} x + 2y = 4 \\ 2x + 4y = 8 \end{cases} \rightarrow \quad x = 4 - 2y$$

$$2(4 - 2y) + 4y = 8 \rightarrow 8 - 4y + 4y = 8 \rightarrow 0y = 0$$

These equations are dependent. Any real number is a solution for y.
The solution of the system is $x = 4 - 2y$, where y is any real number.

23. Multiply each side of the first equation by –5, and add the equations to eliminate x:

$$\begin{cases} 2x - 3y = -1 \quad \xrightarrow{-5} \quad -10x + 15y = 5 \\ 10x + \; y = 11 \quad \longrightarrow \quad \underline{10x + \; y = 11} \end{cases}$$
$$16y = 16$$
$$y = 1$$

Substitute and solve for x:

$$2x - 3(1) = -1 \rightarrow 2x - 3 = -1 \rightarrow 2x = 2 \rightarrow x = 1$$
The solution of the system is $x = 1,\; y = 1$.

25. Solve the second equation for x, substitute into the first equation and solve:

$$\begin{cases} 2x + 3y = 6 \\ x - \; y = \dfrac{1}{2} \end{cases} \rightarrow \quad x = y + \dfrac{1}{2}$$

$$2\left(y + \dfrac{1}{2}\right) + 3y = 6 \rightarrow 2y + 1 + 3y = 6 \rightarrow 5y = 5 \rightarrow y = 1$$

Since $y = 1,\; x = 1 + \dfrac{1}{2} = \dfrac{3}{2}$ The solution of the system is $x = \dfrac{3}{2},\; y = 1$.

27. Multiply each side of the first equation by –6 and each side of the second equation by 12 to eliminate x:

$$\begin{cases} \dfrac{1}{2}x + \dfrac{1}{3}y = 3 \quad \xrightarrow{-6} \quad -3x - 2y = -18 \\ \dfrac{1}{4}x - \dfrac{2}{3}y = -1 \quad \xrightarrow{12} \quad \underline{3x - 8y = -12} \end{cases}$$
$$-10y = -30$$
$$y = 3$$

Substitute and solve for x:

$$\dfrac{1}{2}x + \dfrac{1}{3}(3) = 3 \rightarrow \dfrac{1}{2}x + 1 = 3 \rightarrow \dfrac{1}{2}x = 2 \rightarrow x = 4$$
The solution of the system is $x = 4,\; y = 3$.

29.   Add the equations to eliminate y and solve for x:

$$\begin{cases} 3x - 5y = 3 \\ 15x + 5y = 21 \end{cases}$$
$$\overline{\quad 18x \qquad = 24}$$
$$x \qquad = \frac{4}{3}$$

Substitute and solve for y:

$$3\left(\frac{4}{3}\right) - 5y = 3 \rightarrow 4 - 5y = 3 \rightarrow -5y = -1 \rightarrow y = \frac{1}{5}$$

The solution of the system is $x = \frac{4}{3}, \ y = \frac{1}{5}$.

31.   Rewrite letting $a = \frac{1}{x}, \ b = \frac{1}{y}$:

$$\begin{cases} \dfrac{1}{x} + \dfrac{1}{y} = 8 \\ \dfrac{3}{x} - \dfrac{5}{y} = 0 \end{cases} \begin{array}{c} \longrightarrow \\ \\ \longrightarrow \end{array} \begin{array}{l} a + b = 8 \\ \\ 3a - 5b = 0 \end{array}$$

Solve the first equation for a, substitute into the second equation and solve:

$$\begin{cases} a + b = 8 \quad \rightarrow \quad a = 8 - b \\ 3a - 5b = 0 \end{cases}$$

$$3(8 - b) - 5b = 0 \rightarrow 24 - 3b - 5b = 0 \rightarrow -8b = -24 \rightarrow b = 3$$

Since $b = 3, \ a = 8 - 3 = 5$

Thus, $x = \frac{1}{a} = \frac{1}{5}, \ y = \frac{1}{b} = \frac{1}{3}$

The solution of the system is $x = \frac{1}{5}, \ y = \frac{1}{3}$.

33.   Graph the two equations as y_1 and y_2, and use INTERSECT to solve:

$$\begin{cases} y_1 = \sqrt{2}x - 20\sqrt{7} \\ y_2 = -0.1x + 20 \end{cases}$$

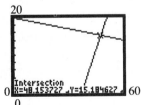

The solution of the system is $x = 48.15, \ y = 15.18$.

35.   Solve for y in each equation, graph the two equations as y_1 and y_2, and use INTERSECT to solve:

$$\begin{cases} \sqrt{2}x + \sqrt{3}y + \sqrt{6} = 0 \\ \sqrt{3}x - \sqrt{2}y + 60 = 0 \end{cases}$$

$$\begin{cases} y_1 = \dfrac{-\sqrt{2}x - \sqrt{6}}{\sqrt{3}} \\ y_2 = \dfrac{\sqrt{3}x + 60}{\sqrt{2}} \end{cases}$$

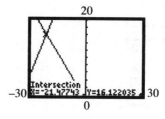

The solution of the system is $x = -21.48,\ y = 16.12$.

37.   Solve for y in each equation, graph the two equations as y_1 and y_2, and use INTERSECT to solve:

$$\begin{cases} \sqrt{3}x + \sqrt{2}y = \sqrt{0.3} \\ 100x - 95y = 20 \end{cases}$$

$$\begin{cases} y_1 = \dfrac{-\sqrt{3}x + \sqrt{0.3}}{\sqrt{2}} \\ y_2 = \dfrac{100x - 20}{95} \end{cases}$$

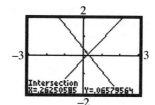

The solution of the system is $x = 0.26,\ y = 0.07$.

39.   Solve the system by substitution:
$$Q_s = Q_d$$
$$-200 + 50p = 1000 - 25p \rightarrow 75p = 1200 \rightarrow p = 16$$
Therefore, $Q_s = -200 + 50(16) = -200 + 800 = 600$
The equilibrium price is \$16 and the equilibrium quantity is 600 T-shirts.

41.   Let l be the length of the rectangle and w be the width of the rectangle. Then:
$$2l + 2w = 90$$
$$l = 2w$$
Solve by substitution:
$$2(2w) + 2w = 90$$
$$4w + 2w = 90 \rightarrow 6w = 90 \rightarrow w = 15 \text{ feet}$$
$$l = 2(15) = 30 \text{ feet}$$
The dimensions of the floor are 15 feet by 30 feet.

43.   Let x = the cost of one cheeseburger and y = the cost of one shake. Then:
$$4x + 2y = 790$$
$$2y = x + 15$$
Solve by substitution:

$$4x + x + 15 = 790 \rightarrow 5x = 775 \rightarrow x = 155$$
$$2y = 155 + 15 \rightarrow 2y = 170 \rightarrow y = 85$$
A cheeseburger cost \$1.55 and a shake costs \$0.85.

45. Let x = the number of pounds of cashews.
Then $x+30$ is the number of pounds in the mixture.
The value of the cashews is $5x$.
The value of the peanuts is $1.50(30) = 45$.
The value of the mixture is $3(x+30)$.
Setting up a value equation:
$$5x+45 = 3(x+30) \rightarrow 5x+45 = 3x+90$$
$$2x = 45 \rightarrow x = 22.5$$
22.5 pounds of cashews should be used in the mixture.

47. Let x = the plane's airspeed and y = the wind speed.

	Rate	Time	Distance
With Wind	$x+y$	3	600
Against	$x-y$	4	600

$(x+y)(3) = 600 \quad \rightarrow \quad x+y = 200$
$(x-y)(4) = 600 \quad \rightarrow \quad x-y = 150$
Solving by elimination:
$$2x = 350 \rightarrow x = 175$$
$$y = 200 - x = 200 - 175 = 25$$
The airspeed of the plane is 175 mph, and the wind speed is 25 mph.

49. Let x = the number of one design.
Let y = the number of the second design.
Then $x+y$ = the total number of sets of dishes.
$25x+45y$ = the cost of the dishes.
Setting up the equations and solving by substitution:
$$\begin{cases} x+ y = 200 \rightarrow y = 200-x \\ 25x+45y = 7400 \end{cases}$$
$$25x+45(200-x) = 7400 \rightarrow 25x+9000-45x = 7400$$
$$-20x = -1600 \rightarrow x = 80$$
$$y = 200-80 = 120$$
80 sets of the \$25 dishes and 120 sets of the \$45 dishes should be ordered.

51. Let x = the cost per package of bacon.
Let y = the cost of a carton of eggs.
Set up a system of equations for the problem:
$$\begin{cases} 3x+2y = 7.45 \\ 2x+3y = 6.45 \end{cases}$$
Multiply each side of the first equation by 3 and each side of the second equation by -2 and solve by elimination:
$$\begin{cases} 3x+2y = 7.45 \xrightarrow{\;3\;} & 9x+6y = 22.35 \\ 2x+3y = 6.45 \xrightarrow{\;-2\;} & -4x-6y = -12.90 \end{cases}$$
$$5x = 9.45$$
$$x = 1.89$$

Substitute and solve for y:
$$3(1.89) + 2y = 7.45$$

$$5.67 + 2y = 7.45 \rightarrow 2y = 1.78 \rightarrow y = 0.89$$

A package of bacon costs $1.89 and a carton of eggs cost $0.89.
The refund for 2 packages of bacon and 2 cartons of eggs will be $5.56.

53. Let x = the # of mg of liquid 1.
Let y = the # of mg of liquid 2.
Setting up the equations and solving by substitution:
$$\begin{cases} 0.2x + 0.4y = 40 & \text{vitamin C} \\ 0.3x + 0.2y = 30 & \text{vitamin D} \end{cases}$$
multiplying each equation by 10 yields
$$\begin{cases} 2x + 4y = 400 & \xrightarrow{} & 2x + 4y = 400 \\ 3x + 2y = 300 & \xrightarrow{2} & 6x + 4y = 600 \end{cases}$$
subtracting the bottom equation from the top equation yields
$$2x + 4y - (6x + 4y) = -200$$

$$2x - 6x = -200 \rightarrow -4x = -200 \rightarrow x = 50$$

$$\rightarrow 2(50) + 4y = 400 \rightarrow 100 + 4y = 400$$

$$\rightarrow 4y = 300 \rightarrow y = \frac{300}{4} = 75$$

So 50 mg of liquid 1 should be mixed with 75 mg of liquid 2.

55. Solve the system by substitution:
$$R = C$$

$$8x = 4.5x + 17500 \rightarrow 3.5x = 17500 \rightarrow x = 5000$$

5000 units must be produced and sold for the firm to break-even.

57. $\begin{cases} y = m_1 x + b_1 \\ y = m_2 x + b_2 \end{cases}$ subtracting the 2 equations yields

$$0 = m_1 x + b_1 - m_2 x + b_2$$

$$-b_2 = x(m_1 - m_2)$$

$$\frac{-b_2}{m_1 - m_2} = x, \text{ provided } m_1 \neq m_2$$

so $y = m_1 \left(\dfrac{-b_2}{m_1 - m_2} \right) + b_1 = \left(\dfrac{-b_2 m_1}{m_1 - m_2} \right) + b_1 = \dfrac{-b_2 m_1 + b_1(m_1 - m_2)}{m_1 - m_2}$

Therefore the solution set is $\left\{ x = \dfrac{-b_2}{m_1 - m_2}, y = \dfrac{-b_2 m_1 + b_1(m_1 - m_2)}{m_1 - m_2} \right\}$, provided $m_1 \neq m_2$.

59. $\begin{cases} y = m_1 x + b_1 \\ y = m_2 x + b_2 \end{cases}$ where $m_1 = m_2 = m$ and $b_1 = b_2$

$\begin{cases} y = mx + b_1 \\ y = mx + b_1 \end{cases}$ subtracting the 2 equations yields

$0 = 0$

Since this statement is always true, there are infinitely many solutions to the system. That is, the system is dependent.

61.   Answers will vary.

Chapter **8**

Systems of Equations and Inequalities

8.2 Systems of Linear Equations: Three Equations Containing Three Variables

1. Substituting the values of the variables:

$$\begin{cases} 3x + 3y + 2z = 4 & \longrightarrow \quad 3(1) + 3(-1) + 2(2) = 3 - 3 + 4 = 4 \\ x - y - z = 0 & \longrightarrow \quad 1 - (-1) - 2 = 1 + 1 - 2 = 0 \\ 2y - 3z = -8 & \longrightarrow \quad 2(-1) - 3(2) = -2 - 6 = -8 \end{cases}$$

Each equation is satisfied, so $x = 1, y = -1, z = 2$ is a solution to the system of equations.

3. Multiply each side of the first equation by -2 and add to the second equation to eliminate x:

$$\begin{cases} x - y = 6 & \xrightarrow{-2} \quad -2x + 2y \qquad = -12 \\ 2x - 3z = 16 & \longrightarrow \quad \underline{2x \qquad - 3z = 16} \\ 2y + z = 4 & \qquad\qquad 2y - 3z = 4 \end{cases}$$

Multiply each side of the result by -1 and add to the original third equation to eliminate y:

$$\begin{aligned} 2y - 3z = 4 & \xrightarrow{-1} \quad -2y + 3z = -4 \\ 2y + z = 4 & \longrightarrow \quad \underline{2y + z = 4} \\ & \qquad\qquad\quad 4z = 0 \\ & \qquad\qquad\quad z = 0 \end{aligned}$$

Substituting and solving for the other variables:

$$\begin{aligned} 2y + 0 &= 4 & 2x - 3(0) &= 16 \\ 2y &= 4 & 2x &= 16 \\ y &= 2 & x &= 8 \end{aligned}$$

The solution is $x = 8, \ y = 2, \ z = 0$.

5. Multiply each side of the first equation by -2 and add to the second equation to eliminate x; and multiply each side of the first equation by 3 and add to the third equation to eliminate x:

$$\begin{cases} x - 2y + 3z = 7 & \xrightarrow{-2} \quad -2x + 4y - 6z = -14 \\ 2x + y + z = 4 & \longrightarrow \quad \underline{2x + y + z = 4} \\ -3x + 2y - 2z = -10 & \qquad\qquad 5y - 5z = -10 \quad \xrightarrow{1/5} \quad y - z = -2 \\ & \xrightarrow{3} \quad 3x - 6y + 9z = 21 \\ & \longrightarrow \quad \underline{-3x + 2y - 2z = -10} \\ & \qquad\qquad -4y + 7z = 11 \end{cases}$$

Multiply each side of the first result by 4 and add to the second result to eliminate y:

$$y - z = -2 \xrightarrow{\ 4\ } \quad 4y - 4z = -8$$
$$-4y + 7z = 11 \longrightarrow \quad \underline{-4y + 7z = \ 11}$$
$$3z = \ 3$$
$$z = 1$$

Substituting and solving for the other variables:

$$y - 1 = -2 \qquad\qquad x - 2(-1) + 3(1) = 7$$
$$y = -1 \qquad\qquad x + 2 + 3 = 7$$
$$x = 2$$

The solution is $x = 2$, $y = -1$, $z = 1$.

7.　Add the first and second equations to eliminate z:

$$\begin{cases} x - y - z = 1 \\ 2x + 3y + z = 2 \\ 3x + 2y \quad = 0 \end{cases} \begin{array}{l} \longrightarrow \quad x - y - z = 1 \\ \longrightarrow \quad \underline{2x + 3y + z = 2} \\ \quad\quad 3x + 2y \quad = 3 \end{array}$$

Multiply each side of the result by −1 and add to the original third equation to eliminate y:

$$3x + 2y = 3 \xrightarrow{\ -1\ } -3x - 2y = -3$$
$$3x + 2y = 0 \longrightarrow \quad \underline{3x + 2y = \ 0}$$
$$0 = -3$$

This result has no solution, so the system is inconsistent.

9.　Add the first and second equations to eliminate x; and multiply the first equation by −3 and add to the third equation to eliminate x:

$$\begin{cases} x - y - z = \ 1 \\ -x + 2y - 3z = -4 \\ 3x - 2y - 7z = \ 0 \end{cases} \begin{array}{l} \longrightarrow \quad x - y - z = \ 1 \\ \longrightarrow \quad \underline{-x + 2y - 3z = -4} \\ \quad\quad y - 4z = -3 \end{array}$$

$$\xrightarrow{\ -3\ } -3x + 3y + 3z = -3$$
$$\longrightarrow \quad \underline{3x - 2y - 7z = \ 0}$$
$$y - 4z = -3$$

Multiply each side of the first result by −1 and add to the second result to eliminate y:

$$y - 4z = -3 \xrightarrow{\ -1\ } -y + 4z = \ 3$$
$$y - 4z = -3 \longrightarrow \quad \underline{y - 4z = -3}$$
$$0 = \ 0$$

The system is dependent. If z is any real number, then $y = 4z - 3$.
Solving for x in terms of z in the first equation:

$$x - (4z - 3) - z = 1$$
$$x - 4z + 3 - z = 1$$
$$x - 5z + 3 = 1$$
$$x = 5z - 2$$

The solution is $x = 5z - 2$, $y = 4z - 3$, z is any real number.

11. Multiply the first equation by –2 and add to the second equation to eliminate x; and add the first and third equations to eliminate x:

$$\begin{cases} 2x - 2y + 3z = 6 \\ 4x - 3y + 2z = 0 \\ -2x + 3y - 7z = 1 \end{cases} \xrightarrow{-2} \begin{array}{r} -4x + 4y - 6z = -12 \\ 4x - 3y + 2z = 0 \\ \hline y - 4z = -12 \end{array}$$

$$\xrightarrow{} \begin{array}{r} 2x - 2y + 3z = 6 \\ -2x + 3y - 7z = 1 \\ \hline y - 4z = 7 \end{array}$$

Multiply each side of the first result by –1 and add to the second result to eliminate y:

$$\begin{array}{r} y - 4z = -12 \\ y - 4z = 7 \end{array} \xrightarrow{-1} \begin{array}{r} -y + 4z = 12 \\ y - 4z = 7 \\ \hline 0 = 19 \end{array}$$

This result has no solution, so the system is inconsistent.

13. Add the first and second equations to eliminate z; and multiply the second equation by 2 and add to the third equation to eliminate z:

$$\begin{cases} x + y - z = 6 \\ 3x - 2y + z = -5 \\ x + 3y - 2z = 14 \end{cases} \xrightarrow{} \begin{array}{r} x + y - z = 6 \\ 3x - 2y + z = -5 \\ \hline 4x - y = 1 \end{array}$$

$$\xrightarrow{2} \begin{array}{r} 6x - 4y + 2z = -10 \\ x + 3y - 2z = 14 \\ \hline 7x - y = 4 \end{array}$$

Multiply each side of the first result by –1 and add to the second result to eliminate y:

$$\begin{array}{r} 4x - y = 1 \\ 7x - y = 4 \end{array} \xrightarrow{-1} \begin{array}{r} -4x + y = -1 \\ 7x - y = 4 \\ \hline 3x = 3 \\ x = 1 \end{array}$$

Substituting and solving for the other variables:

$$\begin{array}{ll} 4(1) - y = 1 & 3(1) - 2(3) + z = -5 \\ -y = -3 & 3 - 6 + z = -5 \\ y = 3 & z = -2 \end{array}$$

The solution is $x = 1$, $y = 3$, $z = -2$.

15. Add the first and second equations to eliminate z; and multiply the second equation by 3 and add to the third equation to eliminate z:

$$\begin{cases} x + 2y - z = -3 \\ 2x - 4y + z = -7 \\ -2x + 2y - 3z = 4 \end{cases} \xrightarrow{} \begin{array}{r} x + 2y - z = -3 \\ 2x - 4y + z = -7 \\ \hline 3x - 2y = -10 \end{array}$$

$$\xrightarrow{\;3\;}\quad 6x - 12y + 3z = -21$$
$$\xrightarrow{\qquad}\quad -2x + 2y - 3z = \quad 4$$
$$\overline{\qquad\qquad 4x - 10y \qquad = -17}$$

Multiply each side of the first result by –5 and add to the second result to eliminate y:

$$3x - 2y = -10 \quad\xrightarrow{\;-5\;}\quad -15x + 10y = \quad 50$$
$$4x - 10y = -17 \quad\xrightarrow{\qquad}\quad \underline{4x - 10y = -17}$$
$$-11x \quad = \quad 33$$
$$x \quad = \quad -3$$

Substituting and solving for the other variables:

$$3(-3) - 2y = -10 \qquad\qquad -3 + 2\left(\frac{1}{2}\right) - z = -3$$
$$-9 - 2y = -10 \qquad\qquad\qquad -3 + 1 - z = -3$$
$$-2y = -1 \qquad\qquad\qquad\qquad -z = -1$$
$$y = \frac{1}{2} \qquad\qquad\qquad\qquad z = 1$$

The solution is $x = -3,\ y = \dfrac{1}{2},\ z = 1$.

17. $y = ax^2 + bx + c$

At $(-1, 4)$ the equation becomes: At $(2, 3)$ the equation becomes:
$$4 = a(-1)^2 + b(-1) + c \qquad\qquad 3 = a(2)^2 + b(2) + c$$
$$4 = a - b + c \qquad\qquad\qquad\qquad 3 = 4a + 2b + c$$
$$a - b + c = 4 \qquad\qquad\qquad 4a + 2b + c = 3$$

At $(0, 1)$ the equation becomes:
$$1 = a(0)^2 + b(0) + c$$
$$c = 1$$

The system of equations is:
$$\begin{cases} a - b + c = 4 \\ 4a + 2b + c = 3 \\ \qquad\quad c = 1 \end{cases}$$

Substitute $c = 1$ into the first and second equations and simplify:
$$\begin{cases} a - b + 1 = 4 \;\rightarrow\; a - b = 3 \;\rightarrow\; a = b + 3 \\ 4a + 2b + 1 = 3 \;\rightarrow\; 4a + 2b = 2 \end{cases}$$

Solve the first equation for a, substitute into the second equation and solve:
$$4(b + 3) + 2b = 2$$
$$4b + 12 + 2b = 2$$
$$6b = -10 \rightarrow b = -\frac{5}{3}$$
$$a = -\frac{5}{3} + 3 = \frac{4}{3}$$

The solution is $a = \dfrac{4}{3},\ b = -\dfrac{5}{3},\ c = 1$. So the equation is $y = \dfrac{4}{3}x^2 - \dfrac{5}{3}x + 1$.

19. Substitute the expression for I_2 into the second and third equations and simplify:

$$\begin{cases} I_2 = I_1 + I_3 \\ 5 - 3I_1 - 5I_2 = 0 \\ 10 - 5I_2 - 7I_3 = 0 \end{cases}$$

$\rightarrow \quad 5 - 3I_1 - 5(I_1 + I_3) = 0 \quad \rightarrow \quad -8I_1 - 5I_3 = -5$

$\rightarrow \quad 10 - 5(I_1 + I_3) - 7I_3 = 0 \quad \rightarrow \quad -5I_1 - 12I_3 = -10$

Multiply both sides of the second equation by 5 and multiply both sides of the third equation by –8 to eliminate I_1:

$$-8I_1 - 5I_3 = -5 \xrightarrow{\quad 5 \quad} -40I_1 - 25I_3 = -25$$

$$-5I_1 - 12I_3 = -10 \xrightarrow{\quad -8 \quad} \underline{\quad 40I_1 + 96I_3 = 80 \quad}$$

$$71I_3 = 55 \rightarrow I_3 = \frac{55}{71}$$

Substituting and solving for the other variables:

$$-8I_1 - 5\left(\frac{55}{71}\right) = -5 \rightarrow -8I_1 - \frac{275}{71} = -5 \rightarrow -8I_1 = -\frac{80}{71} \rightarrow I_1 = \frac{10}{71}$$

$$I_2 = \frac{10}{71} + \frac{55}{71} = \frac{65}{71}$$

The solution is $I_1 = \frac{10}{71}$, $I_2 = \frac{65}{71}$, $I_3 = \frac{55}{71}$.

21. Let x = the number of orchestra seats.
Let y = the number of main seats.
Let z = the number of balcony seats.
Since the total number of seats is 500, $x + y + z = 500$.
Since the total revenue is \$17,100 if all seats are sold, $50x + 35y + 25z = 17,100$.
If only half of the orchestra seats are sold, the revenue is \$14,600. So,

$$50\left(\frac{1}{2}x\right) + 35y + 25z = 14,600 .$$

Multiply each side of the first equation by –25 and add to the second equation to eliminate z; and multiply each side of the third equation by –1 and add to the second equation to eliminate z:

$$\begin{cases} x + y + z = 500 \\ 50x + 35y + 25z = 17100 \\ 25x + 35y + 25z = 14600 \end{cases}$$

$\xrightarrow{\quad -25 \quad} \quad -25x - 25y - 25z = -12500$

$\xrightarrow{\qquad\qquad} \quad \underline{\quad 50x + 35y + 25z = 17100 \quad}$

$25x + 10y = 4600$

$\xrightarrow{\qquad\qquad} \quad 50x + 35y + 25z = 17100$

$\xrightarrow{\quad -1 \quad} \quad \underline{\quad -25x - 35y - 25z = -14600 \quad}$

$25x = 2500$

$x = 100$

Substituting and solving for the other variables:

$25(100) + 10y = 4600 \qquad\qquad 100 + 210 + z = 500$

$2500 + 10y = 4600 \qquad\qquad 310 + z = 500$

$10y = 2100 \qquad\qquad z = 190$

$y = 210$

There are 100 orchestra seats, 210 main seats, and 190 balcony seats.

23. Let x = the number of servings of chicken.
Let y = the number of servings of corn.
Let z = the number of servings of 2% milk.
Protein equation: $30x + 3y + 9z = 66$
Carbohydrate equation: $35x + 16y + 13z = 94.5$
Calcium equation: $200x + 10y + 300z = 910$
Multiply each side of the first equation by –16 and multiply each side of the second
equation by 3 and add them to eliminate y; and multiply each side of the second equation by
–5 and multiply each side of the third equation by 8 and add to eliminate y:

$$\begin{cases} 30x + 3y + 9z = 66 \\ 35x + 16y + 13z = 94.5 \\ 200x + 10y + 300z = 910 \end{cases}$$

$$\xrightarrow{-16} \quad -480x - 48y - 144z = -1056$$
$$\xrightarrow{3} \quad \underline{105x + 48y + 39z = 283.5}$$
$$-375x \quad\quad - 105z = -772.5$$

$$\xrightarrow{-5} \quad -175x - 80y - 65z = -472.5$$
$$\xrightarrow{8} \quad \underline{1600x + 80y + 2400z = 7280}$$
$$1425x \quad\quad + 2335z = 6807.5$$

Multiply each side of the first result by 19 and multiply each side of the second result by 5
to eliminate x:

$$-375x - 105z = -772.5 \xrightarrow{19} -7125x - 1995z = -14677.5$$
$$1425x + 2335z = 6807.5 \xrightarrow{5} \underline{7125x + 11675z = 34037.5}$$
$$9680z = 19360$$
$$z = 2$$

Substituting and solving for the other variables:

$$-375x - 105(2) = -772.5 \qquad\qquad 30(1.5) + 3y + 9(2) = 66$$
$$-375x - 210 = -772.5 \qquad\qquad\quad 45 + 3y + 18 = 66$$
$$-375x = -562.5 \qquad\qquad\qquad\qquad 3y = 3$$
$$x = 1.5 \qquad\qquad\qquad\qquad\quad y = 1$$

The dietitian should serve 1.5 servings of chicken, 1 serving of corn, and 2 servings of 2%
milk.

25. Let x = the price of 1 hamburger.
Let y = the price of 1 order of fries.
Let z = the price of 1 drink.
We can construct the system

$$\begin{cases} 8x + 6y + 6z = 26.10 \\ 10x + 6y + 8z = 31.60 \end{cases}$$

A system involving only 2 equations that contain 3 or more unknowns cannot be solved
uniquely. In other words, we can create as many solutions as we want by choosing a
specific value for one of the variables and then solving the resulting
2 x 2 system.
For example, suppose we know that

$$\$1.75 < \text{hamburger price} < \$2.25$$

$$\$0.75 < \text{fries price} < \$1.00$$

$$\$0.60 < \text{fries price} < \$0.90$$

Pick a specific value for x, y or z	2x2 system	Solution

$x = \$2.00$

$$\begin{cases} 8(2) + 6y + 6z = 26.10 \\ 10(2) + 6y + 8z = 31.60 \end{cases}$$

$x = \$2.00$

$y = \$0.93$

⇓

$$\begin{cases} 16 + 6y + 6z = 26.10 \\ 20 + 6y + 8z = 31.60 \end{cases}$$

$z = \$0.75$

⇓

$$\begin{cases} 6y + 6z = 10.10 \\ 6y + 8z = 11.60 \end{cases}$$

$y = \$0.90$

$$\begin{cases} 8x + 6(0.9) + 6z = 26.10 \\ 10x + 6(0.9) + 8z = 31.60 \end{cases}$$

$x = \$2.00$

$y = \$0.90$

⇓

$$\begin{cases} 8x + 5.4 + 6z = 26.10 \\ 10x + 5.4 + 8z = 31.60 \end{cases}$$

$z = \$0.65$

⇓

$$\begin{cases} 8x + 6z = 20.7 \\ 10x + 8z = 26.2 \end{cases}$$

$z = \$0.80$

$$\begin{cases} 8x + 6y + 6(.8) = 26.10 \\ 10x + 6y + 8(.8) = 31.60 \end{cases}$$

$x = \$1.95$

$y = \$0.95$

⇓

$$\begin{cases} 8x + 6y + 4.8 = 26.10 \\ 10x + 6y + 6.4 = 31.60 \end{cases}$$

$z = \$0.80$

⇓

$$\begin{cases} 8x + 6y = 21.3 \\ 10x + 6y = 25.2 \end{cases}$$

27. Let x = Beth's time working alone.
Let y = Bill's time working alone.
Let z = Edie's time working alone.
We can use the following tables to organize our work:

	Beth	Bill	Edie	Together
Hours to do job	x	y	z	10
Part of job done in 1 hour	$\dfrac{1}{x}$	$\dfrac{1}{y}$	$\dfrac{1}{z}$	$\dfrac{1}{10}$

Equation $\dfrac{1}{x} + \dfrac{1}{y} + \dfrac{1}{z} = \dfrac{1}{10}$

	Bill	Edie	Together
Hours to do job	y	z	15
Part of job done in 1 hour	$\dfrac{1}{y}$	$\dfrac{1}{z}$	$\dfrac{1}{15}$

Equation $\dfrac{1}{y} + \dfrac{1}{z} = \dfrac{1}{15}$

	Beth	Bill	Edie	All three	Beth and Bill
Hours to do job	x	y	z	4	8
Part of job done in 1 hour	$\dfrac{1}{x}$	$\dfrac{1}{y}$	$\dfrac{1}{z}$	$\dfrac{1}{4}$	$\dfrac{1}{8}$

Equation

$$4\left(\frac{1}{x} + \frac{1}{y} + \frac{1}{z}\right) + 8\left(\frac{1}{x} + \frac{1}{y}\right) = 1 \rightarrow \frac{12}{x} + \frac{12}{y} + \frac{4}{z} = 1$$

We can construct the system

$$\begin{cases} \dfrac{1}{x} + \dfrac{1}{y} + \dfrac{1}{z} = \dfrac{1}{10} \\[2mm] \dfrac{1}{y} + \dfrac{1}{z} = \dfrac{1}{15} \\[2mm] \dfrac{12}{x} + \dfrac{12}{y} + \dfrac{4}{z} = 1 \end{cases}$$

subtracting the second equation from the first equation yield

$$\begin{array}{l} \dfrac{1}{x} + \dfrac{1}{y} + \dfrac{1}{z} = \dfrac{1}{10} \\[2mm] \phantom{\dfrac{1}{x} +} \dfrac{1}{y} + \dfrac{1}{z} = \dfrac{1}{15} \\[1mm] \hline \dfrac{1}{x} = \dfrac{1}{10} - \dfrac{1}{15} \end{array} \rightarrow \dfrac{1}{x} = \dfrac{1}{30} \rightarrow x = 30$$

Plugging $x = 30$ into the original system yields

$$\begin{cases} \dfrac{1}{30} + \dfrac{1}{y} + \dfrac{1}{z} = \dfrac{1}{10} \longrightarrow \dfrac{1}{y} + \dfrac{1}{z} = \dfrac{1}{10} - \dfrac{1}{30} \longrightarrow \dfrac{1}{y} + \dfrac{1}{z} = \dfrac{1}{15} \\[2mm] \dfrac{1}{y} + \dfrac{1}{z} = \dfrac{1}{15} \\[2mm] \dfrac{12}{30} + \dfrac{12}{y} + \dfrac{4}{z} = 1 \longrightarrow \dfrac{12}{y} + \dfrac{4}{z} = 1 - \dfrac{12}{30} \longrightarrow \dfrac{12}{y} + \dfrac{4}{z} = \dfrac{3}{5} \end{cases}$$

Now consider the system

$$\begin{cases} \dfrac{1}{y} + \dfrac{1}{z} = \dfrac{1}{15} \xrightarrow{\;-12\;} \dfrac{-12}{y} + \dfrac{-12}{z} = \dfrac{-12}{15} \\[2mm] \dfrac{12}{y} + \dfrac{4}{z} = \dfrac{3}{5} \longrightarrow \quad \dfrac{12}{y} + \dfrac{4}{z} = \dfrac{3}{5} \end{cases}$$

adding these 2 equations yields

$$\dfrac{-12}{y} + \dfrac{-12}{z} = \dfrac{-12}{15}$$

$$\dfrac{\dfrac{12}{y} + \dfrac{4}{z} \qquad = \dfrac{3}{5}}{\dfrac{-12}{z} + \dfrac{4}{z} = \dfrac{-12}{15} + \dfrac{3}{5}} \qquad \rightarrow \dfrac{-8}{z} = \dfrac{-3}{15} \rightarrow \dfrac{8}{z} = \dfrac{1}{5} \rightarrow z = 40$$

plugging $z = 40$ into the equation

$$\dfrac{12}{y} + \dfrac{4}{z} \quad = \dfrac{3}{5} \rightarrow \dfrac{12}{y} + \dfrac{4}{40} \quad = \dfrac{3}{5}$$

$$\dfrac{12}{y} + \dfrac{1}{10} \quad = \dfrac{3}{5} \rightarrow \dfrac{12}{y} = \dfrac{3}{5} - \dfrac{1}{10} \rightarrow \dfrac{12}{y} = \dfrac{1}{2} \rightarrow y = 24$$

So, working alone, it would take Beth 30 hours, Bill 24 hours and Edie 40 hours to finish the job.

Chapter **8**

Systems of Equations and Inequalities

8.3   Systems of Linear Equations: Matrices

1.   Writing the augmented matrix for the system of equations:
$$\begin{cases} x - 5y = 5 \\ 4x + 3y = 6 \end{cases} \rightarrow \begin{bmatrix} 1 & -5 & | & 5 \\ 4 & 3 & | & 6 \end{bmatrix}$$

3.   Writing the augmented matrix for the system of equations:
$$\begin{cases} 2x + 3y - 6 = 0 \\ 4x - 6y + 2 = 0 \end{cases} \rightarrow \begin{cases} 2x + 3y = 6 \\ 4x - 6y = -2 \end{cases} \rightarrow \begin{bmatrix} 2 & 3 & | & 6 \\ 4 & -6 & | & -2 \end{bmatrix}$$

5.   Writing the augmented matrix for the system of equations:
$$\begin{cases} 0.01x - 0.03y = 0.06 \\ 0.13x + 0.10y = 0.20 \end{cases} \rightarrow \begin{bmatrix} 0.01 & -0.03 & | & 0.06 \\ 0.13 & 0.10 & | & 0.20 \end{bmatrix}$$

7.   Writing the augmented matrix for the system of equations:
$$\begin{cases} x - y + z = 10 \\ 3x + 3y \quad = 5 \\ x + y + 2z = 2 \end{cases} \rightarrow \begin{bmatrix} 1 & -1 & 1 & | & 10 \\ 3 & 3 & 0 & | & 5 \\ 1 & 1 & 2 & | & 2 \end{bmatrix}$$

9.   Writing the augmented matrix for the system of equations:
$$\begin{cases} x + y - z = 2 \\ 3x - 2y \quad = 2 \\ 5x + 3y - z = 1 \end{cases} \rightarrow \begin{bmatrix} 1 & 1 & -1 & | & 2 \\ 3 & -2 & 0 & | & 2 \\ 5 & 3 & -1 & | & 1 \end{bmatrix}$$

11.   Writing the augmented matrix for the system of equations:
$$\begin{cases} x - y - z = 10 \\ 2x + y + 2z = -1 \\ -3x + 4y = 5 \\ 4x - 5y + z = 0 \end{cases} \rightarrow \begin{bmatrix} 1 & -1 & -1 & | & 10 \\ 2 & 1 & 2 & | & -1 \\ -3 & 4 & 0 & | & 5 \\ 4 & -5 & 1 & | & 0 \end{bmatrix}$$

13. $\begin{bmatrix} 1 & -3 & | & -2 \\ 2 & -5 & | & 5 \end{bmatrix} \rightarrow \begin{bmatrix} 1 & -3 & | & -2 \\ 0 & 1 & | & 9 \end{bmatrix}$
$$R_2 = -2r_1 + r_2$$

15. $\begin{bmatrix} 1 & -3 & 4 & | & 3 \\ 2 & -5 & 6 & | & 6 \\ -3 & 3 & 4 & | & 6 \end{bmatrix} \rightarrow \begin{bmatrix} 1 & -3 & 4 & | & 3 \\ 0 & 1 & -2 & | & 0 \\ -3 & 3 & 4 & | & 6 \end{bmatrix} \rightarrow \begin{bmatrix} 1 & -3 & 4 & | & 3 \\ 0 & 1 & -2 & | & 0 \\ 0 & -6 & 16 & | & 15 \end{bmatrix}$

(a) $R_2 = -2r_1 + r_2$ (b) $R_3 = 3r_1 + r_3$

17. $\begin{bmatrix} 1 & -3 & 2 & | & -6 \\ 2 & -5 & 3 & | & -4 \\ -3 & -6 & 4 & | & 6 \end{bmatrix} \rightarrow \begin{bmatrix} 1 & -3 & 2 & | & -6 \\ 0 & 1 & -1 & | & 8 \\ -3 & -6 & 4 & | & 6 \end{bmatrix} \rightarrow \begin{bmatrix} 1 & -3 & 2 & | & -6 \\ 0 & 1 & -1 & | & 8 \\ 0 & -15 & 10 & | & -12 \end{bmatrix}$

(a) $R_2 = -2r_1 + r_2$ (b) $R_3 = 3r_1 + r_3$

19. $\begin{bmatrix} 1 & -3 & 1 & | & -2 \\ 2 & -5 & 6 & | & -2 \\ -3 & 1 & 4 & | & 6 \end{bmatrix} \rightarrow \begin{bmatrix} 1 & -3 & 1 & | & -2 \\ 0 & 1 & 4 & | & 2 \\ -3 & 1 & 4 & | & 6 \end{bmatrix} \rightarrow \begin{bmatrix} 1 & -3 & 1 & | & -2 \\ 0 & 1 & 4 & | & 2 \\ 0 & -8 & 7 & | & 0 \end{bmatrix}$

(a) $R_2 = -2r_1 + r_2$ (b) $R_3 = 3r_1 + r_3$

21. $\begin{cases} x = 5 \\ y = -1 \end{cases}$ consistent $x = 5$, $y = -1$

23. $\begin{cases} x = 1 \\ y = 2 \\ 0 = 3 \end{cases}$ inconsistent

25. $\begin{cases} x + 2z = -1 \\ y - 4z = -2 \\ \quad 0 = 0 \end{cases}$ consistent $x = -1 - 2z$, $y = -2 + 4z$, z is any real number

27. $\begin{cases} x_1 = 1 \\ x_2 + x_4 = 2 \\ x_3 + 2x_4 = 3 \end{cases}$ consistent $x_1 = 1, x_2 = 2 - x_4, x_3 = 3 - 2x_4, x_4$ is any real number

29. $\begin{cases} x_1 + 4x_4 = 2 \\ x_2 + + x_3 + 3x_4 = 3 \\ \qquad\qquad 0 = 0 \end{cases}$ consistent $x_1 = 2 - 4x_4, x_2 = 3 - x_3 - 3x_4,$
     x_3, x_4 are any real numbers

31.
$$\begin{cases} x_1 + x_4 = -2 \\ x_2 + 2x_4 = 2 \\ x_3 - x_4 = 0 \\ 0 = 0 \end{cases}$$

consistent $x_1 = -2 - x_4, x_2 = 2 - 2x_4, x_3 = x_4,$
x_4 is any real number

33. $\begin{cases} x + y = 8 \\ x - y = 4 \end{cases}$ can be written as $\begin{bmatrix} 1 & 1 & | & 8 \\ 1 & -1 & | & 4 \end{bmatrix}$

$$\rightarrow \begin{bmatrix} 1 & 1 & | & 8 \\ 0 & -2 & | & -4 \end{bmatrix} \rightarrow \begin{bmatrix} 1 & 1 & | & 8 \\ 0 & 1 & | & 2 \end{bmatrix} \rightarrow \begin{bmatrix} 1 & 0 & | & 6 \\ 0 & 1 & | & 2 \end{bmatrix}$$

$R_2 = -r_1 + r_2 \qquad R_2 = -\frac{1}{2}r_2 \qquad R_1 = -r_2 + r_1$

The solution is $x = 6$, $y = 2$.

35. $\begin{cases} 2x - 4y = -2 \\ 3x + 2y = 3 \end{cases}$ can be written as $\begin{bmatrix} 2 & -4 & | & -2 \\ 3 & 2 & | & 3 \end{bmatrix}$

$$\rightarrow \begin{bmatrix} 1 & -2 & | & -1 \\ 3 & 2 & | & 3 \end{bmatrix} \rightarrow \begin{bmatrix} 1 & -2 & | & -1 \\ 0 & 8 & | & 6 \end{bmatrix} \rightarrow \begin{bmatrix} 1 & -2 & | & -1 \\ 0 & 1 & | & \frac{3}{4} \end{bmatrix} \rightarrow \begin{bmatrix} 1 & 0 & | & \frac{1}{2} \\ 0 & 1 & | & \frac{3}{4} \end{bmatrix}$$

$R_1 = \frac{1}{2}r_1 \qquad R_2 = -3r_1 + r_2 \qquad R_2 = \frac{1}{8}r_2 \qquad R_1 = 2r_2 + r_1$

The solution is $x = \frac{1}{2}, y = \frac{3}{4}$.

37. $\begin{cases} x + 2y = 4 \\ 2x + 4y = 8 \end{cases}$ can be written as $\begin{bmatrix} 1 & 2 & | & 4 \\ 2 & 4 & | & 8 \end{bmatrix}$

$$\rightarrow \begin{bmatrix} 1 & 2 & | & 4 \\ 0 & 0 & | & 0 \end{bmatrix}$$

$R_2 = -2r_1 + r_2$

This is a dependent system and the solution is $x = -2y + 4$, y is any real number.

39. $\begin{cases} 2x + 3y = 6 \\ x - y = \frac{1}{2} \end{cases}$ can be written as: $\begin{bmatrix} 2 & 3 & | & 6 \\ 1 & -1 & | & \frac{1}{2} \end{bmatrix}$

$$\rightarrow \begin{bmatrix} 1 & \frac{3}{2} & | & 3 \\ 1 & -1 & | & \frac{1}{2} \end{bmatrix} \rightarrow \begin{bmatrix} 1 & \frac{3}{2} & | & 3 \\ 0 & -\frac{5}{2} & | & -\frac{5}{2} \end{bmatrix} \rightarrow \begin{bmatrix} 1 & \frac{3}{2} & | & 3 \\ 0 & 1 & | & 1 \end{bmatrix} \rightarrow \begin{bmatrix} 1 & 0 & | & \frac{3}{2} \\ 0 & 1 & | & 1 \end{bmatrix}$$

$R_1 = \frac{1}{2}r_1 \qquad R_2 = -r_1 + r_2 \qquad R_2 = -\frac{2}{5}r_2 \qquad R_1 = -\frac{3}{2}r_2 + r_1$

The solution is $x = \frac{3}{2}, y = 1$.

41. $\begin{cases} 3x - 5y = 3 \\ 15x + 5y = 21 \end{cases}$ can be written as $\begin{bmatrix} 3 & -5 & | & 3 \\ 15 & 5 & | & 21 \end{bmatrix}$

$$\rightarrow \begin{bmatrix} 1 & -\frac{5}{3} & | & 1 \\ 15 & 5 & | & 21 \end{bmatrix} \rightarrow \begin{bmatrix} 1 & -\frac{5}{3} & | & 1 \\ 0 & 30 & | & 6 \end{bmatrix} \rightarrow \begin{bmatrix} 1 & -\frac{5}{3} & | & 1 \\ 0 & 1 & | & \frac{1}{5} \end{bmatrix} \rightarrow \begin{bmatrix} 1 & 0 & | & \frac{4}{3} \\ 0 & 1 & | & \frac{1}{5} \end{bmatrix}$$

$$R_1 = \tfrac{1}{3}r_1 \qquad R_2 = -15r_1 + r_2 \quad R_2 = \tfrac{1}{30}r_2 \quad R_1 = \tfrac{5}{3}r_2 + r_1$$

The solution is $x = \dfrac{4}{3}, y = \dfrac{1}{5}$.

43. $\begin{cases} x - y \quad\;\; = 6 \\ 2x \quad\;\; -3z = 16 \\ \quad\; 2y + z = 4 \end{cases}$ can be written as $\begin{bmatrix} 1 & -1 & 0 & | & 6 \\ 2 & 0 & -3 & | & 16 \\ 0 & 2 & 1 & | & 4 \end{bmatrix}$

$$\rightarrow \begin{bmatrix} 1 & -1 & 0 & | & 6 \\ 0 & 2 & -3 & | & 4 \\ 0 & 2 & 1 & | & 4 \end{bmatrix} \rightarrow \begin{bmatrix} 1 & -1 & 0 & | & 6 \\ 0 & 1 & -\frac{3}{2} & | & 2 \\ 0 & 2 & 1 & | & 4 \end{bmatrix} \rightarrow \begin{bmatrix} 1 & 0 & -\frac{3}{2} & | & 8 \\ 0 & 1 & -\frac{3}{2} & | & 2 \\ 0 & 0 & 4 & | & 0 \end{bmatrix} \rightarrow \begin{bmatrix} 1 & 0 & -\frac{3}{2} & | & 8 \\ 0 & 1 & -\frac{3}{2} & | & 2 \\ 0 & 0 & 1 & | & 0 \end{bmatrix}$$

$$R_2 = -2r_1 + r_2 \qquad R_2 = \tfrac{1}{2}r_2 \qquad R_1 = r_2 + r_1 \qquad\qquad R_3 = \tfrac{1}{4}r_3$$
$$R_3 = -2r_2 + r_3$$

$$\rightarrow \begin{bmatrix} 1 & 0 & 0 & | & 8 \\ 0 & 1 & 0 & | & 2 \\ 0 & 0 & 1 & | & 0 \end{bmatrix}$$

$$R_1 = \tfrac{3}{2}r_3 + r_1$$
$$R_2 = \tfrac{3}{2}r_3 + r_2$$

The solution is $x = 8, y = 2, z = 0$.

45. $\begin{cases} x - 2y + 3z = 7 \\ 2x + y + z = 4 \\ -3x + 2y - 2z = -10 \end{cases}$ can be written as $\begin{bmatrix} 1 & -2 & 3 & | & 7 \\ 2 & 1 & 1 & | & 4 \\ -3 & 2 & -2 & | & -10 \end{bmatrix}$

$$\rightarrow \begin{bmatrix} 1 & -2 & 3 & | & 7 \\ 0 & 5 & -5 & | & -10 \\ 0 & -4 & 7 & | & 11 \end{bmatrix} \rightarrow \begin{bmatrix} 1 & -2 & 3 & | & 7 \\ 0 & 1 & -1 & | & -2 \\ 0 & -4 & 7 & | & 11 \end{bmatrix} \rightarrow \begin{bmatrix} 1 & 0 & 1 & | & 3 \\ 0 & 1 & -1 & | & -2 \\ 0 & 0 & 3 & | & 3 \end{bmatrix}$$

$$R_2 = -2r_1 + r_2 \qquad R_2 = \tfrac{1}{5}r_2 \qquad R_1 = 2r_2 + r_1$$
$$R_3 = 3r_1 + r_3 \qquad\qquad\qquad\qquad R_3 = 4r_2 + r_3$$

$$\rightarrow \begin{bmatrix} 1 & 0 & 1 & | & 3 \\ 0 & 1 & -1 & | & -2 \\ 0 & 0 & 1 & | & 1 \end{bmatrix} \rightarrow \begin{bmatrix} 1 & 0 & 0 & | & 2 \\ 0 & 1 & 0 & | & -1 \\ 0 & 0 & 1 & | & 1 \end{bmatrix}$$

$$R_3 = \tfrac{1}{3}r_3 \qquad\qquad R_1 = -r_3 + r_1$$
$$R_2 = r_3 + r_2$$

The solution is $x = 2, y = -1, z = 1$.

47. $\begin{cases} 2x - 2y - 2z = 2 \\ 2x + 3y + z = 2 \\ 3x + 2y = 0 \end{cases}$ can be written as $\begin{bmatrix} 2 & -2 & -2 & | & 2 \\ 2 & 3 & 1 & | & 2 \\ 3 & 2 & 0 & | & 0 \end{bmatrix}$

$\rightarrow \begin{bmatrix} 1 & -1 & -1 & | & 1 \\ 2 & 3 & 1 & | & 2 \\ 3 & 2 & 0 & | & 0 \end{bmatrix} \rightarrow \begin{bmatrix} 1 & -1 & -1 & | & 1 \\ 0 & 5 & 3 & | & 0 \\ 0 & 5 & 3 & | & -3 \end{bmatrix} \rightarrow \begin{bmatrix} 1 & -1 & -1 & | & 1 \\ 0 & 5 & 3 & | & 0 \\ 0 & 0 & 0 & | & -3 \end{bmatrix}$

$R_1 = \frac{1}{2}r_1$ $\quad\quad$ $R_2 = -2r_1 + r_2$ $\quad$ $R_3 = -r_2 + r_3$

$\quad\quad\quad\quad\quad\quad\quad R_3 = -3r_1 + r_3$

There is no solution. The system is inconsistent.

49. $\begin{cases} -x + y + z = -1 \\ -x + 2y - 3z = -4 \\ 3x - 2y - 7z = 0 \end{cases}$ can be written as $\begin{bmatrix} -1 & 1 & 1 & | & -1 \\ -1 & 2 & -3 & | & -4 \\ 3 & -2 & -7 & | & 0 \end{bmatrix}$

$\rightarrow \begin{bmatrix} 1 & -1 & -1 & | & 1 \\ -1 & 2 & -3 & | & -4 \\ 3 & -2 & -7 & | & 0 \end{bmatrix} \rightarrow \begin{bmatrix} 1 & -1 & -1 & | & 1 \\ 0 & 1 & -4 & | & -3 \\ 0 & 1 & -4 & | & -3 \end{bmatrix} \rightarrow \begin{bmatrix} 1 & 0 & -5 & | & -2 \\ 0 & 1 & -4 & | & -3 \\ 0 & 0 & 0 & | & 0 \end{bmatrix} \rightarrow \begin{matrix} x - 5z = -2 \\ y - 4z = -3 \end{matrix}$

$R_1 = -r_1$ $\quad\quad$ $R_2 = r_1 + r_2$ $\quad\quad$ $R_1 = r_2 + r_1$

$\quad\quad\quad\quad\quad R_3 = -3r_1 + r_3$ $\quad\quad$ $R_3 = -r_2 + r_3$

The solution is $x = 5z - 2$, $y = 4z - 3$, z is any real number.

51. $\begin{cases} 2x - 2y + 3z = 6 \\ 4x - 3y + 2z = 0 \\ -2x + 3y - 7z = 1 \end{cases}$ can be written as $\begin{bmatrix} 2 & -2 & 3 & | & 6 \\ 4 & -3 & 2 & | & 0 \\ -2 & 3 & -7 & | & 1 \end{bmatrix}$

$\rightarrow \begin{bmatrix} 1 & -1 & \frac{3}{2} & | & 3 \\ 4 & -3 & 2 & | & 0 \\ -2 & 3 & -7 & | & 1 \end{bmatrix} \rightarrow \begin{bmatrix} 1 & -1 & \frac{3}{2} & | & 3 \\ 0 & 1 & -4 & | & -12 \\ 0 & 1 & -4 & | & 7 \end{bmatrix} \rightarrow \begin{bmatrix} 1 & 0 & -\frac{5}{2} & | & -9 \\ 0 & 1 & -4 & | & -12 \\ 0 & 0 & 0 & | & 19 \end{bmatrix}$

$R_1 = \frac{1}{2}r_1$ $\quad\quad$ $R_2 = -4r_1 + r_2$ $\quad$ $R_1 = r_2 + r_1$

$\quad\quad\quad\quad\quad R_3 = 2r_1 + r_3$ $\quad\quad$ $R_3 = -r_2 + r_3$

There is no solution. The system is inconsistent.

53. $\begin{cases} x + y - z = 6 \\ 3x - 2y + z = -5 \\ x + 3y - 2z = 14 \end{cases}$ can be written as: $\begin{bmatrix} 1 & 1 & -1 & | & 6 \\ 3 & -2 & 1 & | & -5 \\ 1 & 3 & -2 & | & 14 \end{bmatrix}$

$\rightarrow \begin{bmatrix} 1 & 1 & -1 & | & 6 \\ 0 & -5 & 4 & | & -23 \\ 0 & 2 & -1 & | & 8 \end{bmatrix} \rightarrow \begin{bmatrix} 1 & 1 & -1 & | & 6 \\ 0 & 1 & -\frac{4}{5} & | & \frac{23}{5} \\ 0 & 2 & -1 & | & 8 \end{bmatrix} \rightarrow \begin{bmatrix} 1 & 0 & -\frac{1}{5} & | & \frac{7}{5} \\ 0 & 1 & -\frac{4}{5} & | & \frac{23}{5} \\ 0 & 0 & \frac{3}{5} & | & -\frac{6}{5} \end{bmatrix}$

$R_2 = -3r_1 + r_2$ $\quad\quad$ $R_2 = -\frac{1}{5}r_2$ $\quad\quad$ $R_1 = -r_2 + r_1$

$R_3 = -r_1 + r_3$ $\quad\quad\quad\quad\quad\quad\quad$ $R_3 = -2r_2 + r_3$

$$\rightarrow \begin{bmatrix} 1 & 0 & -\frac{1}{5} & \frac{7}{5} \\ 0 & 1 & -\frac{4}{5} & \frac{23}{5} \\ 0 & 0 & 1 & -2 \end{bmatrix} \rightarrow \begin{bmatrix} 1 & 0 & 0 & 1 \\ 0 & 1 & 0 & 3 \\ 0 & 0 & 1 & -2 \end{bmatrix}$$

$$R_3 = \frac{5}{3} r_3 \qquad\qquad R_1 = \frac{1}{5} r_3 + r_1$$
$$R_2 = \frac{4}{5} r_3 + r_2$$

The solution is $x = 1$, $y = 3$, $z = -2$.

55. $\begin{cases} x + 2y - z = -3 \\ 2x - 4y + z = -7 \\ -2x + 2y - 3z = 4 \end{cases}$ can be written as $\begin{bmatrix} 1 & 2 & -1 & -3 \\ 2 & -4 & 1 & -7 \\ -2 & 2 & -3 & 4 \end{bmatrix}$

$$\rightarrow \begin{bmatrix} 1 & 2 & -1 & -3 \\ 0 & -8 & 3 & -1 \\ 0 & 6 & -5 & -2 \end{bmatrix} \rightarrow \begin{bmatrix} 1 & 2 & -1 & -3 \\ 0 & 1 & -\frac{3}{8} & \frac{1}{8} \\ 0 & 6 & -5 & -2 \end{bmatrix} \rightarrow \begin{bmatrix} 1 & 0 & -\frac{1}{4} & -\frac{13}{4} \\ 0 & 1 & -\frac{3}{8} & \frac{1}{8} \\ 0 & 0 & -\frac{11}{4} & -\frac{11}{4} \end{bmatrix}$$

$$R_2 = -2r_1 + r_2 \qquad R_2 = -\frac{1}{8} r_2 \qquad R_1 = -2r_2 + r_1$$
$$R_3 = 2r_1 + r_3 \qquad\qquad\qquad\qquad R_3 = -6r_2 + r_3$$

$$\rightarrow \begin{bmatrix} 1 & 0 & -\frac{1}{4} & -\frac{13}{4} \\ 0 & 1 & -\frac{3}{8} & \frac{1}{8} \\ 0 & 0 & 1 & 1 \end{bmatrix} \rightarrow \begin{bmatrix} 1 & 0 & 0 & -3 \\ 0 & 1 & 0 & \frac{1}{2} \\ 0 & 0 & 1 & 1 \end{bmatrix}$$

$$R_3 = -\frac{4}{11} r_3 \qquad\qquad R_1 = \frac{1}{4} r_3 + r_1$$
$$R_2 = \frac{3}{8} r_3 + r_2$$

The solution is $x = -3, y = \dfrac{1}{2}, z = 1$

57. $\begin{cases} 3x + y - z = \dfrac{2}{3} \\ 2x - y + z = 1 \\ 4x + 2y = \dfrac{8}{3} \end{cases}$ can be written as: $\begin{bmatrix} 3 & 1 & -1 & \frac{2}{3} \\ 2 & -1 & 1 & 1 \\ 4 & 2 & 0 & \frac{8}{3} \end{bmatrix}$

$$\rightarrow \begin{bmatrix} 1 & \frac{1}{3} & -\frac{1}{3} & \frac{2}{9} \\ 2 & -1 & 1 & 1 \\ 4 & 2 & 0 & \frac{8}{3} \end{bmatrix} \rightarrow \begin{bmatrix} 1 & \frac{1}{3} & -\frac{1}{3} & \frac{2}{9} \\ 0 & -\frac{5}{3} & \frac{5}{3} & \frac{5}{9} \\ 0 & \frac{2}{3} & \frac{4}{3} & \frac{16}{9} \end{bmatrix} \rightarrow \begin{bmatrix} 1 & \frac{1}{3} & -\frac{1}{3} & \frac{2}{9} \\ 0 & 1 & -1 & -\frac{1}{3} \\ 0 & \frac{2}{3} & \frac{4}{3} & \frac{16}{9} \end{bmatrix} \rightarrow \begin{bmatrix} 1 & 0 & 0 & \frac{1}{3} \\ 0 & 1 & -1 & -\frac{1}{3} \\ 0 & 0 & 2 & 2 \end{bmatrix}$$

$$R_1 = \frac{1}{3} r_1 \qquad R_2 = -2r_1 + r_2 \qquad R_2 = -\frac{3}{5} r_2 \qquad R_1 = -\frac{1}{3} r_2 + r_1$$
$$\qquad\qquad R_3 = -4r_1 + r_3 \qquad\qquad\qquad R_3 = -\frac{2}{3} r_2 + r_3$$

$$\rightarrow \begin{bmatrix} 1 & 0 & 0 & \frac{1}{3} \\ 0 & 1 & -1 & -\frac{1}{3} \\ 0 & 0 & 1 & 1 \end{bmatrix} \rightarrow \begin{bmatrix} 1 & 0 & 0 & \frac{1}{3} \\ 0 & 1 & 0 & \frac{2}{3} \\ 0 & 0 & 1 & 1 \end{bmatrix}$$

$$R_3 = \tfrac{1}{2} r_3 \qquad\qquad R_2 = r_3 + r_2$$

The solution is $x = \dfrac{1}{3}, y = \dfrac{2}{3}, z = 1$.

59. $\begin{cases} x + y + z + w = 4 \\ 2x - y + z = 0 \\ 3x + 2y + z - w = 6 \\ x - 2y - 2z + 2w = -1 \end{cases}$ can be written as $\begin{bmatrix} 1 & 1 & 1 & 1 & 4 \\ 2 & -1 & 1 & 0 & 0 \\ 3 & 2 & 1 & -1 & 6 \\ 1 & -2 & -2 & 2 & -1 \end{bmatrix}$

$$\rightarrow \begin{bmatrix} 1 & 1 & 1 & 1 & 4 \\ 0 & -3 & -1 & -2 & -8 \\ 0 & -1 & -2 & -4 & -6 \\ 0 & -3 & -3 & 1 & -5 \end{bmatrix} \rightarrow \begin{bmatrix} 1 & 1 & 1 & 1 & 4 \\ 0 & -1 & -2 & -4 & -6 \\ 0 & -3 & -1 & -2 & -8 \\ 0 & -3 & -3 & 1 & -5 \end{bmatrix} \rightarrow \begin{bmatrix} 1 & 1 & 1 & 1 & 4 \\ 0 & 1 & 2 & 4 & 6 \\ 0 & -3 & -1 & -2 & -8 \\ 0 & -3 & -3 & 1 & -5 \end{bmatrix}$$

$R_2 = -2r_1 + r_2$ Interchange r_2 and r_3 $R_2 = -r_2$

$R_3 = -3r_1 + r_3$

$R_4 = -r_1 + r_4$

$$\rightarrow \begin{bmatrix} 1 & 0 & -1 & -3 & -2 \\ 0 & 1 & 2 & 4 & 6 \\ 0 & 0 & 5 & 10 & 10 \\ 0 & 0 & 3 & 13 & 13 \end{bmatrix} \rightarrow \begin{bmatrix} 1 & 0 & -1 & -3 & -2 \\ 0 & 1 & 2 & 4 & 6 \\ 0 & 0 & 1 & 2 & 2 \\ 0 & 0 & 3 & 13 & 13 \end{bmatrix} \rightarrow \begin{bmatrix} 1 & 0 & 0 & -1 & 0 \\ 0 & 1 & 0 & 0 & 2 \\ 0 & 0 & 1 & 2 & 2 \\ 0 & 0 & 0 & 7 & 7 \end{bmatrix}$$

$R_1 = -r_2 + r_1$ $R_3 = \tfrac{1}{5} r_3$ $R_1 = r_3 + r_1$

$R_3 = 3r_2 + r_3$ $R_2 = -2r_3 + r_2$

$R_4 = 3r_2 + r_4$ $R_4 = -3r_3 + r_4$

$$\rightarrow \begin{bmatrix} 1 & 0 & 0 & -1 & 0 \\ 0 & 1 & 0 & 0 & 2 \\ 0 & 0 & 1 & 2 & 2 \\ 0 & 0 & 0 & 1 & 1 \end{bmatrix} \rightarrow \begin{bmatrix} 1 & 0 & 0 & 0 & 1 \\ 0 & 1 & 0 & 0 & 2 \\ 0 & 0 & 1 & 0 & 0 \\ 0 & 0 & 0 & 1 & 1 \end{bmatrix}$$

$R_4 = \tfrac{1}{7} r_4$ $R_1 = r_4 + r_1$

$R_3 = -2r_4 + r_3$

The solution is $x = 1, y = 2, z = 0, w = 1$.

61. $\begin{cases} x + 2y + z = 1 \\ 2x - y + 2z = 2 \\ 3x + y + 3z = 3 \end{cases}$ can be written as $\begin{bmatrix} 1 & 2 & 1 & | & 1 \\ 2 & -1 & 2 & | & 2 \\ 3 & 1 & 3 & | & 3 \end{bmatrix}$

$$\rightarrow \begin{bmatrix} 1 & 2 & 1 & | & 1 \\ 0 & -5 & 0 & | & 0 \\ 0 & -5 & 0 & | & 0 \end{bmatrix} \rightarrow \begin{bmatrix} 1 & 2 & 1 & | & 1 \\ 0 & -5 & 0 & | & 0 \\ 0 & 0 & 0 & | & 0 \end{bmatrix} \rightarrow \begin{aligned} x + 2y + z &= 1 \\ -5y &= 0 \end{aligned}$$

$R_2 = -2r_1 + r_2 \qquad R_3 = -r_2 + r_3$
$R_3 = -3r_1 + r_3$

Substitute and solve:
$$y = 0$$
$$x + 2(0) + z = 1$$
$$x + z = 1$$
$$x = 1 - z$$

The solution is $y = 0$, $x = 1 - z$, z is any real number.

63. $\begin{cases} x - y + z = 5 \\ 3x + 2y - 2z = 0 \end{cases}$ can be written as: $\begin{bmatrix} 1 & -1 & 1 & | & 5 \\ 3 & 2 & -2 & | & 0 \end{bmatrix}$

$$\rightarrow \begin{bmatrix} 1 & -1 & 1 & | & 5 \\ 0 & 5 & -5 & | & -15 \end{bmatrix} \rightarrow \begin{bmatrix} 1 & -1 & 1 & | & 5 \\ 0 & 1 & -1 & | & -3 \end{bmatrix} \rightarrow \begin{bmatrix} 1 & 0 & 0 & | & 2 \\ 0 & 1 & -1 & | & -3 \end{bmatrix}$$

$R_2 = -3r_1 + r_2 \qquad R_2 = \frac{1}{5}r_2 \qquad R_1 = r_2 + r_1$

The matrix in the third step represents the system $\begin{cases} x = 2 \\ y - z = -3 \end{cases}$

Therefore the solution is $x = 2; y = -3 + z;\ z$ is any real number

or

$$x = 2; z = y + 3;\ y \text{ is any real number}$$

65. $\begin{cases} 2x + 3y - z = 3 \\ x - y - z = 0 \\ -x + y + z = 0 \\ x + y + 3z = 5 \end{cases}$ can be written as: $\begin{bmatrix} 2 & 3 & -1 & | & 3 \\ 1 & -1 & -1 & | & 0 \\ -1 & 1 & 1 & | & 0 \\ 1 & 1 & 3 & | & 5 \end{bmatrix}$

$$\rightarrow \begin{bmatrix} 1 & -1 & -1 & | & 0 \\ 2 & 3 & -1 & | & 3 \\ -1 & 1 & 1 & | & 0 \\ 1 & 1 & 3 & | & 5 \end{bmatrix} \longrightarrow \begin{bmatrix} 1 & -1 & -1 & | & 0 \\ 0 & 5 & 1 & | & 3 \\ 0 & 0 & 0 & | & 0 \\ 0 & 2 & 4 & | & 5 \end{bmatrix} \rightarrow \begin{bmatrix} 1 & -1 & -1 & | & 0 \\ 0 & 5 & 1 & | & 3 \\ 0 & 2 & 4 & | & 5 \\ 0 & 0 & 0 & | & 0 \end{bmatrix}$$

interchange r_1 and r_2 $R_2 = -2r_1 + r_2$ interchange r_3 and r_4
$R_3 = r_1 + r_3$
$R_4 = -r_1 + r_4$

$$\rightarrow \begin{bmatrix} 1 & -1 & -1 & 0 \\ 0 & 1 & -7 & -7 \\ 0 & 2 & 4 & 5 \\ 0 & 0 & 0 & 0 \end{bmatrix} \longrightarrow \begin{bmatrix} 1 & 0 & -8 & -7 \\ 0 & 1 & -7 & -7 \\ 0 & 1 & 18 & 19 \\ 0 & 0 & 0 & 0 \end{bmatrix} \rightarrow \begin{bmatrix} 1 & 0 & -8 & -7 \\ 0 & 1 & -7 & -7 \\ 0 & 0 & 1 & \frac{19}{18} \\ 0 & 0 & 0 & 0 \end{bmatrix}$$

$$R_2 = -2r_3 + r_2 \qquad\qquad R_1 = r_2 + r_1 \qquad R_3 = \tfrac{1}{18}r_3$$
$$R_3 = -2r_2 + r_3$$

The matrix in the last step represents the system
$$\begin{cases} x - 8z = -7 \\ y - 7z = -7 \\ \qquad z = \dfrac{19}{18} \end{cases}$$

Therefore the solution is
$$z = \frac{19}{18}$$

$$x = -7 + 8z = -7 + 8\left(\frac{19}{18}\right) = \frac{13}{9}; \quad y = -7 + 7z = -7 + 7\left(\frac{19}{18}\right) = \frac{7}{18}$$

67. $\begin{cases} 4x + y + z - w = 4 \\ x - y + 2z + 3w = 3 \end{cases}$ can be written as: $\begin{bmatrix} 4 & 1 & 1 & -1 & 4 \\ 1 & -1 & 2 & 3 & 3 \end{bmatrix}$

$$\rightarrow \begin{bmatrix} 1 & -1 & 2 & 3 & 3 \\ 4 & 1 & 1 & -1 & 4 \end{bmatrix} \longrightarrow \begin{bmatrix} 1 & -1 & 2 & 3 & 3 \\ 0 & 5 & -7 & -13 & -8 \end{bmatrix}$$

$\quad$ interchange r_1 and r_2 $\qquad\quad R_2 = -4r_1 + r_2$

The matrix in the last step represents the system $\quad \begin{cases} x - y + 2z + 3w = 3 \\ \quad 5y - 7z - 13w = -8 \end{cases}$

The second equation yields
$$5y - 7z - 13w = -8 \rightarrow 5y = -8 + 7z + 13w \rightarrow y = -\frac{8}{5} + \frac{7}{5}z + \frac{13}{5}w$$

The first equation yields
$$x - y + 2z + 3w = 3 \rightarrow x = 3 + y - 2z - 3w$$

substituting for y

$$x = 3 + \left(-\frac{8}{5} + \frac{7}{5}z + \frac{13}{5}w\right) - 2z - 3w$$

$$x = -\frac{3}{5}z - \frac{2}{5}w + \frac{7}{5}$$

Therefore the solution is

$$x = -\frac{3}{5}z - \frac{2}{5}w + \frac{7}{5}; \quad y = -\frac{8}{5} + \frac{7}{5}z + \frac{13}{5}w$$

$$z \text{ and } w \text{ are any real numbers}$$

69. Each of the points must satisfy the equation $y = ax^2 + bx + c$.

   $(1,2)$: $2 = a + b + c$

   $(-2,-7)$: $-7 = 4a - 2b + c$

   $(2,-3)$: $-3 = 4a + 2b + c$

Set up a matrix and solve:

$$\begin{bmatrix} 1 & 1 & 1 & 2 \\ 4 & -2 & 1 & -7 \\ 4 & 2 & 1 & -3 \end{bmatrix} \rightarrow \begin{bmatrix} 1 & 1 & 1 & 2 \\ 0 & -6 & -3 & -15 \\ 0 & -2 & -3 & -11 \end{bmatrix} \rightarrow \begin{bmatrix} 1 & 1 & 1 & 2 \\ 0 & 1 & \frac{1}{2} & \frac{5}{2} \\ 0 & -2 & -3 & -11 \end{bmatrix} \rightarrow \begin{bmatrix} 1 & 0 & \frac{1}{2} & -\frac{1}{2} \\ 0 & 1 & \frac{1}{2} & \frac{5}{2} \\ 0 & 0 & -2 & -6 \end{bmatrix}$$

$$\begin{array}{cccc} R_2 = -4r_1 + r_2 & R_2 = -\frac{1}{6}r_2 & R_1 = -r_2 + r_1 \\ R_3 = -4r_1 + r_3 & & R_3 = 2r_2 + r_3 \end{array}$$

$$\rightarrow \begin{bmatrix} 1 & 0 & \frac{1}{2} & -\frac{1}{2} \\ 0 & 1 & \frac{1}{2} & \frac{5}{2} \\ 0 & 0 & 1 & 3 \end{bmatrix} \rightarrow \begin{bmatrix} 1 & 0 & 0 & -2 \\ 0 & 1 & 0 & 1 \\ 0 & 0 & 1 & 3 \end{bmatrix}$$

$$\begin{array}{cc} R_3 = -\frac{1}{2}r_3 & R_1 = -\frac{1}{2}r_3 + r_1 \\ & R_2 = -\frac{1}{2}r_3 + r_2 \end{array}$$

The solution is $a = -2, b = 1, c = 3$; so the equation is $y = -2x^2 + x + 3$.

71. Each of the points must satisfy the equation $f(x) = ax^3 + bx^2 + cx + d$.

   $f(-3) = -112$: $-27a + 9b - 3c + d = -112$

   $f(-1) = -2$: $-a + b - c + d = -2$

   $f(1) = 4$: $a + b + c + d = 4$

   $f(2) = 13$: $8a + 4b + 2c + d = 13$

Set up a matrix and solve:

$$\begin{bmatrix} -27 & 9 & -3 & 1 & -112 \\ -1 & 1 & -1 & 1 & -2 \\ 1 & 1 & 1 & 1 & 4 \\ 8 & 4 & 2 & 1 & 13 \end{bmatrix} \rightarrow \begin{bmatrix} 1 & 1 & 1 & 1 & 4 \\ -1 & 1 & -1 & 1 & -2 \\ -27 & 9 & -3 & 1 & -112 \\ 8 & 4 & 2 & 1 & 13 \end{bmatrix} \rightarrow \begin{bmatrix} 1 & 1 & 1 & 1 & 4 \\ 0 & 2 & 0 & 2 & 2 \\ 0 & 36 & 24 & 28 & -4 \\ 0 & -4 & -6 & -7 & -19 \end{bmatrix}$$

$$\begin{array}{ccc} \text{Interchange } r_3 \text{ and } r_1 & R_2 = r_1 + r_2 \\ & R_3 = 27r_1 + r_3 \\ & R_4 = -8r_1 + r_4 \end{array}$$

$$\rightarrow \begin{bmatrix} 1 & 1 & 1 & 1 & 4 \\ 0 & 1 & 0 & 1 & 1 \\ 0 & 36 & 24 & 28 & -4 \\ 0 & -4 & -6 & -7 & -19 \end{bmatrix} \rightarrow \begin{bmatrix} 1 & 0 & 1 & 0 & 3 \\ 0 & 1 & 0 & 1 & 1 \\ 0 & 0 & 24 & -8 & -40 \\ 0 & 0 & -6 & -3 & -15 \end{bmatrix} \rightarrow \begin{bmatrix} 1 & 0 & 1 & 0 & 3 \\ 0 & 1 & 0 & 1 & 1 \\ 0 & 0 & 1 & -\frac{1}{3} & -\frac{5}{3} \\ 0 & 0 & -6 & -3 & -15 \end{bmatrix}$$

$$\begin{array}{ccc} R_2 = \frac{1}{2}r_2 & R_1 = -r_2 + r_1 & R_3 = \frac{1}{24}r_3 \\ & R_3 = -36r_2 + r_3 \\ & R_4 = 4r_2 + r_4 \end{array}$$

$$\rightarrow \begin{bmatrix} 1 & 0 & 0 & \frac{1}{3} & \frac{14}{3} \\ 0 & 1 & 0 & 1 & 1 \\ 0 & 0 & 1 & -\frac{1}{3} & -\frac{5}{3} \\ 0 & 0 & 0 & -5 & -25 \end{bmatrix} \rightarrow \begin{bmatrix} 1 & 0 & 0 & \frac{1}{3} & \frac{14}{3} \\ 0 & 1 & 0 & 1 & 1 \\ 0 & 0 & 1 & -\frac{1}{3} & -\frac{5}{3} \\ 0 & 0 & 0 & 1 & 5 \end{bmatrix} \rightarrow \begin{bmatrix} 1 & 0 & 0 & 0 & 3 \\ 0 & 1 & 0 & 0 & -4 \\ 0 & 0 & 1 & 0 & 0 \\ 0 & 0 & 0 & 1 & 5 \end{bmatrix}$$

$$R_1 = -r_3 + r_1 \qquad R_4 = -\frac{1}{5}r_4 \qquad R_1 = -\frac{1}{3}r_4 + r_1$$
$$R_4 = 6r_3 + r_4 \qquad\qquad\qquad\qquad R_2 = -r_4 + r_2$$
$$R_3 = \frac{1}{3}r_4 + r_3$$

The solution is $a = 3$, $b = -4$, $c = 0$, $d = 5$; so the equation is $f(x) = 3x^3 - 4x^2 + 5$.

73. Let $x =$ the number of servings of salmon steak.
Let $y =$ the number of servings of baked eggs.
Let $z =$ the number of servings of acorn squash.
Protein equation: $30x + 15y + 3z = 78$
Carbohydrate equation: $20x + 2y + 25z = 59$
Vitamin A equation: $2x + 20y + 32z = 75$
Set up a matrix and solve:

$$\begin{bmatrix} 30 & 15 & 3 & 78 \\ 20 & 2 & 25 & 59 \\ 2 & 20 & 32 & 75 \end{bmatrix} \rightarrow \begin{bmatrix} 2 & 20 & 32 & 75 \\ 20 & 2 & 25 & 59 \\ 30 & 15 & 3 & 78 \end{bmatrix} \rightarrow \begin{bmatrix} 1 & 10 & 16 & 37.5 \\ 20 & 2 & 25 & 59 \\ 30 & 15 & 3 & 78 \end{bmatrix}$$

Interchange r_3 and r_1 $R_1 = \frac{1}{2}r_1$

$$\rightarrow \begin{bmatrix} 1 & 10 & 16 & 37.5 \\ 0 & -198 & -295 & -691 \\ 0 & -285 & -477 & -1047 \end{bmatrix} \rightarrow \begin{bmatrix} 1 & 10 & 16 & 37.5 \\ 0 & -198 & -295 & -691 \\ 0 & 0 & -\frac{3457}{66} & -\frac{3457}{66} \end{bmatrix}$$

$$R_2 = -20r_1 + r_2 \qquad\qquad R_3 = -\frac{95}{66}r_2 + r_3$$
$$R_3 = -30r_1 + r_3$$

$$\rightarrow \begin{bmatrix} 1 & 10 & 16 & 37.5 \\ 0 & -198 & -295 & -691 \\ 0 & 0 & 1 & 1 \end{bmatrix}$$

$$R_3 = -\frac{66}{3457}r_3$$

Substitute $z = 1$ and solve:

$$-198y - 295(1) = -691 \qquad\qquad x + 10(2) + 16(1) = 37.5$$
$$-198y = -396 \qquad\qquad\qquad x + 36 = 37.5$$
$$y = 2 \qquad\qquad\qquad\qquad x = 1.5$$

The dietitian should serve 1.5 servings of salmon steak, 2 servings of baked eggs, and 1 serving of acorn squash.

75. Let $x =$ the amount invested in Treasury bills.
Let $y =$ the amount invested in Treasury bonds.
Let $z =$ the amount invested in corporate bonds.
Total investment equation: $x + y + z = 10000$
Annual income equation: $0.06x + 0.07y + 0.08z = 680$

Condition on investment equation: $z = \frac{1}{2}x$

Set up a matrix and solve:

$$\begin{bmatrix} 1 & 1 & 1 & | & 10000 \\ 0.06 & 0.07 & 0.08 & | & 680 \\ 1 & 0 & -2 & | & 0 \end{bmatrix} \rightarrow \begin{bmatrix} 1 & 1 & 1 & | & 10000 \\ 0 & 0.01 & 0.02 & | & 80 \\ 0 & -1 & -3 & | & -10000 \end{bmatrix} \rightarrow \begin{bmatrix} 1 & 1 & 1 & | & 10000 \\ 0 & 1 & 2 & | & 8000 \\ 0 & -1 & -3 & | & -10000 \end{bmatrix}$$

$$R_2 = -0.06\,r_1 + r_2 \qquad\qquad R_2 = 100r_2$$
$$R_3 = -r_1 + r_3$$

$$\rightarrow \begin{bmatrix} 1 & 0 & -1 & | & 2000 \\ 0 & 1 & 2 & | & 8000 \\ 0 & 0 & -1 & | & -2000 \end{bmatrix} \rightarrow \begin{bmatrix} 1 & 0 & -1 & | & 2000 \\ 0 & 1 & 2 & | & 8000 \\ 0 & 0 & 1 & | & 2000 \end{bmatrix} \rightarrow \begin{bmatrix} 1 & 0 & 0 & | & 4000 \\ 0 & 1 & 0 & | & 4000 \\ 0 & 0 & 1 & | & 2000 \end{bmatrix}$$

$$R_1 = -r_2 + r_1 \qquad R_3 = -r_3 \qquad R_1 = r_3 + r_1$$
$$R_3 = r_2 + r_3 \qquad\qquad\qquad R_2 = -2r_3 + r_2$$

Carletta should invest \$4000 in Treasury bills, \$4000 in Treasury bonds, and \$2000 in corporate bonds.

77. Let x = the number of Deltas produced.
     Let y = the number of Betas produced.
     Let z = the number of Sigmas produced.
     Painting equation: $10x + 16y + 8z = 240$
     Drying equation: $3x + 5y + 2z = 69$
     Polishing equation: $2x + 3y + z = 41$
     Set up a matrix and solve:

$$\begin{bmatrix} 10 & 16 & 8 & | & 240 \\ 3 & 5 & 2 & | & 69 \\ 2 & 3 & 1 & | & 41 \end{bmatrix} \rightarrow \begin{bmatrix} 1 & 1 & 2 & | & 33 \\ 3 & 5 & 2 & | & 69 \\ 2 & 3 & 1 & | & 41 \end{bmatrix} \rightarrow \begin{bmatrix} 1 & 1 & 2 & | & 33 \\ 0 & 2 & -4 & | & -30 \\ 0 & 1 & -3 & | & -25 \end{bmatrix} \rightarrow \begin{bmatrix} 1 & 1 & 2 & | & 33 \\ 0 & 1 & -2 & | & -15 \\ 0 & 1 & -3 & | & -25 \end{bmatrix}$$

$$R_1 = -3r_2 + r_1 \qquad R_2 = -3r_1 + r_2 \qquad R_2 = \tfrac{1}{2}r_2$$
$$R_3 = -2r_1 + r_3$$

$$\rightarrow \begin{bmatrix} 1 & 0 & 4 & | & 48 \\ 0 & 1 & -2 & | & -15 \\ 0 & 0 & -1 & | & -10 \end{bmatrix} \rightarrow \begin{bmatrix} 1 & 0 & 4 & | & 48 \\ 0 & 1 & -2 & | & -15 \\ 0 & 0 & 1 & | & 10 \end{bmatrix} \rightarrow \begin{bmatrix} 1 & 0 & 0 & | & 8 \\ 0 & 1 & 0 & | & 5 \\ 0 & 0 & 1 & | & 10 \end{bmatrix}$$

$$R_1 = -r_2 + r_1 \qquad R_3 = -r_3 \qquad R_1 = -4r_3 + r_1$$
$$R_3 = -r_2 + r_3 \qquad\qquad\qquad R_2 = 2r_3 + r_2$$

The company should produce 8 Deltas, 5 Betas, and 10 Sigmas.

79. Rewrite the system as set up and solve the matrix:

$$\begin{cases} -4 + 8 - 2I_2 = 0 \\ 8 = 5I_4 + I_1 \\ 4 = 3I_3 + I_1 \\ I_3 + I_4 = I_1 \end{cases} \rightarrow \begin{cases} 2I_2 = 4 \\ I_1 + 5I_4 = 8 \\ I_1 + 3I_3 = 4 \\ I_1 - I_3 - I_4 = 0 \end{cases}$$

$$\begin{bmatrix} 0 & 2 & 0 & 0 & | & 4 \\ 1 & 0 & 0 & 5 & | & 8 \\ 1 & 0 & 3 & 0 & | & 4 \\ 1 & 0 & -1 & -1 & | & 0 \end{bmatrix} \rightarrow \begin{bmatrix} 1 & 0 & 0 & 5 & | & 8 \\ 0 & 2 & 0 & 0 & | & 4 \\ 1 & 0 & 3 & 0 & | & 4 \\ 1 & 0 & -1 & -1 & | & 0 \end{bmatrix} \rightarrow \begin{bmatrix} 1 & 0 & 0 & 5 & | & 8 \\ 0 & 1 & 0 & 0 & | & 2 \\ 0 & 0 & 3 & -5 & | & -4 \\ 0 & 0 & -1 & -6 & | & -8 \end{bmatrix}$$

Interchange r_2 and r_1 $R_2 = \frac{1}{2}r_2$
$R_3 = -r_1 + r_3$
$R_4 = -r_1 + r_4$

$$\rightarrow \begin{bmatrix} 1 & 0 & 0 & 5 & | & 8 \\ 0 & 1 & 0 & 0 & | & 2 \\ 0 & 0 & -1 & -6 & | & -8 \\ 0 & 0 & 3 & -5 & | & -4 \end{bmatrix} \rightarrow \begin{bmatrix} 1 & 0 & 0 & 5 & | & 8 \\ 0 & 1 & 0 & 0 & | & 2 \\ 0 & 0 & 1 & 6 & | & 8 \\ 0 & 0 & 0 & -23 & | & -28 \end{bmatrix} \rightarrow \begin{bmatrix} 1 & 0 & 0 & 5 & | & 8 \\ 0 & 1 & 0 & 0 & | & 2 \\ 0 & 0 & 1 & 6 & | & 8 \\ 0 & 0 & 0 & 1 & | & \frac{28}{23} \end{bmatrix}$$

Interchange r_3 and r_4 $R_3 = -r_3$ $R_4 = -\frac{1}{23}r_4$
$R_4 = -3r_3 + r_4$

$$\rightarrow \begin{bmatrix} 1 & 0 & 0 & 0 & | & \frac{44}{23} \\ 0 & 1 & 0 & 0 & | & 2 \\ 0 & 0 & 1 & 0 & | & \frac{16}{23} \\ 0 & 0 & 0 & 1 & | & \frac{28}{23} \end{bmatrix}$$

$R_1 = -5r_4 + r_1$
$R_3 = -6r_4 + r_3$

The solution is $I_1 = \dfrac{44}{23},\ I_2 = 2,\ I_3 = \dfrac{16}{23},\ I_4 = \dfrac{28}{23}.$

81.   Let x = the amount invested in Treasury bills.
Let y = the amount invested in Treasury bonds.
Let z = the amount invested in corporate bonds.
(a)   Total investment equation: $x + y + z = 20000$
Annual income equation: $0.07x + 0.09y + 0.11z = 2000$
Set up a matrix and solve:

$$\begin{bmatrix} 1 & 1 & 1 & | & 20000 \\ .07 & .09 & .11 & | & 2000 \end{bmatrix} \rightarrow \begin{bmatrix} 1 & 1 & 1 & | & 20000 \\ 7 & 9 & 11 & | & 200000 \end{bmatrix} \rightarrow \begin{bmatrix} 1 & 1 & 1 & | & 20000 \\ 0 & 2 & 4 & | & 60000 \end{bmatrix}$$

$R_2 = 100r_2$ $R_2 = r_2 - 7r_1$

$$\rightarrow \begin{bmatrix} 1 & 1 & 1 & | & 20000 \\ 0 & 1 & 2 & | & 30000 \end{bmatrix} \rightarrow \begin{bmatrix} 1 & 0 & -1 & | & -10000 \\ 0 & 1 & 2 & | & 30000 \end{bmatrix}$$

$R_2 = \frac{1}{2}r_2$ $R_1 = r_1 - r_2$

The matrix in the last step represents the system $\begin{cases} x - z = -10000 \\ y + 2z = 30000 \end{cases}$

Therefore the solution is

$x = -10000 + z;\ y = 30000 - 2z;\ z$ is any real number

Possible investment strategies:

	Amount invested at	
7%	9%	11%
0	10000	10000
1000	8000	11000
2000	6000	12000
3000	4000	13000
4000	2000	14000
5000	0	15000

(b)   Total investment equation: $x + y + z = 25000$
       Annual income equation: $0.07x + 0.09y + 0.11z = 2000$
       Set up a matrix and solve:

$$\begin{bmatrix} 1 & 1 & 1 & 25000 \\ .07 & .09 & .11 & 2000 \end{bmatrix} \rightarrow \begin{bmatrix} 1 & 1 & 1 & 25000 \\ 7 & 9 & 11 & 200000 \end{bmatrix} \rightarrow \begin{bmatrix} 1 & 1 & 1 & 25000 \\ 0 & 2 & 4 & 25000 \end{bmatrix}$$

$$\qquad\qquad R_2 = 100r_2 \qquad\qquad R_2 = r_2 - 7r_1$$

$$\rightarrow \begin{bmatrix} 1 & 1 & 1 & 25000 \\ 0 & 1 & 2 & 12500 \end{bmatrix} \rightarrow \begin{bmatrix} 1 & 0 & -1 & 12500 \\ 0 & 1 & 2 & 12500 \end{bmatrix}$$

$$\qquad R_2 = \tfrac{1}{2}r_2 \qquad\qquad R_1 = r_1 - r_2$$

The matrix in the last step represents the system $\begin{cases} x - z = 12500 \\ y + 2z = 12500 \end{cases}$

Therefore the solution is

$$x = 12500 + z, \ \ y = 12500 - 2z, \ \ z \text{ is any real number}$$

Possible investment strategies:

	Amount invested at	
7%	9%	11%
12500	12500	0
14500	8500	2000
16500	4500	4000
18750	0	6250

(c)   Total investment equation: $x + y + z = 30000$
       Annual income equation: $0.07x + 0.09y + 0.11z = 2000$
       Set up a matrix and solve:

$$\begin{bmatrix} 1 & 1 & 1 & 30000 \\ .07 & .09 & .11 & 2000 \end{bmatrix} \rightarrow \begin{bmatrix} 1 & 1 & 1 & 30000 \\ 7 & 9 & 11 & 200000 \end{bmatrix} \rightarrow \begin{bmatrix} 1 & 1 & 1 & 30000 \\ 0 & 2 & 4 & -10000 \end{bmatrix}$$

$$\qquad\qquad R_2 = 100r_2 \qquad\qquad R_1 = r_2 - 7r_1$$

$$\rightarrow \begin{bmatrix} 1 & 1 & 1 & 30000 \\ 0 & 1 & 2 & -5000 \end{bmatrix} \rightarrow \begin{bmatrix} 1 & 0 & -1 & 35000 \\ 0 & 1 & 2 & -5000 \end{bmatrix}$$

$$\qquad R_2 = \tfrac{1}{2}r_2 \qquad\qquad R_1 = r_1 - r_2$$

The matrix in the last step represents the system $\begin{cases} x - z = 35000 \\ y + 2z = -5000 \end{cases}$

Therefore the solution is

$$x = 35000 + z; \ y = -5000 - 2z; \ z \text{ is any real number}$$

One possible investment strategy

Amount invested at		
7%	9%	11%
30000	0	0

This will yield ($30000)(.07) = $2100, which is more than the required income.

83. Let $x =$ the amount of liquid 1.
Let $y =$ the amount of liquid 2.
Let $z =$ the amount of liquid 3.
$$.20x + .40y + .30z = 40 \ \text{Vitamin C}$$
$$.30x + .20y + .50z = 30 \ \text{Vitamin D}$$
multiplying each equation by 10 yields
$$2x + 4y + 3z = 400$$
$$3x + 2y + 5z = 300$$

Set up a matrix and solve: $\begin{bmatrix} 2 & 4 & 3 & | & 400 \\ 3 & 2 & 5 & | & 300 \end{bmatrix} \rightarrow \begin{bmatrix} 1 & 2 & \frac{3}{2} & | & 200 \\ 3 & 2 & 5 & | & 300 \end{bmatrix} \rightarrow \begin{bmatrix} 1 & 2 & \frac{3}{2} & | & 200 \\ 0 & -4 & \frac{1}{2} & | & -300 \end{bmatrix}$

$$R_1 = \tfrac{1}{2} r_1 \qquad\qquad R_2 = r_2 - 3r_1$$

$$\rightarrow \begin{bmatrix} 1 & 2 & \frac{3}{2} & | & 200 \\ 0 & 1 & -\frac{1}{8} & | & 75 \end{bmatrix} \rightarrow \begin{bmatrix} 1 & 0 & \frac{7}{4} & | & 50 \\ 0 & 1 & -\frac{1}{8} & | & 75 \end{bmatrix}$$

$$R_2 = -\tfrac{1}{4} r_2 \qquad\qquad R_1 = r_1 - 2r_2$$

The matrix in the last step represents the system $\begin{cases} x + \dfrac{7}{4}z = 50 \\[2mm] y - \dfrac{1}{8}z = 75 \end{cases}$

Therefore the solution is

$$x = 50 - \frac{7}{4}z; \ y = 75 + \frac{1}{8}z; \ z \text{ is any real number}$$

Possible combinations:

Liquid 1	Liquid 2	Liquid 3
50mg	75mg	0mg
36mg	76mg	8mg
22mg	77mg	16mg
8mg	78mg	24mg

85 – 87. Answers will vary.

Chapter **8**

Systems of Equations and Inequalities

8.4   Systems of Linear Equations: Determinants

1.   Evaluating the determinant:
$$\begin{vmatrix} 3 & 1 \\ 4 & 2 \end{vmatrix} = 3(2) - 4(1) = 6 - 4 = 2$$

3.   Evaluating the determinant:
$$\begin{vmatrix} 6 & 4 \\ -1 & 3 \end{vmatrix} = 6(3) - (-1)(4) = 18 + 4 = 22$$

5.   Evaluating the determinant:
$$\begin{vmatrix} -3 & -1 \\ 4 & 2 \end{vmatrix} = -3(2) - 4(-1) = -6 + 4 = -2$$

7.   Evaluating the determinant:
$$\begin{vmatrix} 3 & 4 & 2 \\ 1 & -1 & 5 \\ 1 & 2 & -2 \end{vmatrix} = 3\begin{vmatrix} -1 & 5 \\ 2 & -2 \end{vmatrix} - 4\begin{vmatrix} 1 & 5 \\ 1 & -2 \end{vmatrix} + 2\begin{vmatrix} 1 & -1 \\ 1 & 2 \end{vmatrix}$$

$$= 3\big[(-1)(-2) - 2(5)\big] - 4\big[1(-2) - 1(5)\big] + 2\big[1(2) - 1(-1)\big]$$
$$= 3(2 - 10) - 4(-2 - 5) + 2(2 + 1)$$
$$= 3(-8) - 4(-7) + 2(3) = -24 + 28 + 6 = 10$$

9.   Evaluating the determinant:
$$\begin{vmatrix} 4 & -1 & 2 \\ 6 & -1 & 0 \\ 1 & -3 & 4 \end{vmatrix} = 4\begin{vmatrix} -1 & 0 \\ -3 & 4 \end{vmatrix} - (-1)\begin{vmatrix} 6 & 0 \\ 1 & 4 \end{vmatrix} + 2\begin{vmatrix} 6 & -1 \\ 1 & -3 \end{vmatrix}$$

$$= 4\big[-1(4) - 0(-3)\big] + 1\big[6(4) - 1(0)\big] + 2\big[6(-3) - 1(-1)\big]$$
$$= 4(-4) + 1(24) + 2(-17) = -16 + 24 - 34 = -26$$

11. Set up and evaluate the determinants to use Cramer's Rule:

$$\begin{cases} x + y = 8 \\ x - y = 4 \end{cases}$$

$$D = \begin{vmatrix} 1 & 1 \\ 1 & -1 \end{vmatrix} = 1(-1) - 1(1) = -1 - 1 = -2$$

$$D_x = \begin{vmatrix} 8 & 1 \\ 4 & -1 \end{vmatrix} = 8(-1) - 4(1) = -8 - 4 = -12$$

$$D_y = \begin{vmatrix} 1 & 8 \\ 1 & 4 \end{vmatrix} = 1(4) - 1(8) = 4 - 8 = -4$$

Find the solutions by Cramer's Rule:

$$x = \frac{D_x}{D} = \frac{-12}{-2} = 6 \qquad y = \frac{D_y}{D} = \frac{-4}{-2} = 2$$

13. Set up and evaluate the determinants to use Cramer's Rule:

$$\begin{cases} 5x - y = 13 \\ 2x + 3y = 12 \end{cases}$$

$$D = \begin{vmatrix} 5 & -1 \\ 2 & 3 \end{vmatrix} = 5(3) - 2(-1) = 15 + 2 = 17$$

$$D_x = \begin{vmatrix} 13 & -1 \\ 12 & 3 \end{vmatrix} = 13(3) - 12(-1) = 39 + 12 = 51$$

$$D_y = \begin{vmatrix} 5 & 13 \\ 2 & 12 \end{vmatrix} = 5(12) - 2(13) = 60 - 26 = 34$$

Find the solutions by Cramer's Rule:

$$x = \frac{D_x}{D} = \frac{51}{17} = 3 \qquad y = \frac{D_y}{D} = \frac{34}{17} = 2$$

15. Set up and evaluate the determinants to use Cramer's Rule:

$$\begin{cases} 3x & = 24 \\ x + 2y = & 0 \end{cases}$$

$$D = \begin{vmatrix} 3 & 0 \\ 1 & 2 \end{vmatrix} = 6 - 0 = 6$$

$$D_x = \begin{vmatrix} 24 & 0 \\ 0 & 2 \end{vmatrix} = 48 - 0 = 48$$

$$D_y = \begin{vmatrix} 3 & 24 \\ 1 & 0 \end{vmatrix} = 0 - 24 = -24$$

Find the solutions by Cramer's Rule:

$$x = \frac{D_x}{D} = \frac{48}{6} = 8 \qquad y = \frac{D_y}{D} = \frac{-24}{6} = -4$$

17. Set up and evaluate the determinants to use Cramer's Rule:
$$\begin{cases} 3x - 6y = 24 \\ 5x + 4y = 12 \end{cases}$$

$$D = \begin{vmatrix} 3 & -6 \\ 5 & 4 \end{vmatrix} = 12 - (-30) = 42$$

$$D_x = \begin{vmatrix} 24 & -6 \\ 12 & 4 \end{vmatrix} = 96 - (-72) = 168$$

$$D_y = \begin{vmatrix} 3 & 24 \\ 5 & 12 \end{vmatrix} = 36 - 120 = -84$$

Find the solutions by Cramer's Rule:
$$x = \frac{D_x}{D} = \frac{168}{42} = 4 \qquad y = \frac{D_y}{D} = \frac{-84}{42} = -2$$

19. Set up and evaluate the determinants to use Cramer's Rule:
$$\begin{cases} 3x - 2y = 4 \\ 6x - 4y = 0 \end{cases}$$

$$D = \begin{vmatrix} 3 & -2 \\ 6 & -4 \end{vmatrix} = -12 - (-12) = 0$$

Since $D = 0$, Cramer's Rule does not apply.

21. Set up and evaluate the determinants to use Cramer's Rule:
$$\begin{cases} 2x - 4y = -2 \\ 3x + 2y = 3 \end{cases}$$

$$D = \begin{vmatrix} 2 & -4 \\ 3 & 2 \end{vmatrix} = 4 - (-12) = 16$$

$$D_x = \begin{vmatrix} -2 & -4 \\ 3 & 2 \end{vmatrix} = -4 - (-12) = 8$$

$$D_y = \begin{vmatrix} 2 & -2 \\ 3 & 3 \end{vmatrix} = 6 - (-6) = 12$$

Find the solutions by Cramer's Rule:
$$x = \frac{D_x}{D} = \frac{8}{16} = \frac{1}{2} \qquad y = \frac{D_y}{D} = \frac{12}{16} = \frac{3}{4}$$

23. Set up and evaluate the determinants to use Cramer's Rule:
$$\begin{cases} 2x - 3y = -1 \\ 10x + 10y = 5 \end{cases}$$

$$D = \begin{vmatrix} 2 & -3 \\ 10 & 10 \end{vmatrix} = 20 - (-30) = 50$$

$$D_x = \begin{vmatrix} -1 & -3 \\ 5 & 10 \end{vmatrix} = -10 - (-15) = 5$$

$$D_y = \begin{vmatrix} 2 & -1 \\ 10 & 5 \end{vmatrix} = 10 - (-10) = 20$$

Find the solutions by Cramer's Rule:
$$x = \frac{D_x}{D} = \frac{5}{50} = \frac{1}{10} \qquad y = \frac{D_y}{D} = \frac{20}{50} = \frac{2}{5}$$

25. Set up and evaluate the determinants to use Cramer's Rule:

$$\begin{cases} 2x + 3y = 6 \\ x - y = \dfrac{1}{2} \end{cases}$$

$$D = \begin{vmatrix} 2 & 3 \\ 1 & -1 \end{vmatrix} = -2 - 3 = -5$$

$$D_x = \begin{vmatrix} 6 & 3 \\ \frac{1}{2} & -1 \end{vmatrix} = -6 - \frac{3}{2} = -\frac{15}{2}$$

$$D_y = \begin{vmatrix} 2 & 6 \\ 1 & \frac{1}{2} \end{vmatrix} = 1 - 6 = -5$$

Find the solutions by Cramer's Rule:

$$x = \frac{D_x}{D} = \frac{\left(-\dfrac{15}{2}\right)}{-5} = \frac{3}{2} \qquad y = \frac{D_y}{D} = \frac{-5}{-5} = 1$$

27. Set up and evaluate the determinants to use Cramer's Rule:

$$\begin{cases} 3x - 5y = 3 \\ 15x + 5y = 21 \end{cases}$$

$$D = \begin{vmatrix} 3 & -5 \\ 15 & 5 \end{vmatrix} = 15 - (-75) = 90$$

$$D_x = \begin{vmatrix} 3 & -5 \\ 21 & 5 \end{vmatrix} = 15 - (-105) = 120$$

$$D_y = \begin{vmatrix} 3 & 3 \\ 15 & 21 \end{vmatrix} = 63 - 45 = 18$$

Find the solutions by Cramer's Rule:

$$x = \frac{D_x}{D} = \frac{120}{90} = \frac{4}{3} \qquad y = \frac{D_y}{D} = \frac{18}{90} = \frac{1}{5}$$

29. Set up and evaluate the determinants to use Cramer's Rule:

$$\begin{cases} x + y - z = 6 \\ 3x - 2y + z = -5 \\ x + 3y - 2z = 14 \end{cases}$$

$$D = \begin{vmatrix} 1 & 1 & -1 \\ 3 & -2 & 1 \\ 1 & 3 & -2 \end{vmatrix} = 1 \begin{vmatrix} -2 & 1 \\ 3 & -2 \end{vmatrix} - 1 \begin{vmatrix} 3 & 1 \\ 1 & -2 \end{vmatrix} + (-1) \begin{vmatrix} 3 & -2 \\ 1 & 3 \end{vmatrix}$$

$$= 1(4 - 3) - 1(-6 - 1) - 1(9 + 2) = 1 + 7 - 11 = -3$$

$$D_x = \begin{vmatrix} 6 & 1 & -1 \\ -5 & -2 & 1 \\ 14 & 3 & -2 \end{vmatrix} = 6 \begin{vmatrix} -2 & 1 \\ 3 & -2 \end{vmatrix} - 1 \begin{vmatrix} -5 & 1 \\ 14 & -2 \end{vmatrix} + (-1) \begin{vmatrix} -5 & -2 \\ 14 & 3 \end{vmatrix}$$

$$= 6(4 - 3) - 1(10 - 14) - 1(-15 + 28) = 6 + 4 - 13 = -3$$

$$D_y = \begin{vmatrix} 1 & 6 & -1 \\ 3 & -5 & 1 \\ 1 & 14 & -2 \end{vmatrix} = 1\begin{vmatrix} -5 & 1 \\ 14 & -2 \end{vmatrix} - 6\begin{vmatrix} 3 & 1 \\ 1 & -2 \end{vmatrix} + (-1)\begin{vmatrix} 3 & -5 \\ 1 & 14 \end{vmatrix}$$

$$= 1(10-14) - 6(-6-1) - 1(42+5) = -4 + 42 - 47 = -9$$

$$D_z = \begin{vmatrix} 1 & 1 & 6 \\ 3 & -2 & -5 \\ 1 & 3 & 14 \end{vmatrix} = 1\begin{vmatrix} -2 & -5 \\ 3 & 14 \end{vmatrix} - 1\begin{vmatrix} 3 & -5 \\ 1 & 14 \end{vmatrix} + 6\begin{vmatrix} 3 & -2 \\ 1 & 3 \end{vmatrix}$$

$$= 1(-28+15) - 1(42+5) + 6(9+2) = -13 - 47 + 66 = 6$$

Find the solutions by Cramer's Rule:

$$x = \frac{D_x}{D} = \frac{-3}{-3} = 1 \qquad y = \frac{D_y}{D} = \frac{-9}{-3} = 3 \qquad z = \frac{D_z}{D} = \frac{6}{-3} = -2$$

31.   Set up and evaluate the determinants to use Cramer's Rule:

$$\begin{cases} x + 2y - z = -3 \\ 2x - 4y + z = -7 \\ -2x + 2y - 3z = 4 \end{cases}$$

$$D = \begin{vmatrix} 1 & 2 & -1 \\ 2 & -4 & 1 \\ -2 & 2 & -3 \end{vmatrix} = 1\begin{vmatrix} -4 & 1 \\ 2 & -3 \end{vmatrix} - 2\begin{vmatrix} 2 & 1 \\ -2 & -3 \end{vmatrix} + (-1)\begin{vmatrix} 2 & -4 \\ -2 & 2 \end{vmatrix}$$

$$= 1(12-2) - 2(-6+2) - 1(4-8) = 10 + 8 + 4 = 22$$

$$D_x = \begin{vmatrix} -3 & 2 & -1 \\ -7 & -4 & 1 \\ 4 & 2 & -3 \end{vmatrix} = -3\begin{vmatrix} -4 & 1 \\ 2 & -3 \end{vmatrix} - 2\begin{vmatrix} -7 & 1 \\ 4 & -3 \end{vmatrix} + (-1)\begin{vmatrix} -7 & -4 \\ 4 & 2 \end{vmatrix}$$

$$= -3(12-2) - 2(21-4) - 1(-14+16) = -30 - 34 - 2 = -66$$

$$D_y = \begin{vmatrix} 1 & -3 & -1 \\ 2 & -7 & 1 \\ -2 & 4 & -3 \end{vmatrix} = 1\begin{vmatrix} -7 & 1 \\ 4 & -3 \end{vmatrix} - (-3)\begin{vmatrix} 2 & 1 \\ -2 & -3 \end{vmatrix} + (-1)\begin{vmatrix} 2 & -7 \\ -2 & 4 \end{vmatrix}$$

$$= 1(21-4) + 3(-6+2) - 1(8-14) = 17 - 12 + 6 = 11$$

$$D_z = \begin{vmatrix} 1 & 2 & -3 \\ 2 & -4 & -7 \\ -2 & 2 & 4 \end{vmatrix} = 1\begin{vmatrix} -4 & -7 \\ 2 & 4 \end{vmatrix} - 2\begin{vmatrix} 2 & -7 \\ -2 & 4 \end{vmatrix} + (-3)\begin{vmatrix} 2 & -4 \\ -2 & 2 \end{vmatrix}$$

$$= 1(-16+14) - 2(8-14) - 3(4-8) = -2 + 12 + 12 = 22$$

Find the solutions by Cramer's Rule:

$$x = \frac{D_x}{D} = \frac{-66}{22} = -3 \qquad y = \frac{D_y}{D} = \frac{11}{22} = \frac{1}{2} \qquad z = \frac{D_z}{D} = \frac{22}{22} = 1$$

33. Set up and evaluate the determinants to use Cramer's Rule:

$$\begin{cases} x - 2y + 3z = 1 \\ 3x + y - 2z = 0 \\ 2x - 4y + 6z = 2 \end{cases}$$

$$D = \begin{vmatrix} 1 & -2 & 3 \\ 3 & 1 & -2 \\ 2 & -4 & 6 \end{vmatrix} = 1\begin{vmatrix} 1 & -2 \\ -4 & 6 \end{vmatrix} - (-2)\begin{vmatrix} 3 & -2 \\ 2 & 6 \end{vmatrix} + 3\begin{vmatrix} 3 & 1 \\ 2 & -4 \end{vmatrix}$$

$$= 1(6 - 8) + 2(18 + 4) + 3(-12 - 2) = -2 + 44 - 42 = 0$$

Since $D = 0$, Cramer's Rule does not apply.

35. Set up and evaluate the determinants to use Cramer's Rule:

$$\begin{cases} x + 2y - z = 0 \\ 2x - 4y + z = 0 \\ -2x + 2y - 3z = 0 \end{cases}$$

$$D = \begin{vmatrix} 1 & 2 & -1 \\ 2 & -4 & 1 \\ -2 & 2 & -3 \end{vmatrix} = 1\begin{vmatrix} -4 & 1 \\ 2 & -3 \end{vmatrix} - 2\begin{vmatrix} 2 & 1 \\ -2 & -3 \end{vmatrix} + (-1)\begin{vmatrix} 2 & -4 \\ -2 & 2 \end{vmatrix}$$

$$= 1(12 - 2) - 2(-6 + 2) - 1(4 - 8) = 10 + 8 + 4 = 22$$

$$D_x = \begin{vmatrix} 0 & 2 & -1 \\ 0 & -4 & 1 \\ 0 & 2 & -3 \end{vmatrix} = 0 \quad \text{(By Theorem 12)}$$

$$D_y = \begin{vmatrix} 1 & 0 & -1 \\ 2 & 0 & 1 \\ -2 & 0 & -3 \end{vmatrix} = 0 \quad \text{(By Theorem 12)}$$

$$D_z = \begin{vmatrix} 1 & 2 & 0 \\ 2 & -4 & 0 \\ -2 & 2 & 0 \end{vmatrix} = 0 \quad \text{(By Theorem 12)}$$

Find the solutions by Cramer's Rule:

$$x = \frac{D_x}{D} = \frac{0}{22} = 0 \qquad y = \frac{D_y}{D} = \frac{0}{22} = 0 \qquad z = \frac{D_z}{D} = \frac{0}{22} = 0$$

37. Set up and evaluate the determinants to use Cramer's Rule:

$$\begin{cases} x - 2y + 3z = 0 \\ 3x + y - 2z = 0 \\ 2x - 4y + 6z = 0 \end{cases}$$

$$D = \begin{vmatrix} 1 & -2 & 3 \\ 3 & 1 & -2 \\ 2 & -4 & 6 \end{vmatrix} = 1\begin{vmatrix} 1 & -2 \\ -4 & 6 \end{vmatrix} - (-2)\begin{vmatrix} 3 & -2 \\ 2 & 6 \end{vmatrix} + 3\begin{vmatrix} 3 & 1 \\ 2 & -4 \end{vmatrix}$$

$$= 1(6 - 8) + 2(18 + 4) + 3(-12 - 2) = -2 + 44 - 42 = 0$$

Since $D = 0$, Cramer's Rule does not apply.

39. Rewrite the system letting $u = \dfrac{1}{x}$ and $v = \dfrac{1}{y}$:

$$\begin{cases} \dfrac{1}{x} + \dfrac{1}{y} = 8 \\ \dfrac{3}{x} - \dfrac{5}{y} = 0 \end{cases} \quad \rightarrow \quad \begin{cases} u + v = 8 \\ 3u - 5v = 0 \end{cases}$$

Set up and evaluate the determinants to use Cramer's Rule:

$$D = \begin{vmatrix} 1 & 1 \\ 3 & -5 \end{vmatrix} = -5 - 3 = -8$$

$$D_u = \begin{vmatrix} 8 & 1 \\ 0 & -5 \end{vmatrix} = -40 - 0 = -40$$

$$D_v = \begin{vmatrix} 1 & 8 \\ 3 & 0 \end{vmatrix} = 0 - 24 = -24$$

Find the solutions by Cramer's Rule:

$$u = \frac{D_u}{D} = \frac{-40}{-8} = 5 \qquad v = \frac{D_v}{D} = \frac{-24}{-8} = 3$$

The solutions are $x = \dfrac{1}{5}, \; y = \dfrac{1}{3}$

41. Solve for x:

$$\begin{vmatrix} x & x \\ 4 & 3 \end{vmatrix} = 3x - 4x = -x$$

$$-x = 5 \rightarrow x = -5$$

43. Solve for x:

$$\begin{vmatrix} x & 1 & 1 \\ 4 & 3 & 2 \\ -1 & 2 & 5 \end{vmatrix} = x\begin{vmatrix} 3 & 2 \\ 2 & 5 \end{vmatrix} - 1\begin{vmatrix} 4 & 2 \\ -1 & 5 \end{vmatrix} + 1\begin{vmatrix} 4 & 3 \\ -1 & 2 \end{vmatrix}$$

$$= x(15 - 4) - (20 + 2) + (8 + 3) = 11x - 22 + 11 = 11x - 11$$

So, $11x - 11 = 2 \rightarrow 11x = 13 \rightarrow x = \dfrac{13}{11}$

45. Solve for x:

$$\begin{vmatrix} x & 2 & 3 \\ 1 & x & 0 \\ 6 & 1 & -2 \end{vmatrix} = x\begin{vmatrix} x & 0 \\ 1 & -2 \end{vmatrix} - 2\begin{vmatrix} 1 & 0 \\ 6 & -2 \end{vmatrix} + 3\begin{vmatrix} 1 & x \\ 6 & 1 \end{vmatrix}$$

$$= x(-2x - 0) - 2(-2 - 0) + 3(1 - 6x)$$

$$= -2x^2 + 4 + 3 - 18x = -2x^2 - 18x + 7$$

So, $-2x^2 - 18x + 7 = 7$

$$-2x^2 - 18x = 0 \rightarrow -2x(x + 9) = 0 \rightarrow x = 0 \text{ or } x = -9$$

47.   Let $\begin{vmatrix} x & y & z \\ u & v & w \\ 1 & 2 & 3 \end{vmatrix} = 4$

Then $\begin{vmatrix} 1 & 2 & 3 \\ u & v & w \\ x & y & z \end{vmatrix} = -4$ by Theorem 11 --

The value of the determinant changes sign when two rows are interchanged.

Problems 49 – 54 use the Laws for Determinants in reverse order.

49.   Let $\begin{vmatrix} x & y & z \\ u & v & w \\ 1 & 2 & 3 \end{vmatrix} = 4$

$$\underbrace{\begin{vmatrix} x & y & z \\ -3 & -6 & -9 \\ u & v & w \end{vmatrix} = -3\begin{vmatrix} x & y & z \\ 1 & 2 & 3 \\ u & v & w \end{vmatrix}}_{\text{Theorem 14}} = \underbrace{-3(-1)\begin{vmatrix} x & y & z \\ u & v & w \\ 1 & 2 & 3 \end{vmatrix}}_{\text{Theorem 11}} = 3(4) = 12$$

51.   Let $\begin{vmatrix} x & y & z \\ u & v & w \\ 1 & 2 & 3 \end{vmatrix} = 4$

$$\underbrace{\begin{vmatrix} 1 & 2 & 3 \\ x-3 & y-6 & z-9 \\ 2u & 2v & 2w \end{vmatrix} = 2\begin{vmatrix} 1 & 2 & 3 \\ x-3 & y-6 & z-9 \\ u & v & w \end{vmatrix}}_{\text{Theorem 14}} = \underbrace{2(-1)\begin{vmatrix} x-3 & y-6 & z-9 \\ 1 & 2 & 3 \\ u & v & w \end{vmatrix}}_{\text{Theorem 11}}$$

$$= \underbrace{2(-1)(-1)\begin{vmatrix} x-3 & y-6 & z-9 \\ u & v & w \\ 1 & 2 & 3 \end{vmatrix}}_{\text{Theorem 11}} = \underbrace{2(-1)(-1)\begin{vmatrix} x & y & z \\ u & v & w \\ 1 & 2 & 3 \end{vmatrix} = 2(-1)(-1)(4) = 8}_{\text{Theorem 15}\ \ (R_1 = -3r_3 + r_1)}$$

53.   Let $\begin{vmatrix} x & y & z \\ u & v & w \\ 1 & 2 & 3 \end{vmatrix} = 4$

$$\underbrace{\begin{vmatrix} 1 & 2 & 3 \\ 2x & 2y & 2z \\ u-1 & v-2 & w-3 \end{vmatrix} = 2\begin{vmatrix} 1 & 2 & 3 \\ x & y & z \\ u-1 & v-2 & w-3 \end{vmatrix}}_{\text{Theorem 14}} = \underbrace{2(-1)\begin{vmatrix} x & y & z \\ 1 & 2 & 3 \\ u-1 & v-2 & w-3 \end{vmatrix}}_{\text{Theorem 11}}$$

$$= \underbrace{2(-1)(-1)\begin{vmatrix} x & y & z \\ u-1 & v-2 & w-3 \\ 1 & 2 & 3 \end{vmatrix}}_{\text{Theorem 11}} = \underbrace{2(-1)(-1)\begin{vmatrix} x & y & z \\ u & v & w \\ 1 & 2 & 3 \end{vmatrix} = 2(-1)(-1)(4) = 8}_{\text{Theorem 15}\ \ (R_2 = -r_3 + r_2)}$$

55.　Expanding the determinant:

$$\begin{vmatrix} x & y & 1 \\ x_1 & y_1 & 1 \\ x_2 & y_2 & 1 \end{vmatrix} = x\begin{vmatrix} y_1 & 1 \\ y_2 & 1 \end{vmatrix} - y\begin{vmatrix} x_1 & 1 \\ x_2 & 1 \end{vmatrix} + 1\begin{vmatrix} x_1 & y_1 \\ x_2 & y_2 \end{vmatrix}$$

$$= x(y_1 - y_2) - y(x_1 - x_2) + (x_1 y_2 - x_2 y_1) = 0$$
$$x(y_1 - y_2) + y(x_2 - x_1) = x_2 y_1 - x_1 y_2$$
$$y(x_2 - x_1) = x_2 y_1 - x_1 y_2 + x(y_2 - y_1)$$
$$y(x_2 - x_1) - y_1(x_2 - x_1) = x_2 y_1 - x_1 y_2 + x(y_2 - y_1) - y_1(x_2 - x_1)$$
$$(x_2 - x_1)(y - y_1) = x(y_2 - y_1) + x_2 y_1 - x_1 y_2 - y_1 x_2 + y_1 x_1$$
$$(x_2 - x_1)(y - y_1) = (y_2 - y_1)x - (y_2 - y_1)x_1$$
$$(x_2 - x_1)(y - y_1) = (y_2 - y_1)(x - x_1)$$
$$(y - y_1) = \frac{(y_2 - y_1)}{(x_2 - x_1)}(x - x_1)$$

57.　Expanding the determinant:

$$\begin{vmatrix} x^2 & x & 1 \\ y^2 & y & 1 \\ z^2 & z & 1 \end{vmatrix} = x^2\begin{vmatrix} y & 1 \\ z & 1 \end{vmatrix} - x\begin{vmatrix} y^2 & 1 \\ z^2 & 1 \end{vmatrix} + 1\begin{vmatrix} y^2 & y \\ z^2 & z \end{vmatrix}$$

$$= x^2(y - z) - x(y^2 - z^2) + 1(y^2 z - z^2 y)$$
$$= x^2(y - z) - x(y - z)(y + z) + yz(y - z)$$
$$= (y - z)\left[x^2 - xy - xz + yz \right]$$
$$= (y - z)\left[x(x - y) - z(x - y) \right]$$
$$= (y - z)(x - y)(x - z)$$

59.　Evaluating the determinant to show the relationship:

$$\begin{vmatrix} a_{13} & a_{12} & a_{11} \\ a_{23} & a_{22} & a_{21} \\ a_{33} & a_{32} & a_{31} \end{vmatrix} = a_{13}\begin{vmatrix} a_{22} & a_{21} \\ a_{32} & a_{31} \end{vmatrix} - a_{12}\begin{vmatrix} a_{23} & a_{21} \\ a_{33} & a_{31} \end{vmatrix} + a_{11}\begin{vmatrix} a_{23} & a_{22} \\ a_{33} & a_{32} \end{vmatrix}$$

$$= a_{13}(a_{22}a_{31} - a_{21}a_{32}) - a_{12}(a_{23}a_{31} - a_{21}a_{33}) + a_{11}(a_{23}a_{32} - a_{22}a_{33})$$
$$= a_{13}a_{22}a_{31} - a_{13}a_{21}a_{32} - a_{12}a_{23}a_{31} + a_{12}a_{21}a_{33} + a_{11}a_{23}a_{32} - a_{11}a_{22}a_{33}$$
$$= -a_{11}a_{22}a_{33} + a_{11}a_{23}a_{32} + a_{12}a_{21}a_{33} - a_{12}a_{23}a_{31} - a_{13}a_{21}a_{32} + a_{13}a_{22}a_{31}$$
$$= -a_{11}(a_{22}a_{33} - a_{23}a_{32}) + a_{12}(a_{21}a_{33} - a_{23}a_{31}) - a_{13}(a_{21}a_{32} - a_{22}a_{31})$$
$$= -a_{11}\begin{vmatrix} a_{22} & a_{23} \\ a_{32} & a_{33} \end{vmatrix} + a_{12}\begin{vmatrix} a_{21} & a_{23} \\ a_{31} & a_{33} \end{vmatrix} - a_{13}\begin{vmatrix} a_{21} & a_{22} \\ a_{31} & a_{32} \end{vmatrix}$$
$$= -\left[a_{11}\begin{vmatrix} a_{22} & a_{23} \\ a_{32} & a_{33} \end{vmatrix} - a_{12}\begin{vmatrix} a_{21} & a_{23} \\ a_{31} & a_{33} \end{vmatrix} + a_{13}\begin{vmatrix} a_{21} & a_{22} \\ a_{31} & a_{32} \end{vmatrix} \right]$$
$$= -\begin{vmatrix} a_{11} & a_{12} & a_{13} \\ a_{21} & a_{22} & a_{23} \\ a_{31} & a_{32} & a_{33} \end{vmatrix}$$

61.   Set up a 3 by 3 determinant in which the first column and third column are the same and evaluate:

$$\begin{vmatrix} a & b & a \\ c & d & c \\ e & f & e \end{vmatrix} = -b \begin{vmatrix} c & c \\ e & e \end{vmatrix} + d \begin{vmatrix} a & a \\ e & e \end{vmatrix} - f \begin{vmatrix} a & a \\ c & c \end{vmatrix}$$

$$= -b(ce - ce) + d(ae - ae) - f(ac - ac) = -b(0) + d(0) - f(0) = 0$$

Systems of Equations and Inequalities

8.5 Matrix Algebra

1. $A + B = \begin{bmatrix} 0 & 3 & -5 \\ 1 & 2 & 6 \end{bmatrix} + \begin{bmatrix} 4 & 1 & 0 \\ -2 & 3 & -2 \end{bmatrix} = \begin{bmatrix} 0+4 & 3+1 & -5+0 \\ 1+(-2) & 2+3 & 6+(-2) \end{bmatrix} = \begin{bmatrix} 4 & 4 & -5 \\ -1 & 5 & 4 \end{bmatrix}$

3. $4A = 4\begin{bmatrix} 0 & 3 & -5 \\ 1 & 2 & 6 \end{bmatrix} = \begin{bmatrix} 4 \cdot 0 & 4 \cdot 3 & 4(-5) \\ 4 \cdot 1 & 4 \cdot 2 & 4 \cdot 6 \end{bmatrix} = \begin{bmatrix} 0 & 12 & -20 \\ 4 & 8 & 24 \end{bmatrix}$

5. $3A - 2B = 3\begin{bmatrix} 0 & 3 & -5 \\ 1 & 2 & 6 \end{bmatrix} - 2\begin{bmatrix} 4 & 1 & 0 \\ -2 & 3 & -2 \end{bmatrix}$

   $= \begin{bmatrix} 0 & 9 & -15 \\ 3 & 6 & 18 \end{bmatrix} - \begin{bmatrix} 8 & 2 & 0 \\ -4 & 6 & -4 \end{bmatrix} = \begin{bmatrix} -8 & 7 & -15 \\ 7 & 0 & 22 \end{bmatrix}$

7. $AC = \begin{bmatrix} 0 & 3 & -5 \\ 1 & 2 & 6 \end{bmatrix} \cdot \begin{bmatrix} 4 & 1 \\ 6 & 2 \\ -2 & 3 \end{bmatrix}$

   $= \begin{bmatrix} 0(4)+3(6)+(-5)(-2) & 0(1)+3(2)+(-5)(3) \\ 1(4)+2(6)+6(-2) & 1(1)+2(2)+6(3) \end{bmatrix} = \begin{bmatrix} 28 & -9 \\ 4 & 23 \end{bmatrix}$

9. $CA = \begin{bmatrix} 4 & 1 \\ 6 & 2 \\ -2 & 3 \end{bmatrix} \cdot \begin{bmatrix} 0 & 3 & -5 \\ 1 & 2 & 6 \end{bmatrix}$

   $= \begin{bmatrix} 4(0)+1(1) & 4(3)+1(2) & 4(-5)+1(6) \\ 6(0)+2(1) & 6(3)+2(2) & 6(-5)+2(6) \\ -2(0)+3(1) & -2(3)+3(2) & -2(-5)+3(6) \end{bmatrix} = \begin{bmatrix} 1 & 14 & -14 \\ 2 & 22 & -18 \\ 3 & 0 & 28 \end{bmatrix}$

11. $C(A + B) = \begin{bmatrix} 4 & 1 \\ 6 & 2 \\ -2 & 3 \end{bmatrix} \left(\begin{bmatrix} 0 & 3 & -5 \\ 1 & 2 & 6 \end{bmatrix} + \begin{bmatrix} 4 & 1 & 0 \\ -2 & 3 & -2 \end{bmatrix} \right)$

    $= \begin{bmatrix} 4 & 1 \\ 6 & 2 \\ -2 & 3 \end{bmatrix} \cdot \begin{bmatrix} 4 & 4 & -5 \\ -1 & 5 & 4 \end{bmatrix} = \begin{bmatrix} 15 & 21 & -16 \\ 22 & 34 & -22 \\ -11 & 7 & 22 \end{bmatrix}$

13. $AC - 3I_2 = \begin{bmatrix} 0 & 3 & -5 \\ 1 & 2 & 6 \end{bmatrix} \cdot \begin{bmatrix} 4 & 1 \\ 6 & 2 \\ -2 & 3 \end{bmatrix} - 3 \begin{bmatrix} 1 & 0 \\ 0 & 1 \end{bmatrix} = \begin{bmatrix} 28 & -9 \\ 4 & 23 \end{bmatrix} - \begin{bmatrix} 3 & 0 \\ 0 & 3 \end{bmatrix} = \begin{bmatrix} 25 & -9 \\ 4 & 20 \end{bmatrix}$

15. $CA - CB = \begin{bmatrix} 4 & 1 \\ 6 & 2 \\ -2 & 3 \end{bmatrix} \cdot \begin{bmatrix} 0 & 3 & -5 \\ 1 & 2 & 6 \end{bmatrix} - \begin{bmatrix} 4 & 1 \\ 6 & 2 \\ -2 & 3 \end{bmatrix} \cdot \begin{bmatrix} 4 & 1 & 0 \\ -2 & 3 & -2 \end{bmatrix}$

$= \begin{bmatrix} 1 & 14 & -14 \\ 2 & 22 & -18 \\ 3 & 0 & 28 \end{bmatrix} - \begin{bmatrix} 14 & 7 & -2 \\ 20 & 12 & -4 \\ -14 & 7 & -6 \end{bmatrix} = \begin{bmatrix} -13 & 7 & -12 \\ -18 & 10 & -14 \\ 17 & -7 & 34 \end{bmatrix}$

17. $\begin{bmatrix} 2 & -2 \\ 1 & 0 \end{bmatrix} \begin{bmatrix} 2 & 1 & 4 & 6 \\ 3 & -1 & 3 & 2 \end{bmatrix}$

$= \begin{bmatrix} 2(2) + (-2)(3) & 2(1) + (-2)(-1) & 2(4) + (-2)(3) & 2(6) + (-2)(2) \\ 1(2) + 0(3) & 1(1) + 0(-1) & 1(4) + 0(3) & 1(6) + 0(2) \end{bmatrix}$

$= \begin{bmatrix} -2 & 4 & 2 & 8 \\ 2 & 1 & 4 & 6 \end{bmatrix}$

19. $\begin{bmatrix} 1 & 0 & 1 \\ 2 & 4 & 1 \\ 3 & 6 & 1 \end{bmatrix} \begin{bmatrix} 1 & 3 \\ 6 & 2 \\ 8 & -1 \end{bmatrix} = \begin{bmatrix} 1(1) + 0(6) + 1(8) & 1(3) + 0(2) + 1(-1) \\ 2(1) + 4(6) + 1(8) & 2(3) + 4(2) + 1(-1) \\ 3(1) + 6(6) + 1(8) & 3(3) + 6(2) + 1(-1) \end{bmatrix} = \begin{bmatrix} 9 & 2 \\ 34 & 13 \\ 47 & 20 \end{bmatrix}$

21. Augment the matrix with the identity and use row operations to find the inverse:

$A = \begin{bmatrix} 2 & 1 \\ 1 & 1 \end{bmatrix} \rightarrow \begin{bmatrix} 2 & 1 & | & 1 & 0 \\ 1 & 1 & | & 0 & 1 \end{bmatrix}$

$\rightarrow \begin{bmatrix} 1 & 1 & | & 0 & 1 \\ 2 & 1 & | & 1 & 0 \end{bmatrix} \rightarrow \begin{bmatrix} 1 & 1 & | & 0 & 1 \\ 0 & -1 & | & 1 & -2 \end{bmatrix} \rightarrow \begin{bmatrix} 1 & 1 & | & 0 & 1 \\ 0 & 1 & | & -1 & 2 \end{bmatrix} \rightarrow \begin{bmatrix} 1 & 0 & | & 1 & -1 \\ 0 & 1 & | & -1 & 2 \end{bmatrix}$

Interchange $R_2 = -2r_1 + r_2$ $R_2 = -r_2$ $R_1 = -r_2 + r_1$
r_1 and r_2

$A^{-1} = \begin{bmatrix} 1 & -1 \\ -1 & 2 \end{bmatrix}$

23. Augment the matrix with the identity and use row operations to find the inverse:

$A = \begin{bmatrix} 6 & 5 \\ 2 & 2 \end{bmatrix} \rightarrow \begin{bmatrix} 6 & 5 & | & 1 & 0 \\ 2 & 2 & | & 0 & 1 \end{bmatrix}$

$\rightarrow \begin{bmatrix} 2 & 2 & | & 0 & 1 \\ 6 & 5 & | & 1 & 0 \end{bmatrix} \rightarrow \begin{bmatrix} 2 & 2 & | & 0 & 1 \\ 0 & -1 & | & 1 & -3 \end{bmatrix} \rightarrow \begin{bmatrix} 1 & 1 & | & 0 & \frac{1}{2} \\ 0 & 1 & | & -1 & 3 \end{bmatrix} \rightarrow \begin{bmatrix} 1 & 0 & | & 1 & -\frac{5}{2} \\ 0 & 1 & | & -1 & 3 \end{bmatrix}$

Interchange $R_2 = -3r_1 + r_2$ $R_1 = \frac{1}{2}r_1$ $R_1 = -r_2 + r_1$
r_1 and r_2 $R_2 = -r_2$

$A^{-1} = \begin{bmatrix} 1 & -2.5 \\ -1 & 3 \end{bmatrix}$

25. Augment the matrix with the identity and use row operations to find the inverse:

$$A = \begin{bmatrix} 2 & 1 \\ a & a \end{bmatrix} \;\rightarrow\; \begin{bmatrix} 2 & 1 & | & 1 & 0 \\ a & a & | & 0 & 1 \end{bmatrix} \text{ where } a \neq 0.$$

$$\rightarrow \begin{bmatrix} 1 & \frac{1}{2} & | & \frac{1}{2} & 0 \\ a & a & | & 0 & 1 \end{bmatrix} \rightarrow \begin{bmatrix} 1 & \frac{1}{2} & | & \frac{1}{2} & 0 \\ 0 & \frac{1}{2}a & | & -\frac{1}{2}a & 1 \end{bmatrix} \rightarrow \begin{bmatrix} 1 & \frac{1}{2} & | & \frac{1}{2} & 0 \\ 0 & 1 & | & -1 & \frac{2}{a} \end{bmatrix} \rightarrow \begin{bmatrix} 1 & 0 & | & 1 & -\frac{1}{a} \\ 0 & 1 & | & -1 & \frac{2}{a} \end{bmatrix}$$

$$R_1 = \tfrac{1}{2}r_1 \qquad\qquad R_2 = -ar_1 + r_2 \qquad R_2 = \left(\tfrac{2}{a}\right)r_2 \qquad\qquad R_1 = -\tfrac{1}{2}r_2 + r_1$$

$$A^{-1} = \begin{bmatrix} 1 & -\frac{1}{a} \\ -1 & \frac{2}{a} \end{bmatrix}$$

27. Augment the matrix with the identity and use row operations to find the inverse:

$$A = \begin{bmatrix} 1 & -1 & 1 \\ 0 & -2 & 1 \\ -2 & -3 & 0 \end{bmatrix} \;\rightarrow\; \begin{bmatrix} 1 & -1 & 1 & | & 1 & 0 & 0 \\ 0 & -2 & 1 & | & 0 & 1 & 0 \\ -2 & -3 & 0 & | & 0 & 0 & 1 \end{bmatrix}$$

$$\rightarrow \begin{bmatrix} 1 & -1 & 1 & | & 1 & 0 & 0 \\ 0 & -2 & 1 & | & 0 & 1 & 0 \\ 0 & -5 & 2 & | & 2 & 0 & 1 \end{bmatrix} \rightarrow \begin{bmatrix} 1 & -1 & 1 & | & 1 & 0 & 0 \\ 0 & 1 & -\frac{1}{2} & | & 0 & -\frac{1}{2} & 0 \\ 0 & -5 & 2 & | & 2 & 0 & 1 \end{bmatrix} \rightarrow \begin{bmatrix} 1 & 0 & \frac{1}{2} & | & 1 & -\frac{1}{2} & 0 \\ 0 & 1 & -\frac{1}{2} & | & 0 & -\frac{1}{2} & 0 \\ 0 & 0 & -\frac{1}{2} & | & 2 & -\frac{5}{2} & 1 \end{bmatrix}$$

$$R_3 = 2r_1 + r_3 \qquad\qquad R_2 = -\tfrac{1}{2}r_2 \qquad\qquad\qquad R_1 = r_2 + r_1$$
$$R_3 = 5r_2 + r_3$$

$$\rightarrow \begin{bmatrix} 1 & 0 & \frac{1}{2} & | & 1 & -\frac{1}{2} & 0 \\ 0 & 1 & -\frac{1}{2} & | & 0 & -\frac{1}{2} & 0 \\ 0 & 0 & 1 & | & -4 & 5 & -2 \end{bmatrix} \rightarrow \begin{bmatrix} 1 & 0 & 0 & | & 3 & -3 & 1 \\ 0 & 1 & 0 & | & -2 & 2 & -1 \\ 0 & 0 & 1 & | & -4 & 5 & -2 \end{bmatrix}$$

$$R_3 = -2r_3 \qquad\qquad\qquad R_1 = -\tfrac{1}{2}r_3 + r_1$$
$$R_2 = \tfrac{1}{2}r_3 + r_2$$

$$A^{-1} = \begin{bmatrix} 3 & -3 & 1 \\ -2 & 2 & -1 \\ -4 & 5 & -2 \end{bmatrix}$$

29. Augment the matrix with the identity and use row operations to find the inverse:

$$A = \begin{bmatrix} 1 & 1 & 1 \\ 3 & 2 & -1 \\ 3 & 1 & 2 \end{bmatrix} \;\rightarrow\; \begin{bmatrix} 1 & 1 & 1 & | & 1 & 0 & 0 \\ 3 & 2 & -1 & | & 0 & 1 & 0 \\ 3 & 1 & 2 & | & 0 & 0 & 1 \end{bmatrix}$$

$$\rightarrow \begin{bmatrix} 1 & 1 & 1 & | & 1 & 0 & 0 \\ 0 & -1 & -4 & | & -3 & 1 & 0 \\ 0 & -2 & -1 & | & -3 & 0 & 1 \end{bmatrix} \rightarrow \begin{bmatrix} 1 & 1 & 1 & | & 1 & 0 & 0 \\ 0 & 1 & 4 & | & 3 & -1 & 0 \\ 0 & -2 & -1 & | & -3 & 0 & 1 \end{bmatrix} \rightarrow \begin{bmatrix} 1 & 0 & -3 & | & -2 & 1 & 0 \\ 0 & 1 & 4 & | & 3 & -1 & 0 \\ 0 & 0 & 7 & | & 3 & -2 & 1 \end{bmatrix}$$

$$R_2 = -3r_1 + r_2 \qquad\qquad R_2 = -r_2 \qquad\qquad\qquad R_1 = -r_2 + r_1$$
$$R_3 = -3r_1 + r_3 \qquad\qquad\qquad\qquad\qquad\qquad R_3 = 2r_2 + r_3$$

$$\rightarrow \begin{bmatrix} 1 & 0 & -3 \\ 0 & 1 & 4 \\ 0 & 0 & 1 \end{bmatrix} \begin{array}{|ccc} -2 & 1 & 0 \\ 3 & -1 & 0 \\ \frac{3}{7} & -\frac{2}{7} & \frac{1}{7} \end{array} \rightarrow \begin{bmatrix} 1 & 0 & 0 \\ 0 & 1 & 0 \\ 0 & 0 & 1 \end{bmatrix} \begin{array}{|ccc} -\frac{5}{7} & \frac{1}{7} & \frac{3}{7} \\ \frac{9}{7} & \frac{1}{7} & -\frac{4}{7} \\ \frac{3}{7} & -\frac{2}{7} & \frac{1}{7} \end{array}$$

$$R_3 = \tfrac{1}{7} r_3 \qquad\qquad R_1 = 3r_3 + r_1$$
$$R_2 = -4r_3 + r_2$$

$$A^{-1} = \begin{bmatrix} -\frac{5}{7} & \frac{1}{7} & \frac{3}{7} \\ \frac{9}{7} & \frac{1}{7} & -\frac{4}{7} \\ \frac{3}{7} & -\frac{2}{7} & \frac{1}{7} \end{bmatrix}$$

31. Rewrite the system of equations in matrix form:
$$\begin{cases} 2x + y = 8 \\ x + y = 5 \end{cases} \quad A = \begin{bmatrix} 2 & 1 \\ 1 & 1 \end{bmatrix}, \quad X = \begin{bmatrix} x \\ y \end{bmatrix}, \quad B = \begin{bmatrix} 8 \\ 5 \end{bmatrix}$$
Find the inverse of A and solve $X = A^{-1}B$:

From Problem 21, $A^{-1} = \begin{bmatrix} 1 & -1 \\ -1 & 2 \end{bmatrix}$ and $X = A^{-1}B = \begin{bmatrix} 1 & -1 \\ -1 & 2 \end{bmatrix}\begin{bmatrix} 8 \\ 5 \end{bmatrix} = \begin{bmatrix} 3 \\ 2 \end{bmatrix}$.

The solution is $x = 3, y = 2$.

33. Rewrite the system of equations in matrix form:
$$\begin{cases} 2x + y = 0 \\ x + y = 5 \end{cases} \quad A = \begin{bmatrix} 2 & 1 \\ 1 & 1 \end{bmatrix}, \quad X = \begin{bmatrix} x \\ y \end{bmatrix}, \quad B = \begin{bmatrix} 0 \\ 5 \end{bmatrix}$$
Find the inverse of A and solve $X = A^{-1}B$:

From Problem 21, $A^{-1} = \begin{bmatrix} 1 & -1 \\ -1 & 2 \end{bmatrix}$ and $X = A^{-1}B = \begin{bmatrix} 1 & -1 \\ -1 & 2 \end{bmatrix}\begin{bmatrix} 0 \\ 5 \end{bmatrix} = \begin{bmatrix} -5 \\ 10 \end{bmatrix}$.

The solution is $x = -5, y = 10$.

35. Rewrite the system of equations in matrix form:
$$\begin{cases} 6x + 5y = 7 \\ 2x + 2y = 2 \end{cases} \quad A = \begin{bmatrix} 6 & 5 \\ 2 & 2 \end{bmatrix}, \quad X = \begin{bmatrix} x \\ y \end{bmatrix}, \quad B = \begin{bmatrix} 7 \\ 2 \end{bmatrix}$$
Find the inverse of A and solve $X = A^{-1}B$:

From Problem 23, $A^{-1} = \begin{bmatrix} 1 & -\frac{5}{2} \\ -1 & 3 \end{bmatrix}$ and $X = A^{-1}B = \begin{bmatrix} 1 & -\frac{5}{2} \\ -1 & 3 \end{bmatrix}\begin{bmatrix} 7 \\ 2 \end{bmatrix} = \begin{bmatrix} 2 \\ -1 \end{bmatrix}$

The solution is $x = 2, y = -1$.

37. Rewrite the system of equations in matrix form:
$$\begin{cases} 6x + 5y = 13 \\ 2x + 2y = 5 \end{cases} \quad A = \begin{bmatrix} 6 & 5 \\ 2 & 2 \end{bmatrix}, \quad X = \begin{bmatrix} x \\ y \end{bmatrix}, \quad B = \begin{bmatrix} 13 \\ 5 \end{bmatrix}$$
Find the inverse of A and solve $X = A^{-1}B$:

From Problem 23, $A^{-1} = \begin{bmatrix} 1 & -\frac{5}{2} \\ -1 & 3 \end{bmatrix}$ and $X = A^{-1}B = \begin{bmatrix} 1 & -\frac{5}{2} \\ -1 & 3 \end{bmatrix}\begin{bmatrix} 13 \\ 5 \end{bmatrix} = \begin{bmatrix} \frac{1}{2} \\ 2 \end{bmatrix}$.

The solution is $x = \dfrac{1}{2}, y = 2$.

39. Rewrite the system of equations in matrix form:

$$\begin{cases} 2x + y = -3 \\ ax + ay = -a \end{cases} a \neq 0 \qquad A = \begin{bmatrix} 2 & 1 \\ a & a \end{bmatrix}, \quad X = \begin{bmatrix} x \\ y \end{bmatrix}, \quad B = \begin{bmatrix} -3 \\ -a \end{bmatrix}$$

Find the inverse of A and solve $X = A^{-1}B$:

From Problem 25, $A^{-1} = \begin{bmatrix} 1 & -\frac{1}{a} \\ -1 & \frac{2}{a} \end{bmatrix}$ and $X = A^{-1}B = \begin{bmatrix} 1 & -\frac{1}{a} \\ -1 & \frac{2}{a} \end{bmatrix}\begin{bmatrix} -3 \\ -a \end{bmatrix} = \begin{bmatrix} -2 \\ 1 \end{bmatrix}$.

The solution is $x = -2$, $y = 1$.

41. Rewrite the system of equations in matrix form:

$$\begin{cases} 2x + y = \dfrac{7}{a} \\ ax + ay = 5 \end{cases} a \neq 0 \qquad A = \begin{bmatrix} 2 & 1 \\ a & a \end{bmatrix}, \quad X = \begin{bmatrix} x \\ y \end{bmatrix}, \quad B = \begin{bmatrix} \frac{7}{a} \\ 5 \end{bmatrix}$$

Find the inverse of A and solve $X = A^{-1}B$:

From Problem 25, $A^{-1} = \begin{bmatrix} 1 & -\frac{1}{a} \\ -1 & \frac{2}{a} \end{bmatrix}$ and $X = A^{-1}B = \begin{bmatrix} 1 & -\frac{1}{a} \\ -1 & \frac{2}{a} \end{bmatrix}\begin{bmatrix} \frac{7}{a} \\ 5 \end{bmatrix} = \begin{bmatrix} \frac{2}{a} \\ \frac{3}{a} \end{bmatrix}$.

The solution is $x = \dfrac{2}{a}, y = \dfrac{3}{a}$.

43. Rewrite the system of equations in matrix form:

$$\begin{cases} x - y + z = 0 \\ -2y + z = -1 \\ -2x - 3y = -5 \end{cases} \qquad A = \begin{bmatrix} 1 & -1 & 1 \\ 0 & -2 & 1 \\ -2 & -3 & 0 \end{bmatrix}, \quad X = \begin{bmatrix} x \\ y \\ z \end{bmatrix}, \quad B = \begin{bmatrix} 0 \\ -1 \\ -5 \end{bmatrix}$$

Find the inverse of A and solve $X = A^{-1}B$:

From Problem 27,

$$A^{-1} = \begin{bmatrix} 3 & -3 & 1 \\ -2 & 2 & -1 \\ -4 & 5 & -2 \end{bmatrix} \text{ and } X = A^{-1}B = \begin{bmatrix} 3 & -3 & 1 \\ -2 & 2 & -1 \\ -4 & 5 & -2 \end{bmatrix}\begin{bmatrix} 0 \\ -1 \\ -5 \end{bmatrix} = \begin{bmatrix} -2 \\ 3 \\ 5 \end{bmatrix}$$

The solution is $x = -2$, $y = 3$, $z = 5$.

45. Rewrite the system of equations in matrix form:

$$\begin{cases} x - y + z = 2 \\ -2y + z = 2 \\ -2x - 3y = \dfrac{1}{2} \end{cases} \qquad A = \begin{bmatrix} 1 & -1 & 1 \\ 0 & -2 & 1 \\ -2 & -3 & 0 \end{bmatrix}, \quad X = \begin{bmatrix} x \\ y \\ z \end{bmatrix}, \quad B = \begin{bmatrix} 2 \\ 2 \\ \frac{1}{2} \end{bmatrix}$$

Find the inverse of A and solve $X = A^{-1}B$:

From Problem 27,

$$A^{-1} = \begin{bmatrix} 3 & -3 & 1 \\ -2 & 2 & -1 \\ -4 & 5 & -2 \end{bmatrix} \text{ and } X = A^{-1}B = \begin{bmatrix} 3 & -3 & 1 \\ -2 & 2 & -1 \\ -4 & 5 & -2 \end{bmatrix}\begin{bmatrix} 2 \\ 2 \\ \frac{1}{2} \end{bmatrix} = \begin{bmatrix} \frac{1}{2} \\ -\frac{1}{2} \\ 1 \end{bmatrix}$$

The solution is $x = \dfrac{1}{2}, y = -\dfrac{1}{2}, z = 1$.

47. Rewrite the system of equations in matrix form:

$$\begin{cases} x+\ y+\ z=9 \\ 3x+2y-\ z=8 \\ 3x+\ y+2z=1 \end{cases} \quad A=\begin{bmatrix} 1 & 1 & 1 \\ 3 & 2 & -1 \\ 3 & 1 & 2 \end{bmatrix}, \quad X=\begin{bmatrix} x \\ y \\ z \end{bmatrix}, \quad B=\begin{bmatrix} 9 \\ 8 \\ 1 \end{bmatrix}$$

Find the inverse of A and solve $X = A^{-1}B$:

From Problem 29,

$$A^{-1}=\begin{bmatrix} -\frac{5}{7} & \frac{1}{7} & \frac{3}{7} \\ \frac{9}{7} & \frac{1}{7} & -\frac{4}{7} \\ \frac{3}{7} & -\frac{2}{7} & \frac{1}{7} \end{bmatrix} \text{ and } X=A^{-1}B=\begin{bmatrix} -\frac{5}{7} & \frac{1}{7} & \frac{3}{7} \\ \frac{9}{7} & \frac{1}{7} & -\frac{4}{7} \\ \frac{3}{7} & -\frac{2}{7} & \frac{1}{7} \end{bmatrix}\begin{bmatrix} 9 \\ 8 \\ 1 \end{bmatrix}=\begin{bmatrix} -\frac{34}{7} \\ \frac{85}{7} \\ \frac{12}{7} \end{bmatrix}.$$

The solution is $x=-\dfrac{34}{7}, y=\dfrac{85}{7}, z=\dfrac{12}{7}$.

49. Rewrite the system of equations in matrix form:

$$\begin{cases} x+\ y+z=2 \\ 3x+2y-z=\dfrac{7}{3} \\ 3x+\ y+2z=\dfrac{10}{3} \end{cases} \quad A=\begin{bmatrix} 1 & 1 & 1 \\ 3 & 2 & -1 \\ 3 & 1 & 2 \end{bmatrix}, \quad X=\begin{bmatrix} x \\ y \\ z \end{bmatrix}, \quad B=\begin{bmatrix} 2 \\ \frac{7}{3} \\ \frac{10}{3} \end{bmatrix}$$

Find the inverse of A and solve $X = A^{-1}B$:

From Problem 29,

$$A^{-1}=\begin{bmatrix} -\frac{5}{7} & \frac{1}{7} & \frac{3}{7} \\ \frac{9}{7} & \frac{1}{7} & -\frac{4}{7} \\ \frac{3}{7} & -\frac{2}{7} & \frac{1}{7} \end{bmatrix} \text{ and } X=A^{-1}B=\begin{bmatrix} -\frac{5}{7} & \frac{1}{7} & \frac{3}{7} \\ \frac{9}{7} & \frac{1}{7} & -\frac{4}{7} \\ \frac{3}{7} & -\frac{2}{7} & \frac{1}{7} \end{bmatrix}\begin{bmatrix} 2 \\ \frac{7}{3} \\ \frac{10}{3} \end{bmatrix}=\begin{bmatrix} \frac{1}{3} \\ 1 \\ \frac{2}{3} \end{bmatrix}.$$

The solution is $x=\dfrac{1}{3}, y=1, z=\dfrac{2}{3}$.

51. Augment the matrix with the identity and use row operations to find the inverse:

$$A=\begin{bmatrix} 4 & 2 \\ 2 & 1 \end{bmatrix} \rightarrow \left[\begin{array}{cc|cc} 4 & 2 & 1 & 0 \\ 2 & 1 & 0 & 1 \end{array}\right]$$

$$\rightarrow \left[\begin{array}{cc|cc} 4 & 2 & 1 & 0 \\ 0 & 0 & -\frac{1}{2} & 1 \end{array}\right] \rightarrow \left[\begin{array}{cc|cc} 1 & \frac{1}{2} & \frac{1}{4} & 0 \\ 0 & 0 & -\frac{1}{2} & 1 \end{array}\right]$$

$$R_2=-\tfrac{1}{2}r_1+r_2 \qquad R_1=\tfrac{1}{4}r_1$$

There is no way to obtain the identity matrix on the left; thus, there is no inverse.

53. Augment the matrix with the identity and use row operations to find the inverse:

$$A=\begin{bmatrix} 15 & 3 \\ 10 & 2 \end{bmatrix} \rightarrow \left[\begin{array}{cc|cc} 15 & 3 & 1 & 0 \\ 10 & 2 & 0 & 1 \end{array}\right]$$

$$\rightarrow \left[\begin{array}{cc|cc} 15 & 3 & 1 & 0 \\ 0 & 0 & -\frac{2}{3} & 1 \end{array}\right] \rightarrow \left[\begin{array}{cc|cc} 1 & \frac{1}{5} & \frac{1}{15} & 0 \\ 0 & 0 & -\frac{2}{3} & 1 \end{array}\right]$$

$$R_2=-\tfrac{2}{3}r_1+r_2 \qquad R_1=\tfrac{1}{15}r_1$$

There is no way to obtain the identity matrix on the left; thus, there is no inverse.

55. Augment the matrix with the identity and use row operations to find the inverse:

$$A = \begin{bmatrix} -3 & 1 & -1 \\ 1 & -4 & -7 \\ 1 & 2 & 5 \end{bmatrix} \rightarrow \begin{bmatrix} -3 & 1 & -1 & | & 1 & 0 & 0 \\ 1 & -4 & -7 & | & 0 & 1 & 0 \\ 1 & 2 & 5 & | & 0 & 0 & 1 \end{bmatrix}$$

$$\rightarrow \begin{bmatrix} 1 & 2 & 5 & | & 0 & 0 & 1 \\ 1 & -4 & -7 & | & 0 & 1 & 0 \\ -3 & 1 & -1 & | & 1 & 0 & 0 \end{bmatrix} \rightarrow \begin{bmatrix} 1 & 2 & 5 & | & 0 & 0 & 1 \\ 0 & -6 & -12 & | & 0 & 1 & -1 \\ 0 & 7 & 14 & | & 1 & 0 & 3 \end{bmatrix} \rightarrow \begin{bmatrix} 1 & 2 & 5 & | & 0 & 0 & 1 \\ 0 & 1 & 2 & | & 0 & -\frac{1}{6} & \frac{1}{6} \\ 0 & 7 & 14 & | & 1 & 0 & 3 \end{bmatrix}$$

Interchange r_1 and r_3 $R_2 = -r_1 + r_2$ $R_2 = -\frac{1}{6}r_2$

$R_3 = 3r_1 + r_3$

$$\rightarrow \begin{bmatrix} 1 & 0 & 1 & | & 0 & \frac{1}{3} & \frac{2}{3} \\ 0 & 1 & 2 & | & 0 & -\frac{1}{6} & \frac{1}{6} \\ 0 & 0 & 0 & | & 1 & \frac{7}{6} & \frac{11}{6} \end{bmatrix}$$

$R_1 = -2r_2 + r_1$

$R_3 = -7r_2 + r_3$

There is no way to obtain the identity matrix on the left; thus, there is no inverse.

57.
$$\begin{bmatrix} 0.01 & 0.05 & -0.01 \\ 0.01 & -0.02 & 0.01 \\ -0.02 & 0.01 & 0.03 \end{bmatrix}$$

59.
$$\begin{bmatrix} 0.02 & -0.04 & -0.01 & 0.01 \\ -0.02 & 0.05 & 0.03 & -0.03 \\ 0.02 & 0.01 & -0.04 & 0.00 \\ -0.02 & 0.06 & 0.07 & 0.06 \end{bmatrix}$$

61. $x = 4.57, \ y = -6.44, \ z = -24.07$

63. $x = -1.19, \ y = 2.46, \ z = 8.27$

65. (a) The rows of the 2 by 3 matrix represent stainless steel and aluminum. The columns represent 10-gallon, 5-gallon, and 1-gallon.

The 2 by 3 matrix is: The 3 by 2 matrix is:

$$\begin{bmatrix} 500 & 350 & 400 \\ 700 & 500 & 850 \end{bmatrix} \qquad \begin{bmatrix} 500 & 700 \\ 350 & 500 \\ 400 & 850 \end{bmatrix}$$

(b) The 3 by 1 matrix representing the amount of material is:

$$\begin{bmatrix} 15 \\ 8 \\ 3 \end{bmatrix}$$

(c) The days usage of materials is:

$$\begin{bmatrix} 500 & 350 & 400 \\ 700 & 500 & 850 \end{bmatrix} \cdot \begin{bmatrix} 15 \\ 8 \\ 3 \end{bmatrix} = \begin{bmatrix} 11,500 \\ 17,050 \end{bmatrix}$$

11,500 pounds of stainless steel and 17,050 pounds of aluminum are used each day.

(d)   The 1 by 2 matrix representing cost is:
$$[0.10 \quad 0.05]$$

(e)   The total cost of the days production was:
$$[0.10 \quad 0.05] \cdot \begin{bmatrix} 11,500 \\ 17,050 \end{bmatrix} = [2002.50]$$

The total cost of the days production was $2,002.50.

67.   We need to consider 2 different cases.

Case 1: $a \neq 0$, $D = ad - bc \neq 0$.

$$A = \begin{bmatrix} a & b & | & 1 & 0 \\ c & d & | & 0 & 1 \end{bmatrix} \longrightarrow \begin{bmatrix} 1 & \dfrac{b}{a} & | & \dfrac{1}{a} & 0 \\ c & d & | & 0 & 1 \end{bmatrix} \longrightarrow \begin{bmatrix} 1 & \dfrac{b}{a} & | & \dfrac{1}{a} & 0 \\ c & d - \dfrac{cb}{a} & | & -\dfrac{c}{a} & 1 \end{bmatrix} = \begin{bmatrix} 1 & \dfrac{b}{b} & | & \dfrac{1}{a} & 0 \\ c & \dfrac{ad - cb}{a} & | & -\dfrac{c}{a} & 1 \end{bmatrix}$$

$$R_1 = \tfrac{1}{a} \cdot r_1 \qquad\qquad R_2 = -c \cdot r_1 + r_2$$

$$\longrightarrow \begin{bmatrix} 1 & \dfrac{b}{a} & | & \dfrac{1}{a} & 0 \\ 0 & 1 & | & -\dfrac{c}{ad - bc} & \dfrac{a}{ad - bc} \end{bmatrix} \longrightarrow \begin{bmatrix} 1 & 0 & | & \dfrac{1}{a} + \dfrac{bc}{a(ad - bc)} & \dfrac{-b}{ad - bc} \\ 0 & 1 & | & -\dfrac{c}{ad - bc} & \dfrac{a}{ad - bc} \end{bmatrix}$$

$$R_2 = \left(\dfrac{a}{ad - bc} \right) \cdot r_2 \qquad\qquad R_1 = \left(-\dfrac{b}{a} \right) r_2 + r_1$$

Note that $\dfrac{1}{a} + \dfrac{bc}{a(ad - bc)} = \dfrac{1 \cdot (ad - bc) + bc}{a(ad - bc)} = \dfrac{ad - bc + bc}{a(ad - bc)} = \dfrac{ad}{a(ad - bc)} = \dfrac{d}{ad - bc}$

So, we have $\begin{bmatrix} 1 & 0 & | & \dfrac{1}{a} + \dfrac{bc}{a(ad - bc)} & \dfrac{-b}{ad - bc} \\ 0 & 1 & | & -\dfrac{c}{ad - bc} & \dfrac{a}{ad - bc} \end{bmatrix} = \begin{bmatrix} 1 & 0 & | & \dfrac{d}{ad - bc} & \dfrac{-b}{ad - bc} \\ 0 & 1 & | & -\dfrac{c}{ad - bc} & \dfrac{a}{ad - bc} \end{bmatrix}$

Therefore $A^{-1} = \begin{bmatrix} \dfrac{d}{ad - bc} & \dfrac{-b}{ad - bc} \\ -\dfrac{c}{ad - bc} & \dfrac{a}{ad - bc} \end{bmatrix} = \left(\dfrac{1}{ad - bc} \right) \begin{bmatrix} d & -b \\ -c & a \end{bmatrix} = \left(\dfrac{1}{D} \right) \begin{bmatrix} d & -b \\ -c & a \end{bmatrix},$

where $D = ad - bc$.

Case 2: $a = 0$, $D = ad - bc \neq 0$.

First note that $D = ad - bc = 0 \cdot d - bc = -bc \neq 0 \Rightarrow b \neq 0$ and $c \neq 0$.

$$A = \begin{bmatrix} 0 & b & 1 & 0 \\ c & d & 0 & 1 \end{bmatrix} \longrightarrow \begin{bmatrix} c & d & 0 & 1 \\ 0 & b & 1 & 0 \end{bmatrix} \longrightarrow \begin{bmatrix} 1 & \dfrac{d}{c} & 0 & \dfrac{1}{c} \\ 0 & b & 1 & 0 \end{bmatrix} \longrightarrow \begin{bmatrix} 1 & \dfrac{d}{c} & 0 & \dfrac{1}{c} \\ 0 & 1 & \dfrac{1}{b} & 0 \end{bmatrix}$$

interchange r_1 and r_2 $\qquad$ $R_1 = \dfrac{1}{c} \cdot r_1$ $\qquad$ $R_2 = \dfrac{1}{b} \cdot r_2$

$$\longrightarrow \begin{bmatrix} 1 & 0 & \dfrac{-d}{bc} & \dfrac{1}{c} \\ 0 & 1 & \dfrac{1}{b} & 0 \end{bmatrix}$$

$R_1 = \left(\dfrac{-d}{c} \right) \cdot r_2 + r_1$

Therefore $\qquad A^{-1} = \begin{bmatrix} \dfrac{-d}{bc} & \dfrac{1}{c} \\ \dfrac{1}{b} & 0 \end{bmatrix} = \left(\dfrac{1}{-bc} \right) \begin{bmatrix} d & -b \\ -c & 0 \end{bmatrix} = \left(\dfrac{1}{D} \right) \begin{bmatrix} d & -b \\ -c & 0 \end{bmatrix}$,

where $D = ad - bc = 0 \cdot d - bc = -bc$.

Systems of Equations and Inequalities

8.6   Partial Fraction Decomposition

1.   The rational expression $\dfrac{x}{x^2-1}$ is proper, since the degree of the numerator is less than the degree of the denominator.

3.   The rational expression $\dfrac{x^2+5}{x^2-4}$ is improper, so perform the division:

$$x^2-4\,\overline{\smash{)}\,x^2+5}$$
$$\underline{\,x^2-4}$$
$$\,9$$

with quotient 1.

The proper rational expression is:
$$\frac{x^2+5}{x^2-4}=1+\frac{9}{x^2-4}$$

5.   The rational expression $\dfrac{5x^3+2x-1}{x^2-4}$ is improper, so perform the division:

$$x^2-4\,\overline{\smash{)}\,5x^3+0x^2+\ 2x-1}$$
$$\underline{\,5x^3-20x}$$
$$\,22x-1$$

with quotient $5x$.

The proper rational expression is:
$$\frac{5x^3+2x-1}{x^2-4}=5x+\frac{22x-1}{x^2-4}$$

7.   The rational expression $\dfrac{x(x-1)}{(x+4)(x-3)}=\dfrac{x^2-x}{x^2+x-12}$ is improper, so perform the division:

$$x^2+x-12\,\overline{\smash{)}\,x^2-x+\ 0}$$
$$\underline{\,x^2+x-12}$$
$$\,-2x+12$$

with quotient 1.

The proper rational expression is: $\dfrac{x(x-1)}{(x+4)(x-3)}=1+\dfrac{-2x+12}{x^2+x-12}$

9.   Find the partial fraction decomposition:
$$\frac{4}{x(x-1)}=\frac{A}{x}+\frac{B}{x-1}$$
$$4=A(x-1)+Bx \quad \text{(Multiply both sides by } x(x-1).)$$
Let $x=1$:   then $4=A(0)+B$, or $B=4$
Let $x=0$:   then $4=A(-1)+B(0)$, or $A=-4$
$$\frac{4}{x(x-1)}=\frac{-4}{x}+\frac{4}{x-1}$$

11. Find the partial fraction decomposition:

$$\frac{1}{x(x^2+1)} = \frac{A}{x} + \frac{Bx+C}{x^2+1}$$

$$1 = A(x^2+1) + (Bx+C)x \quad \text{(Multiply both sides by } x(x^2+1).\text{)}$$

Let $x = 0$:   then $1 = A(1) + (B(0)+C)(0)$, or $A = 1$

Let $x = 1$:   then $1 = A(1+1) + (B(1)+C)(1)$,   or $1 = 2A+B+C$

   or $1 = 2(1) + B + C$

   or $-1 = B + C$

Let $x = -1$: then $1 = A(1+1) + (B(-1)+C)(-1)$,   or $1 = 2A + B - C$

   or $1 = 2(1) + B - C$

   or $-1 = B - C$

Solve the system of equations:

$$
\begin{array}{l}
B + C = -1 \\
\underline{B - C = -1} \\
2B \quad\;\; = -2 \qquad -1 + C = -1 \\
\;\; B \quad\;\; = -1 \qquad\quad\; C = 0
\end{array}
$$

$$\frac{1}{x(x^2+1)} = \frac{1}{x} + \frac{-x}{x^2+1}$$

13. Find the partial fraction decomposition:

$$\frac{x}{(x-1)(x-2)} = \frac{A}{x-1} + \frac{B}{x-2} \quad \text{(Multiply both sides by } (x-1)(x-2).\text{)}$$

$$x = A(x-2) + B(x-1)$$

Let $x = 1$:   then $1 = A(1-2) + B(1-1) \;\rightarrow\; 1 = -A \;\rightarrow\; A = -1$

Let $x = 2$:   then $2 = A(2-2) + B(2-1) \;\rightarrow\; 2 = B \;\rightarrow\; B = 2$

$$\frac{x}{(x-1)(x-2)} = \frac{-1}{x-1} + \frac{2}{x-2}$$

15. Find the partial fraction decomposition:

$$\frac{x^2}{(x-1)^2(x+1)} = \frac{A}{x-1} + \frac{B}{(x-1)^2} + \frac{C}{x+1} \quad \text{(Multiply both sides by } (x-1)^2(x+1).\text{)}$$

$$x^2 = A(x-1)(x+1) + B(x+1) + C(x-1)^2$$

Let $x = 1$:   then $1^2 = A(1-1)(1+1) + B(1+1) + C(1-1)^2$

$$\rightarrow 1 = 2B \;\rightarrow\; B = \frac{1}{2}$$

Let $x = -1$:   then $(-1)^2 = A(-1-1)(-1+1) + B(-1+1) + C(-1-1)^2$

$$\rightarrow 1 = 4C \;\rightarrow\; C = \frac{1}{4}$$

Let $x = 0$:   then $0^2 = A(0-1)(0+1) + B(0+1) + C(0-1)^2$

$$\rightarrow 0 = -A + B + C \;\rightarrow\; A = \frac{1}{2} + \frac{1}{4} = \frac{3}{4}$$

$$\frac{x^2}{(x-1)^2(x+1)} = \frac{\left(\dfrac{3}{4}\right)}{x-1} + \frac{\left(\dfrac{1}{2}\right)}{(x-1)^2} + \frac{\left(\dfrac{1}{4}\right)}{x+1}$$

438

17. Find the partial fraction decomposition:

$$\frac{1}{x^3 - 8} = \frac{1}{(x-2)(x^2+2x+4)} = \frac{A}{x-2} + \frac{Bx+C}{x^2+2x+4}$$

(Multiply both sides by $(x-2)(x^2+2x+4)$.)

$$1 = A(x^2+2x+4) + (Bx+C)(x-2)$$

Let $x = 2$: then $1 = A\left(2^2+2(2)+4\right) + (B(2)+C)(2-2)$

$$\rightarrow 1 = 12A \rightarrow A = \frac{1}{12}$$

Let $x = 0$: then $1 = A\left(0^2+2(0)+4\right) + (B(0)+C)(0-2)$

$$\rightarrow 1 = 4A - 2C \rightarrow 1 = 4\left(\frac{1}{12}\right) - 2C$$

$$\rightarrow -2C = \frac{2}{3} \rightarrow C = -\frac{1}{3}$$

Let $x = 1$: then $1 = A\left(1^2+2(1)+4\right) + (B(1)+C)(1-2)$

$$\rightarrow 1 = 7A - B - C \rightarrow 1 = 7\left(\frac{1}{12}\right) - B + \frac{1}{3} \rightarrow B = -\frac{1}{12}$$

$$\frac{1}{x^3-8} = \frac{\left(\frac{1}{12}\right)}{x-2} + \frac{-\left(\frac{1}{12}\right)x - \frac{1}{3}}{x^2+2x+4}$$

19. Find the partial fraction decomposition:

$$\frac{x^2}{(x-1)^2(x+1)^2} = \frac{A}{x-1} + \frac{B}{(x-1)^2} + \frac{C}{x+1} + \frac{D}{(x+1)^2}$$

(Multiply both sides by $(x-1)^2(x+1)^2$.)

$$x^2 = A(x-1)(x+1)^2 + B(x+1)^2 + C(x-1)^2(x+1) + D(x-1)^2$$

Let $x = 1$: then $1^2 = A(1-1)(1+1)^2 + B(1+1)^2 + C(1-1)^2(1+1) + D(1-1)^2$

$$\rightarrow 1 = 4B \rightarrow B = \frac{1}{4}$$

Let $x = -1$: then

$$(-1)^2 = A(-1-1)(-1+1)^2 + B(-1+1)^2 + C(-1-1)^2(-1+1) + D(-1-1)^2$$

$$\rightarrow 1 = 4D \rightarrow D = \frac{1}{4}$$

Let $x = 0$: then

$$0^2 = A(0-1)(0+1)^2 + B(0+1)^2 + C(0-1)^2(0+1) + D(0-1)^2$$

$$\rightarrow 0 = -A + B + C + D \rightarrow A - C = \frac{1}{4} + \frac{1}{4} = \frac{1}{2}$$

Let $x = 2$: then

$$2^2 = A(2-1)(2+1)^2 + B(2+1)^2 + C(2-1)^2(2+1) + D(2-1)^2$$

$$\rightarrow\ 4 = 9A + 9B + 3C + D\ \rightarrow\ 9A + 3C = 4 - \frac{9}{4} - \frac{1}{4} = \frac{3}{2}$$

$$\rightarrow\ 3A + C = \frac{1}{2}$$

Solve the system of equations:

$$A - C = \frac{1}{2}$$

$$3A + C = \frac{1}{2}$$

$$\overline{ 4A = 1}$$

$$A = \frac{1}{4}\ \rightarrow\ \frac{3}{4} + C = \frac{1}{2}\ \rightarrow\ C = -\frac{1}{4}$$

$$\frac{x^2}{(x-1)^2(x+1)^2} = \frac{\left(\frac{1}{4}\right)}{x-1} + \frac{\left(\frac{1}{4}\right)}{(x-1)^2} + \frac{\left(-\frac{1}{4}\right)}{x+1} + \frac{\left(\frac{1}{4}\right)}{(x+1)^2}$$

21. Find the partial fraction decomposition:

$$\frac{x-3}{(x+2)(x+1)^2} = \frac{A}{x+2} + \frac{B}{x+1} + \frac{C}{(x+1)^2}$$

(Multiply both sides by $(x+2)(x+1)^2$.)

$$x - 3 = A(x+1)^2 + B(x+2)(x+1) + C(x+2)$$

Let $x = -2$: then $-2 - 3 = A(-2+1)^2 + B(-2+2)(-2+1) + C(-2+2)$

$$\rightarrow\ -5 = A\ \rightarrow\ A = -5$$

Let $x = -1$: then $-1 - 3 = A(-1+1)^2 + B(-1+2)(-1+1) + C(-1+2)$

$$\rightarrow\ -4 = C\ \rightarrow\ C = -4$$

Let $x = 0$: then

$$0 - 3 = A(0+1)^2 + B(0+2)(0+1) + C(0+2)\ \rightarrow\ -3 = A + 2B + 2C$$

$$\rightarrow\ -3 = -5 + 2B + 2(-4)\ \rightarrow\ 2B = 10\ \rightarrow\ B = 5$$

$$\frac{x-3}{(x+2)(x+1)^2} = \frac{-5}{x+2} + \frac{5}{x+1} + \frac{-4}{(x+1)^2}$$

23. Find the partial fraction decomposition:

$$\frac{x+4}{x^2(x^2+4)} = \frac{A}{x} + \frac{B}{x^2} + \frac{Cx+D}{x^2+4}$$ (Multiply both sides by $x^2(x^2+4)$.)

$$x + 4 = Ax(x^2+4) + B(x^2+4) + (Cx+D)x^2$$

Let $x = 0$: then $0 + 4 = A(0)(0^2+4) + B(0^2+4) + (C0+D)(0)^2$

$$\rightarrow\ 4 = 4B\ \rightarrow\ B = 1$$

Let $x = 1$: then $1 + 4 = A(1)(1^2+4) + B(1^2+4) + (C(1)+D)(1)^2$

$$\rightarrow\ 5 = 5A + 5B + C + D\ \rightarrow\ 5 = 5A + 5 + C + D$$

$$\rightarrow\ 5A + C + D = 0$$

Let $x = -1$: then
$$-1 + 4 = A(-1)((-1)^2 + 4) + B((-1)^2 + 4) + (C(-1) + D)(-1)^2$$
$$\rightarrow 3 = -5A + 5B - C + D \rightarrow 3 = -5A + 5 - C + D$$
$$\rightarrow -5A - C + D = -2$$

Let $x = 2$:   then $2 + 4 = A(2)(2^2 + 4) + B(2^2 + 4) + (C(2) + D)(2)^2$
$$\rightarrow 6 = 16A + 8B + 8C + 4D \rightarrow 6 = 16A + 8 + 8C + 4D$$
$$\rightarrow 16A + 8C + 4D = -2$$

Solve the system of equations:
$$5A + C + D = 0$$
$$\underline{-5A - C + D = -2}$$

$$2D = -2 \qquad\qquad 5A + C - 1 = 0$$
$$D = -1 \qquad\qquad\qquad C = 1 - 5A$$
$$16A + 8(1 - 5A) + 4(-1) = -2$$
$$16A + 8 - 40A - 4 = -2 \qquad C = 1 - 5\left(\frac{1}{4}\right)$$
$$-24A = -6$$
$$A = \frac{1}{4} \qquad\qquad C = 1 - \frac{5}{4} = -\frac{1}{4}$$

$$\frac{x+4}{x^2(x^2+4)} = \frac{\left(\frac{1}{4}\right)}{x} + \frac{1}{x^2} + \frac{\left(-\frac{1}{4}x - 1\right)}{x^2 + 4}$$

25. Find the partial fraction decomposition:
$$\frac{x^2 + 2x + 3}{(x+1)(x^2 + 2x + 4)} = \frac{A}{x+1} + \frac{Bx + C}{x^2 + 2x + 4}$$

(Multiply both sides by $(x+1)(x^2 + 2x + 4)$.)
$$x^2 + 2x + 3 = A(x^2 + 2x + 4) + (Bx + C)(x+1)$$

Let $x = -1$: then
$$(-1)^2 + 2(-1) + 3 = A((-1)^2 + 2(-1) + 4) + (B(-1) + C)(-1 + 1)$$
$$\rightarrow 2 = 3A \rightarrow A = \frac{2}{3}$$

Let $x = 0$:   then $0^2 + 2(0) + 3 = A(0^2 + 2(0) + 4) + (B(0) + C)(0 + 1)$
$$\rightarrow 3 = 4A + C \rightarrow 3 = 4\left(\frac{2}{3}\right) + C \rightarrow C = \frac{1}{3}$$

Let $x = 1$: then $1^2 + 2(1) + 3 = A(1^2 + 2(1) + 4) + (B(1) + C)(1 + 1)$
$$\rightarrow 6 = 7A + 2B + 2C \rightarrow 6 = 7\left(\frac{2}{3}\right) + 2B + 2\left(\frac{1}{3}\right)$$
$$\rightarrow 2B = 6 - \frac{14}{3} - \frac{2}{3} \rightarrow 2B = \frac{2}{3} \rightarrow B = \frac{1}{3}$$

$$\frac{x^2 + 2x + 3}{(x+1)(x^2 + 2x + 4)} = \frac{\left(\frac{2}{3}\right)}{x+1} + \frac{\left(\frac{1}{3}x + \frac{1}{3}\right)}{x^2 + 2x + 4}$$

27.   Find the partial fraction decomposition:

$$\frac{x}{(3x-2)(2x+1)} = \frac{A}{3x-2} + \frac{B}{2x+1} \quad \text{(Multiply both sides by } (3x-2)(2x+1).)$$

$$x = A(2x+1) + B(3x-2)$$

$$\text{Let } x = -\frac{1}{2}: \quad \text{then } -\frac{1}{2} = A\left(2\left(-\frac{1}{2}\right)+1\right) + B\left(3\left(-\frac{1}{2}\right)-2\right)$$

$$\rightarrow \quad -\frac{1}{2} = -\frac{7}{2}B \quad \rightarrow \quad B = \frac{1}{7}$$

$$\text{Let } x = \frac{2}{3}: \quad \text{then } \frac{2}{3} = A\left(2\left(\frac{2}{3}\right)+1\right) + B\left(3\left(\frac{2}{3}\right)-2\right) \rightarrow \frac{2}{3} = \frac{7}{3}A \rightarrow A = \frac{2}{7}$$

$$\frac{x}{(3x-2)(2x+1)} = \frac{\left(\frac{2}{7}\right)}{3x-2} + \frac{\left(\frac{1}{7}\right)}{2x+1}$$

29.   Find the partial fraction decomposition:

$$\frac{x}{x^2+2x-3} = \frac{x}{(x+3)(x-1)} = \frac{A}{x+3} + \frac{B}{x-1}$$

$$\text{(Multiply both sides by } (x+3)(x-1).)$$

$$x = A(x-1) + B(x+3)$$

$$\text{Let } x = 1: \quad \text{then } 1 = A(1-1) + B(1+3) \rightarrow 1 = 4B \rightarrow B = \frac{1}{4}$$

$$\text{Let } x = -3: \quad \text{then } -3 = A(-3-1) + B(-3+3) \rightarrow -3 = -4A \rightarrow A = \frac{3}{4}$$

$$\frac{x}{x^2+2x-3} = \frac{\left(\frac{3}{4}\right)}{x+3} + \frac{\left(\frac{1}{4}\right)}{x-1}$$

31.   Find the partial fraction decomposition:

$$\frac{x^2+2x+3}{(x^2+4)^2} = \frac{Ax+B}{x^2+4} + \frac{Cx+D}{(x^2+4)^2}$$

$$\text{(Multiply both sides by } (x^2+4)^2.)$$

$$x^2+2x+3 = (Ax+B)(x^2+4) + Cx+D$$

$$x^2+2x+3 = Ax^3 + Bx^2 + 4Ax + 4B + Cx + D$$

$$x^2+2x+3 = Ax^3 + Bx^2 + (4A+C)x + 4B + D$$

$$A = 0$$

$$B = 1$$

$$4A+C = 2 \rightarrow 4(0)+C = 2 \rightarrow C = 2$$

$$4B+D = 3 \rightarrow 4(1)+D = 3 \rightarrow D = -1$$

$$\frac{x^2+2x+3}{(x^2+4)^2} = \frac{1}{x^2+4} + \frac{2x-1}{(x^2+4)^2}$$

33. Find the partial fraction decomposition:
$$\frac{7x+3}{x^3-2x^2-3x} = \frac{7x+3}{x(x-3)(x+1)} = \frac{A}{x} + \frac{B}{x-3} + \frac{C}{x+1}$$

(Multiply both sides by $x(x-3)(x+1)$.)
$$7x+3 = A(x-3)(x+1) + Bx(x+1) + Cx(x-3)$$

Let $x=0$: then $7(0)+3 = A(0-3)(0+1) + B(0)(0+1) + C(0)(0-3)$
$$\rightarrow \; 3 = -3A \;\rightarrow\; A=-1$$

Let $x=3$: then $7(3)+3 = A(3-3)(3+1) + B(3)(3+1) + C(3)(3-3)$
$$\rightarrow \; 24 = 12B \;\rightarrow\; B=2$$

Let $x=-1$: then
$$7(-1)+3 = A(-1-3)(-1+1) + B(-1)(-1+1) + C(-1)(-1-3)$$
$$\rightarrow \; -4 = 4C \;\rightarrow\; C=-1$$
$$\frac{7x+3}{x^3-2x^2-3x} = \frac{-1}{x} + \frac{2}{x-3} + \frac{-1}{x+1}$$

35. Perform synthetic division to find a factor:

```
2)1  -4   5  -2
       2  -4   2
   ─────────────
   1  -2   1   0
```

$$x^3-4x^2+5x-2 = (x-2)(x^2-2x+1) = (x-2)(x-1)^2$$

Find the partial fraction decomposition:
$$\frac{x^2}{x^3-4x^2+5x-2} = \frac{x^2}{(x-2)(x-1)^2} = \frac{A}{x-2} + \frac{B}{x-1} + \frac{C}{(x-1)^2}$$

(Multiply both sides by $(x-2)(x-1)^2$.)
$$x^2 = A(x-1)^2 + B(x-2)(x-1) + C(x-2)$$

Let $x=2$: then $2^2 = A(2-1)^2 + B(2-2)(2-1) + C(2-2)$
$$\rightarrow \; 4 = A \;\rightarrow\; A=4$$

Let $x=1$: then $1^2 = A(1-1)^2 + B(1-2)(1-1) + C(1-2)$
$$\rightarrow \; 1 = -C \;\rightarrow\; C=-1$$

Let $x=0$: then $0^2 = A(0-1)^2 + B(0-2)(0-1) + C(0-2)$
$$\rightarrow \; 0 = A+2B-2C \;\rightarrow\; 0 = 4+2B-2(-1)$$
$$\rightarrow \; 2B=-6 \;\rightarrow\; B=-3$$
$$\frac{x^2}{x^3-4x^2+5x-2} = \frac{4}{x-2} + \frac{-3}{x-1} + \frac{-1}{(x-1)^2}$$

37. Find the partial fraction decomposition:
$$\frac{x^3}{(x^2+16)^3} = \frac{Ax+B}{x^2+16} + \frac{Cx+D}{(x^2+16)^2} + \frac{Ex+F}{(x^2+16)^3}$$

(Multiply both sides by $(x^2+16)^3$.)
$$x^3 = (Ax+B)(x^2+16)^2 + (Cx+D)(x^2+16) + Ex+F$$
$$x^3 = (Ax+B)(x^4+32x^2+256) + Cx^3 + Dx^2 + 16Cx + 16D + Ex + F$$

$$x^3 = Ax^5 + Bx^4 + 32Ax^3 + 32Bx^2 + 256Ax + 256B + Cx^3 + Dx^2$$
$$+16Cx + 16D + Ex + F$$

$$x^3 = Ax^5 + Bx^4 + (32A + C)x^3 + (32B + D)x^2 + (256A + 16C + E)x$$
$$+(256B + 16D + F)$$

$$A = 0$$
$$B = 0$$
$$32A + C = 1 \;\rightarrow\; 32(0) + C = 1 \;\rightarrow\; C = 1$$
$$32B + D = 0 \;\rightarrow\; 32(0) + D = 0 \;\rightarrow\; D = 0$$
$$256A + 16C + E = 0 \;\rightarrow\; 256(0) + 16(1) + E = 0 \;\rightarrow\; E = -16$$
$$256B + 16D + F = 0 \;\rightarrow\; 256(0) + 16(0) + F = 0 \;\rightarrow\; F = 0$$

$$\frac{x^3}{(x^2 + 16)^3} = \frac{x}{(x^2 + 16)^2} + \frac{-16x}{(x^2 + 16)^3}$$

39. Find the partial fraction decomposition:

$$\frac{4}{2x^2 - 5x - 3} = \frac{4}{(x - 3)(2x + 1)} = \frac{A}{x - 3} + \frac{B}{2x + 1}$$

(Multiply both sides by $(x - 3)(2x + 1)$.)

$$4 = A(2x + 1) + B(x - 3)$$

Let $x = -\dfrac{1}{2}$: then $4 = A\left(2\left(-\dfrac{1}{2}\right) + 1\right) + B\left(-\dfrac{1}{2} - 3\right)$

$$\rightarrow\; 4 = -\frac{7}{2}B \;\rightarrow\; B = -\frac{8}{7}$$

Let $x = 3$: then $4 = A(2(3) + 1) + B(3 - 3) \;\rightarrow\; 4 = 7A \;\rightarrow\; A = \dfrac{4}{7}$

$$\frac{4}{2x^2 - 5x - 3} = \frac{4}{(x - 3)(2x + 1)} = \frac{\left(\dfrac{4}{7}\right)}{x - 3} + \frac{\left(-\dfrac{8}{7}\right)}{2x + 1}$$

41. Find the partial fraction decomposition:

$$\frac{2x + 3}{x^4 - 9x^2} = \frac{2x + 3}{x^2(x - 3)(x + 3)} = \frac{A}{x} + \frac{B}{x^2} + \frac{C}{x - 3} + \frac{D}{x + 3}$$

(Multiply both sides by $x^2(x - 3)(x + 3)$.)

$$2x + 3 = Ax(x - 3)(x + 3) + B(x - 3)(x + 3) + Cx^2(x + 3) + Dx^2(x - 3)$$

Let $x = 0$: then

$$2 \cdot 0 + 3 = A \cdot 0(0 - 3)(0 + 3) + B(0 - 3)(0 + 3) + C \cdot 0^2(0 + 3) + D \cdot 0^2(0 - 3)$$

$$\rightarrow\; 3 = -9B \;\rightarrow\; B = -\frac{1}{3}$$

Let $x = 3$: then

$$2 \cdot 3 + 3 = A \cdot 3(3 - 3)(3 + 3) + B(3 - 3)(3 + 3) + C \cdot 3^2(3 + 3) + D \cdot 3^2(3 - 3)$$

$$\rightarrow\; 9 = 54C \;\rightarrow\; C = \frac{1}{6}$$

Let $x = -3$: then

$$2(-3) + 3 = A(-3)(-3-3)(-3+3) + B(-3-3)(-3+3) + C(-3)^2(-3+3)$$
$$+ D(-3)^2(-3-3)$$

$$\rightarrow -3 = -54D \rightarrow D = \frac{1}{18}$$

Let $x = 1$: then

$$2 \cdot 1 + 3 = A \cdot 1(1-3)(1+3) + B(1-3)(1+3) + C \cdot 1^2(1+3) + D \cdot 1^2(1-3)$$

$$\rightarrow 5 = -8A - 8B + 4C - 2D$$

$$\rightarrow 5 = -8A - 8\left(-\frac{1}{3}\right) + 4\left(\frac{1}{6}\right) - 2\left(\frac{1}{18}\right)$$

$$\rightarrow 5 = -8A + \frac{8}{3} + \frac{2}{3} - \frac{1}{9} \rightarrow -8A = \frac{16}{9} \rightarrow A = -\frac{2}{9}$$

$$\frac{2x+3}{x^4-9x^2} = \frac{2x+3}{x^2(x-3)(x+3)} = \frac{\left(-\frac{2}{9}\right)}{x} + \frac{\left(-\frac{1}{3}\right)}{x^2} + \frac{\left(\frac{1}{6}\right)}{x-3} + \frac{\left(\frac{1}{18}\right)}{x+3}$$

Chapter 8

Systems of Equations and Inequalities

8.7 Systems of Nonlinear Equations

1. $\begin{cases} y = x^2 + 1 \\ y = x + 1 \end{cases}$

   Graph: $y_1 = x^2 + 1$; $y_2 = x + 1$

   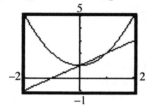

   (0, 1) and (1, 2) are the intersection points.

   Solve by substitution:
   $$x^2 + 1 = x + 1$$
   $$x^2 - x = 0$$
   $$x(x - 1) = 0$$
   $$x = 0 \ \text{ or } \ x = 1$$
   $$y = 1 \qquad y = 2$$
   Solutions: (0, 1) and (1, 2)

3. $\begin{cases} y = \sqrt{36 - x^2} \\ y = 8 - x \end{cases}$

   Graph: $y_1 = \sqrt{36 - x^2}$; $y_2 = 8 - x$

   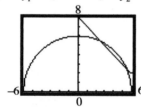

   (2.59, 5.41) and (5.41, 2.59) are the intersection points.

   Solve by substitution:
   $$\sqrt{36 - x^2} = 8 - x$$
   $$36 - x^2 = 64 - 16x + x^2$$
   $$2x^2 - 16x + 28 = 0$$
   $$x^2 - 8x + 14 = 0$$
   $$x = \frac{8 \pm \sqrt{64 - 56}}{2}$$
   $$x = \frac{8 \pm 2\sqrt{2}}{2}$$
   $$x = 4 \pm \sqrt{2}$$

   If $x = 4 + \sqrt{2}$, $y = 8 - \left(4 + \sqrt{2}\right) = 4 - \sqrt{2}$

   If $x = 4 - \sqrt{2}$, $y = 8 - \left(4 - \sqrt{2}\right) = 4 + \sqrt{2}$

   Solutions:
   $$\left(4 + \sqrt{2}, 4 - \sqrt{2}\right) \text{ and } \left(4 - \sqrt{2}, 4 + \sqrt{2}\right)$$

5. $\begin{cases} y = \sqrt{x} \\ y = 2 - x \end{cases}$

Graph: $y_1 = \sqrt{x}$; $y_2 = 2 - x$

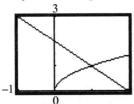

(1, 1) is the intersection point.

Solve by substitution:
$$\sqrt{x} = 2 - x$$
$$x = 4 - 4x + x^2$$
$$x^2 - 5x + 4 = 0$$
$$(x - 4)(x - 1) = 0$$
$$x = 4 \quad \text{or } x = 1$$
$$y = -2 \quad \text{or } y = 1$$

Eliminate (4, –2); it does not check.
Solution: (1, 1)

7. $\begin{cases} x = 2y \\ x = y^2 - 2y \end{cases}$

Solve each equation for y in order to enter it into the graphing utility:
$$y^2 - 2y + 1 = x + 1 \rightarrow (y - 1)^2 = x + 1$$
$$y - 1 = \pm\sqrt{x + 1} \rightarrow y = 1 \pm \sqrt{x + 1}$$

Graph: $y_1 = \dfrac{x}{2}$; $y_2 = 1 + \sqrt{x + 1}$;

$y_3 = 1 - \sqrt{x + 1}$

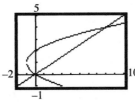

(0, 0) and (8, 4) are the intersection points.

Solve by substitution:
$$2y = y^2 - 2y$$
$$y^2 - 4y = 0$$
$$y(y - 4) = 0$$
$$y = 0 \quad \text{or } y = 4$$
$$x = 0 \quad \text{or } x = 8$$

Solutions: (0, 0) and (8, 4)

9. $\begin{cases} x^2 + y^2 = 4 \\ x^2 + 2x + y^2 = 0 \end{cases}$

Graph: $y_1 = \sqrt{4 - x^2}$; $y_2 = -\sqrt{4 - x^2}$; $y_3 = \sqrt{-x^2 - 2x}$; $y_4 = -\sqrt{-x^2 - 2x}$

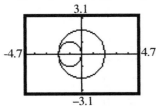

(–2, 0) is the intersection point.
(Note: This intersection point is impossible to find on your graphing utility unless you have just the right window and make an excellent guess.)

Substitute 4 for $x^2 + y^2$ in the second equation:
$$2x + 4 = 0$$
$$2x = -4$$
$$x = -2$$
$$y = \sqrt{4 - (-2)^2} = 0$$

Solution: (–2, 0)

11. $\begin{cases} y = 3x - 5 \\ x^2 + y^2 = 5 \end{cases}$

Graph: $y_1 = 3x - 5$; $y_2 = \sqrt{5 - x^2}$;
$y_3 = -\sqrt{5 - x^2}$

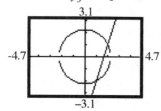

(1, –2) and (2, 1) are the intersection points.

Solve by substitution:
$$x^2 + (3x - 5)^2 = 5$$
$$x^2 + 9x^2 - 30x + 25 = 5$$
$$10x^2 - 30x + 20 = 0$$
$$x^2 - 3x + 2 = 0$$
$$(x - 1)(x - 2) = 0$$
$$x = 1 \qquad \text{or } x = 2$$
$$y = 3(1) - 5 \qquad y = 3(2) - 5$$
$$y = -2 \qquad\quad y = 1$$

Solutions: (1, –2) and (2, 1)

13. $\begin{cases} x^2 + y^2 = 4 \\ y^2 - x = 4 \end{cases}$

Graph: $y_1 = \sqrt{4 - x^2}$; $y_2 = -\sqrt{4 - x^2}$; $y_3 = \sqrt{x + 4}$; $y_4 = -\sqrt{x + 4}$

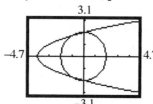

(–1, 1.73), (–1, –1.73), (0, 2), and (0, –2) are the intersection points.

Substitute $x + 4$ for y^2 in the first equation:
$$x^2 + x + 4 = 4$$
$$x^2 + x = 0$$
$$x(x + 1) = 0$$
$$x = 0 \qquad \text{or } x = -1$$
$$y^2 = 4 \qquad\quad y^2 = 3$$
$$y = \pm 2 \qquad y^2 = \pm\sqrt{3}$$

Solutions:
$$(0, -2),\ (0, 2),\ \left(-1,\ \sqrt{3}\right),\ \left(-1,\ -\sqrt{3}\right)$$

15. $\begin{cases} xy = 4 \\ x^2 + y^2 = 8 \end{cases}$

Graph: $y_1 = \dfrac{4}{x}$; $y_2 = \sqrt{8 - x^2}$;
$y_3 = -\sqrt{8 - x^2}$

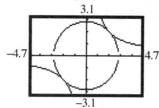

(–2, –2) and (2, 2) are the intersection points.

Solve by substitution:
$$x^2 + \left(\frac{4}{x}\right)^2 = 8$$
$$x^2 + \frac{16}{x^2} = 8$$
$$x^4 + 16 = 8x^2$$
$$x^4 - 8x^2 + 16 = 0$$
$$\left(x^2 - 4\right)^2 = 0$$
$$x^2 - 4 = 0$$
$$x^2 = 4$$
$$x = 2 \text{ or } x = -2$$
$$y = 2 \qquad y = -2$$

Solutions: (–2, –2) and (2, 2)

17. $\begin{cases} x^2 + y^2 = 4 \\ \quad\ y = x^2 - 9 \end{cases}$

Graph: $y_1 = x^2 - 9$; $y_2 = \sqrt{4 - x^2}$;
$$y_3 = -\sqrt{4 - x^2}$$

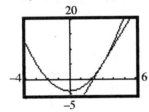

No solution; Inconsistent.

Solve by substitution:
$$x^2 + (x^2 - 9)^2 = 4$$
$$x^2 + x^4 - 18x^2 + 81 = 4$$
$$x^4 - 17x^2 + 77 = 0$$
$$x^2 = \frac{17 \pm \sqrt{289 - 4(77)}}{2}$$
$$x^2 = \frac{17 \pm \sqrt{-19}}{2}$$

There are no real solutions to this expression; Inconsistent.

19. $\begin{cases} y = x^2 - 4 \\ y = 6x - 13 \end{cases}$

Graph: $y_1 = x^2 - 4$; $y_2 = 6x - 13$

(3,5) is the intersection point.

Solve by substitution:
$$x^2 - 4 = 6x - 13$$
$$x^2 - 6x + 9 = 0$$
$$(x - 3)^2 = 0$$
$$x - 3 = 0$$
$$x = 3$$
$$y = 6(3) - 13 = 5$$

Solutions: $(3,5)$

21. Solve the second equation for y, substitute into the first equation and solve:

$\begin{cases} 2x^2 + y^2 = 18 \\ \quad\quad xy = 4 \ \rightarrow \ y = \dfrac{4}{x} \end{cases}$

$$2x^2 + \left(\frac{4}{x}\right)^2 = 18 \rightarrow 2x^2 + \frac{16}{x^2} = 18$$

$$2x^4 + 16 = 18x^2 \rightarrow 2x^4 - 18x^2 + 16 = 0$$

$$x^4 - 9x^2 + 8 = 0 \rightarrow (x^2 - 8)(x^2 - 1) = 0$$

$$x^2 = 8 \ \rightarrow x = \pm\sqrt{8} = \pm 2\sqrt{2}$$

$$x^2 = 1 \rightarrow \ x = \pm 1$$

If $x = 2\sqrt{2}$: $\quad y = \dfrac{4}{2\sqrt{2}} = \sqrt{2}$

If $x = -2\sqrt{2}$: $\quad y = \dfrac{4}{-2\sqrt{2}} = -\sqrt{2}$

If $x = 1$: $\quad\quad y = \dfrac{4}{1} = 4$

If $x = -1$: $\quad\quad y = \dfrac{4}{-1} = -4$

Solutions: $\left(2\sqrt{2}, \sqrt{2}\right), \left(-2\sqrt{2}, -\sqrt{2}\right), (1, 4), (-1, -4)$

23.   Substitute the first equation into the second equation and solve:

$$\begin{cases} y = 2x + 1 \\ 2x^2 + y^2 = 1 \end{cases}$$

$$2x^2 + (2x+1)^2 = 1 \rightarrow 2x^2 + 4x^2 + 4x + 1 = 1$$

$$6x^2 + 4x = 0 \rightarrow 2x(3x+2) = 0$$

$$2x = 0 \quad \text{or} \quad 3x + 2 = 0$$

$$x = 0 \quad \text{or} \qquad x = -\frac{2}{3}$$

If $x = 0$: $y = 2(0) + 1 = 1$

If $x = -\frac{2}{3}$: $y = 2\left(-\frac{2}{3}\right) + 1 = -\frac{4}{3} + 1 = -\frac{1}{3}$

Solutions: $(0, 1), \left(-\frac{2}{3}, -\frac{1}{3}\right)$

25.   Solve the first equation for y, substitute into the second equation and solve:

$$\begin{cases} x + y + 1 = 0 \quad \rightarrow \quad y = -x - 1 \\ x^2 + y^2 + 6y - x = -5 \end{cases}$$

$$x^2 + (-x-1)^2 + 6(-x-1) - x = -5 \rightarrow x^2 + x^2 + 2x + 1 - 6x - 6 - x = -5$$

$$2x^2 - 5x = 0 \rightarrow x(2x - 5) = 0 \rightarrow x = 0 \quad \text{or} \quad x = \frac{5}{2}$$

If $x = 0$: $y = -(0) - 1 = -1$

If $x = \frac{5}{2}$: $y = -\frac{5}{2} - 1 = -\frac{7}{2}$

Solutions: $(0, -1), \left(\frac{5}{2}, -\frac{7}{2}\right)$

27.   Solve the second equation for y, substitute into the first equation and solve:

$$\begin{cases} 4x^2 - 3xy + 9y^2 = 15 \\ \\ 2x + 3y = 5 \quad \rightarrow \quad y = -\frac{2}{3}x + \frac{5}{3} \end{cases}$$

$$4x^2 - 3x\left(-\frac{2}{3}x + \frac{5}{3}\right) + 9\left(-\frac{2}{3}x + \frac{5}{3}\right)^2 = 15 \rightarrow 4x^2 + 2x^2 - 5x + 4x^2 - 20x + 25 = 15$$

$$10x^2 - 25x + 10 = 0 \rightarrow 2x^2 - 5x + 2 = 0$$

$$(2x - 1)(x - 2) = 0 \rightarrow x = \frac{1}{2} \quad \text{or} \quad x = 2$$

If $x = \frac{1}{2}$: $y = -\frac{2}{3}\left(\frac{1}{2}\right) + \frac{5}{3} = \frac{4}{3}$

If $x = 2$: $y = -\frac{2}{3}(2) + \frac{5}{3} = \frac{1}{3}$

Solutions: $\left(\frac{1}{2}, \frac{4}{3}\right), \left(2, \frac{1}{3}\right)$

29. Multiply each side of the second equation by 4 and add the equations to eliminate y:

$$\begin{cases} x^2 - 4y^2 = -7 \\ 3x^2 + y^2 = 31 \end{cases} \xrightarrow[]{} \begin{array}{l} x^2 - 4y^2 = -7 \\ \underline{12x^2 + 4y^2 = 124} \\ 13x^2 = 117 \end{array}$$

$$x^2 = 9$$
$$x = \pm 3$$

If $x = 3$: $3(3)^2 + y^2 = 31 \rightarrow y^2 = 4 \rightarrow y = \pm 2$

If $x = -3$: $3(-3)^2 + y^2 = 31 \rightarrow y^2 = 4 \rightarrow y = \pm 2$

Solutions: $(3, 2), (3, -2), (-3, 2), (-3, -2)$

31. Multiply each side of the first equation by 5 and each side of the second equation by 3 to eliminate y:

$$\begin{cases} 7x^2 - 3y^2 = -5 \\ 3x^2 + 5y^2 = 12 \end{cases} \xrightarrow[3]{5} \begin{array}{l} 35x^2 - 15y^2 = -25 \\ \underline{9x^2 + 15y^2 = 36} \\ 44x^2 = 11 \end{array}$$

$$x^2 = \frac{1}{4} \rightarrow x = \pm\frac{1}{2}$$

If $x = \frac{1}{2}$: $3\left(\frac{1}{2}\right)^2 + 5y^2 = 12 \rightarrow 5y^2 = \frac{45}{4} \rightarrow y^2 = \frac{9}{4} \rightarrow y = \pm\frac{3}{2}$

If $x = -\frac{1}{2}$: $3\left(-\frac{1}{2}\right)^2 + 5y^2 = 12 \rightarrow 5y^2 = \frac{45}{4} \rightarrow y^2 = \frac{9}{4} \rightarrow y = \pm\frac{3}{2}$

Solutions: $\left(\frac{1}{2}, \frac{3}{2}\right), \left(\frac{1}{2}, -\frac{3}{2}\right), \left(-\frac{1}{2}, \frac{3}{2}\right), \left(-\frac{1}{2}, -\frac{3}{2}\right)$

33. Multiply each side of the second equation by 2 and add to eliminate xy:

$$\begin{cases} x^2 + 2xy = 10 \\ 3x^2 - xy = 2 \end{cases} \xrightarrow[2]{} \begin{array}{l} x^2 + 2xy = 10 \\ \underline{6x^2 - 2xy = 4} \\ 7x^2 = 14 \end{array}$$

$$x^2 = 2$$
$$x = \pm\sqrt{2}$$

If $x = \sqrt{2}$: $3\left(\sqrt{2}\right)^2 - \sqrt{2} \cdot y = 2 \rightarrow -\sqrt{2} \cdot y = -4 \rightarrow y = \frac{4}{\sqrt{2}} \rightarrow y = 2\sqrt{2}$

If $x = -\sqrt{2}$: $3\left(-\sqrt{2}\right)^2 - \left(-\sqrt{2}\right)y = 2 \rightarrow \sqrt{2} \cdot y = -4 \rightarrow y = \frac{-4}{\sqrt{2}} \rightarrow y = -2\sqrt{2}$

Solutions: $\left(\sqrt{2}, 2\sqrt{2}\right), \left(-\sqrt{2}, -2\sqrt{2}\right)$

35. Multiply each side of the first equation by 2 and add the equations to eliminate y:

$$\begin{cases} 2x^2 + y^2 = 2 \xrightarrow{\;2\;} 4x^2 + 2y^2 = 4 \\ x^2 - 2y^2 = -8 \longrightarrow \underline{\; x^2 - 2y^2 = -8 \;} \end{cases}$$

$$5x^2 \qquad = -4$$

$$x^2 = -\frac{4}{5}$$

No solution. The system is inconsistent.

37. Multiply each side of the second equation by 2 and add the equations to eliminate y:

$$\begin{cases} x^2 + 2y^2 = 16 \longrightarrow \quad x^2 + 2y^2 = 16 \\ 4x^2 - y^2 = 24 \xrightarrow{\;2\;} \underline{\; 8x^2 - 2y^2 = 48 \;} \end{cases}$$

$$9x^2 \qquad = 64$$

$$x^2 = \frac{64}{9} \quad \rightarrow \quad x = \pm\frac{8}{3}$$

If $x = \frac{8}{3}$: $\left(\frac{8}{3}\right)^2 + 2y^2 = 16 \;\rightarrow\; 2y^2 = \frac{80}{9} \;\rightarrow\; y^2 = \frac{40}{9} \;\rightarrow\; y = \pm\frac{2\sqrt{10}}{3}$

If $x = -\frac{8}{3}$: $\left(-\frac{8}{3}\right)^2 + 2y^2 = 16 \;\rightarrow\; 2y^2 = \frac{80}{9} \;\rightarrow\; y^2 = \frac{40}{9} \;\rightarrow\; y = \pm\frac{2\sqrt{10}}{3}$

Solutions: $\left(\frac{8}{3}, \frac{2\sqrt{10}}{3}\right), \left(\frac{8}{3}, \frac{-2\sqrt{10}}{3}\right), \left(-\frac{8}{3}, \frac{2\sqrt{10}}{3}\right), \left(-\frac{8}{3}, \frac{-2\sqrt{10}}{3}\right)$

39. Multiply each side of the second equation by 2 and add the equations to eliminate y:

$$\begin{cases} \dfrac{5}{x^2} - \dfrac{2}{y^2} = -3 \longrightarrow \dfrac{5}{x^2} - \dfrac{2}{y^2} = -3 \\ \dfrac{3}{x^2} + \dfrac{1}{y^2} = 7 \xrightarrow{\;2\;} \underline{\; \dfrac{6}{x^2} + \dfrac{2}{y^2} = 14 \;} \end{cases}$$

$$\dfrac{11}{x^2} \qquad = 11$$

$$11 = 11x^2 \rightarrow x^2 = 1 \rightarrow x = \pm 1$$

If $x = 1$: $\dfrac{3}{(1)^2} + \dfrac{1}{y^2} = 7 \;\rightarrow\; \dfrac{1}{y^2} = 4 \;\rightarrow\; y^2 = \dfrac{1}{4} \;\rightarrow\; y = \pm\dfrac{1}{2}$

If $x = -1$: $\dfrac{3}{(-1)^2} + \dfrac{1}{y^2} = 7 \;\rightarrow\; \dfrac{1}{y^2} = 4 \;\rightarrow\; y^2 = \dfrac{1}{4} \;\rightarrow\; y = \pm\dfrac{1}{2}$

Solutions: $\left(1, \dfrac{1}{2}\right), \left(1, -\dfrac{1}{2}\right), \left(-1, \dfrac{1}{2}\right), \left(-1, -\dfrac{1}{2}\right)$

41. Multiply each side of the first equation by –2 and add the equations to eliminate x:

$$\begin{cases} \dfrac{1}{x^4} + \dfrac{6}{y^4} = 6 \xrightarrow{-2} \dfrac{-2}{x^4} - \dfrac{12}{y^4} = -12 \\[4mm] \dfrac{2}{x^4} - \dfrac{2}{y^4} = 19 \longrightarrow \dfrac{2}{x^4} - \dfrac{2}{y^4} = 19 \end{cases}$$

$$\dfrac{-14}{y^4} = 7$$

$$-14 = 7y^4 \rightarrow y^4 = -2$$

There are no real solutions. The system is inconsistent.

43. Factor the first equation, solve for x, substitute into the second equation and solve:

$$\begin{cases} x^2 - 3xy + 2y^2 = 0 \ \rightarrow \ (x - 2y)(x - y) = 0 \ \rightarrow \ x = 2y \text{ or } x = y \\ x^2 + xy = 6 \end{cases}$$

Substitute $x = 2y$ and solve:

$$x^2 + xy = 6$$
$$(2y)^2 + (2y)y = 6$$
$$4y^2 + 2y^2 = 6 \rightarrow 6y^2 = 6$$
$$y^2 = 1 \rightarrow y = \pm 1$$

If $y = 1$: $x = 2 \cdot 1 = 2$
If $y = -1$: $x = 2(-1) = -2$

Substitute $x = y$ and solve:

$$x^2 + xy = 6$$
$$y^2 + y \cdot y = 6$$
$$y^2 + y^2 = 6 \rightarrow 2y^2 = 6$$
$$y^2 = 3 \rightarrow y = \pm\sqrt{3}$$

If $y = \sqrt{3}$: $x = \sqrt{3}$
If $y = -\sqrt{3}$: $x = -\sqrt{3}$

Solutions: $(2, 1), (-2, -1), \left(\sqrt{3}, \sqrt{3}\right), \left(-\sqrt{3}, -\sqrt{3}\right)$

45. Multiply each side of the second equation by –y and add the equations to eliminate y:

$$\begin{cases} y^2 + y + x^2 - x - 2 = 0 \longrightarrow y^2 + y + x^2 - x - 2 = 0 \\ y + 1 + \dfrac{x-2}{y} = 0 \xrightarrow{-y} -y^2 - y \quad - x + 2 = 0 \end{cases}$$

$$x^2 - 2x = 0 \rightarrow x(x - 2) = 0$$
$$x = 0 \text{ or } x = 2$$

If $x = 0$: $y^2 + y + 0^2 - 0 - 2 = 0 \ \rightarrow \ y^2 + y - 2 = 0 \ \rightarrow \ (y + 2)(y - 1) = 0$
$$\rightarrow \ y = -2 \text{ or } y = 1$$

If $x = 2$: $y^2 + y + 2^2 - 2 - 2 = 0 \ \rightarrow \ y^2 + y = 0 \ \rightarrow \ y(y + 1) = 0$
$$\rightarrow \ y = 0 \text{ or } y = -1$$

Solutions: $(0, -2), (0, 1), (2, 0), (2, -1)$

47.   Rewrite each equation in exponential form:
$$\begin{cases} \log_x y = 3 \;\rightarrow\; y = x^3 \\ \log_x(4y) = 5 \;\rightarrow\; 4y = x^5 \end{cases}$$
Substitute the first equation into the second and solve:
$$4x^3 = x^5$$
$$x^5 - 4x^3 = 0 \rightarrow x^3(x^2 - 4) = 0 \rightarrow x^3 = 0 \text{ or } x^2 = 4 \rightarrow x = 0 \text{ or } x = \pm 2$$
The base of a logarithm must be positive, thus $x \neq 0$ and $x \neq -2$.
$$\text{If } x = 2\!: \qquad y = 2^3 = 8$$
Solution: $(2, 8)$

49.   Rewrite each equation in exponential form:
$$\begin{cases} \ln x = 4 \ln y \;\rightarrow\; x = e^{4 \ln y} = e^{\ln y^4} = y^4 \\ \log_3 x = 2 + 2\log_3 y \;\rightarrow\; x = 3^{2 + 2\log_3 y} = 3^2 \cdot 3^{2\log_3 y} = 3^2 \cdot 3^{\log_3 y^2} = 9y^2 \end{cases}$$
So we have the system
$$\begin{cases} x = y^4 \\ x = 9y^2 \end{cases}$$
Therefore we have
$$9y^2 = y^4 \rightarrow 9y^2 - y^4 = 0$$
$$y^2(9 - y^2) = 0 \rightarrow y^2(3 + y)(3 - y) = 0$$
$$y = 0 \text{ or } y = -3 \text{ or } y = 3$$
Since $\ln y$ is undefined when $y \leq 0$, the only solution is $y = 3$.
$$\text{If } y = 3\!: \qquad x = y^4 \rightarrow x = 3^4 = 81$$
Solution: $(81, 3)$

51.   Solve the first equation for x, substitute into the second equation and solve:
$$\begin{cases} x + 2y = 0 \;\rightarrow\; x = -2y \\ (x - 1)^2 + (y - 1)^2 = 5 \end{cases}$$
$$(-2y - 1)^2 + (y - 1)^2 = 5$$
$$4y^2 + 4y + 1 + y^2 - 2y + 1 = 5$$
$$5y^2 + 2y - 3 = 0$$
$$(5y - 3)(y + 1) = 0$$
$$y = \frac{3}{5} = 0.6 \text{ or } y = -1$$
$$x = -\frac{6}{5} = -1.2 \text{ or } x = 2$$

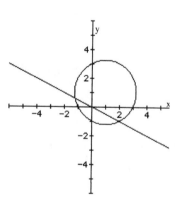

The points of intersection are $(-1.2, 0.6), (2, -1)$.

53. Complete the square on the second equation, substitute into the first equation and solve:

$$\begin{cases} (x-1)^2 + (y+2)^2 = 4 \\ y^2 + 4y - x + 1 = 0 \;\rightarrow\; y^2 + 4y + 4 = x - 1 + 4 \rightarrow (y+2)^2 = x + 3 \end{cases}$$

$$(x-1)^2 + x + 3 = 4$$
$$x^2 - 2x + 1 + x + 3 = 4$$
$$x^2 - x = 0$$
$$x(x-1) = 0$$
$$x = 0 \quad \text{or} \quad x = 1$$

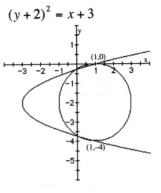

If $x = 0$: $(y+2)^2 = 0 + 3 \;\rightarrow\; y + 2 = \pm\sqrt{3}$
$$\rightarrow\; y = -2 \pm \sqrt{3}$$

If $x = 1$: $(y+2)^2 = 1 + 3 \;\rightarrow\; y + 2 = \pm 2$
$$\rightarrow\; y = -2 \pm 2$$

The points of intersection are:
$$\left(0, -2 - \sqrt{3}\right), \left(0, -2 + \sqrt{3}\right), (1, -4), (1, 0).$$

55. Solve the first equation for x, substitute into the second equation and solve:

$$\begin{cases} \quad y = \dfrac{4}{x-3} \;\rightarrow\; x - 3 = \dfrac{4}{y} \;\rightarrow\; x = \dfrac{4}{y} + 3 \\ x^2 - 6x + y^2 + 1 = 0 \end{cases}$$

$$\left(\frac{4}{y}+3\right)^2 - 6\left(\frac{4}{y}+3\right) + y^2 + 1 = 0$$

$$\frac{16}{y^2} + \frac{24}{y} + 9 - \frac{24}{y} - 18 + y^2 + 1 = 0$$

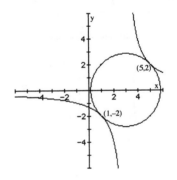

$$\frac{16}{y^2} + y^2 - 8 = 0$$
$$16 + y^4 - 8y^2 = 0$$
$$y^4 - 8y^2 + 16 = 0$$
$$(y^2 - 4)^2 = 0$$
$$y^2 - 4 = 0$$
$$y^2 = 4$$
$$y = \pm 2$$

If $y = 2$: $x = \dfrac{4}{2} + 3 = 5$

If $y = -2$: $x = \dfrac{4}{-2} + 3 = 1$

The points of intersection are: $(1, -2), (5, 2)$.

57.   Graph: $y_1 = x \wedge (2/3); \quad y_2 = e \wedge (-x)$
      Use INTERSECT to solve:

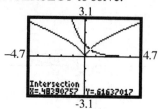

Solution: $(0.48, 0.62)$

59.   Graph: $y_1 = \sqrt[3]{(2 - x^2)}; \quad y_2 = 4/x^3$
      Use INTERSECT to solve:

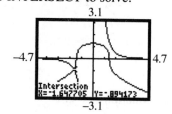

Solution: $(-1.65, -0.89)$

61.   Graph: $y_1 = \sqrt[4]{(12 - x^4)}; \quad y_2 = -\sqrt[4]{(12 - x^4)}; \quad y_3 = \sqrt{2/x}; \quad y_4 = -\sqrt{2/x}$
      Use INTERSECT to solve:

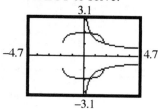

Solutions: $(0.58, 1.86), (1.81, 1.05), (1.81, -1.05), (0.58, -1.86)$

63.   Graph: $y_1 = 2/x; \quad y_2 = \ln x$
      Use INTERSECT to solve:

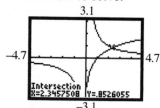

Solution: $(2.35, 0.85)$

65. Let x and y be the two numbers. The system of equations is:

$$\begin{cases} x - y = 2 \\ x^2 + y^2 = 10 \end{cases}$$

Solve the first equation for x, substitute into the second equation and solve:

$$(y+2)^2 + y^2 = 10 \rightarrow y^2 + 4y + 4 + y^2 = 10$$

$$2y^2 + 4y - 6 = 0 \rightarrow y^2 + 2y - 3 = 0 \rightarrow (y+3)(y-1) = 0 \rightarrow y = -3 \text{ or } y = 1$$

If $y = -3$: $x = -3 + 2 = -1$

If $y = 1$: $x = 1 + 2 = 3$

The two numbers are 1 and 3 or -1 and -3.

67. Let x and y be the two numbers. The system of equations is:

$$\begin{cases} xy = 4 \\ x^2 + y^2 = 8 \end{cases}$$

Solve the first equation for x, substitute into the second equation and solve:

$$\left(\frac{4}{y}\right)^2 + y^2 = 8 \rightarrow \frac{16}{y^2} + y^2 = 8 \rightarrow 16 + y^4 = 8y^2$$

$$y^4 - 8y^2 + 16 = 0 \rightarrow (y^2 - 4)^2 = 0 \rightarrow y^2 - 4 = 0 \rightarrow y^2 = 4 \rightarrow y = \pm 2$$

If $y = 2$: $x = \frac{4}{2} = 2$

If $y = -2$: $x = \frac{4}{-2} = -2$

The two numbers are 2 and 2 or -2 and -2.

69. Let x and y be the two numbers. The system of equations is:

$$\begin{cases} x - y = xy \\ \dfrac{1}{x} + \dfrac{1}{y} = 5 \end{cases}$$

Solve the first equation for x, substitute into the second equation and solve:

$$x - xy = y \rightarrow x(1 - y) = y \rightarrow x = \frac{y}{1 - y}$$

$$\frac{1}{\left(\dfrac{y}{1-y}\right)} + \frac{1}{y} = 5 \rightarrow \frac{1-y}{y} + \frac{1}{y} = 5$$

$$\frac{2-y}{y} = 5 \rightarrow 2 - y = 5y \rightarrow 6y = 2 \rightarrow y = \frac{1}{3}$$

If $y = \frac{1}{3}$: $x = \dfrac{\left(\dfrac{1}{3}\right)}{\left(1 - \dfrac{1}{3}\right)} = \dfrac{\left(\dfrac{1}{3}\right)}{\left(\dfrac{2}{3}\right)} = \dfrac{1}{2}$

The two numbers are $\dfrac{1}{2}$ and $\dfrac{1}{3}$.

71. $\begin{cases} \dfrac{a}{b} = \dfrac{2}{3} \\ a + b = 10 \end{cases}$

Solve the second equation for a, substitute into the first equation and solve:

$$\frac{10 - b}{b} = \frac{2}{3} \rightarrow 3(10 - b) = 2b \rightarrow 30 - 3b = 2b \rightarrow 30 = 5b$$

$$b = 6 \rightarrow a = 4$$
$$a + b = 10; \quad b - a = 2$$

The ratio of $a + b$ to $b - a$ is $\dfrac{10}{2} = 5$.

73. Let x = the width of the rectangle.
Let y = the length of the rectangle.

$$\begin{cases} 2x + 2y = 16 \\ xy = 15 \end{cases}$$

Solve the first equation for y, substitute into the second equation and solve:

$$2x + 2y = 16 \qquad\qquad x(8 - x) = 15$$
$$2y = 16 - 2x \qquad\qquad 8x - x^2 = 15$$
$$y = 8 - x$$
$$x^2 - 8x + 15 = 0 \rightarrow (x - 5)(x - 3) = 0$$
$$x = 5 \text{ or } x = 3$$
$$y = 3 \qquad y = 5$$

The dimensions of the rectangle are 3 inches by 5 inches.

75. Let x = the radius of the first circle.
Let y = the radius of the second circle.

$$\begin{cases} 2\pi x + 2\pi y = 12\pi \\ \pi x^2 + \pi y^2 = 20\pi \end{cases}$$

Solve the first equation for y, substitute into the second equation and solve:

$$2\pi x + 2\pi y = 12\pi \qquad\qquad \pi x^2 + \pi y^2 = 20\pi$$
$$x + y = 6 \qquad\qquad\qquad x^2 + y^2 = 20$$
$$y = 6 - x \qquad\qquad\qquad x^2 + (6 - x)^2 = 20$$
$$x^2 + 36 - 12x + x^2 = 20$$
$$2x^2 - 12x + 16 = 0$$
$$x^2 - 6x + 8 = 0$$
$$(x - 4)(x - 2) = 0$$
$$x = 4 \text{ or } x = 2$$
$$y = 2 \qquad y = 4$$

The radii of the circles are 2 centimeters and 4 centimeters.

77. The tortoise takes $9 + 3 = 12$ minutes or 0.2 hour longer to complete the race than the hare.
Let $r =$ the rate of the hare.
Let $t =$ the time for the hare to complete the race.
Then $t + 0.2 =$ the time for the tortoise.
$r - 0.5 =$ the rate for the tortoise.
Since the length of the race is 21 meters, the distance equations are:
$$\begin{cases} rt = 21 \\ (r - 0.5)(t + 0.2) = 21 \end{cases}$$
Solve the first equation for r, substitute into the second equation and solve:
$$\left(\frac{21}{t} - 0.5\right)(t + 0.2) = 21 \rightarrow 21 + \frac{4.2}{t} - 0.5t - 0.1 = 21$$
$$10t \cdot \left(21 + \frac{4.2}{t} - 0.5t - 0.1\right) = 10t \cdot (21)$$
$$210t + 42 - 5t^2 - t = 210t \rightarrow 5t^2 + t - 42 = 0 \rightarrow (5t - 14)(t + 3) = 0$$
$$t = \frac{14}{5} = 2.8 \text{ or } t = -3$$
$t = -3$ makes no sense, since time cannot be negative.

Solve for r:
$$r = \frac{21}{2.8} = 7.5$$
The average speed of the hare is 7.5 meters per hour, and the average speed for the tortoise
is 7 meters per hour.

79. Let $x =$ the width of the cardboard.
Let $y =$ the length of the cardboard.
The width of the box will be $x - 4$, the length of the box will be $y - 4$, and the height is 2.
The volume is $V = (x - 4)(y - 4)(2)$.
Solve the system of equations:
$$\begin{cases} xy = 216 \\ 2(x - 4)(y - 4) = 224 \end{cases}$$
Solve the first equation for y, substitute into the second equation and solve:
$$(2x - 8)\left(\frac{216}{x} - 4\right) = 224 \rightarrow 432 - 8x - \frac{1728}{x} + 32 = 224$$
$$432x - 8x^2 - 1728 + 32x = 224x \rightarrow -8x^2 + 240x - 1728 = 0 \rightarrow x^2 - 30x + 216 = 0$$
$$(x - 12)(x - 18) = 0 \rightarrow x = 12 \text{ or } x = 18$$
$$y = 18 \qquad y = 12$$
The cardboard should be 12 centimeters by 18 centimeters.

81. Find equations relating area and perimeter:
$$\begin{cases} x^2 + y^2 = 4500 \\ 3x + 3y + (x - y) = 300 \end{cases}$$
Solve the second equation for y, substitute into the first equation and solve:
$$4x + 2y = 300$$

$$2y = 300 - 4x \qquad\qquad x^2 + (150 - 2x)^2 = 4500$$
$$y = 150 - 2x \qquad\qquad x^2 + 22500 - 600x + 4x^2 = 4500$$
$$5x^2 - 600x + 18000 = 0 \rightarrow x^2 - 120x + 3600 = 0$$
$$(x - 60)^2 = 0 \rightarrow x - 60 = 0$$
$$x = 60$$
$$y = 150 - 2(60) = 30$$

The sides of the squares are 30 feet and 60 feet.

83. Solve the system for l and w:
$$\begin{cases} 2l + 2w = P \\ \quad lw = A \end{cases}$$
Solve the first equation for l, substitute into the second equation and solve:
$$2l = P - 2w \ \rightarrow\ l = \frac{P}{2} - w$$

$$\left(\frac{P}{2} - w\right)w = A \rightarrow \frac{P}{2}w - w^2 = A \rightarrow w^2 - \frac{P}{2}w + A = 0$$

$$w = \frac{\frac{P}{2} \pm \sqrt{\frac{P^2}{4} - 4A}}{2} = \frac{\frac{P}{2} \pm \sqrt{\frac{P^2 - 16A}{4}}}{2} = \frac{\frac{P}{2} \pm \frac{\sqrt{P^2 - 16A}}{2}}{2}$$

$$w = \frac{P \pm \sqrt{P^2 - 16A}}{4}$$

If $w = \dfrac{P + \sqrt{P^2 - 16A}}{4}$ then $l = \dfrac{P}{2} - \dfrac{P + \sqrt{P^2 - 16A}}{4} = \dfrac{P - \sqrt{P^2 - 16A}}{4}$

If $w = \dfrac{P - \sqrt{P^2 - 16A}}{4}$ then $l = \dfrac{P}{2} - \dfrac{P - \sqrt{P^2 - 16A}}{4} = \dfrac{P + \sqrt{P^2 - 16A}}{4}$

If it is required that length be greater than width, then the solution is:

$$w = \frac{P - \sqrt{P^2 - 16A}}{4} \text{ and } l = \frac{P + \sqrt{P^2 - 16A}}{4}$$

85. Solve the equation:

$$m^2 - 4(2m - 4) = 0 \rightarrow m^2 - 8m + 16 = 0 \rightarrow (m - 4)^2 = 0 \rightarrow m - 4 = 0 \rightarrow m = 4$$
Use the point-slope equation with slope 4 and the point $(2, 4)$ to obtain the equation of the tangent line:

$$y - 4 = 4(x - 2) \rightarrow y - 4 = 4x - 8 \rightarrow y = 4x - 4$$

87. Solve the system:
$$\begin{cases} y = x^2 + 2 \\ y = mx + b \end{cases}$$
Solve the system by substitution:
$$x^2 + 2 = mx + b$$
$$x^2 - mx + 2 - b = 0$$
Note that the tangent line passes through (1, 3). Find the relation between m and b:
$$3 = m(1) + b$$
$$b = 3 - m$$
Substitute into the quadratic to eliminate b:
$$x^2 - mx + 2 - (3 - m) = 0$$
$$x^2 - mx + (m - 1) = 0$$
Find when the discriminant is 0:
$$(-m)^2 - 4(1)(m - 1) = 0 \rightarrow m^2 - 4m + 4 = 0 \rightarrow (m - 2)^2 = 0$$
$$m - 2 = 0 \rightarrow m = 2 \quad \rightarrow \quad b = 3 - 2 = 1$$
The equation of the tangent line is $y = 2x + 1$.

89. Solve the system:
$$\begin{cases} 2x^2 + 3y^2 = 14 \\ \qquad y = mx + b \end{cases}$$
Solve the system by substitution:
$$2x^2 + 3(mx + b)^2 = 14$$
$$2x^2 + 3m^2x^2 + 6mbx + 3b^2 = 14$$
$$(3m^2 + 2)x^2 + 6mbx + 3b^2 - 14 = 0$$
Note that the tangent line passes through (1, 2). Find the relation between m and b:
$$2 = m(1) + b$$
$$b = 2 - m$$
Substitute into the quadratic to eliminate b:
$$(3m^2 + 2)x^2 + 6m(2 - m)x + 3(2 - m)^2 - 14 = 0$$
$$(3m^2 + 2)x^2 + (12m - 6m^2)x + 12 - 12m + 3m^2 - 14 = 0$$
$$(3m^2 + 2)x^2 + (12m - 6m^2)x + (3m^2 - 12m - 2) = 0$$
Find when the discriminant is 0:
$$(12m - 6m^2)^2 - 4(3m^2 + 2)(3m^2 - 12m - 2) = 0$$
$$144m^2 - 144m^3 + 36m^4 - 4(9m^4 - 36m^3 - 24m - 4) = 0$$
$$144m^2 - 144m^3 + 36m^4 - 36m^4 + 144m^3 + 96m + 16 = 0$$
$$144m^2 + 96m + 16 = 0$$
$$9m^2 + 6m + 1 = 0$$
$$(3m + 1)^2 = 0$$
$$3m + 1 = 0$$
$$m = -\frac{1}{3} \qquad b = 2 - \left(-\frac{1}{3}\right) = \frac{7}{3}$$
The equation of the tangent line is $y = -\frac{1}{3}x + \frac{7}{3}$.

91.   Solve the system:
$$\begin{cases} x^2 - y^2 = 3 \\ \quad y = mx + b \end{cases}$$
Solve the system by substitution:

$$x^2 - (mx + b)^2 = 3 \rightarrow x^2 - m^2 x^2 - 2mbx - b^2 = 3 \rightarrow (1 - m^2)x^2 - 2mbx - b^2 - 3 = 0$$

Note that the tangent line passes through (2, 1). Find the relation between m and b:
$$1 = m(2) + b$$
$$b = 1 - 2m$$

Substitute into the quadratic to eliminate b:
$$(1 - m^2)x^2 - 2m(1 - 2m)x - (1 - 2m)^2 - 3 = 0$$
$$(1 - m^2)x^2 + (-2m + 4m^2)x - 1 + 4m - 4m^2 - 3 = 0$$
$$(1 - m^2)x^2 + (-2m + 4m^2)x + (-4m^2 + 4m - 4) = 0$$

Find when the discriminant is 0:
$$(-2m + 4m^2)^2 - 4(1 - m^2)(-4m^2 + 4m - 4) = 0$$

$$4m^2 - 16m^3 + 16m^4 - 4(4m^4 - 4m^3 + 4m - 4) = 0$$

$$4m^2 - 16m^3 + 16m^4 - 16m^4 + 16m^3 - 16m + 16 = 0$$

$$4m^2 - 16m + 16 = 0 \rightarrow m^2 - 4m + 4 = 0$$

$$(m - 2)^2 = 0 \rightarrow m - 2 = 0 \rightarrow m = 2 \rightarrow b = 1 - 2(2) = -3$$

The equation of the tangent line is $y = 2x - 3$.

93.   Solve for r_1 and r_2:
$$\begin{cases} r_1 + r_2 = -\dfrac{b}{a} \\ \quad r_1 r_2 = \dfrac{c}{a} \end{cases}$$

Substitute and solve:

$$r_1 = -r_2 - \frac{b}{a} \rightarrow \left(-r_2 - \frac{b}{a}\right)r_2 = \frac{c}{a}$$

$$-r_2^{\,2} - \frac{b}{a}r_2 - \frac{c}{a} = 0 \rightarrow ar_2^{\,2} + br_2 + c = 0$$

$$r_2 = \frac{-b \pm \sqrt{b^2 - 4ac}}{2a}$$

$$r_1 = -r_2 - \frac{b}{a} = -\left(\frac{-b \pm \sqrt{b^2 - 4ac}}{2a}\right) - \frac{2b}{2a} = \frac{-b \mp \sqrt{b^2 - 4ac}}{2a}$$

The solutions are: $\dfrac{-b + \sqrt{b^2 - 4ac}}{2a}$ and $\dfrac{-b - \sqrt{b^2 - 4ac}}{2a}$

95. Since the area of the square piece of sheet metal is 100 square feet, the sheet's dimensions are 10 feet by 10 feet. Let x = the length of the cut.

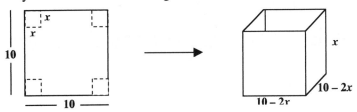

The dimensions of the box are length $= 10 - 2x$; width $= 10 - 2x$, height $= x$

Note that each of these expressions must be positive. So we must have

$x > 0$ and $10 - 2x > 0 \rightarrow x < 5$, that is, $0 < x < 5$.

So the volume of the box is given by

$$V = (length) \cdot (width) \cdot (height) = (10 - 2x)(10 - 2x)(x) = (10 - 2x)^2 (x)$$

(a) In order to get a volume equal to 9 cubic feet, we solve $(10 - 2x)^2 (x) = 9$.

$$(10 - 2x)^2 (x) = 9 \rightarrow (100 - 40x + 4x^2)x = 9 \rightarrow 100x - 40x^2 + 4x^3 = 9$$

So we need to solve the equation $4x^3 - 40x^2 + 100x - 9 = 0$.

Graphing the function $y_1 = 4x^3 - 40x^2 + 100x - 9$ on a calculator yields the graph

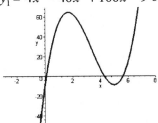

The graph indicates that there three real zeros on the interval [0,6].

Using the ZERO feature of a graphing calculator, we find that the three roots shown occur at $x \approx 0.09$, $x \approx 4.27$ and $x \approx 5.63$.

But we've already noted that we must have $0 < x < 5$, so the only practical values for the cut are $x \approx 0.09$ feet and $x \approx 4.27$ feet.

(b) If the sheet metal has dimensions k feet by k feet, then the volume equation becomes

$$V = (k - 2x)(k - 2x)(x) = (k - 2x)^2 (x) = 9$$

Solving for k we get the quadratic equation

$xk^2 - 4x^2k + 4x^3 - 9 = 0$

$$k = \frac{-(-4x^2) \pm \sqrt{(-4x^2)^2 - 4(x)(4x^3 - 9)}}{2x} = \frac{4x^2 \pm \sqrt{16x^4 - 16x^4 + 36x}}{2x}$$

$$= \frac{4x^2 \pm \sqrt{36x}}{2x} = \frac{4x^2 \pm 6\sqrt{x}}{2x}$$

Therefore, we get a real solution for k provided $x > 0$ and $4x^2 \pm 6\sqrt{x} \geq 0$.

$$4x^2 \pm 6\sqrt{x} \geq 0 \rightarrow 4x^2 \geq 6\sqrt{x} \rightarrow 16x^4 \geq 36x$$

$$16x^4 - 36x \geq 0 \rightarrow 4x(4x^3 - 9) \geq 0$$

This last inequality holds provided $x \geq \sqrt[3]{\dfrac{9}{4}}$.

Systems of Equations and Inequalities

8.8   Systems of Inequalities

1. $x \geq 0$

Graph the line $x = 0$. Use a solid line since the inequality uses $\geq$.

Choose a test point not on the line, such as $(2, 0)$. Since $2 \geq 0$ is true, shade the side of the line containing $(2, 0)$.

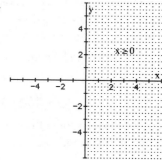

3. $x \geq 4$

Graph the line $x = 4$. Use a solid line since the inequality uses $\geq$.

Choose a test point not on the line, such as $(5, 0)$. Since $5 \geq 0$ is true, shade the side of the line containing $(5, 0)$.

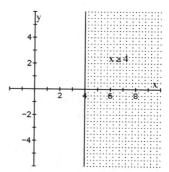

5. $2x + y \geq 6$

Graph the line $2x + y = 6$. Use a solid line since the inequality uses $\geq$.

Choose a test point not on the line, such as $(0, 0)$. Since $2(0) + 0 \geq 6$ is false, shade the opposite side of the line from $(0, 0)$.

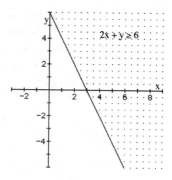

7. $x^2 + y^2 > 1$

Graph the circle $x^2 + y^2 > 1$. Use a dashed line since the inequality uses >.

Choose a test point not on the circle, such As $(0, 0)$. Since $0^2 + 0^2 > 1$ is false, shade the opposite side of the circle from $(0, 0)$.

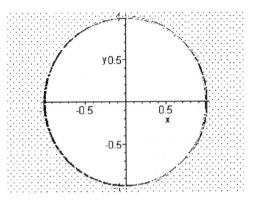

9. $y \leq x^2 - 1$

Graph the parabola $y = x^2 - 1$. Use a solid line since the inequality uses $\leq$.

Choose a test point not on the parabola, such as $(0, 0)$. Since $0 \leq 0^2 - 1$ is false, shade the opposite side of the parabola from $(0, 0)$.

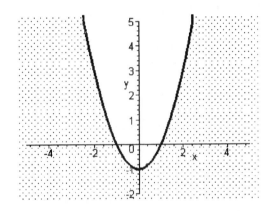

11. $xy \geq 4$

Graph the hyperbola $xy = 4$. Use a solid line since the inequality uses $\geq$.

Choose a test point not on the hyperbola, such as $(0, 0)$. Since $0 \cdot 0 \geq 4$ is false, shade the opposite side of the hyperbola from $(0, 0)$.

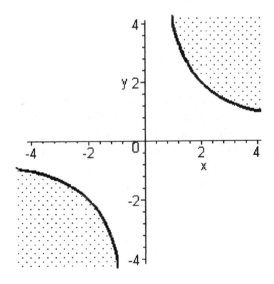

13. $\begin{cases} x + y \le 2 \\ 2x + y \ge 4 \end{cases}$

    (a)   Graph the line $x + y = 2$. Use a solid line since the inequality uses $\le$.

         Choose a test point not on the line, such as $(0, 0)$. Since $0 + 0 \le 2$ is true, shade the side of the line containing $(0, 0)$.

    (b)   Graph the line $2x + y = 4$. Use a solid line since the inequality uses $\ge$.

         Choose a test point not on the line, such as $(0, 0)$. Since $2(0) + 0 \ge 4$ is false, shade the opposite side of the line from $(0, 0)$.

    (c)   The overlapping region is the solution

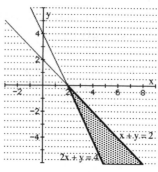

15. $\begin{cases} 2x - y \le 4 \\ 3x + 2y \ge -6 \end{cases}$

    (a)   Graph the line $2x - y = 4$. Use a solid line since the inequality uses $\le$.

         Choose a test point not on the line, such as $(0, 0)$. Since $2(0) - 0 \le 4$ is true, shade the side of the line containing $(0, 0)$.

    (b)   Graph the line $3x + 2y = -6$. Use a solid line since the inequality uses $\ge$.

         Choose a test point not on the line, such as $(0, 0)$. Since $3(0) + 2(0) \ge -6$ is true, shade the side of the line containing $(0, 0)$.

    (c)   The overlapping region is the solution

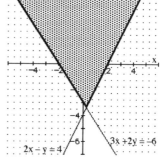

17. $\begin{cases} 2x - 3y \le 0 \\ 3x + 2y \le 6 \end{cases}$

    (a)   Graph the line $2x - 3y = 0$. Use a solid line since the inequality uses $\le$.

         Choose a test point not on the line, such as $(0, 3)$. Since $2(0) - 3(3) \le 0$ is true, shade the side of the line containing $(0, 3)$.

    (b)   Graph the line $3x + 2y = 6$. Use a solid line since the inequality uses $\le$.

         Choose a test point not on the line, such as $(0, 0)$. Since $3(0) + 2(0) \le 6$ is true, shade the side of the line containing $(0, 0)$.

    (c)   The overlapping region is the solution

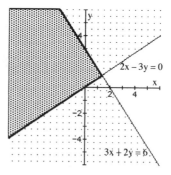

19. $\begin{cases} x^2 + y^2 \le 9 \\ x + y \ge 3 \end{cases}$

(a) Graph the circle $x^2 + y^2 = 9$. Use a
     solid line since the inequality uses $\ge$.
     Choose a test point not on the circle,
     such as $(0, 0)$. Since $0^2 + 0^2 \le 9$ is true,
     shade the same side of the circle as
     $(0, 0)$.

(b) Graph the line $x + y = 3$. Use a solid
     line since the inequality uses $\ge$.
     Choose a test point not on the line,
     such as $(0, 0)$. Since $0 + 0 \ge 3$ is
     false, shade the opposite side of the
     line from $(0, 0)$.

(c) The overlapping region is the solution

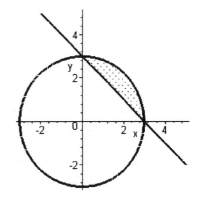

21. $\begin{cases} y \ge x^2 - 4 \\ y \le x - 2 \end{cases}$

(a) Graph the parabola $y = x^2 - 4$.
     Use a solid line since the inequality uses $\ge$.
     Choose a test point not on the parabola, such
     as $(0, 0)$. Since $0 \ge 0^2 - 4$ is true, shade the
     same side of the parabola as $(0, 0)$.

(b) Graph the line $y = x - 2$. Use a solid
     line since the inequality uses $\le$.
     Choose a test point not on the line,
     such as $(0, 0)$. Since $0 \le 0 - 2$ is
     false, shade the opposite side of the
     line from $(0, 0)$.

(c) The overlapping region is the solution

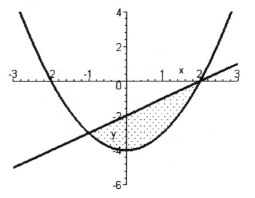

23. $\begin{cases} xy \ge 4 \\ y \ge x^2 + 1 \end{cases}$

(a) Graph the hyperbola $xy = 4$.
     Use a solid line since the inequality uses $\ge$.
     Choose a test point not on the parabola, such as
     $(0, 0)$. Since $0 \cdot 0 \ge 4$ is false, shade the
     opposite side of the hyperbola from $(0, 0)$.

(b) Graph the parabola $y = x^2 + 1$. Use a solid line
     since the inequality uses $\ge$. Choose a test point
     not on the parabola, such as $(0, 0)$. Since
     $0 \ge 0^2 + 1$ is false, shade the opposite
     side of the parabola from $(0, 0)$.

(c) The overlapping region is the solution

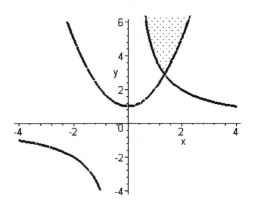

25. $\begin{cases} x - 2y \le 6 \\ 2x - 4y \ge 0 \end{cases}$

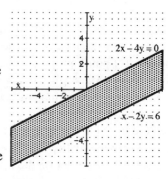

    (a)   Graph the line $x - 2y = 6$. Use a solid line since the inequality uses $\le$.

         Choose a test point not on the line, such as $(0, 0)$. Since $0 - 2(0) \le 6$ is true, shade the side of the line containing $(0, 0)$.

    (b)   Graph the line $2x - 4y = 0$. Use a solid line since the inequality uses $\ge$.

         Choose a test point not on the line, such as $(0, 2)$. Since $2(0) - 4(2) \ge 0$ is false, shade the opposite side of the line from $(0, 2)$.

    (c)   The overlapping region is the solution

27. $\begin{cases} 2x + y \ge -2 \\ 2x + y \ge \;\; 2 \end{cases}$

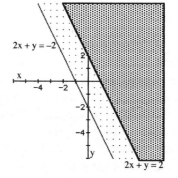

    (a)   Graph the line $2x + y = -2$. Use a solid line since the inequality uses $\ge$.

         Choose a test point not on the line, such as $(0, 0)$. Since $2(0) + 0 \ge -2$ is true, shade the side of the line containing $(0, 0)$.

    (b)   Graph the line $2x + y = 2$. Use a solid line since the inequality uses $\ge$.

         Choose a test point not on the line, such as $(0, 0)$. Since $2(0) + 0 \ge 2$ is false, shade the opposite side of the line from $(0, 0)$.

    (c)   The overlapping region is the solution.

29. $\begin{cases} 2x + 3y \ge 6 \\ 2x + 3y \le 0 \end{cases}$

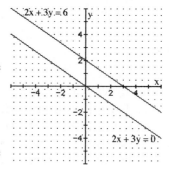

    (a)   Graph the line $2x + 3y = 6$. Use a solid line since the inequality uses $\ge$.

         Choose a test point not on the line, such as $(0, 0)$. Since $2(0) + 3(0) \ge 6$ is false, shade the opposite side of the line from $(0, 0)$.

    (b)   Graph the line $2x + 3y = 0$. Use a solid line since the inequality uses $\le$.

         Choose a test point not on the line, such as $(0, 2)$. Since $2(0) + 3(2) \le 0$ is false, shade the opposite side of the line from $(0, 2)$.

    (c)   Since the regions do not overlap, the solution is an empty set.

31. Graph the system of linear inequalities:
$$\begin{cases} x \geq 0 \\ y \geq 0 \\ 2x + y \leq 6 \\ x + 2y \leq 6 \end{cases}$$

(a) Graph $x \geq 0$; $y \geq 0$. Shaded region is the first quadrant.

(b) Graph the line $2x + y = 6$. Use a solid line since the inequality uses $\leq$.

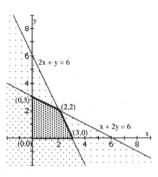

Choose a test point not on the line, such as $(0, 0)$. Since $2(0) + 0 \leq 6$ is true, shade the side of the line containing $(0, 0)$.

(c) Graph the line $x + 2y = 6$. Use a solid line since the inequality uses $\leq$.

Choose a test point not on the line, such as $(0, 0)$. Since $0 + 2(0) \leq 6$ is true, shade the side of the line containing $(0, 0)$.

(d) The overlapping region is the solution.

(e) The graph is bounded.

(f) Find the vertices:

The x-axis and y-axis intersect at $(0, 0)$.

The intersection of $x + 2y = 6$ and the y-axis is $(0, 3)$.

The intersection of $2x + y = 6$ and the x-axis is $(3, 0)$.

To find the intersection of $x + 2y = 6$ and $2x + y = 6$, solve the system:
$$\begin{cases} x + 2y = 6 & \rightarrow & x = 6 - 2y \\ 2x + y = 6 \end{cases}$$

Substitute and solve:
$$2(6 - 2y) + y = 6 \rightarrow 12 - 4y + y = 6 \rightarrow -3y = -6 \rightarrow y = 2$$
$$x = 6 - 2(2) = 6 - 4 = 2$$

The point of intersection is $(2, 2)$.

The four corner points are $(0, 0)$, $(0, 3)$, $(3, 0)$, and $(2, 2$

33.   Graph the system of linear inequalities:

$$\begin{cases} x \geq 0 \\ y \geq 0 \\ x + y \geq 2 \\ 2x + y \geq 4 \end{cases}$$

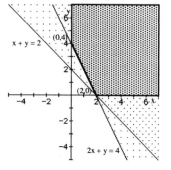

(a)   Graph $x \geq 0$; $y \geq 0$. Shaded region is the first quadrant.

(b)   Graph the line $x + y = 2$. Use a solid line since the inequality uses $\geq$.

Choose a test point not on the line, such as   (0, 0). Since $0 + 0 \geq 2$ is false, shade the opposite side of the line from (0, 0).

(c)   Graph the line $2x + y = 4$. Use a solid line since the inequality uses $\geq$.

Choose a test point not on the line, such as   (0, 0). Since $2(0) + 0 \geq 4$ is false, shade the opposite side of the line from (0, 0).

(d)   The overlapping region is the solution.

(e)   The graph is unbounded.

(f)   Find the vertices:

The intersection of $x + y = 2$ and the x-axis is (2, 0).

The intersection of $2x + y = 4$ and the y-axis is (0, 4).

The two corner points are (2, 0), and (0, 4).

35.   Graph the system of linear inequalities:

$$\begin{cases} x \geq 0 \\ y \geq 0 \\ x + y \geq 2 \\ 2x + 3y \leq 12 \\ 3x + y \leq 12 \end{cases}$$

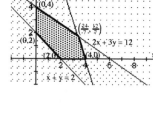

(a)   Graph $x \geq 0$; $y \geq 0$. Shaded region is the first quadrant.

(b)   Graph the line $x + y = 2$. Use a solid line since the inequality uses $\geq$.

Choose a test point not on the line, such as   (0, 0). Since $0 + 0 \geq 2$ is false, shade the opposite side of the line from (0, 0).

(c)   Graph the line $2x + 3y = 12$. Use a solid line since the inequality uses $\leq$.

Choose a test point not on the line, such as   (0, 0). Since $2(0) + 3(0) \leq 12$ is true, shade the side of the line containing (0, 0).

(d)   Graph the line $3x + y = 12$. Use a solid line since the inequality uses $\leq$.

Choose a test point not on the line, such as (0, 0). Since $3(0) + 0 \leq 12$ is true, shade the side of the line containing (0, 0).

(e)   The overlapping region is the solution.

(f)   The graph is bounded.

(g)   Find the vertices:

The intersection of $x + y = 2$ and the y-axis is $(0, 2)$.
The intersection of $x + y = 2$ and the x-axis is $(2, 0)$.
The intersection of $2x + 3y = 12$ and the y-axis is $(0, 4)$.
The intersection of $3x + y = 12$ and the x-axis is $(4, 0)$.
To find the intersection of $2x + 3y = 12$ and $3x + y = 12$, solve the system:
$$\begin{cases} 2x + 3y = 12 \\ 3x + y = 12 \end{cases} \rightarrow \quad y = 12 - 3x$$
Substitute and solve:
$$2x + 3(12 - 3x) = 12 \rightarrow 2x + 36 - 9x = 12$$

$$-7x = -24 \rightarrow x = \frac{24}{7}$$

$$y = 12 - 3\left(\frac{24}{7}\right) = 12 - \frac{72}{2} = \frac{12}{7}$$

The point of intersection is $\left(\dfrac{24}{7}, \dfrac{12}{7}\right)$.

The five corner points are $(0, 2)$, $(0, 4)$, $(2, 0)$, $(4, 0)$, and $\left(\dfrac{24}{7}, \dfrac{12}{7}\right)$.

37. Graph the system of linear inequalities:
$$\begin{cases} x \geq 0 \\ y \geq 0 \\ x + y \geq 2 \\ x + y \leq 8 \\ 2x + y \leq 10 \end{cases}$$

(a) Graph $x \geq 0; y \geq 0$. Shaded region is the first quadrant.

(b) Graph the line $x + y = 2$. Use a solid line since the inequality uses $\geq$.
Choose a test point not on the line, such as $(0, 0)$. Since $0 + 0 \geq 2$ is false, shade the opposite side of the line from $(0, 0)$.

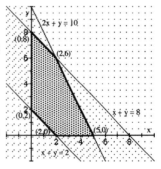

(c) Graph the line $x + y = 8$. Use a solid line since the inequality uses $\leq$.
Choose a test point not on the line, such as $(0, 0)$. Since $0 + 0 \leq 8$ is true, shade the side of the line containing $(0, 0)$.

(d) Graph the line $2x + y = 10$. Use a solid line since the inequality uses $\leq$.
Choose a test point not on the line, such as $(0, 0)$. Since $2(0) + 0 \leq 10$ is true, shade the side of the line containing $(0, 0)$.

(e) The overlapping region is the solution.

(f) The graph is bounded.

(g) Find the vertices:
The intersection of $x + y = 2$ and the y-axis is $(0, 2)$.
The intersection of $x + y = 2$ and the x-axis is $(2, 0)$.
The intersection of $x + y = 8$ and the y-axis is $(0, 8)$.

The intersection of $2x + y = 10$ and the x-axis is $(5, 0)$.

To find the intersection of $x + y = 8$ and $2x + y = 10$, solve the system:

$$\begin{cases} x + y = 8 & \rightarrow \quad y = 8 - x \\ 2x + y = 10 \end{cases}$$

Substitute and solve:

$$2x + 8 - x = 10 \rightarrow x = 2$$

$$y = 8 - 2 = 6$$

The point of intersection is $(2, 6)$.

The five corner points are $(0, 2)$, $(0, 8)$, $(2, 0)$, $(5, 0)$, and $(2, 6)$.

39. Graph the system of linear inequalities:

$$\begin{cases} x \geq 0 \\ y \geq 0 \\ x + 2y \geq 1 \\ x + 2y \leq 10 \end{cases}$$

(a) Graph $x \geq 0$; $y \geq 0$. Shaded region is the first quadrant.

(b) Graph the line $x + 2y = 1$. Use a solid line since the inequality uses $\geq$.

Choose a test point not on the line, such as $(0, 0)$.
Since $0 + 2(0) \geq 1$ is false, shade the opposite side of the line from $(0, 0)$.

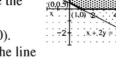

(c) Graph the line $x + 2y = 10$. Use a solid line since the inequality uses $\leq$.

Choose a test point not on the line, such as $(0, 0)$.
Since $0 + 2(0) \leq 10$ is true, shade the side of the line containing $(0, 0)$.

(d) The overlapping region is the solution.

(e) The graph is bounded.

(f) Find the vertices:

The intersection of $x + 2y = 1$ and the y-axis is $(0, 0.5)$.

The intersection of $x + 2y = 1$ and the x-axis is $(1, 0)$.

The intersection of $x + 2y = 10$ and the y-axis is $(0, 5)$.

The intersection of $x + 2y = 10$ and the x-axis is $(10, 0)$.

The four corner points are $(0, 0.5)$, $(0, 5)$, $(1, 0)$, and $(10, 0)$.

41. The system of linear inequalities is:

$$\begin{cases} x \geq 0 \\ y \geq 0 \\ x \leq 4 \\ x + y \leq 6 \end{cases}$$

43. The system of linear inequalities is:

$$\begin{cases} x \geq 0 \\ y \geq 15 \\ x \leq 20 \\ x + y \leq 50 \\ x - y \leq 0 \end{cases}$$

45.   (a)   Let x = the amount invested in Treasury bills.
            Let y = the amount invested in corporate bonds.
      The constraints are:

        $x \geq 0, y \geq 0$ A non-negative amount must be invested.

        $x + y \leq 50000$ Total investment cannot exceed \$50,000.

        $y \leq 10000$ Amount invested in corporate bonds must not exceed
                                       \$10,000.

        $x \geq 35000$ Amount invested in Treasury bills must be at least \$35,000.

        $x > y$ Amount invested in Treasury bills must be greater than the amount
                                         invested in corporate bonds.

(b)   Graph the system $\begin{cases} x \geq 0 \\ y \geq 0 \\ x + y \leq 50000 \\ y \leq 10000 \\ x \geq 35000 \\ x > y \end{cases}$

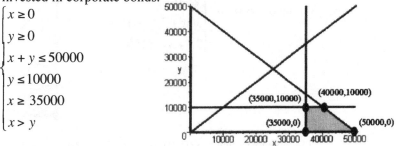

The corner points are (35000, 0), (35000, 10000), (40000, 10000), (50000, 0).

47.   (a)   Let x = the # of packages of the economy blend.
            Let y = the # of packages of the superior blend.
      The constraints are:

        $x \geq 0, y \geq 0$ A non-negative # of packages must be produced.

        $4x + 8y \leq 75 \cdot 16$ Total amount of grade A coffee cannot exceed 75
                                    pounds. (Note: 75 pounds = (75)(16) ounces.)

        $12x + 8y \leq 120 \cdot 16$ Total amount of grade B coffee cannot exceed 120
                                    pounds. (Note: 120 pounds = (120)(16) ounces.)

      We can simplify the equations

        $4x + 8y \leq 75 \cdot 16 \rightarrow x + 2y \leq 75 \cdot 4 \rightarrow x + 2y \leq 300$

        $12x + 8y \leq 120 \cdot 16 \rightarrow 3x + 2y \leq 120 \cdot 4 \rightarrow 3x + 2y \leq 480$

(b)   Graph the system. $\begin{cases} x \geq 0 \\ y \geq 0 \\ x + 2y \leq 300 \\ 3x + 2y \leq 480 \end{cases}$

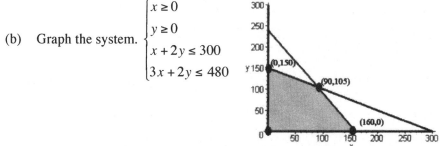

The corner points are (0, 0), (0, 150), (90, 105), (160, 0).

49.   (a)   Let x = the # of microwaves.
            Let y = the # of printers.
      The constraints are:

      $x \geq 0, y \geq 0$ A non-negative # of items must be shipped.
      $30x + 20y \leq 1600$ Total cargo weight cannot exceed 1600 pounds.
      $2x + 3y \leq 150$ Total cargo volume cannot exceed 150 cubic feet.

      (b)   Graph the system. $\begin{cases} x \geq 0 \\ y \geq 0 \\ 30x + 20y \leq 1600 \\ 2x + 3y \leq 150 \end{cases}$

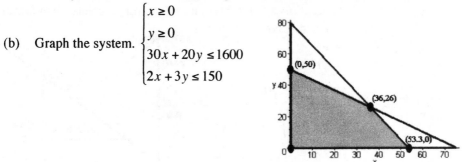

      The corner points are (0, 0), (0, 50), (36, 26), (53.3, 0).

Systems of Equations and Inequalities

8.9   Linear Programming

1. $z = x + y$

Vertex	Value of $z = x + y$
$(0, 3)$	$z = 0 + 3 = 3$
$(0, 6)$	$z = 0 + 6 = 6$
$(5, 6)$	$z = 5 + 6 = 11$
$(5, 2)$	$z = 5 + 2 = 7$
$(4, 0)$	$z = 4 + 0 = 4$

The maximum value is 11 at $(5, 6)$, and the minimum value is 3 at $(0, 3)$.

3. $z = x + 10y$

Vertex	Value of $z = x + 10y$
$(0, 3)$	$z = 0 + 10(3) = 30$
$(0, 6)$	$z = 0 + 10(6) = 60$
$(5, 6)$	$z = 5 + 10(6) = 65$
$(5, 2)$	$z = 5 + 10(2) = 25$
$(4, 0)$	$z = 4 + 10(0) = 4$

The maximum value is 65 at $(5, 6)$, and the minimum value is 4 at $(4, 0)$.

5. $z = 5x + 7y$

Vertex	Value of $z = 5x + 7y$
$(0, 3)$	$z = 5(0) + 7(3) = 21$
$(0, 6)$	$z = 5(0) + 7(6) = 42$
$(5, 6)$	$z = 5(5) + 7(6) = 67$
$(5, 2)$	$z = 5(5) + 7(2) = 39$
$(4, 0)$	$z = 5(4) + 7(0) = 20$

The maximum value is 67 at $(5, 6)$, and the minimum value is 20 at $(4, 0)$.

7. Maximize $z = 2x + y$

Subject to $x \geq 0, \quad y \geq 0, \quad x + y \leq 6, \quad x + y \geq 1$

Graph the constraints.

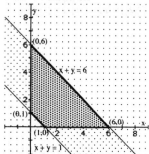

The corner points are $(0, 1), (1, 0), (0, 6), (6, 0)$.

Evaluate the objective function:

Vertex	Value of $z = 2x + y$
(0, 1)	$z = 2(0) + 1 = 1$
(0, 6)	$z = 2(0) + 6 = 6$
(1, 0)	$z = 2(1) + 0 = 2$
(6, 0)	$z = 2(6) + 0 = 12$

The maximum value is 12 at $(6, 0)$.

9. Minimize $z = 2x + 5y$

Subject to $x \geq 0, \quad y \geq 0, \quad x + y \geq 2, \quad x \leq 5, \quad y \leq 3$

Graph the constraints.

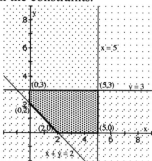

The corner points are $(0, 2), (2, 0), (0, 3), (5, 0), (5, 3)$.

Evaluate the objective function:

Vertex	Value of $z = 2x + 5y$
(0, 2)	$z = 2(0) + 5(2) = 10$
(0, 3)	$z = 2(0) + 5(3) = 15$
(2, 0)	$z = 2(2) + 5(0) = 4$
(5, 0)	$z = 2(5) + 5(0) = 10$
(5, 3)	$z = 2(5) + 5(3) = 25$

The minimum value is 4 at $(2, 0)$.

11. Maximize $z = 3x + 5y$

Subject to $x \geq 0$, $y \geq 0$, $x + y \geq 2$, $2x + 3y \leq 12$, $3x + 2y \leq 12$

Graph the constraints.

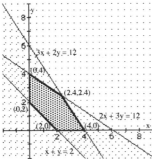

To find the intersection of $2x + 3y = 12$ and $3x + 2y = 12$, solve the system:

$$\begin{cases} 2x + 3y = 12 \\ 3x + 2y = 12 \quad \rightarrow \quad y = 6 - \dfrac{3}{2}x \end{cases}$$

Substitute and solve:

$$2x + 3\left(6 - \frac{3}{2}x\right) = 12 \rightarrow 2x + 18 - \frac{9}{2}x = 12 \rightarrow -\frac{5}{2}x = -6$$

$$x = \frac{12}{5} = 2.4 \qquad y = 6 - \frac{3}{2}\left(\frac{12}{5}\right) = 6 - \frac{18}{5} = \frac{12}{5} = 2.4$$

The point of intersection is $(2.5, 2.4)$.

The corner points are $(0, 2)$, $(2, 0)$, $(0, 4)$, $(4, 0)$, $(2.4, 2.4)$.

Evaluate the objective function:

Vertex	Value of $z = 3x + 5y$
(0, 2)	z = 3(0) + 5(2) = 10
(0, 4)	z = 3(0) + 5(4) = 20
(2, 0)	z = 3(2) + 5(0) = 6
(4, 0)	z = 3(4) + 5(0) = 12
(2.4, 2.4)	z = 3(2.4) + 5(2.4) = 19.2

The maximum value is 20 at $(0, 4)$.

13. Minimize $z = 5x + 4y$

Subject to $x \geq 0$, $y \geq 0$, $x + y \geq 2$, $2x + 3y \leq 12$, $3x + y \leq 12$

Graph the constraints.

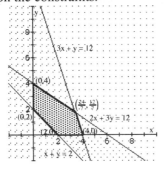

To find the intersection of $2x + 3y = 12$ and $3x + y = 12$, solve the system:
$$\begin{cases} 2x + 3y = 12 \\ 3x + \ y = 12 \end{cases} \rightarrow \quad y = 12 - 3x$$

Substitute and solve:
$$2x + 3(12 - 3x) = 12 \rightarrow 2x + 36 - 9x = 12 \rightarrow -7x = -24 \rightarrow x = \frac{24}{7}$$

$$y = 12 - 3\left(\frac{24}{7}\right) = 12 - \frac{72}{7} = \frac{12}{7}$$

The point of intersection is $\left(\frac{24}{7}, \frac{12}{7}\right)$.

The corner points are $(0, 2)$, $(2, 0)$, $(0, 4)$, $(4, 0)$, $\left(\frac{24}{7}, \frac{12}{7}\right)$.

Evaluate the objective function:

Vertex	Value of $z = 5x + 4y$
$(0, 2)$	$z = 5(0) + 4(2) = 8$
$(0, 4)$	$z = 5(0) + 4(4) = 16$
$(2, 0)$	$z = 5(2) + 4(0) = 10$
$(4, 0)$	$z = 5(4) + 4(0) = 20$
$\left(\frac{24}{7}, \frac{12}{7}\right)$	$z = 5\left(\frac{24}{7}\right) + 4\left(\frac{12}{7}\right) = \frac{120}{7} + \frac{48}{7} = \frac{168}{7} = 24$

The minimum value is 8 at $(0, 2)$.

15. Maximize $z = 5x + 2y$

Subject to $x \ge 0$, $y \ge 0$, $x + y \le 10$, $2x + y \ge 10$, $x + 2y \ge 10$

Graph the constraints.

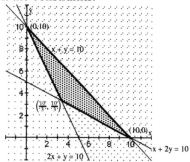

To find the intersection of $2x + y = 10$ and $x + 2y = 10$, solve the system:
$$\begin{cases} 2x + \ y = 10 \quad \rightarrow \quad y = 10 - 2x \\ \ x + 2y = 10 \end{cases}$$

Substitute and solve:
$$x + 2(10 - 2x) = 10 \rightarrow x + 20 - 4x = 10 \rightarrow -3x = -10 \rightarrow x = \frac{10}{3}$$

$$y = 10 - 2\left(\frac{10}{3}\right) = 10 - \frac{20}{3} = \frac{10}{3}$$

The point of intersection is $\left(\dfrac{10}{3}, \dfrac{10}{3}\right)$.

The corner points are $(0, 10)$, $(10, 0)$, $\left(\dfrac{10}{3}, \dfrac{10}{3}\right)$.

Evaluate the objective function:

Vertex	Value of $z = 5x + 2y$
$(0, 10)$	$z = 5(0) + 2(10) = 20$
$(10, 0)$	$z = 5(10) + 2(0) = 50$
$\left(\dfrac{10}{3}, \dfrac{10}{3}\right)$	$z = 5\left(\dfrac{10}{3}\right) + 2\left(\dfrac{10}{3}\right) = \dfrac{50}{3} + \dfrac{20}{3} = \dfrac{70}{3} = 23\dfrac{1}{3}$

The maximum value is 50 at $(10, 0)$.

17. Let x = the number of downhill skis produced.
Let y = the number of cross-country skis produced.
The total profit is: $P = 70x + 50y$. Profit is to be maximized; thus, this is the objective function.
The constraints are:

$x \geq 0, \ y \geq 0$ A positive number of skis must be produced.

$2x + y \leq 40$ Only 40 hours of manufacturing time is available.

$x + y \leq 32$ Only 32 hours of finishing time is available.

Graph the constraints.

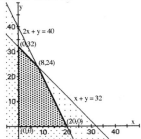

To find the intersection of $x + y = 32$ and $2x + y = 40$, solve the system:

$$\begin{cases} x + y = 32 \ \rightarrow \ \ y = 32 - x \\ 2x + y = 40 \end{cases}$$

Substitute and solve:

$$2x + 32 - x = 40 \rightarrow x = 8 \rightarrow y = 32 - 8 = 24$$

The point of intersection is $(8, 24)$.

The corner points are $(0, 0)$, $(0, 32)$, $(20, 0)$, $(8, 24)$.

Evaluate the objective function:

Vertex	Value of $P = 70x + 50y$
$(0, 0)$	$P = 70(0) + 50(0) = 0$
$(0, 32)$	$P = 70(0) + 50(32) = 1600$
$(20, 0)$	$P = 70(20) + 50(0) = 1400$
$(8, 24)$	$P = 70(8) + 50(24) = 1760$

The maximum profit is \$1760, when 8 downhill skis and 24 cross-country skis are produced.

With the increase of the manufacturing time to 48 hours, we do the following:

The constraints are:

$x \geq 0, \quad y \geq 0$ A positive number of skis must be produced.

$2x + y \leq 48$ Only 48 hours of manufacturing time is available.

$x + y \leq 32$ Only 32 hours of finishing time is available.

Graph the constraints.

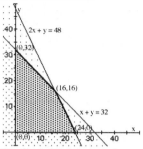

To find the intersection of $x + y = 32$ and $2x + y = 48$, solve the system:

$$\begin{cases} x + y = 32 & \rightarrow \quad y = 32 - x \\ 2x + y = 48 \end{cases}$$

Substitute and solve:

$$2x + 32 - x = 48 \rightarrow x = 16 \rightarrow y = 32 - 16 = 16$$

The point of intersection is (16, 16).

The corner points are (0, 0), (0, 32), (24, 0), (16, 16).

Evaluate the objective function:

Vertex	Value of $P = 70x + 50y$
(0, 0)	$P = 70(0) + 50(0) = 0$
(0, 32)	$P = 70(0) + 50(32) = 1600$
(24, 0)	$P = 70(24) + 50(0) = 1680$
(16, 16)	$P = 70(16) + 50(16) = 1920$

The maximum profit is $1920, when 16 downhill skis and 16 cross-country skis are produced.

19. Let x = the number of acres of corn planted.

Let y = the number of acres of soybeans planted.

The total profit is: $P = 250x + 200y$. Profit is to be maximized; thus, this is the objective function.

The constraints are:

$x \geq 0, \quad y \geq 0$ A non-negative number of acres must be planted.

$x + y \leq 100$ Acres available to plant.

$60x + 40y \leq 1800$ Money available for cultivation costs.

$60x + 60y \leq 2400$ Money available for labor costs.

Graph the constraints.

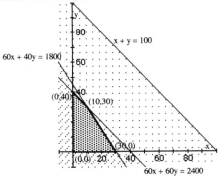

To find the intersection of $60x + 40y = 1800$ and $60x + 60y = 2400$, solve the system:

$$\begin{cases} 60x + 40y = 1800 & \rightarrow \quad 60x = 1800 - 40y \\ 60x + 60y = 2400 \end{cases}$$

Substitute and solve:

$$1800 - 40y + 60y = 2400 \rightarrow 20y = 600 \rightarrow y = 30$$

$$60x = 1800 - 40(30) \rightarrow 60x = 600 \rightarrow x = 10$$

The point of intersection is (10, 30).

The corner points are (0, 0), (0, 40), (30, 0), (10, 30).

Evaluate the objective function:

Vertex	Value of $P = 250x + 200y$
(0, 0)	$P = 250(0) + 200(0) = 0$
(0, 40)	$P = 250(0) + 200(40) = 8000$
(30, 0)	$P = 250(30) + 200(0) = 7500$
(10, 30)	$P = 250(10) + 200(30) = 8500$

The maximum profit is \$8500, when 10 acres of corn and 30 acres of soybeans are planted.

21. Let x = the number of hours that machine 1 is operated.

Let y = the number of hours that machine 2 is operated.

The total cost is: $C = 50x + 30y$. Cost is to be minimized; thus, this is the objective function.

The constraints are:

$x \geq 0, \; y \geq 0$ A positive number of hours must be used.

$x \leq 10$ 10 hours available on machine 1.

$y \leq 10$ 10 hours available on machine 2.

$60x + 40y \geq 240$ At least 240 8-inch plyers must be produced.

$70x + 20y \geq 140$ At least 140 6-inch plyers must be produced.

Graph the constraints.

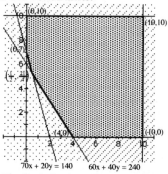

$$70x + 20y = 140 \qquad 60x + 40y = 240$$

To find the intersection of $60x + 40y = 240$ and $70x + 20y = 140$, solve the system:

$$\begin{cases} 60x + 40y = 240 \\ 70x + 20y = 140 \quad \rightarrow \quad 20y = 140 - 70x \end{cases}$$

Substitute and solve:

$$60x + 2(140 - 70x) = 240 \rightarrow 60x + 280 - 140x = 240$$

$$-80x = -40 \rightarrow x = 0.5$$

$$20y = 140 - 70(0.5) \rightarrow 20y = 105 \rightarrow y = 5.25$$

The point of intersection is $(0.5, 5.25)$.

The corner points are $(0, 7)$, $(0, 10)$, $(4, 0)$, $(10, 0)$, $(10, 10)$, $(0.5, 5.25)$.

Evaluate the objective function:

Vertex	Value of $C = 50x + 30y$
$(0, 7)$	$C = 50(0) + 30(7) = 210$
$(0, 10)$	$C = 50(0) + 30(10) = 300$
$(4, 0)$	$C = 50(4) + 30(0) = 200$
$(10, 0)$	$C = 50(10) + 30(0) = 500$
$(10, 10)$	$C = 50(10) + 30(10) = 800$
$(0.5, 5.25)$	$C = 50(0.5) + 30(5.25) = 182.50$

The minimum cost is $182.50, when machine 1 is used for 0.5 hours and machine 2 is used for 5.25 hours.

23.　Let x = the number of pounds of ground beef.
Let y = the number of pounds of ground pork.
The total cost is: $C = 0.75x + 0.45y$. Cost is to be minimized; thus, this is the objective function.

The constraints are:

$x \geq 0, \quad y \geq 0$　　　　A positive number of pounds must be used.
$x \leq 200$　　　　　　　Only 200 pounds of ground beef are available.
$y \geq 50$　　　　　　　At least 50 pounds of ground pork must be used.
$0.75x + 0.60y \geq 0.70(x + y) \rightarrow 0.05x \geq 0.10y$　　Leanness condition to be met.

Graph the constraints.

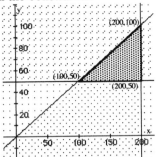

The corner points are (100, 50), (200, 50), (200, 100).

Evaluate the objective function:

Vertex	Value of $C = 0.75x + 0.45y$
(100, 50)	$C = 0.75(100) + 0.45(50) = 97.50$
(200, 50)	$C = 0.75(200) + 0.45(50) = 172.50$
(200,100)	$C = 0.75(200) + 0.45(100) = 195.00$

The minimum cost is $97.50, when 100 pounds of ground beef and 50 pounds of ground pork are used.

25. Let x = the number of racing skates manufactured.

Let y = the number of figure skates manufactured.

The total profit is: $P = 10x + 12y$. Profit is to be maximized; thus, this is the objective function.

The constraints are:

$x \geq 0, \ y \geq 0$	A positive number of skates must be manufactured.
$6x + 4y \leq 120$	Only 120 hours are available for fabrication.
$x + 2y \leq 40$	Only 40 hours are available for finishing.

Graph the constraints.

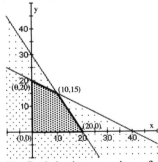

To find the intersection of $6x + 4y = 120$ and $x + 2y = 40$, solve the system:

$$\begin{cases} 6x + 4y = 120 \\ x + 2y = 40 \end{cases} \rightarrow \quad x = 40 - 2y$$

Substitute and solve:

$$6(40 - 2y) + 4y = 120 \rightarrow 240 - 12y + 4y = 120$$

$$-8y = -120 \rightarrow y = 15 \rightarrow x = 40 - 2(15) = 10$$

The point of intersection is (10, 15).

The corner points are (0, 0), (0, 20), (20, 0), (10, 15).

Evaluate the objective function:

Vertex	Value of $P = 10x + 12y$
(0, 0)	$P = 10(0) + 12(0) = 0$
(0, 20)	$P = 10(0) + 12(20) = 240$
(20, 0)	$P = 10(20) + 12(0) = 200$
(10, 15)	$P = 10(10) + 12(15) = 280$

The maximum profit is \$280, when 10 racing skates and 15 figure skates are produced.

27. Let x = the number of metal fasteners.
Let y = the number of plastic fasteners.
The total cost is: $C = 9x + 4y$. Cost is to be minimized; thus, this is the objective function.
The constraints are:

$x \geq 2, \; y \geq 2$ At least 2 of each fastener must be made.

$x + y \geq 6$ At least 6 fasteners are needed.

$4x + 2y \leq 24$ Only 24 hours are available.

Graph the constraints.

The corner points are (2, 4), (2, 8), (4, 2), (5, 2).
Evaluate the objective function:

Vertex	Value of $C = 9x + 4y$
(2, 4)	$C = 9(2) + 4(4) = 34$
(2, 8)	$C = 9(2) + 4(8) = 50$
(4, 2)	$C = 9(4) + 4(2) = 44$
(5, 2)	$C = 9(5) + 4(2) = 53$

The minimum cost is \$34, when 2 metal fasteners and 4 plastic fasteners are ordered.

29. Let x = the number of first-class seats.
Let y = the number of coach seats.
The constraints are:

$8 \leq x \leq 16$ Restriction on first-class seats.

$80 \leq y \leq 120$ Restriction on coach seats.

(a) $\dfrac{x}{y} \leq \dfrac{1}{12}$ Ratio of seats.

If $y = 120$, then $\dfrac{x}{120} \leq \dfrac{1}{12} \rightarrow 12x \leq 120 \rightarrow x \leq 10$

The maximum revenue will be obtained with 120 coach seats and 10 first-class seats.
(Note that the first-class seats meet their constraint.)

(b) $\dfrac{x}{y} \leq \dfrac{1}{8}$ Ratio of seats.

If $y = 120$, then $\dfrac{x}{120} \leq \dfrac{1}{8} \rightarrow 8x \leq 120 \rightarrow x \leq 15$

The maximum revenue will be obtained with 120 coach seats and 15 first-class seats.
(Note that the first-class seats meet their constraint.)

Systems of Equations and Inequalities

8.R Chapter Review

1. Solve the first equation for y, substitute into the second equation and solve:

$$\begin{cases} 2x - y = 5 & \to \quad y = 2x - 5 \\ 5x + 2y = 8 \end{cases}$$

$$5x + 2(2x - 5) = 8 \to 5x + 4x - 10 = 8$$

$$9x = 18 \to x = 2 \to y = 2(2) - 5 = 4 - 5 = -1$$

The solution is $x = 2, \ y = -1$.

3. Solve the second equation for x, substitute into the first equation and solve:

$$\begin{cases} 3x - 4y = 4 \\ x - 3y = \dfrac{1}{2} & \to \quad x = 3y + \dfrac{1}{2} \end{cases}$$

$$3\left(3y + \frac{1}{2}\right) - 4y = 4 \to 9y + \frac{3}{2} - 4y = 4 \to 5y = \frac{5}{2} \to y = \frac{1}{2} \to x = 3\left(\frac{1}{2}\right) + \frac{1}{2} = 2$$

The solution is $x = 2, \ y = \dfrac{1}{2}$.

5. Solve the first equation for x, substitute into the second equation and solve:

$$\begin{cases} x - 2y - 4 = 0 & \to \quad x = 2y + 4 \\ 3x + 2y - 4 = 0 \end{cases}$$

$$3(2y + 4) + 2y - 4 = 0 \to 6y + 12 + 2y - 4 = 0$$

$$8y = -8 \to y = -1 \to x = 2(-1) + 4 = 2$$

The solution is $x = 2, \ y = -1$.

7. Substitute the first equation into the second equation and solve:

$$\begin{cases} y = 2x - 5 \\ x = 3y + 4 \end{cases}$$

$$x = 3(2x - 5) + 4 \to x = 6x - 15 + 4$$

$$-5x = -11 \to x = \frac{11}{5} \to y = 2\left(\frac{11}{5}\right) - 5 = -\frac{3}{5}$$

The solution is $x = \dfrac{11}{5}, \ y = -\dfrac{3}{5}$.

9.   Multiply each side of the first equation by 5 and each side of the second equation by 30 and add to eliminate y:

$$\begin{cases} x - y + 4 = 0 \quad \xrightarrow{\ 5\ } \quad 5x - 5y + 20 = 0 \\ \dfrac{1}{2}x + \dfrac{1}{6}y + \dfrac{2}{5} = 0 \quad \xrightarrow{\ 30\ } \quad \dfrac{15x + 5y + 12 = 0}{20x \quad\quad + 32 = 0} \end{cases}$$

$$20x = -32 \to x = -\dfrac{8}{5} \qquad \text{Substitute and solve for y:} \quad -\dfrac{8}{5} - y + 4 = 0 \;\to\; y = \dfrac{12}{5}$$

The solution of the system is $x = -\dfrac{8}{5},\; y = \dfrac{12}{5}$.

11. Rewrite each equation and add to eliminate y:

$$\begin{cases} x - 2y - 8 = 0 \quad \longrightarrow \quad x - 2y = 8 \\ 2x + 2y - 10 = 0 \quad \longrightarrow \quad \dfrac{2x + 2y = 10}{\quad} \end{cases}$$
$$3x \quad\quad = 18$$
$$x = 6$$

Substitute and solve for y:

$$6 - 2y = 8 \to -2y = 2 \to y = -1$$
The solution of the system is $x = 6,\; y = -1$.

13. Solve the first equation for y, substitute into the second equation and solve:

$$\begin{cases} y - 2x = 11 \quad \to \quad y = 2x + 11 \\ 2y - 3x = 18 \end{cases}$$
$$2(2x + 11) - 3x = 18$$
$$4x + 22 - 3x = 18 \to x = -4 \to y = 2(-4) + 11 = 3$$
The solution is $x = -4,\; y = 3$.

15. Multiply each side of the first equation by 2 and each side of the second equation by 3 and add to eliminate y:

$$\begin{cases} 2x + 3y - 13 = 0 \quad \xrightarrow{\ 2\ } \quad 4x + 6y - 26 = 0 \\ 3x - 2y \quad\quad = 0 \quad \xrightarrow{\ 3\ } \quad \dfrac{9x - 6y \quad\quad = 0}{\quad} \end{cases}$$
$$13x \quad\quad - 26 = 0$$
$$13x = 26$$
$$x = 2$$

Substitute and solve for y:
$$3(2) - 2y = 0$$
$$-2y = -6$$
$$y = 3$$
The solution of the system is $x = 2,\; y = 3$.

17. Multiply each side of the second equation by –3 and add to eliminate x:

$$\begin{cases} 3x - 2y = 8 \\ x - \frac{2}{3}y = 12 \end{cases} \xrightarrow{} \begin{array}{r} 3x - 2y = 8 \\ -3x + 2y = -36 \\ \hline 0 = -28 \end{array}$$

The system has no solution, so the system is inconsistent.

19. Multiply each side of the first equation by –2 and add to the second equation to eliminate x; and multiply each side of the first equation by –3 and add to the third equation to eliminate x:

$$\begin{cases} x + 2y - z = 6 \\ 2x - y + 3z = -13 \\ 3x - 2y + 3z = -16 \end{cases}$$

$$\xrightarrow{-2} \begin{array}{r} -2x - 4y + 2z = -12 \\ 2x - y + 3z = -13 \\ \hline -5y + 5z = -25 \end{array} \xrightarrow{-1/5} y - z = 5$$

$$\xrightarrow{-3} \begin{array}{r} -3x - 6y + 3z = -18 \\ 3x - 2y + 3z = -16 \\ \hline -8y + 6z = -34 \end{array}$$

Multiply each side of the first result by 8 and add to the second result to eliminate y:

$$\begin{array}{r} y - z = 5 \xrightarrow{8} 8y - 8z = 40 \\ -8y + 6z = -34 \xrightarrow{} -8y + 6z = -34 \\ \hline -2z = 6 \\ z = -3 \end{array}$$

Substituting and solving for the other variables:

$$\begin{array}{ll} y - (-3) = 5 & x + 2(2) - (-3) = 6 \\ y = 2 & x + 4 + 3 = 6 \\ & x = -1 \end{array}$$

The solution is $x = -1$, $y = 2$, $z = -3$.

21. $A + C = \begin{bmatrix} 1 & 0 \\ 2 & 4 \\ -1 & 2 \end{bmatrix} + \begin{bmatrix} 3 & -4 \\ 1 & 5 \\ 5 & -2 \end{bmatrix} = \begin{bmatrix} 4 & -4 \\ 3 & 9 \\ 4 & 0 \end{bmatrix}$

23. $6A = 6 \cdot \begin{bmatrix} 1 & 0 \\ 2 & 4 \\ -1 & 2 \end{bmatrix} = \begin{bmatrix} 6 & 0 \\ 12 & 24 \\ -6 & 12 \end{bmatrix}$

25. $AB = \begin{bmatrix} 1 & 0 \\ 2 & 4 \\ -1 & 2 \end{bmatrix} \cdot \begin{bmatrix} 4 & -3 & 0 \\ 1 & 1 & -2 \end{bmatrix} = \begin{bmatrix} 4 & -3 & 0 \\ 12 & -2 & -8 \\ -2 & 5 & -4 \end{bmatrix}$

27. $CB = \begin{bmatrix} 3 & -4 \\ 1 & 5 \\ 5 & -2 \end{bmatrix} \cdot \begin{bmatrix} 4 & -3 & 0 \\ 1 & 1 & -2 \end{bmatrix} = \begin{bmatrix} 8 & -13 & 8 \\ 9 & 2 & -10 \\ 18 & -17 & 4 \end{bmatrix}$

29. Augment the matrix with the identity and use row operations to find the inverse:

$$A = \begin{bmatrix} 4 & 6 \\ 1 & 3 \end{bmatrix} \rightarrow \begin{bmatrix} 4 & 6 & | & 1 & 0 \\ 1 & 3 & | & 0 & 1 \end{bmatrix}$$

$$\rightarrow \begin{bmatrix} 1 & 3 & | & 0 & 1 \\ 4 & 6 & | & 1 & 0 \end{bmatrix} \rightarrow \begin{bmatrix} 1 & 3 & | & 0 & 1 \\ 0 & -6 & | & 1 & -4 \end{bmatrix} \rightarrow \begin{bmatrix} 1 & 3 & | & 0 & 1 \\ 0 & 1 & | & -\frac{1}{6} & \frac{2}{3} \end{bmatrix} \rightarrow \begin{bmatrix} 1 & 0 & | & \frac{1}{2} & -1 \\ 0 & 1 & | & -\frac{1}{6} & \frac{2}{3} \end{bmatrix}$$

Interchange $R_2 = -4r_1 + r_2$ $R_2 = -\frac{1}{6}r_2$ $R_1 = -3r_2 + r_1$
r_1 and r_2

$$A^{-1} = \begin{bmatrix} \frac{1}{2} & -1 \\ -\frac{1}{6} & \frac{2}{3} \end{bmatrix}$$

31. Augment the matrix with the identity and use row operations to find the inverse:

$$A = \begin{bmatrix} 1 & 3 & 3 \\ 1 & 2 & 1 \\ 1 & -1 & 2 \end{bmatrix} \rightarrow \begin{bmatrix} 1 & 3 & 3 & | & 1 & 0 & 0 \\ 1 & 2 & 1 & | & 0 & 1 & 0 \\ 1 & -1 & 2 & | & 0 & 0 & 1 \end{bmatrix}$$

$$\rightarrow \begin{bmatrix} 1 & 3 & 3 & | & 1 & 0 & 0 \\ 0 & -1 & -2 & | & -1 & 1 & 0 \\ 0 & -4 & -1 & | & -1 & 0 & 1 \end{bmatrix} \rightarrow \begin{bmatrix} 1 & 3 & 3 & | & 1 & 0 & 0 \\ 0 & 1 & 2 & | & 1 & -1 & 0 \\ 0 & -4 & -1 & | & -1 & 0 & 1 \end{bmatrix} \rightarrow \begin{bmatrix} 1 & 0 & -3 & | & -2 & 3 & 0 \\ 0 & 1 & 2 & | & 1 & -1 & 0 \\ 0 & 0 & 7 & | & 3 & -4 & 1 \end{bmatrix}$$

$R_2 = -r_1 + r_2$ $R_2 = -r_2$ $R_1 = -3r_2 + r_1$
$R_3 = -r_1 + r_3$ $R_3 = 4r_2 + r_3$

$$\rightarrow \begin{bmatrix} 1 & 0 & -3 & | & -2 & 3 & 0 \\ 0 & 1 & 2 & | & 1 & -1 & 0 \\ 0 & 0 & 1 & | & \frac{3}{7} & -\frac{4}{7} & \frac{1}{7} \end{bmatrix} \rightarrow \begin{bmatrix} 1 & 0 & 0 & | & -\frac{5}{7} & \frac{9}{7} & \frac{3}{7} \\ 0 & 1 & 0 & | & \frac{1}{7} & \frac{1}{7} & -\frac{2}{7} \\ 0 & 0 & 1 & | & \frac{3}{7} & -\frac{4}{7} & \frac{1}{7} \end{bmatrix} \longrightarrow A^{-1} = \begin{bmatrix} -\frac{5}{7} & \frac{9}{7} & \frac{3}{7} \\ \frac{1}{7} & \frac{1}{7} & -\frac{2}{7} \\ \frac{3}{7} & -\frac{4}{7} & \frac{1}{7} \end{bmatrix}$$

$R_3 = \frac{1}{7}r_3$ $R_1 = 3r_3 + r_1$
$R_2 = -2r_3 + r_2$

33. Augment the matrix with the identity and use row operations to find the inverse:

$$A = \begin{bmatrix} 4 & -8 \\ -1 & 2 \end{bmatrix} \rightarrow \begin{bmatrix} 4 & -8 & | & 1 & 0 \\ -1 & 2 & | & 0 & 1 \end{bmatrix}$$

$$\rightarrow \begin{bmatrix} -1 & 2 & | & 0 & 1 \\ 4 & -8 & | & 1 & 0 \end{bmatrix} \rightarrow \begin{bmatrix} -1 & 2 & | & 0 & 1 \\ 0 & 0 & | & 1 & 4 \end{bmatrix} \rightarrow \begin{bmatrix} 1 & -2 & | & 0 & -1 \\ 0 & 0 & | & 1 & 4 \end{bmatrix}$$

Interchange $R_2 = 4r_1 + r_2$ $R_1 = -r_1$
r_1 and r_2

There is no inverse because there is no way to obtain the identity on the left side.
The matrix is singular.

35. $\begin{cases} 3x - 2y = 1 \\ 10x + 10y = 5 \end{cases}$ can be written as: $\begin{bmatrix} 3 & -2 & | & 1 \\ 10 & 10 & | & 5 \end{bmatrix}$

$\rightarrow \begin{bmatrix} 3 & -2 & | & 1 \\ 1 & 16 & | & 2 \end{bmatrix} \rightarrow \begin{bmatrix} 1 & 16 & | & 2 \\ 3 & -2 & | & 1 \end{bmatrix} \rightarrow \begin{bmatrix} 1 & 16 & | & 2 \\ 0 & -50 & | & -5 \end{bmatrix} \rightarrow \begin{bmatrix} 1 & 16 & | & 2 \\ 0 & 1 & | & \frac{1}{10} \end{bmatrix} \rightarrow \begin{bmatrix} 1 & 0 & | & \frac{2}{5} \\ 0 & 1 & | & \frac{1}{10} \end{bmatrix}$

$R_2 = -3r_1 + r_2$ Interchange $R_2 = -3r_1 + r_2$ $R_2 = -\frac{1}{50}r_2$ $R_1 = -16r_2 + r_1$

r_1 and r_2

The solution is $x = \dfrac{2}{5}, y = \dfrac{1}{10}$.

37. $\begin{cases} 5x + 6y - 3z = 6 \\ 4x - 7y - 2z = -3 \\ 3x + y - 7z = 1 \end{cases}$ can be written as $\begin{bmatrix} 5 & 6 & -3 & | & 6 \\ 4 & -7 & -2 & | & -3 \\ 3 & 1 & -7 & | & 1 \end{bmatrix}$

$\rightarrow \begin{bmatrix} 1 & 13 & -1 & | & 9 \\ 4 & -7 & -2 & | & -3 \\ 3 & 1 & -7 & | & 1 \end{bmatrix} \rightarrow \begin{bmatrix} 1 & 13 & -1 & | & 9 \\ 0 & -59 & 2 & | & -39 \\ 0 & -38 & -4 & | & -26 \end{bmatrix} \rightarrow \begin{bmatrix} 1 & 13 & -1 & | & 9 \\ 0 & 1 & -\frac{2}{59} & | & \frac{39}{59} \\ 0 & -38 & -4 & | & -26 \end{bmatrix}$

$R_1 = -r_2 + r_1$ $R_2 = -4r_1 + r_2$ $R_2 = -\frac{1}{59}r_2$

$R_3 = -3r_1 + r_3$

$\rightarrow \begin{bmatrix} 1 & 0 & -\frac{33}{59} & | & \frac{24}{59} \\ 0 & 1 & -\frac{2}{59} & | & \frac{39}{59} \\ 0 & 0 & -\frac{312}{59} & | & -\frac{52}{59} \end{bmatrix} \rightarrow \begin{bmatrix} 1 & 0 & -\frac{33}{59} & | & \frac{24}{59} \\ 0 & 1 & -\frac{2}{59} & | & \frac{39}{59} \\ 0 & 0 & 1 & | & \frac{1}{6} \end{bmatrix} \rightarrow \begin{bmatrix} 1 & 0 & 0 & | & \frac{1}{2} \\ 0 & 1 & 0 & | & \frac{2}{3} \\ 0 & 0 & 1 & | & \frac{1}{6} \end{bmatrix}$

$R_1 = -13r_2 + r_1$ $R_3 = -\frac{59}{312}r_3$ $R_1 = \frac{33}{59}r_3 + r_1$

$R_3 = 38r_2 + r_3$ $R_2 = \frac{2}{59}r_3 + r_2$

The solution is $x = \dfrac{1}{2}, y = \dfrac{2}{3}, z = \dfrac{1}{6}$.

39. $\begin{cases} x - 2z = 1 \\ 2x + 3y = -3 \\ 4x - 3y - 4z = 3 \end{cases}$ can be written as $\begin{bmatrix} 1 & 0 & -2 & | & 1 \\ 2 & 3 & 0 & | & -3 \\ 4 & -3 & -4 & | & 3 \end{bmatrix}$

$\rightarrow \begin{bmatrix} 1 & 0 & -2 & | & 1 \\ 0 & 3 & 4 & | & -5 \\ 0 & -3 & 4 & | & -1 \end{bmatrix} \rightarrow \begin{bmatrix} 1 & 0 & -2 & | & 1 \\ 0 & 1 & \frac{4}{3} & | & -\frac{5}{3} \\ 0 & -3 & 4 & | & -1 \end{bmatrix} \rightarrow \begin{bmatrix} 1 & 0 & -2 & | & 1 \\ 0 & 1 & \frac{4}{3} & | & -\frac{5}{3} \\ 0 & 0 & 8 & | & -6 \end{bmatrix}$

$R_2 = -2r_1 + r_2$ $R_2 = \frac{1}{3}r_2$ $R_3 = 3r_2 + r_3$

$R_3 = -4r_1 + r_3$

$\rightarrow \begin{bmatrix} 1 & 0 & -2 & | & 1 \\ 0 & 1 & \frac{4}{3} & | & -\frac{5}{3} \\ 0 & 0 & 1 & | & -\frac{3}{4} \end{bmatrix} \rightarrow \begin{bmatrix} 1 & 0 & 0 & | & -\frac{1}{2} \\ 0 & 1 & 0 & | & -\frac{2}{3} \\ 0 & 0 & 1 & | & -\frac{3}{4} \end{bmatrix}$

$R_3 = \frac{1}{8}r_3$ $R_1 = 2r_3 + r_1$

$R_2 = -\frac{4}{3}r_3 + r_2$

The solution is $x = -\dfrac{1}{2}, y = -\dfrac{2}{3}, z = -\dfrac{3}{4}$.

41. $\begin{cases} x - y + z = 0 \\ x - y - 5z = 6 \\ 2x - 2y + z = 1 \end{cases}$ can be written as: $\begin{bmatrix} 1 & -1 & 1 & | & 0 \\ 1 & -1 & -5 & | & 6 \\ 2 & -2 & 1 & | & 1 \end{bmatrix}$

$\rightarrow \begin{bmatrix} 1 & -1 & 1 & | & 0 \\ 0 & 0 & -6 & | & 6 \\ 0 & 0 & -1 & | & 1 \end{bmatrix} \rightarrow \begin{bmatrix} 1 & -1 & 1 & | & 0 \\ 0 & 0 & 1 & | & -1 \\ 0 & 0 & -1 & | & 1 \end{bmatrix} \rightarrow \begin{bmatrix} 1 & -1 & 0 & | & 1 \\ 0 & 0 & 1 & | & -1 \\ 0 & 0 & 0 & | & 0 \end{bmatrix} \rightarrow \begin{cases} x = y + 1 \\ z = -1 \end{cases}$

$R_2 = -r_1 + r_2$ $R_2 = -\frac{1}{6}r_2$ $R_1 = -r_2 + r_1$
$R_3 = -2r_1 + r_3$ $R_3 = r_2 + r_3$

The solution is $x = y + 1, z = -1, y$ is any real number..

43. $\begin{cases} x - y - z - t = 1 \\ 2x + y + z + 2t = 3 \\ x - 2y - 2z - 3t = 0 \\ 3x - 4y + z + 5t = -3 \end{cases}$ can be written as $\begin{bmatrix} 1 & -1 & -1 & -1 & | & 1 \\ 2 & 1 & 1 & 2 & | & 3 \\ 1 & -2 & -2 & -3 & | & 0 \\ 3 & -4 & 1 & 5 & | & -3 \end{bmatrix}$

$\rightarrow \begin{bmatrix} 1 & -1 & -1 & -1 & | & 1 \\ 0 & 3 & 3 & 4 & | & 1 \\ 0 & -1 & -1 & -2 & | & -1 \\ 0 & -1 & 4 & 8 & | & -6 \end{bmatrix} \rightarrow \begin{bmatrix} 1 & -1 & -1 & -1 & | & 1 \\ 0 & -1 & -1 & -2 & | & -1 \\ 0 & 3 & 3 & 4 & | & 1 \\ 0 & -1 & 4 & 8 & | & -6 \end{bmatrix} \rightarrow \begin{bmatrix} 1 & -1 & -1 & -1 & | & 1 \\ 0 & 1 & 1 & 2 & | & 1 \\ 0 & 3 & 3 & 4 & | & 1 \\ 0 & -1 & 4 & 8 & | & -6 \end{bmatrix}$

$R_2 = -2r_1 + r_2$ Interchange r_2 and r_3 $R_2 = -r_2$
$R_3 = -r_1 + r_3$
$R_4 = -3r_1 + r_4$

$\rightarrow \begin{bmatrix} 1 & 0 & 0 & 1 & | & 2 \\ 0 & 1 & 1 & 2 & | & 1 \\ 0 & 0 & 0 & -2 & | & -2 \\ 0 & 0 & 5 & 10 & | & -5 \end{bmatrix} \rightarrow \begin{bmatrix} 1 & 0 & 0 & 1 & | & 2 \\ 0 & 1 & 1 & 2 & | & 1 \\ 0 & 0 & 0 & 1 & | & 1 \\ 0 & 0 & 1 & 2 & | & -1 \end{bmatrix} \rightarrow \begin{bmatrix} 1 & 0 & 0 & 1 & | & 2 \\ 0 & 1 & 1 & 2 & | & 1 \\ 0 & 0 & 1 & 2 & | & -1 \\ 0 & 0 & 0 & 1 & | & 1 \end{bmatrix}$

$R_1 = r_2 + r_1$ $R_3 = -\frac{1}{2}r_3$ Interchange r_3 and r_4
$R_3 = -3r_2 + r_3$ $R_4 = \frac{1}{5}r_4$
$R_4 = r_2 + r_4$

$\rightarrow \begin{bmatrix} 1 & 0 & 0 & 1 & | & 2 \\ 0 & 1 & 0 & 0 & | & 2 \\ 0 & 0 & 1 & 2 & | & -1 \\ 0 & 0 & 0 & 1 & | & 1 \end{bmatrix} \rightarrow \begin{bmatrix} 1 & 0 & 0 & 0 & | & 1 \\ 0 & 1 & 0 & 0 & | & 2 \\ 0 & 0 & 1 & 0 & | & -3 \\ 0 & 0 & 0 & 1 & | & 1 \end{bmatrix}$

$R_2 = -r_3 + r_2$ $R_1 = -r_4 + r_1$
                         $R_3 = -2r_4 + r_3$

The solution is $x = 1, y = 2, z = -3, t = 1$.

45. Evaluating the determinant:

$\begin{vmatrix} 3 & 4 \\ 1 & 3 \end{vmatrix} = 3(3) - 4(1) = 9 - 4 = 5$

47. Evaluating the determinant:

$$\begin{vmatrix} 1 & 4 & 0 \\ -1 & 2 & 6 \\ 4 & 1 & 3 \end{vmatrix} = 1\begin{vmatrix} 2 & 6 \\ 1 & 3 \end{vmatrix} - 4\begin{vmatrix} -1 & 6 \\ 4 & 3 \end{vmatrix} + 0\begin{vmatrix} -1 & 2 \\ 4 & 1 \end{vmatrix}$$

$$= 1[2(3) - 6(1)] - 4[-1(3) - 6(4)] + 0[-1(1) - 2(4)]$$

$$= 1(6 - 6) - 4(-3 - 24) + 0(-1 - 8)$$

$$= 1(0) - 4(-27) + 0(-9) = 0 + 108 + 0 = 108$$

49. Evaluating the determinant:

$$\begin{vmatrix} 2 & 1 & -3 \\ 5 & 0 & 1 \\ 2 & 6 & 0 \end{vmatrix} = 2\begin{vmatrix} 0 & 1 \\ 6 & 0 \end{vmatrix} - 1\begin{vmatrix} 5 & 1 \\ 2 & 0 \end{vmatrix} + (-3)\begin{vmatrix} 5 & 0 \\ 2 & 6 \end{vmatrix}$$

$$= 2(0 - 6) - 1(0 - 2) + (-3)(30 - 0) = -12 + 2 - 90 = -100$$

51. Set up and evaluate the determinants to use Cramer's Rule:

$$\begin{cases} x - 2y = 4 \\ 3x + 2y = 4 \end{cases}$$

$$D = \begin{vmatrix} 1 & -2 \\ 3 & 2 \end{vmatrix} = 1(2) - 3(-2) = 2 + 6 = 8$$

$$D_x = \begin{vmatrix} 4 & -2 \\ 4 & 2 \end{vmatrix} = 4(2) - 4(-2) = 8 + 8 = 16$$

$$D_y = \begin{vmatrix} 1 & 4 \\ 3 & 4 \end{vmatrix} = 1(4) - 4(3) = 4 - 12 = -8$$

Find the solutions by Cramer's Rule: $x = \dfrac{D_x}{D} = \dfrac{16}{8} = 2 \qquad y = \dfrac{D_y}{D} = \dfrac{-8}{8} = -1$

53. Set up and evaluate the determinants to use Cramer's Rule:

$$\begin{cases} 2x + 3y = 13 \\ 3x - 2y = 0 \end{cases}$$

$$D = \begin{vmatrix} 2 & 3 \\ 3 & -2 \end{vmatrix} = -4 - 9 = -13$$

$$D_x = \begin{vmatrix} 13 & 3 \\ 0 & -2 \end{vmatrix} = -26 - 0 = -26$$

$$D_y = \begin{vmatrix} 2 & 13 \\ 3 & 0 \end{vmatrix} = 0 - 39 = -39$$

Find the solutions by Cramer's Rule: $x = \dfrac{D_x}{D} = \dfrac{-26}{-13} = 2 \qquad y = \dfrac{D_y}{D} = \dfrac{-39}{-13} = 3$

55. Set up and evaluate the determinants to use Cramer's Rule:

$$\begin{cases} x + 2y - z = 6 \\ 2x - y + 3z = -13 \\ 3x - 2y + 3z = -16 \end{cases}$$

$$D = \begin{vmatrix} 1 & 2 & -1 \\ 2 & -1 & 3 \\ 3 & -2 & 3 \end{vmatrix} = 1 \begin{vmatrix} -1 & 3 \\ -2 & 3 \end{vmatrix} - 2 \begin{vmatrix} 2 & 3 \\ 3 & 3 \end{vmatrix} + (-1) \begin{vmatrix} 2 & -1 \\ 3 & -2 \end{vmatrix}$$

$$= 1(-3 + 6) - 2(6 - 9) - 1(-4 + 3) = 3 + 6 + 1 = 10$$

$$D_x = \begin{vmatrix} 6 & 2 & -1 \\ -13 & -1 & 3 \\ -16 & -2 & 3 \end{vmatrix} = 6 \begin{vmatrix} -1 & 3 \\ -2 & 3 \end{vmatrix} - 2 \begin{vmatrix} -13 & 3 \\ -16 & 3 \end{vmatrix} + (-1) \begin{vmatrix} -13 & -1 \\ -16 & -2 \end{vmatrix}$$

$$= 6(-3 + 6) - 2(-39 + 48) - 1(26 - 16) = 18 - 18 - 10 = -10$$

$$D_y = \begin{vmatrix} 1 & 6 & -1 \\ 2 & -13 & 3 \\ 3 & -16 & 3 \end{vmatrix} = 1 \begin{vmatrix} -13 & 3 \\ -16 & 3 \end{vmatrix} - 6 \begin{vmatrix} 2 & 3 \\ 3 & 3 \end{vmatrix} + (-1) \begin{vmatrix} 2 & -13 \\ 3 & -16 \end{vmatrix}$$

$$= 1(-39 + 48) - 6(6 - 9) - 1(-32 + 39) = 9 + 18 - 7 = 20$$

$$D_z = \begin{vmatrix} 1 & 2 & 6 \\ 2 & -1 & -13 \\ 3 & -2 & -16 \end{vmatrix} = 1 \begin{vmatrix} -1 & -13 \\ -2 & -16 \end{vmatrix} - 2 \begin{vmatrix} 2 & -13 \\ 3 & -16 \end{vmatrix} + 6 \begin{vmatrix} 2 & -1 \\ 3 & -2 \end{vmatrix}$$

$$= 1(16 - 26) - 2(-32 + 39) + 6(-4 + 3) = -10 - 14 - 6 = -30$$

Find the solutions by Cramer's Rule:

$$x = \frac{D_x}{D} = \frac{-10}{10} = -1 \qquad y = \frac{D_y}{D} = \frac{20}{10} = 2 \qquad z = \frac{D_z}{D} = \frac{-30}{10} = -3$$

57. Find the partial fraction decomposition:

$$\frac{6}{x(x - 4)} = \frac{A}{x} + \frac{B}{x - 4} \quad \text{(Multiply both sides by } x(x - 4).\text{)}$$

$$6 = A(x - 4) + Bx$$

Let $x = 4$: then $6 = A(4 - 4) + B(4) \ \rightarrow \ 4B = 6 \ \rightarrow \ B = \dfrac{3}{2}$

Let $x = 0$: then $6 = A(0 - 4) + B(0) \ \rightarrow \ -4A = 6 \ \rightarrow \ A = -\dfrac{3}{2}$

$$\frac{6}{x(x - 4)} = \frac{\left(-\dfrac{3}{2}\right)}{x} + \frac{\left(\dfrac{3}{2}\right)}{x - 4}$$

59. Find the partial fraction decomposition:

$$\frac{x - 4}{x^2(x - 1)} = \frac{A}{x} + \frac{B}{x^2} + \frac{C}{x - 1} \text{(Multiply both sides by } x^2(x - 1).\text{)}$$

$$x - 4 = Ax(x - 1) + B(x - 1) + Cx^2$$

Let $x = 1$: then $1 - 4 = A(1)(1 - 1) + B(1 - 1) + C(1)^2 \rightarrow -3 = C \rightarrow C = -3$

Let $x = 0$: then $0 - 4 = A(0)(0 - 1) + B(0 - 1) + C(0)^2 \rightarrow -4 = -B \rightarrow B = 4$

Let $x = 2$: then $2 - 4 = A(2)(2 - 1) + B(2 - 1) + C(2)^2 \rightarrow -2 = 2A + B + 4C$

$$\rightarrow 2A = -2 - 4 - 4(-3) \rightarrow 2A = 6 \rightarrow A = 3$$

$$\frac{x - 4}{x^2(x - 1)} = \frac{3}{x} + \frac{4}{x^2} + \frac{-3}{x - 1}$$

61. Find the partial fraction decomposition:

$$\frac{x}{(x^2 + 9)(x + 1)} = \frac{A}{x + 1} + \frac{Bx + C}{x^2 + 9} \quad \text{(Multiply both sides by } (x + 1)(x^2 + 9).\text{)}$$

$$x = A(x^2 + 9) + (Bx + C)(x + 1)$$

Let $x = -1$: then $-1 = A((-1)^2 + 9) + (B(-1) + C)(-1 + 1)$

$$\rightarrow -1 = A(10) + (-B + C)(0) \rightarrow -1 = 10A \rightarrow A = -\frac{1}{10}$$

Let $x = 1$: then $1 = A(1^2 + 9) + (B(1) + C)(1 + 1) \rightarrow 1 = 10A + 2B + 2C$

$$\rightarrow 1 = 10\left(-\frac{1}{10}\right) + 2B + 2C \rightarrow 2 = 2B + 2C \rightarrow B + C = 1$$

Let $x = 0$: then $0 = A(0^2 + 9) + (B(0) + C)(0 + 1) \rightarrow 0 = 9A + C$

$$\rightarrow 0 = 9\left(-\frac{1}{10}\right) + C \rightarrow C = \frac{9}{10} B = 1 - C \rightarrow B = 1 - \frac{9}{10} \rightarrow B = \frac{1}{10}$$

$$\frac{x}{(x^2 + 9)(x + 1)} = \frac{-\left(\frac{1}{10}\right)}{x + 1} + \frac{\left(\frac{1}{10}x + \frac{9}{10}\right)}{x^2 + 9}$$

63. Find the partial fraction decomposition:

$$\frac{x^3}{(x^2 + 4)^2} = \frac{Ax + B}{x^2 + 4} + \frac{Cx + D}{(x^2 + 4)^2} \quad \text{(Multiply both sides by } (x^2 + 4)^2.\text{)}$$

$$x^3 = (Ax + B)(x^2 + 4) + Cx + D$$

$$x^3 = Ax^3 + Bx^2 + 4Ax + 4B + Cx + D$$

$$x^3 = Ax^3 + Bx^2 + (4A + C)x + 4B + D$$

$$A = 1$$

$$B = 0$$

$$4A + C = 0 \rightarrow 4(1) + C = 0 \rightarrow C = -4$$

$$4B + D = 0 \rightarrow 4(0) + D = 0 \rightarrow D = 0$$

$$\frac{x^3}{(x^2 + 4)^2} = \frac{x}{x^2 + 4} + \frac{-4x}{(x^2 + 4)^2}$$

65. Find the partial fraction decomposition:

$$\frac{x^2}{(x^2+1)(x^2-1)} = \frac{x^2}{(x^2+1)(x-1)(x+1)} = \frac{A}{x-1} + \frac{B}{x+1} + \frac{Cx+D}{x^2+1}$$

(Multiply both sides by $(x-1)(x+1)(x^2+1)$.)

$$x^2 = A(x+1)(x^2+1) + B(x-1)(x^2+1) + (Cx+D)(x-1)(x+1)$$

Let $x=1$: then $1^2 = A(1+1)(1^2+1) + B(1-1)(1^2+1) + (C(1)+D)(1-1)(1+1)$

$$\to 1 = 4A \to A = \frac{1}{4}$$

Let $x=-1$: then

$$(-1)^2 = A(-1+1)((-1)^2+1) + B(-1-1)((-1)^2+1) + (C(-1)$$
$$+ D)(-1-1)(-1+1)$$

$$\to 1 = -4B \to B = -\frac{1}{4}$$

Let $x=0$: then

$$0^2 = A(0+1)(0^2+1) + B(0-1)(0^2+1) + (C(0)+D)(0-1)(0+1)$$

$$\to 0 = A - B - D \to 0 = \frac{1}{4} - \left(-\frac{1}{4}\right) - D \to D = \frac{1}{2}$$

Let $x=2$: then

$$2^2 = A(2+1)(2^2+1) + B(2-1)(2^2+1) + (C(2)+D)(2-1)(2+1)$$

$$\to 4 = 15A + 5B + 6C + 3D \to 4 = 15\left(\frac{1}{4}\right) + 5\left(-\frac{1}{4}\right) + 6C + 3\left(\frac{1}{2}\right)$$

$$\to 6C = 4 - \frac{15}{4} + \frac{5}{4} - \frac{3}{2} \to 6C = 0 \to C = 0$$

$$\frac{x^2}{(x^2+1)(x^2-1)} = \frac{x^2}{(x^2+1)(x-1)(x+1)} = \frac{\left(\frac{1}{4}\right)}{x-1} + \frac{-\left(\frac{1}{4}\right)}{x+1} + \frac{\left(\frac{1}{2}\right)}{x^2+1}$$

67. Solve the first equation for y, substitute into the second equation and solve:

$$\begin{cases} 2x + y + 3 = 0 \to y = -2x - 3 \\ x^2 + y^2 = 5 \end{cases}$$

$$x^2 + (-2x-3)^2 = 5 \to x^2 + 4x^2 + 12x + 9 = 5$$

$$5x^2 + 12x + 4 = 0 \to (5x+2)(x+2) = 0$$

$$x = -\frac{2}{5} \quad \text{or} \quad x = -2$$

$$y = -\frac{11}{5} \qquad y = 1$$

Solutions: $\left(-\frac{2}{5}, -\frac{11}{5}\right), (-2, 1)$.

69. Multiply each side of the second equation by 2 and add the equations to eliminate xy:

$$\begin{cases} 2xy + y^2 = 10 \\ -xy + 3y^2 = 2 \end{cases} \xrightarrow{} \begin{array}{l} 2xy + y^2 = 10 \\ \underline{-2xy + 6y^2 = 4} \end{array}$$

$$7y^2 = 14 \to y^2 = 2 \to y = \pm\sqrt{2}$$

If $y = \sqrt{2}$: $2x\left(\sqrt{2}\right) + \left(\sqrt{2}\right)^2 = 10 \to 2\sqrt{2}x = 8 \to x = \dfrac{8}{2\sqrt{2}} = 2\sqrt{2}$

If $y = -\sqrt{2}$: $2x\left(-\sqrt{2}\right) + \left(-\sqrt{2}\right)^2 = 10 \to -2\sqrt{2}x = 8 \to x = \dfrac{8}{-2\sqrt{2}} = -2\sqrt{2}$

Solutions: $\left(2\sqrt{2}, \sqrt{2}\right), \left(-2\sqrt{2}, -\sqrt{2}\right)$

71. Substitute into the second equation into the first equation and solve:

$$\begin{cases} x^2 + y^2 = 6y \\ x^2 = 3y \end{cases}$$

$3y + y^2 = 6y \to y^2 - 3y = 0 \to y(y - 3) = 0 \to y = 0$ or $y = 3$

If $y = 0$: $x^2 = 3(0) \to x^2 = 0 \to x = 0$

If $y = 3$: $x^2 = 3(3) \to x^2 = 9 \to x = \pm 3$

Solutions: $(0, 0), (-3, 3), (3, 3)$

73. Factor the second equation, solve for x, substitute into the first equation and solve:

$$\begin{cases} 3x^2 + 4xy + 5y^2 = 8 \\ x^2 + 3xy + 2y^2 = 0 \end{cases} \to (x + 2y)(x + y) = 0 \to x = -2y \text{ or } x = -y$$

Substitute $x = -2y$ and solve: Substitute $x = -y$ and solve:

$$\begin{aligned} 3x^2 + 4xy + 5y^2 &= 8 \\ 3(-2y)^2 + 4(-2y)y + 5y^2 &= 8 \\ 12y^2 - 8y^2 + 5y^2 &= 8 \\ 9y^2 &= 8 \\ y^2 &= \frac{8}{9} \\ y &= \pm\frac{2\sqrt{2}}{3} \end{aligned}$$

$$\begin{aligned} 3x^2 + 4xy + 5y^2 &= 8 \\ 3(-y)^2 + 4(-y)y + 5y^2 &= 8 \\ 3y^2 - 4y^2 + 5y^2 &= 8 \\ 4y^2 &= 8 \\ y^2 &= 2 \\ y &= \pm\sqrt{2} \end{aligned}$$

If $y = \dfrac{2\sqrt{2}}{3}$: $x = -2\left(\dfrac{2\sqrt{2}}{3}\right) = \dfrac{-4\sqrt{2}}{3}$

If $y = \sqrt{2}$: $x = -\sqrt{2}$

If $y = -\sqrt{2}$: $x = \sqrt{2}$

If $y = \dfrac{-2\sqrt{2}}{3}$: $x = -2\left(\dfrac{-2\sqrt{2}}{3}\right) = \dfrac{4\sqrt{2}}{3}$

Solutions: $\left(\dfrac{-4\sqrt{2}}{3}, \dfrac{2\sqrt{2}}{3}\right), \left(\dfrac{4\sqrt{2}}{3}, \dfrac{-2\sqrt{2}}{3}\right), \left(-\sqrt{2}, \sqrt{2}\right), \left(\sqrt{2}, -\sqrt{2}\right)$

75. Multiply each side of the second equation by $-y$ and add the equations to eliminate y:

$$\begin{cases} x^2 - 3x + y^2 + y = -2 & \longrightarrow & x^2 - 3x + y^2 + y = -2 \\ \dfrac{x^2 - x}{y} + y + 1 = 0 & \xrightarrow{-y} & -x^2 + x - y^2 - y = 0 \end{cases}$$

$$-2x \qquad\qquad = -2$$
$$x = 1$$

If $x = 1$: $1^2 - 3(1) + y^2 + y = -2 \;\rightarrow\; y^2 + y = 0 \;\rightarrow\; y(y+1) = 0$
$$\rightarrow\; y = 0 \text{ or } y = -1$$

Note that $y \neq 0$ because that would cause division by zero in the original equation.
Solution: $(1, -1)$

77. Graph the system of linear inequalities:
$$\begin{cases} -2x + y \le 2 \\ x + y \ge 2 \end{cases}$$

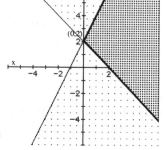

(a) Graph the line $-2x + y = 2$. Use a solid line since the
inequality uses $\le$.
Choose a test point not on the line, such as $(0, 0)$.
Since $-2(0) + 0 \le 2$ is true, shade the side of the line
containing $(0, 0)$.

(b) Graph the line $x + y = 2$. Use a solid line since the
inequality uses $\ge$.
Choose a test point not on the line, such as $(0, 0)$.
Since $0 + 0 \ge 2$ is false, shade the opposite side of the
line from $(0, 0)$.

(c) The overlapping region is the solution.

(d) The graph is unbounded.

(e) Find the vertices:
To find the intersection of $x + y = 2$ and $-2x + y = 2$, solve the system:
$$\begin{cases} x + y = 2 & \rightarrow & x = 2 - y \\ -2x + y = 2 \end{cases}$$

Substitute and solve:
$$-2(2 - y) + y = 2 \rightarrow -4 + 2y + y = 2 \rightarrow 3y = 6 \rightarrow y = 2$$
$$x = 2 - 2 = 0$$
The point of intersection is $(0, 2)$.
The corner point is $(0, 2)$.

79. Graph the system of linear inequalities:

$$\begin{cases} x \geq 0 \\ y \geq 0 \\ x + y \leq 4 \\ 2x + 3y \leq 6 \end{cases}$$

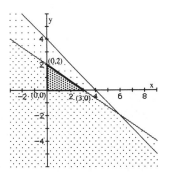

(a) Graph $x \geq 0$; $y \geq 0$. Shaded region is the first quadrant.

(b) Graph the line $x + y = 4$. Use a solid line since the inequality uses $\leq$.
Choose a test point not on the line, such as $(0, 0)$. Since $0 + 0 \leq 4$ is true, shade the side of the line containing $(0, 0)$.

(c) Graph the line $2x + 3y = 6$. Use a solid line since the inequality uses $\leq$.
Choose a test point not on the line, such as $(0, 0)$. Since $2(0) + 3(0) \leq 6$ is true, shade the side of the line containing $(0, 0)$.

(d) The overlapping region is the solution.

(e) The graph is bounded.

(f) Find the vertices:
The x-axis and y-axis intersect at $(0, 0)$.
The intersection of $2x + 3y = 6$ and the y-axis is $(0, 2)$.
The intersection of $2x + 3y = 6$ and the x-axis is $(3, 0)$.
The three corner points are $(0, 0)$, $(0, 2)$, and $(3, 0)$.

81. Graph the system of linear inequalities:

$$\begin{cases} x \geq 0 \\ y \geq 0 \\ 2x + y \leq 8 \\ x + 2y \geq 2 \end{cases}$$

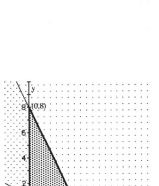

(a) Graph $x \geq 0$; $y \geq 0$. Shaded region is the first quadrant.

(b) Graph the line $2x + y = 8$. Use a solid line since the inequality uses $\leq$.
Choose a test point not on the line, such as $(0, 0)$. Since $2(0) + 0 \leq 8$ is true, shade the side of the line containing $(0, 0)$.

(c) Graph the line $x + 2y = 2$. Use a solid line since the inequality uses $\geq$.
Choose a test point not on the line, such as $(0, 0)$. Since $0 + 2(0) \geq 2$ is false, shade the opposite side of the line from $(0, 0)$.

(d) The overlapping region is the solution.

(e) The graph is bounded.

(f) Find the vertices:

The intersection of $x + 2y = 2$ and the y-axis is $(0, 1)$.
The intersection of $x + 2y = 2$ and the x-axis is $(2, 0)$.
The intersection of $2x + y = 8$ and the y-axis is $(0, 8)$.
The intersection of $2x + y = 8$ and the x-axis is $(4, 0)$.
The four corner points are $(0, 1)$, $(0, 8)$, $(2, 0)$, and $(4, 0)$.

83. Graph the system of inequalities:
$$\begin{cases} x^2 + y^2 \le 16 \\ x + y \ge 2 \end{cases}$$

(a) Graph the circle $x^2 + y^2 = 16$. Use a solid line since the inequality uses $\le$. Choose a test point not on the circle, such as $(0, 0)$. Since $0^2 + 0^2 \le 16$ is true, shade the side of the circle containing $(0, 0)$.

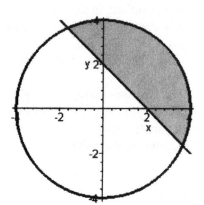

(b) Graph the line $x + y = 2$. Use a solid line since the inequality uses $\ge$. Choose a test point not on the line, such as $(0, 0)$. Since $0 + 0 \ge 2$ is false, shade the opposite side of the line from $(0, 0)$.

(c) The overlapping region is the solution.

85. Graph the system of inequalities:
$$\begin{cases} y \le x^2 \\ xy \le 4 \end{cases}$$

(a) Graph the parabola $y = x^2$. Use a solid line since the inequality uses $\le$. Choose a test point not on the parabola, such as $(1, 2)$. Since $2 \le 1^2$ is false, shade the opposite side of the parabola from $(1, 2)$.
(b) Graph the hyperbola $xy = 4$. Use a solid line since the inequality uses $\le$.

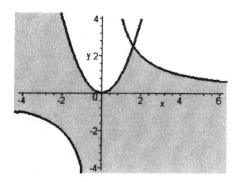

Choose a test point not on the hyperbola, such as $(1, 2)$. Since $1 \cdot 2 \le 4$ is true, shade the same side of the hyperbola as $(1, 2)$.

(c) The overlapping region is the solution.

87. Maximize $z = 3x + 4y$ Subject to $x \geq 0,\ y \geq 0,\ 3x + 2y \geq 6,\ x + y \leq 8$
     Graph the constraints.

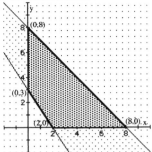

The corner points are $(0, 3),\ (2, 0),\ (0, 8),\ (8, 0)$.
Evaluate the objective function:

Vertex	Value of $z = 3x + 4y$
$(0, 3)$	$z = 3(0) + 4(3) = 12$
$(0, 8)$	$z = 3(0) + 4(8) = 32$
$(2, 0)$	$z = 3(2) + 4(0) = 6$
$(8, 0)$	$z = 3(8) + 4(0) = 24$

The maximum value is 32 at $(0, 8)$.

89. Minimize $z = 3x + 5y$
     Subject to $x \geq 0,\ y \geq 0,\ x + y \geq 1,\ 3x + 2y \leq 12,\ x + 3y \leq 12$
     Graph the constraints.

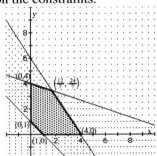

To find the intersection of $3x + 2y = 12$ and $x + 3y = 12$, solve the system:
$$\begin{cases} 3x + 2y = 12 \\ x + 3y = 12 \end{cases} \quad \rightarrow \quad x = 12 - 3y$$

Substitute and solve:

$$3(12 - 3y) + 2y = 12 \rightarrow 36 - 9y + 2y = 12 \rightarrow -7y = -24 \rightarrow y = \frac{24}{7}$$

$$x = 12 - 3\left(\frac{24}{7}\right) = 12 - \frac{72}{7} = \frac{12}{7}$$

The point of intersection is $\left(\frac{12}{7}, \frac{24}{7}\right)$.

The corner points are $(0, 1),\ (1, 0),\ (0, 4),\ (4, 0),\ \left(\frac{12}{7}, \frac{24}{7}\right)$.

Evaluate the objective function:

Vertex	Value of $z = 3x + 5y$
$(0, 1)$	$z = 3(0) + 5(1) = 5$
$(0, 4)$	$z = 3(0) + 5(4) = 20$
$(1, 0)$	$z = 3(1) + 5(0) = 3$
$(4, 0)$	$z = 3(4) + 5(0) = 12$
$\left(\dfrac{12}{7}, \dfrac{24}{7}\right)$	$z =$

$$3\left(\frac{12}{7}\right) + 5\left(\frac{24}{7}\right) = \frac{36}{7} + \frac{120}{7} = \frac{156}{7}$$

The minimum value is 3 at $(1, 0)$.

91. Maximize $z = 5x + 4y$ Subject to $x \geq 0,\ y \geq 0,\ x + 2y \geq 2,\ 3x + 4y \leq 12,\ y \geq x$
     Graph the constraints.

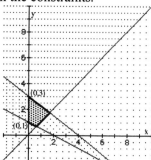

To find the intersection of $x + 2y = 2$ and $y = x$, substitute and solve:

$$x + 2x = 2 \rightarrow 3x = 2 \rightarrow x = \frac{2}{3} \rightarrow y = \frac{2}{3}$$

The point of intersection is $\left(\dfrac{2}{3}, \dfrac{2}{3}\right)$.

To find the intersection of $y = x$ and $3x + 4y = 12$, substitute and solve:

$$3x + 4x = 12 \rightarrow 7x = 12 \rightarrow x = \frac{12}{7} \rightarrow y = \frac{12}{7}$$

The point of intersection is $\left(\dfrac{12}{7}, \dfrac{12}{7}\right)$.

The corner points are $(0, 1)$, $(0, 3)$, $\left(\dfrac{2}{3}, \dfrac{2}{3}\right)$, $\left(\dfrac{12}{7}, \dfrac{12}{7}\right)$.

Evaluate the objective function:

Vertex	Value of $z = 5x + 4y$
$(0, 1)$	$z = 5(0) + 4(1) = 4$
$(0, 3)$	$z = 5(0) + 4(3) = 12$
$\left(\dfrac{2}{3}, \dfrac{2}{3}\right)$	$z = 5\left(\dfrac{2}{3}\right) + 4\left(\dfrac{2}{3}\right) = \dfrac{18}{3} = 6$
$\left(\dfrac{12}{7}, \dfrac{12}{7}\right)$	$z = 5\left(\dfrac{12}{7}\right) + 4\left(\dfrac{12}{7}\right) = \dfrac{108}{7} \approx 15.43$

The maximum value is $\dfrac{108}{7}$ at $\left(\dfrac{12}{7}, \dfrac{12}{7}\right)$.

93. Multiply each side of the first equation by –2 and eliminate x:

$$\begin{cases} 2x + 5y = 5 \\ 4x + 10y = A \end{cases} \xrightarrow{-2} \quad \begin{array}{l} -4x - 10y = -10 \\ \underline{4x + 10y = \quad A} \\ \quad\quad 0 = A - 10 \end{array}$$

If there are to be infinitely many solutions, the sum in elimination should be $0 = 0$. Therefore, $A - 10 = 0$ or $A = 10$.

95. when $x = 1$, $y = (1)^2 + b(1) + c = 2 \to 1 + b + c = 2 \to b + c = 1$

when $x = -1$, $y = (-1)^2 + b(-1) + c = 3 \to 1 - b + c = 3 \to -b + c = 2$

so we have the system $\begin{cases} b + c = 1 \\ -b + c = 2 \end{cases}$

subtracting the first equation from the second equation yields

$$\begin{array}{l} b + c = 1 \\ \underline{- (-b + c = 2)} \quad \therefore b = -0.5 \\ \quad 2b = -1 \end{array}$$

Back-substituting we get: $-0.5 + c = 1 \to c = 1.5$

Therefore, $y = x^2 - 0.5x + 1.5$, which satisfies the given conditions.

97. $y = ax^2 + bx + c$

At (0, 1) the equation becomes:

$1 = a(0)^2 + b(0) + c$

$c = 1$

At (1, 0) the equation becomes:

$0 = a(1)^2 + b(1) + c$

$0 = a + b + c$

$a + b + c = 0$

At (–2, 1) the equation becomes:

$1 = a(-2)^2 + b(-2) + c$

$1 = 4a - 2b + c$

$4a - 2b + c = 1$

The system of equations is:

$$\begin{cases} a + b + c = 0 \\ 4a - 2b + c = 1 \\ \quad\quad\quad c = 1 \end{cases}$$

Substitute $c = 1$ into the first and second equations and simplify:

$$\begin{cases} a + b + 1 = 0 & \to & a + b = -1 & \to & a = -b - 1 \\ 4a - 2b + 1 = 1 & \to & 4a - 2b = 0 \end{cases}$$

Solve the first equation for a, substitute into the second equation and solve:

$4(-b - 1) - 2b = 0$

$-4b - 4 - 2b = 0$

$-6b = 4 \to b = -\dfrac{2}{3} \to a = \dfrac{2}{3} - 1 = -\dfrac{1}{3}$

The quadratic function is $y = -\dfrac{1}{3}x^2 - \dfrac{2}{3}x + 1$.

99. Let x = the number of pounds of coffee that costs \$3.00 per pound.
    Let y = the number of pounds of coffee that costs \$6.00 per pound.
    Then $x + y = 100$ represents the total amount of coffee in the blend.
    The value of the blend will be represented by the equation: $3x + 6y = 3.90(100)$.
    Solve the system of equations:
    $$\begin{cases} x + y = 100 \\ 3x + 6y = 390 \end{cases} \rightarrow \quad y = 100 - x$$
    Solve by substitution:
    $$3x + 6(100 - x) = 390 \rightarrow 3x + 600 - 6x = 390$$
    $$-3x = -210 \rightarrow x = 70$$
    $$y = 100 - 70 = 30$$
    The blend is made up of 70 pounds of the \$3 per pound coffee and 30 pounds of the \$6 per pound coffee.

101. Let x = the number of small boxes.
     Let y = the number of medium boxes.
     Let z = the number of large boxes.
     Oatmeal raisin equation: $x + 2y + 2z = 15$
     Chocolate chip equation: $x + y + 2z = 10$
     Shortbread equation: $y + 3z = 11$
     Multiply each side of the second equation by -1 and add to the first equation to eliminate x:
     $$\begin{cases} x + 2y + 2z = 15 \\ x + y + 2z = 10 \\ y + 3z = 11 \end{cases} \xrightarrow{\quad -1 \quad} \begin{aligned} x + 2y + 2z &= 15 \\ -x - y - 2z &= -10 \\ \hline y &= 5 \end{aligned}$$
     Substituting and solving for the other variables:
     $$5 + 3z = 11 \qquad\qquad x + 5 + 2(2) = 10$$
     $$3z = 6 \qquad\qquad\qquad x + 9 = 10$$
     $$z = 2 \qquad\qquad\qquad\quad x = 1$$
     1 small box, 5 medium boxes, and 2 large boxes of cookies should be purchased.

103. Let x = the length of the lot.
     Let y = the width of the lot.
     Perimeter equation: $2x + 2y = 68$
     Diagonal equation: $x^2 + y^2 = 26^2$
     Solve the system of equations:
     $$\begin{cases} 2x + 2y = 68 \\ x^2 + y^2 = 676 \end{cases} \rightarrow \quad y = 34 - x$$
     Solve by substitution:

$$x^2 + (34-x)^2 = 676 \rightarrow x^2 + 1156 - 68x + x^2 = 676$$
$$2x^2 - 68x + 480 = 0 \rightarrow x^2 - 34x + 240 = 0$$
$$(x-24)(x-10) = 0 \rightarrow x = 24 \text{ or } x = 10$$
$$y = 10 \text{ or } y = 24$$

The dimensions of the lot are 24 feet by 10 feet.

105. Let x = the length of one leg.
Let y = the length of the other leg.
Perimeter equation: $x + y + 6 = 14$
Pythagorean equation: $x^2 + y^2 = 6^2$
Solve the system of equations:
$$\begin{cases} x + y = 8 \quad \rightarrow \quad y = 8 - x \\ x^2 + y^2 = 36 \end{cases}$$
Solve by substitution:
$$x^2 + (8-x)^2 = 36 \rightarrow x^2 + 64 - 16x + x^2 = 36$$
$$2x^2 - 16x + 28 = 0 \rightarrow x^2 - 8x + 14 = 0$$
$$x = \frac{8 \pm \sqrt{64-56}}{2} = \frac{8 \pm \sqrt{8}}{2} = \frac{8 \pm 2\sqrt{2}}{2} = 4 \pm \sqrt{2}$$
If $x = 4 - \sqrt{2}$, then $y = 8 - 4 + \sqrt{2} = 4 + \sqrt{2}$
If $x = 4 + \sqrt{2}$, then $y = 8 - 4 - \sqrt{2} = 4 - \sqrt{2}$
The legs are $4 + \sqrt{2}$ and $4 - \sqrt{2}$.

107. Let x = the length of the side of the smaller square.
Then $2x$ = the length of the side of the larger square.
The needed fencing is $4x + 8x = 12x$.
Solve the area equation:
$$x^2 + (2x)^2 = 5000 \rightarrow 5x^2 = 5000 \rightarrow x^2 = 1000 \rightarrow x = 10\sqrt{10}$$
$$12x = 120\sqrt{10} \approx 379.5 \text{ feet of fence are needed.}$$

$$x + y + z + w = 45$$
$$y = 2x$$
$$w = x$$
$$z = \frac{1}{2}x$$

109. Let x = the speed of the boat in still water.
Let y = the speed of the river current.
Let d = the distance from Chiritza to the Flotel Orellana (100 kilometers)

	Rate	Time	Distance
trip downstream	$x+y$	$\frac{5}{2}$	100
trip downstream	$x-y$	3	100

The system of equations is:

$$\begin{cases} (x+y)\left(\dfrac{5}{2}\right) = 100 & \rightarrow \quad 5x+5y=200 \\ (x-y)(3)=d & \rightarrow \quad 3x-3y=100 \end{cases}$$

$$5x+5y=200 \xrightarrow{\;3\;} \quad 15x+15y=600$$

$$3x-3y=100 \xrightarrow{\;5\;} \underline{+\; 15x-15y=500}$$

$$30x=1100$$

$$\therefore x = \frac{1100}{30} = \frac{110}{3}$$

$$\rightarrow 3\left(\frac{110}{3}\right) - 3y = 100 \rightarrow 110 - 3y = 100 \rightarrow 10 = 3y \rightarrow y = \frac{10}{3}$$

The speed of the boat $= \dfrac{110}{3} \approx 36.67$ km/hr and the speed of the river

current $= \dfrac{10}{3} \approx 3.33$ km/hr.

111. Let $x =$ the number of hours for Bruce to do the job alone.
Let $y =$ the number of hours for Bryce to do the job alone.
Let $z =$ the number of hours for Marty to do the job alone.
Then $\dfrac{1}{x}$ represents the fraction of the job that Bruce does in one hour.

$\dfrac{1}{y}$ represents the fraction of the job that Bryce does in one hour.

$\dfrac{1}{z}$ represents the fraction of the job that Marty does in one hour.

The equation representing Bruce and Bryce working together is:

$$\frac{1}{x} + \frac{1}{y} = \frac{1}{\left(\dfrac{4}{3}\right)} = \frac{3}{4} = 0.75$$

The equation representing Bryce and Marty working together is:

$$\frac{1}{y} + \frac{1}{z} = \frac{1}{\left(\dfrac{8}{5}\right)} = \frac{5}{8} = 0.675$$

The equation representing Bruce and Marty working together is:

$$\frac{1}{x} + \frac{1}{z} = \frac{1}{\left(\dfrac{8}{3}\right)} = 0.375$$

Solve the system of equations: Let
$$\begin{cases} x^{-1} + y^{-1} = 0.75 \\ y^{-1} + z^{-1} = 0.675 \\ x^{-1} + z^{-1} = 0.375 \end{cases}$$

$$u = x^{-1},\; v = y^{-1},\; w = z^{-1}$$
$$\begin{cases} u+v = 0.75 & \rightarrow \quad u = 0.75 - v \\ v+w = 0.675 & \rightarrow \quad w = 0.675 - v \\ u+w = 0.375 \end{cases}$$

Substitute into the third equation and solve:
$$0.75 - v + 0.675 - v = 0.375 \rightarrow -2v = -1 \rightarrow v = 0.5$$

$$u = 0.75 - 0.5 = 0.25$$

$$w = 0.675 - 0.5 = 0.125$$

Solve for x, y, and z:

$x = 4$, $y = 2$, $z = 8$ (reciprocals)

Bruce can do the job in 4 hours, Bryce in 2 hours, and Marty in 8 hours.

113. Let x = the number of gasoline engines produced each week.
Let y = the number of diesel engines produced each week.
The total cost is: $C = 450x + 550y$. Cost is to be minimized; thus, this is the objective function.
The constraints are:

$20 \leq x \leq 60$ number of gasoline engines needed and capacity each week.

$15 \leq y \leq 40$ number of diesel engines needed and capacity each week.

$x + y \geq 50$ number of engines produced to prevent layoffs.

Graph the constraints.

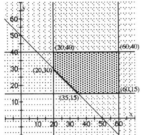

The corner points are (20, 30), (20, 40), (35, 15), (60, 15), (60, 40).
Evaluate the objective function:

Vertex	Value of $C = 450x + 550y$
(20, 30)	$C = 450(20) + 550(30) = 25{,}500$
(20, 40)	$C = 450(20) + 550(40) = 31{,}000$
(35, 15)	$C = 450(35) + 550(15) = 24{,}000$
(60, 15)	$C = 450(60) + 550(15) = 35{,}250$
(60, 40)	$C = 450(60) + 550(40) = 49{,}000$

The minimum cost is \$24,000, when 35 gasoline engines and 15 diesel engines are produced.
The excess capacity is 15 gasoline engines, since only 20 gasoline engines had to be delivered.

Chapter 9

Sequences; Induction; The Binomial Theorem

9.1 Sequences

1. $a_1 = 1,\ a_2 = 2,\ a_3 = 3,\ a_4 = 4,\ a_5 = 5$

3. $a_1 = \dfrac{1}{1+2} = \dfrac{1}{3},\ a_2 = \dfrac{2}{2+2} = \dfrac{2}{4} = \dfrac{1}{2},\ a_3 = \dfrac{3}{3+2} = \dfrac{3}{5},\ a_4 = \dfrac{4}{4+2} = \dfrac{4}{6} = \dfrac{2}{3},$
    $$a_5 = \dfrac{5}{5+2} = \dfrac{5}{7}$$

5. $a_1 = (-1)^{1+1}(1^2) = 1,\ a_2 = (-1)^{2+1}(2^2) = -4,\ a_3 = (-1)^{3+1}(3^2) = 9,$
    $$a_4 = (-1)^{4+1}(4^2) = -16,\ a_5 = (-1)^{5+1}(5^2) = 25$$

7. $a_1 = \dfrac{2^1}{3^1+1} = \dfrac{2}{4} = \dfrac{1}{2},\ a_2 = \dfrac{2^2}{3^2+1} = \dfrac{4}{10} = \dfrac{2}{5},\ a_3 = \dfrac{2^3}{3^3+1} = \dfrac{8}{28} = \dfrac{2}{7},$
    $$a_4 = \dfrac{2^4}{3^4+1} = \dfrac{16}{82} = \dfrac{8}{41},\ a_5 = \dfrac{2^5}{3^5+1} = \dfrac{32}{244} = \dfrac{8}{61}$$

9. $a_1 = \dfrac{(-1)^1}{(1+1)(1+2)} = \dfrac{-1}{2\cdot 3} = \dfrac{-1}{6},\ a_2 = \dfrac{(-1)^2}{(2+1)(2+2)} = \dfrac{1}{3\cdot 4} = \dfrac{1}{12},$
    $$a_3 = \dfrac{(-1)^3}{(3+1)(3+2)} = \dfrac{-1}{4\cdot 5} = \dfrac{-1}{20},\ a_4 = \dfrac{(-1)^4}{(4+1)(4+2)} = \dfrac{1}{5\cdot 6} = \dfrac{1}{30},$$
    $$a_5 = \dfrac{(-1)^5}{(5+1)(5+2)} = \dfrac{-1}{6\cdot 7} = -\dfrac{1}{42}$$

11. $a_1 = \dfrac{1}{e^1} = \dfrac{1}{e},\ a_2 = \dfrac{2}{e^2},\ a_3 = \dfrac{3}{e^3},\ a_4 = \dfrac{4}{e^4},\ a_5 = \dfrac{5}{e^5}$

13. $\dfrac{n}{n+1}$ 15. $\dfrac{1}{2^{n-1}}$ 17. $(-1)^{n+1}$ 19. $(-1)^{n+1}n$

21. $a_1 = 2,\ a_2 = 3+2 = 5,\ a_3 = 3+5 = 8,\ a_4 = 3+8 = 11,\ a_5 = 3+11 = 14$

23. $a_1 = -2,\ a_2 = 2+(-2) = 0,\ a_3 = 3+0 = 3,\ a_4 = 4+3 = 7,\ a_5 = 5+7 = 12$

25. $a_1 = 5,\ a_2 = 2\cdot 5 = 10,\ a_3 = 2\cdot 10 = 20,\ a_4 = 2\cdot 20 = 40,\ a_5 = 2\cdot 40 = 80$

27. $a_1 = 3$, $a_2 = \dfrac{3}{2}$, $a_3 = \dfrac{\left(\dfrac{3}{2}\right)}{3} = \dfrac{1}{2}$, $a_4 = \dfrac{\left(\dfrac{1}{2}\right)}{4} = \dfrac{1}{8}$, $a_5 = \dfrac{\left(\dfrac{1}{8}\right)}{5} = \dfrac{1}{40}$

29. $a_1 = 1$, $a_2 = 2$, $a_3 = 2 \cdot 1 = 2$, $a_4 = 2 \cdot 2 = 4$, $a_5 = 4 \cdot 2 = 8$

31. $a_1 = A$, $a_2 = A + d$, $a_3 = (A + d) + d = A + 2d$, $a_4 = (A + 2d) + d = A + 3d$,
$a_5 = (A + 3d) + d = A + 4d$

33. $a_1 = \sqrt{2}$, $a_2 = \sqrt{2 + \sqrt{2}}$, $a_3 = \sqrt{2 + \sqrt{2 + \sqrt{2}}}$, $a_4 = \sqrt{2 + \sqrt{2 + \sqrt{2 + \sqrt{2}}}}$,
$a_5 = \sqrt{2 + \sqrt{2 + \sqrt{2 + \sqrt{2 + \sqrt{2}}}}}$

35. $\displaystyle\sum_{k=1}^{10} 5 = \underbrace{5 + 5 + 5 + \ldots + 5}_{10 \text{ times}} = 50$

37. $\displaystyle\sum_{k=1}^{6} k = 1 + 2 + 3 + 4 + 5 + 6 = 21$

39. $\displaystyle\sum_{k=1}^{5} (5k + 3) = 8 + 13 + 18 + 23 + 28 = 90$

41. $\displaystyle\sum_{k=1}^{3} (k^2 + 4) = 5 + 8 + 13 = 26$

43. $\displaystyle\sum_{k=1}^{6} (-1)^k 2^k = (-1)^1 \cdot 2^1 + (-1)^2 \cdot 2^2 + (-1)^3 \cdot 2^3 + (-1)^4 \cdot 2^4 + (-1)^5 \cdot 2^5 + (-1)^6 \cdot 2^6$
$= -2 + 4 - 8 + 16 - 32 + 64 = 42$

45. $\displaystyle\sum_{k=1}^{4} (k^3 - 1) = 0 + 7 + 26 + 63 = 96$

47. $\displaystyle\sum_{k=1}^{n} (k + 2) = 3 + 4 + 5 + 6 + \cdots + (n + 2)$

49. $\displaystyle\sum_{k=1}^{n} \dfrac{k^2}{2} = \dfrac{1}{2} + 2 + \dfrac{9}{2} + 8 + \dfrac{25}{2} + \cdots + \dfrac{n^2}{2}$

51. $\displaystyle\sum_{k=0}^{n} \dfrac{1}{3^k} = 1 + \dfrac{1}{3} + \dfrac{1}{9} + \dfrac{1}{27} + \cdots + \dfrac{1}{3^n}$

53. $\displaystyle\sum_{k=0}^{n-1} \dfrac{1}{3^{k+1}} = \dfrac{1}{3} + \dfrac{1}{9} + \dfrac{1}{27} + \cdots + \dfrac{1}{3^n}$

55. $\displaystyle\sum_{k=2}^{n}(-1)^{k}\ln k = \ln 2 - \ln 3 + \ln 4 - \ln 5 + \cdots + (-1)^{n}\ln n$

57. $1 + 2 + 3 + \cdots + 20 = \displaystyle\sum_{k=1}^{20}k$

59. $\dfrac{1}{2} + \dfrac{2}{3} + \dfrac{3}{4} + \cdots + \dfrac{13}{13+1} = \displaystyle\sum_{k=1}^{13}\dfrac{k}{k+1}$

61. $1 - \dfrac{1}{3} + \dfrac{1}{9} - \dfrac{1}{27} + \cdots + (-1)^{6}\left(\dfrac{1}{3^{6}}\right) = \displaystyle\sum_{k=0}^{6}(-1)^{k}\left(\dfrac{1}{3^{k}}\right)$

63. $3 + \dfrac{3^{2}}{2} + \dfrac{3^{3}}{3} + \cdots + \dfrac{3^{n}}{n} = \displaystyle\sum_{k=1}^{n}\dfrac{3^{k}}{k}$

65. $a + (a+d) + (a+2d) + \cdots + (a+nd) = \displaystyle\sum_{k=0}^{n}(a+kd)$

67. $B_{1} = 1.01(3000) - 100 = \$2930$

69. $p_{1} = 1.03(2000) + 20 = 2080;\qquad p_{2} = 1.03(2080) + 20 = 2162.4$

71. $a_{1} = 1,\ a_{2} = 1,\ a_{3} = 2,\ a_{4} = 3,\ a_{5} = 5,\ a_{6} = 8,\ a_{7} = 13,\ a_{8} = 21,\ a_{n} = a_{n-1} + a_{n-2}$
    $a_{8} = a_{7} + a_{6} = 13 + 8 = 21$
    After 7 months there are 21 mature pairs of rabbits.

73. 1, 1, 2, 3, 5, 8, 13   This is the Fibonacci sequence.

75. To show that $\quad 1 + 2 + 3 + \ldots + (n-1) + n = \dfrac{n(n+1)}{2}$

    Let
    $$S = 1 + 2 + 3 + \ldots\ldots\ldots + (n-1) + n,\ \text{we can reverse the order to get}$$
    $$+S = n + (n-1) + (n-2) + \ldots + 2 + 1,\ \text{now add these two lines to get}$$
    $$2S = [1+n] + [2+(n-1)] + [3+(n-2)] + \ldots\ldots + [(n-1)+2] + [n+1]$$

    n terms

    So we have

    $$2S = [1+n] + [1+n] + [1+n] + \ldots + [n+1] + [n+1]$$

    n terms

    $$2S = n \cdot [n+1] \rightarrow S = \dfrac{n \cdot (n+1)}{2}$$

Chapter 9

Sequences; Induction; The Binomial Theorem

9.2 Arithmetic Sequences

1. $d = a_{n+1} - a_n = (n+1+4) - (n+4) = n+5-n-4 = 1$
   $a_1 = 1+4 = 5, \ a_2 = 2+4 = 6, \ a_3 = 3+4 = 7, \ a_4 = 4+4 = 8$

3. $d = a_{n+1} - a_n = (2(n+1) - 5) - (2n-5) = 2n+2-5-2n+5 = 2$
   $a_1 = 2 \cdot 1 - 5 = -3, \ a_2 = 2 \cdot 2 - 5 = -1, \ a_3 = 2 \cdot 3 - 5 = 1, \ a_4 = 2 \cdot 4 - 5 = 3$

5. $d = a_{n+1} - a_n = (6 - 2(n+1)) - (6 - 2n) = 6-2n-2-6+2n = -2$
   $a_1 = 6 - 2 \cdot 1 = 4, \ a_2 = 6 - 2 \cdot 2 = 2, \ a_3 = 6 - 2 \cdot 3 = 0, \ a_4 = 6 - 2 \cdot 4 = -2$

7. $d = a_{n+1} - a_n = \left(\dfrac{1}{2} - \dfrac{1}{3}(n+1) \right) - \left(\dfrac{1}{2} - \dfrac{1}{3}n \right) = \dfrac{1}{2} - \dfrac{1}{3}n - \dfrac{1}{3} - \dfrac{1}{2} + \dfrac{1}{3}n = -\dfrac{1}{3}$
   $a_1 = \dfrac{1}{2} - \dfrac{1}{3} \cdot 1 = \dfrac{1}{6}, \ a_2 = \dfrac{1}{2} - \dfrac{1}{3} \cdot 2 = -\dfrac{1}{6}, \ a_3 = \dfrac{1}{2} - \dfrac{1}{3} \cdot 3 = -\dfrac{1}{2}, \ a_4 = \dfrac{1}{2} - \dfrac{1}{3} \cdot 4 = -\dfrac{5}{6}$

9. $d = a_{n+1} - a_n = \ln 3^{n+1} - \ln 3^n = (n+1)\ln 3 - n\ln 3 = \ln 3 (n+1-n) = \ln 3$
   $a_1 = \ln 3^1 = \ln 3, \ a_2 = \ln 3^2 = 2\ln 3, \ a_3 = \ln 3^3 = 3\ln 3, \ a_4 = \ln 3^4 = 4\ln 3$

11. $a_n = a + (n-1)d = 2 + (n-1)3 = 2 + 3n - 3 = 3n - 1$
    $a_5 = 3 \cdot 5 - 1 = 14$

13. $a_n = a + (n-1)d = 5 + (n-1)(-3) = 5 - 3n + 3 = 8 - 3n$
    $a_5 = 8 - 3 \cdot 5 = -7$

15. $a_n = a + (n-1)d = 0 + (n-1)\dfrac{1}{2} = \dfrac{1}{2}n - \dfrac{1}{2}$
    $a_5 = \dfrac{1}{2} \cdot 5 - \dfrac{1}{2} = 2$

17. $a_n = a + (n-1)d = \sqrt{2} + (n-1)\sqrt{2} = \sqrt{2} + \sqrt{2}n - \sqrt{2} = \sqrt{2}n$
    $a_5 = 5\sqrt{2}$

19. $a_1 = 2, \ d = 2, \ a_n = a + (n-1)d$
    $a_{12} = 2 + (12-1)2 = 2 + 11(2) = 2 + 22 = 24$

21. $a_1 = 1, \ d = -2 - 1 = -3, \ a_n = a + (n-1)d$
$a_{10} = 1 + (10 - 1)(-3) = 1 + 9(-3) = 1 - 27 = -26$

23. $a_1 = a, \ d = (a+b) - a = b, \ a_n = a + (n-1)d$
$a_8 = a + (8-1)b = a + 7b$

25. $a_8 = a + 7d = 8 \qquad a_{20} = a + 19d = 44$
Solve the system of equations:
$8 - 7d + 19d = 44$

$12d = 36 \rightarrow d = 3 \rightarrow a = 8 - 7(3) = 8 - 21 = -13$
Recursive formula: $a_1 = -13 \qquad a_n = a_{n-1} + 3$

27. $a_9 = a + 8d = -5 \qquad a_{15} = a + 14d = 31$
Solve the system of equations:
$-5 - 8d + 14d = 31 \rightarrow 6d = 36 \rightarrow d = 6$

$a = -5 - 8(6) = -5 - 48 = -53$
Recursive formula: $a_1 = -53 \qquad a_n = a_{n-1} + 6$

29. $a_{15} = a + 14d = 0 \qquad a_{40} = a + 39d = -50$
Solve the system of equations:
$-14d + 39d = -50 \rightarrow 25d = -50 \rightarrow d = -2$

$a = -14(-2) = 28$
Recursive formula: $a_1 = 28 \qquad a_n = a_{n-1} - 2$

31. $a_{14} = a + 13d = -1 \qquad a_{18} = a + 17d = -9$
Solve the system of equations:
$-1 - 13d + 17d = -9$

$4d = -8 \rightarrow d = -2 \rightarrow a = -1 - 13(-2) = -1 + 26 = 25$
Recursive formula: $a_1 = 25 \qquad a_n = a_{n-1} - 2$

33. $S_n = \dfrac{n}{2}(a + a_n) = \dfrac{n}{2}(1 + (2n - 1)) = \dfrac{n}{2}(2n) = n^2$

35. $S_n = \dfrac{n}{2}(a + a_n) = \dfrac{n}{2}(7 + (2 + 5n)) = \dfrac{n}{2}(9 + 5n) = \dfrac{9}{2}n + \dfrac{5}{2}n^2$

37. $a_1 = 2, \ d = 4 - 2 = 2, \ a_n = a + (n-1)d$

$70 = 2 + (n-1)2 \rightarrow 70 = 2 + 2n - 2 \rightarrow 70 = 2n \rightarrow n = 35$
$S_n = \dfrac{n}{2}(a + a_n) = \dfrac{35}{2}(2 + 70) = \dfrac{35}{2}(72) = 35(36) = 1260$

39. $a_1 = 5$, $d = 9 - 5 = 4$, $a_n = a + (n-1)d$

$$49 = 5 + (n-1)4 \to 49 = 5 + 4n - 4 \to 48 = 4n \to n = 12$$
$$S_n = \frac{n}{2}(a + a_n) = \frac{12}{2}(5 + 49) = 6(54) = 324$$

41. Using the sum of the sequence feature:

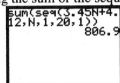

43. $d = 5.2 - 2.8 = 2.4$
    $a = 2.8$
$36.4 = 2.8 + (n-1)2.4$
$36.4 = 2.8 + 2.4n - 2.4$
   $36 = 2.4n$
   $n = 15$
   $a_n = 2.8 + (n-1)2.4 = 2.8 + 2.4n - 2.4 = 2.4n + 0.4$

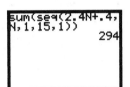

45. $d = 7.48 - 4.9 = 2.58$
    $a = 4.9$
$66.82 = 4.9 + (n-1)2.58$
$66.82 = 4.9 + 2.58n - 2.58$
  $64.5 = 2.58n$
    $n = 25$
    $a_n = 4.9 + (n-1)2.58 = 4.9 + 2.58n - 2.58$
    $a_n = 2.58n + 2.32$

47. Find the common difference of the terms and solve the system of equations:
$$(2x + 1) - (x + 3) = d \;\to\; x - 2 = d$$
$$(5x + 2) - (2x + 1) = d \;\to\; 3x + 1 = d$$
$$3x + 1 = x - 2 \to 2x = -3 \to x = -1.5$$

49. The total number of seats is: $S = 25 + 26 + 27 + \cdots$
This is the sum of an arithmetic sequence with $d = 1$, $a = 25$, and $n = 30$.
Find the sum of the sequence:
$$S_{30} = \frac{30}{2}[2(25) + (30 - 1)(1)] = 15(50 + 29) = 15(79) = 1185$$
There are 1185 seats in the theater.

51. The lighter colored tiles have 20 tiles in the bottom row and 1 tile in the top row. The number decreases by 1 as we move up the triangle. This is an arithmetic sequence with $a_1 = 20$, $d = -1$, and $n = 20$. Find the sum:
$$S = \frac{20}{2}[2(20) + (20 - 1)(-1)] = 10(40 - 19) = 10(21) = 210 \text{ lighter tiles.}$$

The darker colored tiles have 19 tiles in the bottom row and 1 tile in the top row. The number decreases by 1 as we move up the triangle. This is an arithmetic sequence with $a_1 = 19$, $d = -1$, and $n = 19$. Find the sum:

$$S = \frac{19}{2}[2(19) + (19-1)(-1)] = \frac{19}{2}(38-18) = \frac{19}{2}(20) = 190 \text{ darker tiles.}$$

53. Find n in an arithmetic sequence with $a_1 = 10$, $d = 4$, $s_n = 2040$.

$$s_n = \frac{n}{2}[2a_1 + (n-1)d] \to 2040 = \frac{n}{2}[2(10) + (n-1)4]$$

$$4080 = n[20 + 4n - 4] \to 4080 = n(4n + 16)$$

$$4080 = 4n^2 + 16n \to 1020 = n^2 + 4n$$

$$n^2 + 4n - 1020 = 0 \to (n+34)(n-30) = 0 \to n = -34 \text{ or } n = 30$$

There are 30 rows in the corner section of the stadium.

55. Answers will vary.

Sequences; Induction; The Binomial Theorem

9.3   Geometric Sequences; Geometric Series

1. $r = \dfrac{3^{n+1}}{3^n} = 3^{n+1-n} = 3$

$a_1 = 3^1 = 3, \ a_2 = 3^2 = 9, \ a_3 = 3^3 = 27, \ a_4 = 3^4 = 81$

3. $r = \dfrac{-3\left(\dfrac{1}{2}\right)^{n+1}}{-3\left(\dfrac{1}{2}\right)^n} = \left(\dfrac{1}{2}\right)^{n+1-n} = \dfrac{1}{2}$

$a_1 = -3\left(\dfrac{1}{2}\right)^1 = -\dfrac{3}{2}, \ a_2 = -3\left(\dfrac{1}{2}\right)^2 = -\dfrac{3}{4}, \ a_3 = -3\left(\dfrac{1}{2}\right)^3 = -\dfrac{3}{8}, \ a_4 = -3\left(\dfrac{1}{2}\right)^4 = -\dfrac{3}{16}$

5. $r = \dfrac{\left(\dfrac{2^{n+1-1}}{4}\right)}{\left(\dfrac{2^{n-1}}{4}\right)} = \dfrac{2^n}{2^{n-1}} = 2^{n-(n-1)} = 2$

$a_1 = \dfrac{2^{1-1}}{4} = \dfrac{2^0}{2^2} = 2^{-2} = \dfrac{1}{4}, \ a_2 = \dfrac{2^{2-1}}{4} = \dfrac{2^1}{2^2} = 2^{-1} = \dfrac{1}{2}, \ a_3 = \dfrac{2^{3-1}}{4} = \dfrac{2^2}{2^2} = 1,$

$a_4 = \dfrac{2^{4-1}}{4} = \dfrac{2^3}{2^2} = 2$

7. $r = \dfrac{2^{\left(\frac{n+1}{3}\right)}}{2^{\left(\frac{n}{3}\right)}} = 2^{\left(\frac{n+1}{3} - \frac{n}{3}\right)} = 2^{1/3}$

$a_1 = 2^{1/3}, \ a_2 = 2^{2/3}, \ a_3 = 2^{3/3} = 2, \ a_4 = 2^{4/3}$

9. $r = \dfrac{\left(\dfrac{3^{n+1-1}}{2^{n+1}}\right)}{\left(\dfrac{3^{n-1}}{2^{n}}\right)} = \dfrac{3^{n}}{3^{n-1}} \cdot \dfrac{2^{n}}{2^{n+1}} = 3^{n-(n-1)} \cdot 2^{n-(n+1)} = 3 \cdot 2^{-1} = \dfrac{3}{2}$

$a_1 = \dfrac{3^{1-1}}{2^{1}} = \dfrac{3^{0}}{2} = \dfrac{1}{2}$, $a_2 = \dfrac{3^{2-1}}{2^{2}} = \dfrac{3^{1}}{2^{2}} = \dfrac{3}{4}$, $a_3 = \dfrac{3^{3-1}}{2^{3}} = \dfrac{3^{2}}{2^{3}} = \dfrac{9}{8}$,

$a_4 = \dfrac{3^{4-1}}{2^{4}} = \dfrac{3^{3}}{2^{4}} = \dfrac{27}{16}$

11. $\{n + 2\}$ Arithmetic
$d = (n + 1 + 2) - (n + 2) = n + 3 - n - 2 = 1$

13. $\{4n^2\}$ Examine the terms of the sequence: 4, 16, 36, 64, 100, ...
There is no common difference; there is no common ratio; neither.

15. $\left\{3 - \dfrac{2}{3}n\right\}$ Arithmetic
$d = \left(3 - \dfrac{2}{3}(n+1)\right) - \left(3 - \dfrac{2}{3}n\right) = 3 - \dfrac{2}{3}n - \dfrac{2}{3} - 3 + \dfrac{2}{3}n = -\dfrac{2}{3}$

17. 1, 3, 6, 10, ...   Neither
There is no common difference or common ratio.

19. $\left\{\left(\dfrac{2}{3}\right)^{n}\right\}$ Geometric
$r = \dfrac{\left(\dfrac{2}{3}\right)^{n+1}}{\left(\dfrac{2}{3}\right)^{n}} = \left(\dfrac{2}{3}\right)^{n+1-n} = \dfrac{2}{3}$

21. $-1, -2, -4, -8, ...$ Geometric $r = \dfrac{-2}{-1} = \dfrac{-4}{-2} = \dfrac{-8}{-4} = 2$

23. $\{3^{n/2}\}$ Geometric
$r = \dfrac{3^{\left(\frac{n+1}{2}\right)}}{3^{\left(\frac{n}{2}\right)}} = 3^{\left(\frac{n+1}{2} - \frac{n}{2}\right)} = 3^{1/2}$

25. $a_5 = 2 \cdot 3^{5-1} = 2 \cdot 3^{4} = 2 \cdot 81 = 162$ $a_n = 2 \cdot 3^{n-1}$

27. $a_5 = 5(-1)^{5-1} = 5(-1)^{4} = 5 \cdot 1 = 5$ $a_n = 5 \cdot (-1)^{n-1}$

29. $a_5 = 0 \cdot \left(\dfrac{1}{2}\right)^{5-1} = 0 \cdot \left(\dfrac{1}{2}\right)^{4} = 0$ $a_n = 0 \cdot \left(\dfrac{1}{2}\right)^{n-1} = 0$

31. $a_5 = \sqrt{2} \cdot \sqrt{2}^{5-1} = \sqrt{2} \cdot \sqrt{2}^{4} = \sqrt{2} \cdot 4 = 4\sqrt{2}$ $a_n = \sqrt{2} \cdot \sqrt{2}^{n-1} = \sqrt{2}^{n}$

33. $a = 1, \ r = \dfrac{1}{2}, \ n = 7 \qquad a_7 = 1 \cdot \left(\dfrac{1}{2}\right)^{7-1} = \left(\dfrac{1}{2}\right)^6 = \dfrac{1}{64}$

35. $a = 1, \ r = -1, \ n = 9 \qquad a_7 = 1 \cdot (-1)^{9-1} = (-1)^8 = 1$

37. $a = 0.4, \ r = 0.1, \ n = 8 \qquad a_7 = 0.4 \cdot (0.1)^{8-1} = 0.4(0.1)^7 = 0.00000004$

39. $a = \dfrac{1}{4}, \ r = 2 \qquad S_n = a\left(\dfrac{1-r^n}{1-r}\right) = \dfrac{1}{4}\left(\dfrac{1-2^n}{1-2}\right) = -\dfrac{1}{4}\left(1-2^n\right)$

41. $a = \dfrac{2}{3}, \ r = \dfrac{2}{3} \qquad S_n = a\left(\dfrac{1-r^n}{1-r}\right) = \dfrac{2}{3}\left(\dfrac{1-\left(\frac{2}{3}\right)^n}{1-\frac{2}{3}}\right) = \dfrac{2}{3}\left(\dfrac{1-\left(\frac{2}{3}\right)^n}{\frac{1}{3}}\right) = 2\left(1-\left(\dfrac{2}{3}\right)^n\right)$

43. $a = -1, \ r = 2 \qquad S_n = a\left(\dfrac{1-r^n}{1-r}\right) = -1\left(\dfrac{1-2^n}{1-2}\right) = 1-2^n$

45. Using the sum of the sequence feature:

```
sum(seq(2^N/4,N,
0,14,1))
           8191.75
```

47. Using the sum of the sequence feature:

```
sum(seq((2/3)^N,
N,1,15,1))
        1.995432683
```

49. Using the sum of the sequence feature:

```
sum(seq(-1*2^N,N
,0,14,1))
           -32767
```

51.

$a = 1, \ r = \dfrac{1}{3} \qquad$ Since $|r| < 1, \ S_n = \dfrac{a}{1-r} = \dfrac{1}{\left(1-\frac{1}{3}\right)} = \dfrac{1}{\left(\frac{2}{3}\right)} = \dfrac{3}{2}$

53.

$$a = 8, \ r = \frac{1}{2} \quad \text{Since } |r| < 1, \ S_n = \frac{a}{1-r} = \frac{8}{\left(1 - \frac{1}{2}\right)} = \frac{8}{\left(\frac{1}{2}\right)} = 16$$

55.

$$a = 2, \ r = -\frac{1}{4} \quad \text{Since } |r| < 1, \ S_n = \frac{a}{1-r} = \frac{2}{\left(1 - \left(-\frac{1}{4}\right)\right)} = \frac{2}{\left(\frac{5}{4}\right)} = \frac{8}{5}$$

57.

$$a = 5, \ r = \frac{1}{4} \quad \text{Since } |r| < 1, \ S_n = \frac{a}{1-r} = \frac{5}{\left(1 - \frac{1}{4}\right)} = \frac{5}{\left(\frac{3}{4}\right)} = \frac{20}{3}$$

59.

$$a = 6, \ r = -\frac{2}{3} \quad \text{Since } |r| < 1, \ S_n = \frac{a}{1-r} = \frac{6}{\left(1 - \left(-\frac{2}{3}\right)\right)} = \frac{6}{\left(\frac{5}{3}\right)} = \frac{18}{5}$$

61. Find the common ratio of the terms and solve the system of equations:

$$\frac{x+2}{x} = r$$

$$\frac{x+3}{x+2} = r \rightarrow \frac{x+2}{x} = \frac{x+3}{x+2} \rightarrow x^2 + 4x + 4 = x^2 + 3x \rightarrow x = -4$$

63. This is a geometric series with $a = \$18,000, \ r = 1.05, \ n = 5$. Find the 5th term:

$$a_5 = 18000(1.05)^{5-1} = 18000(1.05)^4 = \$21,879.11$$

65. (a) Find the 10th term of the geometric sequence:

$$a = 2, \ r = 0.9, \ n = 10 \qquad a_{10} = 2(0.9)^{10-1} = 2(0.9)^9 = 0.775 \text{ feet}$$

    (b) Find n when $a_n < 1$:

$$2(0.9)^{n-1} < 1 \rightarrow 0.9^{n-1} < 0.5$$

$$(n-1)\log 0.9 < \log 0.5 \rightarrow n-1 > \frac{\log 0.5}{\log 0.9} \rightarrow n > \frac{\log 0.5}{\log 0.9} + 1 = 7.58$$

On the 8th swing the arc is less than 1 foot.

    (c) Find the sum of the first 15 swings:

$$S_{15} = 2\left(\frac{1 - (0.9)^{15}}{1 - 0.9}\right) = 2\left(\frac{1 - 0.9^{15}}{0.1}\right) = 20\left(1 - 0.9^{15}\right) = 15.88 \text{ feet}$$

    (d) Find the infinite sum of the geometric series:

$$S = \frac{2}{1 - 0.9} = \frac{2}{0.1} = 20 \text{ feet}$$

67. This is an ordinary annuity with $P = \$100$ and $n = (12)(30) = 360$ payment periods.

The interest rate per period is $\dfrac{.12}{12} = .01$. Thus,

$$A = 100\left[\dfrac{\left[1+\dfrac{.12}{12}\right]^{360}-1}{\left(\dfrac{.12}{12}\right)}\right] = \$349496.41$$

69. This is an ordinary annuity with $P = \$500$ and $n = (4)(20) = 80$ payment periods.

The interest rate per period is $\dfrac{.08}{4} = .02$. Thus,

$$A = 500\left[\dfrac{\left[1+\dfrac{.08}{4}\right]^{80}-1}{\left(\dfrac{.08}{4}\right)}\right] = \$96885.98$$

71. This is an ordinary annuity with $A = \$50000$ and $n = (12)(10) = 120$ payment periods. The interest rate per period is $\dfrac{.06}{12} = .005$. Thus,

$$50000 = P\left[\dfrac{\left[1+\dfrac{.06}{12}\right]^{120}-1}{\left(\dfrac{.06}{12}\right)}\right] \longrightarrow P = 50000\left[\dfrac{\left(\dfrac{.06}{12}\right)}{\left[1+\dfrac{.06}{12}\right]^{120}-1}\right] = \$305.10$$

73. Both options are geometric sequences:

Option A: $a = \$20,000$; $r = 1.06$; $n = 5$
$$a_5 = 20,000(1.06)^{5-1} = 20,000(1.06)^4 = \$25,250$$
$$S_5 = 20000\left(\dfrac{1-1.06^5}{1-1.06}\right) = \$112,742$$

Option B: $a = \$22,000$; $r = 1.03$; $n = 5$
$$a_5 = 22,000(1.03)^{5-1} = 22,000(1.03)^4 = \$24,761$$
$$S_5 = 22000\left(\dfrac{1-1.03^5}{1-1.03}\right) = \$116,801$$

Option A provides more money in the 5th year, while Option B provides the greatest total amount of money over the 5 year period.

75. Option 1:   Total Salary = $\$2,000,000(7) + \$100,000(7) = \$14,700,000$
Option 2:   Geometric series with: $a = \$2,000,000$, $r = 1.045$, $n = 7$
Find the sum of the geometric series:
$$S = 2,000,000\left(\dfrac{1-1.045^7}{1-1.045}\right) = \$16,038,304$$

Option 3:   Arithmetic series with: $a = \$2,000,000$, $d = \$95,000$, $n = 7$

Find the sum of the arithmetic series:
$$S_7 = \frac{7}{2}(2(2,000,000) + (7-1)(95,000)) = \$15,995,000$$
Option 2 provides the most money; Option 1 provides the least money.

77. This is a geometric sequence with $a = 1$, $r = 2$, $n = 64$.
Find the sum of the geometric series:
$$S_{64} = 1\left(\frac{1 - 2^{64}}{1 - 2}\right) = \frac{1 - 2^{64}}{-1} = 2^{64} - 1 = 1.845 \times 10^{19} \text{ grains}$$

79. The common ratio, $r = 0.90 < 1$. The sum is: $S = \dfrac{1}{1 - 0.9} = \dfrac{1}{0.10} = 10$.
The multiplier is 10.

81. This is an infinite geometric series with $a = 4$, and $r = \dfrac{1.03}{1.09}$.

Find the sum: Price $= \dfrac{4}{\left(1 - \dfrac{1.03}{1.09}\right)} = \$72.67$.

83. – 85. Answers will vary.

Chapter 9

Sequences; Induction; The Binomial Theorem

9.4 Mathematical Induction

1. I: $n = 1$: $2 \cdot 1 = 2$ and $1(1 + 1) = 2$
    II: If $2 + 4 + 6 + \cdots + 2k = k(k + 1)$
         then $2 + 4 + 6 + \cdots + 2k + 2(k + 1)$
    $$= [2 + 4 + 6 + \cdots + 2k] + 2(k + 1) = k(k + 1) + 2(k + 1)$$
    $$= (k + 1)(k + 2)$$

    Conditions I and II are satisfied; the statement is true.

3. I: $n = 1$: $1 + 2 = 3$ and $\dfrac{1}{2} \cdot 1(1 + 5) = 3$

    II: If $3 + 4 + 5 + \cdots + (k + 2) = \dfrac{1}{2} \cdot k(k + 5)$

         then $3 + 4 + 5 + \cdots + (k + 2) + [(k + 1) + 2]$

    $$= [3 + 4 + 5 + \cdots + (k + 2)] + (k + 3) = \frac{1}{2} \cdot k(k + 5) + (k + 3)$$

    $$= \frac{1}{2}k^2 + \frac{5}{2}k + k + 3 = \frac{1}{2}k^2 + \frac{7}{2}k + 3 = \frac{1}{2} \cdot \left(k^2 + 7k + 6\right)$$

    $$= \frac{1}{2} \cdot (k + 1)(k + 6)$$

    Conditions I and II are satisfied; the statement is true.

5. I: $n = 1$: $3 \cdot 1 - 1 = 2$ and $\dfrac{1}{2} \cdot 1(3 \cdot 1 + 1) = 2$

    II: If $2 + 5 + 8 + \cdots + (3k - 1) = \dfrac{1}{2} \cdot k(3k + 1)$

         then $2 + 5 + 8 + \cdots + (3k - 1) + [3(k + 1) - 1]$

    $$= [2 + 5 + 8 + \cdots + (3k - 1)] + (3k + 2) = \frac{1}{2} \cdot k(3k + 1) + (3k + 2)$$

    $$= \frac{3}{2}k^2 + \frac{1}{2}k + 3k + 2 = \frac{3}{2}k^2 + \frac{7}{2}k + 2 = \frac{1}{2} \cdot \left(3k^2 + 7k + 4\right)$$

    $$= \frac{1}{2} \cdot (k + 1)(3k + 4)$$

    Conditions I and II are satisfied; the statement is true.

7. I: $n = 1$: $2^{1-1} = 1$ and $2^1 - 1 = 1$

    II: If $1 + 2 + 2^2 + \cdots + 2^{k-1} = 2^k - 1$

    then $1 + 2 + 2^2 + \cdots + 2^{k-1} + 2^{k+1-1}$

    $$= \left[1 + 2 + 2^2 + \cdots + 2^{k-1}\right] + 2^k = 2^k - 1 + 2^k$$

    $$= 2 \cdot 2^k - 1 = 2^{k+1} - 1$$

Conditions I and II are satisfied; the statement is true.

9. I: $n = 1$: $4^{1-1} = 1$ and $\dfrac{1}{3} \cdot \left(4^1 - 1\right) = 1$

    II: If $1 + 4 + 4^2 + \cdots + 4^{k-1} = \dfrac{1}{3} \cdot \left(4^k - 1\right)$

    then $1 + 4 + 4^2 + \cdots + 4^{k-1} + 4^{k+1-1}$

    $$= \left[1 + 4 + 4^2 + \cdots + 4^{k-1}\right] + 4^k = \frac{1}{3} \cdot \left(4^k - 1\right) + 4^k$$

    $$= \frac{1}{3} \cdot 4^k - \frac{1}{3} + 4^k = \frac{4}{3} \cdot 4^k - \frac{1}{3} = \frac{1}{3}\left(4 \cdot 4^k - 1\right) = \frac{1}{3} \cdot \left(4^{k+1} - 1\right)$$

Conditions I and II are satisfied; the statement is true.

11. I: $n = 1$: $\dfrac{1}{1(1+1)} = \dfrac{1}{2}$ and $\dfrac{1}{1+1} = \dfrac{1}{2}$

    II: If $\dfrac{1}{1 \cdot 2} + \dfrac{1}{2 \cdot 3} + \dfrac{1}{3 \cdot 4} + \cdots + \dfrac{1}{k(k+1)} = \dfrac{k}{k+1}$

    then $\dfrac{1}{1 \cdot 2} + \dfrac{1}{2 \cdot 3} + \dfrac{1}{3 \cdot 4} + \cdots + \dfrac{1}{k(k+1)} + \dfrac{1}{(k+1)(k+1+1)}$

    $$= \left[\frac{1}{1 \cdot 2} + \frac{1}{2 \cdot 3} + \frac{1}{3 \cdot 4} + \cdots + \frac{1}{k(k+1)}\right] + \frac{1}{(k+1)(k+2)}$$

    $$= \frac{k}{k+1} + \frac{1}{(k+1)(k+2)} = \frac{k}{k+1} \cdot \frac{k+2}{k+2} + \frac{1}{(k+1)(k+2)}$$

    $$= \frac{k^2 + 2k + 1}{(k+1)(k+2)} = \frac{(k+1)(k+1)}{(k+1)(k+2)} = \frac{k+1}{k+2}$$

Conditions I and II are satisfied; the statement is true.

13. I: $n = 1$: $1^2 = 1$ and $\dfrac{1}{6} \cdot 1(1+1)(2 \cdot 1 + 1) = 1$

    II: If $1^2 + 2^2 + 3^2 + \cdots + k^2 = \dfrac{1}{6} \cdot k(k+1)(2k+1)$

    then $1^2 + 2^2 + 3^2 + \cdots + k^2 + (k+1)^2$

    $$= \left[1^2 + 2^2 + 3^2 + \cdots + k^2\right] + (k+1)^2 = \frac{1}{6}k(k+1)(2k+1) + (k+1)^2$$

    $$= (k+1)\left[\frac{1}{6}k(2k+1) + k + 1\right] = (k+1)\left[\frac{1}{3}k^2 + \frac{1}{6}k + k + 1\right]$$

$$= (k+1)\left[\frac{1}{3}k^2 + \frac{7}{6}k + 1\right] = \frac{1}{6}(k+1)\left[2k^2 + 7k + 6\right]$$

$$= \frac{1}{6} \cdot (k+1)(k+2)(2k+3)$$

Conditions I and II are satisfied; the statement is true.

15. I: $n = 1$: $5 - 1 = 4$ and $\frac{1}{2} \cdot 1(9-1) = 4$

   II: If $4 + 3 + 2 + \cdots + (5-k) = \frac{1}{2} \cdot k(9-k)$

   then $4 + 3 + 2 + \cdots + (5-k) + (5-(k+1))$

$$= \left[4 + 3 + 2 + \cdots + (5-k)\right] + (4-k) = \frac{1}{2}k(9-k) + (4-k)$$

$$= \frac{9}{2}k - \frac{1}{2}k^2 + 4 - k = -\frac{1}{2}k^2 + \frac{7}{2}k + 4 = -\frac{1}{2} \cdot \left[k^2 - 7k - 8\right]$$

$$= -\frac{1}{2} \cdot (k+1)(k-8) = \frac{1}{2} \cdot (k+1)(8-k) = \frac{1}{2} \cdot (k+1)\left[9 - (k+1)\right]$$

Conditions I and II are satisfied; the statement is true.

17. I: $n = 1$: $1(1+1) = 2$ and $\frac{1}{3} \cdot 1(1+1)(1+2) = 2$

   II: If $1 \cdot 2 + 2 \cdot 3 + 3 \cdot 4 + \cdots + k(k+1) = \frac{1}{3} \cdot k(k+1)(k+2)$

   then $1 \cdot 2 + 2 \cdot 3 + 3 \cdot 4 + \cdots + k(k+1) + (k+1)(k+1+1)$

$$= \left[1 \cdot 2 + 2 \cdot 3 + 3 \cdot 4 + \cdots + k(k+1)\right] + (k+1)(k+2)$$

$$= \frac{1}{3} \cdot k(k+1)(k+2) + (k+1)(k+2) = (k+1)(k+2)\left[\frac{1}{3}k + 1\right]$$

$$= \frac{1}{3} \cdot (k+1)(k+2)(k+3)$$

Conditions I and II are satisfied; the statement is true.

19. I: $n = 1$: $1^2 + 1 = 2$ is divisible by 2
   II: If $k^2 + k$ is divisible by 2
      then $(k+1)^2 + (k+1) = k^2 + 2k + 1 + k + 1 = (k^2 + k) + (2k+2)$
      Since $k^2 + k$ is divisible by 2 and $2k + 2$ is divisible by 2, then $(k+1)^2 + (k+1)$
      is divisible by 2.
Conditions I and II are satisfied; the statement is true.

21. I: $n = 1$: $1^2 - 1 + 2 = 2$ is divisible by 2
    II: If $k^2 - k + 2$ is divisible by 2
        then $(k+1)^2 - (k+1) + 2 = k^2 + 2k + 1 - k - 1 + 2 = (k^2 - k + 2) + (2k)$
        Since $k^2 - k + 2$ is divisible by 2 and $2k$ is divisible by 2, then
        $(k+1)^2 - (k+1) + 2$ is divisible by 2.
    Conditions I and II are satisfied; the statement is true.

23. I: $n = 1$: If $x > 1$ then $x^1 = x > 1$.
    II: Assume, for any natural number k, that if $x > 1$, then $x^k > 1$.
        Show that if $x^k > 1$, then $x^{k+1} > 1$:
        $$x^{k+1} = x^k \cdot x > 1 \cdot x = x > 1$$
        $$\uparrow$$
        $$(x^k > 1)$$
    Conditions I and II are satisfied; the statement is true.

25. I: $n = 1$: $a - b$ is a factor of $a^1 - b^1 = a - b$.
    II: If $a - b$ is a factor of $a^k - b^k$
        Show that $a - b$ is a factor of $a^{k+1} - b^{k+1} = a \cdot a^k - b \cdot b^k$
        $$= a \cdot a^k - a \cdot b^k + a \cdot b^k - b \cdot b^k = a(a^k - b^k) + b^k(a - b)$$
        Since $a - b$ is a factor of $a^k - b^k$ and $a - b$ is a factor of $a - b$, then
        $a - b$ is a factor of $a^{k+1} - b^{k+1}$.
    Conditions I and II are satisfied; the statement is true.

27. $n = 1$: $1^2 - 1 + 41 = 41$ is a prime number.
    $n = 41$: $41^2 - 41 + 41 = 41^2$ is not a prime number.

29. I: $n = 1$: $ar^{1-1} = a$ and $a\left(\dfrac{1 - r^1}{1 - r}\right) = a$

    II: If $a + ar + ar^2 + \cdots + ar^{k-1} = a\left(\dfrac{1 - r^k}{1 - r}\right)$

        then $a + ar + ar^2 + \cdots + ar^{k-1} + ar^{k+1-1}$

        $$= \left[a + ar + ar^2 + \cdots + ar^{k-1}\right] + ar^k = a\left(\frac{1 - r^k}{1 - r}\right) + ar^k$$

        $$= \frac{a(1 - r^k) + ar^k(1 - r)}{1 - r} = \frac{a - ar^k + ar^k - ar^{k+1}}{1 - r} = a\left(\frac{1 - r^{k+1}}{1 - r}\right)$$

    Conditions I and II are satisfied; the statement is true.

31. I: $n = 4$:   The number of diagonals of a quadrilateral is $\frac{1}{2} \cdot 4(4-3) = 2$

II: Assume that for any integer k the number of diagonals of a convex polygon

with k sides (k vertices) is $\frac{1}{2} \cdot k(k-3)$. A convex polygon with $k+1$ sides

($k+1$ vertices) consists of a convex polygon with k sides (k vertices) plus

a triangle for a total of $k+1$ vertices. The number of diagonals of this

convex polygon consists of the original ones plus $k-1$ additional ones,

namely, $\frac{1}{2} \cdot k(k-3) + (k-1) = \frac{1}{2}k^2 - \frac{3}{2}k + k - 1 = \frac{1}{2}k^2 - \frac{1}{2}k - 1$

$$= \frac{1}{2} \cdot \left(k^2 - k - 2\right) = \frac{1}{2} \cdot (k+1)(k-2)$$

Conditions I and II are satisfied; the statement is true.

33. Answers will vary.

Sequences; Induction; The Binomial Theorem

9.5 The Binomial Theorem

1. $\dbinom{5}{3} = \dfrac{5!}{3!\,2!} = \dfrac{5\cdot4\cdot3\cdot2\cdot1}{3\cdot2\cdot1\cdot2\cdot1} = \dfrac{5\cdot4}{2\cdot1} = 10$

3. $\dbinom{7}{5} = \dfrac{7!}{5!\,2!} = \dfrac{7\cdot6\cdot5\cdot4\cdot3\cdot2\cdot1}{5\cdot4\cdot3\cdot2\cdot1\cdot2\cdot1} = \dfrac{7\cdot6}{2\cdot1} = 21$

5. $\dbinom{50}{49} = \dfrac{50!}{49!\,1!} = \dfrac{50\cdot49!}{49!\cdot1} = \dfrac{50}{1} = 50$

7. $\dbinom{1000}{1000} = \dfrac{1000!}{1000!\,0!} = \dfrac{1}{1} = 1$

9. $\dbinom{55}{23} = \dfrac{55!}{23!\,32!} = 1.866442159 \times 10^{15}$

11. $\dbinom{47}{25} = \dfrac{47!}{25!\,22!} = 1.483389769 \times 10^{13}$

13. $(x+1)^5 = \dbinom{5}{0}x^5 + \dbinom{5}{1}x^4 + \dbinom{5}{2}x^3 + \dbinom{5}{3}x^2 + \dbinom{5}{4}x^1 + \dbinom{5}{5}x^0$

$\qquad = x^5 + 5x^4 + 10x^3 + 10x^2 + 5x + 1$

15. $(x-2)^6 = \dbinom{6}{0}x^6 + \dbinom{6}{1}x^5(-2) + \dbinom{6}{2}x^4(-2)^2 + \dbinom{6}{3}x^3(-2)^3 + \dbinom{6}{4}x^2(-2)^4$

$\qquad\quad + \dbinom{6}{5}x(-2)^5 + \dbinom{6}{6}x^0(-2)^6$

$\qquad = x^6 + 6x^5(-2) + 15x^4\cdot4 + 20x^3(-8) + 15x^2\cdot16 + 6x\cdot(-32) + 64$

$\qquad = x^6 - 12x^5 + 60x^4 - 160x^3 + 240x - 192x + 64$

17. $(3x+1)^4 = \dbinom{4}{0}(3x)^4 + \dbinom{4}{1}(3x)^3 + \dbinom{4}{2}(3x)^2 + \dbinom{4}{3}(3x) + \dbinom{4}{4}$

$\qquad = 81x^4 + 4\cdot27x^3 + 6\cdot9x^2 + 4\cdot3x + 1 = 81x^4 + 108x^3 + 54x^2 + 12x + 1$

19. $\left(x^2 + y^2\right)^5 = \binom{5}{0}\left(x^2\right)^5\left(y^2\right)^0 + \binom{5}{1}\left(x^2\right)^4\left(y^2\right) + \binom{5}{2}\left(x^2\right)^3\left(y^2\right)^2 + \binom{5}{3}\left(x^2\right)^2\left(y^2\right)^3$

$\qquad\qquad\qquad + \binom{5}{4}x^2\left(y^2\right)^4 + \binom{5}{5}\left(y^2\right)^5$

$\qquad = x^{10} + 5x^8 y^2 + 10x^6 y^4 + 10x^4 y^6 + 5x^2 y^8 + y^{10}$

21. $\left(\sqrt{x} + \sqrt{2}\right)^6 = \binom{6}{0}\left(\sqrt{x}\right)^6\left(\sqrt{2}\right)^0 + \binom{6}{1}\left(\sqrt{x}\right)^5\left(\sqrt{2}\right)^1 + \binom{6}{2}\left(\sqrt{x}\right)^4\left(\sqrt{2}\right)^2 + \binom{6}{3}\left(\sqrt{x}\right)^3\left(\sqrt{2}\right)^3$

$\qquad\qquad\quad \binom{6}{4}\left(\sqrt{x}\right)^2\left(\sqrt{2}\right)^4 + \binom{6}{5}\left(\sqrt{x}\right)\left(\sqrt{2}\right)^5 + \binom{6}{6}\left(\sqrt{x}\right)^0\left(\sqrt{2}\right)^6$

$\qquad = x^3 + 6\sqrt{2}x^{5/2} + 15\cdot 2x^2 + 20\cdot 2\sqrt{2}x^{3/2} + 15\cdot 4x + 6\cdot 4\sqrt{2}x^{1/2} + 8$

$\qquad = x^3 + 6\sqrt{2}x^{5/2} + 30x^2 + 40\sqrt{2}x^{3/2} + 60x + 24\sqrt{2}x^{1/2} + 8$

23. $\left(ax + by\right)^5 = \binom{5}{0}\left(ax\right)^5 + \binom{5}{1}\left(ax\right)^4\cdot by + \binom{5}{2}\left(ax\right)^3\left(by\right)^2 + \binom{5}{3}\left(ax\right)^2\left(by\right)^3$

$\qquad\qquad\qquad + \binom{5}{4}ax\left(by\right)^4 + \binom{5}{5}\left(by\right)^5$

$\qquad = a^5 x^5 + 5a^4 x^4 by + 10a^3 x^3 b^2 y^2 + 10a^2 x^2 b^3 y^3 + 5axb^4 y^4 + b^5 y^5$

25. $n = 10$, $j = 4$, $x = x$, $a = 3$

$\qquad \binom{10}{4}x^6\cdot 3^4 = \dfrac{10!}{4!\,6!}\cdot 81x^6 = \dfrac{10\cdot 9\cdot 8\cdot 7}{4\cdot 3\cdot 2\cdot 1}\cdot 81x^6 = 17{,}010x^6$

The coefficient of x^6 is $17{,}010$.

27. $n = 12$, $j = 5$, $x = 2x$, $a = -1$

$\qquad \binom{12}{5}(2x)^7\cdot(-1)^5 = \dfrac{12!}{5!\,7!}\cdot 128x^7(-1) = \dfrac{12\cdot 11\cdot 10\cdot 9\cdot 8}{5\cdot 4\cdot 3\cdot 2\cdot 1}\cdot(-128)x^7 = -101{,}376x^7$

The coefficient of x^7 is $-101{,}376$.

29. $n = 9$, $j = 2$, $x = 2x$, $a = 3$

$\qquad \binom{9}{2}(2x)^7\cdot 3^2 = \dfrac{9!}{2!\,7!}\cdot 128x^7(9) = \dfrac{9\cdot 8}{2\cdot 1}\cdot 128x^7\cdot 9 = 41{,}472x^7$

The coefficient of x^7 is $41{,}472$.

31. $n = 7$, $j = 4$, $x = x$, $a = 3$

$\qquad \binom{7}{4}x^3\cdot 3^4 = \dfrac{7!}{4!\,3!}\cdot 81x^3 = \dfrac{7\cdot 6\cdot 5}{3\cdot 2\cdot 1}\cdot 81x^3 = 2835x^3$

33. $n = 9$, $j = 2$, $x = 3x$, $a = -2$

$\qquad \binom{9}{2}(3x)^7\cdot(-2)^2 = \dfrac{9!}{2!\,7!}\cdot 2187x^7\cdot 4 = \dfrac{9\cdot 8}{2\cdot 1}\cdot 8748x^7 = 314{,}928x^7$

35. The constant term in $\binom{12}{j}(x^2)^{12-j}\left(\frac{1}{x}\right)^j$ occurs when:

$$2(12-j)=j \;\rightarrow\; 24-2j=j \;\rightarrow\; 3j=24 \;\rightarrow\; j=8.$$

Evaluate the 9th term:

$$\binom{12}{8}(x^2)^4\cdot\left(\frac{1}{x}\right)^8=\frac{12!}{8!\,4!}x^8\cdot\frac{1}{x^8}=\frac{12\cdot11\cdot10\cdot9}{4\cdot3\cdot2\cdot1}x^0=495$$

37. The x^4 term in $\binom{10}{j}(x)^{10-j}\left(\frac{-2}{\sqrt{x}}\right)^j$ occurs when:

$$10-j-\tfrac{1}{2}j=4 \;\rightarrow\; -\tfrac{3}{2}j=-6 \;\rightarrow\; j=4.$$

Evaluate the 5th term:

$$\binom{10}{4}(x)^6\cdot\left(\frac{-2}{\sqrt{x}}\right)^4=\frac{10!}{6!\,4!}x^6\cdot\frac{16}{x^2}=\frac{10\cdot9\cdot8\cdot7}{4\cdot3\cdot2\cdot1}\cdot16x^4=3360x^4$$

The coefficient is 3360.

39. $(1.001)^5=\left(1+10^{-3}\right)^5=\binom{5}{0}\cdot1^5+\binom{5}{1}\cdot1^4\cdot10^{-3}+\binom{5}{2}\cdot1^3\cdot\left(10^{-3}\right)^2+\binom{5}{3}\cdot1^2\cdot\left(10^{-3}\right)^3+\ldots$

$$=1+5(0.001)+10(0.000001)+10(0.000000001)+\ldots$$
$$=1+0.005+0.000010+0.000000010+\ldots$$
$$=1.00501 \quad\text{(correct to 5 decimal places)}$$

41. $\binom{n}{n-1}=\dfrac{n!}{(n-1)!(n-(n-1))!}=\dfrac{n!}{(n-1)!(1)!}=n$

$\binom{n}{n}=\dfrac{n!}{n!(n-n)!}=\dfrac{n!}{n!\,0!}=\dfrac{n!}{n!\cdot1}=\dfrac{n!}{n!}=1$

43. Show that $\binom{n}{0}+\binom{n}{1}+\ldots+\binom{n}{n}=2^n$

$$2^n=(1+1)^n$$
$$=\binom{n}{0}\cdot1^n+\binom{n}{1}\cdot1^{n-1}\cdot1+\binom{n}{2}\cdot1^{n-2}\cdot1^2+\ldots+\binom{n}{n}\cdot1^{n-n}\cdot1^n$$
$$=\binom{n}{0}+\binom{n}{1}+\ldots+\binom{n}{n}$$

45. $\binom{5}{0}\left(\frac{1}{4}\right)^5+\binom{5}{1}\left(\frac{1}{4}\right)^4\left(\frac{3}{4}\right)+\binom{5}{2}\left(\frac{1}{4}\right)^3\left(\frac{3}{4}\right)^2+\binom{5}{3}\left(\frac{1}{4}\right)^2\left(\frac{3}{4}\right)^3$

$$+\binom{5}{4}\left(\frac{1}{4}\right)\left(\frac{3}{4}\right)^4+\binom{5}{5}\left(\frac{3}{4}\right)^5=\left(\frac{1}{4}+\frac{3}{4}\right)^5=(1)^5=1$$

Sequences; Induction; The Binomial Theorem

9.R Chapter Review

1. $a_1 = (-1)^1 \dfrac{1+3}{1+2} = -\dfrac{4}{3}$, $a_2 = (-1)^2 \dfrac{2+3}{2+2} = \dfrac{5}{4}$, $a_3 = (-1)^3 \dfrac{3+3}{3+2} = -\dfrac{6}{5}$,

   $a_4 = (-1)^4 \dfrac{4+3}{4+2} = \dfrac{7}{6}$, $a_5 = (-1)^5 \dfrac{5+3}{5+2} = -\dfrac{8}{7}$

3. $a_1 = \dfrac{2^1}{1^2} = \dfrac{2}{1} = 2$, $a_2 = \dfrac{2^2}{2^2} = \dfrac{4}{4} = 1$, $a_3 = \dfrac{2^3}{3^2} = \dfrac{8}{9}$, $a_4 = \dfrac{2^4}{4^2} = \dfrac{16}{16} = 1$, $a_5 = \dfrac{2^5}{5^2} = \dfrac{32}{25}$

5. $a_1 = 3$, $a_2 = \dfrac{2}{3} \cdot 3 = 2$, $a_3 = \dfrac{2}{3} \cdot 2 = \dfrac{4}{3}$, $a_4 = \dfrac{2}{3} \cdot \dfrac{4}{3} = \dfrac{8}{9}$, $a_5 = \dfrac{2}{3} \cdot \dfrac{8}{9} = \dfrac{16}{27}$

7. $a_1 = 2$, $a_2 = 2 - 2 = 0$, $a_3 = 2 - 0 = 2$, $a_4 = 2 - 2 = 0$, $a_5 = 2 - 0 = 2$

9. $\{n+5\}$ Arithmetic

   $d = (n+1+5) - (n+5) = n+6-n-5 = 1$

   $S_n = \dfrac{n}{2}[6 + n + 5] = \dfrac{n}{2}(n+11)$

11. $\{2n^3\}$ Examine the terms of the sequence: 2, 16, 54, 128, 250, ...

    There is no common difference; there is no common ratio; neither.

13. $\{2^{3n}\}$ Geometric $\quad r = \dfrac{2^{3(n+1)}}{2^{3n}} = \dfrac{2^{3n+3}}{2^{3n}} = 2^{3n+3-3n} = 2^3 = 8$

    $S_n = 8\left(\dfrac{1-8^n}{1-8}\right) = 8\left(\dfrac{1-8^n}{-7}\right) = \dfrac{8}{7}\left(8^n - 1\right)$

15. 0, 4, 8, 12, ... Arithmetic $\quad d = 4 - 0 = 4$

    $S_n = \dfrac{n}{2}(2(0) + (n-1)4) = \dfrac{n}{2}(4(n-1)) = 2n(n-1)$

17. $3, \dfrac{3}{2}, \dfrac{3}{4}, \dfrac{3}{5}, \dfrac{3}{16}, \cdots$ Geometric $r = \dfrac{\left(\dfrac{3}{2}\right)}{3} = \dfrac{3}{2} \cdot \dfrac{1}{3} = \dfrac{1}{2}$

$$S_n = 3\left\{\dfrac{1-\left(\dfrac{1}{2}\right)^n}{1-\dfrac{1}{2}}\right\} = 3\left\{\dfrac{1-\left(\dfrac{1}{2}\right)^n}{\left(\dfrac{1}{2}\right)}\right\} = 6\left(1-\left(\dfrac{1}{2}\right)^n\right)$$

19. Neither.   There is no common difference or common ratio.

21. $\displaystyle\sum_{k=1}^{5}(k^2+12) = 13+16+21+28+37 = 115$

23. $\displaystyle\sum_{k=1}^{10}(3k-9) = \sum_{k=1}^{10}3k - \sum_{k=1}^{10}9 = 3\sum_{k=1}^{10}k - \sum_{k=1}^{10}9 = 3\left(\dfrac{10(10+1)}{2}\right) - 10(9) = 165 - 90 = 75$

25. $\displaystyle\sum_{k=1}^{7}\left(\dfrac{1}{3}\right)^k = \dfrac{1}{3}\left\{\dfrac{1-\left(\dfrac{1}{3}\right)^7}{\left(1-\dfrac{1}{3}\right)}\right\} = \dfrac{1}{3}\left\{\dfrac{1-\left(\dfrac{1}{3}\right)^7}{\left(\dfrac{2}{3}\right)}\right\} = \dfrac{1}{2}\left(1-\dfrac{1}{2187}\right) = \dfrac{1}{2}\cdot\dfrac{2186}{2187} = \dfrac{1093}{2187}$

27. Arithmetic $a_1 = 3, \; d = 4, \; a_n = a+(n-1)d$
$a_9 = 3+(9-1)4 = 3+8(4) = 3+32 = 35$

29. Geometric $a=1, \; r=\dfrac{1}{10}, \; n=11$ $a_{11} = 1\cdot\left(\dfrac{1}{10}\right)^{11-1} = \left(\dfrac{1}{10}\right)^{10} = \dfrac{1}{10,000,000,000}$

31. Arithmetic $a_1 = \sqrt{2}, \; d = \sqrt{2}, \; n=9, \; a_n = a+(n-1)d$
$a_9 = \sqrt{2}+(9-1)\sqrt{2} = \sqrt{2}+8\sqrt{2} = 9\sqrt{2}$

33. $a_7 = a+6d = 31$ $a_{20} = a+19d = 96$
Solve the system of equations:
$31-6d+19d = 96$
$13d = 65$
$d = 5$ General formula: $\{5n-4\}$
$a = 31-6(5) = 31-30 = 1$

35. $a_{10} = a+9d = 0$ $a_{18} = a+17d = 8$
Solve the system of equations:
$-9d+17d = 8$
$8d = 8$
$d = 1$ General formula: $\{n-10\}$
$a = -9(1) = -9$

37.

$$a = 3, \ r = \frac{1}{3} \quad \text{Since } |r| < 1, \ S_n = \frac{a}{1-r} = \frac{3}{\left(1 - \frac{1}{3}\right)} = \frac{3}{\left(\frac{2}{3}\right)} = \frac{9}{2}$$

39.

$$a = 2, \ r = -\frac{1}{2} \quad \text{Since } |r| < 1, \ S_n = \frac{a}{1-r} = \frac{2}{\left(1 - \left(-\frac{1}{2}\right)\right)} = \frac{2}{\left(\frac{3}{2}\right)} = \frac{4}{3}$$

41.

$$a = 4, \ r = \frac{1}{2} \quad \text{Since } |r| < 1, \ S_n = \frac{a}{1-r} = \frac{4}{\left(1 - \frac{1}{2}\right)} = \frac{4}{\left(\frac{1}{2}\right)} = 8$$

43. I: $n = 1$: $3 \cdot 1 = 3$ and $\dfrac{3 \cdot 1}{2}(1 + 1) = 3$

II: If $3 + 6 + 9 + \cdots + 3k = \dfrac{3k}{2}(k + 1)$

then $3 + 6 + 9 + \cdots + 3k + 3(k + 1)$

$$= \left[3 + 6 + 9 + \cdots + 3k\right] + 3(k + 1) = \frac{3k}{2}(k + 1) + 3(k + 1)$$

$$= (k + 1)\left(\frac{3k}{2} + 3\right) = \frac{3}{2}(k + 1)(k + 2)$$

Conditions I and II are satisfied; the statement is true.

45. I: $n = 1$: $2 \cdot 3^{1-1} = 2$ and $3^1 - 1 = 2$

II: If $2 + 6 + 18 + \cdots + 2 \cdot 3^{k-1} = 3^k - 1$

then $2 + 6 + 18 + \cdots + 2 \cdot 3^{k-1} + 2 \cdot 3^{k+1-1}$

$$= \left[2 + 6 + 18 + \cdots + 2 \cdot 3^{k-1}\right] + 2 \cdot 3^k = 3^k - 1 + 2 \cdot 3^k$$

$$= 3 \cdot 3^k - 1 = 3^{k+1} - 1$$

Conditions I and II are satisfied; the statement is true.

47. I: $n = 1$: $(3 \cdot 1 - 2)^2 = 1$ and $\dfrac{1}{2} \cdot 1(6 \cdot 1^2 - 3 \cdot 1 - 1) = 1$

II: If $1^2 + 4^2 + 7^2 + \cdots + (3k - 2)^2 = \dfrac{1}{2} \cdot k\left(6k^2 - 3k - 1\right)$

then $1^2 + 4^2 + 7^2 + \cdots + (3k - 2)^2 + \left(3(k + 1) - 2\right)^2$

$$= \left[1^2 + 4^2 + 7^2 + \cdots + (3k - 2)^2\right] + (3k + 1)^2$$

$$= \frac{1}{2} \cdot k\left(6k^2 - 3k - 1\right) + (3k + 1)^2$$

$$= \frac{1}{2} \cdot \left[6k^3 - 3k^2 - k + 18k^2 + 12k + 2\right] = \frac{1}{2} \cdot \left[6k^3 + 15k^2 + 11k + 2\right]$$

$$= \frac{1}{2} \cdot (k+1)\left[6k^2 + 9k + 2\right] = \frac{1}{2} \cdot (k+1)\left[6k^2 + 12k + 6 - 3k - 3 - 1\right]$$

$$= \frac{1}{2} \cdot (k+1)\left[6(k^2 + 2k + 1) - 3(k+1) - 1\right]$$

$$= \frac{1}{2} \cdot (k+1)\left[6(k+1)^2 - 3(k+1) - 1\right]$$

Conditions I and II are satisfied; the statement is true.

49. $(x+2)^5 = \binom{5}{0}x^5 + \binom{5}{1}x^4 \cdot 2 + \binom{5}{2}x^3 \cdot 2^2 + \binom{5}{3}x^2 \cdot 2^3 + \binom{5}{4}x^1 \cdot 2^4 + \binom{5}{5} \cdot 2^5$

$= x^5 + 5 \cdot 2x^4 + 10 \cdot 4x^3 + 10 \cdot 8x^2 + 5 \cdot 16x + 1 \cdot 32$

$= x^5 + 10x^4 + 40x^3 + 80x^2 + 80x + 32$

51. $(2x+3)^5 = \binom{5}{0}(2x)^5 + \binom{5}{1}(2x)^4 \cdot 3 + \binom{5}{2}(2x)^3 \cdot 3^2 + \binom{5}{3}(2x)^2 \cdot 3^3$

$$+ \binom{5}{4}(2x)^1 \cdot 3^4 + \binom{5}{5} \cdot 3^5$$

$= 32x^5 + 5 \cdot 16x^4 \cdot 3 + 10 \cdot 8x^3 \cdot 9 + 10 \cdot 4x^2 \cdot 27 + 5 \cdot 2x \cdot 81 + 1 \cdot 243$

$= 32x^5 + 240x^4 + 720x^3 + 1080x^2 + 810x + 243$

53. $n = 9, \ j = 2, \ x = x, \ a = 2$

$$\binom{9}{2}x^7 \cdot 2^2 = \frac{9!}{2! \, 7!} \cdot 4x^7 = \frac{9 \cdot 8}{2 \cdot 1} \cdot 4x^7 = 144x^7$$

The coefficient of x^7 is 144.

55. $n = 7, \ j = 5, \ x = 2x, \ a = 1$

$$\binom{7}{5}(2x)^2 \cdot 1^5 = \frac{7!}{5! \, 2!} \cdot 4x^2(1) = \frac{7 \cdot 6}{2 \cdot 1} \cdot 4x^2 = 84x^2$$

The coefficient of x^2 is 84.

57. This is an arithmetic sequence with $a = 80, \ d = -3, \ n = 25$

(a) $a_{25} = 80 + (25 - 1)(-3) = 80 - 72 = 8$ bricks

(b) $S_{25} = \frac{25}{2}(80 + 8) = 25(44) = 1100$ bricks

1100 bricks are needed to build the steps.

59. This is an ordinary annuity with $P = \$200$ and $n = (12)(20) = 240$ payment periods.

The interest rate per period is $\frac{.10}{12} = .008\overline{3}$. Thus,

$$A = 200\left[\frac{\left[1 + \frac{.10}{12}\right]^{240} - 1}{\left(\frac{.10}{12}\right)}\right] = \$151873.77$$

61. This is a geometric sequence with $a = 20, \ r = \dfrac{3}{4}$.

   (a) After striking the ground the third time, the height is $20\left(\dfrac{3}{4}\right)^3 = \dfrac{135}{16} \approx 8.44$ feet.

   (b) After striking the ground the nth time, the height is $20\left(\dfrac{3}{4}\right)^n$ feet.

   (c) If the height is less than 6 inches or 0.5 feet, then:

   $$0.5 = 20\left(\dfrac{3}{4}\right)^n \rightarrow 0.025 = \left(\dfrac{3}{4}\right)^n \rightarrow \log 0.025 = n\log\left(\dfrac{3}{4}\right) \rightarrow n = \dfrac{\log 0.025}{\log\left(\dfrac{3}{4}\right)} = 12.82$$

   The height is less than 6 inches after the 13th strike.

   (d) Since this is a geometric sequence with $|r| < 1$, the distance is the sum of the two infinite geometric series - the distances going down plus the distances going up.

   Distance going down: $S_{down} = \dfrac{20}{\left(1 - \dfrac{3}{4}\right)} = \dfrac{20}{\left(\dfrac{1}{4}\right)} = 80$ feet.

   Distance going up: $S_{up} = \dfrac{15}{\left(1 - \dfrac{3}{4}\right)} = \dfrac{15}{\left(\dfrac{1}{4}\right)} = 60$ feet.

   The total distance traveled is 140 feet.

Chapter 10

Counting and Probability

10.1 Sets and Counting

1. $A \cup B = \{1, 3, 5, 7, 9\} \cup \{1, 5, 6, 7\} = \{1, 3, 5, 6, 7, 9\}$

3. $A \cap B = \{1, 3, 5, 7, 9\} \cap \{1, 5, 6, 7\} = \{1, 5, 7\}$

5. $(A \cup B) \cap C = (\{1, 3, 5, 7, 9\} \cup \{1, 5, 6, 7\}) \cap \{1, 2, 4, 6, 8, 9\}$
   $= \{1, 3, 5, 6, 7, 9\} \cap \{1, 2, 4, 6, 8, 9\}$
   $= \{1, 6, 9\}$

7. $(A \cap B) \cup C = (\{1, 3, 5, 7, 9\} \cap \{1, 5, 6, 7\}) \cup \{1, 2, 4, 6, 8, 9\}$
   $= \{1, 5, 7\} \cup \{1, 2, 4, 6, 8, 9\}$
   $= \{1, 2, 4, 5, 6, 7, 8, 9\}$

9. $(A \cup C) \cap (B \cup C)$
   $= (\{1, 3, 5, 7, 9\} \cup \{1, 2, 4, 6, 8, 9\}) \cap (\{1, 5, 6, 7\} \cup \{1, 2, 4, 6, 8, 9\})$
   $= \{1, 2, 3, 4, 5, 6, 7, 8, 9\} \cap \{1, 2, 4, 5, 6, 7, 8, 9\}$
   $= \{1, 2, 4, 5, 6, 7, 8, 9\}$

11. $\overline{A} = \{0, 2, 6, 7, 8\}$

13. $\overline{A \cap B} = \overline{\{1, 3, 4, 5, 9\} \cap \{2, 4, 6, 7, 8\}} = \overline{\{4\}} = \{0, 1, 2, 3, 5, 6, 7, 8, 9\}$

15. $\overline{A} \cup \overline{B} = \{0, 2, 6, 7, 8\} \cup \{0, 1, 3, 5, 9\} = \{0, 1, 2, 3, 5, 6, 7, 8, 9\}$

17. $\overline{A \cap \overline{C}} = \overline{\{1, 3, 4, 5, 9\} \cap \{0, 2, 5, 7, 8, 9\}} = \overline{\{5, 9\}} = \{0, 1, 2, 3, 4, 6, 7, 8\}$

19. $\overline{A \cup B \cup C} = \overline{\{1, 3, 4, 5, 9\} \cup \{2, 4, 6, 7, 8\} \cup \{1, 3, 4, 6\}}$
    $= \overline{\{1, 2, 3, 4, 5, 6, 7, 8, 9\}} = \{0\}$

21. $\{a\}, \{b\}, \{c\}, \{d\}, \{a, b\}, \{a, c\}, \{a, d\}, \{b, c\}, \{b, d\}, \{c, d\}, \{a, b, c\}, \{a, b, d\},$
    $\{a, c, d\}, \{b, c, d\}, \{a, b, c, d\}, \varnothing$

23. $n(A) = 15, n(B) = 20, n(A \cap B) = 10$
$n(A \cup B) = n(A) + n(B) - n(A \cap B) = 15 + 20 - 10 = 25$

25. $n(A \cup B) = 50, n(A \cap B) = 10, n(B) = 20$
$n(A \cup B) = n(A) + n(B) - n(A \cap B)$
$50 = n(A) + 20 - 10 \rightarrow 40 = n(A)$

27. From the figure:
$n(A) = 15 + 3 + 5 + 2 = 25$

29. From the figure:
$n(A \text{ or } B) = n(A \cup B) = n(A) + n(B) - n(A \cap B) = 25 + 20 - 8 = 37$

31. From the figure:
$n(A \text{ but not } C) = n(A) - n(A \cap C) = 25 - 7 = 18$

33. From the figure:
$n(A \text{ and } B \text{ and } C) = n(A \cap B \cap C) = 5$

35. Let $A = \{$those who will purchase a major appliance$\}$
$B = \{$those who will buy a car$\}$
$n(U) = 500, \ n(A) = 200, \ n(B) = 150, \ n(A \cap B) = 25$
$n(A \cup B) = n(A) + n(B) - n(A \cap B) = 200 + 150 - 25 = 325$
$n(\text{purchase neither}) = 500 - 325 = 175$
$n(\text{purchase only a car}) = 150 - 25 = 125$

37. Construct a Venn diagram:

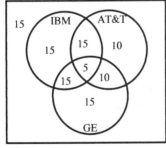

(a)   15
(b)   15
(c)   15
(d)   25
(e)   40

39. (a) $n(\text{married}) = n(\text{married, spouse present}) + n(\text{married, spouse absent})$
$= 54,654 + 3,232 = 57,886 \text{ thousand}$
     (b) $n(\text{widowed or divorced}) = n(\text{widowed}) + n(\text{divorced})$
$= 2,686 + 8,208 = 10,894 \text{ thousand}$
     (c) $n(\text{married, spouse absent or widowed or divorced})$
$= n(\text{married, spouse absent}) + n(\text{widowed}) + n(\text{divorced})$
$= 3,232 + 2,686 + 8,208 = 14,126 \text{ thousand}$

41. Answers will vary.

Chapter 10

Counting and Probability

10.2 Permutations and Combinations

1. $P(6, 2) = \dfrac{6!}{(6-2)!} = \dfrac{6!}{4!} = \dfrac{6 \cdot 5 \cdot 4!}{4!} = 30$

3. $P(4, 4) = \dfrac{4!}{(4-4)!} = \dfrac{4!}{0!} = \dfrac{4 \cdot 3 \cdot 2 \cdot 1}{1} = 24$

5. $P(7, 0) = \dfrac{7!}{(7-0)!} = \dfrac{7!}{7!} = 1$

7. $P(8, 4) = \dfrac{8!}{(8-4)!} = \dfrac{8!}{4!} = \dfrac{8 \cdot 7 \cdot 6 \cdot 5 \cdot 4!}{4!} = 1680$

9. $C(8, 2) = \dfrac{8!}{(8-2)!\, 2!} = \dfrac{8!}{6!\, 2!} = \dfrac{8 \cdot 7 \cdot 6!}{6! \cdot 2 \cdot 1} = 28$

11. $C(7, 4) = \dfrac{7!}{(7-4)!\, 4!} = \dfrac{7!}{3!\, 4!} = \dfrac{7 \cdot 6 \cdot 5 \cdot 4!}{4! \cdot 3 \cdot 2 \cdot 1} = 35$

13. $C(15, 15) = \dfrac{15!}{(15-15)!\, 15!} = \dfrac{15!}{0!\, 15!} = \dfrac{15!}{15! \cdot 1} = 1$

15. $C(26, 13) = \dfrac{26!}{(26-13)!\, 13!} = \dfrac{26!}{13!\, 13!} = 10,400,600$

17. {*abc, abd, abe, acb, acd, ace, adb, adc, ade, aeb, aec, aed, bac, bad, bae, bca, bcd, bce, bda, bdc, bde, bea, bec, bed, cab, cad, cae, cba, cbd, cbe, cda, cdb, cde, cea, ceb, ced, dab, dac, dae, dba, dbc, dbe, dca, dcb, dce, dea, deb, dec, eab, eac, ead, eba, ebc, ebd, eca, ecb, ecd, eda, edb, edc*}

$$P(5,3) = \dfrac{5!}{(5-3)!} = \dfrac{5!}{2!} = \dfrac{5 \cdot 4 \cdot 3 \cdot 2!}{2!} = 60$$

19. {123, 124, 132, 134, 142, 143, 213, 214, 231, 234, 241, 243, 312, 314, 321, 324, 341, 342, 412, 413, 421, 423, 431, 432}

$$P(4,3) = \dfrac{4!}{(4-3)!} = \dfrac{4!}{1!} = \dfrac{4 \cdot 3 \cdot 2 \cdot 1}{1} = 24$$

21. {abc, abd, abe, acd, ace, ade, bcd, bce, bde, cde}

$$C(5,3) = \frac{5!}{(5-3)!3!} = \frac{5 \cdot 4 \cdot 3!}{2 \cdot 1 \cdot 3!} = 10$$

23. {123, 124, 134, 234} $C(4,3) = \frac{4!}{(4-3)!3!} = \frac{4 \cdot 3!}{1!3!} = 4$

25. There are 5 choices of shirts and 3 choices of ties; there are (5)(3) = 15 combinations.

27. There are 4 choices for the first letter in the code and 4 choices for the second letter in the code; there are (4)(4) = 16 possible two-letter codes.

29. There are two choices for each of three positions; there are (2)(2)(2) = 8 possible three-digit numbers.

31. To line up the four people, there are 4 choices for the first position, 3 choices for the second position, 2 choices for the third position, and 1 choice for the fourth position. Thus there are (4)(3)(2)(1) = 24 possible ways four people can be lined up.

33. Since no letter can be repeated, there are 5 choices for the first letter, 4 choices for the second letter, and 3 choices for the third letter. Thus, there are (5)(4)(3) = 60 possible three-letter codes.

35. There are 26 possible one-letter names. There are (26)(26) = 676 possible two-letter names. There are (26)(26)(26) = 17576 possible three-letter names. Thus, there are 26 + 676 + 17576 = 18,278 possible companies that can be listed on the New York Stock Exchange.

37. A committee of 4 from a total of 7 students is given by:

$$C(7,4) = \frac{7!}{(7-4)!4!} = \frac{7!}{3!4!} = \frac{7 \cdot 6 \cdot 5 \cdot 4!}{3 \cdot 2 \cdot 1 \cdot 4!} = 35$$

35 committees are possible.

39. There are 2 possible answers for each question. Therefore, there are 2^{10} = 1024 different possible arrangements of the answers.

41. There are 9 choices for the first digit, and 10 choices for each of the other three digits. Thus, there are (9)(10)(10)(10) = 9000 possible four-digit numbers.

43. There are 5 choices for the first position, 4 choices for the second position, 3 choices for the third position, 2 choices for the fourth position, and 1 choice for the fifth position. Thus, there are (5)(4)(3)(2)(1) = 120 possible arrangements of the books.

45. There are 8 choices for the DOW stocks, 15 choices for the NASDAQ stocks, and 4 choices for the global stocks. Thus, there are (8)(15)(4) = 480 different portfolios.

47. The first person can have any of 365 days, the second person can have any of the remaining 364 days. Thus, there are $(365)(364) = 132,860$ possible ways two people can have different birthdays.

49. Choosing 2 boys from the 4 boys can be done $C(4,2)$ ways, and choosing 3 girls from the 8 girls can be done in $C(8,3)$ ways. Thus, there are a total of:
$$C(4,2) \cdot C(8,3) = \frac{4!}{(4-2)!\,2!} \cdot \frac{8!}{(8-3)!\,3!} = \frac{4!}{2!\,2!} \cdot \frac{8!}{5!\,3!}$$
$$= \frac{4 \cdot 3!}{2 \cdot 1 \cdot 2 \cdot 1} \cdot \frac{8 \cdot 7 \cdot 6 \cdot 5!}{5!\,3!} = 336$$

51. This is a permutation with repetition. There are $\dfrac{9!}{2!\,2!} = 90,720$ different words.

53. (a) $C(7,2) \cdot C(3,1) = 21 \cdot 3 = 63$
     (b) $C(7,3) = 35$
     (c) $C(3,3) = 1$

Chapter 10

Counting and Probability

10.3 Probability

1. Probabilities must be between 0 and 1, inclusive. Thus, 0, 0.01, 0.35, and 1 are probabilities.

3. All the probabilities are between 0 and 1.
   The sum of the probabilities is $0.2 + 0.3 + 0.1 + 0.4 = 1$.
   This is a probability model.

5. All the probabilities are between 0 and 1.
   The sum of the probabilities is $0.3 + 0.2 + 0.1 + 0.3 = 0.9$.
   This is not a probability model.

7. The sample space is: $S = \{HH, HT, TH, TT\}$.
   Each outcome is equally likely to occur; so $P(E) = \dfrac{n(E)}{n(S)}$.
   The probabilities are: $P(HH) = \dfrac{1}{4}$, $P(HT) = \dfrac{1}{4}$, $P(TH) = \dfrac{1}{4}$, $P(TT) = \dfrac{1}{4}$.

9. The sample space of tossing two fair coins and a fair die is:
   $$S = \{HH1, HH2, HH3, HH4, HH5, HH6, HT1, HT2, HT3, HT4, HT5,$$
   $$HT6, TH1, TH2, TH3, TH4, TH5, TH6, TT1, TT2, TT3, TT4, TT5, TT6\}$$
   There are 24 equally likely outcomes and the probability of each is $\dfrac{1}{24}$.

11. The sample space for tossing three fair coins is:
    $$S = \{HHH, HHT, HTH, THH, HTT, THT, TTH, TTT\}$$
    There are 8 equally likely outcomes and the probability of each is $\dfrac{1}{8}$.

13. The sample space is:
    $$S = \{1\text{ Yellow, }1\text{ Red, }1\text{ Green, }2\text{ Yellow, }2\text{ Red, }2\text{ Green, }3\text{ Yellow, }3\text{ Red,}$$
    $$3\text{ Green, }4\text{ Yellow, }4\text{ Red, }4\text{ Green}\}$$
    There are 12 equally likely events and the probability of each is $\dfrac{1}{12}$. The probability of getting a 2 or 4 followed by a Red is $P(2\text{ Red}) + P(4\text{ Red}) = \dfrac{1}{12} + \dfrac{1}{12} = \dfrac{1}{6}$.

15. The sample space is:

    S = {1 Yellow Forward, 1 Yellow Backward, 1 Red Forward, 1 Red Backward, 1 Green Forward, 1 Green Backward, 2 Yellow Forward, 2 Yellow Backward, 2 Red Forward, 2 Red Backward, 2 Green Forward, 2 Green Backward, 3 Yellow Forward, 3 Yellow Backward, 3 Red Forward, 3 Red Backward, 3 Green Forward, 3 Green Backward, 4 Yellow Forward, 4 Yellow Backward, 4 Red Forward, 4 Red Backward, 4 Green Forward, 4 Green Backward}

    There are 24 equally likely events and the probability of each is $\frac{1}{24}$. The probability of getting a 1, followed by a Red or Green, followed by a Backward is

    $$P(1\text{ Red Backward}) + P(1\text{ Green Backward}) = \frac{1}{24} + \frac{1}{24} = \frac{1}{12}.$$

17. The sample space is:

    S = {1 1 Yellow, 1 1 Red, 1 1 Green, 1 2 Yellow, 1 2 Red, 1 2 Green, 1 3 Yellow, 1 3 Red, 1 3 Green, 1 4 Yellow, 1 4 Red, 1 4 Green, 2 1 Yellow, 2 1 Red, 2 1 Green, 2 2 Yellow, 2 2 Red, 2 2 Green, 2 3 Yellow, 2 3 Red, 2 3 Green, 2 4 Yellow, 2 4 Red, 2 4 Green, 3 1 Yellow, 3 1 Red, 3 1 Green, 3 2 Yellow, 3 2 Red, 3 2 Green, 3 3 Yellow, 3 3 Red, 3 3 Green, 3 4 Yellow, 3 4 Red, 3 4 Green, 4 1 Yellow, 4 1 Red, 4 1 Green, 4 2 Yellow, 4 2 Red, 4 2 Green,   4 3 Yellow, 4 3 Red, 4 3 Green, 4 4 Yellow, 4 4 Red, 4 4 Green}

    There are 48 equally likely events and the probability of each is $\frac{1}{48}$. The probability of getting a 2, followed by a 2 or 4, followed by a Red or Green is

    $$P(2\ 2\text{ Red}) + P(2\ 4\text{ Red}) + P(2\ 2\text{ Green}) + P(2\ 4\text{ Green}) = \frac{1}{48} + \frac{1}{48} + \frac{1}{48} + \frac{1}{48} = \frac{1}{12}$$

19. A, B, C, F   21. B

23. Let $P(\text{tails}) = x$, then $P(\text{heads}) = 4x$

    $$x + 4x = 1 \rightarrow 5x = 1 \rightarrow x = \frac{1}{5} \qquad P(\text{tails}) = \frac{1}{5}, \quad P(\text{heads}) = \frac{4}{5}$$

25. $P(2) = P(4) = P(6) = x \qquad P(1) = P(3) = P(5) = 2x$

    $P(1) + P(2) + P(3) + P(4) + P(5) + P(6) = 1$

    $$2x + x + 2x + x + 2x + x = 1 \rightarrow 9x = 1 \rightarrow x = \frac{1}{9}$$

    $$P(2) = P(4) = P(6) = \frac{1}{9} \qquad P(1) = P(3) = P(5) = \frac{2}{9}$$

27. $P(E) = \dfrac{n(E)}{n(S)} = \dfrac{n\{1,2,3\}}{10} = \dfrac{3}{10}$

29. $P(E) = \dfrac{n(E)}{n(S)} = \dfrac{n\{2,4,6,8,10\}}{10} = \dfrac{5}{10} = \dfrac{1}{2}$

31. $P(\text{white}) = \dfrac{n(\text{white})}{n(S)} = \dfrac{5}{5 + 10 + 8 + 7} = \dfrac{5}{30} = \dfrac{1}{6}$

33.   The sample space is: S = {BBB, BBG, BGB, GBB, BGG, GBG, GGB, GGG}

$P(3 \text{ boys}) = \dfrac{n(3 \text{ boys})}{n(S)} = \dfrac{1}{8}$

35.   The sample space is:

S = {BBBB, BBBG, BBGB, BGBB, GBBB, BBGG, BGBG, GBBG, BGGB, GBGB, GGBB, BGGG, GBGG, GGBG, GGGB, GGGG}

$P(1 \text{ girl, } 3 \text{ boys}) = \dfrac{n(1 \text{ girl, } 3 \text{ boys})}{n(S)} = \dfrac{4}{16} = \dfrac{1}{4}$

37. $P(\text{sum of two die is } 7) = \dfrac{n(\text{sum of two die is } 7)}{n(S)}$

$= \dfrac{n\{1,6 \text{ or } 2,5 \text{ or } 3,4 \text{ or } 4,3 \text{ or } 5,2 \text{ or } 6,1\}}{n(S)} = \dfrac{6}{36} = \dfrac{1}{6}$

39. $P(\text{sum of two die is } 3) = \dfrac{n(\text{sum of two die is } 3)}{n(S)} = \dfrac{n\{1,2 \text{ or } 2,1\}}{n(S)} = \dfrac{2}{36} = \dfrac{1}{18}$

41. $P(A \cup B) = P(A) + P(B) - P(A \cap B) = 0.25 + 0.45 - 0.15 = 0.55$

43. $P(A \cup B) = P(A) + P(B) = 0.25 + 0.45 = 0.70$

45. $P(A \cup B) = P(A) + P(B) - P(A \cap B)$
       $0.85 = 0.60 + P(B) - 0.05$
       $P(B) = 0.85 - 0.60 + 0.05 = 0.30$

47. $P(\text{not victim}) = 1 - P(\text{victim}) = 1 - 0.253 = 0.747$

49. $P(\text{not in } 70\text{'s}) = 1 - P(\text{in } 70\text{'s}) = 1 - 0.3 = 0.7$

51. $P(\text{white or green}) = P(\text{white}) + P(\text{green}) = \dfrac{n(\text{white}) + n(\text{green})}{n(S)} = \dfrac{9+8}{9+8+3} = \dfrac{17}{20}$

53. $P(\text{not white}) = 1 - P(\text{white}) = 1 - \dfrac{n(\text{white})}{n(S)} = 1 - \dfrac{9}{20} = \dfrac{11}{20}$

55. $P(\text{strike or one}) = P(\text{strike}) + P(\text{one}) = \dfrac{n(\text{strike}) + n(\text{one})}{n(S)} = \dfrac{3+1}{8} = \dfrac{4}{8} = \dfrac{1}{2}$

57.   There are 30 households out of 100 with an income of $30,000 or more.

$P(E) = \dfrac{n(E)}{n(S)} = \dfrac{n(30,000 \text{ or more})}{n(\text{total households})} = \dfrac{30}{100} = \dfrac{3}{10}$

59.   There are 40 households out of 100 with an income of less than $20,000.

$P(E) = \dfrac{n(E)}{n(S)} = \dfrac{n(\text{less than } \$20,000)}{n(\text{total households})} = \dfrac{40}{100} = \dfrac{2}{5}$

61.   (a) $P(1 \text{ or } 2) = P(1) + P(2) = 0.24 + 0.33 = 0.57$
      (b) $P(1 \text{ or more}) = P(1) + P(2) + P(3) + P(4 \text{ or more})$
$$= 0.24 + 0.33 + 0.21 + 0.17 = 0.95$$
      (c) $P(3 \text{ or fewer}) = P(0) + P(1) + P(2) + P(3) = 0.05 + 0.24 + 0.33 + 0.21 = 0.83$
      (d) $P(3 \text{ or more}) = P(3) + P(4 \text{ or more}) = 0.21 + 0.17 = 0.38$
      (e) $P(\text{less than } 2) = P(0) + P(1) = 0.05 + 0.24 = 0.29$
      (f) $P(\text{less than } 1) = P(0) = 0.05$
      (g) $P(1, 2, \text{ or } 3) = P(1) + P(2) + P(3) = 0.24 + 0.33 + 0.21 = 0.78$
      (h) $P(2 \text{ or more}) = P(2) + P(3) + P(4 \text{ or more}) = 0.33 + 0.21 + 0.17 = 0.71$

63.   (a) $P(\text{freshman or female}) = P(\text{freshman}) + P(\text{female}) - P(\text{freshman and female})$
$$= \frac{n(\text{freshman}) + n(\text{female}) - n(\text{freshman and female})}{n(S)}$$
$$= \frac{18 + 15 - 8}{33} = \frac{25}{33}$$
      (b) $P(\text{sophomore or male}) = P(\text{sophomore}) + P(\text{male}) - P(\text{sophomore and male})$
$$= \frac{n(\text{sophomore}) + n(\text{male}) - n(\text{sophomore and male})}{n(S)}$$
$$= \frac{15 + 18 - 8}{33} = \frac{25}{33}$$

65. $P(\text{at least 2 with same birthday}) = 1 - P(\text{none with same birthday})$
$$= 1 - \frac{n(\text{different birthdays})}{n(S)}$$
$$= 1 - \frac{365 \cdot 364 \cdot 363 \cdot 362 \cdot 361 \cdot 360 \cdot \ldots \cdot 354}{365^{12}}$$
$$= 1 - 0.833$$
$$= 0.167$$

67.   The sample space for picking 5 out of 10 numbers in a particular order contains
$$P(10,5) = \frac{10!}{(10-5)!} = \frac{10!}{5!} = 30,240 \text{ possible outcomes.}$$

One of these is the desired outcome. Thus, the probability of winning is:
$$P(E) = \frac{n(E)}{n(S)} = \frac{n(\text{winning})}{n(\text{total possible outcomes})} = \frac{1}{30240}$$

69.   (a) $P(3 \text{ heads}) = \dfrac{C(5,3)}{2^5} = \dfrac{10}{32} = \dfrac{5}{16}$ (b) $P(0 \text{ heads}) = \dfrac{C(5,0)}{2^5} = \dfrac{1}{32}$

71.   (a) $P(\text{sum} = 7 \text{ three times}) = P(\text{sum} = 7) \cdot P(\text{sum} = 7) \cdot P(\text{sum} = 7)$
$$= \frac{1}{6} \cdot \frac{1}{6} \cdot \frac{1}{6} = \frac{1}{216}$$

      (b) $P(\text{sum} = 7 \text{ or } 11 \text{ at least twice})$
$$= P(\text{sum} = 7 \text{ or } 11) \cdot P(\text{sum} = 7 \text{ or } 11) \cdot P(\text{sum} \neq 7 \text{ or } 11) +$$
$$P(\text{sum} = 7 \text{ or } 11) \cdot P(\text{sum} = 7 \text{ or } 11) \cdot P(\text{sum} = 7 \text{ or } 11)$$
$$= \frac{8}{36} \cdot \frac{8}{36} \cdot \frac{28}{36} + \frac{8}{36} \cdot \frac{8}{36} \cdot \frac{8}{36} = 0.049$$

73. $P(\text{all 5 defective}) = \dfrac{n(5 \text{ defective})}{n(S)} = \dfrac{1}{C(30,5)} = 7.02 \times 10^{-6}$

$P(\text{at least 2 defective}) = 1 - (P(\text{none defective}) + P(\text{one defective}))$

$$= 1 - \left(\frac{C(5,0) \cdot C(25,5)}{C(30,5)} + \frac{C(5,1) \cdot C(25,4)}{C(30,5)} \right) = 1 - 0.817 = 0.183$$

75. $P(\text{one of 5 coins is valued at more than \$10,000}) = \dfrac{C(49,4) \cdot C(1,1)}{C(50,5)} = 0.1$

Chapter 10

Counting and Probability

10.R Chapter Review

1. $A \cup B = \{1, 3, 5, 7\} \cup \{3, 5, 6, 7, 8\} = \{1, 3, 5, 6, 7, 8\}$

3. $A \cap C = \{1, 3, 5, 7\} \cap \{2, 3, 7, 8, 9\} = \{3, 7\}$

5. $\overline{A} \cup \overline{B} = \overline{\{1, 3, 5, 7\}} \cup \overline{\{3, 5, 6, 7, 8\}} = \{2, 4, 6, 8, 9\} \cup \{1, 2, 4, 9\} = \{1, 2, 4, 6, 8, 9\}$

7. $\overline{B \cap C} = \overline{\{3, 5, 6, 7, 8\} \cap \{2, 3, 7, 8, 9\}} = \overline{\{3, 7, 8\}} = \{1, 2, 4, 5, 6, 9\}$

9. $n(A) = 8, \ n(B) = 12, \ n(A \cap B) = 3$
    $n(A \cup B) = n(A) + n(B) - n(A \cap B) = 8 + 12 - 3 = 17$

11. From the figure:
    $n(A) = 20 + 2 + 6 + 1 = 29$

13. From the figure:
    $n(A \text{ and } C) = n(A \cap C) = 1 + 6 = 7$

15. From the figure:
    $n(\text{neither in } A \text{ nor in } C) = n(\overline{A \cup C}) = 20 + 5 = 25$

17. $5! = 5 \cdot 4 \cdot 3 \cdot 2 \cdot 1 = 120$

19. $P(8,3) = \dfrac{8!}{(8-3)!} = \dfrac{8!}{5!} = \dfrac{8 \cdot 7 \cdot 6 \cdot 5!}{5!} = 336$

21. $C(8,3) = \dfrac{8!}{(8-3)!\,3!} = \dfrac{8!}{5!\,3!} = \dfrac{8 \cdot 7 \cdot 6 \cdot 5!}{5! \cdot 3 \cdot 2 \cdot 1} = 56$

23. There are 2 choices of material, 3 choices of color, and 10 choices of size. The complete assortment would have: $2 \cdot 3 \cdot 10 = 60$ suits.

25. There are two possible outcomes for each game or
    $2 \cdot 2 \cdot 2 \cdot 2 \cdot 2 \cdot 2 \cdot 2 = 2^7 = 128$ outcomes for 7 games.

27. Since order is significant, this is a permutation.
    $P(9,4) = \dfrac{9!}{(9-4)!} = \dfrac{9!}{5!} = \dfrac{9 \cdot 8 \cdot 7 \cdot 6 \cdot 5!}{5!} = 3024$ ways to seat 4 people in 9 seats.

29. Choose 4 runners - order is not significant:
$$C(8,4) = \frac{8!}{(8-4)!4!} = \frac{8!}{4!4!} = \frac{8 \cdot 7 \cdot 6 \cdot 5 \cdot 4!}{4 \cdot 3 \cdot 2 \cdot 1 \cdot 4!} = 70 \text{ ways a squad can be chosen.}$$

31. Choose 14 teams 2 at a time:
$$C(14,2) = \frac{14!}{(14-2)!2!} = \frac{14!}{12!2!} = \frac{14 \cdot 13 \cdot 12!}{12! \cdot 2 \cdot 1} = 91 \text{ ways to pair 14 teams.}$$

33. There are $8 \cdot 10 \cdot 10 \cdot 10 \cdot 10 \cdot 2 = 1,600,000$ possible phone numbers.

35. There are $24 \cdot 9 \cdot 10 \cdot 10 \cdot 10 = 216,000$ possible license plates.

37. Since there are repeated letters:
$$\frac{7!}{2! \cdot 2!} = \frac{7 \cdot 6 \cdot 5 \cdot 4 \cdot 3 \cdot 2 \cdot 1}{2 \cdot 1 \cdot 2 \cdot 1} = 1260 \text{ different words can be formed.}$$

39. (a) $C(9,4) \cdot C(9,3) \cdot C(9,2) = 126 \cdot 84 \cdot 36 = 381,024$ committees can be formed.
    (b) $C(9,4) \cdot C(5,3) \cdot C(2,2) = 126 \cdot 10 \cdot 1 = 1260$ committees can be formed.

41. (a) $365 \cdot 364 \cdot 363 \cdot 362 \cdot \ldots \cdot 348 = 8.634628387 \times 10^{45}$
    (b) $P(\text{no one has same birthday}) = \dfrac{365 \cdot 364 \cdot 363 \cdot 362 \cdot \ldots \cdot 348}{365^{18}} = 0.6531 = 65.31\%$
    (c) $P(\text{at least 2 have same birthday}) = 1 - P(\text{no one has same birthday})$
         $$= 1 - 0.6531 = 0.3469 = 34.69\%$$

43. (a) $P(\text{unemployed}) = 0.054 = 5.4\%$
    (b) $P(\text{not unemployed}) = 1 - P(\text{unemployed}) = 1 - 0.054 = 0.946 = 94.6\%$

45. $P(\$1 \text{ bill}) = \dfrac{n(\$1 \text{ bill})}{n(S)} = \dfrac{4}{9}$

47. Let S be all possible selections, let D be a card that is divisible by 5, and let PN be a 1 or a prime number.

    $n(S) = 100$

    $n(D) = 20$ (There are 20 numbers divisible by 5 between 1 and 100.)

    $n(PN) = 26$ (There are 25 prime numbers less than or equal to 100.)

    $$P(D) = \frac{n(D)}{n(S)} = \frac{20}{100} = \frac{1}{5} = 0.2$$

    $$P(PN) = \frac{n(PN)}{n(S)} = \frac{26}{100} = \frac{13}{50} = 0.26$$

49. (a) $P(5 \text{ heads}) = \dfrac{n(5 \text{ heads})}{n(S)} = \dfrac{C(10,5)}{2^{10}} = \dfrac{\frac{10!}{5!5!}}{1024} = \dfrac{252}{1024} = 0.2461$
    (b) $P(\text{all heads}) = \dfrac{n(\text{all heads})}{n(S)} = \dfrac{1}{2^{10}} = \dfrac{1}{1024} = 0.00098$

Appendix

Graphing Utilities

A.1 The Viewing Rectangle

1. $(-1, 4)$

3. $(3, 1)$

5.
$X \min = -6$
$X \max = 6$
$X \operatorname{scl} = 2$
$Y \min = -4$
$Y \max = 4$
$Y \operatorname{scl} = 2$

7.
$X \min = -6$
$X \max = 6$
$X \operatorname{scl} = 2$
$Y \min = -1$
$Y \max = 3$
$Y \operatorname{scl} = 1$

9.
$X \min = 3$
$X \max = 9$
$X \operatorname{scl} = 1$
$Y \min = 2$
$Y \max = 10$
$Y \operatorname{scl} = 2$

11.
$X \min = -11$
$X \max = 5$
$X \operatorname{scl} = 1$
$Y \min = -3$
$Y \max = 6$
$Y \operatorname{scl} = 1$

13.
$X \min = -30$
$X \max = 50$
$X \operatorname{scl} = 10$
$Y \min = -90$
$Y \max = 50$
$Y \operatorname{scl} = 10$

15.
$X \min = -10$
$X \max = 110$
$X \operatorname{scl} = 10$
$Y \min = -10$
$Y \max = 160$
$Y \operatorname{scl} = 10$

17. $P_1 = (1,3); P_2 = (5,15)$

$$d(P_1, P_2) = \sqrt{(5-1)^2 + (15-3)^2}$$
$$= \sqrt{(4)^2 + (12)^2}$$
$$= \sqrt{16 + 144}$$
$$= \sqrt{160} = 2\sqrt{10}$$

19. $P_1 = (-4,6); P_2 = (4,-8)$

$$d(P_1, P_2) = \sqrt{(4-(-4))^2 + (-8-6)^2}$$
$$= \sqrt{(8)^2 + (-14)^2}$$
$$= \sqrt{64 + 196}$$
$$= \sqrt{260} = 2\sqrt{65}$$

Graphing Utilities

A.2   Using a Graphing Utility to Graph Equations

1. (a) $y = x + 2$

$X \min = -5$
$X \max = 5$
$X \text{ scl} = 1$
$Y \min = -4$
$Y \max = 4$
$Y \text{ scl} = 1$

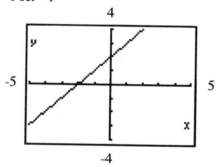

(b)

$X \min = -10$
$X \max = 10$
$X \text{ scl} = 1$
$Y \min = -8$
$Y \max = 8$
$Y \text{ scl} = 1$

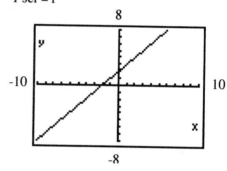

(c)

$X \min = -10$
$X \max = 10$
$X \text{ scl} = 2$
$Y \min = -8$
$Y \max = 8$
$Y \text{ scl} = 2$

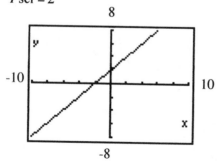

(d)

$X \min = -5$
$X \max = 5$
$X \text{ scl} = 1$
$Y \min = -20$
$Y \max = 20$
$Y \text{ scl} = 5$

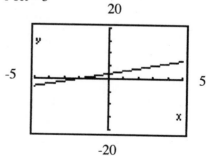

3. (a) $y = -x + 2$

X min $= -5$

X max $= 5$

X scl $= 1$

Y min $= -4$

Y max $= 4$

Y scl $= 1$

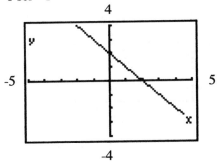

(b)

X min $= -10$

X max $= 10$

X scl $= 1$

Y min $= -8$

Y max $= 8$

Y scl $= 1$

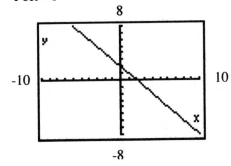

(c)

X min $= -10$

X max $= 10$

X scl $= 2$

Y min $= -8$

Y max $= 8$

Y scl $= 2$

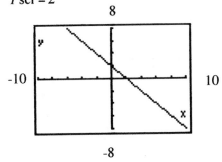

(d)

X min $= -5$

X max $= 5$

X scl $= 1$

Y min $= -20$

Y max $= 20$

Y scl $= 5$

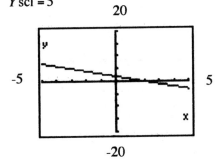

5. (a) $y = 2x + 2$

$X \min = -5$

$X \max = 5$

$X \text{scl} = 1$

$Y \min = -4$

$Y \max = 4$

$Y \text{scl} = 1$

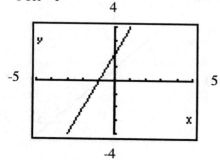

(b)

$X \min = -10$

$X \max = 10$

$X \text{scl} = 1$

$Y \min = -8$

$Y \max = 8$

$Y \text{scl} = 1$

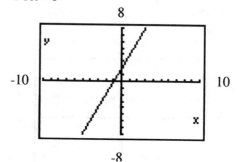

(c)

$X \min = -10$

$X \max = 10$

$X \text{scl} = 2$

$Y \min = -8$

$Y \max = 8$

$Y \text{scl} = 2$

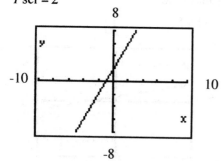

(d)

$X \min = -5$

$X \max = 5$

$X \text{scl} = 1$

$Y \min = -20$

$Y \max = 20$

$Y \text{scl} = 5$

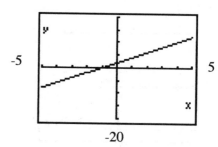

7. (a) $y = -2x + 2$

$X \min = -5$

$X \max = 5$

$X \operatorname{scl} = 1$

$Y \min = -4$

$Y \max = 4$

$Y \operatorname{scl} = 1$

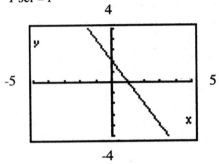

(b)

$X \min = -10$

$X \max = 10$

$X \operatorname{scl} = 1$

$Y \min = -8$

$Y \max = 8$

$Y \operatorname{scl} = 1$

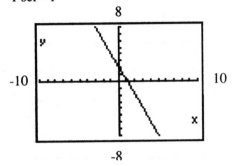

(c)

$X \min = -10$

$X \max = 10$

$X \operatorname{scl} = 2$

$Y \min = -8$

$Y \max = 8$

$Y \operatorname{scl} = 2$

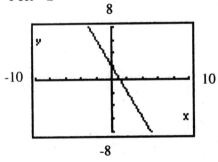

(d)

$X \min = -5$

$X \max = 5$

$X \operatorname{scl} = 1$

$Y \min = -20$

$Y \max = 20$

$Y \operatorname{scl} = 5$

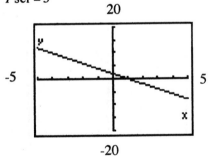

9. (a) $y = x^2 + 2$

$X \min = -5$
$X \max = 5$
$X \text{ scl} = 1$
$Y \min = -4$
$Y \max = 4$
$Y \text{ scl} = 1$

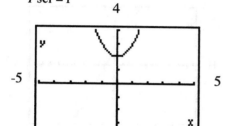

(b)

$X \min = -10$
$X \max = 10$
$X \text{ scl} = 1$
$Y \min = -8$
$Y \max = 8$
$Y \text{ scl} = 1$

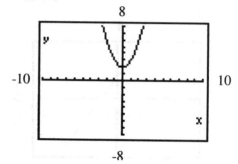

(c)

$X \min = -10$
$X \max = 10$
$X \text{ scl} = 2$
$Y \min = -8$
$Y \max = 8$
$Y \text{ scl} = 2$

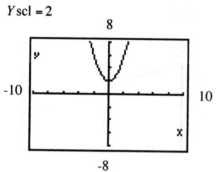

(d)

$X \min = -5$
$X \max = 5$
$X \text{ scl} = 1$
$Y \min = -20$
$Y \max = 20$
$Y \text{ scl} = 5$

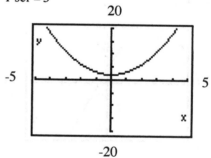

550

11. (a) $y = -x^2 + 2$

$X \min = -5$

$X \max = 5$

$X \operatorname{scl} = 1$

$Y \min = -4$

$Y \max = 4$

$Y \operatorname{scl} = 1$

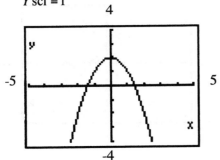

(b)

$X \min = -10$

$X \max = 10$

$X \operatorname{scl} = 1$

$Y \min = -8$

$Y \max = 8$

$Y \operatorname{scl} = 1$

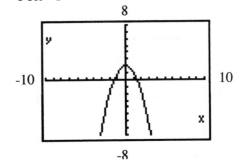

(c)

$X \min = -10$

$X \max = 10$

$X \operatorname{scl} = 2$

$Y \min = -8$

$Y \max = 8$

$Y \operatorname{scl} = 2$

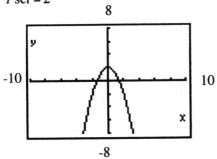

(d)

$X \min = -5$

$X \max = 5$

$X \operatorname{scl} = 1$

$Y \min = -20$

$Y \max = 20$

$Y \operatorname{scl} = 5$

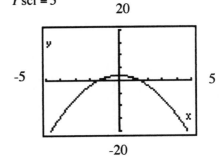

13. (a) $3x + 2y = 6$

$X \min = -5$

$X \max = 5$

$X \operatorname{scl} = 1$

$Y \min = -4$

$Y \max = 4$

$Y \operatorname{scl} = 1$

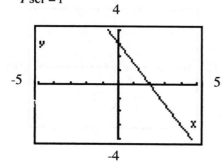

(b)

$X \min = -10$

$X \max = 10$

$X \operatorname{scl} = 1$

$Y \min = -8$

$Y \max = 8$

$Y \operatorname{scl} = 1$

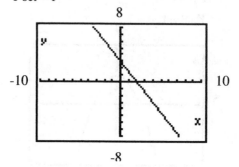

(c)

$X \min = -10$

$X \max = 10$

$X \operatorname{scl} = 2$

$Y \min = -8$

$Y \max = 8$

$Y \operatorname{scl} = 2$

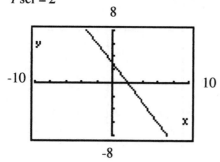

(d)

$X \min = -5$

$X \max = 5$

$X \operatorname{scl} = 1$

$Y \min = -20$

$Y \max = 20$

$Y \operatorname{scl} = 5$

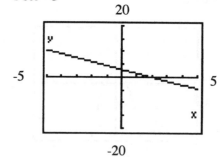

15. (a) $-3x + 2y = 6$

$X \min = -5$
$X \max = 5$
$X \text{scl} = 1$
$Y \min = -4$
$Y \max = 4$
$Y \text{scl} = 1$

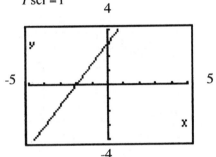

(b)

$X \min = -10$
$X \max = 10$
$X \text{scl} = 1$
$Y \min = -8$
$Y \max = 8$
$Y \text{scl} = 1$

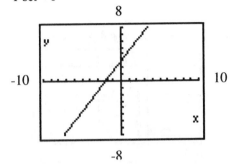

(c)

$X \min = -10$
$X \max = 10$
$X \text{scl} = 2$
$Y \min = -8$
$Y \max = 8$
$Y \text{scl} = 2$

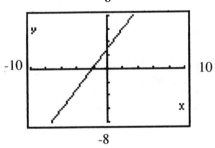

(d)

$X \min = -5$
$X \max = 5$
$X \text{scl} = 1$
$Y \min = -20$
$Y \max = 20$
$Y \text{scl} = 5$

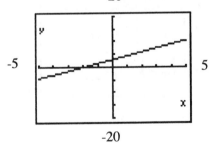

17. $y = x + 2;$ $-3 \le x \le 3$

X	Y1
-3	-1
-2	0
-1	1
0	2
1	3
2	4
3	5

X=3

19. $y = -x + 2;$ $-3 \le x \le 3$

X	Y1
-3	5
-2	4
-1	3
0	2
1	1
2	0
3	-1

X=3

21. $y = 2x + 2;$ $-3 \le x \le 3$

X	Y1
-3	-4
-2	-2
-1	0
0	2
1	4
2	6
3	8

X=3

23. $y = -2x + 2;$ $-3 \le x \le 3$

X	Y1
-3	8
-2	6
-1	4
0	2
1	0
2	-2
3	-4

X=3

25. $y = x^2 + 2;$ $-3 \le x \le 3$

X	Y1
-3	11
-2	6
-1	3
0	2
1	3
2	6
3	11

X=3

27. $y = -x^2 + 2;$ $-3 \le x \le 3$

X	Y1
-3	-7
-2	-2
-1	1
0	2
1	1
2	-2
3	-7

X=3

29. $3x + 2y = 6;$ $-3 \le x \le 3$

X	Y1
-3	7.5
-2	6
-1	4.5
0	3
1	1.5
2	0
3	-1.5

X=3

31. $-3x + 2y = 6;$ $-3 \le x \le 3$

X	Y1
-3	-1.5
-2	0
-1	1.5
0	3
1	4.5
2	6
3	7.5

X=3

Graphing Utilities

A.3 Using a Graphing Utility to Locate Intercepts and Check for Symmetry

1. $y = x^2 + 4x + 2$

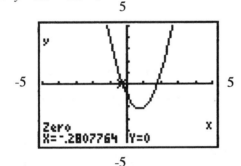

The smaller x-intercept is $x \approx -3.41$.

3. $y = 2x^2 + 4x + 1$

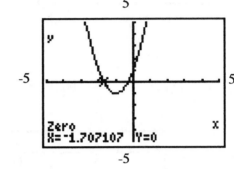

The smaller x-intercept is $x \approx -1.71$.

5. $y = 2x^2 - 3x - 1$

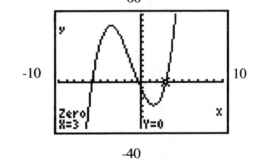

The smaller x-intercept is $x \approx -0.28$.

7. $y = x^3 + 3.2x^2 - 16.83x - 5.31$

The positive x-intercept is $x = 3$.

9. $y = x^4 - 1.4x^3 - 33.71x^2 + 23.94x + 292.41$ We zoom in on the positive x-intercept:

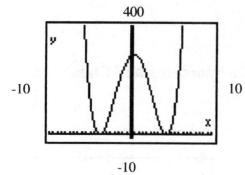

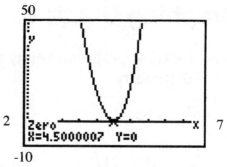

The positive x-intercept is $x \approx 4.50$.

11. $y = \pi x^3 - (8.88\pi + 1)x^2 - (42.066\pi - 8.88)x + 42.066$

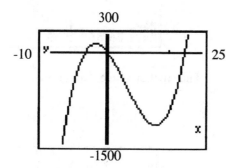

We zoom in on the positive x-intercepts:

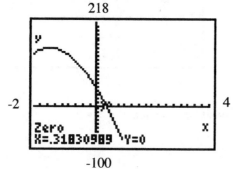

The smallest positive x-intercept is $x \approx 0.32$.

We zoom in on the positive x-intercepts:

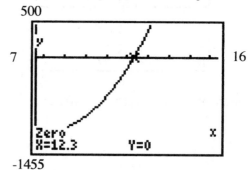

The largest positive x-intercept is $x \approx 12.3$.

13. $y = x^3 + 19.5x^2 - 1021x + 1000.5$

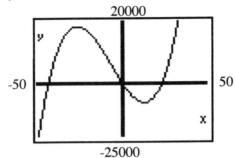

We zoom in on the positive x-intercepts:

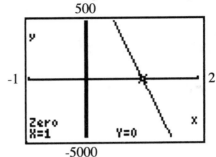

The smallest positive x-intercept is $x = 1$.

We zoom in on the positive x-intercepts:

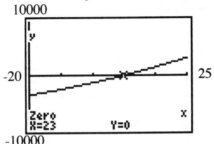

The largest positive x-intercept is $x = 23$.

15. x-intercepts: $(-1.5, 0); (1.5, 0)$

   y-intercept: $(0, -2)$

   y-axis symmetry

17. x-intercepts: none

   y-intercept: none

   origin symmetry

Graphing Utilities

A.5   Square Screens

1. yes

$X\min = -3$
$X\max = 3$
$X\operatorname{scl} = 2$
$Y\min = -2$
$Y\max = 2$
$Y\operatorname{scl} = 2$

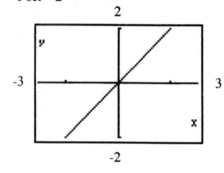

3. yes

$X\min = 0$
$X\max = 9$
$X\operatorname{scl} = 3$
$Y\min = -2$
$Y\max = 4$
$Y\operatorname{scl} = 2$

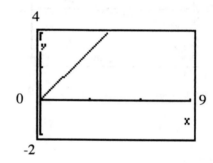

5. no

$X \min = -6$
$X \max = 6$
$X \operatorname{scl} = 1$
$Y \min = -2$
$Y \max = 2$
$Y \operatorname{scl} = 0.5$

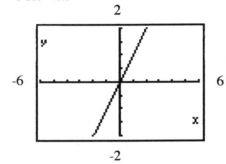

7. yes

$X \min = 0$
$X \max = 9$
$X \operatorname{scl} = 1$
$Y \min = -2$
$Y \max = 4$
$Y \operatorname{scl} = 1$

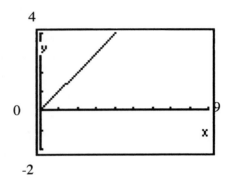

9. One possible answer:

$X \min = -4$
$X \max = 8$
$X \operatorname{scl} = 1$
$Y \min = 4$
$Y \max = 12$
$Y \operatorname{scl} = 1$